Burke&Wills

PETER FITZSIMONS

Burke&Wills

The triumph and tragedy of Australia's
most famous explorers

CONSTABLE

CONSTABLE

First published in the Australia and New Zealand in 2017 by Hachette Australia,
an imprint of Hachette Australia Pty Limited

First published in Great Britain in 2018 by Constable

3 5 7 9 10 8 6 4 2

Images are from the State Library of Victoria (SLV) unless otherwise acknowledged.

Front cover, top: The departure of the Burke and Wills expedition, lithograph from the
Illustrated Australian News, 4 May 1881 (SLV IAN04/05/81/sup)

Front cover, bottom: Portraits of Burke (*left*) and Wills (*right*) from wood engraving in the
Illustrated London News, 1 February 1862 (Trove, National Library of Australia, nla.obj-
135907470); Departure of the expedition from the Royal Park, Melbourne, Aug. 20, 1860,
wood engraving from *Illustrated London News*, 1 February 1862 (Trove, National Library
of Australia, nla.obj-135907585)

Map on p. x by Dave Phoenix; internal maps by Jane Macaulay

Back cover: The Dig Tree (photo © Dave Phoenix, 2008)

Author photo courtesy Peter Morris/Sydney Heads

Aboriginal readers: Please note that this book contains names and images of people
who are deceased or who may be deceased.

A CIP catalogue record for this book is available from the British Library.

ISBN: 978-1-47212-899-7

Printed and bound in Great Britain by Clays Ltd, Elcograf S.p.A.

Papers used by Robinson are from well-managed forests and other responsible sources.

MIX
Paper from
responsible sources
FSC
www.fsc.org   FSC® C104740

Constable
An imprint of
Little, Brown Book Group
Carmelite House
50 Victoria Embankment
London EC4Y 0DZ

An Hachette UK Company
www.hachette.co.uk
www.littlebrown.co.uk

To Dave Phoenix, and those like him,

who have laboured long and hard,

driven by an overwhelming passion

to keep this story alive ever since 1860.

We owe them all a great debt.

CONTENTS

List of Maps ix

Dramatis Personae xi

Background and Acknowledgements xiii

Prologue xvii

One 'A Ghastly Blank . . .' 1

Two A Herd of Camels, A Winnowing of Explorers 26

Three Help Wanted 49

Four Miles of Supplies for the Miles Ahead 72

Five Northwards Bound 100

Six 'Push, Push, Push . . .' 123

Seven The Sting and the Policeman 148

Eight Menindee Madness 181

Nine Cooper's Creek Calling 216

Ten Pushing North 250

Eleven Once More unto the Breach, Dear Friends . . . 287

Twelve Homeward Bound 317

Thirteen A Departure and an Arrival 360

Fourteen Full Circle 405

Fifteen Off to the Rescue 451

Sixteen Long Live the King! 487

Seventeen Royal Commission 523

Eighteen The Verdict, the Funeral 564

Epilogue 599

Endnotes 625

Bibliography 673

Index 681

LIST OF MAPS

The Burke and Wills expedition   x
Australian explorers 1844–1860   3
Possible alternative route for Burke's supplies   89
The Victorian Exploring Expedition: The first week   115
Tragowel to Balranald   126
The Darling River and Menindee   184
Lyons and MacPherson   230
Following the Diamantina   276
From the Selwyn Range to the Gulf of Carpentaria   315
Return from the Gulf   338
Position of the three parties, 4 April 1861   348
Burke's return to the Depot   354
Wright's supply party, Torowoto to Bulloo   389
Burke's northbound trip and Brahe's return   392
Wright and Brahe return to Dig Tree   409
Burke, Wills and King on Cooper's Creek   448
Burke and Wills relief expeditions   474

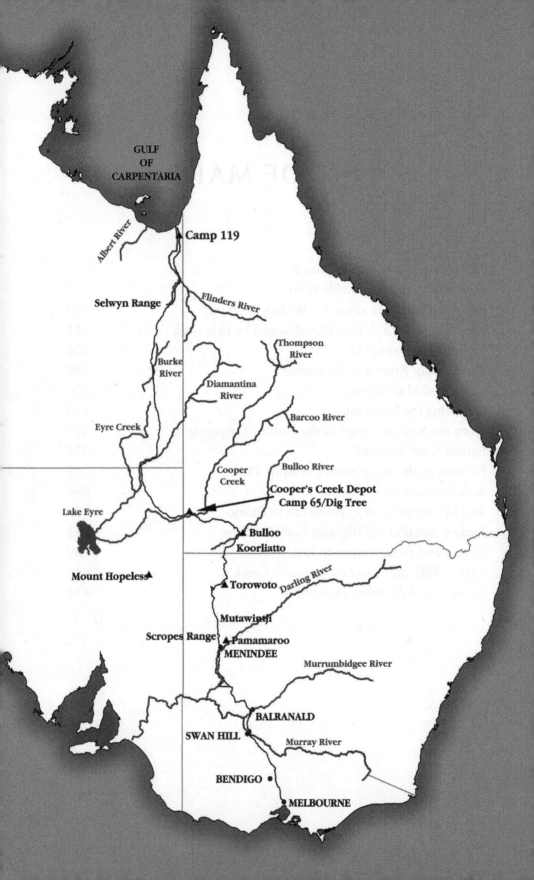

DRAMATIS PERSONAE

1. *Robert O'Hara Burke*, leader of the expedition. An officer and a gentleman, born in a stately ancestral home in Ireland. Served in the Irish constabulary and Austrian army before arriving in Australia and becoming a police inspector and superintendent in Victoria.
2. *William John Wills*, surveyor, observer (astronomical). As a precocious teenager, he assisted his doctor father in his surgery, distributing medicines and occasionally helping with minor medical procedures, before deciding his true calling was in the world of science and the continent of Australia.
3. *William Wright*, bushman and station overseer; became third in command. Met Burke near his property at Kinchega, one day out from Menindee.
4. *George Landells*, in charge of the camels, initial second officer of the expedition. Born in Barbados in 1825, then lived in India from 1842. Arrived in Australia in 1856. A horse trader who became a camel master.
5. *Dr Ludwig Becker*, artist. Born in Germany. Officer, official artist and naturalist for the expedition. A doctor of philosophy, his wonderful sketches and drawings of the journey are on display today in the State Library of Victoria.
6. *Dr Hermann Beckler*, also born in Germany. Official medical officer and botanist for the expedition, unofficial artist and chronicler.
7. *Charles Ferguson*, American adventurer. He had spent two years in the California goldfields before coming to Australia to dig for more gold. Arrested at Eureka Stockade, talked his way out of it, one of his many brushes with the law. The foreman of the expedition as it left Royal Park.

8. *William Brahe*, German, arrived in Victoria in 1852, employed as gold digger, drover, storekeeper and wagon driver.

9. *Thomas McDonough*, his family knew Burke in Ireland, appointed to the expedition as assistant on Burke's request.

10. *William Patten*, Irish blacksmith, submitted by Robert Burke on his list of men to serve on the expedition.

11. *John King*, Irish, joined the 70th Regiment in 1853 when 14 years old, and was then posted to India. Met Mr Landells while convalescing, sailed from India to Australia with his camels. Of his many attributes, one was that he could speak the language – 'Indostanee' – of the camel drivers.

12. *William 'Billy' Hodgkinson*, journalist for the *Age* who became an expedition assistant after being summoned from Melbourne by Mr Burke while already on the road.

13. *Charley Gray*, Scottish, runaway sailor, hired at Swan Hill as expedition assistant.

14. *Dr John Macadam*, polymath, politician, physician, university lecturer, the first VFL umpire and the Hon. Secretary of the Exploration Committee of the Royal Society of Victoria.

15. *Sir William Stawell*, Chief Justice of Victoria and the Chairman of the Exploration Committee.

16. *Julia Matthews*, singer and actress. The young rising star of the Victorian stage, acclaimed for her voice, her dramatic gifts and her beauty. Sweetheart of Robert Burke.

17. *Richard Birnie*, barrister and lecturer, the son of a knight and graduate of Oxford and Cambridge. Friend of Thackeray and Dickens. Lived with and mentored William Wills, his intimate companion and friend.

18. *Professor Georg Neumayer*, brilliant scientist and head of Melbourne Observatory. Employer and sponsor of his protégé William Wills.

19. *Alfred Howitt*, explorer, naturalist, social scientist and Victorian adventurer.

20. *Edwin Welch*, surveyor, wit and writer.

21. *Dr William Wills*, physician and father of William Wills the explorer.

22. *William Lockhart Morton*, inventor, member of the Royal Society of Victoria, would-be exploration leader.

BACKGROUND AND
ACKNOWLEDGEMENTS

My father, Peter McCloy FitzSimons, gave all of his children a love of stories and storytelling. All seven of us have benefited from it, but by strange happenstance this is the second book I've done where the one to inspire me to turn the story into a book was my eldest brother, David. About ten years ago, I sat there transfixed as Davo told me the yarn of Burke and Wills, just as he had done with the story of Mawson a couple of years earlier. Both times he and I agreed, 'There's a book in this . . .' and both times we were right.

I was stunned that there was much more to Burke and Wills than I had imagined, that it was not simply two blokes running out of steam in the desert and wilting, that there was the whole back-story drama of Melbourne, of the Dig Tree, of the Indigenous people, of the rescue attempt and so on . . .

Once embarked with my four brilliant researchers going hard, I was equally amazed at just how much material was available to fulfil my motto to 'make the skeletons dance', to bring back to life in these pages not only the people themselves, but accurate renditions of the conversations they had.

The whole thing was, in short, right up my alley, from first to last, and I can honestly say I've never enjoyed doing a book more. What a *story*!

As ever, I have tried to bring the *story* part of this hi*story* alive, by putting it in the present tense, and constructing it in the manner of a novel, albeit with 2500 footnotes, give or take, as the pinpoint pillars on which the story rests. For the sake of the storytelling, I have put it in strong, though not strict, chronological order of events and, just as

I did with my recent Great War trilogy, I have occasionally created a direct quote from reported speech in a newspaper, diary or letter, and changed pronouns and tenses to put that reported speech in the present tense. Equally, every now and then I have assumed generic emotions where it is obvious, even though that emotion is not necessarily recorded in the diary entries, letter, etc.

Always, my goal has been to determine what were the words used, based on the primary documentary evidence presented, and what the feel of the situation was. For the same reason of remaining faithful to the language of the day, I have stayed with the imperial system of measurement and used the contemporary spelling, with only the odd exception where it would create too much confusion otherwise.

There are words and terms used by the men in this book to describe Aboriginal people that today are correctly regarded as offensive. It is one of the fascinating aspects of this story to see how the hostile and at best contemptuous attitudes that the explorers had towards this country's first inhabitants changed when they met reality. Of all the explorers only Ludwig Becker had a consistent attitude of respect, sympathy and fascination with Aboriginal culture and people. To read the 1860s nomenclature used to describe Aboriginal people can still be jolting, as can the attitudes and opinions of the men of the Victorian era, and I hope the reader will understand that their quotation and use in this work in no way reflects my opinions or the language any modern Australian would employ.

All books used are listed in the Bibliography, but here I cite most particularly the late Sarah Murgatroyd's book *The Dig Tree*. I frequently came to entirely different conclusions to her as to what actually happened, but found her account wonderfully compelling and an excellent guide.

For the last decade I have relied heavily on a great team of researchers, and this book owes them as great a debt as ever. *Mein freund*, Sonja Goernitz, a dual German–Australian citizen, was as useful as ever getting to the bottom of the German angle in this book, which is considerable, thanks to the strong German contingent who headed off with Burke.

My warm thanks also to Dr Peter Williams, the Canberra military historian who first started working with me on my book on Gallipoli, and has stayed with me thereafter.

For the first time, my cousin, Angus FitzSimons, worked on the project from first to last, from top to bottom, and there are few parts of this whole saga not stronger for his input. Long after my own intellectual resources were spent, trying to get to the bottom of something from the frequently conflicting primary accounts, Angus worked on into the night and when I woke up in the morning, there it was! (King *did* put the broken bits of bottle above the stockade!)

Dr Libby Effeney has worked with me on the last five books, and as a researcher and friend is as good as it gets – she is hard-working, and, curiously, as intellectually strict as she is creative in working out how the story can be told better while still remaining within the parameters of *what happened*. On this one, our common intellectual journey turned into a real-world journey when, in late January 2017, we rented a four-wheel drive and traced the bottom half of the expedition's course, from Melbourne all the way to Birdsville, something that opened both our eyes as to just how extraordinary the whole expedition was, how wild and fabulous and *empty* the country was, even to this day. (Trust me, when you blow a tyre on the Birdsville Track in late January, and can't work out how to get the spare wheel off, you know lonely.)

In all of my books, I like to have whoever the foremost expert in the field is on my side, and in this case I was very lucky to secure the services of Dave Phoenix, President of the Burke and Wills Historical Society, who, time and again, I found to be the last word to beat all last words when it came to knowing and providing documentary proof of what happened.

As ever, I also relied on other specialists in their fields, including Dr Michael Cooper for all matters medical, from scurvy through to syphilis to starvation; while Aaron Paterson, the descendant of two of the characters you will meet, was wonderfully strong on the Indigenous angle of the book.

I am once more indebted to Jane Macaulay for the maps, which you will see throughout.

This time, for the first time, my eldest son Jake did the preliminary sub-editing giving me frank counsel about what worked and what didn't, where I had to turn the volume up or down, where I had too much dull detail or too little to make the story live and breathe, and I was not only grateful for the astute input, but thrilled at how good he proved to be at it.

My long-time sub-editor meanwhile, Harriet Veitch, took the fine-tooth comb to the whole thing, untangling hopelessly twisted sentences, eliminating many grammatical errors and giving my stuff a sheen which does not properly belong to it. She has strengthened my work for three decades now, and I warmly thank her for it.

My thanks also, as ever, to my highly skilled editor Deonie Fiford, who has honoured my request that she preserve most of the sometimes odd way I write, while only occasionally insisting that something come out because it just doesn't work.

I am grateful, as ever, to my friend and publisher, Matthew Kelly of Hachette, who I have worked with many times over the last three decades, and who was enthusiastic and supportive throughout, always giving great guidance.

None, however, has been more supportive than my wife, Lisa. We've been married 25 years this year, and for much of that time, I have not only been somewhere in the house, with my 'head in a book', but even when I put it down, afterwards, that book has been in my head! It has made me somewhat distracted for the last quarter-century but she understands, and it is one of the many things I love about her.

Peter FitzSimons
Neutral Bay, Sydney
19 February 2017

PROLOGUE

He was greatly liked by all classes, and though somewhat of a martinet, he was adored by his men. In truth, although he was a strange and even eccentric man, he was what we may call very loveable. Amiable, though hasty in disposition; brave as a lion; an enthusiast about music; an ardent lover of his native country, a devoted admirer of the fair sex, with whom he was a universal favourite, a gentleman by birth, and a soldier by profession, it was no wonder that with him strangers speedily became acquaintances, acquaintances friends, and friends brothers. Always burning for some great enterprise, yearning for glory and distinction, he yet had the heart of a woman – melting at a tale of distress, or at the story of some heroic deed.[1]

A Beechworth local recalls Robert O'Hara Burke in the
Ovens and Murray Advertiser, 1880

Burke . . . an enthusiastic lover of music, indeed a musician and a devoted admirer of the fair sex, and it [is] known to his intimate friends, that: although . . . a great favourite with women, whatever part the spirit of adventure which burned within him had to do with his final journey, there was something due also to the sadness of an unrequited passion.[2]

Ovens and Murray Advertiser, 9 July 1874

How very strange.

It is somewhat muffled, but you can still hear it.

Coming from 87 Ford Street in the Victorian town of Beechworth are the strains of 'Sweet Spirit, Hear My Prayer', a very popular song in this winter of 1858.

And there, through the window, you can see him, an enormous man with piercing blue eyes and a bushy beard, pounding away at an old piano which, curiously, has heavy blankets draped all over it.

Despite playing violin in the Beechworth band, *Liedertafel,* at this instrument he is not skilled.

His fingers do not fly lightly over the ivory like a practised pianist and in fact have a relationship to the keys more akin to that of an elephant hunter to his fallen prey . . . they hack and bash, rather than tickle and tinkle; they pound and press, rather than patter and prance.

And look at those fingers! They are not long and delicate, reserved for piano playing only. They are worn and calloused, and bear one or two knobbly knuckles that show they have been broken.

Yes, these are not the hands of a soft man, but a hard man. These fingers are made to hold truncheons, to clench for a fistfight and hit recalcitrant skulls, to pull triggers.

And yes, look closer. It is exactly that man, Police Inspector Robert O'Hara Burke. Originally from Ireland, born into a family of Protestant gentry and landowners, he began his career with the Hungarian Hussars and moved on to a stint in the Irish constabulary. Leaving Europe behind, he came out to Australia to find his fortune and is now the highest-ranking policeman in our northern Victorian town.

The blankets are to try to deaden the sound for the family next door, who have a new baby, for despite his sometimes rough background he is a considerate, likeable man. As to the rough piano playing and dreadful singing, he is a man with a broken heart.

Just a couple of months ago, the burlesque show *Aladdin* came through town, and after attending every performance on every day and then following it to the next town and the town after that, Burke has become ever more smitten, ever more *stricken,* 'falling head over ears in love with the prima donna',[3] Julia Matthews . . .

But could one such as her ever fall for one such as him, a man of modest means, a man with a trail of debts behind him, a man so uncaring of fashion that despite his senior position in the police force he didn't even possess 'a dress suit, nor even a white shirt'[4], a man who is over two decades her senior?

The answer, she tells him is . . . *no.*

Which he takes to mean, *not yet*.

But perhaps, if he *proves* his love, by learning the songs she sings in *Aladdin*, that might sway her?

He can only hope, and, as later recounted by a friend, 'he bought a piano, and took daily lessons from a little German teacher, so that he might learn to play the airs Julia used to sing'.[5]

He continues to practise, night after night after night, and on his rare days off. Sarah, his very respectable housekeeper, tries to keep herself up the other end of the house, just as she does every morning after Inspector Burke has his bath, and insists on drying his stark naked body in the hallway, while calling for her to get his breakfast.

Ah, but long before he gets to breakfast, he *must* master his favourite Julia song, 'Sweet Spirit, Hear My Prayer'.

And again, and again, and again . . .

> *Oh! thou to whom my thoughts are known,*
> *Calm, oh, calm these trembling fears!*
> *Ah! turn away the world's cold frown,*
> *And dry these falling tears.*
> *Oh! leave me not alone in grief,*
> *Send this blighted heart relief . . .*[6]

For yes, as another friend of his would ruefully recount, 'her song of "Sweet Spirit, Hear My Prayer", in *Aladdin*, so curled around the susceptible Irish heart of Robert O'Hara Burke, that he wanted to do a Great Deed or Die . . .'[7]

Which is fine.

But all up, though well regarded in his tiny community of Beechworth, and highly thought of by his family, the truth of it is that in 1858, in the midst of his thirty-seventh cold winter on this earth, Burke is a singularly unlikely character to do any kind of Great Deed, let alone arise within three years to the position of the most famous man on the Australian continent, to have a statue raised in his honour in Melbourne, to have a legendary status that would endure at least most of the next two centuries.

How did that *happen*?

Ah, friends, therein lies a tale.

CHAPTER ONE

'A GHASTLY BLANK...'

I have played like a child with the pebbles on the shore while the
great ocean of truth lies unexplored before me.[1]

Dr Ferdinand Mueller quotes Isaac Newton in his address to the
Philosophical Institute about the history of explorations of Australia,
25 November 1857

A ghastly blank will no longer stare us in the face when we bend
our eyes upon the map of this continent, and the track of the
explorers, winding over that white plain, may become one of the
highways of commerce, dotted with centres of population, and
vital with the ebb and flow of a periodical tide of travellers ...[2]

The Argus, 1 September 1858

While, famously, a journey of a thousand miles must start with a single step, so too did a famous journey of much longer distance start with a stray thought, at first idly expressed, which soon assumed a momentum of its own ...

For it is Dr David Wilkie of the venerable Philosophical Institute of Victoria – devoted to the promotion of science and discovery – who, in 1857 in Melbourne Town, after talking it over with friends, first crystallises an idea that has been loosely abroad among the wider public for some time.

Why not, says he, at a meeting of the Philosophical Institute on 21 October, send an expedition to cross our continent? His proposition is well received, and an Exploration Committee is formed on the spot.

Dr Wilkie returns to the subject three weeks later, at the institute's next meeting.

Hear him now, as he rises to speak.

1

'The geographical exploration of the interior,' says the bow-tie wearing 42-year-old medico from Edinburgh, 'is a subject of great national importance. On scientific grounds it is the province of the Institute to promote this great object. The proposed search for [the missing explorer, Ludwig] Leichhardt would, I am sure, command the warmest sympathy of the members and the public. In no part of the world is there so wide an extent of available country for the future settlement of the surplus population of the Old World. The exploration of the interior is, therefore, fraught with the most important results.'[3]

Intriguing! There is even, that rarest of all things at such meetings, a rustle of genuine excitement around the room at his remarks. This is not dull discussion of arcane concepts, this is nothing less than a call to action to the great and good of the day, who are quite capable of making it happen. Sir William Stawell, the Chief Justice of Victoria, leans in close, as does Dr John Macadam, the political powerhouse and polymath, who, everyone knows, will soon be premier if they can't work out how to stop him first. Dr Ferdinand Mueller, the explorer and botanist, is particularly fascinated – this is his field. One of the newest members of the institute, Mr William Lockhart Morton, is entranced. Hanging on every word, his eyes sparkle, his soul sings. Oh, how he has long dreamt of leading just such an expedition! Yes, he already has a certain measure of renown and respect as the inventor of the sheep dip and the swing gate. But what are they, compared to what this would be, the glory of a grand exploration! An expedition into the heart of the country, into the unknown, into . . . eternal fame.

Continue, Dr Wilkie, we are all listening.

Yes, well, Dr Wilkie's idea is to start the proposed expedition from Curtis Bay on the east coast of the continent, some 300 miles north of Brisbane, and to then push directly west, staying broadly on the line of the Tropic of Capricorn all the way to Shark Bay, 500 miles north of Perth, while 'embracing at the same time, any fitting opportunity of exploring the interior both to the north and south of this line'[4].

Dr Wilkie refers to the valuable results of previous exploring expeditions under Charles Sturt, who plunged deeper into Australia's interior than any other, discovering rivers and deserts, but no inland sea, as

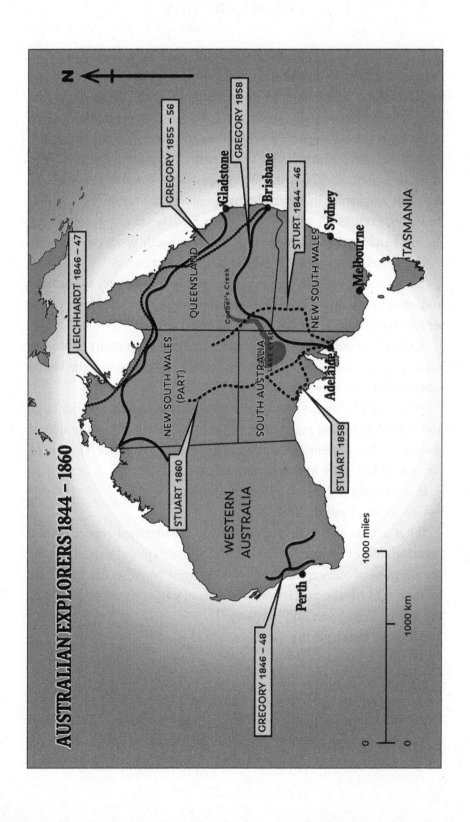

he had always hoped. And the successes of Ludwig Leichhardt, the Prussian explorer who travelled north-west from the Darling Downs in Queensland's south-east to Port Essington in the country's north-west, discovering pastoral lands along the way, before going missing in the Queensland wilderness with all hands. And who can forget the great Sir Thomas Mitchell, one of the earliest explorers and surveyors of south-eastern Australia? Dr Wilkie speaks most warmly, though, of the great Augustus Gregory, who has explored the north of Australia, and who, even as we speak, is about to bravely set out to search for the lost Leichhardt, at the request of the New South Wales government.

The projected expense, Wilkie insists, is manageable.

'Six thousand pounds,' he estimates, 'would be necessary to organise and maintain a suitable exploring party for a period of two years, which would suffice for the proposed objects.'[5]

After all, he notes, New South Wales had fitted out many exploring parties, as had the Royal Geographic Society of London and the Home Government. So why not Victoria?

'[Our colony],' he says, 'from her unexampled wealth, and her large and rapidly increasing population, ought to take the lead in geographical discovery. The present is the most auspicious occasion for Victoria to contribute her share in this honourable work . . .'[6]

It is a strong argument, and well received.

Gentlemen, I put the motion:

'That a Committee be appointed to consider and report on the practicability of fitting out, in Victoria, a geographical expedition for the purpose of . . . exploring the vast interior of Australia from east to west, and for the purpose, if possible, of gathering some tidings of the fate of Leichhardt and his party.'[7]

All those in favour say 'Aye'.

Aye. Aye. Aye.

I ask that the record show, it is passed by acclamation.

No matter that the Philosophical Institute is rich in philosophy alone and cannot actually fund such a trip themselves. Surely, such a prosperous colony as ours can raise the money so long as the right people come to believe in the project?

It is with this in mind that the Exploration Committee – consisting of 32 leading members of the scientific, mercantile, professional, academic and political worlds – is given its first task: to explore just how such an expedition might be mounted.

At the Committee's first meeting, on 14 November 1857, at the famed Mechanics' Institute in Collins Street, Melbourne, the enthusiasm is palpable as different segments of the community embrace the idea, each for their own reasons.

The scientific community, of whom the leaders are mostly German-born and raised, are led on this Committee by Professor Georg Neumayer – the brilliant scientist and astronomer who has a particular passion for studying the earth's magnetic fields. The scientists are eager to penetrate the interior and so expand the frontiers of science. At this time, more is known about what lies on the moon than what lies in the centre of this continent, and for that reason the centre is widely referred to as a 'ghastly blank'[8] and *terra incognita*. A well-equipped expedition would undoubtedly return with maps of mountains, rivers, deserts, perhaps an inland sea, not to mention hundreds of new species of animal, bird and plant life, together with precious meteorological and magnetic data.

Science is fine, but the mercantile and political worlds represented on the Committee have an eye on *land* – both that which is fertile, and that which might contain gold. Back in the 1830s, the first settlers in the lush central land of Victoria had become 'squatters', establishing 'runs' where they and their cattle grew fat off the bounty of the land. In the 1850s, the first men to find gold at Ballarat had become many times richer even than the squatters. The gold had been pretty much *lying around*! Perhaps another rival to El Dorado lies in the interior? Just how much more rich and powerful might that make us all?

For the wealth from that Ballarat gold has built Melbourne – funding the construction of such venerable institutions as the parliament, the State Library and the University of Melbourne – and made it one of the finest, grandest cities on earth. What was wilderness just 30 years ago is now, as the *Geelong Advertiser* proudly notes of its big brother, 'transformed into a great city, as comfortable, as elegant, as luxurious ... as any place out of London or Paris'.[9]

Why, in the space of less than a decade since the discovery of gold, our city's population has gone from 30,000 to four times that number! Melbourne now outstrips even Sydney in size to have become the fastest growing city in the British Empire. We Victorians, meanwhile, boast everything from the first telegraph lines to the first railway tracks, and are the continent's most powerful colony.

Or are we? South Australia and New South Wales have launched many expeditions and discovered many things, but neither has managed anything so grand as crossing the entire continent. We must do this for civic pride!

A final bonus is that such an expedition could lead to the establishment of a telegraph line across the continent, linked to London, that would come straight to Melbourne. It would make our fair city the most modern metropolis on the continent, instantly aware of news and market prices for our export industry, instead of waiting three months for often out-of-date information to arrive here by ship.

And so it is that another key decision taken in early meetings is to agree to the motion, 'That this Committee, as representing Victoria, do not seek the co-operation of other colonies, but act alone . . .'[10]

This is to be a solely Victorian expedition. It is a matter of pride.

But what direction should the expedition head?

The original suggestion from Dr Wilkie, that it head east to west, is quickly countered by influential Committee member Ferdinand Mueller.

'It seems inadvisable,' the government's brilliant botanist explains, 'to send a simultaneous expedition from Victoria to the subtropical east coast, whilst the New South Wales Government has already entrusted to Mr Gregory the command of an expedition in search of Dr Leichhardt . . . By adopting the Darling as a starting point,' he goes on, 'a new and large portion of country in close proximity to the northern goldfields of the colony of Victoria, and probably in part available for pastures, would be opened.'[11]

Mueller would know, as he has just presented his paper on the history of explorations of Australia to the institute. It is his strong feeling that the Darling would make the finest starting point. The transit of stores could then be furnished by the Murray steamers, almost to the point of unexplored country.

At the next meeting, on 7 December 1857, the entire agenda is consumed with arguments about direction, with the only resolution being a rough agreement to send a small party to the Darling, basing themselves up around Menindee, and leave to them the decision as to which direction a larger party should go.

That can, perhaps, be resolved at the next meeting. So it goes. Resolutions are passed, motions debated, more meetings called, with little progress made to an actual expedition being launched, until . . . nearly a year later, on 18 August 1858, a significant breakthrough is made.

•

The Antarctic winds that whistle over Port Phillip Bay this morning first knock the tops off the 'white horses' that canter across the dark waters, and then career and careen up the streets, around the buildings, along cobbled laneways of the city centre, before doing their most dastardly work of all – lashing the residents' ruddy faces, their hands clenching into icy fists.

An interesting character – as odd, as earnest, as he is curious – is ushered into the presence of the second most esteemed man in the colony, after His Excellency the Governor, and that is Sir William Stawell, Chief Justice and President of the Philosophical Institute.

With the smooth assurance of one who is used to being greeted warmly wherever he goes, the visitor unbuttons his overcoat, doffs his hat, and reveals himself as, *hulloa!*, Ambrose Kyte, the Irish merchant, businessman, theatre owner and property speculator, who after starting his illustrious career selling hay, currently has an annual income of £15,000 from rents alone.

He has an interesting offer to make. He will commit, he tells Sir William, £1000 towards the cost of the expedition, so long as 'a sum of £2000 should be raised within a year from the present time by public subscription'.[12]

With, thus, £3000 raised the Philosophical Institute could have a great start to getting the funds they need to get the expedition off the ground!

'The idea was given to me from above,' the devout Anglican tells Sir William. 'I believe that I am an instrument in God's hand.'[13]

Despite such a glorious inspiration for his generosity, Kyte also makes clear that, for the moment at least, he wishes to remain anonymous. For, should he put his name to the donation all sorts of charges may be levelled at him, besmirching his motivation.

No, better this way, and the *Age* soon simply announces on page one:

EXPLORATION OF AUSTRALIA.

A citizen of Melbourne having signified to Sir W. Stawell, President of the Philosophical Institute, his intention of subscribing £1000 to the purpose of the exploration of Australia, on condition of a certain further sum being subscribed by the public towards the same object, a Public Meeting will be held at the Mechanics' Institute, on Tuesday, August 31st, at four o'clock p.m., to consider the above proposal. Sir William Stawell will be present.[14]

And so Chief Justice Stawell *is* present, together with 50 others, and an 'Exploration Fund Committee' is quickly established, setting itself the first task of raising matching funds. It is decided that once that has been accomplished, an application could be made to the Colonial Legislature (which contains more than a few members of the institute) for a further £6000, at which point planning proper for the expedition could get underway. As easily as that, an anonymous £1000 offer has now turned into the hope of a £9000 expedition, the largest and most expensive in Australia's history.

In order to get the word out to the public, John Macadam, the honorary secretary of the fundraising committee, as well as of the Philosophical Institute, puts out a note to possible donors, making his plea, which encompasses all the major reasons for the expedition in one paragraph:

'To open up a communication with the northern shores of this Continent, is an enterprise which should engage the sympathies and command the support of the merchant, the squatter and the miner, no less than those of the man of science; for such an enterprise promises to abridge the distance which separates us from the old world; to bring us, at an early date, in telegraphic communication with India and Europe; to open new avenues of commerce; to indicate how we may obtain access to vast areas of pastoral land, from which we are at present cut off, owing to our ignorance of the intervening country; and to solve a geological problem, which is as important as it is interesting.'[15]

Another point brought up at the public meeting of 31 August is the desirability of importing camels with a view to future explorations, as it seems the arid heat of the interior proper will be entirely unsuitable for horses.

Victorian MP Thomas Embling – long determined to solve the problem of the 'Australian Sahara'[16] by using camels to establish an overland trade route with Asia – had put it rather well back in March, in a letter to the editor of the *Argus*:

'Our desert could be crossed in 10 days, north to south, and all we need is to leave in Europe that curse of our race – namely, doing only as our fathers have done, from wearing a black hat and black woollen garments, to trying to travel a desert with a horse.'[17]

The *Argus* broadly agrees: 'The camel, with a load of five to six hundred pounds upon its back, will, with the greatest facility proceed at a rate of forty or fifty miles a day, and, if necessary, will go without water for a period of from ten to fourteen days . . . What might not be expected from an exploring party provided with these "ships of the desert?"'[18]

Make no mistake, Embling says in a follow-up letter: the camel, too, is part of God's rich plan.

'Civilised man tests his puny powers on horseback against the desert in its aridity, and perishes on its threshold . . . Would we cross the Southern Ocean in a cockle-boat? Why then, attempt to find our way across a desert except on a desert-ship – the gift of Heaven for that undertaking?'[19]

This is not just any letter writer, this is a member of the Victorian government, and he is happy to put his views to all the key decision-makers. In fact, his argument is so compelling that the Victorian Parliament agrees to accept the offer of the well-known local horse-trader George Landells, who will shortly be heading to India – with a contingent of 150 Victorian brumbies (specially bred cavalry and artillery horses, not the wild kind) to sell to the British military stationed in India – to buy 24 camels while there, and bring them back as his return cargo.

Rising proudly in the manner of one who has just been knighted by Queen Victoria herself, Dr Embling addresses the public meeting of 31 August – held in the august halls of the Mechanics' Institute on Collins Street, in a room lined by rich mahogany, grand portraits and esteemed gentlemen – to reveal the welcome, if tentative, news from the government. Either the camels can be used for the expedition, or as part of a breeding program so that Victoria can have the finest camels in all Australia, and be set up for future explorations. Landells, who stands in the crowd looking very tanned next to the pinkish scientists – more brawn than brain – claims to have no fewer than 14 years experience in handling camels, and so should be perfect for the task. In fact, they even ask him to hire some sepoys, Indian soldiers serving under the British Empire and past masters of handling camels.

•

Mr Landells leaves for India in October 1858.

Although the camels are to be bought by the Government of Victoria for future exploration in general, the men of the Philosophical Institute can't help but think what a boon it would be if they were able to use the new desert fleet on their great venture to cross the continent. Alas, the camels are not expected to arrive in Melbourne until early in 1860 – more than a year away – and surely the Exploration Committee will have raised the funds and started, well, exploring, long before then.

In the meantime, how to raise the £2000 required to match Kyte's offer?

Exactly.

It is one thing for the community as a whole, led by the newspapers, to agree it is a good idea. It is quite another for people to actually reach into their wallets and purses to provide the money.

Late 1858, Melbourne, the Committee explores the explorers

Now, as is the way of such things, the best way of finding a worthy leader for the expedition is to start by asking the most obvious candidate of the lot, and that is Augustus Gregory.

Perhaps the most accomplished explorer in the country, Augustus Gregory, a noted inventor, surveyor and expert in bushcraft – not to mention fine leader of men – may just be available, too. Recently returned from his unsuccessful attempt to find the remains of Leichhardt, he is first approached by Mueller, with an invitation to become the leader.

The exhausted Gregory, however – who is set to take up the post as the first Surveyor-General of Queensland – refuses the exhortations of Dr Mueller, writing that 'even under the most favourable circumstances, the results [of the expedition] must fall far short of public expectation'. He also suggests that it be a Victorian resident who is given lead of the expedition; someone, he explains, who 'would be more closely identified with the community than a non-resident like myself'.[20]

Gregory does, however, offer his sage advice on the best route and some of the logistics, based on his recent travels along Cooper's and Strzelecki creeks on his Leichhardt search expedition:[21]

'Taking everything into consideration,' he writes, 'the most eligible point [for a depot] is where the Strzelecki Creek branches off from the Cooper [Creek] . . . Here there is a fine reach of water in the River, and sufficient grass for the stock even if detained through the dry season. Were a depot formed at this place the stores and equipment could easily be brought up from Port Augusta, as only 150 miles of desert intervene between the out-stations of South Australia and Cooper River, and, by following the channel of Strzelecki Creek, water would probably be found . . . From this depot, two days' journey would take a party into the unexplored country, nearer the centre of the *Terra Incognita* than any other that could be selected, with a due regard to the existing facilities of approach.'[22]

Now that *is* interesting. A depot at Cooper's Creek. Right on the spot where another watercourse, Strzelecki Creek, branches off from it. It makes sense, and the Exploration Committee takes due note. While they are a long way away from discussing routes, let alone the site of depots, advice from a man of Gregory's experience and expertise carries such weight that, in all the bluster, buffeting and ballyhoo that might come, it is unlikely to be easily shifted. *Cooper's Creek, indeed . . .*

For all the excitement of some members, however, at their next meeting, the Exploration Committee can't help but notice that not only have donations been drying up, but so has attendance, as interest wanes, both inside and outside the Committee room.

In fact, by early May 1859, interest has fallen away so markedly a bare half-a-dozen men make it to the meeting of the Exploration Committee and the Exploration Fund Committee. Among the absentees, most notable, and deplorable, is the Committee's honorary secretary, who has engagements elsewhere. (Typical. Macadam *always* has engagements elsewhere, from delivering the inaugural lecture on analytical chemistry at the University of Melbourne to acting as umpire and bouncing the first ball at the first match of the curious new game of Victorian Football. Macadam is like a moth drawn to whichever flame in Melbourne is burning brightest at the time, and his absence from the meeting on this day is a fair indication that its light has dimmed.)

In sum, the project is still alive, but only just. Sir William Stawell cautions if there is not a good turn-up for the next meeting 'in my opinion it would be far better to abandon the project altogether, than to be constantly putting off action'[23].

Somehow, the meetings struggle on, but it is not until two months later that a further prompt is given. On 20 July 1859 the government of the fine colony of South Australia proposes in its House of Assembly 'that a reward of £1000 might be given to the first person who should penetrate to the north-western or northern shore of this continent'.

It is passed, with an amendment to the effect that the said penetration must be 'from Port Augusta to between 115 and 143 degrees longitude'[24].

(In sum, to claim the prize the explorer must keep his explorations in the area directly above South Australia – ideally suited to positioning the overland telegraph – giving South Australia a financial reward far beyond the mere pittance they'd be paying.)

Beyond merely sponsoring the prize, however, the South Australians already have one of their own nearly ready to get started – none other than John McDouall Stuart, who had learnt his craft at the shoulder of Captain Charles Sturt, and gone on to his own exploring glories since.

The *Argus* puts it stingingly, in an editorial: 'By the time the inhabitants of this colony have subscribed the £2,000 necessary to secure the promised donation of £1,000, and by the time the camels ordered from India for exploring purposes have been shipped to this port, the probability is that Mr Stuart will have reached the Gulf of Carpentaria, and secured a lasting reputation as the pioneer of an over-land route to the northern shores of this continent . . .'[25]

Suddenly, courtesy of the keen rivalry between the two adjacent southern colonies, Victoria stirs. Three notable donations of £100 come in, including one from the man thought to be the richest in the colony, the railway contractor John Bruce.

Soon, the money surging forth into Victorian coffers is enough that the Exploration Committee begins to discuss the composition of the expedition. There is a basic notion from the first that there must be one leader in overall charge, perhaps half-a-dozen officers in charge of specific aspects of the expedition, together with another dozen or so workers to provide the grunt necessary.

One particularly influential Exploration Committee member, Professor Georg Neumayer of Flagstaff Observatory, is insistent that the expedition have a strong scientific quotient. If they are to navigate and map what lies in the middle of Australia, north of the Murray–Darling – that combined tributary that runs 915 miles across New South Wales, Victoria and South Australia like a flowing boundary to European settlement – they must send men of considerable knowledge and expertise.

With this in mind, Neumayer suggests that a position be reserved for his brilliant young offsider, the 25-year-old William Wills, who can take carriage of all scientific matters on the expedition. The suggestion receives a broadly positive response, but not positive enough for young Wills to be officially confirmed.

•

Oh, the thrill of it!

When William Wills hears that the suggestion of his name has been well received by the Committee he is beside himself with joy. In many ways, he feels he was born for just such an expedition. For Wills is a refined fellow, boasting a curious combination of passions not frequently found in the same breast – for physics, chemistry, pathology, astronomy *and* for art, literature and poetry.

His appetite for knowledge is innate, pure, a defining aspect of his character since early childhood. Ah, yes, Willy had been speaking in clear sentences before turning one, and many of those sentences had been questions.

He was further educated in the grammar school of Ashburton in Devonshire before working for three years in his father's medical practice, helping out in any manner he could, distributing medicines and occasionally being allowed to extract a tooth or breathe a vein. Wills sailed for Victoria in 1852, in the company of his brother and just ahead of their father, who gravitated to the goldfields and even helped patch together one of those who had been wounded by the Redcoats at the Eureka Stockade.

Nineteen-year-old William Wills, meantime, continued to widen his experience in Australia, doing everything from working as a shepherd on a station near Deniliquin, to trying his own luck as a prospector on the goldfields, before the call of intellectual pursuits became too strong. After studying surveying in Ballarat, and gaining practical experience over three years under the tutelage of a master of the field, Frederick John Byerly, Wills returned to Melbourne and a new challenge. For after taking up an appointment at the new Magnetic Observatory at Flagstaff Hill, he was seduced by astronomy and meteorology while working as an assistant to Government Meteorologist and Observatory Director Professor Neumayer, who admires him greatly. Wills is a quiet, loyal, endlessly methodical young man of an ability that is matched only by his humility.

But beneath such humility – an impression perhaps enhanced by his slight *sp-sp-sp*-speech impediment – the young man bursts with many, and growing, passions.

Wills is living in a comfortable boarding house in Gertrude Street, Fitzroy, where he has formed a close bond with another remarkable resident, Melbourne barrister, Richard Birnie, the son of an English knight.

'We gravitated to each other by mutual attraction, though I was double his age,' Birnie would chronicle. 'More and more he impressed me with his rare and beautiful character. Seldom, if ever, have I known such a harmony of firmness, gentleness, refinement, application, and ardent desire of knowledge.'[26]

Closer than close, the two talk for hours, night after night, of anything and everything – theatre, philosophy, gossip, the ancient Greeks, literature, astronomy, religion ... their learning mixed with laughter, on and on into the wee hours.

Educated at Oxford *and* Cambridge, Birnie is an impressively learned man, worldly, a brilliant wit with more than a hint of scepticism, a genius in most matters of the mind except the management of money, and the law – the last a particular pity as that is his profession. When still in London, Birnie had been a friend of such literary luminaries as Charles Dickens and William Thackeray. Tellingly, young Wills is particularly enamoured of Dickens's two sunniest characters – Mr Micawber, who is always hoping 'something will turn up'[27], and Mark Tapley, a character from *Martin Chuzzlewit*, who is always eager to seek out miserable circumstances so he can prove happiness can exist anywhere, and to show that he can 'come out strong under circumstances as would keep other men down'[28] – and he hangs on Birnie's every word about what Mr Dickens is really *like*.

Most wonderfully, Birnie returns Wills's deep affection in kind, and devotes himself to teaching the young scientist everything he knows, to act as his mentor, guide and loving wise hand on the younger man's development.

Yes, William's 'heart [is] in science, especially in astronomy', but under the tutelage of Richard Birnie, he thirsts for so much more, don't you see?

Soon, the thoughts and opinions of Richard Birnie begin to fill William's letters home to England, back to the mother who remained to take care of his young sisters. Now the Wills women read of the things he and Richard have done together, the excursions they have made, the discussions they have embarked upon (even, worryingly for the devout Mrs Wills, discussions on what faith and religion *really* mean).

Wills just can't get enough. He can *learn* from this man, and though he is more frank with his father than his mother when it comes to his new questioning of faith, Birnie is an intellectual drug that he cannot turn away from.

And nor can Richard Birnie turn from William, later describing him: 'A clear (perhaps too clear) complexion, an expressive eye that always outstripped his tongue (for he fought with, and partly subdued, a slight stammer), golden hair, a thick, tawny beard, a smile at once intellectual and sympathising, a light, clean, agile frame, prompt spontaneous movements, and a handsomeness such as is often seen in a young girl . . . propriety of dress, an easy geniality, tempered with a becoming self-respect . . . He [has], moreover, a keen and deep sense of the humorous, no less than of the ridiculous; and I used often to contrast his disfiguring bursts of laughter with the intellectual beauty of his smile in repose.'[29]

Indeed, it is those very wild guffaws of mirth that are among the things Birnie enjoys most about his young admirer.

'[William],' says Birnie jocularly many a'time, 'you have a god-like smile, but a bumpkin laugh.'[30]

The most thrilling thing is that if William could be accepted on this expedition as the official astronomical and meteorological observer as well as surveyor, so many of his passions could be indulged at once.

To tread where no European has gone before, to witness things never before recorded, to discover new worlds . . . what joy!

This is not a passing whim; this is something he has been yearning to do for the last *five years*.

'So long ago as 1855,' Richard Birnie would attest of his dear friend, '[William] frequently spoke . . . of a longing desire to explore the interior of Australia. He also expressed at this time a belief that he should be among the first who ever should succeed in crossing to the Gulf of Carpentaria.'[31]

Back in 1856, when Wills had first heard tell of such an expedition being mounted, by a Dr Catherwood of Ballarat, he had walked the 90 miles to that city to see if he could join, only to find it a fundraising scam. But this new expedition, clearly, is serious and, as news of the opportunity spreads by way of newspaper stories and word of mouth, he is one of an astonishing number of prospective expedition members to put in his application. And he is quick to write to his brother Charles in England to tell him the wonderful news, when it indeed breaks,

that the Committee has raised the money to match the anonymous
donation, just in time!

Melbourne, September 15th, 1859.

> *MY DEAR CHARLEY,*
> *... They have just succeeded in raising the two thousand pounds here,*
> *by subscription, that was wanted towards an exploration fund, for fitting*
> *out an expedition that will probably start for the interior of our continent*
> *next March. Camels have been sent for, to be used in places where horses*
> *cannot go. You would be astonished at the number of applications that*
> *are being made by people anxious to join the expedition. Nine-tenths*
> *of them would wish themselves home again before they had been out*
> *three months.*
>
> *Give my love to the two girls,*
> *and believe me,*
> *my dear Charley,*
>   *Your affectionate brother,*
>   *WILLIAM J. WILLS.*[32]

•

The press, it must be said, is a little less impressed, with the *Argus*,
for one, noting archly on 15 October 1859:

> The Exploration Committee are apparently having a short nap.
> We may echo the cry, which has been more than once raised in
> our columns – what are the Committee about? ... The map of
> Australia is a curiosity of the nineteenth century. Perhaps nothing
> approaching nearer to an absolute blank [exists].[33]

Still, for the moment, the Committee are not particularly fussed, for
they are on the edge of announcing the wonderful news, and come
8 November 1859, they can finally break it.

For it is on this momentous day that the Philosophical Institute
officially receives its long-sought Royal Charter – the imprimatur of
Queen Victoria herself – and will henceforth be known as the 'Royal
Society of Victoria'.

It is serendipitous synchronicity that sees them shortly thereafter move into their new premises at 8 La Trobe Street, an imposing Victorian building, constructed specifically for their purpose. For there it stands, an august red brick building of solid, stately splendour. Inside, the vaulted ceiling rises high above the single-level meeting hall, with imposing arch windows all around. It is a grand building fit for grand men to hatch grand plans.

For the Empire.

For Victoria.

For Queen Victoria.

Surely, the now *Royal* Society will be able to organise and launch what has confounded the mere *Philosophical* Institute?

Young William Wills is one who thinks so, taking his pen on a quiet night at Melbourne's Flagstaff Observatory ten days later to tell his beloved sister, Bessy, back in England,

> *It seems very likely that I shall be leaving Melbourne in March, to accompany the expedition for the exploration of the interior of this continent. It is calculated that we shall be away for about three years. It may be more, but it is not likely to be much less. It is not yet certain that I shall go. In fact, nothing is decided, not even who will be the leader; but I thought it would be as well to mention it to you now, as your answer to this cannot reach me until March . . . It is quite possible that I may not go, but it is more likely that I shall, as Professor Neumayer is very anxious that I should, to make magnetic and meteorological observations, and he is on the Exploration Committee. . .*[34]

And yet, while there really is progress in organising a possible expedition, the process of choosing a leader for it seems to have come to a dead stop.

John McDouall Stuart is surely the most industrious of explorers in Australia at this time, and he is demonstrably worth his salt, having been the right-hand man of the great explorer Charles Sturt. However, he is out in the interior right now, promising to better his teacher's efforts and reach the centre, if not all the way up to the northern coast of the continent. What's more, he is a South Australian.

The leader must be a Victorian.

Keep thinking, gentlemen . . .

•

The good news is that with £3000 raised towards the expedition, the Exploration Fund Committee is indeed able to approach the Victorian government for a further £6000, and on 20 January 1860, the money is approved by the Victorian Legislative Assembly! Now, *now* things start to move. For one, the fundraising committee is promptly dissolved.

25 January '60, Melbourne, in the beginning

At the first meeting of the new Exploration Committee of the Royal Society of Victoria, Sir William Stawell is voted in as chairman, with the former Mayor of Melbourne, John Hodgson, as vice chair, Dr David Wilkie as treasurer and Dr John Macadam as secretary. It is true that in the whole 18-man Committee there are just three members – Ferdinand Mueller, the government botanist and director of the Botanical Gardens; Clement Hodgkinson, the Victorian deputy surveyor-general; and Angus McMillan, a pioneer pastoralist – who have any background that touches on exploration, but that is simply the nature of a rich urban society – explorers are not thick on the ground.

The chief object of the discussion, and it goes for two hours on this alone, is who should lead the expedition, with Mueller being quick to suggest that Major Peter Warburton, the Police Commissioner of South Australia, with a strong record of exploration in that state, be interviewed as leader.

Ferdinand Mueller notes that Major Warburton is the obvious candidate because of his demonstrated 'zeal, untiring energy, and past experience in Australian exploration' and points out that, 'as Chief Commissioner of Police, and as a soldier, he is accustomed to direct and see his orders carried out'[35]. All that, and he has experience in travelling with camels in India, with no disasters. To top it all off, Augustus Gregory himself has 'given Warburton his warmest recommendation for the post'[36].

Now, it is true that Major Warburton – like Stuart – is not from the right colony, but does the Committee have any choice? No other particular candidates have emerged from Victoria and they must find *someone.* Warburton is, at least, a competent explorer – not to mention a man of impeccable pedigree, from an old aristocratic English family, the second son of a lord, with a fine Parisian education and good grasp of scientific matters. But a little too sure of himself? And more than a tad on the born-to-rule side of things? The Committee is aware of that.

After Warburton had rescued the lost explorer Benjamin Babbage in 1858, he had been more than free with his views – which had quickly reached the newspapers – that Babbage had brought water tanks that were 'rubbish' and 'utterly useless', that he was 'incurring great danger without the smallest real benefit', was 'erratic', 'injudicious', and he had left his own camp which was 'an act of insanity' and didn't care about 'the men he had deserted'[37]. In case the reader hadn't decided how Warburton felt about Babbage, he further explained, 'I am amazed when I consider Mr Babbage's ignorance, indifference and rashness.'[38]

Herein lies a possible problem. The Committee are after a 'gentleman' in the tradition of British exploration and, though Major Warburton has that pedigree by birth, his comments about Babbage show he does not quite make the grade in person. Still, Ferdinand Mueller, at least, is insistent that Commissioner Warburton is the best man for the job and – strongly supported by the great river explorer and society member, Captain Francis Cadell – Dr John Macadam, the ambitious young politician, seconds the motion 'with much pleasure'[39].

Motion carried.

Commissioner Warburton will be invited to 'an interview', from which point his appointment, everyone understands, will be a mere formality and the expedition can soon be on its way!

25 January '60, St Kilda, Mr Bruce makes up Macadam's mind

John Macadam?

Mr Bruce is here.

Well, show him in!

When politicians meet men whose wealth is at least a match for their own influence – and both sides want something from the other – crate-loads of courtesy may be counted on. Both men fit the part. John Macadam, the recently elected Member for Castlemaine, is a huge

Scot, whose barrel chest is only marginally more impressive than his full-flowing red beard and mane – and slightly less imposing than the rich cadence of his always eloquent words. Rare is the man of deep scientific background – the Scot is a chemist by training – whose skill in language at least matches it, but Macadam is that man. No matter that at just 32 he is younger than many of his Royal Society colleagues. As huge in physical stature as in vocabulary and ambitious energy, Macadam comes across as one who could out-debate most men in his big booming voice, while also beating them in an arm-wrestle, even while using his other hand to write out a dissertation on the finer points of analytical chemistry, which is his field of specialty. A force of nature, he has recently become a rising force in politics, courtesy, in no small way, beyond his undoubted talents, to the patronage of one of the most influential, and certainly the richest, men in Victoria . . .

For John Bruce, the well-known railway contractor from Castlemaine, as well as being a constant donor to great public causes such as the expedition fund, also happens to be the chief financial backer for Macadam's political career. (Now as financial backers go, they don't come much stronger than Mr Bruce, as he holds a contract for just under £3.5 million to construct the first leg of the Melbourne to Bendigo[40] railway – the biggest contract in the history of the Australian continent. It is true that Mr Bruce often courts controversy, as he is regularly accused of bribing politicians to get such contracts, and then bribing officials to turn a blind eye when his constructions might not technically fulfil every particular of them, but . . . powerful? Yes. And interested in opening up new lands, to which railways may well be built? Definitely!)

Mr Bruce – who is a member of the Royal Society and privy to most of the deliberations about the expedition – presents an idea to John Macadam, who is quickly convinced of its genius. Leave it with me, Mr Bruce, leave it with *me*.[41]

Yes, not for nothing is it Mr Bruce's boast to intimates that 'any man might be bought for money'[42], and it is for equally good reason that it will be said of him in the Victorian Parliament that he 'circulated more money and more patronage than the government or any individual in the colony'[43].

Mr Bruce is a man used to getting what he wants.

What he wants is the role of leader to be given to his 'personal friend'[44], Robert O'Hara Burke. Nobody else. Not even Major Warburton, the experienced explorer. Put simply, Burke is Bruce's kind of man. Well-born, but a man's man, he is charming and garrulous all at once, supremely well connected and a dreamer of dreams – all descriptions Mr Bruce answers to himself.

'If an angel from heaven had come down and volunteered to be leader,' the *Yeoman and Australian Acclimatiser* would later remark, 'he, too, would have been objected to.'[45]

Yes, it is quite true that Mr Burke has no experience in exploration and is a little on the eccentric side, a strange mix of otherwise contrary parts . . . Though a gentleman, he dresses like a peasant as a point of pride. Though careful with the safety of his men, he seems to delight in putting his own life in careless danger. Though he longs for family and stability, he is still a hopeless, impractical romantic when it comes to women, mooning over an actress half his age and beneath his station. While well educated and voraciously intelligent, he cannot discipline his mind to pass any practical exam. Though mostly loved by his men, he can be ruthless. Though he has travelled the world and speaks four languages, he now commands a provincial police force in an Antipodean backwater. Though the key upholder of the law in his region, one of his favourite activities is to travel to Benalla, for the sole purpose of swinging on the gate of a police magistrate who once displeased him. This magistrate, known as 'Pompous Piper'[46], is eccentric in himself, and it is known that while 'you might cut his flowers, pull his fruit, and run your dog through the grape vines, and he would hardly, even by look, express his displeasure, but if any one swung on his gate the whole concentrated indignation of his system burst forth'[47]. Ah, then, how many times would Pompous Piper look out from his front door to see Inspector Burke swinging steadily back and forth, staring straight at him!

'Actions of this sort in a grown man,' a colleague would note, 'can only indicate that there is something wrong with the brain.'[48]

But, you know what? Perhaps that is precisely what is required? After all, is it not mad in itself to think you could walk across a continent? Confronted with obstacles north of Cooper's Creek, hadn't

Thomas Mitchell, Charles Sturt, John McDouall Stuart and Augustus Gregory decided to a man, rationally, that it couldn't be done, and so had turned around? Perhaps, this time, what is needed is one who just refuses to bow to anyone or anything. Perhaps mad Mr Burke might be that very man?

And let's not forget his pedigree! Despite his, let's face it, rather devil-may-care slovenly appearance, he is of a fine family, and he is a gentleman with the courage we need and . . . maybe the madness.

•

It is the most remarkable thing, is it not?

At the meeting of the Exploration Committee on 30 January, John Macadam appears to have had a complete change of heart. No matter that he had championed the cause of Major Warburton just five days earlier, now he wants applications from new candidates for the post to be considered. What? New candidates? *Applications* for a filled position? 'Have you received any applications for the leadership?'[49] asks a startled Dr Mueller.

'I have received many applications for every department in the expedition,'[50] replies Dr Macadam smoothly.

Privately, Dr Macadam has already begun his campaigning to secure the role for Mr Bruce's favourite. *Between ourselves* – Mr Bruce considers Mr Burke no less than 'a personal friend' and I can tell you, any friend of Mr Bruce should be a friend to us all. Mr Bruce would very much appreciate Committee members – *no pressure, you understand?* – supporting his friend, and just the other day Mr Bruce said to Dr Macadam that, 'No other man living should lead the Victorian Expedition.'[51]

Dr Macadam, now that he comes to think of it, could not agree more! Mr Burke *is* the only man living who is fit for the job, and – no matter that just a few days ago they were robustly supporting Mr Warburton – other Committee members are soon equally enthusiastic.

How to get around the fact that Warburton has already been proposed?

Simple! Dr Macadam has thought of that, and now reveals it to all, including an alarmed Dr Mueller, shocked at how quickly everything is moving.

We will, Dr Macadam says, advertise the position in Victorian papers – but *certainly* not in South Australia or New South Wales. Yes, we will write to Major Warburton, inviting him to apply, but our advertisements will hopefully generate applications allowing us to go through a whole selection process. (At that point, the best man for the job, by which I mean the worthy Mr Burke – You understand? We have your support? I shall personally inform Mr Bruce of your excellent judgement – shall rise to the post.)

But now, Dr Macadam is careful, and as cunning as a digger on the Eureka with a 10-pound nugget hidden in his swag. What he says in the hallways of the Royal Society is not what he says in the meeting hall itself.

At meeting's end, a motion is passed: 'That public intimation be given to gentlemen desirous to offer their services for leadership of the Victorian Exploration, to put themselves in communication with the Secretary to the Exploration Committee on or before the first day of March of the present year.'[52]

It is agreed also 'that a special communication be forwarded to Major Warburton on the same subject'.[53]

To some of the press watching, whatever John Macadam's desire to be discreet about it all, it is quite strange that the same man who at the meeting on 25 January had seconded the nomination of Major Warburton 'with much pleasure'[54], is now backing an advertisement for a leader. As the *Age* comments:

> They are in a strange position ... They have invited Major Warburton to accept the appointment, and they have also asked others to apply for it. It remains to be seen whether this does not turn out to be a very characteristic blunder. Will Major Warburton not hesitate to accept under those circumstances, and may not other persons fully competent be prevented from offering themselves while the invitation to the Major remains open?[55]

For its part, the Melbourne *Herald* is outraged, sniffing at the very notion.

'Men of science, of enterprise, and with some knowledge of the ways of the world,' it thunders, 'do not relish the notion of being advertised for, as the keeper of a registry office advertises for a butler, housemaid or a cook.'[56]

That, dear friends, is the *point*, as far as Dr Macadam is concerned. Hopefully, Major Warburton will take precisely the same view and regard answering an ad, just like a washerwoman, as well beneath his dignity. And the problem will be solved. Major Warburton will step back, Mr Burke will step forward, and Mr Bruce will be *happy*. Yes, though it is not obvious at the time, it will later become clear:

> A powerful clique, embracing a few members of the Committee and some persons outside of it, entered into something like a conspiracy that one man, and he only, should obtain the appointment as leader.[57]

That clique is indeed led by Dr John Macadam, the Member for Castlemaine, and soon has such influential backers as Sir William Stawell himself. As to the one man they want, he is the new toast of the Melbourne Club. Gentlemen, please lift your glasses to . . . Robert O'Hara Burke!

CHAPTER TWO

A HERD OF CAMELS, A WINNOWING OF EXPLORERS

I have only one ambition, which is to do some deed before I die, that shall entitle me to have my name honourably inscribed on the page of history. If I succeed in that I care not what death, or when I die.[1]

Robert O'Hara Burke to a friend, 1860

Let any man lay the map of Australia before him, and regard the blank upon its surface, and then let me ask him if it would not be an honourable achievement to be the first to place foot in its centre. Men of undoubted perseverance and energy in vain had tried to work their way to that distant and shrouded spot. A veil hung over Central Australia that could neither be pierced or raised. Girt round about by deserts, it almost appeared as if Nature had intentionally closed it upon civilized man, that she might have one domain on the earth's wide field over which the savage might roam in freedom.[2]

Charles Sturt reflecting on his previous expeditions to the interior in 1844–46 in his *Narrative of an Expedition into Central Australia*, 1849

Beechworth and Castlemaine, early '60, the writing on the wall

Perhaps you can tell something of a man by what he chooses to put on his walls?

Fine art bespeaks a certain sophistication.

Books, a desire for learning.

Other shelving, a utilitarianism.

Blank walls, either poverty, a certain spartan nature, or both.

Robert O'Hara Burke has on his walls something no one has ever seen before.

They are pasted scraps of paper, filled with 'quotations from Byron, Heine, Berger, and other poets, forage accounts, musical scores of mild and touching airs, brands of lost cattle, sketches of friends and foes, designs for a service boot or a camp kettle . . .'[3] Right in the middle of them all hangs a sign, in large black letters:

Visitors are requested not to read the memoranda on these walls.
I cannot keep any record in a systematic manner, so I jot things down like this.[4]

As strange as that is, stranger still is that every month all the notices are taken down, the walls are whitewashed, and then, bit by bit a fresh slew of signs goes up, with fresh quotations, followed soon enough, by the sign.

The only thing besides the sign that doesn't change is an article published in 1854, written by the war correspondent of the *Times* and faithfully reprinted by Australian papers, including Castlemaine's *Mount Alexander Mail*, of what had happened to Burke's beloved brother, James, in the Crimean War.

> When he first leapt on shore: from the boat six soldiers charged him. Two he shot with his revolver, one he cut down with his sword – the rest turned and fled. [Next] a number of riflemen advanced from behind a ditch, and took deliberate aim at him. Poor Burke charged them with headlong gallantry. As he got near he was struck by a ball, which broke his jawbone, but he rushed on, shot three men dead at close quarters with his revolver and cleft two men through helmet and all into the brain with his sword.
>
> He was then surrounded, and while engaged in cutting his way with heroic courage through the ranks of the enemy, a sabre cut from behind, given by a dragoon as he went by, nearly severed his head from his body; and he fell dead covered with bayonet

wounds, sabre gashes, and marked with lance thrusts and bullet holes. Mr Burke's body was found after the action in which he had lost his life, with no less than 33 wounds upon it.[5]

When first apprised of the news of his brother's death – the first British officer killed in the Crimean War – Burke had been found, clutching the letter, still in tears.

'I have just learned the particulars of my brother's fate,' he told the policeman who happened upon him, 'but it is not his dying that moves me in this way, but the glory of his death.'[6]

Burke can only dream of such a glorious end. His own attempt to join the British war effort in the Crimea, sailing from Australia in March 1856 to share in his brother's glory, was abruptly aborted – he had arrived *just that little bit too late*. There had been nothing for it but to return to Australia and resume where he had left off.

But his obsession with his brother's death certainly worries his colleagues, one of them later noting, 'Burke's intellect was unhinged . . . the apparent reason for it a sabre wound and a disappointment in love . . . I think that the insanity was intensified . . . by the illustrated account of the death of Burke's brother. Burke always kept the picture of the tragic death of his brother in a top drawer, from which I have seen him over and over again take it out, and, placing it on the table before him, sit down and study it closely without speaking a word for perhaps twenty minutes. His elbows would be on the table and his head supported by both hands, whilst his wild-looking eyes bulged and flashed, keeping time to the surging thoughts that crowded through his brain . . . I am satisfied that the constant contemplation of the picture I refer to sensibly aggravated the irritation from which his brain unquestionably suffered.'[7]

Perhaps driven by such mental aggravation, Burke continues to search for something that will soak up his restless, roving energy.

'I wish I had something to do that would take the sting out of me,'[8] he was often heard to cry.

Yes, a strange man Robert O'Hara Burke, and a shambolic one, in all things bar the way he led his men, where, as one colleague would later recall, 'to a very large extent [he] was a rigid disciplinarian, bordering on the martinet . . .'[9]

Not that he is despised, by any means. For Robert O'Hara Burke has long had a way with his men, which means that, on a good day, they love him well.

In a story that would long be told by those there at the time, there had been an occasion a few years ago while he was still at Beechworth, on the morning of St Patrick's Day when, in jocular homage to him and his well-known passion for the Emerald Isle of his birth, his constables – all of the constables, English, Irish, Welsh and Scotch – had formed up in the courtyard of Beechworth Police Station sporting shamrocks in their caps, and . . .

And here he comes now!

Grinning from ear to ear, proudly bearing their shamrocks, his men had stood to attention, waiting for Inspector Burke to notice. Alas, as he emerges from his bath – shambling and ambling his way back to his quarters – in his shirtsleeves, his braces hanging loose, his hair uncombed, saliva hanging like a spring from his beard, he walks by with his head down and doesn't even notice! His face is all thunder and lightning, with troubles unknown.

The sergeant, as sergeants have always been wont to do, takes charge. 'Atten-SHUN!' he calls.

Burke, sure enough, looks up to see the cause of the fuss and, in an instant, takes it all in, his men are paying him homage in an unexpected and charming fashion. Taking the sergeant aside, he says, 'Let the man stand easy till I return', before marching off to his quarters.

Just five minutes later he is back in his regular daily uniform, but this time complete with a shamrock in his cap.

The men cheer, even before he can say 'Right face, Dismiss . . .' and in short order the cadets are in his quarters, knocking back whiskey, given by Burke, 'With his compliments, to drown their shamrocks . . .'[10]

It is typical of him.

On the occasion of the Buckland riots in the winter of 1857, the first detachment of 24 police to arrive on the scene – to try to quell the violent rising of some 700 European miners against the detested 'Celestials', the Chinese miners – was under the command of Inspector

Robert O'Hara Burke. He and another mounted man led the two dozen constables in coaches forward. Just as they arrived on the outskirts of Buckland, a man came galloping up to advise, 'the rioters have shot Constable Duffy!'[11] and have set up barricades along the road.

As later recounted by the *Ovens and Murray Advertiser*, 'Mr Burke ordered the men to dismount from the coaches, to fall in and load, and then directed the [only other] mounted man to take one side of the road in front while he took the other. The second in command expostulated with him, saying he ought to look to himself for the sake of the men as there were known to be from 400 to 500 rioters. His answer was "forward; if there is any danger my place is in front".'[12]

Far from being afraid of death, there is even something a little fatalistic about Burke.

Once, when his duties required him to forge the raging torrent of a river, after extremely heavy overnight rain, one of his fellow officers begged him to wait till the waters subsided, Burke laughed off the very suggestion.

'No,' said he, 'it does not do for a commanding officer to shirk a danger that you are constantly obliged to face in the ordinary course of duty. But ... you may come with me to the crossing, as should I be drowned, I would like someone to see the last of me.'[13]

It was almost as if he knew more about the mystical nature of death than most.

'He had that peculiar far off look,' it would be said of him, 'as if he saw something beyond, which the superstitious have attributed to persons who are destined to die a strange death ...'[14]

He is a rough, tough, shambolic bastard, but not a bad one. Indeed, when the officers under his command in Beechworth were informed of his transfer to Castlemaine, back in 1858, they had petitioned for him to be able to stay. Their efforts failed, so to show their regard for the departing leader, they presented him with a pair of fine pistols bearing the inscription, 'Presented to R. O'Hara Burke Esq. Supt. of Police by the Officers of the district on his transfer from Beechworth, November 1858'.

While such respect keeps Burke satiated, it is far from the glory he craves.

But just in the last ten days, he has been focused as rarely before, for the very thing to take that sting out of him might suddenly and propitiously have emerged.

First, he had been approached by his dear friend, Mr John Vans Agnew Bruce, with the idea that *he* should apply to lead the Victorian Expedition across Australia. The Royal Society's Honorary Secretary, John Macadam, has agreed to push him, as has none other than the chair of the Exploration Committee, Sir William Stawell, both of whom Burke knows through the Melbourne Club. John Bruce is determined to make this happen, so long as Burke agrees.

('With respect to Burke,' Bruce would later note, 'I take credit for myself for being the first to invite him to strive for the leadership. I went to town with him, worked hard to get him the appointment . . .'[15])

Burke is interested from the first. He had been an early modest donor to the fundraising, contributing 10 shillings, and had subsequently noted the advertisements appearing in the paper, from 1 February on – appearing every day thereafter in the *Argus*, and twice a week in the *Age* – just as Mr Bruce had told him there would be. He knows all about the expedition, and is impressed to have such powerful sponsors behind him. It is a worthwhile thing to do, with one enormous bonus.

'If I get the leadership and come out successful,' he tells a friend, 'I have no doubt but that Julia will accept my offer of marriage.'[16]

Now, at his behest, a friend and colleague from the Victoria Police, Inspecting Superintendent Peter Henry Smithe, is putting forward Burke's name to lead the expedition across the country! It is for Burke himself to oversee its writing . . .

Castlemaine
7th February 1860

My dear Dr,

My friend and brother Officer Mr Robt O'Hara Burke, Supt. of Police in charge of this district is most anxious to obtain command of the Expln. Party. Sir Wm. Stawell is acquainted with Mr Burke, and I believe will give him his vote and interest. Mr Burke is an honourable man, was for many years Captn. in a Dragoon Regt. in Austria where

he distinguished himself, subsequently held a Commission in the Irish
Constabulary and is now a Supt. in our own Police.

Mr Burke speaks and writes French, German and Italian. He is a
most active man and very strong – most temperate in his habits – and is
kind and gentle in his manners, but possessing a strong will – ambitious
– and had been accustomed to command from boyhood. Mr Burke is
prepared to give up his present appointment to succeed to that of yours.

In conclusion, I am confident from my knowledge of Mr Burke that
there is not another Gentleman in this Colony possessing so many of the
qualifications necessary to the success of the undertaking in question as
my friend Burke.

I remain,
my dear Dr
Yours truly,
P. N. Smithe.[17]

•

Meantime?

Meantime, even as the plans of the Victorian Exploration Committee
twist in the wind, over in South Australia, John McDouall Stuart has
smoothly put his plans in place and sets off for the northern coast,
using the small depot he has established 400 miles north of Adelaide as
his jumping off point. (He is travelling light, with just two companions
on horseback and a bare minimum of rations – a little flour, sugar
and dried beef – but a maximum capacity to live off the land, carrying
guns, ammunition and fishing lines. No luxury tents for them. Why
bother, when it is as good to sleep in a swag and spare yourself the
colossal weight and time-wasting activity represented by having canvas
over your head?)

The news that Stuart is on his way throws the total *lack* of movement
in Victoria into stark relief, a fact that the *Argus* is quick to point out:
'The Exploration Fund Committee are in an embarrassing position.
Time presses. The season of the year at which the expedition should
set out is rapidly passing away; the camels have not yet arrived; and
no leader has been appointed.'[18]

Clearly what the Exploration Committee must do is *get moving*, just as Stuart is now moving, and within days, a sub-committee convenes in the Royal Society's hall and begins the process of going through the 14 serious applications for leader that have been winnowed down from the 18 applications received.

•

For the most part, the applications are a depressing mixture of the absurd and the irrelevant, sent by the clearly unqualified. But one application, from a Mr John Frizzell, is of particular interest:

> As the 'Camels' are now in all probability purchased for the expedition,
> [I] would have them with keepers (who should be natives or 'Coolies'
> accustomed to manage or drive them) landed, not in Melbourne – but on
> the North Shore of Australia Say at Port Essington – or at the mouth
> of the Albert River mentioned by Stokes with the positive instructions to
> remain there until called upon, I would then 'Ship' the Exploring party
> with the necessary provisions, implements, Boats, &, &, and dispatch
> them, to the appointed rendezvous. I would follow up the river to its
> source, and there establish a permanent Depot, and when all would be in
> readiness I would start on the exploration direct South . . .
>   [Heading thus, and with the] 'Northerly Sirocco' blowing not in their
> faces as with former explorers starting from the South, but in the backs
> of the party and assisting them forward, and what would still further
> stimulate their efforts, would be the consideration that every day would
> bring them nearer to the Abodes of Civilization, their homes, and the
> Cities of the South, this idea would stimulate them to go forward over
> the 'Sahara Australis' – if such they would meet with – invigorated
> minds to the performance of their duties . . . [19]

Mr Frizzel generously adds in a postscript: 'I shall write you again on the probable route – you are at liberty to make the best use of this letter. JF'[20]

Which is as well. Because he does, and they do.

There is, too, an application from Royal Society member and pastoralist William Lockhart Morton, who has a little experience in exploring, having led last year a small expedition north of Rockhampton looking for grazing runs, but no one takes that quite seriously.

Major Warburton maintains a stony silence. He is the Commissioner of the South Australian Police Force and a *gentleman*. He does not (*sniff*) answer Positions Vacant ads. He finds the whole idea *well* beneath him.

February '60, Melbourne, the best test designed for future failure

What though, of this application from Superintendent Robert Burke, of Castlemaine, the one whose name keeps being pushed by Dr Macadam, our honorary secretary, and Sir William Stawell, our chair?

It is, in truth, as one of the Committee members will later describe it, 'no application worthy of the name'[21], but at least that senior officer of the Victoria Police had bolstered it somewhat with his personal testament that waxes lyrical about Burke's many desirable attributes. He is, thus, one worth considering – which is something, given there really are so few other applications with *anything* commending them.

For now, there is much deliberation, much impassioned argument with many meetings and several votes taken with no clear majority for any applicant, as other names, too, have powerful backers on the Committee, with Major Warburton still being strongly pushed by the likes of Ferdinand Mueller and the riverboat captain and explorer Captain Francis Cadell.

Some think Cadell himself could do the job. After all, this is a bloke with a military past, who is used to command, who has taken his own vessel up the Amazon River, who penetrated the River Murray further than any before, opening up steam navigation and commerce with the Riverina squatters. His courage is beyond question, his skill there for all to see, his zeal for adventure precisely what we are looking for?

Whatever else, he *looks* the part.

'He wore a prolonged sort of Norfolk jacket', a contemporary would describe him, 'gathered in at the waist with a broad leather belt, and continuations of blue dungaree, which partially obscured a pair of dainty patent leather shoes, the whole finished off on top with an irreproachable black bell-topper . . . With pistols in his belt he would have passed muster as a medieval pirate . . . But when he started talking all sense of the incongruous vanished, and he appeared in his true light, as a man who had been almost everywhere, done most things that a man may do and keep his name sweet, and lost large sums of money in doing some of them. But always with a clean record, a light heart, and a smile that held his audience as with a grapnel.'[22]

So when Cadell speaks, passionately, in favour of Warburton – and he does – he is worth listening to.

But is it all a waste of time? Is the fix already in?

Why, look here, as on 16 February, a most telling article appears in the *Bendigo Advertiser*:

> **THE GOVERNMENT EXPLORING EXPEDITION.**
> We understand that Mr Bourke, Chief Superintendent of Police at Castlemaine, has been appointed to the command of the proposed exploration party. From the recognised ability of the gentleman and his experience of the country, we may augur a successful result to the undertaking.[23]

Outrageous!

Dr Mueller for one is appalled by the presumption and sincerely trusts that he can stop the manifestly unqualified Mr Burke becoming the leader, but the question is, *how*?

A close observer of proceedings is the German artist and scientist Dr Ludwig Becker – himself a member of the Royal Society, and noted by his acquaintance Lady Denison, the wife of the Governor of Van Diemen's Land, as 'one of those universal geniuses who can do anything; a very good naturalist, geologist, &c., draws and plays and sings, conjures and ventriloquises and imitates the notes of birds so accurately that the wild birds will come to him at the sound of the call'[24]. Becker is, further, all but confirmed as an officer on the expedition, and in a letter to his friend Dr Mueller, he suggests a solution, one that will get them back to the most obvious candidate all along, Major Warburton:

'My plan is: No leader has to be elected from among those 14 men as no one can be elected among them: this will become evident in the course of an examination of the candidates.'

A test! One that Burke is sure to fail. Excellent solution. The candidates will all be questioned on

1) Astronomical knowledge, taking the meridian etc.
2) Surveying and map-making.
3) Knowledge about the nature of the country

Ludwig Becker lays out nine separate categories to bedazzle Burke.

'As I am certain that there is nobody among these 14 who would obtain No 1 in all these 9 points; their claim falls away, time is won, and Warburton will be asked to take command, and so the damaging consequences of the stupid advertising will be avoided . . .'[25]

Dr Mueller is delighted at this elegant and practical solution to the problem of Mr Burke. It makes sense! Within a week, the *Argus* reports: 'We are informed that the Exploration Committee have resolved to defer their proposed expedition into the interior for three months.' Why? Well, 'none of the candidates who have applied for the leadership are in all respects suitable, chiefly through their want of astronomical knowledge'. Just as Becker suggested, the *Argus* notes an impending test. 'In the course of three months, one or two of the candidates now applying for the leadership, and in all other respects eligible, will have learnt, it is hoped, to take "lunars".'[26]

(This grasp of the basics of astronomy, of being able to determine longitude and latitude from the position of the sun and the moon at given times of day, is regarded by many as the *sine qua non* of being the expedition leader. For without being able to determine precisely where on earth you are, the leader himself will soon become lost. And, frankly, the whole discussion scares Burke a little. If you ask his former officers back in Beechworth, they'll be quick to remark that 'he could not tell the north from the south in broad daylight, and the Southern Cross as a guide was a never ending puzzle to him. If he were not closely looked after on a bad track, somebody else had to find him as he would certainly lose himself.'[27])

•

'You will be glad to learn,' William Wills writes to his worried mother, 'that the Exploring Expedition is postponed . . . for want of a suitable leader, as none of the candidates who offered their services were thought qualified in a scientific point of view.'[28]

So, his mother may stay calm for now, as his departure is not as imminent as supposed.

But it will come. There are well over a dozen men who will embark on the expedition and William Wills is insistent that he will be among their number. On that subject he wishes for his beloved mother to understand his reasoning.

'You need not work yourself up to such a state of excitement at the bare idea of my going,' he writes, 'but should rather rejoice that the opportunity presents itself. The actual danger is nothing, and the positive advantages very great. Besides, my dear mother, what avails your faith if you terrify yourself about such trifles? Were we born, think you, to be locked up in comfortable rooms, and never to incur the hazard of a mishap? If things were at the worst, I trust I could meet death with as much resignation as others, even if it came tonight. I am often disgusted at hearing young people I know, declare that they are afraid of doing this or that, because they *might* be killed. Were I in some of their shoes I should be glad to hail the chance of departing this life fairly in the execution of an honourable duty.'[29]

10 April '60, Collins St, Melbourne, His Excellency's excellent remarks

Sparkles from the chandeliers, sparkle from the wine, sparkles in the eyes, sparkles in the repartee. It is the inaugural annual dinner of the Royal Society of Victoria, if you please, held at the Criterion Hotel in Collins Street, and we are now at the climactic moment, the address to be given by Sir Henry Barkly, the Governor of Victoria who is also the President of our *Royal* Society, did we mention that Her Majesty has conferred that extraordinary honour upon us?

'Gentlemen of the Royal Society of Victoria,' the great man begins, before warming to the virtues of coming together to support, for the purpose of scientific inquiry ' . . . the exploration of the interior. I rejoice that this Colony is at length about to take its share in this important

National duty. Our very presence here tonight may be said to be attributable to the love of science and of maritime discovery which the Anglo-Saxon race has always displayed, for you will remember that it was to observe the transit of Venus over the Sun that Captain Cook was dispatched on his first voyage to the Southern Ocean, and but for his subsequent exploration of the east coast of Australia, this continent might never have been colonised by the British nation.

'It seems but right, then, that this, the wealthiest and most civilised of the communities which have hence sprung into existence, should make some effort to advance the cause to which it owes its origin.

'I trust that every pains will be taken in the spring to organise and equip an expedition worthy of this colony, and that by the commencement of the ensuing summer it will be on its way, under a leader of approved ability, to the Depot selected upon Cooper's Creek – which marks the northern frontier of the land explored by white men – as the basis of its operations, so as to be ready to take advantage of the first rains that may fall, to prosecute its researches.

'The precise direction of these must necessarily be left a good deal to the discretion of the leader to be chosen ... My own opinion has, however, always been in favour of directing the earlier efforts of the expedition to ascertaining the exact eastern limits of the Great Desert, with a view to crossing as directly as possible to the Gulf of Carpentaria.'[30]

Hear, hear.

Oh, *hear, hear*!

Still, bemused at such carry-on when the Victorians have no means of transport, no settled plan, no leader, no supplies, all while their own hero is well on his way, South Australia's leading paper, the *South Australian Advertiser*, can't resist firing a friendly jibe:

> Only let the Victorian explorers look out for their laurels. It is quite possible and by no means improbable that at this moment the problem of the interior is solved and that John McDouall Stuart will be back in time to show the camels a beaten track through the heart of the Australian mainland.[31]

14 June '60, Hobson's Bay, Melbourne, one hump or two?

They are here! They are *here*!

It has taken over a year and a half to organise, and 10 weeks on the high seas, but on this fine day, not only are the 25 camels unloaded – by using a steam-driven crane with massive slings – from the good ship *Chinsurah* onto the Railway Pier at Hobson's Bay, but now they are led through the streets of Melbourne, the passage kept clear by the constables lining the route! Get back, get *back*! The population, completely agog, do indeed stand back, cheer, stare, gasp and applaud, even as police continue to press the crowd back.

Just look at those extraordinary creatures! It is said of the Australian platypus, you'll recall, that it was made of all the pieces that God had left over on the sixth day, and these camels are much the same . . . but it is not until you see them up close that you get any idea of the *size* of them! The grotesque heads! The wooden pegs through their noses! Their grimaces! The 'nurrr, *nurrr*, NURRRRRR' noise they make!

Some observers notice that any horse within coo-ee suddenly shies away. Apparently Australian horses react the opposite way to Australian people; they are *terrified* by the camels.

'The camels marched in procession,' the *Argus* reports, 'each of the swifter kind with its turbaned rider on its back, picturesquely attired in white and red, followed by the burden-bearing-animals . . .'[32]

They are, in sum, quite the sensation. Melburnians – who had recently been flocking to an exhibition of a stuffed gorilla – thought they had seen it all. But never like *this*.

And doesn't Mr Landells know it, as he somehow sits securely upon the single hump of his favourite camel, Golah. Out in front, 'in his Oriental costume'[33], leading the procession triumphantly into Melbourne, surely Napoleon returning to Paris after the successful conquest of Egypt did not muster such sheer élan.

Not long ago a mere horse-trader, this now Emperor of the Exotic and Quixotic, who has even begun signing his official reports 'Camel Agent to the Government of Victoria',[34] is gracious enough on this day to occasionally offer a languid hand of acknowledgement to the roaring crowds. What does it matter that he has spent double the budget given him by the Committee and is arriving some months later than scheduled, when you get a reception like this?

Following Mr Landells closely – wide-eyed at the roar of the crowd – are the nine Indian sepoys, each on a camel of his own, who are now finding themselves in a mysterious land, and are clearly not at all happy with it. The sepoys, like the camels, have been recruited by Mr Landells from as far afield as deep northern India and Afghanistan, and have never felt so far from home.

And now, who are the three white men coming right up the back, one of whom is much younger, and distinctly wide-eyed? No one knows him, as he has never been in our fair city before, but it is in fact young John King, a 21-year-old Irishman who has seen service with the British Army in India and speaks the same language as the sepoys. King had been discharged by his 70th Regiment after contracting 'fever of a bad type'[35], and Mr Landells had promptly hired him to accompany him to Australia, and look after the sepoys, who had never been to sea before.

The *Argus* warmly approves of the whole thing.

'They certainly are magnificent animals,' the paper notes, and makes a firm prediction. 'Years hence, Australia will boast of its race of camels as England does now of her horse.'[36]

As to the Exploration Committee, they are so caught up in the excitement of the camels that on this very day they pass a motion to buy half-a-dozen camels from the local menagerie of George Coppin at £50 a head, to be added to the newly arrived Indian herd. It will give the expedition as many as 30 camels to depart with, bound to cross Australia!

Still, it is not as if everyone is impressed.

As one newspaper correspondent writes, one puzzled gold digger, after having quite a few drinks at a Melbourne pub, strolled down to take a gander at the new arrivals. The old soak gazed upon the famous camels then wondered out loud, in his slurred tones, what all the fuss *ish* about? Surely, horses would be better anyways?

At this point 'a kindly old gentleman explained that, as the centre of Australia was an arid, waterless country, they were the more suitable animals as they could go without a drink for a week. The horrified digger replied, "Well, who wants to be a camel, anyway?"'[37]

20 June '60, Royal Society of Victoria, a gentlemanly vote: full, fair and fixed

The initial applications have been whittled down to six by a sub-committee, and now a final decision must be made. The Governor of Victoria, His Excellency Sir Henry Barkly, is in attendance for the occasion, while it is Sir William Stawell who presides over the process. Some members of the Committee, Warburton's strongest backers, are notably *not* in attendance – no Ferdinand Mueller, no Captain Cadell.

Why not?

For the simple reason that, in their view, the whole affair is a sham, a charade and a shameful corruption all in one. Having observed the machinations of Dr Macadam and his cronies over the last months, they know all too well what the result of the so-called 'election' is going to be. With strong feeling abroad that there are 'base and shameless personal motives at work'[38], they have better things to do with their time than take part in a puppet show. It is a *disgrace* – did they mention? – to reduce science to such politicking and petty games. (Not that Mueller is above such games himself. It was he, after all, who took up Dr Ludwig Becker's suggestion of an astronomy test, which they knew Mr Burke would fail. In fact, they had simply been out-manoeuvred as Mr Bruce and Dr Macadam are old hands at the science of politics and had neatly bypassed Mueller's scientific gambit. Mr Burke has learnt nothing of the stars, but he is about to be one.)

The actual vote will be based on the 'Australian ballot', sometimes known as 'a secret ballot' – a way of voting in private introduced as a result of the political reforms ushered in by the Eureka Stockade. The final list of six nominations is led by Mr Robert O'Hara Burke and Major Peter Warburton, with *Herr* Gustavus von Tempsky next on the list, along with three more, each with some exploration experience: Mr Samuel Parry, Mr Baldwin Fraser and Mr Lockhart Morton.

Then begins a long discussion. Alas for Major Warburton, without Ferdinand Mueller or Captain Cadell in the room, he has no hope. Even though Macadam reads a letter from the explorer addressing the Committee, the pre-vote discussion tends to remain focused on the relative merits of Robert O'Hara Burke and von Tempsky.

One by one, each man on the Committee writes the name of one of the candidates on a piece of paper, which he then folds and gravely places in the slot of the ballot box.

And the winner is – just as the *Bendigo Advertiser* had rather peremptorily, but *accurately*, announced back in February – Superintendent Robert O'Hara Burke!

It is in fact, not even close.

Burke receives 10 votes, and Warburton five, while . . . the number of votes for Gustavus von Tempsky could be counted on the fingers of a double amputee. A thumping triumph for Robert O'Hara Burke! (Oh. And Dr Macadam and Mr Bruce.)

The *Mount Alexander Mail*, Burke's local paper, greets the news with proud acclaim that their man – who has spent no time in the Australian bush and has neither scientific nor navigational skills – has been accorded such an honour.

THE LEADER OF THE EXPLORING EXPEDITION.

Mr Burke has been elected in a manner that not only silences all cavil, but that shows conclusively the committee's conviction of his pre-eminent suitability . . . Mr Burke is a gentleman in the prime of life, a perfect centaur as to horsemanship, they say; and accustomed to command . . . His personal qualities as an officer are thus stated by his commander, Captain Standish: 'Mr Burke possesses indomitable pluck, energy, great powers of endurance, and the by no means useless talent of making himself beloved by those serving with or under him, without relaxing the rules of discipline.'[39]

•

For the most part, Burke's colleagues, while pleased for him, are somewhere between bemused and . . . concerned. Even those who actively love Burke as a man and a leader of men are not always sure it is a wise choice. For, we must face this. There is the very real issue that, beyond merely his eccentricity, some question his . . . sanity. No, not that he is insane, *per se*, just that he might not be, you know, quite all there.

In reference to the sabre wound he had received in Austria – reportedly in a duel 'over a Hungarian beauty', who, not for the first time, had broken his heart – one of his fellow officers would be frank.

'I believe [it] affected his brain ever afterwards,' he would note. 'I was often struck by the fact that Burke was absolutely destitute of fear . . . Either he did not realise danger, or his mind was unhinged to that extent that he revelled in it. [But he] was decidedly eccentric to a degree which caused numbers of his friends to suspect that he was not quite sane – an opinion I share myself . . .'[40]

Another man, a bank manager who had come to know Burke well over several years, was later to note, 'I never discovered in him the qualities for such a leadership. He was a careless, daredevil sort of Irishman of very ordinary physique. He wore a long beard, over which he dribbled his saliva. When he was off duty he often wore a slouching sombrero-like hat, and as he did not wear braces his breeches hung in rolls about his heels, and he looked all together untidy . . . It was told of him as a good joke, but true nevertheless, that when he was returning from Yakanandah to Beechworth, he lost his way, although the track was well beaten and frequented, and did not arrive at his destination until many hours after he was due. He was in no sense a bushman.'[41]

For the cadets who are in on the running joke, which morphs into a new version with every telling – 'Burke had once lost himself on the main road between Kyneton and Bendigo, and turned up just as an expedition was being organised to search for him'[42] – his appointment as leader, though applauded, has a perplexing whiff about it.

To be sure – despite his many charms, however considerable they might be – no one ever said he was organised. Why, look at his erratic wall of notes – apparently the only way he knows how to keep track of things. Just look at the way he presents himself!

One acquaintance is frank, later noting of the man he calls a 'privileged Bohemian', that 'Burke prided himself on slovenliness . . . I have seen him wearing an old worn out slouch felt hat, odd boots, trousers – the legs of which were of different lengths, and a coat which never could have come in its then shape from any sane tailor. Burke was only known to have worn his uniform on one occasion, that being the visit of Governor to the Ovens, and even then he only sported it for half an hour.'[43]

Systematically shambolic, anything that connotes attention to detail is simply not in Burke's nature. Witness his attendance at church. Instead of sitting alone, as befits an officer, he usually sits among the men, simply so he can read the prayer book of the constable next to him, 'for, of course, he had no prayer-book of his own'[44].

But, for all that, he has pedigree, and is, most importantly of all, a gentleman. And that counts for a lot!

The Melbourne *Herald*, previously bitterly critical of the Exploration Committee for its treatment of Major Warburton and its endless dilly-dallying, now commends the Committee's selection process, lauding it as 'exhaustive . . . conducted throughout with strict impartiality'[45].

For Burke personally, the news is extremely welcome, even if he is more than a little put out by how forcefully the likes of Captain Cadell have been in speaking of the risks the Committee takes in picking him. Such criticism stings, but it is an irritant with which Mr Burke soon becomes all too familiar.

But, for the moment, that trouble is as nothing to his triumph.

Now, will the delectable Julia Matthews give him the attention, the love, he deserves? Well, perhaps, if he returns as he intends as the conquering hero.

One friend, at least, hopes that the prestigious appointment, the monumental opportunity and challenge that presents itself, will snap Burke out of his generally depressed state due to his 'monomania'[46] over Julia Matthews.

'Burke was a changed man,' John Sadleir would record of his colleague's state over the unrequited romance. 'He seemed to lose all his interest in life, and his eagerness to lead the expedition to the Gulf of Carpentaria seemed to all who knew his story nothing but the desire of a man suffering severe mental anguish to seek forgetfulness.'[47]

But looking at him now, striding victoriously around Melbourne Town, onlookers could surely not fathom his former anguish and despair. He seems unstoppable.

Before anything else, Burke is quick to have a portrait taken of himself with that new-fangled photography thing, then placed in a locket which he offers to young Julia and she accepts, she *accepts*.

No, it is no testament of her undying love for him, which he still must earn, but it is *some* sign that her estimation of him has risen since he became the talk of all the colony. Burke's heart sings with the wonder of it all, no doubt often with Julia's favourite song that he knows so well, 'Sweet Spirit, Hear My Prayer'.[48]

News that his contract with the Exploration Committee will see him on a £500 per annum salary is more than welcome. It is true that the taking of the portrait and the purchase of the locket has left him with just a little over seven shillings in his bank account, hardly enough to meet his pressing debts . . .

(*Quietly?* Superintendent Burke is a heavy gambler, most particularly playing the card game cribbage at the Melbourne Club, and is in more than a mere spot of financial bother. For all the powerful connections he makes at 'the club', and he certainly does, the thing is . . . the promissory notes he has been in the habit of writing can only go so far. His debts currently add up to just a little under £500, meaning that if he can pull off this trip, he could return just about debt free.)

Late June '60, Melbourne, poison pens, Justinian jibes, anonymous antagonists

The selection of Burke for the important role of expedition leader soon begins to receive its fair share of criticism, with no barbs more pointed than a letter published in the *Argus* at the end of June, written by 'Justitia', but widely believed to be by Major Peter Warburton, whose own qualifications for the role were ample, self-evident, and yet denied.

> When the lives of so many men are at stake, placed in the power of
> an incompetent man – as I shall endeavour to show the gentleman
> nominated is – it is time that something were done to prevent the
> destruction, ruin, and disgrace certain to follow . . .

These prove to be merely Justitia's opening remarks, for he goes on . . .

. . . he has not had the slightest experience as a bush-traveller . . . he knows nothing about exploring, and has never attempted to try anything of the kind; in short, has had no practice whatever as a bushman, never having camped even in the bush, and never been in any part of Australia where there are no roads . . . He cannot construct a map of his course, should he be sent with the party . . . he is altogether ignorant of any of the physical sciences . . . his literary ability is so small that he could not write an intelligent account of the journey . . . he knows nothing whatever of astronomical science – cannot take even the sun's elevation to find his latitude! Surely a more incompetent man never in the world's history entered upon an enterprise so great and responsible. With such facts before me, I have, as a citizen of Victoria, fulfilled my duty in thus exposing a shameless trans-action, and removed from my door the blood of those that must perish under such leadership . . .

Justitia[49]

Good heavens! Such an unexpected attack.

And yet, there is more to come, with another letter by 'Scientia', appearing in the Melbourne press shortly afterwards, taking specific aim at Burke's lack of scientific expertise, as well.

THE EXPLORATORY EXPEDITION — IS THE RIGHT MAN IN THE RIGHT PLACE?

TO THE EDITOR OF THE AGE.

Sir,— . . . It is right for us to expect in the person chosen some acquaintance with the natural sciences; for in the course of his operations he will be called upon to make reports upon the botanical, geological, meteorological and kindred phenomena that he may meet with. It is desirable also that he should be in some degree a draftsman; and able to determine his position with tolerable accuracy . . .

If Mr B.'s scientific attainments are equal to the task, let the public know them; if they are not, the public will protest against a piece of cliqueism in which the interests of the country are again sacrificed to please and serve the purposes of an unscrupulous and dangerous party.

Yours, &c.,

SCIENTIA.[50]

It seems the editor of the *Age* agrees! For in an Editor's PostScript beneath the letter, that learned gentleman notes drolly that 'Scientia' must be naive indeed if he does not realise that in Melbourne Town this is simply the way things are done and it is connections, rather than capabilities, which count most when it comes to selecting a leader:

> It is an affair of cliquery altogether ... A certain ex-minister, it is said, and his satellites, to wit a railway contractor, and two doctors ... have manufactured the business in a way to insure the election of the successful candidates without reference to fitness or unfitness for the arduous post. The appointment may turn out well; but if so, it will be a lucky accident. — ED. AGE.[51]

Dr John Macadam himself is, make no mistake, outraged at such poison pen letters and is convinced the authors are two disappointed rivals for leadership of the expedition.

Yes, with such unbridled sneering, one is likely Major Warburton, a man talented at attack and invective on paper and in the papers – he, who had never hesitated to savage Babbage – now hiding behind anonymity to pretend to be a sneering Victorian gentleman. The other is more than likely an enemy within, a Victorian gentleman used to being patronised and ignored within the walls of the Royal Society of which he is a member – making it double the treachery – Mr Lockhart Morton himself!

Come hell or high water, Dr Macadam resolves to unveil the two traitors and hold them responsible for this damned perfidy.

Yet, whoever it is, it is clear that, even before beginning, Burke has a growing circle of critics – and a vicious circle at that – only too eager to fall upon any mistake he makes and denounce him at the first opportunity.

Apart from these press attacks, Macadam worries about Burke's chances of beating John McDouall Stuart across the continent. Stuart, after all, left his base camp at Chambers Creek, in the middle of South Australia, in early March, and is surely nearly to the north coast by now.

In fact, though no one in Melbourne knows it yet, on this very day, Stuart is suffering an enormous setback. Yes, two months earlier, he and his companion William Kekwick had climbed the bump of land Stuart named 'Mt Sturt' in honour of his mentor, firmly taken the mighty Union Jack in his hands, and planted it in what he judged to be the middle of Australia, claiming this *terra nullius* as a new outpost of the British Empire, before heading north. But today, 26 June 1860, the local Aboriginal tribe – fiercely unaware that their *terra* is *nullius* – are attacking him and his men in force.

'They were,' Stuart would recount, 'tall, powerful, muscular men – bold, daring and courageous; not at all frightened by either us or the horses, but rushing boldly to the charge . . . The moment we entered the scrub they were upon us. Every bush seemed to have hidden a man, and upwards of thirty attacked us in front, and how many more there were endeavouring to surround us and cut us off from our pack horses I cannot tell. If I proceeded I should leave enemies behind and in all probability meet with enemies in front. Thus would I have to fight my way to the coast and back again. To do that with only two men and myself, and having six pack horses to look after, would be utterly impossible.'[52]

Feeling he has no choice but to turn back to Adelaide to get more men, more supplies and more weaponry, he gives the orders for exactly that . . .

CHAPTER THREE

HELP WANTED

The Committee and – more so – the subcommittee is that old spinster who has won an elephant in the lottery and does not know now what to do with it.[1]

Dr Ludwig Becker in a letter to Ferdinand Mueller, 1860

The 'busy haunts of men' had no attraction for him. He preferred the society of a few to that of many, but the study of nature was his passion. His love was fixed on animals, plants, and the starry firmament.[2]

Dr William Wills, on his son William

Late June '60, Richmond, grand plans and visions splendid

His pale blue eyes flashing at the sheer *injustice* of it, Robert O'Hara Burke quietly notes the bitter criticism of his appointment, but the saving grace is that he is now too busy to dwell on it. There is an expedition to organise! There are supplies to be purchased, men to be employed and a route to be worked out.

'I will do it or die,'[3] he firmly tells friends, his thick Galway accent somehow managing to add resolution to the strong words. Quickly moving digs to Melbourne, he drops his kit at the barracks of Richmond Police, girds his loins, gathers his scattered thoughts, and begins the tremendous task of preparation; the first task of which is to decide just *how* to cross the continent.

With police colleagues, he is frank on his intent from the first.

The way he sees it, there are two ways of organising it.

One is 'the idea of a rapid dash by a light party'.[4]

The other is 'the advance of the exploring party in great strength and equipped after the military style of Hannibal or Julius Caesar, or rather that of "Congo" Stanley on his present relieving trip through Central Africa'.[5]

Perhaps the best method will be to combine the two?

That is, form up a huge expedition party, supplied with everything, get to Cooper's Creek and then advance at pace from there with a light party.

As to who will join Burke, it is for the Royal Society to now appoint the 'officers', who will act as senior members, each assigned specific tasks to do with both science and stewardship of the whole expedition. Meanwhile, it is for Burke himself – albeit in consultation with the Committee – to appoint the common workers.

Quickly proposed as the obvious candidate to be Burke's second-in-command is the impressive George Landells, who has brought the camels over. He is, obviously, a man of great capacity.

When one of the sepoys had proven insubordinate, Landells had given him what the 'coolie' so richly deserved, a damn good thrashing followed by a dismissal. The *Age* approved: 'DISORDERLIES. *Tuttie Khan*, a swarthy son of India, was discharged on a charge of using abusive language and improper conduct to his master, Mr Landells.'[6]

Yes, on the one hand, George Landells is perfect for the job, able to keep both the camels and the men who mind them in line. But he has no experience in the Australian bush, and wouldn't know a latitude from a longitude from bacon and eggs for breakfast.

Robert Burke doesn't care about that. He is convinced, even anxious, that Landells must come along to look after the camels, and the Committee falls into line, resolving to make him an offer.

30 June '60, Victoria, positions vacant and heroes for hire

The search for the workers to join the expedition, meanwhile, ramps up. On the morning of 30 June, another German man, William Brahe, is one of many men who happen to come across an interesting notice on page seven in the *Argus*:

VICTORIAN EXPLORATION EXPEDITION. —
Persons desiring to JOIN the EXPEDITION will APPLY
PERSONALLY on Wednesday, the 4th of July, at the Hall of
the Royal Society, Victoria Street, at 9 o'clock. The leader, Mr
Burke, will be in attendance. After that date no further applica-
tions will be entertained.
     JOHN MACADAM, M.D., Hon. Sec.[7]

Brahe – who had arrived in Australia eight years earlier, in pursuit of the
gold rush – resolves to go to the interview, *um sein Glück zu versuchen*,
well, you never know your luck. After all, it is well known there is a
strong German contingent among the organisers of the expedition, and
Brahe's own connections to the highest echelons of that community are
strong, thanks to his solicitor brother, who co-founded Melbourne's
Deutschen Verein, or German Club.

Mary Street, Richmond, 2nd July 1860.

R. O'Hara Burke Esq.
Sir,

*I beg to tender you my services as labourer in the Victorian Exploring
Expedition, which is now being formed under your leadership. I am
a Prussian by birth and 25 years of age. I arrived in this Colony in
1852 and was for the first 2 years engaged as carrier and digger. From
1854 up to the present time I have had engagements as stockkeeper at
Glenormeston in the Warrnambool district, Mr Neil Black's station,
and at Barwidgee near Beechworth, Mr R. Box's station, and have had
much experience in travelling with stock. With the handling of horses
and the management of cattle I deem myself thoroughly acquainted and
can do any work which can be required from a bushman.*

*Professor Neumayer and Mr Kauerau have permitted me to refer
you to them as to my general character and habits. I enclose letters from
both gentlemen.*

I am, Sir, your obedient servant,
William Brahe.[8]

Early July '60, Melbourne, all at sea in study time

In the meantime, Burke devotes himself, in whatever spare time he can muster, to what will be described by his earliest biographer, Andrew Jackson, as 'an active examination of the records of previous explorers'[9]. William Wills, of far more bookish disposition, though *still* not confirmed, does the same.

Through reading newspaper accounts, and such works as Sturt's lucid book, *Narrative of an Expedition into Central Australia*, which chronicles his trips in 1844–46, they try to grasp the essence of the Australian experience when it comes to exploring.

From the first it is obvious that Charles Sturt – an English gentleman soldier who had fought alongside the Duke of Wellington and then escorted convicts all the way to New South Wales – is the one from whom they can learn most. In the course of Sturt's travels towards the interior, he had become convinced that right in the middle of Australia 'there may be a central sea not far from the Darling . . . and I should be prepared to go for a *voyage*'[10].

Determined to find out, in 1844 at the age of 49, Sturt mustered 16 men, 11 horses, 30 bullocks, 200 sheep and two kangaroo dogs (for hunting 'roos), together with a wooden boat on a carriage, and set off for the north.

Leaving from Adelaide, Sturt and his men followed the Murray River until it met the Darling, which they followed northwards until a bend in the river towards the east, at a spot known as Menindee – a corruption of the native Barkindji people's name for it, *Minandichee*, meaning many waters.

From there, Sturt and his men needed to keep heading north, and eventually west, if they were to ever hit the centre of the continent, so they left the Darling and pushed north to a large waterhole on a creek. There they built Depot Glen, a manned and defended depot they could use as a base. So began the probe proper, Sturt and his party heading out into a summer so hot that it was nigh on beyond human imagining – 157 degrees Fahrenheit in the sun at its worst and 132 in the shade. It was so hot that Sturt seriously struggled to record their journey, as ink dried up immediately and the lead fell from his pencils as he picked them up. They were driven nearly mad by heat and light, with even the night bringing little respite, as 'the dazzling brightness of the moon was one of the most distressing things we had to endure. It was impossible indeed to shut out its light whichever way one turned, and its irritating effects were remarkable.'[11]

Not far from the spot where the three colonies of New South Wales, Queensland and South Australia come together in one junction, Sturt discovered an arid stretch, which he named the Strzelecki Desert after the Polish-born explorer Pawel Strzelecki, who had climbed and named Australia's highest peak, Mount Koscuiszko. At a rare water source he found therein, a small lake, he established another manned depot – a stockade – which he called 'Fort Grey', and then kept pushing broadly north, sure that his inland sea must be close. First up, the closest he found was a sad creek, which he also named the Strzelecki, and followed it until . . . Up ahead!

Not the sea, true, but something even more welcome. Gradually the shimmering horizon of hell gives way to a fleck of green that grew larger as they approached. It was a coolabah tree! And there is another! And *another*!

Within hours they have discovered an entire chain of waterholes in the desert, linked by a watercourse that runs when there is rain enough; a beautiful if finely balanced river system that lay about 400 miles north of where the key outpost of Menindee now lies. Sturt names it 'Cooper's Creek' after a well-known South Australian lawyer and friend, Charles Cooper.

Leaving Cooper's Creek and heading north once more, Sturt enters a desert he names the 'Stony Desert' because the horses' hooves are cut up terribly by the endless 'gibber plains': sun burned, hard ground covered with purplish-red flint stones so numerous that the men and their beasts leave no tracks that can be followed. It is a strange, other-worldly place. Every now and then Sturt and his party hear 'explosions as of a distant gun'[12], which they work out must be due to 'gaseous influences'[13], most probably caused by chunks of rock being split by the huge differences in temperature between day and night. Exhausted, waterless, desperate to find the inland sea he knows must be here . . .

But the desert – as deserts have been wont to do since the dawn of time – beats the intruders in the end. Sturt must finally accept the inland sea he'd been expecting to discover simply isn't there, and they head back to Fort Grey – only to find, after a brutal journey of 49 days – that it is abandoned. The men they had left there had *not* waited!

'With the bitter feelings of disappointment with which I was returning home,' Sturt would record, 'I could calmly have laid my head on that desert, never to raise it again.'[14]

Digging under a pre-designated cache tree they find a bottle with a note from the man who'd been left in charge of the depot, Harris-Browne, saying that he'd been compelled to move back to the waterhole at Depot Glen 67 miles away due to dysentery, caused by putrid water at Fort Grey. The next day, Sturt and his faithful lieutenant, John McDouall Stuart, following the directions on the note, rode that huge distance in a day, 20 hours of straight riding, and collapsed upon arrival.

Sturt's muscles were horribly contracted, his skin turned black. He suffered severe lethargy, bleeding gums, shortness of breath and agonisingly sore limbs, signalling the onset of scurvy, that terrible disease known too well to sailors and convicts, that strikes down those who go too long without fruit and vegetables.

Sturt limped slowly for home, reaching Adelaide, strapped to his horse, a year and a half after he had left, more dead than alive.

A slew of other explorations also capture Burke's attention, including – as Burke scribbles mindlessly on an application letter: '*Leicherd, Leichard, Leicherd, Leichard*'[15] . . . the German fellow, who, with a party of six men, including two Aboriginal guides, had left Moreton Bay in October 1844, heading west, only to disappear and then re-appear in December 1845, 3000 miles away through uncharted territory, at Port Essington, 100 miles north-east of Darwin.

In 1847 the intrepid German explorer had again set off, from the Darling Downs in Queensland, intending to cross the entire continent to the west, only to have to turn back due to heavy rain and a malaria outbreak. The next year he started off again, with four Europeans, two Aboriginal guides, seven horses, 20 mules, with 270 goats and 50 bullocks for them to eat on the way . . . and had never been seen since.

Augustus Gregory had, of course, been sent to look for Leichhardt, but found no trace. Of particular interest to Robert Burke is that, while Gregory was out, he had attempted to get north of Cooper's Creek, but, like Sturt, found the country impenetrable. Once Gregory had found himself at Cooper's Creek, running short of supplies, and needing to get back to civilisation, he had come up with an interesting solution. Instead of going directly south towards Menindee on the Darling, as Sturt had done, he travelled to the south-west to get to the nearest settlement, which was just 150 miles or so away in the colony of South Australia, a cattle station near Mount Hopeless (a stony rise so named because another explorer, Edward Eyre, had discovered it while fruitlessly trying to conquer the interior himself in 1840 and had recorded of the view from atop the hill, 'Cheerless and hopeless indeed was the prospect before us. I had now a view before me that would have damped the ardour of the most enthusiastic, or dissipated the doubt of the most sceptical . . .'[16])

To Robert O'Hara Burke one thing is becoming obvious: Augustus Gregory's original advice to the Committee – that the best thing will be to get to Cooper's Creek and there establish a Depot – is very likely the right plan. Once that Depot is established, the next thing will be to gird their loins and try to get through the searing barren country lying just to the north that had defeated both Gregory and Sturt. Perhaps they can navigate between their courses, to see if there really is a manageable way north.

To get there, Burke will need his own team of first-rate officers and good men, and much of his energies in the latter part of June and early July are spent in selecting them – starting with sending out missives to one or two men he knows he wants . . .

Late June '60, Kiandra, Eureka, they found him!

At his digs in Kiandra in the Snowy Mountains in late June – 'the roughest and coldest part of the colony I had yet found'[17] – Charles Ferguson, an American goldminer who had been at the heart of the battle of the Eureka Stockade back in December of 1854, noting it as 'the most exciting time I had ever witnessed'[18], is surprised to receive a formal letter, with elegant handwriting on the front.

Opening it, he finds it comes from a 'Dr John Macadam', none other than the Secretary of the Royal Society at Melbourne, Victoria. His proposal is simple:

> MR. CHARLES D. FERGUSON:
> Sir—There is a vacancy in the Victoria Exploring Expedition which will be held open for you up to its leaving Melbourne. If you think favourably of it, come to Melbourne as soon as convenient, as it intends to leave on the first of August.
> JOHN MACADAM, Secretary.[19]

A letter from Robert Burke received in the same batch of mail confirms the offer. Burke knows Ferguson from Beechworth, and has specifically requested that he joins the expedition as foreman, to be in charge of the working men as opposed to the scientists and officers.

'I am anxious for you to join the expedition,' Burke writes, 'and would like you to come to Melbourne at once. Salary is a second consideration.'[20]

Ferguson, keen from the first, sets off on foot, heading for Albury, the closest major outpost of civilisation . . .

William Patten, meanwhile, an Irishman with a splendid build who is already friendly with Mr Burke from Castlemaine, is hired, first to start collecting the stores, and then appointed blacksmith and armourer, to look after all their firearms. Thomas McDonough, another Burke intimate – for he had known Mr Burke's family in the old country and is proud to call Burke his 'particular friend'[21] – is also hired, despite being no bushman.

Others though, even when they are one of Burke's few close friends, and even when he knows them to be capable, and *even* when they are keen to go . . . are rejected. One of them is Sub-Inspector John Sadleir, Burke's colleague at Beechworth police. Sadleir would later recount, 'His answer to my offer [to join the expedition] was short. "You have got to look after your wife and children. You cannot come."'[22]

One man, William Hodgkinson, a 25-year-old journalist for the *Age* who Burke had come to know a little during the time they both spent in Castlemaine – press and police operating in respectful and reciprocal sympathy – is as interested in going as Burke is keen on having him. Mr Hodgkinson is a clever and able, if abrasive, young man, with a noted capacity for finding favour with his superiors which he does not always return with loyalty in kind, but we'll see . . .

Like Mr Landells, Mr Burke trusts his own instincts on these things and invites the young man to join them to fill an unspecified role, but perhaps to draft the dispatches and diaries that Mr Burke as leader will be expected to produce. As it happens, the journalist cannot extricate himself from his commitment to his paper at this time, but Burke promises to send for him if an opportunity arises.

Truthfully, so many men on the Committee have their own favourites they would like to see taken, regardless of qualifications, that by the time Burke has added his own, there are few positions remaining.

For the sake of form, more than anything, on the morning of 4 July – even as the good Lord blows up a tempest, providing, as the *Age* puts it, 'fitting accessories of thunder, lightning, and rain'[23] – Burke goes through with the process of nominally interviewing 300 applicants in just three hours at the rooms of the Royal Society, all of them eager to take part in something that will 'constitute for long years if not ages to come, the highest glory of the colony of Victoria'[24].

They are not just the rag-tag itinerants with nothing better to do.

'Many fine stalwart men were there,' one journalist notes, 'evidently inured to the hardships of the bush. Many overlanders modestly solicited employment, speaking with bushy faces and bronzed skin of nights of camping and days of travel.'[25]

Nearly to a man, those bushies are shown the door only shortly after being interviewed.

In short order, the list of expedition members is compiled. William Brahe, the German wagon driver and horse-handler with the well-connected brother, is among the lucky men; he has his application accepted.

Names of eminently qualified men who *don't* make it onto the growing list, despite having expressed interest, include one Robert Bowman, who has extensive experience exploring with Augustus Gregory; an F. Schmidt, who had explored the interior of Africa between 1847 and

1851; Colour Sergeant Dennis Kenny, who'd accompanied Charles Sturt along the Murray River in 1844; and James Knight, who'd also explored with Gregory in Western Australia. Outstanding, experienced bushmen, all. But with no connection of note to the decision-makers they simply did not make the cut.

6 July '60, Castlemaine, the toast of the town

Castlemaine can do no better than this, to hold a dinner for their newfound hero, Mr Robert O'Hara Burke, to 'bid [him] farewell, and wish him God speed'[26].

The affair, replete with a three-course dinner of local fare and the finest wines, is held at the town hall, and boasts *le tout* Castlemaine. All the leading figures of the town are present, the local paper will report, most particularly in the fields of 'law, physic [medicine], divinity, the leading commercial firms, storekeepers, farmers, and, in fact, every grade found representatives, and the enthusiasm shown by all was unbounded'[27] with a waiting list of many other notable figures who would love to come, but just can't be squeezed in.

It is Chairman William Froomes who has the honour of doing the honours, offering first the loyal toasts – 'to the Queen and Royal Family . . . and to the Governor, Sir Henry Barkly . . . the best Governor the colony ever had . . .' – and it is he who proposes the toast to their honoured guest, Robert O'Hara Burke, which is met by enormous cheering from the assembled gathering.

'I was quite prepared for that burst of cheering,' Mr Froomes acknowledges happily, 'for Mr Burke during his residence in Castlemaine, had gained the esteem of all (*cheers*). I have never heard a syllable breathed against that gentleman, whose cordiality of demeanour, and urbane and frank manner, would ever ensure him the possession of the public respect . . . I could relate many acts performed by Mr Burke alike honourable to his humanity and his understanding, but they had been done privately and unostentatiously, and a public recital of them would give no pleasure to the doer . . . But I cannot allow this opportunity to pass without publicly acknowledging the very valuable services Mr Burke had rendered to the community as superintendent of the police force, which under him has attained the highest degree of efficiency.'[28] (*Cheers.*)

Warming to his task now, the good gentleman feels obliged to raise a delicate subject, knowing that the issue must be aired, and settled, and there will likely never be a better time than before this supportive gathering.

'It has been said that Mr Burke is the second best man . . .' he begins, pausing just long enough for the diners to cry, *No! No!* '. . . and as always happens when an individual becomes prominent, some envious people have by anonymous attacks endeavoured to detract from his good name. I have the most implicit confidence in Mr Burke's ability to answer these detractors, in the best possible way, by carrying the expedition through successfully (*cheers*), and I call on this company to show their concurrence by drinking this toast.'[29] Gentlemen, a toast! To Superintendent Burke!

Superintendent Burke . . .

Superintendent Burke . . .

Superintendent Burke . . .

So tumultuous are the cheers, so long do they go, that it is some time before the great man can respond, noting to begin with that he is about to make the first speech of his life.

Ah, but what a grand job he does, as the room falls completely silent to hang on every word.

'It is unnecessary for me,' Mr Burke says in a voice as rich and rolling as the green hills of Ireland, 'to say how proud, how flattered, I am, by the proofs of warm sympathy with which I have this evening been honoured.'[30]

The room falls still more silent now, as Burke makes his first and only public answer to his critics, most particularly as it pertains to Major Warburton.

'As my friend the Chairman has alluded to charges made against me, and he seems to think they require explanation, I will briefly refer to them. In the first place, my conduct in going to town before my election has been contrasted unfavourably with that of the gentleman opposed to me. Well, gentlemen, it was fortunate for me that I did go to town, for upon my arrival there I found that a statement had been made by one of that gentleman's supporters . . .'[31]

Name him, name him! cries the gathering.

'. . . Captain Cadell, that I had informed him that I would accept the second place under Major Warburton. Captain Cadell subsequently explained this statement, by saying that he had mistaken me for another person; but it was a very awkward mistake, at a very critical period, and might have endangered my election if I had not been on the spot to correct it. (*Cheers.*)'[32]

Ah, but still he is only warming up!

'It is also asserted that I belong to a political party or clique,' Burke says. 'But the fact is that political disputes have no charm for me. I do not know the difference between one political party and the other; and the only recent attempt I have made to increase my political knowledge was in reading the Land Bill the other day (*laughter*), and I must confess it was a failure, for I was as wise at the beginning as I was at the end.'[33] (*Laughter.*)

More, Mr Burke, more!

'It has been stated, too, that I am an illiterate man. Well, gentlemen, if writing cowardly, scurrilous, anonymous letters . . . (*Hear! Hear!*) . . . is a necessary literary qualification, then I certainly admit that I am most illiterate, and glory in my ignorance. (*Cheers.*) Gentlemen, I fear I have allowed myself to be carried away by the subject. Upon the whole I have really very little to grumble at, as generally I have received the most kind and generous support. (*Cheers.*) I now conclude by tendering my heartiest thanks to all, and to the people of Castlemaine particularly, for their courtesy and kindness, assuring you that I will strain every nerve to carry the expedition through successfully.'[34]

Cheers, and standing ovation!

So wild is the cheering, so sincere are the good wishes, that Superintendent Burke feels obliged to rise, to acknowledge such wonderful warmth. As a special treat, he even gives some insight to his plans.

'I am not certain whether we will be able to leave Cooper's Creek, or even the Darling, this year as the season is so advanced . . . I must be guided by circumstances. I won't go forward for fear of being called a coward, nor remain behind to be called a fool. If I don't succeed, there will be a good reason for it.'[35]

As the gathering breaks up, Mr Burke is 'perfectly overwhelmed with the good wishes of the departing guests'[36].

9 July '60, Melbourne, Burke's personnel

Do go on, Mr Burke. With little more than a month until the great day of departure, he finds himself addressing the Exploration Committee. The newly appointed leader now reads out the list of people he has chosen to join the expedition, that he would like to be confirmed.

'Mr G. G. Landells, Mr Ferguson, Mr Fletcher, Mr Cowen, Mr Patten, Mr Langan, Mr Creber, Mr Brahe, and Mr Elliott.'[37]

Of the men on Burke's list, few are more pleased than Mr Henry Creber and Mr Robert Fletcher, two Englishmen who are those rarest of all things among the expedition party – men who have *genuinely* been chosen on their *merits*! Neither of them knows Mr Burke personally. No, they are simply two of the 700 applicants whose resumes have been as impressive as their face-to-face interview with Mr Burke, and space has been made for them.

A veteran chief officer of steamboats on the Brazilian coast trade, the softly spoken Henry Creber has the useful skill of being able, unlike Mr Burke, to take astronomic observations. Mr Fletcher, on the other hand, is something of a gentleman all-rounder, a former medical student who has found his way to the colonies, and over the last four years spent his time in the bush, riding horses, shooting and living rough – precisely what expedition members will need to be doing in coming months.

And so to the next order of business . . .

Now it is proposed that 'Mr Wills, Senior Assistant to Professor Neumayer at the Flagstaff Observatory, as Astronomer and Meteorologist to the Expedition'[38], also be appointed.

To the clear delight of Professor Neumayer, who regards Wills almost with fatherly pride, the Committee nods and 'aye, aye, aye' their agreement, as they also do, shortly afterwards to Dr Hermann Beckler, as

'Medical Officer and Botanist'[39], and a Dr Ludwig Becker, as artist and naturalist.

Four days later, on 13 July, after meeting once again in the Royal Society Hall, the Committee will announce its decisions.

It is also proposed that Mr Landells is to be appointed as second officer, though his conditions for joining the party – including his insistence that he be given full carriage over the camels, and his exorbitant salary demands – remain to be resolved. So, although the Committee and Burke are behind him, Landells himself is not yet committed.

9 July '60, Melbourne, the camel-cade cometh
More mayhem!

As the camels are moved from Parliament House to their new quarters at Royal Park, their appearance on the streets of Melbourne once again frightens the 'horses to such an extent that riding and driving became a work of serious difficulty'[40].

The primary danger to the camels, and their attendant sepoys, comes from the Melburnians. They find themselves 'in some little danger, from the too great kindness of their visitors . . . Hundreds of persons find their way daily to the stables . . . to satisfy their curiosity as to these uncouth, but very useful and interesting animals, and having no other manner of showing their desire to fraternise with the Indian attendants, invitations to what we may mildly term "refreshment" were common. Little as these turbaned strangers may be supposed to know of the Queen's English, as it is spoken in Melbourne, it is curious how readily they understand the offers made to them; and as they are no more exempt than white-faced people from the over-stimulating properties of beer and brandy, it is not, perhaps, surprising that intoxication overtakes them to a greater extent than those who take an interest in the camels considered at all desirable for the safety of the animals . . .'[41]

•

It is quietly noted among those who know that, 'Burke probably had not walked five miles in a stretch within five years'[42].

Yes, 'he had been at all times an accomplished and daring horseman'[43], his first biographer Andrew Jackson would recount, but hardly one to focus on his fitness out of the saddle. So it is that Burke enters 'upon a course of regular training, taking severe pedestrian exercise, and accustoming himself to fatigue and privation of every possible kind that an attempt to traverse the vast untrodden wilds of Australia was likely to bring to his experience'[44].

•

The lost and lonely figure lying by the road outside Albury on this cold and sleety evening? It is none other than Charles Ferguson – the veteran of the Eureka Stockade – who, after covering an extraordinary 40 miles a day over the last four days has just had a bad mishap. Just as darkness had fallen, so had he – badly spraining his ankle, leaving him in excruciating pain and facing a freezing night. But, wait!

Suddenly he hears the sound of a cart approaching, and soon in the moonlight it appears, driven by a hawker.

Ferguson cries out for him to stop.

The hawker reaches for his whip, to lash the horse to go faster.

Desperate, Ferguson grabs the horse's bridle with one hand as it tries to pass, while bringing his pistol to bear on the driver with the other. He said he wanted a ride, and he *means* it. As few things are so persuasive as the barrel of a gun pointed right at you, the driver instantly changes his mind, and Ferguson is carried the rest of the way to a hotel in Albury – and is even taken to his door by the hawker, who *insists* on being helpful!

'I then treated him to a glass of brandy,' Ferguson would recount, 'and tendered him five shillings for my ride. He declined to take it but accepted a glass of hot brandy.'[45]

The next morning, at Albury's Exchange Hotel, there is a knock on the door and Ferguson hobbles to it, slips the bolt and . . . oh dear, oh dear . . . finds a policeman standing there.

'Your name?' the policeman asks.

'Charles Ferguson.'

To the American's surprise he is not quickly arrested. Instead, the policeman advises that he has a letter for him, and though it had taken some time to track him down, he is glad to have finally found him.

The letter proves to be from Superintendent Burke's replacement at Beechworth, Inspector Bookey, telling him that the Royal Society is looking for him, as they are concerned another missive sent might not have reached him. He is wanted in Melbourne. There is a big expedition going!

Ferguson is on his way south again the next morning, this time by coach.

13 July '60, Melbourne, no latitude for error as the expedition comes together

His dearest wish has come true!

To the infinite delight of William John Wills, on this day, he is officially confirmed as all of third officer, astronomer, meteorologist and surveyor on the Victorian Exploring Expedition. It will be his job to carefully note the route of the expedition, making detailed maps as they proceed. Firstly, as his soon-to-be formalised instructions insist, 'Every opportunity should be taken to ascertain the geograph-ical position of the party, referring it to some well marked point, as offered by an easily recognisable mountain, the junction of rivers, creek &c.'[46] Latitude and longitude must be calculated whenever possible. Wills must also record observations on 'all astronomical phenomena of particular interest' as well as 'the variations of the compass'[47]. The movements of the stars and 'observations on Zodiacal light'[48] will be of utmost importance for Wills, as well as more typical measurements on their earthly trail: air pressure, wind force and temperature, duration and intensity of rain, so on and so forth, on into the endless etcetera of the scientifically obsessed – up to and including collecting whatever bubbles of gas might rise from rivers, lakes or creeks, 'in small glasses prepared for the purpose, in order to have them analysed afterwards'[49].

But with this long list of things to do, one thing is paramount: the map. The penultimate lines of formal instructions make clear: 'scientific observations should be subordinate to the mapping of the country'[50].

He will at least have help in such endeavours, as some of the officers have great scientific expertise, such as the German medico, Dr Hermann Beckler, trained in Germany's prestigious Munich University, and another very different fellow German, Ludwig Becker, is the expedition's artist.

The 52-year-old Becker is a man who has already made quite an impression on some parts of Australian high society, during his extended stay in Hobart, Lady Denison noted of him, 'He is a most amusing person, talks English badly, but very energetically. I have sometimes great difficulty in keeping my countenance when I see him struggling between the rapidity of his ideas and the difficulty of giving them utterance . . .'[51]

It remains to be seen whether this portly, bespectacled 52-year-old will be up to such an arduous exercise. Dr Beckler, on the other hand, is a slim 32 years old, but *both* men have large question marks over them from the beginning, at least as far as Burke is concerned. They are not his choices, they have been imposed on him. They are not men of action, but men of mind, they are part of the scientific section of the expedition, which from Burke's point of view is wholly secondary. It already seems to him that the scientific quotient of this journey might prove a distraction from the main goal.

•

As proud as his father Dr Wills and Richard Birnie are of William, however, it is not as if this appointment is without criticism. One of Birnie's acquaintances even approaches him to wonder out loud, and loudly at that, 'How they came to appoint a beardless boy to duties that exact medical, no less than scientific, knowledge?'

Birnie, a man with rapier wit and razor-sharp intellect, rises to the occasion.

'I cannot solve the problem, but pray accept these palliations,' says he. 'First, he has an ample tawny beard, and is 27 years old. Second, his father, a prosperous physician, avers that his son knows far more of medicine, of pharmacy, and of pathology than himself, and for further particulars I must refer you to Professor Neumayer.'[52]

It is a good enough response for the said gentleman to accept it.

Meanwhile, a fellow tenant at their boarding house, Mr Philister, is equally critical of Wills's appointment to such important positions, but Richard Birnie is untroubled. A short time later, the lawyer takes the curmudgeon aside, and is so bold as to make a prediction.

'Sir, before your head is more grizzled,' says he, then gesturing to Wills, 'his statue will be seen in our widest street, his photo in every shop window, and his name coupled with that of his colleague heard on almost every tongue.'[53]

In the time that Wills and Birnie have left together, they become even closer, oft times ignoring entirely the subject of their forthcoming split, and instead focusing on the finer things.

'Many a walk and many an evening,' Birnie would recount, 'was devoted to Shakespeare and the philosophical analysis of his master-pieces was a perennial source of novelty and delight.'[54]

Now, many a young man about to head to the wilderness for a year might be disposed to head to places where some of his more base, common desires might be sated.

But not Wills, never Wills!

'Vulgar vices came not near him,' Richard Birnie would note proudly. 'His aspirations were noble, and his strength drawn from purity of soul.'[55]

17 July '60, Melbourne, trying to keep the blunders at bay

Ah, the excitement for many of the journalists now assembled in the gallery of the Royal Society. For the man of the moment, Robert O'Hara Burke, the leader of the expedition, is present at their deliberations, and for the first time they are able to get a good look at this hero of the hour who has suddenly burst across the Melbourne firmament like a meteor of glory.

Whatever else, there is no doubt that the Irishman certainly *looks* the part. A quite tall man, all of five feet nine inches high, he has a lean and lanky frame that suggests both power and endurance. And that beard! Burke's extraordinary black beard appears to have a life of its own. Other men grow beards; this beard is so munificent however, so black, so *fertile*, it very much appears that it might have grown Burke! (The fact that he has grown it – it is known – to hide a deep duelling scar from his opponent's sabre only adds to the sense of romance.)

'There was such a daring reckless look about him!'[56] Lady Stawell would later record her own impressions.

And it is true. It is the look of a man who other men just want to follow.

In what direction, exactly?

That, as it turns out, is precisely what this meeting has been convened to determine . . . and therein lies a story.

For if a camel, as they say, is 'a horse designed by a committee', might it not then be that a committee can be a decision-making body that sometimes makes decisions worthy of a camel? As it happens, on this day from the very bowels of this Committee – in any case, many would assert, as far from the head as it is possible to get, and certainly somewhere very close to the bowels – emerges . . . let's call it . . . an idea.

Even though the departure date for the expedition is now less than a month away, it is suddenly proposed that instead of heading south to north, the whole expedition should be put on a ship, landed in Northern Australia, and proceed south from there!

Messrs Embling, Macadam and Bleasdale are behind it – and it is proposed on a day when Sir William Stawell happens to be absent. It has taken some time, but the idea of one of the unsuccessful applicants, John Frizzell, that proceeding thus would see the 'Northerly Sirocco' blowing at their backs[57] has taken hold. An added bonus – beyond the fact that they'd only have to cross Australia once, not twice – is that if they did start from the north and head south, they might have a better chance of claiming all the newly discovered land for Victoria, rather than by going north through New South Wales and then dipping into South Australia.

As pushed most particularly by Dr Macadam, the recently arrived camels will be put back on a ship, with the expedition team, and taken all the way to Blunder Bay in Northern Australia, and then go south from there.

After all, the most brutal country to traverse is thought to be the unknown country between the Gulf and Cooper's Creek, so why not knock that over while still fresh, rather than arrive at Cooper's exhausted, and have to tackle it from there? The SS *Chinsurah*, which had brought the camels in the first place, would cost just £300 per month and could get them there in six weeks. It is available until October, but after that the monsoon would set in and it would be unsafe.

Burke, while not passionately in favour of the proposal, is not strongly against it. For him, as he privately notes, it is simply a choice between 'Starting to go to a dangerous spot, or starting from a dangerous spot.'[58]

Typical of Burke, his notes are not taken on a fresh piece of paper, but on the other side of a letter he has received, recommending a particular police trooper as a good recruit for the expedition. Any old piece of paper would do, and it might even be that any old route will do.

Nevertheless, after the discussion goes on for some time, as recorded in minutes, 'Mr Burke stated that on full consideration . . . he believed the route by Blunder Bay to be the best.'[59]

Mr Landells, meanwhile, affirms that the camels are in good form, ready to go and if they do land at Blunder Bay, he says, 'A rest of a fortnight or three weeks will be sufficient for resting the camels.'[60]

But, from there, once they are underway, 'the camels could . . . go thirty miles a day but only twenty if the country be difficult . . .'[61]

To the general murmurs of satisfaction, Mr Landells follows up with information that causes gasps of astonishment.

'Some of my Camels could go eighty miles a day.'[62]

It is all much better than they had hoped for.

And yes, there are objections to this new route. Professor Neumayer is against it on the grounds that the season itself, with its attendant monsoons, will be against landing at that time, while Dr David Wilkie thinks that such an important decision should be approved by the entire Royal Society, while others suggest Port Augusta and Kings Sound in Dampier's Land as better places. But still there is enough support in the room for Dr Macadam to put it to the vote. All those in favour of the motion 'That the expedition start from Hobson's Bay, and shall commence the land journey from Blunder Bay . . . proceeding thence by the most direct practicable route southward to Cooper's Creek . . .'[63]

It is quickly passed!

Nearly all that remains will be for the government – whose public monies are attendant on what amounts to a right of veto – to approve the new route.

Ah, but there is one last delicate issue that must be resolved, the matter of Mr Landells's conditions.

'I should be entirely charged,' he has demanded in his letter to the Committee, 'with all matters relating to the treatment of the camels and be responsible for their health.'[64]

That is, he is to be the boss of the camels, even to the exclusion of Mr Burke.

What choice do they have? Maybe none . . .

Still, the Committee decides it needs time to consider, and the meeting is closed.

All up, the feeling is that much has been accomplished, most particularly the decision to go to Blunder Bay!

•

Meanwhile, the sepoys – sometimes known in the press as 'coolie assistants'[65] – are on board, and settling in. Though Landells had arrived in Melbourne with nine, he ends up selecting just four to join the expedition. Known simply as Samla, Dost Mahomet, Hassan Khan and Belooch Khan, they are seen as 'Indian' men by the Europeans, though they come from various regions of British India and Afghanistan. They stick close to each other and their camels. They speak Hindustani among themselves – the common language of Northern India – and it is only George Landells and his offsider, John King, with whom they can easily converse. Still, they are generally happy characters and one word the others do pick up is *salaam* – meaning 'Peace be unto you' – while some of the Europeans also learn such basic words as *kamat* for a male camel, and *datchi* for a female.

Generally, Robert O'Hara Burke is happy with the sepoys and requests permission, successfully, that the Committee doubles their wages – 'two shillings (2s) per day instead of one shilling as at present'[66]. Yes, this is still less than a third of what the other workers are getting, but the sepoys are happy with it.

•

Alas, alas, enthusiasm for the Committee's new plan to head to Blunder Bay proves to extend no further than beyond the very committee room where it was hatched and approved.

Ferdinand Mueller and Sir William Stawell – who had both been absent on the evening – are appalled when they find out, with the latter even going so far as to make public his distress.

'It seems to me,' he thunders to the *Age*, 'that we are fated to do nothing at all, and at every meeting I grow more desponding from the extreme dilatoriness of our proceedings.'[67]

The venerable newspaper could not agree more, but it is the *Argus* that is likely most outraged and does not delay to weigh into the fray.

> The recent determination of the Royal Society to alter the route of the Exploring Expedition, and to give a totally new character to the undertaking, will be unhesitatingly condemned by a vast majority of the Victorian public as a most unwarrantable departure from the original project. We cannot conceive what were the powerful motives which induced the Committee thus to stultify itself and bring ridicule upon the Expedition . . .
>
> What, in the name of all the dromedaries, has Victoria to do with an expedition to discover the interior *from* Blunder Bay? . . .
>
> We believe the resolution to form a depot at Cooper's Creek, as the centre of operations, was adopted on the suggestion of our latest explorer, Mr GREGORY . . . We believe [everyone] will now . . . universally consider it a blunder to go to Blunder Bay.[68]

Once reported, one interested reader of the *Argus* can stand the madness no more, and writes his views in a Letter to the Editor:

> Sir, if the proposition is attempted to be carried out the immediate failure *in toto* of the expedition is certain. The idea is plain and simple madness and ignorance . . . It must here be recollected that [the camels] were landed with every possible care, and by a vessel alongside a jetty. If Mr Landells understands camels, he well knows that, to make them efficient and useful, they must ere they commence their long and severe journey be in a healthy,

strong state – not suffering from the effects of shipboard; that they must by degrees be seasoned to their work; and, above all, not bruised nor suffering from any bodily accident . . . So sure as the attempt is made, so sure will it fail. Mr Landells ought to know it; and if Mr Inspector Burke does not wish the total destruction of the enterprise on its commencement, he ought at once to object to so mad a scheme. If the expedition is to succeed, as it now ought, let it start from the Royal Park . . .

AN INDIAN OFFICER.[69]

Now, whether it is this letter, or other wise heads that prevail is never sure, but within days of the letter being published, the plan is changed once more. It is decided that the expedition will indeed start from Melbourne's Royal Park, head north to the Gulf of Carpentaria, and then return.

The decision to revert to the original plan brings widespread relief, but still the general criticism continues, with the *Argus* now putting a question that seems to be arising with ever greater frequency.

It seems late in the day to inquire for what purpose we have organized an exploring expedition; yet it appears that this is the question which is just now beginning to dawn on the minds of some of the Exploration Committee. Having got out of Blunder Bay by a miracle, and having steered clear of Shark's Bay and the monsoons, the more practical of the committee think it as well to ask, what is the object of the journey?[70]

CHAPTER FOUR

MILES OF SUPPLIES FOR THE MILES AHEAD

The Exploration Committee [has] got superabundance of money, an excellent stud of camels, a leader and a party of their own choice, and an open field for their exertions. They are just beginning to find out that they know not what to do with these things, and while they have been entering upon the discussion of the matter, Autumn has merged into Winter, and Winter is giving way to Spring. The captain and his mates are hanging about Melbourne, the camels are browsing lazily with the town herd, and the money is beginning to melt away.[1]

Edward Bulwer-Lytton, *Geelong Advertiser*, July, 1860

You cannot fail to like [William Wills]. He is a thorough Englishman, self-relying and self-contained; a well-bred gentleman without a jot of effeminacy. Plucky as a mastiff, high-blooded as a racer, enterprising but reflective, cool, keen, and as composed as daring. Few men talk less; few by manner and conduct suggest more.[2]

Richard Birnie, on his dear friend

July '60, Melbourne, an inland sea of stores

Robert Burke half suspects there is a problem. The expedition's supplies, procured carefully at first, have expanded to the point they now need a veritable wagon-train! It looks like they'll need at least two more expensive wagons to add to the three costly wagons the Committee has already bought.

The procurement of supplies is guided by Dr Ferdinand Mueller, who was with Augustus Gregory on his northern Exploring Expedition, and has been quick to list everything Gregory had used, together with everything they wished they'd had. Burke has formed up a list of his own, as have others. These lists have been combined – Mueller and Burke both finding it is easier to allow something onto the list than to leave it off – before being approved by the Expedition Committee, then 'submitted to the Chief Secretary'[3], who adds his own mark of approval before the government storekeeper, Richard Nash, is given orders to fund the purchases.

The inevitable result is that the net weight increases exponentially.

Not least of that which must be carried is scientific in nature, and therein lies something of a tale, pertaining to the key scientific officer . . .

For, long ago back in England, Dr Wills had taken his son, wee Willy, on a horse and buggy ride to Devonport, and they had stayed the night at that fair city's Royal Hotel, only to find the following morning that the young lad had gone missing! The hotel had been turned upside down to no avail.

'After a twenty minutes' search in all directions by the whole establishment,' Dr Wills would later recount, 'he was discovered at the window of a nautical instrument maker's shop . . . gazing in riveted attention on the attractive display before him. The owner told me that he had noticed him for more than an hour in the same place, examining the instruments with the eye of a connoisseur, as if he understood them.'[4]

So what a pleasure it is for Wills to now take his pick of some of Professor Neumayer's best instruments from the Flagstaff Observatory, starting with a gloriously crafted seven-inch sextant, made by the famous Julius Lohmeier of Hamburg, to measure the positions of the stars and the planets. And let's add two prismatic compasses to aid the determination of the course taken; two barometers to calculate altitude, two gold watches to precisely determine the time wherever they are – which, with the nautical almanacs Wills also purchases, will allow him to calculate their longitude. A theodolite will measure angles when surveying, and a telescope will allow him to engage in his greatest passion of all, gazing at the stars. Beyond that he also buys many notebooks on which he can record all the measurements he intends to take, together with sketchbooks and specimen jars with preserving fluids so whatever new species of reptiles or birds or the like that they discover can be safely brought back to Melbourne.

Other officers are buying their own supplies with the wild abandon peculiar to those who don't actually have to pay it for themselves. Becker and Beckler also organise sketchbooks and specimen jars with preserving fluids. Other purchases include a 'Stationary cabinet'[5], 'Frying pans'[6], 'Camp Ovens'[7], 'Corkscrews'[8], 'Turkey Stone'[9], 'Spring Balance Scales'[10], 'Looking Glasses'[11] and beads to impress the natives. Oh yes, and matches. Plenty of matches! Huge ones with large red phosphorous heads are chosen. They stink like sulphur when struck, but the flame is sure and steady. True, as a box of 50 costs as much as one shilling and six pence, they are not cheap . . . but worth it. Just like the beads and looking glasses, they, too, might impress the natives. And if the natives get dangerous? Well, at a cost of £62 the expedition purchases 10 'Double barrel guns with slings'[12], as a bare beginning to what will be an extensive array of weaponry and enormous amounts of ammunition.

In terms of provisions to keep body and soul together – and in the case of the double-barrel guns, to separate body from soul, if the heathen natives have souls – Sir William Stawell is one who comes forward to assist Mr Burke. It is he who works out exactly what needs to be purchased to ensure that they will have everything needed for the 2600 miles trip to the Gulf and back, which is estimated to take as long as a year. It is true that Sir William claims no particular expertise in the needs of an exploration, but, against that, neither does Burke and neither does Macadam (non-expertise in exploring being the only qualification all parties share). Dr Macadam also has a very strong input though, in terms of making arrangements for the expedition, 'he always deferred to Burke whenever any difficulty arose'[13]. As it is, the only difficulty Mr Burke has is stopping the damn stores and supplies from accumulating.

At least the idea of driving cattle with them is soon abandoned as it is resolved to go instead with a concept invented and used by Augustus Gregory. That is, to mix dried meat and meat juice with flour, before baking to make small flat 'meat biscuits' that can be packed into barrels, preserved, and eaten at your convenience. As extraordinary as it may seem, just over a ton of it is prepared (and no less than the Chief Justice Sir William Stawell personally supervises the work), placed in barrels, and stacked away, ready to head north.

There is also 320 pounds of pure pemmican, a high calorie concentrated mix of meat and fat that is also packed away into barrels. Historically, pemmican had been a wonderful boon to explorers on Arctic expeditions. But will it work in the desert?

Beyond that, they pack away 600 pounds of salt pork, 400 pounds of bacon, and 60 pounds of potted mutton. Now, together with this, we will be needing – to feed 19 men for some 18 months – 7100 pounds of flour, 200 pounds of Captain's biscuits and 3000 pounds of sugar.

What to eat the meals *on*, though? Burke is prevailed upon to include a cedar-topped oak table, with matching 'Oak Camp Stools . . .'[14] together with the requisite cutlery. Miscellaneous items include a large iron bathtub, bells for the horses so they can be found when they stray, 'an ample supply of rockets and blue lights'[15] to send up in the night if they are lost from each other, a Union Jack to plant on the Gulf of Carpentaria when they get there, not to forget a Chinese gong to bring the men together for mealtimes, and a dozen dandruff brushes to groom the animals. For dinners to be eaten by candlelight, let's get 150 pounds of sperm candles, made with wax 'spermaceti' from the head cavity of a sperm whale. And then there are tailor's scissors, 10 pounds of tea '(for Asiatics)'[16] and 20 gallons of lime juice which, it has been thought for over a century, will help to stop scurvy (citric acid and preserved vegetables are brought for the same broad purpose). Ah, and let's not forget to issue each expedition member a state-of-the-art charcoal filter, 'by means of which he will be able to obtain drinkable water under the most unfavourable circumstances'[17]. For removing even greater impurities, a state-of-the-art 'enema syringe' – don't ask – is provided. And don't forget we need plenty of sets of camel shoes. Fifty sets? No, let's go with 80 sets, to be safe. And not just any camel shoes, either. No, these ones are specially made to get across the likes of the Stony Desert and consist 'of several folds of leather, and shod with iron'[18]. Several sets of specially designed waterproof rugs with holes in the middle to fit neatly over the camels' humps are also included.

Mr Landells also insists that they take a staggering 60 gallons of rum to administer to the camels to keep them in rude good health. With a good dosing of rum, or pepper, or both, he says, a tired camel could be stimulated to perform above and beyond the call of duty – and they will help to prevent the camels from getting scurvy. Burke, personally, is sceptical that such a substance could be of much benefit to the animals. And as a long-time policeman who knows better than most the oft devastating consequences of mixing men with gallons of rum, he is highly reluctant to head to the middle of Australia with such a combination on board. But so insistent is Mr Landells that the camels *must* have the rum, for he knows all about camels, yes he does, Mr Burke feels obliged to accede.

Now, how to move such an array of men, supplies and animals across whatever bodies of water they might come across?

That, too, has been thought of!

'Two new wagons,' the *Herald* rather breathlessly reports, had been 'built expressly for the expedition, and one of them is so constructed, that at a very short notice it can have its wheels removed, and put to all the uses of a river punt, carrying an immense load high and dry on the water. If it be necessary to swim the camels, air bags are provided to be lashed under their jowls, so as to keep their heads clear when crossing deep streams.'[19]

(Which seems fabulous. What is not so fabulous is that Charles Ferguson insists that the horses must get used to pulling the custom wagon, and so every day takes one of them on the streets of Melbourne – meaning 'the repairs made to this new wagon during two weeks of use cost £83!'[20] It is yet another expense that hasn't been factored in, but must be paid regardless. Ferguson also spends many days at Pentridge prison, overseeing the prisoners as they fit out the expedition's wagons to his specifications, shoe the horses, and even manufacture the clothes and boots the expedition members will wear, based on a rough uniform of ruby red serge shirt and moleskin trousers.

What if someone gets ill? They've thought of that, *too*, and a 'hospital camel' has been designated, with a specially constructed and enclosed pannier that will hang from its hump to 'afford capital accommodation for invalids, should sickness unfortunately visit the party'[21].

How to organise all the supplies?

The Committee decides to allow each field of endeavour within the expedition – from wagoners, cooks, scientists, blacksmiths and botanists – to make their own orders, and have them all delivered to the government stores at King Street, where Hermann Beckler will take overall charge.

'Mr Becker,' Hermann Beckler would recount by way of example, 'ordered a not inconsiderable stock of sketch-books, notebooks, steel-nibs, inks and pencils. A farrier, putting his tools together, started off with a portable forge, bellows and anvil. What else could the poor man do? One day even a grindstone with frame, stand and crank was received at our warehouse! . . . Ordering and buying is so easy and enjoyable, and this activity is doubly seductive when someone else is paying for it.'[22]

The result is that, every day, ever more boxes, packages and ironworks are received. Hermann Beckler himself is quickly over-whelmed – endlessly writing out receipts for new packages received, then finding a place to put them – but then gets into the spirit of it.

'I myself had put together a very modest list of medicaments,' he would recount. 'How ashamed I was of my modesty when I saw the list of medications that had been prepared for the horses by our leading carter, Ferguson, a Yankee! Was I perhaps to let myself be reproached for taking less care of my patients than the horse-doctor of his? I made larger orders at once . . .'[23]

All up, the cost of the provisions is '£4,585.2s.10d'[24], which is a little over half of the overall budget – something that rather shocks the Exploration Committee's treasurer, Dr David Wilkie. But it is his brow alone that is furrowed on this account, as all the others are caught up in the frenzy of preparation and purchase. The size and frequency of the bills may make Dr Wilkie sweat, but the grandness of the bills merely speaks to the grandness of the enterprise, and the grandees of the Committee are little concerned with trifles such as expense.

But far more concerning to Burke personally – he has never been too fussed with money – is the sheer weight and bulk of it all! All 20 tons of it! Yes, he had wanted a Hannibal-like cavalcade, a very well-provi-sioned one, but *not* 20 tons of provisions, not such ludicrous extras as punt wagons. (Yes, a punt! To take to the desert! Mr Burke can scarcely believe it, but he is assured by the learned scientific gentlemen of the Royal Society that a punt is essential for crossing rivers, should they not find another way – or perhaps an inland sea, as Sturt had prepared for? Mr Burke could, of course, note how strange it was that Captain Cook was not obliged to take a carriage with him on the *Endeavour*, just in case an outland island had been discovered that had to be crossed, but refrains. Agreed then, gentlemen. We will haul a boat across the continent.)

Every evening Burke returns to his new Melbourne dwelling at Alfred Ford's Royal Artillery Hotel at 616 Elizabeth Street – the one he is sharing with Dr Hermann Beckler – ever more exhausted, and frequently says to the German, 'What are we going to do with all of this, how are we going to move it?'[25]

One move that Mr Burke makes to help keep things organised is to change Robert Fletcher, the well-heeled Englishman, from being his personal messenger to now being one of the storekeepers, helping Dr Beckler to look after the flood of supplies coming in, tabulating them, registering them, working out just how much of everything they have, and recording where it can all be found. The Eley cartridges – the high quality London-made ammunition – should be stored with the separately imported Eley wadding, and all of them kept close to our growing store of guns. The whole goatskin waterbags, so finely stitched, the ones that hold 35 pints each, with four straps coming from where the four legs used to be, and a spout where the neck used to be? Put them over here, right by the India-rubber water-bottles and I will take a note.

27 July '60, Melbourne, a date declared
When, exactly, will they get underway?

Mr Burke is consulted both about just when things will be ready, and whether there will be a problem with starting the camels at a time when the season is relatively cold. Upon the Exploration Committee being advised – at a meeting held on 27 July – that he needs a little more than three weeks, and as to camels in the cold, 'no great difficulty would be encountered from that source'[26], the motion is put. 'That the Expedition start on the 20th August – Carried.'[27]

•

How extraordinary an opportunity it is for young Wills to have been picked to go on this expedition. How grateful he is to have had his name pushed by Professor Neumayer. And yet, how sad he knows he will be when the day comes to part from his most cherished friend in the world, dear Richard Birnie. All such emotions come together on this extraordinary evening when, after dining at Professor Neumayer's home – to discuss the things he must take with him on the trip, the things he must look for, the charts, the almanacs – the two are walking back to their Fitzroy boarding house. As ever, after the sparkle comes the sadness, the growing realisation that soon they must part from each other, and after chatting happily all evening, young William suddenly falls into silence.

And yet now he sparks to life as he gazes to the sparkling stars above on this resplendent evening, and exclaims, 'What an astronomer he would have made!'

'Whom do you mean?' asks the older man.

'Whom should I mean,' says Wills, 'but Shakespeare, the myriad-minded. The stars brought him up to my mind, he was thrown away at that Globe Theatre.'[28]

Arriving home, Wills begs his mentor – perhaps the Antonio to his Bassanio, à la Shakespeare's masterpiece, The Merchant of Venice – just one simple request.

'Give me as much Shakespearanity as you can, but nothing else.'[29]

Ah, as if in a mid-summer night's dream, Richard could not be more delighted at the request, holding forth into the starry, starry night . . .

> If this fall into thy hand, revolve. In my stars I am above thee, but be not afraid of greatness.
> Some are born great, some achieve greatness, and some have greatness thrust upon 'em.
> Thy Fates open their hands. Let thy blood and spirit embrace them.[30]

1 August '60, Melbourne, mammon and magnanimity

For a fortnight now, since Mr Landells has been announced as the second-in-command of the expedition, he, like Mr Burke, has been attending and speaking at meetings of the Exploration Committee, giving his thoughts on the many issues that arise, but today, on this first day of August, just three weeks before scheduled departure, the final issue regarding his own contract must be settled.

For Landells has demanded an annual salary of £600 whereas Mr Burke has already agreed to a salary of just £500.

Yes, well. Their finances are already rather stretched – of the £9000 raised, £4585 has already been splurged on supplies, and the salary bill is estimated to cost another £3000 per annum. The cost is already half again as much as Dr Wilkie had initially envisioned in his speech that had acted as a catalyst for this whole project – and it means they now have very little for unforeseen circumstances, and for buying supplies along the way.

But, against that, there is little choice. Mr Landells is resolute that he will not agree to less and there is no time to find someone else with his specialised skills with the camels and the sepoys. And, equally, there is little choice but to raise Mr Burke's salary to £600 as well, as it is simply not *proper* that the leader be paid less, but now that the Committee is about to debate that motion an extraordinary thing happens. (And all the more extraordinary, if anyone could but know how deeply in debt the Irishman is.)

'Mr Burke,' the *Argus* reports, 'very generously waived this point, and declined to allow a motion for the increase of his own salary to be discussed. He also expressed great anxiety to have the co-operation of Mr Landells, and, after some discussion, it was unanimously agreed that that gentleman's offer should be accepted.'[31]

Such has always been Burke's way. From the beginning, Dr Macadam would later note, the Irishman had been 'utterly indifferent'[32] to what he was to be paid.

As to Landells having full charge of the camels, the Committee finally, formally agrees, at least after a manner . . . informing him that while he is to follow Burke's instructions, his own special duty is to have 'Charge of Camels'.[33]

To close observers, the situation seems made to fail, with one of them, William Lockhart Morton, later noting: 'It was just as absurd as if the command of a ship were given to a captain, whilst full control over the sails remained in the hands of the first mate.'[34]

•

Charles Ferguson knows a thing or two about rough men, hard men, bushmen, and is such a valuable addition that Mr Burke had even paid well over the odds for his services – at a salary of £200 plus expenses (a wage Mr Burke insisted on for him, £80 more than the ordinary men) – to keep the workers under control.

The problem the 28-year-old Ferguson has right now, however, as he drops his kit at Royal Park where the men of the expedition are assembling – he knows he is at the right spot when he sees an array of tents set up beneath gum trees, with extraordinarily high and newly constructed camel stables right behind them – is that he can't actually see any. *Hard* men. *Bush*men. He can see rather well-dressed officers, certainly, some with neatly trimmed beards, glasses, who are surely Germans. He can see dark men, the sepoys, fussing around the camels. (And by God, he can smell the rich, pungent aroma coming from the camels.) Here and there are delivery people with drays, loaded with supplies, heading up to the expedition encampment, where they are soon heaving long and strong to lift the heavy boxes off the back. And yes, he can see the men who are the workers, most of them clothed in a rough kind of expeditionary uniform with thick flannel trousers and scarlet jumpers for protection against the cold, and wide-brimmed hats, taking the boxes from the drays and stacking them wherever one of the officers so directs them.

But *hard* men? *Bush*men? He keeps looking for men, like him, with unruly beards, big shoulders, scarred knuckles, leathery skin and the oft squinty eyes that come from spending years surviving and *prospering* in environments where the only shade that might come is when you find yourself shaping up to a bastard so big he blocks out the sun.

They just don't appear to be there!

And so, when Burke asks him, presently, what he thinks of the crew that has been assembled, Ferguson, as is his way – in his thick Midwestern American accent – has no hesitation in telling the leader.

'If I could have my way,' he says flatly, 'I would select my men from some of the old experienced bush-men in the prison, rather than start out across the continent with such raw recruits . . . I do not believe one-half of them could harness up a team and drive it.'[35]

Mr Burke, not a bushman himself, not by a long stretch, is not worried about the lack of bushmen. Mr Burke is an officer, and his firm belief is he needs fewer bushmen and more solid men he knows and can trust, men who will follow orders. Any drover, farmer or stockman can hold himself out as a 'bushman', but his men are going to cross a continent, into the unknown, through vast deserts – not roaming around in the bush. And so copious are their supplies that they will, in any case, be taking many of the city comforts with them.

His real concerns are primarily with the officers who have been *foisted* on him by the Committee, such as the 52-year-old German artist, Dr Becker, and his countryman Dr Beckler – his junior by 20 years – a high-handed, self-important and insufferably pompous botanist and medico. Both have that German manner about them of innate superiority to all those who are *not* German, exacerbated in their case by their high degree of education, unmatched by anyone else in the party, except Mr Wills.

Well, let's just see how far these two Germans last on the long trip across the entire continent of Australia. Either way, once the journey has started, Burke has scrawled another note to himself on what he suspects he will need to do with some of his compulsory retinue, as he embarks on a process of 'Weeding out the Party'[36].

For, whatever else, this will be no gentle stroll for gentleman scientists, as they will all have to steel themselves for the 'long privations we will have to meet'[37].

For the moment, Dr Beckler is himself distinctly unimpressed with the leader.

'Burke, with whom I am residing,' he writes to his brother Carl back home in Germany, 'is an ordinary person, certainly not an unattractive leader for me, but is no way adequate to his office. Leader of an expedition, but completely ignorant of the land, totally blind as to geography and astronomy. And this complete lack is not unknown to the Committee, or the Royal Society, or the Government or even the public . . .'[38]

It is certainly not unknown to Charles Ferguson. For him, however, Burke's own ignorance of such matters is less a problem than the fact that ignorance is widespread.

Heading off into the wilderness for such a long time with such a large group, the American gets more worried the more he finds out.

And the problem is not just with the men. Mr Nash, the government storekeeper, has provided 23 horses for the expedition, but as revealed by the *Age*, they 'appear to have been selected for no other purpose than as far as possible to rid the Melbourne market of all the unsightly and ill-conditioned animals that generally frequent it . . . and there is scarcely a serviceable-looking one amongst the lot, the majority of them appearing to be broken-down cab or light draught horses, the age of which it would be unsafe even to guess.'[39]

Worse still, only two of them have been broken in!

In the absence of anyone else capable of doing it, it falls to Ferguson to do the honours. Dressed in his usual dungarees and calico shirt, for he outright refuses to wear the expedition uniform that the other working men do – he climbs astride one bucking nag and holds on for his life until it finally submits to his will, before quickly climbing onto the next, and so on. Yes, it will take many sessions before they are finally broken in, but at least the horses now know they have a boss, and his name is Ferguson.

Beyond that, he decides that the most important of his tasks, in the weeks that remain, will be to turn these 'new chum explorers' into men who can cope in the bush, who can contribute to the expedition, and if he overdoes it on occasion, what does he care?

Now, men, get CRACKING!

Shortly thereafter, loud rifle shots echo around Royal Park.

It proves to be the men of the expedition who are now being trained by Colonel Pitt of the Victorian Volunteer Forces on how to aim your rifle by looking down the barrel, lining up the notch on the end with your target, even as you hold the barrel steady with one hand, while gently squeezing the trigger with the other.

With the officers, Ferguson is a little more genteel, but, happily, Mr Wills needs no instruction at all, as he had been taught by his father from the age of 11 how to shoot, and shoot well. The other standout is the quiet young Irishman, John King, Mr Landells's offsider – who has also been formally hired at a salary of £120 a year. Having served in the British Army in India during the Indian Mutiny, the tanned, thin, admittedly rather sickly looking fellow has served with the 70th Regiment in India, and knows just how to handle the newly purchased double-barrelled shotguns.

Yes, he is nominally only here to handle the camels, but both Ferguson and Mr Burke are impressed regardless. And King also proves to be even better at what will become a keenly required skill: chasing after the camels like a mad thing, as – in this case, alarmed by the shots – they indulge in one of their favourite habits, running away like even madder things.

Meantime, the members of the expedition also receive instructions from the likes of Mr Landells and King in how to look after those camels; how to groom them; make them sit to be loaded up; make them rise up again; and, most crucially, how to hobble them at night, to make sure they don't wander for miles searching for feed in the bush. Again, some of the men take to it, others don't. The preparations for a 20 August departure continue apace.

•

As to how to shift all the men and supplies to the north, a wonderful offer has been made by Captain Francis Cadell to give the expedition a flying start.

If the bulk of supplies can be gathered and transported to Adelaide, he says, then he will personally undertake to put them on one of his paddle-steamers, and transport it from there to any tributary of the Murray the Committee cares to name, at which convenient point Burke and his men and animals could gather them in. It is a handsome offer, from the man most expert in the country to make it. Why, just 120 miles north of the junction between the Darling and the Murray, Captain

Cadell had only the year before personally established the small outpost of Menindee – the northernmost point of the settled districts and the very spot the Burke party will be heading to – where his steamers took supplies from Adelaide and took back bales of wool from the settlers. He knows the area, knows the river. And if he says he can get Mr Burke's supplies at least to the Murray–Darling junction, and perhaps all the way to Menindee if the river is in full flood at the time, he *can*. This would save the Victorian Expedition the terrible burden of unnecessarily carrying their heaviest supplies 460 miles. And Captain Cadell will do it for the extraordinarily cheap fee of £500 and ... !

And let the minutes of the 10 August meeting tell the story:

'Mr Burke strongly objected to Captain Cadell having anything whatever to do with the transport of the goods or stores. He stated that he was prepared to give the Committee substantive reasons for his objection.'[40]

Whatever the views of some, Burke, the man ultimately responsible for the success of the expedition, has no confidence that Captain Cadell can deliver the supplies to the spot he says, at the time he says. Mr Burke has no wish to have his whole expedition dependent on the performance of a man who has never supported his own leadership of the expedition in the first place and would no doubt not mind seeing him fail! For, yes, Mr Burke has not forgotten: Captain Cadell had been one of the more outspoken opponents to his appointment, and even if he can deliver the goods to the right spot on time, the Irishman wishes the riverboat captain to have *no* part of the glory.

As it happens, the Committee are not terribly bothered by Mr Burke's objection. Mr Richard Selwyn, the Geological Surveyor of Victoria, moves and Mr Embling seconds the motion that Macadam contact Cadell about terms.

In short, Mr Burke is miffed, but stiffed: the Committee holds sway for the moment. At least, it is not as if it will *definitely* happen, just that the Committee is asserting its rights to explore the possibilities. With a little more time, Burke is confident he can have it stopped.

•

One evening, the men are dining on bread and tea when Mr Burke stops at the Royal Park 'camp'. He does not like what he sees. His men, the men who man the biggest expedition in Australia's history, are practically being served bread and water! For dinner! 'Mr Fletcher, what is the reason for this?'[41] barks Mr Burke.

Mr Fletcher starts to remind Mr Burke of their conversation about stretching the rations, the other day . . . but Mr Burke will have none of it.

'The blame lies with you, Mr Fletcher,'[42] he says and promptly orders the cook to take control of all rations in the future. But, but . . . that is Mr Fletcher's job! Not anymore. Mr Fletcher is now demoted to camel attendant, attending five of the beasts to be precise. It is not, perhaps, the most glamorous position that an English gentleman might aspire to, but . . . is that an order? Then, yes, Mr Burke. (Fletcher has heard that Mr Burke told the Exploration Committee that 'in the event of any of the men disobeying his orders, he would nail his ears to a tree and give him twenty-four lashes,'[43] and doesn't want to find out if the leader would be true to his word.)

On a roll, Burke instructs Mr Henry Creber, who was on camel duty for some time at first, to take charge of the new tents, which with all their odd rigging and ropes is just the sort of thing a sailing man like Mr Creber is a dab hand at.

(The truth of Burke's impetuous behaviour? Well, it is later alleged to be far more calculated than the two working men know. For the Irishman, their leader, is in fact *trying* to get rid of the two Englishmen who the Committee have picked for him and that he does not want.

Mr Burke, it is later asserted, has asked Mr Landells to find fault with them, whether real or imagined, and give Mr Burke his trigger to end their employment.

'I urge you to find fault with them,' he had instructed his second officer. 'They have been forced upon me and I want men of my own choosing.'[44]

Mr Landells finds both the request and Mr Burke's conduct a trifle 'strange'[45], but agrees to play his part in the quite devious plan. This is only the beginning for Fletcher and Creber.)

18 August '60, Melbourne, being of (reasonably) sound mind and body

Now, over the last few months, Victorian government storekeeper Richard Nash has prepared and signed many official documents for his new friend, Robert Burke. But this particular document is something else again, and it greatly concerns him. For this document is nothing less than Mr Burke's will, and rather a surprising one it is. John Macadam and he exchange a glance as the soon-to-depart expedition leader reads it to them.

> This is my last will and testament. That I Robert O'Hara Burke do here direct Mr R. Nash in case of my death whilst in charge of the Expedition to pay all monies belonging to me (after debts have been defrayed) to Miss Julia Matthews (Actress) now of Melbourne and presently engaged at the Princess Theatre in this colony. And all of my other effects to the said Julia Matthews.[46]

Have I got this right?

You, Robert, are leaving what you are pleased to call your 'estate' – mostly debts, but we'll get to that – to . . . an *actress* . . . a young girl not even half your age?

Richard Nash is stunned. Yes, he knows that his friend is completely smitten with the young woman, and is practically a caricature of the stage-door johnny – sitting in the front row with owl eyes every performance he can, learning her songs on his piano – but this is going too far! Burke is a gentleman of a fine family, with a cousin married to a peer of the realm, Edward Lawless, 3rd Baron of Cloncurry. And a gentleman does not bypass all familial heirs to leave his estate to a young actress, most particularly when the said gentleman has four sisters and one surviving brother. Robert, my friend, don't you understand this is scandalous, or it will be if anyone finds out about it?

But Robert O'Hara Burke will not be moved.

He has made up his mind, and that is that. He allows it must be kept secret, but his primary desire is to finish the formalities so he can get back to heading up the grandest expedition in Australian history. They have much to do in the time that remains, including an important ceremony with the chief justice in just a few hours. He insists on the will.

Mr Burke signs. Mr Nash signs. Dr Macadam witnesses the document and it is done with the three men agreeing to keep this sensational news wisely to themselves.

There remains one more document to sign, however, giving Nash the power of attorney for Burke – essentially meaning he will have the power to keep those many creditors who want Mr Burke to pay off his debts (gambling and otherwise) at bay. If all works well, and the leader of the expedition returns from climes where he couldn't lose money if he wanted to, and has a year's salary owing, there will be money enough to deal with these insistent gentlemen.

Satisfied, Mr Nash puts the signed and witnessed will, together with the power of attorney document, in the bulging Burke file with all the bills, promissory notes and angry letters. And now Mr Burke and Dr Macadam must head off to an important meeting in the hall of the Royal Society.

For on this day, just two days prior to their scheduled departure, it is time for the members of the expedition to come together with the leading lights of the Committee – including the Chief Justice of Victoria, Sir William Stawell, and the Mayor of Melbourne, Richard Eades – in the hall of the Royal Society, all in the presence of the press, to enact an important ceremony.

But first we must get through a paper to be read by Lockhart Morton, the very man who many on the Committee, led by Dr John Macadam, believe is quite possibly the author of the treacherous 'Scientia' letter!

To then begin the main business of the day, in front of the assembled dignitaries, Robert O'Hara Burke takes the floor and calls on the expedition members to 'fall in'.

As described by the *Argus*, all 15 members of the expedition party 'walked up the room, and drew up in order at the back of the president's chair'[47]. (The sepoys, of course, have not been invited. Their loyalty is presumed as a matter of duty. They will do as they are told.) They are an impressive-looking bunch, all bar Ferguson in their rugged uniforms. Each one of them has passed a 'rigid medical examination', with 'all of them appearing to possess excellent constitutions'[48], and today they really *look* the part of men ready to take on anything. The possible exception is one rather rotund older fellow – I think that must

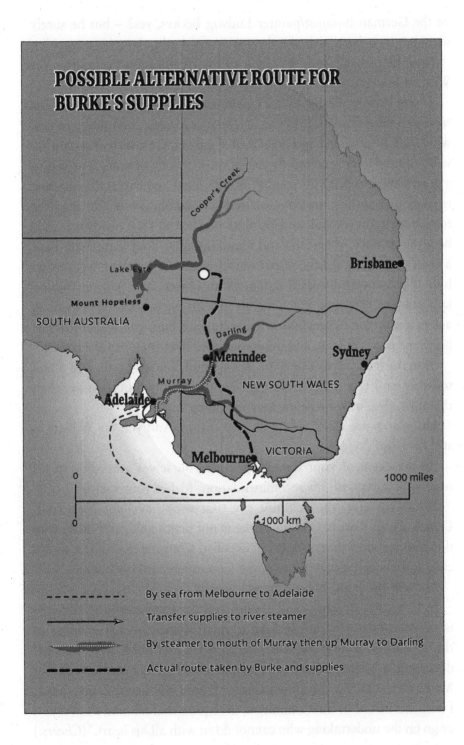

POSSIBLE ALTERNATIVE ROUTE FOR
BURKE'S SUPPLIES

Cooper's Creek

Lake Eyre

Mount Hopeless

SOUTH AUSTRALIA

Brisbane

Darling

Menindee

Sydney

Murray

NEW SOUTH WALES

Adelaide

Melbourne

VICTORIA

0

1000 miles

0

1000 km

– – – – – – – – – – By sea from Melbourne to Adelaide

————————▶ Transfer supplies to river steamer

~~~~~~~~~~~~ By steamer to mouth of Murray then up Murray to Darling

– – – – – – – – Actual route taken by Burke and supplies

be the German botanist/painter Ludwig Becker, yes? – but he surely wouldn't have been picked if there was any doubt about his capacities.

Now let us hear from the Chair of the Exploration Committee, Sir William Stawell.

'I have been requested by the Committee,' he begins in his stentorian tones, 'to say a few words to you in reference to your undertaking, a task which will be attended by a great deal of danger, but which, if successful, will redound very much to the credit of every one of you . . . It will to a great extent depend on your all being united and cheerfully assisting in carrying out the object of your leader, to whom you will be required to give the most implicit and absolute obedience. That obedience must be given at once, cheerfully and unhesitatingly. Your leader will have a great deal to do. All the responsibility of the undertaking will rest on him. If you cheerfully assist him in all his objects, you will very materially aid him, whereas, if you merely give an eye-service – an unwilling assent – and don't cheerfully co-operate with him, you will embarrass him very much indeed, and even your own lives may pay the forfeit.

'You must all act as one man. A long pull, a strong pull, and a pull together, and you will pull through every difficulty. But to insure that, the most absolute obedience must be given . . .'

His words are stark, and a clear warning. And yet, Sir William is still far from done.

'In the event of your not comporting yourselves according to his orders, you may, on his recommendation, forfeit your salaries . . .'[49]

Whatever else, they cannot say that they have not been told. Obedience to Robert O'Hara Burke is not negotiable, and those who don't understand that, risk being expelled from the expedition on his call, and his call alone. Be told, the Committee will back *him*.

But *still* the point must be made, *legally*.

In front of everyone – and almost as if the Exploration Committee is *expecting* trouble, and seeking to quell it early – each member of the expedition is now asked to step forward and publicly sign a legal document, a Memorandum of Agreement, binding them to the orders of Mr Burke, or facing the consequences. 'Before you sign this agreement, I wish, on behalf of the Committee, to request that no man shall sign it or go on the undertaking who cannot do so with all his heart.' (*Cheers.*)

'If any of you do not go into the expedition with all your heart, it is not yet too late; and it would be much more open, and manly, and honest that you should now say you don't like to go; and any man who has that lurking feeling in his heart had much better say so now, or, if not, for ever after hold his peace.' (*Cheers.*)[50]

Led by Mr Landells, each member steps forward, takes the proffered quill, and is invited to sign the agreement.

All proceeds smoothly, until it is the turn of the rather irascible Charles Ferguson to sign. Perhaps tiring of browbeating all the men lower than him in the hierarchy, he turns his attention to those above him, starting with the man at the top – Sir William Stawell. For Ferguson, as recorded by the *Argus*, appears '*very much excited*'[51], and refuses to sign the agreement until the society agrees to pay any monies owing him to his daughter.

There is a pause as the Chief Justice of Victoria engages in an 'animated conversation'[52] with this one-time arrestee from the battle of the Eureka Stockade, as they haggle over pay conditions, but soon enough it is resolved.

For now, striking the table rather dramatically, and reaching for the quill, Ferguson declares, 'Well, if I never get a penny, I'll go.'[53]

His signature is quickly affixed, followed by the others, and it is done, with every man signed, and committed.

Memorandum of Agreement
Made the eighteenth day of August, in the year of our Lord eighteen hundred and sixty . . .

The said persons forming an expedition about to explore the interior of Australia under Robert O'Hara Burke, hereby agree with the said David Elliott Wilkie faithfully to discharge the special duties described opposite to their respective names, and also to perform whatever in the opinion of the said Robert O'Hara Burke, as leader, or in the event of his death, in the opinion of the leader for the time being, may be necessary to promote the success of the expedition: and they hereby further agree to place themselves unreservedly under the orders of the leader, recognizing George James Landells as second, William John Wills as third; and their right of succession in the order stated.

In witness whereof the said parties have hereunto set their hands the day and year above written,

	Name	At the rate per annum	Special duties
1	George James Landells	£ 600 -	Charge of camels
2	William John Wills	£ 300 -	Surveyor and astronomical observer
3	Hermann Beckler	£ 300 -	Medical Officer and Botanist
4	Ludwig Becker	£ 300 -	Artist, Naturalist and Geologist
5	Charles J Ferguson	£ 200 -	Foreman
6	Thomas F McDonagh [McDonough]	£ 120 -	Assistant
7	William Patton [Patten]	£ 120 -	– do –
8	Patrick Langan	£ 120 -	– do –
9	Owen Cowen	£ 120 -	– do –
10	William Brahe	£ 120 -	– do –
11	Robert Fletcher	£ 120 -	– do –
12	John King	£ 120 -	– do –
13	Henry Creber	£ 120 -	– do –
14	John Dickford [Drakeford]	£ 120 -	– do –
15	[And three Sepoys]		

Signed by all the above
in the presence of
Robert Dickson.

John Macadam, MD., Hon. Sec.

Exploration Committee of the Royal Society of Victoria.[54]

To conclude proceedings, Dr Richard Eades wishes the party 'God speed'[55] and after a few further words of encouragement moves along the line, 'shaking each man heartily by the hand and wishing him a prosperous journey'[56].

The men now depart, to get on with their preparations, while Robert O'Hara Burke has one more matter to attend to. For today is the day, at last, that he receives his formal orders.

Exploration Committee
Royal Society of Victoria
Melbourne, Aug 18th 60

Sir,

*I am directed by the Committee to convey to you the instructions and views
which have been adopted in connection with the duties which devolve upon you
as Leader of the party now organized to Explore the interior of Australia.*

*The Committee having decided upon Cooper's Creek, of Sturt's, as
the basis of your operations, request that you will proceed thither, form a
depot of provisions and stores and make arrangements for keeping open a
communication in your rear to the Darling, if in your opinion advisable
and thence to Melbourne so that you may be enabled to keep the Committee
informed of your movements, and receive in return the assistance in stores and
advice of which you may stand in need . . .*

*In your route to Cooper's Creek you will avail yourself of any opportunity
that may present itself for examining and reporting on, the Character of the
country East and West of the Darling . . .*

*The Committee is fully aware of the difficulty of the Country you are
called on to traverse; and in giving you these instructions has placed these
routes before you more as an indication of what it has been deemed desirable
to have accomplished than as indicating any exact course for you to pursue . . .*

*The Committee entrusts you with the largest discretion as regards the
forming of depots, and your movements generally, but request that you will
mark your routes as permanently as possible by leaving records, sowing seeds,
building cairns and marking trees at as many points as possible, consistently
with your various other duties . . .*

*The Committee also requests that you would address all your
communications on subjects connected with the Exploration to the Hon.
Secretary; and that all persons acting with you should forward their
communications on the same subject through you . . .*

I have the honour to be,
Sir,
Your most obedient Servant,
John Macadam
Hon. Sec.
E. C. R. S. V. [57]

Formal orders are all very well, but Burke knows exactly what he wants to do and will do. As he says to one friend, he wants to go 'slap across'[58] the continent. From Melbourne to the Gulf, with a depot at Cooper's Creek halfway across. Simple as that and anything else will not be enough.

Still, the receipt of the orders focuses a nagging worry for Burke and, typical of him, he takes action.

To this point, working in the government stores, Hermann Beckler has been carefully labelling all heavy equipment and stores unlikely to be needed in the settled districts – all ironmongery, ropes and heavy crates – as per ship to Adelaide, meaning it is to be taken to the docks, and sent to Adelaide, so that one of Captain Cadell's steamers can take it all the way up the Murray River, then as far up the Darling as possible. But suddenly, now, just two days before departure, Mr Burke, in a seeming fit of pique, has managed to kill off the whole idea. He will not give *any* of their stores to Captain Cadell, and for one simple reason.

'Captain Cadell did not support my election as leader of the expedition,' he tells Dr Hermann Beckler by way of explanation, if not expiation, 'and will lay all sorts of obstacles in our way, delaying his promised transport of our stores to the Darling.'[59]

In Burke's view, Cadell simply can not be relied upon, and they will have to take the material themselves. Beckler is stunned, but Burke will not be swayed. The only way to cope with this sudden increase in tonnage to be transported is to complement the punt wagon and the two American wagons already purchased and manned by the Exploration Committee and hire two additional wagons – with notably long trays, two small wheels at the front and two at the back, they are capable of carrying a much larger load than normal wagons – complete with drivers and six horses. These two wagons will accompany them as far as Swan Hill, when they can return to Melbourne and the supplies they bear be transferred to the camels. It will be hideously expensive to hire the wagons to take them even as far as that, some £200[60] per wagon, but . . . so be it. Having declined Captain Cadell's offer, there is simply no choice but to mount a major exercise like this.

In the meantime, though not yet formally ratified, the Committee's instructions for the scientific officers continue to be composed. Ludwig

Becker, as artist, naturalist and geologist, your diary must 'be kept regularly, and all observations made during the day to be entered before the next day'[61]. Further, please collect and categorise geological specimens, taking care – for reasons of weight – to only take with you new types, while sketching the others, and on that subject ... 'A sketch of each *camp* and its environs should, if possible, be made before quitting it [and] also outline views of *mountain ranges, remarkable hills,* and other *physical features* on either side of the line of route, also of all objects of *Natural History and Natives* (Aborigines).'[62]

In your role as a naturalist, please collect fossils, record detailed observations of all animal forms you come across, including sketches, and collect samples of fish.

'The larger fishes may be skinned, by the removal of one-half of the fish, leaving the fins of the mid-line perfect; if then washed with solution of corrosive sublimate in spirit, the specimen can be packed flat between papers without injury.'[63]

As to you, Dr Beckler, your medical duties are to be matched by your botanical responsibilities. We require medical notes on the daily health of the men and also 'the principal botanical features of the country should be noted,' as well as 'any plant either remarkable or observed for the first time'[64]. Any specimens collected, 'should be pressed into papers always immediately and dried as speedily as circumstances will permit, a label should be fixed, containing note of the day of collecting, the habitat of the plant, the soil of its locality, the colour and perhaps odour of the flower, the nature of the bark and of the wood of any arboreous species, and ... forwarded to the Secretary of the Exploration Committee always at the very earliest opportunity afforded for transmission.'[65]

Also, please observe what the natives eat, noting what you can of the 'plants which may prove of utility for food or otherwise, or which are drawn into use by the Aborigines'[66].

There is much, too much practically, for each officer to do each day. But do your best, gentlemen. This is not a mere canter across the country such as (*sniff*) Mr Stuart may indulge in, this is an expedition of the Royal Society, a journey of discovery for science as much as territory.

Nevertheless, we do bring one more thing to your attention, and – at the request of Mr Burke – it is important all scientific officers understand this, which is why we are in the process of formalising it.

General Instructions

Scientific observations or work that would cause hindrance or otherwise interfere with the progress, or necessary work of the expedition [is] never to be undertaken if contrary to the instructions of the Leader.[67]

So, yes, gentlemen, your scientific tasks are important, but they are to be conducted only subject to the pleasure of Mr Burke.

18 August '60, Royal Park, plots thicken, as Englishmen thin and camels fatten

Henry Creber is ready. While others have struggled in working out how best to set up the heavy canvas tents of the expedition expeditiously, his background as a sailor has given him such a proficiency with ropes and knots, not to mention serious physical strength, that he is confident he can now dismantle and construct the tents quicker than anyone. It is as well, as it will be one of his prime tasks once they get underway, which is now just two days away!

And what now? Hulloa! Here is his beloved brother, John, an articled clerk in town who has suddenly turned up at Royal Park, no doubt to bid him fond farewell. But no, John brings troubling news. The thing is, Henry, John received a visit from Mr Landells at the office today – he is a client of the company – and in the course of conversation made a staggering allegation. He said, Henry, that you had been . . . 'drunk and disorderly!'[68]

Drunk! *Never.* Disorderly? Well, he is about to be. For, far more than merely offended, Henry Creber is *outraged* at this entirely baseless slur on his good name. Baseless!

He immediately asks those men standing near whether any of them, any time, has ever seen him drunk?

Never once, they assure him.

Exactly! His dander up, his dudgeon high, his umbrage tucked under his arm, Mr Creber marches with forceful purpose straight to

Mr Burke's tent – for Burke is now spending more time at the camp, as their departure is imminent – to seek satisfaction on this outrage. He finds Mr Burke talking with Mr Landells and Mr Nash, the government storekeeper, and wastes no time on preliminaries.

'Mr Landells,' he interrupts them. 'Can I say a few words to you, sir?'[69]

A curious Mr Landells steps outside the tent.

'My brother has informed me, sir, that you have accused me, behind my back, of drunkenness! Did you say such things, sir? And if you did what foundation have you to make a charge such as . . .'[70]

Creber suddenly stops. There is no point in continuing, when the instant Mr Landells had understood the subject matter of discussion he turns on his heels and heads back to Burke's tent.

'I will not bandy words with the likes of you,'[71] shouts Landells over his shoulder as he retreats.

Mr Creber appeals to the men curiously observing the scene.

'Fletcher, was I ever drunk in your presence?'[72] asks Creber plaintively.

'No,' replies Mr Fletcher. 'And I am a very sober man myself. I drink very little and so I can judge these matters. You were not drunk!'[73]

Mr Landells, hearing the conversation, rushes back outside.

'Mr Creber,' he barks. 'I am *not* going to have my conduct canvassed by you. Go and look after the camels!'[74]

Go and *what* . . . ?

'Mr Landells,' he replies, seething. 'I was placed in charge of the tents by Mr Burke.'[75]

'I shall take it upon myself to order you off that duty,' counters Landells. 'Go and look after the camels!'[76]

It is a close-run thing. In front of his own brother, in front of Mr Fletcher, Henry Creber has been humiliated by the very man who is the source of the whole grievance. With commendable self-discipline, Mr Creber, choking fury and checking his tongue, storms away to the camels, all rumbling thunder and crackling lightning.

A few hours later, a surly man looms at Henry Creber's shoulder and, without even pausing to introduce himself, gets to it.

'Mr Creber,' says he. 'You are suspended.'

'By whose orders, sir?' asks Creber.

'By Mr Burke's orders,' the nameless official replies. 'He has sent me to see that you now give up everything belonging to the Government. If you refuse, you will be placed in custody of the police.'[77]

Stunned, but still resilient, Mr Creber hands back such meagre property of the government as he has, and waits his moment. It comes the next morning, sure enough, when after a restless night and much stalking about the camp in the morning light, he is at last summoned by Mr Burke, who is standing with Mr Landells – who now insists that Creber has been drunk and disorderly.

With the vehemence of a severely aggrieved innocent who finds himself falsely accused, Henry Creber denies it with every fibre of his being, clearly questioning the integrity of Mr Landells that he could make such a false charge.

'I do not wish to talk about this matter further,' Mr Landells bristles. 'You are insolent, sir, and not only that I can never get you to do any work, you are always at the tents.'[78]

'You have never complained about my work before, sir,' responds Creber. 'Even though I have the four worst camels of the lot to look after.'[79]

'Do you remember, Mr Burke,' asks Creber, changing tack, 'what you stated to me in the stable? You said, "Creber seems to get on first rate with the camels; *they look much better than when Landells had them*!"'[80]

A low blow! A calculated insult!

'You, sir, are not a fit person to go in this party!'[81] Mr Landells bellows.

Mr Burke is left with no choice. In this wild dispute between his second officer, the overseer of the camels, and a relatively lowly worker, he must summarily dismiss Creber or throw the whole expedition into turmoil – and does so. Henry Creber would have been sent packing, had he not, already, effectively packed, but he is gone within the hour.

Later that bright Sunday morning, Robert Fletcher is cleaning the camels in their stables, when he looks up to see Mr Burke and Mr Landells approaching from the starboard quarter, cutlasses flashing, and clearly preparing to board.

'Mr Fletcher,' says Mr Burke. 'Mr Landells tells me you are incompetent to perform your duties. As such, I must discharge you.'[82]

Incompetent? At cleaning camels? Really? It is so transparently absurd, Fletcher is quick with his response, and let the devil take the hindmost.

'Is that the real charge, sir?' he says. 'Or is this not in consequence of a conversation I had with Mr Creber?[83] If that is so,' continues Fletcher steadily, 'I have only spoken the truth and I would be sorry to do otherwise.'[84]

'No,' replies Mr Burke, equally steadily. 'The charge was incompetency. You are ordered to give up your travelling clothes and remove yourself from this ground.'[85]

And so it is done. Just hours after formally signing on to join the expedition, two men have been fired on highly contested charges, lacking any independent witness to their outrages, and the whole thing just one day before departure. It is more than passing odd, worrying unstable, and a certain chill sets over the camp.

Yes, it is clear that one way or another, Mr Burke will get *his* way and *his* men, but at what cost? And what will the public make of it? Both Creber and Fletcher are quick to write letters to the newspaper detailing the gross injustices they have suffered, and Fletcher ends his own passionate and well-reasoned missive with a dire prediction.

'I am afraid that Mr Burke is too hasty, and as such is likely to prove tyrannical ... In my case he has shown at the outset such a want of ordinary principles of justice to the rights and feelings of the party, that unless a great change takes place, all the efforts of the Society will be a failure ...'[86]

CHAPTER FIVE

NORTHWARDS BOUND

Burke's qualifications were a well-knit frame, a brave heart, and a chivalrous spirit that would ensure thorough loyalty to friends and companions in any circumstances of danger or difficulty; but he had no knowledge whatever of the resources by which an experienced bushman might find a living in an Australian desert.[1]

Superintendent John Sadleir, the key policeman in the arrest of Ned Kelly, reminiscing about his friend, Robert Burke, 1898

It has always appeared to me that in the equipment and organisation of an exploring party left to the ideas of professors and purely scientific men in Melbourne to fit out, a bungle is sure to be made of it, as a huge bungle they certainly made in their equipment of the Burke and Wills expedition. I remember it from start to finish.[2]

Richard Bennett, manager of Canally station on the Murrumbidgee, 1891

20 August '60, Royal Park, Melbourne, crowds, camels, confusion

On this sparkling morning, the cry rings out around the strangely deserted streets of downtown Melbourne: 'Royal Park camels!'[3]

The problem for the hansom drivers, of course, is that having already taken so many people out there from dawn onwards, by now in the late morning there are few left to go . . . but that cry remains their best chance of getting a few more.

'Royal Park camels!'

100

For as everyone knows, today is the day, the long-awaited moment in history when the Victorian Exploring Expedition sets off from Royal Park with its wonderful camels!

'*Royal Park camels!*'

For those who do answer the cabbies' cry, it is not long before they are caught up in the madness, which gets ever more intense the closer they get to the source.

'Long before noon,' one journalist would recount, '"traps" of every description were running to the park, and the road was a scene of animation such as nothing has equalled since the champion race day. There were thousands of people there – men, women, and children. Horses, spring carts, carriages, and all things else with wheels. In fact it was a grand gala, and the day was of the very finest description.'[4]

Still people keep arriving – streaming down the boulevards, up the avenues – and by noon it is estimated that no fewer than 15,000 Melburnians have turned up. The police do what they can to prevent the crowd getting too close to the men of the expedition, who must be allowed to continue their preparations without interference.

The press, however, are allowed that certain dispensation common to their craft.

'A busy scene was there presented,' the man from the *Herald* would report, after wandering around on the other side of the ropes. 'Men and horses, and camels and drays and goods were scattered here and there amongst the tents, in the sheds and on the [green sward] in picturesque confusion – everything promised a departure ... Artists, reporters and favoured visitors were all the time hurrying and scurrying hither and thither to sketch this, to take a note of that and to ask a question concerning t'other.'[5] Earnestly, the pencils of the artists dance across their sketch-books trying to capture the colour, the movement, the excitement, the exotic animals, the pressing crowds, the sheer, staggering, historic nature of the day. And we are *here*!

Look there! One of the grinning sepoys takes a camel for a trot 'about the park, to the immense enjoyment of the myriad of juveniles collected thither'[6]. And here are the fine ladies, dressed in their grand finery for this grandest of occasions, and over there, harried mothers with squalling children who have not been fed for hours and have no expectation of food any time soon, as the starting point still seems *hours* away.

There, too, are favoured family members, and dearest friends – none dearer to young William Wills, of course, than Richard Birnie.

'All was bustle and wonder,' the well-known, if not highly regarded, barrister would chronicle. 'Burke galloping up and down, here and there, on his fine-spirited horse; Wills, covered with dust, flashed and eager, cording, packing, arranging, and working as only a man of spirit and high blood can work.'[7]

Complicating matters is that the Committee has decided it wants to display to the public just how well equipped the expedition is, and so all of the equipment has been put out on display, in the tents. There is only one man who knows where everything is, and where everything is to go – Dr Hermann Beckler – and the fact that the wagons are still empty with just hours before departure, and now must be loaded amid the pressing throng, gives him what he will describe as 'the sourest day of my life'.

And for good reason . . .

'No member of the expedition could see another,' he would recall, 'no member could work with another, no one could even call to another – such was the crush among the thousands who thronged to see our departure.'[8]

In desperation, Beckler and Burke call for the mounted police to keep the crowd back from the wagons, and the laborious loading commences, as the flurried and hot workers of the expedition – dark wet patches showing up at the back and front of their bright red shirts – set to with a will. Oh, how the huge brims of their enormous cabbage-tree hats flap back and forth as they work!

As the loads are being carefully dispensed to each vehicle, an intense argument now takes place, occasioning raised voices.

For those close enough in this early afternoon, it proves to be a tense exchange between Mr Landells and Mr Burke, with the leader telling the second officer they have no choice but to load up the camels with around three hundredweight (336 pounds) each. After all, this should hardly be too taxing on Mr Landells's mighty 'ships of the desert', the very ones he has previously boasted can carry between six and eight hundredweight each, without problem, as much as 900 pounds!

The response of Mr Landells, however, is shocking.

No.

He wants the camels, *his* camels, the ones he has been given carriage of by the Committee, to carry a far lighter load at the outset of their journey, and will not budge from a maximum one hundredweight (112 pounds) per camel previously agreed to.

Mr Burke does not like to be disagreed with, *especially* not in public with a reporter nearby, but Mr Landells, as the veritable Master of the Camels, is equally insistent that the strength of the camels must not be called upon and depleted until such times as they get to the desert.

Finally, Mr Burke gives way; the camels will halve their load and, on the spot, he agrees to hire one more wagon, with six horses and a driver, who can move the heavy supplies left over after everything has been packed. (This includes, ironically, the wooden camel boxes, which at three feet by three feet by 18 inches are supposed to hang either side of the camels. Now they will be part of the carried goods.) It is going to be expensive to get the wagon at such short notice, very expensive, but there is no choice. Certainly Mr Ferguson expresses his concern that, even with the three extra wagons they have hired over the past days, the ones they have will still be dangerously overloaded, but Mr Burke makes clear they have no choice. They must move. *Now*, Mr Ferguson, if you please.

●

The crowd at Royal Park swells even further, and the preparations go on.

'Orders are being rapidly issued and rapidly executed, and there is, indeed, every indication of the approach of a movement of an extraordinary character.'[9]

Now – as is the way of these things – if embarking on a journey from Melbourne to the likes of Geelong means there are always a few last-minute things to attend to that delay your departure, then surely before heading off to the Gulf of Carpentaria, those last-minute things can add up to hours?

And so it does. No matter how much it might frustrate Mr Burke, it is clear that their departure is going to be *just that little bit late.*

It is also the way of such things that one or two of the expedition members make one too many visits to one of the sly-grog shops that have sprung up behind the stables, and help themselves to several too many beers on the fair reckoning they are unlikely to have too many more opportunities to do so in the next year. (This, notwithstanding what happened to Fletcher and Creber the day before.)

The result, as described by Charles Ferguson, is that one or two 'became a little too hilarious through excess of beer . . .'

Fair enough?

Not according to Robert O'Hara Burke. As soon as he hears of it, he sends for his foreman, Charles Ferguson, and orders him to 'discharge [the drunk men] and send them out of the park'.

Not for the first time, and not for the last, Ferguson declines to follow Burke's directive.

'I have not the power to do that,' says he. 'I can only suspend them from duty and report them to you. It is *your* province to discharge them . . .'[10]

Burke proceeds to do exactly that, and in short order, at least Owen Cowen – a former policeman, no less, whom Burke had personally signed up – is dismissed and is on his way home.

And perhaps, just perhaps, he will not be the only one.

The fact that Ferguson has not done what Burke has ordered him to do, does not sit well with the leader. As it happens, Ferguson is already a standout problem for several keen observers, including Dr Wills, who has come to farewell his son. Having already visited his lad several times, Dr Wills is familiar with the foreman, his unruly presentation and wild ways, and sees that on this day he looks as wild as ever.

Noting as much to one of the Exploration Committee members, that gentleman turns to Dr Wills and replies, 'I have just told Burke he will have to shoot him yet.'[11]

For now, Burke exercises restraint, and continues to pace and bark orders, until, at last, as the shadows of late afternoon start to lengthen, it is nearly time to get going. Burke tries to gather together his team, so otherwise dispersed among a crowd that presses in on them from all sides, but at last manages it . . . no . . . WAIT!

One of the camels is loose, cantering through the crowd, sending people flying, even as a panicked sepoy races after it. The camel, in turn, begins chasing a rotund constable who suddenly takes off like an emu bitten on the bottom by a bee as the crowd roars with laughter! And so it goes, as the camel keeps going . . .

'The horses kicked, the females screamed and there was general confusion for a time, but at length order was restored, and, the camels being duly loaded, Mr Burke, the leader of the expedition, announced that everything was ready for a start.'[12]

Let us say a few words before you go, Mr Burke, now that your party is ready to depart and you have changed into your most magnificent explorer's attire – light tan trousers, boots, dark blue jacket, red shirt, and black high-peaked hat known as a Garibaldi – and really *look* the part, your black beard as magnificent as ever in the sun.

'Mr Burke,' booms Mayor Dr Richard Eades, in a rich Dublin accent, from his position atop one of the expedition's drays, 'I am fully aware that the grand assemblage, this day, while it has impeded your movements in starting, is at the same time a source of much gratification to you. It assures you of the most sincere sympathy of the citizens.'[13]

(*Hear, hear.*)

'I will not detain you, but for this great crowd, and on behalf of the colony at large, I say, God speed you!'[14] (*Cheers.*)

'Three cheers for Mr Burke!' (*Hip-Hip-Hurrah!*)

'Three cheers for Mr Landells!' (*Hip-Hip-Hurrah!*)

'Three cheers for the party itself!' (*Hip-Hip-Hurrah!*)

'God speed and bless you,'[15] the mayor finishes with a flourish.

And now Burke replies . . .

'Mr Mayor,' he says, in ringing, earnest tones, rising to the grand occasion. 'On behalf of myself and the Expedition, I beg to return to you my most sincere thanks. No expedition has ever started under such favourable circumstances as this. The people, the Government, the Committee – they all have done heartily what they could do. It is now our turn, and we shall never do well till we justify what you have done in showing what we can do!'[16] (*Cheers.*)

It is the moment, the time for the last farewells.

In a quiet corner, Richard Birnie has a hurried embrace with young William, and the two promise to write to each other, both feeling a great deal of emotion, so deep is the bond between them. It is now that William gives Richard a surprise present, a 'portrait [of himself], a miniature about three inches square'[17], beautifully framed in its 'well-made plush padded and gilt mounted case'[18]. Richard is so moved he can barely speak.

Nearby, Mr Burke is shaking hands with the many dignitaries who have come to farewell them, their number including Mary Stawell, the wife of the chief justice. As warm as ever, his brilliant blue eyes a-sparkle, Burke takes her by the hand, and says words she will never forget: 'I may fail, but I promise you it will not be an ignoble failure.'[19]

To his great friend, Richard Nash, Burke also now has a quiet word.

'I am very sorry, Nash,' he says, 'that my circumstances will not allow me to present you with a souvenir for all the trouble I have given you, and the further trouble I have imposed upon you during my absence, but, present my portrait to your wife, and call at Ford's Royal Artillery Hotel, Elizabeth Street. You will there find a pistol, which was presented to me by the police at Beechworth. Get it, and take care of it. If I return I shall expect it back again. If I do not, then keep it in remembrance of me.'[20]

●

Meanwhile, as the clock ticks on to the moment they've all been waiting for, the entire scene is so stunning that one little lad in the front row, holding hands with his father, will also be able to recall, 74 years later, the whole thing.

'I had never seen or heard of camels and the great, ungainly creatures seemed as big as a house,' he would recount. 'They had just been loaded up . . . and were very restless, and groaning miserably. Each was held by [a sepoy].'

And now the little lad and his father, and all of the madding crowd that presses in, are told to move back a little, so the men can get into marching order. And look there, young fellow, at the two men with 'big wide hats and leggings', giving all the orders!

'One of them, a dark-complexioned man with a heavy beard, had . . . a pistol stuck in his belt.'

There is a pause, and now as he will ever after recall, a gun fires.

'The leaders in the front lifted their hats, appearing to be waving a farewell; the crowd was cheering, and off they went . . .'[21]

Adding to the splendid gaiety of the occasion, the band strikes up that magnificent tune, 'Cheer, Boys, Cheer'.

Ah yes, cheer, boys, cheer, and everyone sing!

> *Cheer, boys, cheer! We'll march away to battle!*
> *Cheer, boys, cheer, for our sweethearts and our wives!*
> *Cheer, boys, cheer! We'll nobly do our duty,*
> *And give to the South our hearts, our arms, our lives.*[22]

Now, for such an occasion as this, one might expect, that the highest and mightiest, guiding them north through the gates, would be the leader, Robert O'Hara Burke, but no . . .

Instead, while Mr Burke sits modestly atop 'his pretty little grey at the head'[23] – which is to say his favourite horse – right behind him, atop the biggest bull camel of the lot, and looking magnificent, is George Landells. True, a tad odd, that a man so insistent that the camels remain unburdened should then place his own hefty frame upon one of them just hours later, but there it is. As they proceed to the gates, Landells graciously acknowledges the raucous cheers of the crowd, like a king acknowledging his loyal subjects. Napoleon is leaving Paris once more, off to conquer new worlds, in the vanguard of a cavalcade over 500 yards long! He is clearly a man who is not only comfortable with such attention, but actively *seeks* it and, in this circumstance, Burke looks less like the leader than the servant on the humble horse clearing a passage through the crowd for the emperor.

So be it. Mr Burke is not fussed.

Right behind these two in the lead come several of the common men on foot, leading heavily laden pack horses, followed by three of the fabulously attired Indian sepoys – shining with their bright red turbans and white robes – leading, also on foot, four or five of their wonderful camels! In fact, trying to keep calm those camels – most with exotic names like Mochrani, Matvala, Gobin, Golah Singh and

Tschibik – amid the madding crowd is no small thing, and the sepoys only just manage it as fresh bursts of raucous cheering break out as they pass along the line.

And now come the scientists like Ludwig Becker, the portly 52-year-old German, followed by yet more packhorses and, last of all, the six wagons, hauled along by six horses each, with one sepoy in the rear mounted on the twenty-seventh and last camel . . . .

And wait!

Some of the wagons get bogged in the mud, and another breaks down entirely, as 'the pole [connected to the horses] broke in attempting to start it'[24].

Ferguson fumes and curses, without naming those who had not listened to his warnings that *exactly* this thing would happen. (*He did tell you, Mr Burke, but you wouldn't listen. And so, yes, now your expedition is underway, but, only just, and after such a staggered start, who can doubt but that it will remain a staggered procession?*)

There is a pause as one of the wagons, at least, is dragged out again and now they are on their way once more – less William Wills, Hermann Beckler and Charles Ferguson, who must stay behind for what will likely be several hours to sort the wounded wagons, repair and reload them.

Richard Birnie stands alone, watching them go, straining for a last glimpse of William, and is overwhelmed with emotion.

'As the cavalcade slowly vanished from my straining sight,' he would chronicle, 'I felt a sad presentiment that I had looked my last upon the eye that had never been turned upon and met mine but with deep esteem and the warm friendship of a pure and noble mind.'[25]

Will he ever see young William again?

The barrister's overwhelming sadness, however, is certainly the minority sentiment on the day.

Oh, all together sing as we bid them farewell and . . .

> *Cheer, boys, cheer . . .*
> *Tho' to the homes we never may return,*
> *Ne'er press again our lov'd ones in our arms,*

O'er our lone graves their faithful hearts will mourn,
Then cheer, boys, cheer! Such death hath no alarms.[26]

The last of the cavalcade passes through the gates of Royal Park, right by the large pile of camel manure that lies there. Yet another wagon, however, breaks down just beyond it.

As early evening deepens to night, the crowd has dispersed, and all that is left in Royal Park are the men fixing the wagons, and the others laboriously striking the tents. They can catch up later tonight.

In the meantime, many journalists are racing to file their copy, few more enthusiastic than a journalist from the Melbourne *Herald*.

'Never,' he reports, 'have we seen such a manifestation of heart-felt interest in any public undertaking of the kind as on this occasion. The oldest dwellers in Australia have experienced nothing to equal it.'[27]

True, but one old dweller, the Grand Old Man of Melbourne, John Pascoe Fawkner – one of the two founding fathers of Melbourne, who had established the town's first pub and first newspaper all the way back in 1845 – does not share the enthusiasm. Now rising 70, he certainly looks the part, with his wavy leonine locks glistening white in the evening glow, and yet he is nothing less than stunned at what he has witnessed, and as he makes his way home is already mentally composing the letter which will appear the next day in the *Age*.

> Sir,—If we are to infer what will be the performance of the camel-provided exploration party from . . . yesterday's start, — it will be an unmitigated failure. A camel-party, with tremendously ponderous wagons, and rather expensively large decorated tents, which require a great waste of time to take down, pack up, and then unload and reset up, all within a space of two hours, threatens ill for ultimate success, and foretells disaster, if not ruin, to all concerned in the journey . . .
>
> Oh, the futility of such conduct. What marks it? Why incapacity, and therefore waste of money, aye, and loss of life. The whole matter has been mismanaged all through.
>
> JOHN P. FAWKNER.
> 21st August, 1860.[28]

Evening, 20 August '60, Essendon, the end of the beginning

So delayed has the start been on this day, so many distractions and problems, that by the time the expedition makes camp for the night, they are no more than four miles from where they started, right on a green field by St John's Presbyterian Church at Essendon.

It is the equivalent of a train leaving a platform crowded with well-wishers and giving many cheery toots as it departs to thunderous cheers ... only ... only ... only for it to stop before it has disappeared around the bend.

As more well-wishers variously amble, trot and run north towards the Essendon camp, a horseman thunders past at a quick gallop, going the other way ... It is none other than Robert O'Hara Burke, racing back to the theatre, where Julia Matthews, with a fetching new locket around her neck, is performing at the Princess Theatre, on the opening night of a double bill, *The Carnival Hall* and *The Lonely Man of the Ocean*. A horseman in the moonlight, Burke spurs his horse down the Mount Alexander Road, right past Melbourne General Cemetery, filled with men who've had their own dreams and are now turned to dust, but his dream might still come true!

Mr Burke does not arrive in time for the final scene where the male lead with the notably bushy beard, in this case 'The Lonely Man of the Ocean', stands alone on the moonlit deck, with his dead crew lying all around him, but it is perhaps just as well ...

The main thing is that this lonely man and his lovely lady are able to meet, backstage, and briefly talk, and even embrace, before he must a'gallop, a'gallop, a'gallop awaaaaay ... once more.

Ideally, the expedition will be able to make an early start on the morrow.

21 August '60, Essendon, morning, mud and the martinet

Alas, the following morning, the party is delayed; a horse that ran away the previous night is still to be caught, and some of the broken-down wagons are yet to arrive; the loud oaths of Mr Ferguson become gradually coarser and louder throughout the morning.

The delay does give well-wishers and sticky-beaks the opportunity to keep pouring in around them. Among those who do so is Dr Wills, who cannot shake a sudden sense of gloom and foreboding that has come over him, and cannot quite bear to be parted from his son, young William, and so takes the opportunity to have just a little more precious time with him.

But first, Dr Wills gravitates to the expedition's leader, Mr Burke, whom he has come to know just a little over the last weeks.

True, Mr Burke is not in the best of moods, as he is beginning to realise that they are as much a tourist attraction as an expedition, but at the sight of the father of his third officer, Burke softens, and the two talk briefly. In fact, there is enough good fellowship between them that Dr Wills even confides to the leader some of his fears.

'If it were in my power,' Dr Wills says frankly, 'I would even now prevent his going.'

After pausing for a moment, wondering if he should say it, but realising he will long regret it if he doesn't, Dr Wills continues.

'If [my son] knew what I am about to say,' the old man says gravely, 'he would not, I think, be well pleased. But if you ever happen to want my son's advice or opinion, you must ask it, for he will not offer it unasked. No matter what course you may adopt, he will follow without remonstrance or murmur.'

In response, Mr Burke rises to the occasion, shakes Dr Wills warmly by the hand, and replies: 'There is nothing you can say will raise him higher in my estimation than he stands at present; I will do as you desire.'[29]

Soon enough, hail fellow well met once again, William himself drifts over. And now a photographer is pressing Dr Wills and his son to stand still so they may take a portrait shot for future use in their papers.

William, ever modest, declines, and politely waves them away.

'Should it ever be worth while,' he says cheerily, pointing out his pater, 'my father has an excellent one, which you can copy from.'

As ever, Dr Wills is proud of his son's humility. The two embrace, and say their heartfelt goodbyes.

Truthfully?

Despite all the excitement, even young William Wills has his concerns, noting in a letter to Richard Birnie that their first day had been nothing less than a 'miserable start ... I hope that start will not prove a datum from which our future proceedings may be estimated, but that it will rather act as a stimulus to excite more energetic action in future.'[30]

Which it is to be, only time will tell.

Speaking of time ... it is not until the crack of mid-afternoon that the whole party is underway, travelling as far as the Inverness Hotel, some 10 miles to the north.

The next morning, another delay. For there has been yet another ... issue.

And it is George Landells who must resolve it. One of the sepoys, Samla, a Hindu, has decided that he cannot go on and so begs Mr Landells to allow him to return to Melbourne. As a Hindu, he cannot eat beef, making his situation untenable as the rations they are handed every day are heavy on exactly that.

'The poor fellow looked very poorly indeed,' Ludwig Becker would record in his diary, 'having had nothing for the last three days but bread and plenty of work. He saw it was impossible for him to remain with us without breaking his faith.'[31]

Mr Landells has little choice but to cede to the request, and after working things out, hands over to Samla his wages due in the form of a promissory note written by Mr Burke to the account of the Royal Society.

With tears in his eyes, the Indian man, so far from home, so relieved, pockets the note, bends to touch mother earth with his fingers before straightening to touch his forehead. In the curious manner of people of his faith – essentially flicking the fingers of his right hand three times as if he is trying to remove water – he blesses Mr Landells, his fellow sepoys, and the men of the expedition close to him. And now he turns on his heel, and heads back in the direction whence they came.

The rest of them push on ...

Into what, exactly?

Rain and mud and the curses of foreman Ferguson to move faster.

For not long after Samla leaves, the heavens themselves begin to weep, the black soil the expeditioners are pushing through on the rough tracks up around Bolinda, 32 miles north of Melbourne, turns into a sticky mass of mess, and as Ludwig Becker records in his journal, 'and ere night had set in [the rain] came down in torrents. No tea, no fire; we slept in the wet.'[32]

By the following morning, a new problem is apparent, even beyond their frozen state and the fact that everything is sodden, heavy and even more difficult to pack up.

It is one thing, too, to have camels, who are, in the felicitous phrase of Thomas Embling MP, 'the gift of Heaven'[33] for crossing sand, but they are no such gift on these muddy tracks.

'Within five days,' Dr Hermann Beckler chronicles, 'the camels began to show the effects of continual rain, the gradual change of feed and the camping in the open . . . They developed catarrhs and diarrhoea and their faeces contained their hitherto customary feed . . . in an undigested state.'[34]

It is clear to him, and more particularly, Mr Landells, that Mr Burke is pushing the camels too hard through this impossible country, not allowing them to graze, to rest, to replenish their stores. And there is no respite in sight.

'The black soil . . .' Ludwig Becker notes, 'was in consequence of the heavy fall of rain, last night turned into a sort of mud . . . dangerous and difficult for a camel's foot and a great hindrance to our wagons. It was a very tedious and tiring work to lead on foot a camel through such ground, and at the same time taking good care that no branch overhead or on the ground interferes with walking or rather skating.'[35]

Making the heaviest weather of it all are the newly hired wagons, and Burke quickly decides to let them drift behind the convoy . . . and then well behind . . . . . . and soon . . . . to catch up when they can.

Whether or not an inland sea awaits them, they are not sure. But right now they are trudging ankle-deep through an inland sea of mud that saps their spirits and energy in equal measure.

But it is not just the exhaustion that troubles them.

It is quickly becoming apparent that Mr Burke is not an easy-going man. Yes, it is clear he is a leader of men, and there is a confident, generous, garrulous side to him. On occasion he can be fine company around the campfire.

But the other side to him – the martinet, giving sharp orders as though he is Captain Burke and they are all stumbling, bumbling recruits in his personal army – is harder to cope with, let alone warm to. For those who fancy themselves on a scientific expedition, it is particularly jarring to be taking such orders from a man with loaded pistols on each hip. In the same abrupt manner that Ferguson orders the men around, Mr Burke considers the likes of officers such as Becker and Beckler at his beck and call and orders them around like underlings. The difference is that while Ferguson's men are used to being so ordered, the officers have for the most part *never* been spoken to like that in their lives, let alone having the capacity to follow such orders quickly and to the letter.

Mr Ferguson at least thinks he has found the way to manage his leader, and to cope with Burke's style of handing out a series of fast and firm orders that are not necessarily part of a cohesive whole.

'Often,' Ferguson would recount, 'he would come to me with an order which to me seemed erroneous. I would simply say, "Very well, Mr Burke" – that was enough for him to know that I did not approve of it. He would at once ask if I did not think it best to do so, when I would suggest whether it would not be preferable to do so and so, and he would at once say, "You are right; do as you like"', when, if one had said to him that his was not the best way, he would have it done his way, let it result as it might. Landells would have made a better leader than Mr Burke, being a cooler and more calculative man, with a good deal of Indian experience before coming over with the camels.'[36]

28 August '60, Barnadown, roll up and roll on, the carnival is passing

For the Bendigo locals, who walk, ride and race to cheer, wave and stare at the passing 'camel-cade'[37], as the local paper calls it, there are many things of wonder about the Victorian Exploring Expedition as it passes nearby at Knowsley and heads up to Barnadown ... not all of them good.

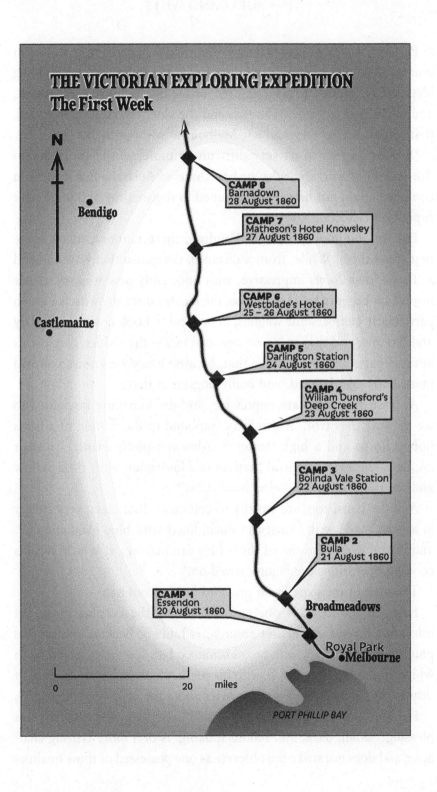

Perhaps the most compelling is the maps. A messenger has been sent into Bendigo requesting maps of the north Australian coast giving 'detailed information respecting the whole of the north, north-west, and north-east coast of Australia, and the chief rivers upon it'[38]. Yes, that's right. Seems they had left Melbourne without them!

'It does appear to us very difficult to understand,' the *Bendigo Advertiser* notes archly, 'why the best charts of Australia that have been compiled could not have been obtained in the wealthy and important capital of Victoria . . .'[39]

But for the good people of Bendigo, there is more, much more that stuns them. While, from a distance, the expedition now camped at Barnadown *looks* impressive, with noticeably new wagons, closer inspection beggars belief. Up close, the locals notice the wheels on two particularly cumbersome wagons, in particular. Look how narrow they are! No one, and they mean *no one*, can tackle the sodden grey plains in these parts with wheels like that, because everyone knows you will immediately get bogged, and badly bogged at that.

At least the camels are impressive, and the locals are fascinated to see the way they trot, 'which is a compound of the motion of a boy's hobby horse and a high trotter'[40]. Almost equally exotic are their minders, the ever colourful 'natives of Hindostan, with their yellow and red ponchos and peculiar head dress'[41].

And the tents, too, are worthy of comment: first class, very cheery in aspect, made with 'American duck, lined with blue blanketing . . . and at the front of some of them fires are blazing, at which various cooking operations are being carried on.'

The men of the expedition prove to be a mixed bag.

Here, at the front of one tent, discussing the evening meal, the journalist for the *Advertiser* records, is Ludwig Becker, 'the natural philosopher and artist, with broad brimmed hat, spectacles, and reddish whiskers and moustaches . . . with his peering look and harmless love of display, but looking somewhat smarter about the nether habiliments'[42].

His German companion, Dr Hermann Beckler, is somewhat less pleasing: 'small, dark, and bilious looking, is of a more retiring character, and does not strike the observer as one possessed of those qualities of mind which lead men to engage in such enterprises, and which have caused his selection by the Royal Society.'

Mr Wills and Mr Landells are much more to the journalist's taste, the former striking him as 'a young, slim, fair complexioned man, with the air of the student, but evidently intelligent and clear headed', while the latter is 'a quiet, unassuming man, who improves very much upon acquaintance ... he seems to be the only man of the lot thoroughly at his ease'[43].

'A robust man, with a large dark beard and black peaked California hat, and with the air of a leader about him, is pointed out to us as Mr Burke.'[44]

But it is not just reporters with notebooks who observe the camp, as many locals within a 20-mile radius flock to see the strange beasts and the famous expedition. Mr Burke's expedition moves off slowly, chased and followed, up through Victoria's settled districts, by eager locals making a day of it, seeing the spectacle, cheering them on ... and slowing them down.

'We were all glad to have [the environs of Bendigo] behind us,' Dr Beckler notes, 'for we and the entire party had descended to the level of exhibits displayed for the curious colonists ...'[45]

Besides which, for naturalists such as he and Ludwig Becker, the joys of this expedition are not to be found within the settled areas, but rather in the open countryside that they head into now, which has visual joys all its own.

'It was a magnificent panorama ...' Dr Beckler records. 'The play of sunlight and clouds produced wonderful effects on the wide plain; light and shadow alternated in quick succession as in a diorama. Miles of land were lit up, only to be cast into deepest shadow within a few seconds. Huge clouds sailed across the sky and their shadows rolled over the land like the tatters of a gigantic, torn veil.'[46]

•

For his part, Robert Burke has much bigger worries than mere opinions expressed in the newspaper. No, his problems are rather more material in nature, and are to be found in a sphere all too familiar to him – money, or the lack thereof.

On arrival to Bendigo he had sent a note to Dr Macadam stating simply: 'Chequebook required immediately.'[47]

For, you see, to meet inevitable expenses along the way in the absence of the chequebook that has been long promised, but never delivered, he has had to sign a series of promissory notes. It is an unsatisfactory and messy way of conducting financial affairs, and as Mr Burke is more expert than most on the dangers and worries attendant to financial messes in his personal life – his own debts back in Melbourne continue to worry him – he is insistent that this expedition avoid it. He so needs that chequebook!

Oh, and one more thing, Dr Macadam, if you please: 'Inform Mr Hodgkinson . . . that there will be a vacancy for him at Swan Hill . . . Inform [him] immediately I require him.'[48]

30 August '60, Melbourne, a scorpion summoned

A message for you, William Hodgkinson.

It proves be from no less than the leader of the Victorian Exploring Expedition – the former police superintendent whom Mr Hodgkinson reported on back in Castlemaine days, when he was a journalist for the local paper.

Well, then!

Mr Hodgkinson likes to be required. From an English grammar school to the Maryborough Goldfield, whether as a midshipman or as a clerk to the War Office in London, to a life of journalism, lately with the *Age*, Hodgkinson has always excelled at being thought of by his superiors as excellent.

True, his peers tend to have a different view, as a malicious and mischievous streak appears when his superiors' backs are turned, while his abrasiveness is legendary. At school he had been known as 'fighting Billy', so strong was his 'combative instinct', and the fact that 'at any age he was prepared to wrestle or fight'[49]. It is just *in* him.

'The Berserker blood thirst of some ancient Norse ancestor,' one schoolmate would recall, 'impelled him towards the arena of prospective battle.'[50]

Could there be a better arena of battle currently in Australia than this, a better struggle than trying to cross the entire continent, and a more glorious venture available, with perhaps better stories to write about?

Hodgkinson is on his way north by the following day. Heading north, too, is Professor Neumayer of the Flagstaff Observatory, who is also joining the expedition, but only for 'some 200 or 300 miles in order to assist in the organisation of systematic observations in the various branches of physical science and astronomy'[51].

(While William Wills is most eager for his scientific mentor's help, Mr Burke is simply eager to keep Professor Neumayer onside, thanks to his unspoken role as temporary observer from the Royal Society. Yes, Mr Burke remains in total control, but it is equally obvious Professor Neumayer will have a word to say back in Melbourne on how it is all going, and Mr Burke is eager that his report card be first class.)

Hodgkinson and Professor Neumayer will be joining an expedition now realising that their journey proper, away from what they regard as the civilised coastal fringe, is beginning in earnest . . .

'There is nothing more interesting than this sharp frontier between the coastal land and the inland, continental regions,' Dr Hermann Beckler notes. No more are they passing happy settlements and excited people who line the highways and byways they have been proceeding triumphantly along. Such comforting things are now left in their wake, replaced by . . . plains . . . just . . . miles . . . . . . and . . . . . . *miles* . . . . of plains, covered by saltbush, with other dense vegetation hiding in the rocks and crevices of the land, the only way it can survive in this harsh environ. Such tracks as there are meander along through the path of least resistance. This area is known as the Terrick-Terrick Plains, surely by virtue of an Aboriginal word meaning *dull and bloody endless, you know?*, and the mood of the expedition members dims a little as they settle to the first of the hard slog that awaits, through what Ludwig Becker describes as looking like 'a calm ocean . . . with green water . . . On you go, miles and miles, a single tree, a belt of timber appeared at the horizon affected by the mirage; you reach that belt of small trees, a Wallaby, a kangaroo-rat disturbs for a moment the monotony, and a few steps further on you are again on the green calm ocean.'[52]

All too soon, alas, this mirage of a green calm ocean turns into an all too real sea of mud as heavy rain falls, drenching the expedition, and making every step forward an exhausting process of extricating one foot from the last sodden step to take the next one.

'The poor camels, completely soaked and shivering with cold, slipped at most every step and sank deep into the mud . . . One could not help but feel for these animals when they stopped now and then for a moment to rest. They looked at us so miserably.'[53]

All the men can do is maintain the course, hour after hour, day after day, comforted that at least one good-sized town, Swan Hill – at least 30 people, maybe 20 – lies up ahead, at the only spot within 50 miles in any direction that you can cross the mighty Murray River, that marks the border with New South Wales, on a punt.

31 August '60, Dr Rowe's station, rest for the rest at Terrick-Terrick

The pleasure is very nearly as exquisite as the painting. After so much rain, on this glorious day of fine, warm weather, Ludwig Becker takes the opportunity on this rare day of rest to engage in some sketching and painting. And yet as interested as he is in trying to capture the immensity and flatness of the Terrick-Terrick Plains, their party strung out to a vanishing point off in the distance, he realises it is as nothing to the fascination the local blacks have for the animals the expedition is travelling with. '4 natives, among them a lubra, went their steps slowly towards the camp. With eyes and mouths wide open, speechless they stared at the *Bunjibs*, our camels, but refused to go nearer than a spear's throw. Although no strangers at Dr Rowe's station, and notwithstanding our assurance that the camels were only harmless "big sheep", they turned their back towards them and squatted soon round a far off camp fire of their own, conversing in their native tongue; probably about the character of these illustrious strangers. If this first interview between natives and camels might be used as a criterion when coming in contact with the blacks in the course of our future journeys, then, surely, we might spare the gunpowder as long as the mesmeric power of our Bunjibs remain with them.'[54]

•

A horse in motion moves its rider backwards and forwards, while a camel sways its rider side to side, meaning the ship of the desert sometimes causes sea-sickness. But not in William Wills.

'Riding on camels is a much more pleasant process than I anticipated,' he writes from the Terrick-Terrick Plains on the last day of August to his former boss and mentor for all things surveying and cartography, Frederick Byerley. He explains to his mentor just how he is making his observations: 'and for my work I find it much better than riding on horseback. The saddles, as you are aware, are double, so I sit on the back portion behind the hump, and pack my instruments in front. I can thus ride on, keeping my journal and making calculations; and need only stop the camel when I want to take any bearings carefully; but the barometers must be read and registered without halting.'[55]

It is as well, for, whatever else, William Wills is the most ever-and-always active man on the entire expedition, constantly conquering new territory for the scientific world, even as he leads the way and guides the course through the previously uncharted geographic world. From first to last – and despite the Exploration Committee's view that the expedition would start their scientific work in earnest only from crossing the Darling onwards – with the camel's hump as his desk and workspace, he is busy recording as many as 15 meteorological readings a day on the chalky pale blue pages of his surveyor's field book: marking down everything from magnetic variations, the temperature and humidity at any given time, to the wind direction, air pressure, altitude, cloud patterns and even bird paths.

4 September '60, Tragowel, new man, old hand

Some 50 miles short of the Murray River, on 4 September, they stop at Tragowel station, where Burke happens upon a new recruit. For an expedition that is simply crying out for the expertise of a bushman, Robert Bowman is the answer. Rejected in the first round of applications – despite the fact that he had been a valued member of *both* of Gregory's Queensland expeditions, meaning he had not only been to the Gulf of Carpentaria on one trip and Cooper's Creek on another, but had also travelled the route from Cooper's Creek to Mount Hopeless via Strzelecki Creek – Mr Burke hires him on the spot. Bowman is soon being ordered around by Mr Ferguson like all the rest, which is to say . . . constantly, as, all day long and into the night, the American foreman barks coercion, correction, suggestion and, on the rarest of occasions, approval.

CHAPTER SIX

'PUSH, PUSH, PUSH ...'

Burke was the worst bushman I ever met, and I have known him to lose himself even on a blazed track – not because he could not follow the blazes, but because the idea would come into his head that he could make a shorter cut by leaving it. He always admitted, and even boasted that he could never cross a 5-mile forest or a hill without losing himself; but this again was an eccentric exaggeration.[1]

A friend and colleague of Robert Burke at Beechworth, 1887

6 September '60, not like ducks to water at Swan Hill

They're coming! They're *coming!*

For the good folk in the tiny hamlet of Swan Hill – which is centred on the punt crossing of the Murray River, which brings travellers their way – it is the most exciting thing that has happened since, well ... since forever.

To think that such a grand expedition, on such a noble cause, is coming through their fair burgh is nothing less than an exquisite honour, and the citizenry turn out in such force as they can muster to welcome the arrivals, gazing at the grimy, sweaty men with their horses and their ... *extraordinary* camels as if they are visitors from another world. It is noted that, 'with the exception of a sepoy, they appeared in good health and spirits, and thoroughly united amongst themselves'.[2]

And the expedition members, of course, gaze back, simply glad to have arrived at this outpost of civilisation in a region not particularly blessed with it.

It is mid-afternoon on 6 September, and Burke and his men are soon guided to 'the hospital reserve' right by the banks of the beautiful Murray River, some half a mile outside the township. (It has to be that far removed, for every horse in Swan Hill only has to catch sight of the camels before they bolt.)

The men begin the ever laborious task of pitching the enormous tents for the officers, pausing only to curse at the sheer gut-busting and time-consuming nature of it.

Of the pleasures that await the new arrivals, one of them is mail, which has just arrived. Mr Burke retreats to the tent that has been set up for himself and Mr Landells, so as to read his letters, and . . .

Oh dear.

Oh dear, oh dear.

For Robert O'Hara Burke, it is one thing to handle the pressure of leading a huge expedition upon which hangs the pride of a colony, but it is quite another thing to handle the pressure that descends upon a man's shoulders when he finds that a warrant for his arrest is pending.

And yet that is apparently the case. He is informed by a letter from his friend with power of attorney, Mr Richard Nash, that a cheque for £74, which he had written more than a month before his departure to a James Montgomery to honour a debt . . . had in fact been dishonoured . . . and Montgomery had been feeling rather grim about it all.

Burke's hands quiver with 'distress'[3], his face flushes with a curious combination of anger, confusion and panic, his neck tightens, his brilliant blue eyes turn a steely grey. This is no small thing. He is the leader of the Victorian Expedition, a police superintendent, and a member of the Melbourne Club with powerful men as friends, who have backed him all the way. And now he is to be known as one whose cheques are not honoured? This fellow Montgomery, a lawyer, is threatening his *arrest*? What will Julia think? It is unthinkable.

He *must* put a stop to it and tries now to do so, getting his reply letter to Nash done before the outgoing mail leaves shortly:

Swan Hill, September 6, 1860.

. . . I certainly do not know under what circumstances a man can be arrested for not meeting his cheque, but if Mr Montgomery, as I suspect,

for the sake of his fee, meant to insinuate that I had committed myself
in any way, that is to say, that I had done anything wilfully to mislead,
if I live to return I will make it a caution to him.[4]

Burke urges Nash to have the matter cleared up by whatever means, otherwise 'I shall suffer in the opinion of the Chief Justice . . . Pray write to me again upon the subject. You have no idea how this has troubled me. R OH B'[5]

He remains deeply, deeply troubled. To have the spectre of your own bankruptcy and disgrace hanging over your head, *while* you are being lauded wherever you go as a great hero; the mental agony is exquisite.

As to young William Wills, as the expedition girds itself over the next few days at Swan Hill to make the next big push, he writes to his dear friend, Richard Birnie in Fitzroy, giving – very quietly – some of his impressions of two of the key characters on the trip, after their first three weeks or so pushing north.

'As to Burke and Landells whose characters I know you will be interested to hear something about, the first is an energetic, good-natured, rough, gentlemanly fellow; the last two characteristics appear to disagree, but I mean rough in manner and gentlemanly in feeling. Landells is quite different, nothing of a gentleman, either in manner or feeling, he is sentimentally good-natured, more particularly towards the animals, [suited to them] in the extreme, mildly persevering and perseveringly mild; but at the same time he must always make people dislike him, from his unmannerly distance and want of substance . . .'[6]

•

The Victorian Exploring Expedition's early days around Swan Hill sees their numbers grow by two, with one permanent arrival in William Hodgkinson, who had caught up with them just before they got to the town, and one temporary addition in Professor Georg Neumayer, who appears in camp four days after their arrival.

Hodgkinson throws down his kit as a freshly minted member of the party, ready to serve as clerk to the leader and do whatever else is required. He brings with him the latest dispatches from the Exploration Committee, and most importantly, that long-awaited chequebook from

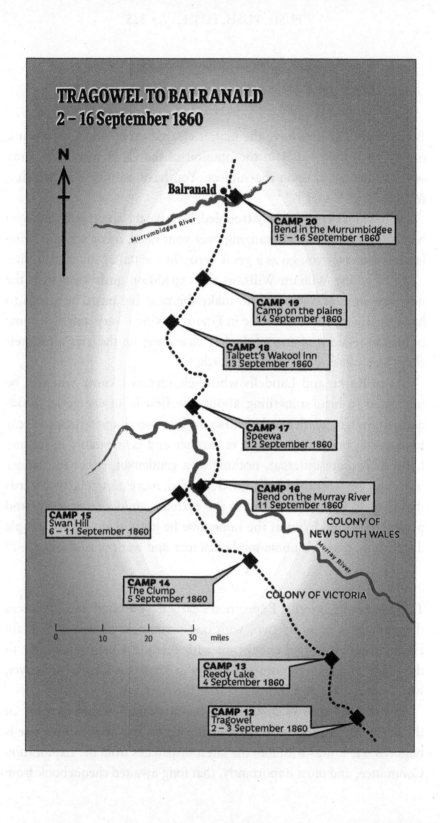

TRAGOWEL TO BALRANALD
2 – 16 September 1860

N

Balranald

Murrumbidgee River

CAMP 20
Bend in the Murrumbidgee
15 – 16 September 1860

CAMP 19
Camp on the plains
14 September 1860

CAMP 18
Talbett's Wakool Inn
13 September 1860

CAMP 17
Speewa
12 September 1860

CAMP 16
Bend on the Murray River
11 September 1860

CAMP 15
Swan Hill
6 – 11 September 1860

COLONY OF
NEW SOUTH WALES

Murray River

CAMP 14
The Clump
5 September 1860

COLONY OF VICTORIA

0   10   20   30   miles

CAMP 13
Reedy Lake
4 September 1860

CAMP 12
Tragowel
2 – 3 September 1860

the National Bank of Australasia, for Mr Burke. It couldn't have been more timely!

For his part, Professor Neumayer heads over to settle into his own tent, already quickly set up by his servant, Mr Marks, who now trails closely behind, bearing the professor's valise.

While the two German scientific officers are pleased to see their countryman, Mr Wills is delighted. Well aware that he owes his present position to being Professor Neumayer's former assistant, Wills effectively becomes his assistant again, as they set out to calibrate the two gold watches, barometers and the accuracy of magnetic observations. They remain a few days yet at Swan Hill to enjoy the hospitality of its residents and the opportunity for some stationary science.

10 September '60, Swan Hill, debts, disobedient dispatches and financial fiddling?

Feverishly, fearfully, in his tent, Burke goes through the dispatches of the Committee. Are they aware of his ... let's call it ... *financial embarrassment* ... back in Melbourne? Has a complaint been made by one or many of his creditors? The fact that Professor Neumayer has greeted him warmly is an indication that there is not yet an issue, but still he is nervous.

To his relief there is no such missive, but still there are financial problems. The Exploration Committee urgently desires to bring to his attention that all the invoices from the government storekeeper that have come in, so far, amount to over £4000! And, Mr Burke? Still more bills are arriving. At the heart of this financial disaster, specifically, are the extra wagons ordered by Mr Burke, the ones drawn by six increasingly expensive horses each, together with cantankerous and even more expensive wagon drivers. The Committee seeks to draw his attention to a recent resolution of the Committee that these new wagons be dispensed with.

Mr Burke reels, just to read it. After all, this crisp missive has been sent to him before the Committee even find out that he has just agreed to *double* the wages of the wagoners! Whereas the weekly salary of the men and officers on the expedition is £66 combined, the wagon hire, negotiated by the savvy driver William Cole, is costing them £110 a week! In a new twist on highway robbery, this time it is wagon drivers themselves who are saying 'stick 'em up!'

But what can he do? No one resents the cost of the wagons more than he does, not to mention their cumbersome nature and infernal slowness. But as the only choice is to load up the camels instead, and Mr Landells is fiercely insistent that the camels remain unburdened, the wagons *must* remain at all costs – the Committee's costs included.

And so now, personally *and* professionally, Mr Burke is under severe financial strain.

All he can do is to write a carefully worded explanation to the Committee, explaining why he must stay with the wagons, at double the price, despite their resolution.

> *The Camp, Swan Hill,*
> *September 10, 1860.*
>
> *. . . I have made arrangements with the draymen for conveying our stores to the Darling . . . I consider it absolutely necessary to make this arrangement, notwithstanding my being in possession of the resolution of the Committee objecting to the transfer of the stores by hired assistance . . .*
>
> *I am well aware that our baggage is too cumbersome, and that a time will, I hope, soon come when we shall be obliged to leave the greater part of it behind us, but to do so now before having established our Depot upon the Darling . . . would, I think, be a most* ~~dangerous and~~ *injudicious proceeding . . .*[7]

Money matters spin around in Mr Burke's mind, just as the flies and mosquitoes buzz around his person. His only relief is when other, sometimes bigger, problems intrude, and here is one now . . .

It is Charles Ferguson, come to see Mr Burke to tell him that he is 'quite prepared to leave at once'[8], to depart from the expedition and go back to Melbourne. Since the beginning his concern at their lack of bushmen in the party has only grown, compounded by the fact that he has felt a growing resistance by the men to his rule, and even a lack of support from the officers, like Mr Burke? He is happy to go.

'I did not think this of you,' Mr Burke replies. 'I thought I could depend upon you.'

'Do you wish me to go on with the expedition? I am confident others don't.'

'I don't know,' the leader says, 'how I should get on without you?'

And yet, despite this declaration, Mr Burke now proceeds to ask his invaluable foreman if he would mind a cut in wages?

'The Royal Society has told me to reduce my expenses,' Burke explains. 'And how I am to do that without lowering the salaries, I do not understand. As you have a larger one than the rest, what do you think about its being reduced?'

'I cannot accede to any such proposal,' the stunned American says firmly, 'as my salary [of £200] is already less than I was getting . . .'[9]

'My hands are tied [financially],' Burke offers by way of expiation, 'and I cannot do what I like. But I have made up my mind not to discharge any man who had signed the agreement in Melbourne, except for misbehaviour.'[10]

For the moment, that is where the matter is left. Ferguson will stay on, but he has given Mr Burke fair warning that he is not happy. Another four men, despite Burke's claim to Ferguson, are dismissed for varying reasons, requiring more men to be hired . . .

Why not, suggests Superintendent Henry Foster of the Swan Hill Police over lunch with Burke at the Lower Murray Inn, try Charley[11] Gray, a local in his early forties, with an interesting background. A Scot, he is a 'run away sailor'[12] – he'd jumped ship in Melbourne to try his luck on the Bendigo goldfields – now a jack-of-all-trades, caring for the horses of travellers who pass through this very inn. True, it is whispered that he hits the bottle too hard, but only on the occasion of payday, and, despite that, his employer at the inn for the last 15 months, Mr Thomas Dick – who Mr Burke consults – swears by him. After all, only getting three sheets to the wind once a month makes him practically a teetotaller by local standards.

Most importantly, Foster advises, Gray's time on the goldfields has taught him bush skills, and when Thomas Dick's cattle had recently gone missing in the mallee scrub, Charley Gray had gone out on his own, tracked them, found them, and turned them for home, all without turning a hair.

Upon meeting him, Burke offers him one of the available jobs on the spot, and Gray, or 'Charley' as he is instantly known to all, accepts with enthusiasm, which proves to be almost infectious. Even so formal a man as Professor Neumayer immediately warms to him.

By 11 September it is clearly time that they get moving once more, and on this day a farewell lunch is given to the officers of the expedition, together with Professor Neumayer, on the veranda of Raines's Royal Hotel.

Mr Landells and his offsider, the shy young Irishman, John King, busy themselves with getting the camels across the Murray and by 5 pm it is done. They set up camp a quarter mile on the north side of the Murray.

Neumayer and the other officers, led by Mr Burke, now have a farewell dinner to attend that evening as well, hosted by Superintendent Foster.

Nearing the dinner's end, Mr Foster publicly gives Mr Burke the gift of 'a highly finished pair of handcuffs . . .'[13]

For who knows just what trouble lies ahead? Either with the natives who might attack, or Burke's own men rising in mutiny? (*General merriment all round.*)

After a little dancing with the fine ladies of Swan Hill for 'a small ball was improvised'[14], it is time for rest.

The next morning, the residents visit once more, as the expedition sets off.

Three hearty cheers are given by the good burghers of Swan Hill as they leave, with perhaps an extra cheer, or at least coo-ee, for the one of their own who has joined them – Charley Gray!

Go well, Charley! Bon voyage! Hip-hip! Hurrah!

The expedition members, in turn, give 'three cheers for the ladies' and then another three cheers for all the inhabitants of Swan Hill, with the mermaids on Charley's bulging biceps dancing a voluptuous jig for the occasion. And now they are on their way!

(All except Mr Burke, who in fact slips back across the river to send some last dispatches to the Committee, including assurances that he really is economising, and that 'any man in future joining the party will supply themselves with clothing at their own cost and any additional article of clothing requested by any member of the party will be deducted from their pay'[15].)

The next day, the town turns out again, this time to farewell the expedition leader for good.

As he rides off, with cheers ringing in his ears once more, he does so 'amid a perfect shower of old shoes', a local custom to wish the traveller well on his journey.[16]

Burke is visibly affected by the tremendous warmth of the send-off, and, as the *Swan Hill Guardian* would later report, 'with tears in his eyes said, "Thank you for all your kindness, we haven't deserved it".

'"It is nothing to the welcome we shall give you on your return," came the quick response ...'[17]

Three days of exhausting travel await, through what is known as 'mallee country' – harsh scrub densely populated by the many types of low-growing mallee eucalyptus, an all but impenetrable territory of clinging trees that hinder progress more surely than any English maze.

They reach Speewa on the first night, camping not far from 'a native camp full of blacks'[18], natives who are stunned, and unsettled, by the sight of the camels. 'The black fellows ...' Professor Neumayer notes, 'call them white [fellow's] emus and said they would sooner ride any "buck jumper" than mount them.'[19]

The next day, the expedition is back tripping its way through the mallee. It is tough to navigate at the best of times, and the fact that heavy rain turns the track into a gluey swamp means, as Hermann Beckler chronicles, 'the horses had lost weight and were exhausted and the carters insisted that the loads be made lighter'[20].

Mercifully, another short rest-stop is up ahead as at four o'clock on the afternoon of 15 September 1860, the flocks of white cockatoos rising in alarm, squawking a deafening cacophony, presages the arrival of the expedition at the mighty Murrumbidgee River – to another punt, on the other side of which lies a small hamlet gracelessly clinging to the red soil plains of the Riverina in far western New South Wales. The hamlet, Balranald, Ludwig Becker notes, proves to be 'about 24 buildings, such as a Store, Hotel, Black Smith shops etc., the building material is bark and timber, calico and paper'[21].

15 September '60, Balranald, surplus stock: everything must ghee . . .

Not long after they arrive, the expedition is visited by one of the leading station owners in the area, Richard Bennett, who is all but instantly stunned at what he sees.

For he is, as he would recount, 'not . . . amused, but amazed, at the enormous quantity of utterly useless lumber they had with them . . . a large bullock wagon fitted up with materials for a complete black-smith's forge . . . camp bedsteads, and other articles too numerous to particularise, but I must not omit two or three large kegs of horseshoes and a boat . . .'

What are they *thinking*, heading off into the wilderness with that kind of useless cargo?

'The expedition,' he chronicles, 'had more the appearance of an army on the march than a party of bushmen going out exploring. There was not, strictly speaking, a bushman among the leaders . . .'

Bennett resolves to do what he can to help them, first steering them to pitch their camp on a plain just at the rear of Balranald, where their animals can easily get feed and water, before inviting Burke to come back to his station homestead to spend the night. Burke declines, for fear of what the men might get up to without him – they have already had a little trouble with the workers slipping away from their camps to drink with settlers – but at least Bennett is able to have 'a quiet talk'[22] with the leader.

As it happens, by now Mr Bennett is definitely preaching to the converted, for Burke's thoughts have been turning exactly this way, and never more so than since leaving Swan Hill. Bennett's words that 'the less impediments you are encumbered with the better'[23], have a logic all their own. After all, having covered less than 300 miles in nearly four weeks, it really is clear *something* must be done.

The next day, Burke gathers what Bennett calls 'a council of war', where it is 'decided to leave fully the half of the outfit with Messrs.

Sparkes and Cramsie, the storekeepers at Balranald, to await instructions from the Victorian Government', and the rest of the day is spent working out what to take, and what to leave.

Burke begins by giving orders to his men to leave behind many of their huge sacks of sugar, many of their guns and their ammunition. Oh, and all those barrels of lime juice must go, too. Yes, Burke is aware of the theory that taking lime juice will prevent scurvy. It is true that the Royal Navy had practically wiped out the condition – marked by bleeding gums, the opening of old wounds, loosening of teeth, lethargy, shooting pains, shortness of breath, easy bruising and eventual death – but it is Burke's judgement that the barrels are simply too heavy for the good they do. And so out they go.

(Somewhere, Captain Cook is turning in his watery grave. He had been convinced of the virtues of sauerkraut and lime juice to ward off scurvy and certainly every ship under his command from 1768 onwards had embraced those preventatives, together with exercising, ensuring dry quarters and clothes, and eating as much fresh food as possible.)

One thing that does attract Burke's overwhelming ire is the fact that they are carrying a staggering 993 pounds of *ghee*, Indian clarified butter that Mr Landells had insisted be brought along, to be mixed with the oatmeal and fed to the camels – nearly half a *ton* of it!

Well, Burke will no longer countenance it. The whole point of camels, as he understood it, is that they could live off the land for the most part – eating just about anything – and then live off their humps for long periods at a time, when going over the desert.

As such, he makes his pointed pronouncement. 'The *ghee* and the oatmeal are to be left behind.'[24]

Mr Landells is stunned.

'That will not give me a fair chance for working the animals when the tug comes,'[25] he says, referring to the time when they will need to rely on the camels to get them over wretched territory.

'If they cannot do without those things,' Burke snarls, 'we should proceed without them. The camels are like the wagons – nothing but a drag [on us]. And it is because of you and the camels that we have the wagons.'[26]

Landells bristles but defers. The ghee and oatmeal will be left behind, and that is that. (Well, not quite. Landells still manages to secrete a fair bit. After all, ghee is the hard-working John King's favourite food and he ensures the young man still has a supply.)

•

After nearly a month together, the men are all getting to know each other, and if one of them stands out for both extreme kindness and excessive uselessness when it comes to doing the hard work, it is Dr Ludwig Becker, the artist.

'A very genial man,' Ferguson would record, 'he was always trying to assist someone, not as yet having had the opportunity to display his artistic skill. He often asked me to find him something to do so he could assist the poor men.'[27]

On this day, Ferguson agrees and asks the Irishman, Patrick Langan, if, perchance, he does not have a task for Dr Becker? Langan glances over at the German with the horn-rim glasses, wearing his ludicrous moleskin pants, which just about swallow him whole so large are they, and doesn't hesitate.

'Yes, sur, of coorse I have,' says the Irishman in his thick County Mayo accent.

'*Vat* is it?' asks the German.

'Groom that camel,'[28] Langan replies, handing him a brush and pointing to one of the camels that Ferguson knows to be perhaps the most vicious of the lot. Conscripted to this cause in India, transported to these infernal climes in the cramped, wet and shuddering hold of a stinking boat, poked, prodded and pushed thereafter, this camel is *not* a happy camper. To this point, he has not been able to make anyone properly pay for the indignities he has suffered, but lives in hope. And so he cannot restrain his joy at the vision of the portly fellow approaching, brush in hand, wearing on his feet the hide of *another* animal that has no doubt been treated even worse than him, and lets out a joyous cry of 'nuuuuur, *nuuuuur*, NUUUUUR'.

True, there are many translations in English for this basic camel utterance, depending on the intonation with which it is uttered, but on this occasion, even the German seems to grasp its central meaning: 'bring the fat one closer, as I want to bite him'.

Dr Becker stops.

Turns to Langan.

'*Ist das Kamel lieb*, is this camel kind?'[29] he asks.

'Kind as a lamb, sur,' says Langon, mildly.

'Nuuuuur, *nuuuuur*, NUUUUUUUUR.'

Falteringly, the doctor – raised on art lessons, lithography practices and the study of the sciences, but now holding a brush before a raging beast in the Australian wilderness – takes a few steps back.

'Just say, *salaam, salaam*, to him,' says Langan, 'and he will be kind as a kitten, sur.'[30]

Again, Dr Becker goes forward – '*Salaam, salaaaam, salaaaaaaam*'[31] – and to his amazement, the camel really does seem to calm somewhat, even allowing him to kneel down before its nobbly knees and start to brush its foreleg. The idea is to brush away all possibility of an insect infestation, to ensure that bites cannot become infected. Dr Becker's first few strokes are tentative, but he appears to be growing in confidence.

Ferguson turns to go, but on the instant hears a cry of 'Help! Help! *Hilfe! HILFEEE!*'[32]

Turning, he sees Dr Becker, 10 feet in the air, the camel holding him between his teeth by the seat of the doctor's massive pants as he shakes him, furiously up and down.

Fifteen feet . . . five feet . . . 15 feet . . . five feet.

'Help! Help! *Hilfe! HILFEEE!*'

'Nuuuuur, *nuuuuur*, NUUUUUUUUR.'

Something has to give, and it proves to be the doctor's pants, right at the point Becker is at the height of both his arc, and his panic.

He hits the ground, landing miraculously on all fours, and hurtles forth like a scalded – if disabled – rabbit.

It is all Ferguson can do not to shriek with laughter, but he manages to compose himself long enough to do what must be done. Of course – no, really – he must reprove Langan.

'Why,' he asks, 'did you select *that* vicious camel for the doctor?'[33]

In reply, Ferguson would recount, Langan looks 'as solemn and sedate as a judge'[34], before giving his considered reply.

'I never saw him do the likes of that before, sur.'

Neither has Ferguson.

'However,' as the American would finish his account, 'the good doctor never applied for any more jobs.'[35]

17 September '60, Balranald, an American revolution

There has been rising disquiet among the men over Burke's high-handedness, his manner of dealing with them. Ferguson, whom Burke had personally sought, has even threatened to leave the expedition altogether.

'Mr Burke was an Irishman, and a gentleman in every sense of the word . . .' Ferguson would note, 'but he had the hasty impulses of his countrymen, and was not calculated, for that reason, for an unwarlike expedition of that kind. He was kind and generous to a fault, but, let anything happen out of the common routine, he was confused, then excited, till finally he would lose all control of his better judgment.'[36]

And this, friends, well, this is a case in point. For on this sparkling morning, Burke calls for officers and men alike to gather around him, so he can make an announcement.

'I have received instructions from the Committee,' he advises the men without preamble, 'that render it impossible for me to take all you men along with me at present.'[37]

There is a stirring at the rather stunning news. Set to cross the entire continent, some of them are going to get no further than *Balranald*?

'I believe however,' the leader continues, 'that I should be able to send eventually for you and bring [you on to the Darling].'[38]

Have they heard correctly? He *believes*, they *should* . . . ?

It all sounds to Charles Ferguson, for one, very much like Mr Burke has no confidence at all that that is what is going to occur.

As it happens, Ferguson is atop Mr Burke's list of those he wishes to leave behind – no doubt thanks to the American's threats to leave – together with Dr Becker, Brahe, McIlwaine, Langan and the sepoy Belooch. He announces they must remain at Balranald, with four of the camels and two horses, to take care of some of the stores that are no longer required.

Dismissed.

Dumbfounded, most of the men drift away. But Ferguson picks his moment to approach Burke alone to find out what is really going on. Typically, Ferguson asks the question that *needs* to be asked. 'Mr Burrrke,' he says, unbidden, his American tongue caressing the 'r' sound. 'Is the case really as you have stated, or are we to be left behind and subsequently told our services are not required?'

'I am only acting in accordance with the instructions of the Royal Society, Mr Ferguson,'[39] says Burke quickly and he goes on to tell the American that 'I shall write to the Committee and say the best men were left behind.'[40]

'I am satisfied,' says Ferguson in a sudden, uncharacteristically conciliatory tone, 'but if I am to be discharged, I should like to know it at once, and not be kept waiting here, and then be told.'[41]

But, not at all! Mr Burke simply shakes hands with him, looks him in the eye, and reassuringly says, 'Goodbye for a week or so'[42], before riding off.

Reassured, Ferguson gets back to work sorting out the stores, when only a short time later he looks up at an approaching horseman, to find it is Mr Burke once more, who now – he is waving him over – wishes to speak to him alone.

'On my conscience I cannot deceive you,' he says. 'You are right. My instructions are to discharge you and others, and I can do nothing.'[43]

Which is as maybe, but Ferguson is outraged regardless. Feeling for him, Mr Burke offers a less humiliating manner of departure, saying, 'I'll give you a chance of resigning.'[44]

Oh, really?

Here they have committed *them*selves, signing documents with great theatricality, to do the right thing by the expedition and its leader, but now, on a whim, the leader can walk away from *his* commitment to them?

It is outrageous and Ferguson can stand it no more.

'No,' he replies icily, 'I demand a thorough discharge. You know I did not wish to go, unless I was wanted, and I prefer a thorough discharge to a dishonourable resignation.'[45]

And now it is a stung Mr Burke who is in for a taste of humiliation; for, after Ferguson demands and receives a cheque for his wages, the leader offers him a written 'recommendation'[46], a reference for his future employment purposes.

'No,' Ferguson replies sternly. 'I refuse to accept. I have my own strong arms to fall back upon, and do not need it.'[47]

Ah, but the American is not done there.

For now, in the presence of Mr Burke, he asks all the men to gather round, and when they have done so, tells them, 'I wish to make a statement, and I ask Mr Burke to say if there is anything I have done wrong.'[48]

As Mr Burke listens carefully, Ferguson takes them all through his story as concerning this expedition, stating 'from beginning to end the way in which he had been treated'[49]. With forensic force, he lists all of the deceptions, what they were promised, what they have since received, and now the last-minute admission of Mr Burke that he was under orders to let them go from the first. Ever and always, his eyes are on the men, but with every verbal blow landed on Burke he looks to see the effect. Will the leader duck and weave, and deny the truth, or will he stand and take it like a man?

Burke stands, at least, and does not interrupt.

'Will you contradict it, Mr Burke?'[50] Ferguson *invites* him to speak.

Burke does not.

'Can you give us a reason why you dismissed us?'

'I cannot give you one,'[51] Mr Burke replies.

And now he rides off.

Now that is that. Or is it?

For only a short time later, Mr Burke gallops back to them.

'Ferguson,' he says, 'this is a very unpleasant affair. I have no fault to find with any of you.'[52]

And it is with this in mind he proposes a solution, a compromise.

If Ferguson and Mr Langan agree to a reduced salary, they can stay with the expedition at least until they get to the Darling.

Langan accepts on the spot, only for Ferguson to descend upon him like an avenging angel of death. 'If you agree to this, Langan, you are not the man I have taken you to be. As for myself, faith has been broken with me, and I will not go with you, Mr Burke, under any circumstances.'[53]

Shamed, Langan declares he will go with Ferguson after all.

Tempers become so frayed there even seems some chance of a real donnybrook, a fist-fight between Mr Ferguson and Mr Burke. Mercifully, in the end it does not come to that, but it is equally clear that Ferguson must prepare to leave immediately, and so he does, in high dudgeon – the only real bushman who left with the original expedition party, getting ready to go. He will be accompanied by Patrick Langan, James McIlwaine and the sepoy Belooch, the last of whom has decided – in his gentle manner – he has had enough.

Burke immediately calls for Dr Becker, and informs him that he must stay behind to arrange the stores with the local storekeeper, Thomas Sparkes. When those stores have been all stowed and everything accounted for, then, and only then, should he come forward.

•

Riding away, a sense of purpose crystallises in Mr Burke's mind: he is to get to the Gulf and back, and as quickly as possible at that. Scientific matters that slow them down will just have to fit in. And now that they have lightened their load he is a little surer of himself, reckoning that they can get to Cooper's Creek in time to make a dash before the searing summer bites ...

Speaking of a dash ... only a short time after Mr Burke has ridden off heading north, he hears something from behind. It proves to be a thundering Charles Ferguson, accompanied by the men who have been dismissed that morning.

The storekeeper is refusing to honour Mr Burke's cheques to pay the men.

Oh.

Oh dear.

It will take some sorting, and Burke is obliged to write an order to Thomas Sparkes requesting he accept the cheques.

Now, that really *is* that. As a bonus, the sepoy Belooch changes his mind, and decides to stay with the expedition. It is a reappearance that greatly relieves Dr Beckler, as Belooch is 'without doubt the best of us all at handling the camels, especially the obstinate ones'[54].

And they are, clearly, going to be needing those camels if Mr Burke's dash to the north before the hot season bites is to be successful. One to whom Mr Burke has confided his plans is young Mr Wills, who had even written to his mother from Balranald: 'It seems probable that we shall finish our work in a much shorter period than was anticipated; very likely in ten or twelve months.'[55]

They could be back in Melbourne, triumphant, as soon as July next year!

There is only one way they can do that, and one order that Mr Burke puts out above all others, and characterised by William Brahe, is: 'Push, push, push!'[56]

And the hard push starts sooner than the men expect, as only a few miles north of Balranald, the gut-busting and back-breaking work must begin. Instead of staying on the well-trodden station tracks, which lead to the Darling River, Burke decides to push across country – 'slap across'[57] – to save time.

But herein lies a problem. For the country is covered in yet more dense mallee scrub, interspersed with soft, deep sand. While the camels can cope in this kind of country, it is hell on earth for the wagoners to keep going – meaning they inevitably lag, badly.

Very well, let them.

20 September '60, Terekencom, a morning brings a mourning

Arising early on this morning – as Mr Burke has insisted they must get away soon after first light to reach Prungle outstation that day – Ludwig Becker is pleased to hear the horses have strayed overnight. It means he has a little time to walk around, to leave the exploration of the continent aside for a moment, in favour of exploring his surrounds, as he always likes to do.

Here now, behind some bushes, he is fascinated to see some natives gazing curiously at the expedition's camp. Among them, two native women stand out in particular, their faces 'painted in such a manner as to give the head the appearance of a skull, when seen from a distance; round the eyes was drawn with white paint, a circle, an inch broad, and the hair of one woman tied up closely and covered with a piece of cloth, while the other lubra had her hair painted or rather smeared over with the same white colour, giving her head a still more skull-like appearance'[58].

They are, Becker comes to understand, in mourning. He quickly takes his pencil to sketch them, now ...[59]

Now the horses have been found. The expedition is on the move. A brutal day unfolds, moving through yet more thick mallee scrub. Though they have recruited a black fellow to guide them, 'the old track was visible enough even for a white fellow's eye'[60], not that it is much easier because of it. When they finally stop, exhausted, at 6.30 pm at an open spot in the bush, a grim and waterless evening beckons, only saved by the fact that just half a mile away, the new man, Bowman, has managed to find a small pool of water – amazing what these true bushmen can do – and as Becker would note, 'although thick and dirty it gave us some relief'[61].

22 September '60, Goowall, when every day is Monday

Mr Burke has had quite enough of the lagging, sagging wagons, which continue to crawl over the brutal terrain. From now they can do it on their own, as he has decided to split the party. Yes, while he, with a small party including Mr Landells and Mr Wills, will go ahead on the camels, the wagons and the rest of the party can bring up the rear with a tear for all he cares.

Alas, those coming on behind ('led' by Dr Beckler and Ludwig Becker, if one can 'lead' from so far back) soon find themselves in 'pathless mallee scrub'[62], with such 'deep, loose sand'[63] that it sucks at the wheels of the wagons, the hoofs of the horses and indeed their own boots, as they sink in up to their ankles. Every step forward saps them all, and their pace slows to little more than one mile an hour.

Next come plains of what is known as porcupine grass, 'a species ...' Dr Beckler notes, 'with the most uncanny appearance and unfriendly character ... it could not have been better named'[64].

The pace and the demands are relentless, but as the following day is a Sunday, Dr Beckler is hoping the wagons, horses and drivers can all have a much-needed day of rest. After all, Mr Burke is many miles ahead in his own camp, and can hardly complain of them stopping on the Sabbath, which . . .

Which is where you are wrong on two counts, Dr Beckler. For, fearing that the German might take exactly this decision, Mr Burke has ridden back, and now expressly orders them forward, to get to Cole's waterhole by nightfall! As to it being the Sabbath, that simply does not register as a factor in the Irishman's decision-making. George Landells had already found this out when, on a recent active Day of the Lord, he had inquired whether Burke felt it was appropriate to not recognise the Sabbath, or any religious rite in camp, for that matter? Mr Burke, as Landells later described it, 'smiled contemptuously'[65].

This time Burke's smile is of grim satisfaction, as he sees the exhausted Dr Beckler and his men get underway once more.

Before long, it is obvious they are in the toughest country yet.

It's thirsty, horrible work, with no shade for relief from the surprisingly biting spring sun, and certainly no water beyond that which they are carrying. The wagoners curse, they shout, they whip their horses who, as Dr Beckler describes it, are 'already half worked to death . . .'[66]

Yes, there is the skeleton of a narrow track that marks where other local traffic has every month or so pushed this way, but it is little more than a scratch in the timeless landscape. And the resistance of the soft sand to all who dare venture here is at least matched by 'the thickest mallee conceivable . . . [as] overhanging boughs tore our wagon covers to shreds. It was the wildest land imaginable.'[67]

'No one knows who invented the mallee,' the local saying runs, 'but the Devil is strongly suspected.'[68]

Time and again the wagons come to a shuddering halt as either the wheels or the horses sink so deep they must be laboriously dug out. The horses grunt and grind, the men groan, grimace and curse ever louder as they put their shoulders to the wheel, whip the horses and try to shift a wagon forward from its rut, invariably succeeding . . . only for the horses to stop again, completely exhausted. And so there is more shouting still.

'The wagoners,' Dr Beckler would recount, 'all became so hoarse that they could hardly utter an audible word. Dozens of times the horses had to be unharnessed from one wagon in order to help another out . . .'[69]

There is only one solace in the general agony of the wagoners: the fact that Burke had already agreed to their absolutely extortionate rates. But, even at those rates, such is their agony, it is surely only just worth it.

Now, while Dr Beckler and Ludwig Becker are inevitably distracted by their interest in recording, from both a scientific and artistic perspective, the country they are passing through, much of the weight of actual leadership falls onto the slender shoulders of the Prussian, and Warrnambool stockman, William Brahe, a quietly spoken 25-year-old of great fortitude. And while that worthy does the best he can to keep the wagon-train moving, it remains slow going, sometimes as slow as one or two miles only, in an hour.

It is, and Beckler knows it, madness, all brought on by the decision of Mr Burke to go cross country.

'The character of this desert was such that travel was severely impeded without a made road,' he would chronicle, 'seen from the fact that the wagons of the neighbouring stations hardly ever took this route, preferring to make a detour of many miles. Why did we have to experiment just here? It was the "shortest route", the straight line, that once again led Mr Burke into temptation. The account given us of the quality of the land was enough; the picture painted for us of the wild bush should have prevented us from taking this route.'[70]

The next day brings much of the same, though at least Ludwig Becker doesn't mind as much as, with the arrival of two Aboriginal guides, he has finally found a worthy subject for his artistic abilities. While one of the guides is very young, the other is old and fabulous, 'Watpipa' by name, and delightfully picturesque as he walks in front of them with a yam stick in one hand, and a firestick in the other.

'This "old man",' Becker will recount, 'appeared to be of the age of 70; his hair is not white but has a peculiar pale greenish-yellow tint, and is beautifully curled by the hand of nature.'[71]

•

Up ahead, on this same day, Mr Burke is also being guided by an Aboriginal man, Simon, who in late morning brings the forward party to a spot known to the local blacks as 'Kompang', where Mr Burke calls a halt by the 'muddy waterhole' which is its key feature. God's answer to weary travellers it isn't, with Wills recording in his diary that it 'both looks and tastes what one would suppose would be the taste of chalk and water with a little ink in it'[72].

It is, however, worse where there is none, particularly for men like them who are still only halfway through the hottest day of the trip so far, going over the toughest terrain so far. It is clearly a good place to wait for the wagons which . . . even by sundown have not arrived. (Unknown to Mr Burke they are not even close.)

Frustrated beyond measure, Mr Burke has his men moving the next morning at sun-up regardless, verbally whipping them forward another 30 miles for the day, over sand-hills as high as 40 feet. Now, how the wagons will get over such obstacles is anyone's guess, but that is not Mr Burke's problem, it is for Dr Beckler to work out. Mr Burke and his men keep going regardless, over wide saltbush plains, through a thunderstorm that sends the animals skittish, and despite the fearful heat which soon returns. Their reward is to make it all the way to the Darling River, making camp after dark, shattered with exhaustion near the outpost of Tarcoola station.

•

The old Irishwoman dressed in black who sets foot on the arrival dock in Melbourne on this crisp September day attracts little attention. There is no one awaiting to give her a tearful welcoming embrace, nor even someone to help carry the bag which contains all her worldly possessions. Slowly, hobbling, Ellen Dogherty simply totters down the long walkway and asks a porter for directions for a coach to Castlemaine, where she hopes to find Master . . . no, Superintendent Robert O'Hara Burke.

Robert O'Hara Burke? The explorer, one and the same?

No, Robert is a police superintendent at Castlemaine . . .

No, madam. Mr Burke is one of the most famous men in the land, and to get to him, a carriage will not do, and you'd be better off finding a camel!

It takes a little while but, soon enough, the bewildered old Colleen comes to understand that she is *just that little bit late*, that the little boy she nursed, who had written to his old nanny earlier in the year asking her to come to Australia to live with him once more, had, in the meantime, headed to points north with the Victorian Exploring Expedition. She is stunned but somehow not surprised. To have come so close to seeing him in the flesh, to being able to hold him in her arms once more! But that he has gone off, suddenly, somewhat erratically, at the head of a famous expedition? Yes, that is her Master Robert.

Still, fussing and frantic, she is taken to the Royal Society – *you did say you are close to Burke the famous explorer, yes?* – where a rather stunned himself Dr John Macadam must bow to her bluster and blarney, and allow her to move into his house, for the moment.

Where, she asks Dr Macadam every day, would Master Robert likely be now?

The good doctor, of course, has no idea. He is soon of the view, however, that this old woman from the Emerald Isle won't be leaving his house until such times as Mr Burke returns, and so wishes Mr Burke even speedier travels than before.

25 September '60, 60 miles south of the Darling, *sturm und drang*

Now three, and perhaps four days hard travelling adrift of Mr Burke's lead party, *das deutsche duo*, Becker and Beckler, are essaying to settle down for the night, but it is not easy. Having been caught in exactly the same fiercely wet tempest as Mr Burke and his men, they are now drenched clear to the bone, as are their clothes, their tent, their supplies, the very ground upon which they are trying to rest.

As Ludwig Becker would recall, 'hail and rain were blown by the gale in a nearly horizontal direction ... so dense was the shower that no object further than a few yards was visible'[73].

Both of them are officers, both are from Germany, both are intellectuals, and from a distance at least they seem as natural tent-mates as if everyone had been assigned on alphabetic alignment alone.

And yet, they are entirely different kinds of men . . .

For when a cyclonic-like wind suddenly hits their camp at Linklinkwho waterhole, their tent is blown down in seconds, taking with it the saplings they had strung the supporting rope between, bringing the whole structure down upon them!

Ludwig Becker only narrowly survives calamity, twice, as one of the heavy poles just misses his head, before he nearly suffocates under the weight of the heavy canvas before he just manages to struggle free . . . to find an enraged Dr Beckler sitting in the open air, shivering in the rain.

'The scene was one of great confusion,' Ludwig Becker records, 'at the same time to me so ludicrous that I could not help laughing, while the Doctor held a different opinion.'[74]

27 September '60, Bilbarka, Bowman to bow . . . or bow out?

Up front, now three miles north of Tarcoola, at a placed called Bilbarka on the banks of the Darling River, and still waiting for his expedition to be reunited, Mr Burke is having yet one more difference of opinion himself, with Robert Bowman.

For you see, Mr Bowman had been exploring with Mr Gregory, did he mention? And he might also note, and does at some length, the enormous difference between the way Mr Gregory had done things, and the way (*sniff*) Mr Burke carries on. Mr Gregory treated his animals with care, not as beasts of burden to be worked till they dropped – for drop they would. Mr Gregory was careful in his relations with his men, and never abrupt. Mr Gregory had a clear idea of what he wanted done, and gave concise, consistent orders to make it happen. Mr Burke does none of those.

On this evening, when Mr Burke orders the men to be sure not to unsaddle their horses for at least five minutes after stopping for the day so that their backs do not cool quickly, Mr Bowman can't help himself.

Did Mr Burke know that Mr Gregory *never* made his men do that? No, Mr Burke does not know that, but does Mr Bowman know that he is now free to go exploring with Mr Gregory again if he wishes, for he is now dismissed? The conversation does not quite go like that, but the upshot is the same. Mr Bowman is soon on his way south, and one of the few experienced bushmen they have is lost to them, due to a clash with the leader.

One thing that likely contributes to Mr Burke's high emotions at this time is his rising frustration with the fact that the wagons have *still* not appeared! What on *earth* can Dr Beckler and Ludwig Becker be doing?

(As it happens, quite a lot . . . it is just that they are not helping the wagons move forward at all. On this particular day, 27 September, 34 miles away at Arumpo, Dr Beckler has had a wonderful time collecting botanical specimens which he carefully places in the pouches, bags, envelopes and notebooks (for pressing) he has brought for the purposes, while Ludwig Becker has been equally avidly doing his sketching. They have enjoyed this 'rest day' so much, even if it was mostly for the exhausted wagon horses, and accomplished so much they agree to have another one the next day!)

CHAPTER SEVEN

THE STING AND THE POLICEMAN

What we have done up to this will cause a great sensation as we have passed some very fine sheep grazing country not before known for which when my report goes down immediate application will be made. We are now encamped upon a creek not before known. Grass nearly fit to mow ...[1]

Robert O'Hara Burke, in a letter to his Uncle John, 30 October 1860

Landells's basic principle was to watch over and care for the camels as long as possible and not to over burden them, in order to have them as strong and fresh as possible when forced marches, principally resulting from lack of water, would become necessary. This strategy was, without doubt, correct. However, Burke was not just impatient with the progress of the expedition in general but, as he often complained to me, with the camels in particular ...[2]

Dr Hermann Beckler, early October 1860

A race! A race! So great a one
The world ne'er saw before;
A race! A race! Across this land,
From South to northern shore!

A race between two colonies!
Each has a stalwart band,
Sent out beyond the settled bounds,
Into the unknown land.

The horseman hails from Adelaide,
The camel rider's ours:—
Now let the steed maintain his speed,
Against the camel's powers . . . [3]

Melbourne Punch magazine, 8 November 1860

28 September '60, VEE Camp 30 at Bilbarka, a ship on the horizon

Voices in the night.

Even as he tries to get to sleep after yet one more exhausting day, Tom McDonough – sharing a tent with the quiet camel-handler, John King – is aware of the important conversation taking place in the next tent. It is led by the rich Irish brogue of his friend, Mr Burke, with some input from Professor Neumayer, who has been with them now for over two weeks – and has spent the last two days and nights making seemingly endless astronomical and magnetic observations with Mr Wills – and is about to head back to Melbourne on the morrow. Occasionally, McDonough can hear the soft, educated tones of Mr Wills breaking in, though always deferential to his two superiors in different fields – at the observatory, and on this expedition.

On and on they go, discussing the journey to date, the journey to come, the problems with the camels, the costs that have blown out, the state of the scientific endeavours and . . . and . . . what's this?

Something very interesting indeed . . .

Mr Burke is saying, 'I am determined to proceed towards the southernmost point of the Gulf of Carpentaria, on or near the Albert River.'[4]

Neumayer agrees this is a good idea.

'I intend to propose to the Government,' Burke says, 'sending a vessel round to that part of the coast. I hope that the Exploration Committee will support the suggestion.'[5]

'I hope to meet you, Burke,' Professor Neumayer says to the expedition leader in his thick German accent, 'in *zee* vessel.'[6]

McDonough's ears prick up from his languid almost-sleep. A vessel?

'No direct steps should be taken in the matter,' Burke says to Neumayer in a clear voice, 'unless it comes first from me, in which case I shall send a dispatch from Menindee to convey my views on the subject to the Chief Secretary and the Exploration Committee.'[7]

Understood.

The next morning, Professor Neumayer and Mr Wills must say their fond farewells, as the professor will accompany Mr Burke and Landells, together with three men and the sepoys, to meet the wagon party, wherever they may be, before continuing south to Melbourne alone.

The two shake hands warmly, Mr Wills wishing him a safe voyage, and that he may be confident that the whole expedition will be a complete success. With that, they are off, with Mr Burke and Professor Neumayer on horseback, driving eight packhorses before them, while Landells and the sepoys escort the camels, and the professor's manservant follows with the spring-cart carrying his luggage.

Freed from the cumbersome wagons, the party travel quickly over the 27 miles, arriving back at their old camp at Kompang at three o'clock that afternoon to find Beckler, Becker and the wagons 'in a great bustle, preparing for a general advance which was to take place the next morning'[8].

Mr Burke is determined that the rear of the expedition, the wagons that drag and drag, will advance. More desperate than ever to increase their rate of progress, and knowing that the terrain ahead is 'desert-like sandy ground'[9], Burke decides that *extreme* measures are necessary. As the wagons are the things that slow them down most, the answer must be to take some of the load from them, and transfer it to the camels who, for the most part to this point, have been only lightly burdened.

Now, each camel will carry 400 pounds upon its back – nearly 75 pounds more than Mr Burke had wanted them to carry in the first place! – and they will need to leave yet more things behind.

What is more, Burke orders the men to transfer from their horses to 'Shanks' pony'. From here on in, the men can *walk* so the horses can carry supplies.

As these rearrangements are made, Professor Neumayer is departing for Melbourne, off to report on their progress.

Still, before he heads off, Mr Burke has one request of the German scientist, to whom he has become quite close in the last three weeks.

'If I should get lost, Professor, I ask for your promise that no one but you should undertake the task to find me.'[10]

The Professor is *bewegt*, very touched. From this gruff soldier, there could be no higher compliment. He is not being treated like either a scientific nuisance, or a Committee observer, but as one of the party, and a highly regarded one at that. In his typically convoluted way, Professor Neumayer is proud to respond: 'Mr Burke, so far as its fulfilment can depend upon myself, I freely grant this promise!'[11]

Farewell, Professor Neumayer. *Auf Wiederseh'n*, Mr Burke.

. . . . . .

Right. Now that the professor is gone, Mr Burke has some fresh orders for his remaining German officers. 'No man, belonging to the Exploring Expedition, from this day will take more luggage with him than 30 lbs weight.'[12]

What? That is correct, in the interest of further lightening the load, personal luggage is restricted to a paltry 30 pounds! The excess will be sent back to Melbourne, and they can collect it upon their return.

There is, to be sure, no little outrage at such high-handedness from Burke by the men and officers alike – particularly the latter, as they are the ones who have the most weighty of the personal effects and equipment.

'In consequence of this order,' Ludwig Becker will note, *mit knirschenden Zähnen*, through gritted teeth, 'I was forced to leave behind a number of the most useful things besides half of the clothings we were supplied with when leaving Melbourne.'[13]

Alas, there is worse to come.

The following morning Dr Beckler and Ludwig Becker are up and working at 5 am and are soon perspiring profusely, despite the bitter cold. First they put the light blue camel rugs over the backs of the camels, followed by the camel pads – essentially, hefty cushions stuffed with horsehair to prevent chafing. And now they must laboriously load all the boxes and bags onto the packsaddles, being ever vigilant that the massive 400-pound load is perfectly balanced. The easiest ones to balance are the huge canvas bags of flour and sugar, *each* weighing 200 pounds. But even lifting them is hell, as the bags must be placed either side of the packsaddle, tied together, secured and only then – and *heaaaaave!* – can the whole thing be hoisted up by no fewer than four men, and lowered gently on to the back of the groaning camel.

'It is a most exhausting kind of labour,' Becker records, 'and the new canvas bags soon told upon our fingernails – half of mine were split and bent.'[14] Indeed, of them all, it is clearly the 52-year-old artist cum naturalist who suffers most, and Burke, when he arrives, finds him as red as a ruby if not quite so felicitous to gaze upon. That, at least, must be the opinion of *Herr* Burke, who has suddenly appeared and is glaring at both men?

'Now, gentlemen,' says he to the Germans, 'from this time you have to give up your scientific investigations [and] work like the rest of the men, as long as you are on the road or not free from camp-duties; at the same time you have to limit your materials and other things required for your investigating.'[15]

Why, why, why . . . what Burke is saying to them is outrageous. In the first place, they *are* working, as witness what they are doing right now! But to say they can *only* do that is a serious breach of the agreement they signed. Both of them have been specifically employed by the Royal Society to come on this expedition to expand scientific frontiers in just the same way as this trek will extend the boundaries of cartography. And suddenly they have to stop, be no more than working men?

In sum, *ja*.

And one more thing.

'From today,' Mr Burke says firmly, 'you have to *walk*, inch for inch, all the way up to the Gulf of Carpentaria.'[16]

And *that* is one for the scientists!

For Burke's attitude is clear, and getting clearer by the day. Science is fine, in its place, if it knows its place, but the expedition leader is far from convinced that it has a place in this place in the first place. The gathering of scientific information, the constant measuring, collecting, notating, is slow – and does nothing to advance either the expedition, or their cause.

And . . . truly?

The likes of Becker getting all the way to the Gulf of Carpentaria and back – that's right, even as a portly and bookish 52-year-old! – would undercut the glory of the whole trip. If the fat and bespectacled German red-beard could make it, it means that *anyone* could have done it. No, far better that he be broken now, to hopefully resign, or just be left behind, and this might be just the trick to do it.

Just one glance at 'old Becker' makes it clear that it shouldn't take long.

The truth is, the doc hasn't slept well the past two nights, and given the exertions of culling and repacking all their stores over the past days, and now a gut-busting *six hours* spent loading the camels, he really is spent.

By 11 o'clock, thankfully, all the camels are loaded and ready, with the several lead camels secured by a wooden nose-peg and a neck halter with a lead rope in front – ready to be taken in hand by a sepoy or worker when the time comes – while the rope from the camel in front is linked to the nose-peg of the camel that follows and so on. An expeditious expedition, it is not. In the meanwhile, the strains of a singularly intense conversation can be heard by some of the men, once again between the leader and his first officer, Mr Landells. Now that the camels are loaded, the former would like the latter to take them directly across country, across the sand-hills, back to Bilbarka, while Mr Burke and a couple of the men keep the wagons on the track, and take the longer route, to be sure they won't break down again, or get bogged. Mr Landells agrees so far.

But now?

Mr Burke asking him to take the packhorses too, across country *with* the camels?

No. The camels are the responsibility of Mr Landells, and Mr Landells alone. And just as Mr Burke has no carriage over the camels, so too does Mr Landells have no carriage over the horses. He cannot be expected to take responsibility for both at once. *No*, Mr Burke.

Mr Burke can barely stand it, but does so once more.

But only once more.

The day is hard for everyone. Burke has pushed them hard before, but never like this. As William Brahe would recall, 'we marched the long stages that meant exhaustion. Sometimes we went into camp as late as 11 o'clock at night, having passed good camping water late in the afternoon. Delay of any kind chafed Burke.'[17]

And it really does.

At one point, Brahe stops off from the relentless push for a small time to adjust the packs on the horses, to redistribute the weight to make them more comfortable. Suddenly he is confronted by an angry and impatient Burke, thundering back on horseback to angrily remonstrate with his delay.

'What is wrong?' he demands.

Brahe explains, finishing with, 'It's all right . . .'

'It's not all right!' Mr Burke snarls, before riding off, and tossing back over his shoulder, 'It's all wrong!'

This, too, is typical of Mr Burke.

For two hours later, here is Mr Burke again, saying kindly to him, 'You must be very tired, Brahe. Ride my horse for a while.'[18]

Brahe has learnt to live with, and even respect, such mercurial bursts.

'He would blaze up into a temper very quickly,' Brahe would recount, 'but soon got over it.'[19]

Once underway, at least, as the group following Mr Landells tackle sand-hills as high as 100 feet, things go exactly as planned by Mr Burke.

For Ludwig Becker is soon completely shattered with exhaustion. He walks despondently in the lead of three camels, his meagre breakfast long disappeared from his *bauch*, tummy. They have not been told how far they have to go on the day, how long before the next stop, they just march. Up the side of the sand-hills they labour mightily, before heading down the other side; up the side of the sand-hills, down the other side. On and on into a hundred hazy horizons.

By sunset, feeling as if he will faint, Becker asks Mr Landells if they can stop for just five minutes so he can recover himself.

'I cannot stop,' Landells replies grimly. 'Loaded camels won't rise again when once allowed to lie down; give me your camels, take rest if you require it, and follow at leisure.'[20]

Becker does just that, and is soon alone in the Australian wilderness, an old German artist, some 9000 miles from his homeland. For water, he at least has a gunpowder flask that has a little left, and by sipping that and traipsing his sand-filled boots slowly forward, following the shouts up ahead, he is able to make ground, to get to Mr Landells's camp, just in time to hear the cry, 'Now then, Mr Becker, look sharp, unload your camels!'[21]

Verdammt noch mal! Damn your eyes!

The long laborious process of getting the loads off the camels now takes place, and it is nearing midnight before they are able to take a little tea and cold mutton under a drizzling rain, before falling onto the camel pads and into a dreamless sleep, smashed at five o'*early* with the cry to load their camels once more!

At least this time the loading goes a little quicker and they are on their way by half past nine, but that just means they must traverse even more exhausting sand-hills than the day before, as they keep pressing towards Tarcoola station on the Darling River.

At least the shattered Ludwig Becker has learnt a valuable lesson from yesterday's march. A day wiser, he is sure to put a chunk of bread in his pocket and fill his flask with fresh rainwater before setting off. And now, with the rope over his shoulder, he first pulls, and then leads his three camels 'through the most dismal country we had passed yet . . . Sand-hills over hundred feet high . . . one behind the other, like gigantic sand ripples. They stretched as far as I could see . . .'[22]

By the end of this day, it is clearer than ever that Mr Burke's object has nearly been achieved. Becker and Beckler are both shattered with exhaustion. How much longer can the poor brutes last?

For their part, they are simply glad that their time dragging the camels over the sand-hills is at an end. As Beckler notes, Tarcoola station, by the Darling River, that little outpost of civilisation and port of rest is a sudden and welcome sight for two sets of very sore eyes: 'The extensive red, hilly and sandy country ended abruptly at the edge of the Darling valley . . . We greeted the waters of the Darling from afar – the high green wall of splendid eucalypts on the edge of the river and the unassuming but attractive station . . . on its bank.'[23]

Typically, his German companion, Ludwig Becker, looks at this most welcome vision from the perspective of an artist, and describes it accordingly: 'River Darling is rising, its waters are of a coffee and plenty of milk-colour.'[24]

3 October '60, Tarcoola, punting the punt, ditching the drays, leaving the luggage

As the party with Landells settles into their camp for the night, Robert Burke and his lot are still out there, making their ever slow progress across the scrubby plains with their wagons.

It is not until the next morning that they hit the Darling, at a place some 20 miles south of Tarcoola, and a little further still from the men at Bilbarka.

Burke is fed up. The wagons are a pain in their side, and will only get more cumbersome as they head north into the sandy, desert areas. Sick of it, he decides to leave the damned things where they are for now, and proceed upstream with the packhorses only. He will return tomorrow with more men to bring the wagons up to Tarcoola, unload them and be rid of them for good. They will strip down to the bare essentials, if they must. What matters is they get a move on.

And so he rides upstream, accompanied by William Brahe and the packhorses, and finds his men in camp at Bilbarka, resting from the previous day's exertions.

The next morning, in the company of Dr Beckler, Burke heads south again, along the river road, to fetch the wagons. Though Burke rides out in a frustrated huff – his resentment of the wagons swells with every passing minute – Beckler is excited for the side-trip, to see a different aspect of the Darling.

And what a delight it is! 'The river made numerous and often very short windings and its bed lay mostly between high, steep banks of the same smooth, bare, canal-like nature . . . Magnificent stands of eucalypts with conspicuously luxuriant foliage shaded the banks and I passed several picturesque spots.'[25]

Fetching the beat-up wagons and horses, they arrive back at Tarcoola station in the early evening, and immediately have the wagons unloaded, and the supplies stored.

And so it is that Burke, now the wagons have at last made it to the Darling, makes the final decision to get rid of them. The three exorbitant hired wagons are sent packing, together with their driver highwaymen, *and* their 18 hideously expensive wagon horses Mr Burke had been obliged to hire. As for the three wagons that the Committee owns, they will be left, too. It is the remaining horses and camels that can finally bear the load for what they have decided is still necessary to take forward. But there will be a whole lot less of that, too, as Burke begins a ruthless culling process of useless things.

Like the punt wagon! Good God, Jesus, Mary and Joseph, is *anything* more symbolic of the useless things Mr Burke has been obliged by the Committee to take on this trip than this wretched boat? It can stay behind, together with six sets of wagon harnesses, a spare wagon axle and two spare rear wagon wheels. They can all stay here with much, much more until such times as the Exploration Committee can explore ways to get the damn things back to Melbourne. Good riddance.

•

Feeling like prisoners who have suddenly been liberated from the ball and chain they have been dragging around for months, Burke and Beckler continue on the three-mile ride to the expedition's camp at Bilbarka.

They arrive back at camp to find Mr Wills and Mr Landells preparing to set off to Tarcoola station to post some letters, as this will be one of their last opportunities to send missives to loved ones, and the station has a regular mail steamer heading down the Darling and Murray to Euston, from where it can be sent on to Melbourne.

Before they go, Burke dashes off a quick letter of his own, to his good friend Captain Standish, back in Melbourne fulfilling his duties as chief police commissioner.

On the Darling,
4th October 1860.

My Dear Standish,

. . . We have been resting here a few days, awaiting the arrival of our baggage, which has just come up. To-morrow we proceed on, and I shall not delay anywhere until I reach Cooper's Creek – being an Irishman I must add, unless I can help it.

I leave the hired wagons and my own behind. The accursed implements, the ruin of so many expeditions, I am determined shall not ruin me.

Then with some relish, Burke adds,

You should have seen old Becker's face, upon my announcing that all the officers would have to act as working men, and that we should only carry 30. lbs weight of baggage for each man.

Loading camels and then marching twenty miles is no joke. The first two days nearly cooked poor Becker, and I think he will not be able to stand it much longer.[26]

Burke is frank with his old friend, on how he himself is coping with the arduous nature of the trek,

I am confident of success and willing to accept the inevitable alternative of success or disgrace, although failure is possible . . . I think it will take the sting out of me for some time if I see it out . . .[27]

After briefly scanning his own words, he folds the paper into the standard neat rectangle – or at least as neat as he can make it, which is 'not very' – before warming a stick of wax over an open flame, and pouring a blob onto the loose edge, then stamping his seal upon it. Dashing off the captain's address above the wax seal, he hands his missive to William Wills, who is shortly on his way.

(It must be said that Mr Wills is becoming a little unsure of his friend Mr Landells. Look, he doesn't like to say anything . . . but a rather odd thing happened today, concerning the camels. After one of the fully laden camels had fallen awkwardly a couple of days earlier, as Mr Landells was making his way to their Bilbarka camp, the camel master had given a quick, grave diagnosis: 'It is a dislocation of the shoulder, and nothing can be done. This camel must be left behind as a perfect cripple.'[28]

At the time, Mr Wills had listened attentively, and taken the camel expert's word for it, that, yes, leaving the poor beast behind likely was the best course.

And yet . . .

And yet . . .

After the camel's heavy load had been shared among the others and the poor brute left behind, an extraordinary thing had happened. The camel had still managed to limp along behind them for the next 20 miles! Indeed, the beast had arrived into camp this very day.

William Wills, for one, is confused. In his inexpert opinion, it is a fair effort indeed for one with a limb clear out of a socket to hobble 20 whole miles. Surely it is less a dislocation – with one leg having come completely out of its socket – as a mere strain?

'But that's merely my idea,' he later notes in a letter to Neumayer. 'Mr L ought to know best.'[29]

Ought to, yes. But does Mr Landells actually know as much about camels as he professes?

Wills's doubts will grow.)

As they ride and chatter, Mr Wills is given further reason to wonder about the capacity and character of Mr Landells, as the camel overseer and second-in-command of the whole expedition feels free to make many disparaging remarks about Mr Burke and the way things are done, remarks that the younger man finds 'quite uncalled for'[30].

'It would seem,' one near-contemporary account would have it, 'that Mr Landells had laid such stress on the importance of the position he himself held in the expedition, that he was unable to control certain feelings of impatience at the exercise of authority on the part of Mr Burke.'[31]

Mr Landells, considering himself the better man, and a more capable leader, has bridled under the yoke of Burke's authority from the first and has only just managed to hold his tongue at a series of decisions taken by the Irishman. But, now alone with a companion he trusts,

William Wills, he feels no reason to hold his tongue and gives full vent to his feelings.

Landells is particularly insistent that 'Mr [Burke] has no right to interfere about the camels, as I have agreements with the Committee, even if Mr Burke is ignorant of them.'[32]

Landells is just warming up.

'[Under Burke],' he says, 'everything is mismanaged; and, in fact, if Mr Burke had his way everything would go to the devil.'[33]

Wills says nothing, but is profoundly shocked at the disloyalty. He does not see Mr Burke like that at all, and even if he did, would keep his tongue in check.

5 October '60, Camp 30 at Bilbarka, Darling River, the eye of the needle

This morning at Bilbarka, the two German scientists, Hermann Beckler and Ludwig Becker, request an audience with Mr Burke. The best they can, they attempt to persuade the Irishman that he needs to be a little more lenient, to calm the growing resentment felt by the men.

Mr Burke hears them out.

Quietly, he is surprised that both men are still here, as he has embarked on a deliberate policy to break them, to get them and their infernal equipment, their time-wasting activities, and their entire *persons*, off the expedition. But still, they *do* go on, both in terms of the expedition, and their remarks. So passionate are they, Burke may even allow himself to be a little persuaded.

Finally – perhaps even as the best way to ensure *zey vill shtopp* talking – Burke allows another 10 pounds can be added to each man's ration. But let this be a warning.

'If anyone,' he says to the men, whom he soon orders to gather before him, 'whoever he may be, takes one *ounce* more than 40 lbs weight of private luggage with him, I shall leave this luggage behind and the man too – now you know it.'[34]

There is one saving grace to this outrageous high-handedness, and Dr Beckler would note it: '[Mr Burke] did not exclude himself from this harsh, but in fact necessary, rule although we would all have happily seen him make an exception for himself.'[35]

As it happens, today is one of those rarest of days, a day when Mr Burke is actually in the mood for granting concessions, like an extra 10 pounds of personal luggage. For today is going to be a *great* day, the day he has been waiting for. At long last, the expedition proper can begin.

Once Mr Landells heads down with some of the camels to fetch up the required stores that are still at Tarcoola station, they will be ready to pack up and head north as one group.

Ah, but Mr Burke should have known – once again, there is a problem.

For where *are* all the camels, now that they need to be taken downstream and loaded up? It is a distressed sepoy, Belooch, who brings them the news, arriving on the back of a male camel, a *kamat*, to report, 'Camels gone, all the *datchi* (she-camels) gone, *datchi* plenty no good!'[36] He has searched around, but found only a camel blanket.

In short order the men scatter to try to find them, going in all directions from the camp. By sunset Burke's plans of being quickly on their way appear shot. Not only are the camels still at large, but now, three men have failed to return to camp and are presumed lost, too. John King, Tom McDonough and William Hodgkinson join most of the dozen camels on the missing list.

'You and I,' Becker suggests to Mr Burke, by the light of the fire, 'should go in the bush and take with us the [Chinese] Gong and firearms to make signals with them for the three men.'[37]

Burke concedes and they head out into the bush in the twilight of dusk in the direction the three men were last seen heading, carrying the Chinese gong, which has miraculously survived the cull. They shall guide the men home by noise alone. John King – who has proved to be a serious young fellow and one of the few who has impressed Mr Burke so far – finds his way to them shortly afterwards but has no idea where the other two are.

After a quick supper back at camp, some of the men head east to make a large fire on a nearby hill, and this brings McDonough home just before another of the sepoys, Dost Mahomet, arrives driving some of the runaway camels into the camp, leaving nine missing.

'All the men returned to Bilbarka,' Becker records in his diary, 'with the exception of Hodgkinson, who was not to be found.'[38]

Mr Burke suspects that Hodgkinson is likely 'lost' at Tarcoola station helping himself to some grog and gambling on the sly.

He will just have to be 'found' on the morrow. At least, during the night, the rest of the camels are found and brought to camp.

The next morning, Mr Landells and Dr Beckler gather together a few men, along with 17 camels, to head to the station to fetch the stores unpacked from the wagons. Easy enough. But by late evening, Mr Burke is disgusted on two counts. Firstly that Mr Landells did not return from the station until well after dark, and secondly, that while he was away, as Wills would recount, 'the nine remaining camels had travelled off, and could not be found anywhere'[39].

Two days, *two* camel breakouts! This is *intolerable*. Whatever the problems with the infernal wagons, however frustrating their eternal breakdown, at least if you turn your back on them they stay put! This is testing Mr Burke's temper as never before on this expedition, which is saying something – and it is tested still further when a dishevelled Hodgkinson arrives at midday, with no meaningful account of himself other than he was 'lost'. Suspecting him lost only at the bottom of a bottle, Mr Burke puts him on a charge of being absent without leave, and does not leave the wordsmith unacquainted with some of the more extravagant words and phrases he has learnt himself over the years. The way he is feeling, if the camels come back right now, he will probably charge *them* too.

Or, better still, *shoot* the brutes.

The next day, 7 October, is a quiet Sunday morning and Mr Burke has let the men know he would like to head out, if possible.

Mr Landells tends to the camels in camp, when . . . suddenly it is not so quiet anymore. For here is Mr Burke arriving back from Tarcoola station in a great rage, his face red, his lips snarling, his every word an accusatory slap in the face of Mr Landells, as the two stand toe to toe in front of their common tent.

'Some of [the station's] people are drunk on our rum!' he roars. Mr Burke refers, of course, to the camels' rum, the 60 gallons that Mr Landells had *insisted* on bringing along despite Mr Burke's doubts about the temptation it offered to the men.

'I said that and I heard so,' Landells replies mildly, 'but had been informed that they got it from a Hawker's cart that was encamped near our wagons.'[40]

'I do not believe it, Sir, and I shall leave all the Rum at [Tarcoola],' says Mr Burke, not mollified for a moment. 'Not one drop shall go with us.'[41]

'I hope, Mr Burke, you will allow me to retain some of it for medicinal purposes.'[42]

Not a bit of it.

'You are always advising me wrong,' Mr Burke snarls in reply, 'and you are constantly doing wrong.'[43]

Landells is stunned, but still the tirade is not over.

'I shall have no more of your friendship, Sir,' Mr Burke adds. 'Duty, duty, nothing but duty between you and me.'[44]

Landells professes himself dismayed. 'I have always done my duty to the best of my ability, and I have never refused any orders you have given me.'[45]

'No! But you are always wrong and advising me wrong.'[46]

'Mr Burke,' Landells says, choosing his words carefully, but purposefully loud enough that the men can hear, 'as I cannot do anything to please you, I think it would be better for both parties that I resigned.'[47]

'Do as you like,'[48] says Burke.

'Have I your consent to resign?'[49]

'Yes!' snarls Burke, 'and I shall recommend it.'[50]

The two have reached an impasse. They glare at each other.

The only way forward, however temporarily, is for Mr Landells to return to his duties. He may not have his dismissal, but his formal resignation will be placed in Mr Burke's hand as soon as it is written.

To the men watching from a distance, it is as engaging a spectacle as they have seen in six weeks – *full of sound and fury*, signifying a great deal – and some are sorry when it's over, as the major protagonists leave the stage now that the climax has been reached.

Mr Burke heads back to his tent, emerging shortly afterwards to snarl at a few of the men to take the packhorses already loaded that morning and head upriver about four miles. It will allow the expedition to salvage something good from a bad day, with at least some of the party making progress.

Mr Landells, meantime, seeks out Mr Wills.

Informing the third officer that he has resigned, Landells wishes to do the proper thing by placing in the surveyor's care those articles belonging to the government, things like the hobbles, blankets, knives, feed, ropes, goatskin waterbags, ammunition and clipping scissors.

In his worked-up state he can't help but add, 'I never knew such a man as Burke; he does not know his own mind ten minutes. He has no confidence in himself nor any about him; in fact, I am afraid to sleep in the same tent with him, for at all hours he springs up and calls out as though he were going to be murdered.'[51]

In response, Wills remains discreetly silent, wishing to neither add to the disloyal opprobrium heaped upon Mr Burke, or remonstrate with the man who is still his superior, the second officer. Finally spent, Mr Landells rises up and storms off in all directions, muttering only as he leaves, 'I will deliver over the camels as soon as I can find them.'[52]

After all, there are still several camels – *his* camels, under *his* protective charge – out in the bush somewhere. But there remains one task he must get underway first, and so he calls to William Hodgkinson, who, among other duties, fulfils the role as Mr Burke's clerk when letters and the like need to be sent.

'I will be departing for Melbourne,' Mr Landells says, 'is there anything you would like me to execute there for you?'[53]

'Merely the posting of a letter,'[54] Hodgkinson replies. 'When do you propose to return? You may take a red blanket of mine for your use on the way?'

'I am going for good,' says Mr Landells firmly. 'I cannot agree with Mr Burke [on anything].'[55]

Carefully, conspiratorially, Hodgkinson confides in Mr Landells his own grievance.

'I am near resigning myself,' he whispers to Mr Landells, glancing every which way to ensure he is not overheard. 'Mr Burke has not treated me fair in charging me with staying away all night wilfully . . .'[56]

With this assurance that Mr Hodgkinson is that most precious of all things in this situation – an *ally* – Mr Landells asks him to write a letter of resignation for him.

Hodgkinson would be delighted.

And now the fuming Landells leaves the camp. And the news of his imminent departure travels with him, for Mr Landells does not care who knows it, even telling the men he passes on his way to search for the camels at the station that he is about to leave the expedition.

It will be a long night for Mr Landells. For now, as Ludwig Becker documents in his diary, 'There were still 8 camels missing and Mr Landells again [went] in search of them, but returned unsuccessfully at night.'[57]

Obeying the orders of the man who is, after all, still the second officer, Hodgkinson sets to, penning the fairly straightforward letter, with the key demand being from Mr Landells that he be paid for the two weeks it will take him to get back to Melbourne, where he hopes to be issued 'a certificate that I have performed my duties well up to this date . . .'[58]

After writing the letter, however, Mr Hodgkinson can't help but wonder how Mr Burke might react when he hears that he has been penning the resignation of the second officer . . .

Momentarily panicked, he seeks out the third officer, Mr Wills, to ask his opinion as to whether his writing of Mr Landells's letter, 'would in any way be prejudicial to me in Mr Burke's opinion?'[59]

Mr Wills manages to calm him. It will not be a problem, he assures Hodgkinson. Mr Burke may be angry, but he is fair, and could hardly hold it against Hodgkinson that he has helped pen the very resignation letter for the very man that Mr Burke most wants to see a resignation letter *from*, whatever it says.

The camp *seethes* with intrigue, with many being very strong in their opinion that one or other is at fault. A notable exception is John King, Mr Landells's offsider. The young Irishman's primary loyalty is to neither man, so much as to his camels. A quiet fellow, he wants no part of any power struggles and simply wishes to get on with his work, and does so with a characteristic sense of duty.

(In truth? By nature a quiet young man, King's experience in India had made him even more withdrawn. His 70th Regiment had been at the prow of the British suppression of the Indian Mutiny – up to and including strapping the worst of the Indian mutineers across the gaping maws of cannons, to see them 'blown away' as the cannons fired. Oh, the horror, John. Not long afterwards, he had become so debilitated by a 'severe attack of illness'[60] that he had spent 16 months convalescing in the Murree Hills in northern India, which is where he had met Mr Landells, who had convinced him to purchase his discharge and come on this new venture. And now he is to be involved in a new power struggle in the middle of Australia? No, thank you.)

Landells returns to camp, empty-handed but still enraged, soon winding up in the tent of Hodgkinson – who always lends a friendly and gossipy ear – to confide his plans. He wants to call all the officers together, see, explain the situation to them and then, together, they can go and see Mr Burke, and *demand* Landells be reinstated and given full control of the camels.

After all, as he tells Hodgkinson, 'the expedition will not succeed without me – no one is qualified to take charge of the camels – and the [sepoys] will leave immediately I do. I have often recommended to Mr Burke to increase their pay.'[61]

Oh, and one more thing.

Does Hodgkinson know that, back at Balranald, Mr Burke 'asked me to find fault with you, so that he could dismiss you'[62], but he, Mr Landells, had refused to do so?

No? Well, that is the case.

Hodgkinson is suitably appalled, as trouble continues to spread throughout the camp. Still, Landells makes him promise not to tell Mr Burke what he has just been told, before going off himself to find the leader, who is sitting by the fire with Wills. As it happens, Mr Landells has some fire of his own and quickly brings it to bear on Mr Burke.

In as high dudgeon as he has ever risen to in his life – the very *impertinence* of the man! – Landells cannot resist coming right out with it.

'Dismiss me!'[63]

Ah, but Burke is too canny for that. Dismiss him, in front of witnesses, and allow Landells to play the wounded party in the piece? No.

'I will forward your resignation, if you wish,'[64] the leader says to his second officer and adds, 'with a recommendation that you receive your pay up to this time.'[65]

The first and second officer are both choosing their words very carefully indeed, for the issue of whether Mr Landells resigns or is dismissed is a key distinction. Clearly, the departure of the second officer so early in the expedition is a serious matter. So who should bear primary responsibility for it, who must answer for it before the Committee and, likely later, the public?

If Mr Burke dismisses Mr Landells, it is the leader who will have to explain himself.

If Mr Landells resigns, the burden will fall on he who has chosen to abandon the expedition.

And there is also the matter of money. With a resignation, there will be no need to pay him beyond the time he has served. With a dismissal, there may be onerous financial obligations that go with it, likely a claim for unjust dismissal and lost wages.

So they are stuck at this delicate impasse of fury and responsibility. They back off.

Later that evening, Landells pays another visit to Wills.

'Mr Burke,' Landells wants it known, 'is a rash, mad man. He does not know what he is doing. He will make a mess of the whole thing, and ruin all of us.'[66]

Dr Beckler, for one, is not surprised at the flare-up. For it has long been clear to him that 'Burke was not just impatient with the progress of the expedition in general but, as he often complained to me, with the camels in particular. Because until now they had run away frequently, because they had moved more slowly than the horses and because they naturally took a greater length of time to load, he no longer placed much confidence with them.'[67]

Or in Mr Landells it seems.

And Mr Landells returns the favour in kind.

'I shall leave at once,' he continues to Mr Wills, 'and I will not accompany the party any further on any consideration.'[68]

William Wills is never in any doubt as to whose side he is on. He follows his leader, is loyal to him, and the next day – while they are *still* at Bilbarka – strongly suggests to Mr Landells that, 'you might be placing yourself in an unpleasant position by leaving without having given proper notice . . .'[69]

'I have written out some conditions,' Mr Landells replies, 'and *only* if they are fulfilled will I go on.'[70]

He desires written agreement whereby Mr Burke confirms that Mr Landells will have 'full and unqualified control of the camels'.

The camels will, further, every day, 'travel just as many miles and no more than [I] think proper.

'They will start and stop when I choose, and I will be allowed to take whatever stores I deem necessary for their use up to the amount of four camels burden.'[71]

Wills remains, as ever, loyally silent.

Ludwig Becker?

He is far more interested in other things, in any case.

Having captured one of the small predatory beetles that abound in these parts, he sets about drawing it, while also carefully noting its extraordinary change of colours. 'Colour beautiful steel blue (which in the sun changed to brilliant green) and orange . . . When dead the brilliant green hue disappeared altogether.'[72]

•

On this Monday afternoon, 8 October, it is not quite that Mr Burke has changed his attitude, but certainly he seems less openly enraged than he was. Oh, he is still expecting to see the back of Mr Landells, it is just that he seems calmer about it, at least in person. Having sent for Mr Landells, the two now meet in Burke's tent, to allow the second officer to, formally, give his reasons for this resignation:

'It was my understanding,' Landells begins, 'that the stores were to be sent up to Cooper's Creek by conveyance and that the camels were not to be loaded until they arrived there.'[73]

Indeed? 'I have a separate agreement which renders me quite independent of you, Mr Burke, in the management of the camels.'[74]

Burke hears him out, even managing to listen to, yes, his 'conditions' without blowing up. This is not the volcanic figure Mr Landells had been expecting, and the camel overseer is not quite sure what to expect after he finally finishes.

In response, Mr Burke simply takes out a copy of the letter *he* has dictated to Hodgkinson, which he intends to send to the Committee in Melbourne, detailing the fact that Mr Landells has resigned and something of the circumstances – and, in a surprisingly emotional voice, reads it to him. Most of the language is relatively neutral – or at least benign enough that Landells does not protest – until the last.

'Mr Landells leaves me disgracefully . . .' the expedition leader trails off.

'Mr Burke,' Landells says with a combination of wounded dignity and genuine surprise at such a nasty finish, 'I never did a disgraceful act in my life.'[75]

Instead of Mr Burke's volcano blowing, as Landells had been expecting, it is his dam that bursts.

Yes, instead of rising to rage once more, Mr Burke suddenly tears up the letter, and bursts into tears, and does nothing less than fall to his knees and grip his camel overseer around the waist before *pleading* with him not to leave:

'I do not think you could, Landells. I like you, because I know you are an honest man . . . My God! I never thought you would leave me, as I have great dependence in you. Come on, I hope none of the men have seen this!'[76]

Instantly mollified, and pitying that his former persecutor could now so reduce himself as to be on his knees begging him to stay, Landells has no choice.

'Mr Burke,' says he, with a suddenly much lighter air, 'do not cut yourself up so, I will go [north with you, even] should you shoot me.'

'I will not shoot you, Landells,'[77] Burke forlornly tries his own version of lightness in reply.

And this is where the matter is left.

At least for Mr Burke and Mr Landells . . .

But not for Mr Hodgkinson.

For, after reflecting on the troubling conversation he'd had with Mr Landells the previous evening, on the possibility of his own sacking, he insists he should raise this subject with Mr Burke, whereupon it is Mr Landells who is suddenly alarmed.

'Mr Landells said I had promised to not tell what he said,' Hodgkinson would recount, 'that he had resolved not to resign; was good friends with Mr Burke, and that my tattling would only make mischief and injure myself. I remarked that if I was discharged at Menindee I should immediately tell Mr Burke what Mr Landells had repeated to me, and have the matter inquired into.'[78]

But along with such private drama, the day-to-day business of the camp goes on in the usual fashion as the diary of Ludwig Becker attests:

Monday, 8 October 1860.
The cook, who was sent yesterday on horse-back, to [Tarcoola] returned today without hat and horse, saying he lost both last night during the rain and he did not know how. Mr Brahe was ordered to find the horse. Mr Burke returned from [Tarcoola] station, telling us that a steamer was approaching which would take stores up to Menindee. Mr Landells again went out for the lost animals and mounted for that purpose a camel taking behind him a 'black-fellow,' I think this was the first time that an Australian aboriginal rode on a camel . . .[79]

And what's that you say about a steamer approaching? Could some of our transport issues be resolved, at least in the short term?

We will see. For, sure enough, the steamer *Moolgewanke* soon heaves into view, the rhythmic beat of its steam engine rolling pleasantly to them over the muddy waters, now being churned by the rotating paddles at the back of the vessel.

Hello, sailor! In short order Mr Burke is able to come to an agreement with the *Moolgewanke's* captain, George Johnson. For the relatively moderate sum of just £48 – thank you, he'll take a cheque – Captain Johnson will see the stores onto his steamer and indeed take them upriver to Menindee where they can be unloaded. *Hooray*. Burke's men roll up their sleeves, as do the men of the steamer, and the *Moolgewanke* is soon lying a little lower in the water as no less than eight tons of supplies, including 'leather water-bags, casks of biscuits and tackle for the camels and horses'[80], are loaded onto it. True, the joy at hearing the steamer whistle blow just before the vessel puffs, steams and paddles its way up around the bend is tempered, a little, by the thought of how much easier it might have been if a steamer had taken the bulk of their supplies to Menindee from the beginning – as Captain Cadell had offered – but they'll take it!

•

In the meantime, their only remaining problem is the missing camels. Oh – and John King and Belooch, who went out looking for them yesterday and are now missing themselves.

'Several of our men and some black fellows,' Ludwig Becker would recount, 'went now in search of camels and to look for King and Belooch.'[81]

Mr Burke's frustration at the delay is palpable, he even confides to a local settler who pops by for a chat, 'I am thinking of setting out at once to Cooper's Creek . . . without waiting any longer for the lost camels.'[82]

By the next morning, when *still* there is no sign, his impatience begins to turn to rage.

'The following,' Becker records, 'were out searching: King and Belooch, Brahe and native, Charley and black fellow, and today Mr Landells started also with Dost Mahomet.'[83]

With eight men and as many camels missing, and now three days *lost* forever, Burke barks with frustration, angrily stalking back and forth, cursing and looking in every direction, hopeful for their return. What makes things more urgent than ever that they get going is that Mr Burke has now had the time to read some of the newspapers carried by the *Moolgewanke*, and one story, in particular, is goading him. It seems that although the South Australian John McDouall Stuart had to turn back to the settled districts on his bid to reach the north coast – because of a clash with the blacks – he intends to stay only a short time, before pushing off again. It means that, while there is an opportunity, after all, for the Victorian Exploring Expedition to triumph, it is not an opportunity that will be there for long. They must move!

'From that point on,' Brahe would note, 'there was only one thought in Burke's mind, to push on and make the record of being the first.'[84]

Which means they need the camels and men back, *now*, did he mention?

At least, over the course of the day, some of the men do indeed begin to drift back, but Mr Burke cannot help but notice that they are irredeemably . . . camel-less.

At last, however, with the darkness comes the light. Just on sunset John King and Belooch ride in with . . . all the missing camels.

'They were found about 20 miles north-eastwards from our camp,' Becker records, 'quietly grazing.'[85]

At long last, they are in shape to get moving again, and can do so at first light.

•

Dr Wilkie?

There is an angry American outside, who would like to see you.

It is, oh dear, Charles Ferguson, freshly arrived in Melbourne, and among other things, tired, dishevelled and *bursting* with indignation.

For you see, Dr Wilkie, not only have I been dismissed, but I have been obliged to WALK back, bouncing Mr Burke's cheque for £16 all the way! Yes, all the way from Balranald where I first tried to cash it, it has been refused, so I could not even purchase a ticket on the coach!

So furious is Ferguson it is obvious that litigation is a likelihood, together with enormous public embarrassment for the expedition and the Committee. When it comes to the latter, Wilkie does his best to settle the American down, promising he will consult his colleagues – *Good God, what has Burke done now? We have a very upset American on our hands* – and see if they can arrange satisfaction for him in some manner.

On the possibility of litigation, however, Dr Wilkie decides it can only be prudent to get legal advice from the best qualified member of the Committee, none other than the Chief Justice of Victoria, Sir

William Stawell, and quickly departs in search of the famous jurist, for that purpose.

11 October '60, Bilbarka, barking blazing Burke

Time to move on. If there is a difference about this one, Camp 30, at Bilbarka, it is that for the first time – now that they are embarked on the unknown, where their every step blazes a trail – Burke gives the order to 'blaze' one of the trees by their camp, following the Committee's written instructions to mark their route 'as permanently as possible, by leaving records, sowing seeds, building cairns, and marking trees at as many points as possible'[86].

Taking an axe, Wills, with a few swift blows, cuts away the bark of a gum tree close to the riverbank in a square shape, and now carves into the outer flesh of the trunk the letters VEE (Victorian Exploring Expedition) and beneath it uses the Roman numerals XXX to mark Camp 30 – for the simple reason that it is easier to blaze in straight lines in that manner than carve the curves of the digits 3 and 0. There is a growing sense, now that Balranald and the towns that can fairly be called a town are soon to be behind them, that they are starting to reach territory that needs to be marked if anyone is to find them.

Mr Burke, as impatient as ever, rides out of camp first, closely followed by Brahe, Patten and Hodgkinson. The plan is for them to make camp some 20 miles upstream, while Burke has left it 'to Landells's discretion to follow with the camels'[87].

As it happens, discretion is not Landells's strong suit, and, far more given to rather noisy bluster – in this case he is determined to show Mr Burke the worth of both the camels and himself – so he is instantly at his men to get going and load, so they can 'follow the horses as quickly as possible'[88].

By 2 pm they are on their way, but it is no easy matter. One of the large Indian camels, now even more heavily burdened, with a 500-pound load, tries to buck free, succeeding only in falling to the ground. It not only sends that load everywhere, not only breaks his saddle-girth and nose-string, but also manages to dislodge part of the load of the camel behind him.

Christ Almighty! Why hast Thou forsaken us?

As the others go ahead, Landells and Becker remain behind to reload their three camels, mend the tackle and get underway once more, only succeeding in doing so just as darkness falls.

What to do? After all, they have no food, no water and no *moon*.

But they have matches and that is enough. Lighting a few, his face suddenly ghostly in the flare, Landells finds the track, and they set off – across the scrubby terrain, through the night. Quickly, their eyes adjust to the darkness, with blurry shadows now taking sharp form. Here, a tree. There, a rock. Just up ahead, a bush, and now a dip in the track, and now a large boulder they must divert around. In this ethereal world, their other senses sharpen, too, as they take it all in, the sounds, the smells, of the night, of the desert air, as the camels continue their march 'neath the starry, starry sky, the punctuation points of their progress being the rhythmical plop of their feet endlessly falling, one after the other as the miles fall away. Mr Landells takes the lead, and is soon so exhausted he keeps staggering, almost as if he is falling asleep though walking. Right behind him comes Becker, leading his camels.

Trudging. Trudging. Trudging along in the sombre darkness. And now it happens . . .

Like a visitation from the heavens, like a sign from, yes, Christ Almighty!

'Suddenly,' Becker would recount, 'the whole firmament and the country underneath it was lit up by a day-like light: a splendid meteor fell in the west.'[89]

In an instant, both his artistic and his scientific eye take it all in.

'It made its appearance in a bright part of the milky way near the tail of Scorpio,' he would recount, 'to the right of it, but, to the left of the Ecliptic . . . Green colour; after disappearance red sparks.'[90]

It is the largest meteor Becker has ever seen.

'I never before observed one which from apparently a most minute point increased to such a size during so short a time and within so small a space on the firmament. For half an hour that colossal shooting star gave us some matter for conversation, but soon the previous dullness prevailed again.'[91]

From the sublime to the mundane, and Landells and Becker once again are left to battle on. How far until they reach camp and rest? Ludwig Becker thinks he sees it at last:

'Hallo! There is the camp-fire, how lovely it flickers through the twigs of the underwood; at last we are near it – we whistled, called and [coo-eed] – and received an answer from a lonely shepherd on the other side of the Darling.'[92]

Oh, Lord. This is not us.

Pushing on, they see another sparkle ahead, which *must* be the campfire, and quicken their shambling pace . . . only to find it is a setting star.

Finally, it is 12.30 in the morning before what they think might be a campfire actually *is* a campfire, and after a quickly knocked together dinner, and a drop of tea, it is rising two o'clock in the morning 'before our overtaxed limbs were allowed to rest. We had travelled this day 22 miles.'[93]

The next morning, at least, Mr Burke, in a rare moment of munificence, invites the officers of the expedition to ride with him, an offer that Ludwig Becker is quick to take up. Dr Beckler, however, declines, preferring to stay with the camels and Mr Landells, who he has found some affinity with.

Once again in the rear with the gear, this time with camels bearing it rather than wagons, Beckler is finding the going and the vehicles themselves particularly difficult:

'The camels,' Dr Beckler would chronicle, 'which had already caused us some trouble by running away unexpectedly, became completely uncontrollable as if they could smell the nearby edge of the masterless land . . .'[94]

But it is not just the camels that present problems for Mr Burke's capacity to control. For as the party pushes on to Menindee, William Hodgkinson profits from the fact that Mr Landells is far away with the camels, to get tightly in the ear of William Wills. It's about some things, Mr Wills, that Mr Landells said to me . . . when the big blow-up over the rum occurred. I shouldn't tell you this, because Mr Landells said he'd sack me if I didn't keep my mouth shut, but . . .

But he said some terrible things about the leader, about him being a *rash madman*, who refused to recognise that he, Mr Landells, had *a special agreement with the Committee all his own*.

William Wills is stunned to hear it. To this point he had hoped that Mr Landells's own harsh words to him on the subject of Mr Burke was simply the second officer blowing off steam to the third officer. But now, it is clear Landells is saying such things to the men as well? That is perilously close to 'plain sedition'[95]. Or it will be, if something is not done.

Wills, considering himself 'duty bound'[96] under the circumstances, reports to his leader the things that Landells has said about him. After all, as he would describe those things in a letter to his father, they are 'opinions . . . which would not tend, if listened to, to raise a leader in the estimation of his officers'[97].

The stunned Burke, in turn, reports some of the things that Landells has previously said about Wills . . .

'Whereupon,' Wills would recount, 'it came out that Mr Landells had been playing a fine game, trying to set us altogether by the ears. To Mr Burke he has been abusing and finding fault with all of us, so much so, that Mr B. tells me that Landells positively hates me.'

The expedition's third officer is, again, shocked.

'We have, apparently, been the best of friends. To me he has been abusing Mr Burke, and has always spoken as if he hated the doctor and Mr Becker; whereas with them he has been all milk and honey. There is scarcely a man in the party whom he has not urged Mr Burke to dismiss.'[98]

There is no way around it. Mr Burke is now more certain than ever that Mr Landells must leave the expedition as soon as possible. He can promote Mr Wills to the position of second officer, leaving a vacancy for the position of third. That can be resolved . . .

13 October '60, Royal Society Building, Melbourne, too little, too late

The issue before the Exploration Committee meeting on this day is every bit as neatly and concisely expressed in the minutes – 'To consider the propriety of communicating to Mr Burke the results obtained by Mr Stuart'[99] – as its actual discussion is untidy and drawn out.

The Mayor of Melbourne, Dr Richard Eades, has already made the point very strongly to Dr Macadam that a matter of importance is 'putting Mr Burke in possession of the intelligence that Stuart had nearly crossed the continent'[100], and Dr Macadam agrees. For while Stuart has returned to Adelaide to recuperate, and replenish supplies, it is known he will not stay there long, and will soon be on his way once more on what is now a beaten path. Mr Burke has an opportunity to grasp the laurels for himself, and for Victoria, but only if he moves, *now*!

Now, they just have to get the learned and languid gentlemen of the Exploration Committee to agree with them, for they view Mr Burke as leading a stately scientific endeavour, not competing in anything so vulgar as a (*sniff*) common running race. But as John Macadam knows all too well, and indicates as such in his carefully tailored remarks to the Committee . . . it *is* a race. Everyone knows it, and the public certainly regards it as exactly that. And don't you *see*? Burke's rival has stumbled! In fact, more than stumbled, he has been forced into a humiliating retreat after being attacked by the natives!

The opportunity is too golden to ignore. All Burke must do now is *proceed*, not tarry, and the prize will be his, the battle won, the wreaths preserved for Victoria and this very Committee!

But, say. If Mr Burke is to be informed of this new development, the next question is *how*? A police trooper is the obvious answer to Dr Macadam, they can be ordered by a telegram to pursue Mr Burke quickly from the farthest reaches of the colony. However, although he is a friend and colleague of Mr Burke, Chief Police Commissioner Standish has been very clear that he will not allow policemen to be used as mailmen for the Royal Society. Despite repeated requests from Macadam, Standish is firm; he 'cannot permit the Police to leave their regular duties'[101].

But don't you see? *This is a matter of the greatest urgency!* We must get the message through to Mr Burke! But it can't be done!

And so, once more, the Melbourne cognoscenti become aware that the Royal Society is doing once more what it has always done best – arguing with itself.

And the quarrel drags on and on and on and on . . .

So it goes, until Macadam steps in.

'Gentlemen,' he booms, his red mane framing his powerful words as perfectly as ever, 'the only fear of Mr Burke when he was in town was that the continent should be crossed before him.'

Ipso facto . . .

They are morally *beholden* to inform Mr Burke that if he tarries, he risks that very thing occurring!

'He must be made to know that £2,000 has been voted for Stuart's assistance, that Stuart is likely to leave again at once, and that Stuart will be all the more anxious to do so knowing of Mr Burke's progress. The best thing to be done is to send a special messenger on to Mr Burke, or at any rate to Swan Hill, to take on a letter to the exploring party.'[102]

It makes sense. But, as ever with the Exploration Committee, that in itself is not enough.

'I think,' says Dr Gillbee, Royal Society vice-president, 'that if we could get the assistance of the police it would be far the best.'[103]

With a tired air, Dr Macadam explains one more time for the road, that Police Commissioner Standish and the Chief Secretary William Nicholson have been firm on this matter – with only a scant few policemen in Swan Hill, they will not be used for delivering someone's mail, no matter how grand that person might be.

But perhaps there is another way?

The thought strikes Dr Wilkie that they can make this more than a mere letter, more than just a casual missive. Yes, it needs to be more urgent than that. Perhaps a dispatch containing . . . new orders?

'Are we prepared to issue, now,' Dr Wilkie proposes to the meeting, 'instructions to Mr Burke, in the view of Stuart's discoveries? If that is the case, that is a very forcible reason for sending a messenger!'[104]

Indeed. And it *is* a very delicately nuanced way of doing it. Of course you can't have a policeman reduced to the role of a postman. That would contravene his role, and be an abuse of public resources. But having a policeman find Superintendent Burke, to deliver important new orders, is not only within the bounds of propriety, it is the way things should be done!

Dr Macadam takes up the fray.

'I move a resolution,' he states, 'that Mr Burke ought to be put in possession, at the earliest possible moment, of the facts of Stuart's recent journey, as far as they are known to the Committee.'[105]

'I second,' joins Dr Gillbee. Passed unanimously. Action at last, to urge Mr Burke to action!

•

Could this be the very man he is looking for?

For it is at an outpost of Tolarno station – its homestead perched above the steep banks of the Darling, where the *Moolgewanke* is anchored below, stationary for the Sabbath – on the morning of 14 October, that Mr Burke comes across a local, William Wright. He introduces himself as the manager of a cattle station on the river Darling, not far upstream from where they are now. Now, if he does say so himself, Mr Burke, it so happens that Mr Wright knows more about the country from here to Torowoto[106] – about halfway to Cooper's Creek – than any white man on the Darling. What is more, he is 'quite confident'[107] that Mr Burke will be able to take the whole party up to Cooper's Creek and form a Depot.

Burke likes the cut of his jib from the first, the sense of strength he projects, his obvious know-how, his local knowledge. Most importantly, he likes the sound of Wright's professed capacity with animals. Might he be the very man to fill the gap that is soon to be left by Landells? It is worth considering, quietly, as for now Wright offers to show Burke the best place on the Darling, not far from here, to get your horses across and on to the northern shore. In fact, let me show you the spot.

Just 20 minutes ride upriver, they are there, at a spot where the Darling widens and, most importantly, shallows – right across from Wright's own homestead on Kinchega station. Within minutes, Burke's packhorses are safely across, and setting up camp.

It is all so easy, when you have someone with local knowledge.

And on that subject, Mr Wright is clear, as he would later be wont to say: 'I have travelled [all] over the country, and know more of it than any other man on the Darling . . .'[108]

Most importantly, he knows the country north of Menindee, and has been as far as 200 miles up, to a place he calls Torowoto Swamp, where there is a supply of water. Yes, here in Wright, Mr Burke has a white man who is good with animals, used to exercising authority, and can guide them at least halfway to Cooper's Creek.

He needs to think about it, certainly, but, *prima facie*, it makes sense!

CHAPTER EIGHT

MENINDEE MADNESS

The Exploring Expedition, as it recedes from the confines of the peopled districts, and approaches the solitude of the unknown interior, is gradually casting off the 'Barnacles' which clung to it, so long as its progress was a mere affair of parade and holiday work. The silent wilderness has terrors for the faint of heart; and any excuse is gladly seized on by them, in order to retreat without open concession of cowardice . . .[1]

The Age, 16 November 1860

[Landells] casts about him for ways and means of bringing about his withdrawal from the Expedition in such a way as to free himself from blame or suspicion of 'having shown the white feather'.[2]

The Age, 7 November 1860

15 October '60, Menindee, nothing lonesome, morbid or drear here . . .

Ah, but how strange it is how two months of oft brutal travel can change a man's perspective. When they had left the grand metropolis of Melbourne back in August, Menindee on the River Darling was no more than a flyspeck on the map, if that. And back then, had they known what that flyspeck consisted of – no more than half-a-dozen hovels of timber and calico, 'one hotel, one store, a kitchen and two native huts'[3], occupied for the most part by stunted men with squinty eyes, trying to see through the glare – they would have groaned in despair at the thought of spending time there.

181

As it is though?

After 470 miles of gut-busting, soul-destroying, blister-inducing foot-slogging and riding, at least half of that through a great nothingness, the heart of Wills – who hitches a ride on the *Moolgewanke*, while Mr Burke follows with the horses – soars, just to see this last frontier outpost of civilisation, right on the edge of the badlands, which press close. Yes, hovels to some, but so comfortable, so stable, so . . . unmoving.

For perhaps, more than anything, that is what the men of the expedition now most desire for themselves. To stop. To rest. To sleep. Perchance, to dream.

The last two months have completely exhausted them, drained their supplies, weakened their animals, and blown a hole in their budget. Yes, by now, Burke might have some regrets about not accepting Captain Cadell's offer to transport the bulk of his supplies right to the very doorstep of Menindee – so they could have started near fresh from here – but it is too late now.

And where better to quiet such regrets than in a pub, and the happy circumstance is that Menindee has one!

'A bush public house, perched on the top of a sand-hill,' one evocative newspaper account would describe it, 'down which its patrons could, and did, roll when they found it inconvenient to walk, and if they frequently adopted the former method of descending, it was doubtless attributable to the fact that some of the refreshments provided were more remarkable for their destruction of motive power than for their nutritious qualities.'[4]

As Burke and his men take in the odd brew – in truth, some take in much more than that, and Burke is aware that drinking too much might be an issue, but lets it pass for the moment – there is much to contemplate, not all of it pleasing. They have arrived here, at what is effectively the most northerly point of settlement on this meridian, very late in the season for ones contemplating pushing on. Summer is just six weeks away, and yet the expedition is *still* in the bottom third of Australia. In fact, despite all their hard work, all their agonies, a fast stagecoach could get them back to Melbourne in just two weeks.

Despite Burke's eagerness to get going as soon as possible, even he recognises that some pause must be taken to sort a few things out.

For now, the men begin unloading the stores and setting up Camp 34 right by the river, that . . .

That smell?

Oh, dear Lord. It proves to be the boxes of dried pemmican meat which have rotted in this infernal heat. No less than 320 pounds of it! It is a bitter blow, reducing by almost a quarter the amount of available meat supplies they had been counting on to sustain them in the difficult months ahead in the Australian wilderness.

15 October '60, Menindee, a duel in the desert . . .

For the past week, things seem to have settled between Landells and Burke, and the former has actually been looking forward to heading into the middle of this extraordinary continent. And yet, only shortly after arriving at Menindee it is apparent that the mercury of the remarkably mercurial Burke has risen once more to boiling point.

Approaching him to report the safe arrival of the camels – Landells has instructed the sepoys to take their time herding the camels, and allow them to graze as they go along – it is indeed clear to Landells that Mr Burke is disturbed, as the expedition leader refuses to speak to him. He even goes so far as to go and lie on his bed and turn his back on Landells!

'Mr Burke,' Landells says, 'I hope there is nothing wrong.'[5]

His words are like the prick of a sword to the haunches of a bull.

For immediately, Mr Burke springs to his feet and snarls, 'Yes, sir, what is this you have been saying to Wills and Hodgkinson?'[6]

Oh. Hodgkinson, too? Still, Landells does not blanche.

'If you call them up I shall know what charges they have been making against me.'[7]

'You are a *scoundrel*, sir!' Mr Burke bursts back. 'I will now give you satisfaction, and waive all leadership, and meet you.'[8]

And so, it has come to this.

Burke, the leader of the expedition, the one charged with guiding them successfully from one side of the continent to the other, seems to

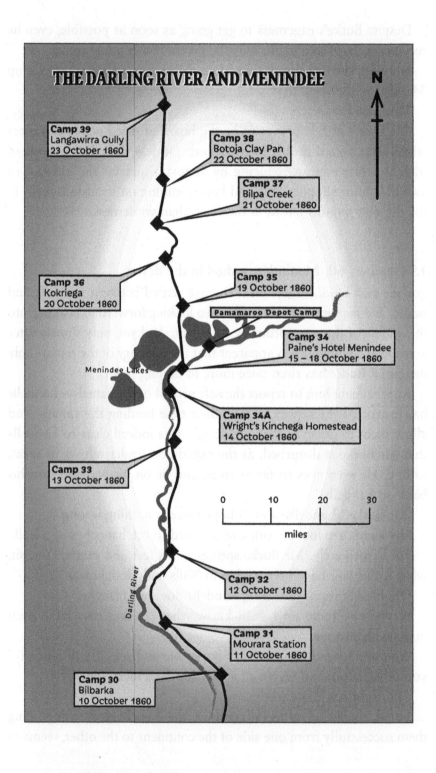

THE DARLING RIVER AND MENINDEE

N

Camp 39
Langawirra Gully
23 October 1860

Camp 38
Botoja Clay Pan
22 October 1860

Camp 37
Bilpa Creek
21 October 1860

Camp 36
Kokriega
20 October 1860

Camp 35
19 October 1860

Pamamaroo Depot Camp

Camp 34
Paine's Hotel Menindee
15 – 18 October 1860

Menindee Lakes

Camp 34A
Wright's Kinchega Homestead
14 October 1860

Camp 33
13 October 1860

0   10   20   30

miles

Camp 32
12 October 1860

Darling River

Camp 31
Mourara Station
11 October 1860

Camp 30
Bilbarka
10 October 1860

actually be inviting Landells to have a duel in the Australian wilderness – for each to forget their rank for the duration, pick a second, to stand back to back with pistols in hand, walk an agreed number of paces, turn and fire on each other.

Landells, stupefied, declines to give Burke the satisfaction he seeks.

'Mr Burke,' says he with some dignity, 'when I left Melbourne it was not to fight you with either words or weapons, but to fight the desert: will you now allow me to resign?'[9]

His face a picture of the most complete contempt, Burke scowls back and simply says, 'Yes!'[10]

And that is *nearly* the end of it, for as yet Landells does not formally hand over his letter of resignation. Rather, he begins to foment dissent, starting by telling Dr Beckler of the terrible situation and adding that he has 'been accused by Wills, in Burke's presence, of pursuing separatist aims'[11].

Dr Beckler is stunned. Mr Burke challenging officers to a duel? Mr Wills making terrible allegations? The second officer and King of the Camels to be cast aside? This is clearly an expedition teetering on total collapse and when Mr Landells says he is going to resign, Dr Beckler takes pause. Clearly, things are so spinning out of control that Dr Beckler feels that he, too, must 'take this step'[12], and absent himself from the whirligig that is Mr Burke. Perhaps, now, things will calm?

A few hours later, however, in the early evening, just as Landells is packing up, the camel overseer hears Burke call out to the one man on the expedition he knows he can rely on, his every word a human bark: 'Wills, you see the camels taken across [the river] tomorrow . . .'[13]

As Menindee has no punt, and no suitable vessel to transport such ungainly animals as camels, Mr Burke has come up with the idea of stringing a long rope from one side of the Darling River to the other, and then having the camels swim across – in part pulled forward by the use of another rope which could be attached to the wooden peg in their noses, and hauled from the other side.

Landells is appalled, nay appalled . . . *and* disgusted!

He has said all along that the camels can only be taken over on a vessel, and has been trying to convince Mr Burke that the answer is to take them over on a barge.

'This Mr Burke refused,' the loyal Wills observes, 'because the captain and everyone else said that it would be a very dangerous experiment from the difficulty of getting them on or off, which is no easy matter to do safely, even on a punt arranged for the purpose; and as for the barge, it can scarcely be brought within six feet of the bank, so Mr Burke insisted on their swimming the river at Kinchica.'[14]

Landells cannot bear it. He actually *cares* for the camels, and cannot bear the thought of them being sent on a difficult and dangerous crossing.

'It is too late,' he says quietly to Burke, for much of his anger has now passed, and he is simply sad. 'I will cross them at 10 o'clock tomorrow morning. And there is no rope here.'[15]

Oh?

'I have just brought a rope across with us,'[16] Wills offers.

Landells rounds on him, all his sadness gone now.

'What business do *you* have to say *anything*?'[17] he roars, even as the conflagration once again erupts into savage life.

More than anything, Wills is stunned that Landells is carrying on in such a manner, making 'a great fool of himself'[18], not only in front of 'several of the men'[19], but also that local fellow, the man who selected the spot for the camels to cross, the proper bushman who Mr Burke has just met the day before, Mr William Wright, who until a few days before has been the manager of nearby Kinchega station.

For his trouble, Landells is given another assessment of his character by Burke, unlikely to make the mother of either man blush with pride, but the expedition leader does at least allow that the crossing can be delayed until 10 am tomorrow . . .

Under the supervision of Mr Wills.

In response, Mr Landells once more jumps to his feet in rage.

'Do you,' Landells demands of Burke, 'intend that Mr Wills supervise the swimming of the camels [across the Darling]?'[20]

'I shall not tell you, sir!' Mr Burke rasps back, to the man he considers has no further authority on the matter. 'Why do you ask such an impertinent question?'[21]

'Because,' Landells replies reasonably, 'I wish to know who will be responsible for them.'[22]

'If you knew your place,' Mr Burke replies, 'you would not ask such a question. You have no right to ask it. I will give such orders as I think proper to my officers, without considering myself responsible to you. Your conduct is insolent and improper, and I will have no more of it.'[23]

Caught by a rage that is somewhere between apoplectic and apocalyptic, Burke finishes by roaring at him, 'O, my boy, I shall soon get rid of you!'[24]

'The entire want of self-respect and self-control evinced in his challenge to fight [me],' Landells would note, 'showed me that his leadership was no longer safe.'[25]

Others in the party agree.

Even MacPherson, the saddler engaged for that purpose by Mr Burke at Swan Hill – the most independent observer of the lot – would say that the men with Mr Burke's expedition were 'treated like convicts'[26].

Compounding Landells's high sense of grievance is that it has come to his ears that long before the subject of his resignation had come up, Mr Wills had been canvassing the other men about whether they felt they could take over the camels without the second officer there to supervise? And Mr Wills had even said he could do it himself . . .

Oh, the infamy!

To have Wills acting behind his back in this manner seems the height of betrayal.

And yet, it is perhaps a measure of Landells's genuine care for the camels that, even though outraged by Mr Burke and Mr Wills, the following morning when the camels are formed up to be swum across in the manner prescribed by Mr Burke, he is there to help, getting into the river himself – the only man who does so, and as he would remark, 'without any interference from Burke or Wills'[27] – while John King and John Drakeford haul hard from the other side. The result is that 'all the camels were swum across the Darling without accident'[28].

Landells is supported by Dr Hermann Beckler, who has broadcast his own disgust at 'the manner in which Mr Burke spoke to Mr Landells', further noting that he does 'not consider that the party . . . safe without Mr Landells to manage the camels'[29].

In sum, as Dr Beckler writes in his own letter of resignation, 'I wish to impress upon you, that the principal reason for my resignation is the way in which Mr Landells was treated by you yesterday evening and his consequent resignation, and it is these two points which determine me not to accompany the party under your charge beyond the occupied districts of New South Wales.'[30]

Once handed the resignation, Mr Burke professes not to be particularly bothered, telling Dr Beckler that, in any case, 'You are unfit for your position.'[31] Against that, Burke also declines to accept the resignation until the Committee at Melbourne can be advised, and a replacement sent north, so despite having resigned, Beckler agrees to remain to oversee the Menindee camp until this new officer arrives. Clearly, far more than just the loss of a senior officer, what Burke faces at this point is something like the beginnings of a full-blown mutiny on his hands . . .

16 October, '60, Menindee, Wright man for the job

Despite it all, there is good news for Mr Burke on the day. As it turns out, that rugged local bushman he'd liked the look of, the one who'd been so hospitable to the explorers, Mr William Wright, has declared himself available. With his employment at Kinchega station coming to an end, the timing is right, and he readily agrees to guide them 100 miles to the north, and will even bring two blacks from the station with him – men who know the area, and are good with horses. One of them, Dick, is of the Barkindji people, who live along the Darling River and speak the Paakantyi language. He is a notably clever, strong, handsome and bearded 20-year-old who had been raised in a traditional tribal environment but in his teen years had started working at Kinchega, where he seems to have picked up a very basic kind of English.

Burke is keen to take just enough supplies with them that they will be able to get to the Gulf and back, while leaving the bulk of the supplies here at Menindee.

'I need to take on provisions for six months for six men,'[32] Mr Burke had already told Tom McDonough. But now they must add provisions for three more, being William Wright, and his two Aboriginal guides, Dick already becoming a quick favourite of the party.

16 October '60, Melbourne, rancour in the ranks and a dispatch dispatched

Order. Order!

The room quietens appropriately as Professor Neumayer stands, ready to give his progress report to the Exploration Committee, assembled in the hall of the Royal Society for the occasion.

And yet, despite the respectful silence the good professor feels a sudden sense of disquiet, as he notices an unexpected face in the public gallery – an angry, glowering one, belonging to the sacked foreman, Charles Ferguson. Dr Wilkie, too, has noticed him, and though he had been relieved to receive advice from the chief justice that, in terms of legal recourse, Ferguson has 'not a leg to stand upon'[33], still he is concerned as to what might happen if Ferguson might stand on both legs now and make a scene, especially as a ravenous press would surely report every word of what is likely to be an outburst.

Is that what the man is playing at?

In the meantime, Professor Neumayer gives a scientific and soothing report on Mr Burke's progress. 'I was highly pleased at the manner and disposition of the officers with one another,' the professor says. 'They were thoroughly inspired with the best feelings regarding the object in view. All the officers and men were exceedingly pleased with their excellent leader . . .'

He particularly cites Mr Wills, and 'the king of the camels', Mr Landells.

When it comes to the assistants, he lauds Mr Hodgkinson as 'one of the most valuable members of the party' as well as 'a sailor named Charley . . .'[34] Oh, and one other fellow drew his attention, 'another member of the expedition, named King, who also showed great skill in managing [the camels] and was otherwise a very serviceable man'[35].

Thank you, Professor Neumayer. Any questions?

Yes, Dr Macadam would like to know what the good professor made of the statement by Charles Ferguson (*Good Lord! Macadam is going to bring this to a head right now!*) both at this meeting and previously in the papers, to the effect that Mr Burke always intended to discharge certain members of the party at the Darling, whatever their worth?

'Mr Burke,' the professor replies with some wounded dignity, 'always expressed to me his great desire to take on the whole of the party as far as it was at all possible for them to go . . . In conclusion, I would say that I do not believe there is any foundation for that statement.'[36] (*Hear, hear.*)

Here now is Charles Ferguson, who can bear it no more, and stands to roar his own question.

'Do you not remember,' he asks furiously of the professor, 'Mr Burke calling me and Langan together at Balranald and saying –'

'Mr Ferguson,' the Chair, Dr Eades, interrupts him sharply, 'no person [who is] not a member of the society can be permitted to put a question.'[37]

Nevertheless, as Mr Ferguson has commenced the question, he may as well conclude, and the American does so, saying surely the professor remembers, at Balranald, Mr Burke *specifically admitting*, 'that he intended to leave certain men at the Darling'?

'I have frequently seen Mr Burke talking to the men,' Professor Neumayer replies, hotly, 'but I never heard of any such conversation having taken place, neither do I think that anything of the sort has been said.'

Ferguson fumes, while Dr Macadam preens just to hear such a comprehensive denial from one who was there, he was *there*! Following up, Dr Macadam asks the professor what he made of one of Ferguson's other statements to the papers, 'that there was great jealousy amongst the officials in the camp, and all that is wanting to bring matters to a rupture is a fitting occasion. I wish to know, Professor Neumayer, have you ever observed anything of the sort?'[38]

'I am very sorry any such remarks should have been made,' Professor Neumayer replies. 'There was no such thing as jealousy existing amongst the members of the expedition . . . I can assure you that there was the very best understanding existing between the whole of the party, and I feel satisfied that they will succeed as far as lies in their power.'[39] (*Cheers.*)

Charles Ferguson can bear it no more, and stalks out angrier than he began. If he cannot gain satisfaction in this forum, he really will seek it elsewhere.

As the meeting draws to a close, Professor Neumayer advises that he will soon be returning to Swan Hill and 'will be happy . . . to take charge of any dispatches and forward them as soon as possible [to the expedition party]'[40]. Indeed, the Hon. Secretary reminds members that this will be the last opportunity to send a message to Mr Burke or his officers before they move beyond the settled districts . . .

'I will be happy to receive any letters for them up until Thursday afternoon at 4 o'clock,'[41] finishes Dr Macadam.

In short order it is the Hon. Secretary who writes the official letter, on behalf of the Committee, that is to be sent north to Mr Burke, courtesy of Superintendent Foster of Swan Hill, who has agreed to send his best trooper north to carry this vital dispatch that Professor Neumayer will bring him – informing Mr Burke of the crucial development that he simply must know. Dr Macadam frames his words to the leader of the expedition carefully:

> *I have now to communicate to you a fact of considerable importance in the History of Australian Exploration. Mr Stuart has returned to South Australia . . . it would appear that he only failed in reaching the Northern Coast from the smallness of his party (only 3 men in all) and the number and ferocity of the natives in the locality of the point arrived at.*

Lest Mr Burke miss the point, that Stuart is to head back immediately, Dr Macadam follows up, as delicately as he can manage . . .

> *The Committee does not think that this circumstance need necessarily interfere in any way with the course of the Expedition, but only hopes it will prove, if possible, an additional stimulus to you to secure at as early a period as may be the objects of the enterprise which you have so auspiciously entered upon . . .'[42]*

Rush, rush, rush, Mr Burke!

No, really, they don't wish to add any pressure on Mr Burke. But look, Dr Macadam also feels he must add a purely personal note, with a little reminder of just how much Julia Matthews would be thrilled if Burke wins the race:

My dearest Burke,
Every success; all well – one especially – you know who. Everyone
wishes you well. The honour of Victoria is in your hands. We know
and feel assured that you will vindicate the confidence reposed in you.
May God bless and preserve you. Yours ever, J. M.[43]

Oh, and Sir William Stawell would also like a word:

My dear Sir,
I have just returned . . . and heard of Stuart's expedition . . . As he is
now to start with an increased number – 12 in all and 36 horses – it
will to a certain extent be a race between you and him – now I know
how exciting this must be to you or anyone with a spark of spirit and
now will come the time of trial for your coolness and caution . . .
Adieu my dear Burke,
    Your sincere friend,
        William F. Stawell [44]

17 October '60, Menindee, the parting of the parties

For his part, Burke, specifically, is keen to resume rushing north as
soon as possible. And yet even he recognises that some pause must be
taken to sort a few things out.

And so he comes to something of a compromise solution.

Travelling light, he will forge ahead with half the expedition, guided
part of the way by Mr Wright, and when they get to Cooper's Creek,
he will send Brahe, Dost Mahomet and some of the camels back to
bring the others forward on the path that they will have established.

Despite his resignation, and even his humiliation, Dr Beckler has
kindly agreed to stay on at Menindee until a replacement for him can
be secured from Melbourne, and he will remain in charge, overseeing
the men who are definitely remaining – MacPherson, Belooch and
Hodgkinson – and ensuring that the remaining seven horses and ten
camels can rest and fatten up.

And what of *you*, Ludwig Becker, with your badly injured foot –
courtesy of being recently trodden on by a horse – which sees you
limping around like the old cripple you are?

'Do you like to stay in the depot,' Mr Burke now asks him disingenuously, 'or to go on with me now to Cooper's Creek? If you like to be with the party, you are welcome, but I must tell you, there is no time for scientific researches, nor a horse or camel to ride on, you will have to tramp all the way, and must do the work like the other men.'

In reply, the German man does not have to consider long.

'Sir,' he says with some dignity, 'I am not afraid to work, although you will find men possessed of greater physical power than I can boast of – but to walk all the way, you see, Mr Burke, is impossible. In consequence of the accident I met with, I am lame at present and can hardly stand. So I think it is better for you and me when I remain here for some time in the depot, where I shall find time to work up the matter and material I gathered in reference to natural sciences.'

'Very well. Now listen, I intend to look for a road up to Cooper's Creek, and how the way is, and about the water; and as soon as I have found a spot where to form a depot, I shall send for you to come up with the others and with such things as wanted.'[45]

18 October '60, Menindee, cross correspondents and rats in the ranks

It doesn't take long for the denizens of Menindee to find out about the departure of Landells and Beckler, and they are quickly on the side of the dear departed, with one noting that 'these persons took the best course they could take under the circumstances in which they were placed; for it would be madness to go with a man whose only recommendation is that he is a strict disciplinarian'[46].

The thing that stuns them most, however, is what Burke does to dispose of the goods he has decided he does not wish to take north. The obvious thing is to order them 'left at one of the out-stations passed in the day time, or where they camped at night . . .'

Instead he effectively dumps it all by the side of the road!

The reason he hastens to depart so quickly, they reckon, is that once the news gets to Melbourne of the resignations of Mr Landells and Dr Beckler, it would be Burke who would be 'fearing his recall'[47].

In sum, the impression that the expedition leader makes upon the Menindee locals is not one that would make him blush with pleasure.

'If I were to give you the opinion people have of the chief,' one of the Menindee locals will write to the *Pastoral News*, 'it would be anything but flattering to that gentleman. We are surprised that the people of Melbourne came to choose him for a leader, and it is a riddle to many besides myself. The man is no bushman, no surveyor, no doctor; nothing could in reality be said in his favour.'[48]

19 October '60, Menindee, time, gentlemen please

Up, up and away! Today is the day of leaving Menindee, of beginning the long haul through the wild country, to get to Cooper's Creek, some 470 miles to the north. As such, the camp is up early with the camels being loaded once more, the horses being checked thoroughly to see which ones are fit to depart. All is movement and purpose ... with one notable exception.

For some unaccountable reason, John Drakeford, the cook who had come all the way from India with George Landells and his other offsider, John King, is not yet up, and not only is Mr Burke appalled to note it, he says so, volubly, opening his remarks by stating, 'You're drunk!'

For his part, though Drakeford would ever after claim he was no such thing, he is not particularly concerned with Mr Burke's anger.

'You've threatened to sack me before,' says he, evenly. 'You can do it now if you like.'

'Damn your eyes,' Mr Burke bursts back, 'you shan't go further with me.'

'How will I get back?'

Without blinking, Burke slashes his signature on a cheque for £5, and hands it over, saying, 'This will take you to Melbourne, and when you reach there you will be paid the balance.'[49]

It is time to get to grips, to get ready to make the hard country that lies between them and Cooper's Creek bow to their will, with the main task for Burke remaining before starting, being to write to the Committee, updating them, via the Hon. Secretary Dr John Macadam:

*Menindee
October 16, 1860.*

Sir,

It is my intention to form a Depot upon the river somewhere in this neighbourhood and to proceed on towards Cooper's Creek with a small party by a route which will be shown to me by Mr Wright, manager for Mr Baker, and which I have every reason to believe is quite practicable but I shall not incur any risk . . .[50]

Yes, the German medico has resigned, but he is no loss.

I believe Dr Beckler to be an honest well-intentioned man but very easily acted upon, and very unfit for his present position.[51]

And even less loss is his second officer.

Mr Landells has as yet, had no difficulties to contend with and at the first station where I proposed to load the camels and begin the real work he tenders his resignation. I believe that the expedition is far better without him . . .

I shall not allow the secession of the Doctor or Mr Landells to retard the progress of the party a moment, and I still feel as confident as ever in the success of the main object of the expedition.

*I have the honour to be, Sir,
Your most obedient servant.
R. O'Hara Burke
Leader*[52]

The letter completed, his hands officially washed of Mr Landells and Dr Beckler, Mr Burke focuses on final preparations, before leaving Menindee. Helping him pack his clothing is Tom McDonough, who is not surprised to see Mr Burke has few shirts left as – in some of his typically inconsistent bursts of generosity, before the ferocity returns – he often hands them over to admiring natives. The friendly Irishman chidingly points out that he is now giving Mr Burke two of his own flannel shirts to make up the difference. Really, it is too bad, Mr Burke!

'I do not care, McDonough,' answers Burke, 'if I get on board the vessel with only a shirt on me, if I get through.'[53]

Ah, yes, the vessel. There has been little talk of that, which is why McDonough notes the remark as curious – though he well recalls the conversation Mr Burke had had with Professor Neumayer and Mr Wills three weeks earlier, on the same subject. Clearly, the leader has not totally abandoned the idea of a nautical return altogether. But enough of that for now. The time for departure is nigh, and Tom McDonough finishes packing the last of Mr Burke's clothes, ready to sling on the camel's back.

19 October '60, The Outback, heads up and hearts full

Onwards.

On this morning, Burke takes the lead alongside Wright once more, with Wills in tight behind, followed by their party consisting of Messrs William Brahe, William Patten, Tom McDonough, John King, Charley Gray and Dost Mahomet, together with 15 horses and 16 camels and such supplies as they think they will need to last them for the three months that Mr Burke estimates it will take.

Mr Becker observes their departure, going on to report to Dr Macadam that, 'Mr Wright is with the party as a volunteer; that gentleman has been once before in the direction and near Cooper's Creek and will be therefore of good service to Mr Burke.'[54]

To Burke's delight, the trip is not nearly so fearsome as he had imagined.

Much of the country is open and fertile, and is nothing less than 'fine, sheep-grazing country'[55], which will clearly be of huge interest to the Committee, for whoever settles here first will do as well, if not better, than the first squatters to settle Victoria's central highlands of rolling grass plains.

Most impressively of all, they have no difficulty in getting fresh water, as creeks and waterholes abound, and they are never more than 20 miles apart. It is good country, *great* country, 'a fine open tract of country, well grassed'[56], and the men are able to advance at the rate of 20 miles a day, which is close to as fast as they have travelled on the whole trip to date.

On the third day out, after climbing over a range – named by Sturt the 'Scropes Range' back in 1844 – they find much the same well-grassed country, albeit with more trees, and fewer stones, which they again easily traverse before some 40 miles later another lump in the landscape presents itself, the Mount Doubeny Ranges. The most wonderful surprise is the plentiful water supply, with billabongs and creeks appearing every few hours. Yes, Mr Wright insists that much of the water is not permanent, but when gulping from a pleasingly tangy spring at Kokriega or delighting in the 'nice clear water'[57] at Bilpa Creek, it is hard to believe they could disappear altogether. Finally, it seems, the weather, the water and luck are going their way. And from here, the pastoral country is simply mouth-watering.

'From these ranges . . .' the ever-vigilant Wills records, still making notes while upright in his saddle, 'we have passed over as good grazing country as one would wish to see. Salt bushes of every kind, grass in abundance and plenty of water. Amongst the ranges we found kangaroo grass as high as our shoulders, and on the plains the spear grass up to our knees.'[58]

Adding to their general sense of well-being is the benign temperatures, with Wills also happily noting, 'the thermometer has never risen above 88.5 degrees in the shade and has seldom been below 50 degrees. The average daily range having been from 58.0 to 80.0 degrees . . .'[59]

•

Trooper Lyons.

Superintendent Foster wishes to see you immediately.

As dutiful as ever, Trooper Myles Lyons is quick to report to the superintendent, who is equally quick to give him some rather surprising orders. You are to go in pursuit of Mr Burke and his Victorian Exploring Expedition. You are to take with you this sealed missive we have just received from Melbourne, containing an urgent change of orders for the leader – and be sure to give it to him, and him alone.

Yes, sir.

Drop everything, leave my love, my friends, my whole life, and head off into the trackless wilderness to deliver this missive just because you say so?

Yes, sir.

Shortly thereafter, the ever dutiful 36-year-old trooper – Superintendent Foster's best and most reliable man – is on his way.

24 October '60, Mutawintji, a short-lived piece of paradise

After traipsing up and up through a hot and sticky valley, the sweat blending the red dust into their sunburnt necks, their cavalcade comes to a strange oasis of silence, shade, water and beauty. Unknown to them, they have come to a place of enormous significance to the local Wilyakali, Milpulo and Maljangapa peoples, who have been in these parts for 40,000 years – a place of the spirits, of initiation ceremonies, of trading, and even of inter-tribal marriage. The ranges in which Mutawintji[60] lies, surrounded by dry plains, were created by the Kurlawirra snake-man. After his sisters disobeyed him, they were banished to the sky, and the local tribe ordered to gather the entrails of a kangaroo into a pile, which turned into the largest mountain on the ranges, the one with bands of white running through the rock face. The locals who disobeyed were turned into stone.

Those who reach its heights can see for dozens of miles in every direction. Ah, but it is not what you can see in this world that is most impressive, so much as in the spiritual world. Over thousands of years the natives have left their mark in their sacred sites, much of it beneath overhangs and on rock walls by shady pools that never empty; their steep, stately descending rock faces, their twisting gorges, their hidden caverns, their depictions of their world, the place of their ancestors. All are engraved and emblazoned with the colours of the earth, with yellow clay and red ochres, the deeper imprints made by the one tribe member, known as 'the clever man', pecking away at the rock with smaller, harder rocks, tracing the outlines of their world over the centuries.

Now, there have been, and will be, times when the Victorian Exploring Expedition barely blinks in face of things that are of enormous cultural and scientific significance. Not this time . . .

Nigh to a man, the expedition members are taken in by the cool beauty of the place, the respite from the heat outside, the wonder of the entire place, with William Wills leading the way, describing 'a romantic gorge in which the creek takes its rise . . . There is a large deep water-hole the whole breadth between the rocks which are perpendicular all round, beyond this there is a narrow chasm just broad enough for a man to pass through. This chasm can only be approached by swimming across the waterhole . . .'[61]

It is with great reluctance that it is decided they don't have time to do that and must keep going.

•

Such is the nature of this extraordinary continent, however, that within just 200 *yards* of leaving the wonders of Mutawintji Gorge, the Victorian Exploring Expedition finds itself back in the desert once more, with glaring red sands, rolling 'hairy panics' – Charles Ferguson would have called them 'tumbleweeds' – and a bitterly dry wind.

There may be drier, more miserable places in Australia, it is just that Mr Wills has not seen them yet.

'This last season,' Mr Wills records in his journal, after talking to William Wright, 'is said to have been the most rainy that they have had for several years; yet everything looked so parched up that I should have imagined it had been an exceedingly dry one.'[62]

Yes, it is tough country, but at least they have Mr Wright with them, and he continues to make a very favourable impression on Mr Burke, particularly. Many of the Menindee mob had insisted it would be madness to push towards Cooper's Creek at this time of year, but fortunately, he had listened to Mr Wright, and they are clearly going to get through! Their daily progress has been unruffled and steady, just like Mr Wright himself. Mr Wright is a man with the know-how they need. He knows how to pick the best native guides, he knows how to pick a route that goes via waterholes, and he definitely knows how to show respect for a first officer.

29 October '60, Torowoto, a plant that will never grow

As good as his word!

Mr Wright had said it would take 10 days or so to get to Torowoto, and sure enough on this morning, 10 days after leaving Menindee, they indeed arrive at this wonderful outpost of green midst the blazing brown, halfway between Menindee and Cooper's Creek. It proves to be a flowery swamp, peppered by tall trees and criss-crossed with small rivulets and channels, in places gathering themselves to become small waterholes.

Delighted, Mr Burke can't help but wonder if this fellow Wright might just be the man he is looking for, a bushman with no scientific pretensions or passions, a man who he could rely on to get a job done. In fact, now that he thinks of it, might he be the very one needed to take charge of bringing up the remaining stores from Menindee? At the moment that job is earmarked for Dr Beckler (if he even remains with the party), or (God help us all) Ludwig Becker if there is no other choice. But Wright easily outstrips both men when it comes to capabilities in these climes. Perhaps he could fill the officer vacancy left by the departed Landells? Mr Wills, of course, had taken over as second officer the moment Mr Landells had handed in his resignation, creating a vacancy for third officer. After all, Wright has successfully managed a station, with many employees and thousands of animals, so taking charge of four men, 10 camels and seven horses and getting them to Cooper's Creek should be an easy matter – or at least easier than it would be for a German botanist or artist? It is true that Burke has not known Wright for long, but rather more to the point is that he has known Beckler and Becker long enough to know they are nowhere near Mr Wright's proven capabilities. So what about you, Mr Wright, how does the proposition strike you?

Oh.

You would like how much? *That* much?

Oh.

Four hundred pounds is £100 more than Mr Wills or any other officer is receiving ... making Wright rather like Mr Landells had been, which is to say very mercenary about it. But, in this case, Mr Burke is of the view that Mr Wright will actually be worth it. So much so, in fact, he not only promises to write to the Committee asking them to meet Wright's salary demands, but even says he'll pay the difference from his own salary if they don't!

Do we have an agreement, sir?

We do.

(The Menindee mob, when they get word, are quite stunned at Mr Burke's choice for third officer, in William Wright. You mean the former superintendent of Kinchega station? The locals can barely believe it, as one letter writer would express in a very dismissive letter to the *Bendigo Advertiser*.

'This is the man elected to [follow in the footsteps of] Sturt and Mitchell!'[63]

After all, Sturt had been educated at Harrow, Mitchell at Oxford University. They are *gentlemen*. Now Burke has hired Mr Wright as an officer – naught but a local yob.

'I think,' the letter writer notes with a certain savage confidence, 'there is no reason to fear that either of these great explorers will be eclipsed by O'Hara Burke.'[64])

Meanwhile, preparing to leave Torowoto, Mr Burke decides to make 'a plant' – bury a cache of edible supplies for the use of any member of the party who passes here in the future. Personally supervised by Mr Burke, a secluded spot by the sand-hills near the lake is marked out, and a box filled with flour, pork, biscuits and tea lowered into it before just as carefully being covered up again. No disturbance on the surface can tell where it lies, so that no blacks might find it. Mr Burke does not even trust their own blacks and they have been purposefully kept away from the burial site. This includes Mr Wright's right-hand man, Dick. He is one of us for now, but he is still one of them for good. And, as a breed, Mr Burke simply does not trust the Aborigines, and never has. Mr Wills feels much the same.

'The Blacks are a lazy set,' the younger man had written home, shortly after arriving in Australia. 'I do not like them at all; the only good they are is to catch fish & ducks and cut wood, for which you give them some damper, after they have done it; they will do no work – if one of them was to [work], the others would kill him. They are continually killing one another, which is a very good thing – they will soon be extinct.'[65]

Nothing either man has seen since has changed their minds, and only a few days ago, Mr Wills had noted finding 'small creeks and ponds at every half mile some of these Mountain [Aboriginal guides] said were permanent but one cannot rely on what any of these blacks say'[66].

So yes, while Dick seems fine, it is much safer not to trust him, and hide the place of burial.

And yet, typical of Burke, despite his general antipathy to the blacks, he also demonstrates bursts of kindness, again presenting one of the natives with one of his shirts, occasioning such delight from the newly splendidly attired native there is little doubt Mr Burke, happy to give anyone the shirt off his back when in the mood, will do it again, soon. The clothing of the 'Chief' of the expedition tribe becomes a repeated diplomatic gift that depletes the official flannel stores as much as it increases native goodwill.

30 October '60, conditional promises, arguable agreements and a parting of the ways . . .

As Burke stands gazing at the Torowoto, he knows it is time for a decision. For this is the point that Mr Wright had agreed to guide them to, and it is now his intent to keep to that, and head back to his family. But Mr Burke has other ideas.

'I wish you could go on farther with me, Mr Wright,'[67] he says in the friendly manner used towards one who he cannot yet *order* to do anything. But Mr Burke wants Wright to come, all right. To keep going, to come with them to Cooper's Creek and perhaps, even, go on with them all the way to the Gulf. This next push, all else being equal, will be less brutal.

Will you come with us, sir?

'Mr Burke,' Wright demurs, 'I cannot possibly do it at this time, I am anxious to get back. I want to send my wife and family down the river to Adelaide, by the paddle steamer.'

Ah-ha. Mr Wright is a family man, the very kind that Mr Burke had sought to avoid when picking who to take on this expedition, but he understands the pull of kith and kin.

At least, Wright tells Burke, Dick has received word from the local blacks that the waterholes to the north, much of the way to Cooper's Creek, are plentiful and reliable and he will even find a native guide for them who can help steer them to that water. For his part, Burke tells Wright that he intends to camp at the waterholes 'a short distance ahead, and rest there for about 14 days'[68]. This will allow the animals to graze and recuperate, and they will then stop for at least as long at Cooper's Creek.

'But you will take the remainder of the party out, [and come on to Cooper's Creek] as soon as you return? I have your word?'[69] presses Burke.

'You have my word, Mr Burke,'[70] declares Mr Wright.

For his part, Burke equally makes a promise to Wright.

'When I get to Cooper's Creek,' he says, 'my intention is to send back [some] horses and camels to Menindee. If you meet the horses and camels coming up – if you start before they get to Menindee – either stop at one of the permanent waters, or go back with those horses, and load them with stores, such as tea, sugar, and flour, and what you think will be the most necessary stores to fetch up to Cooper's Creek.'[71]

The situation, and their agreement, seems clear to both men, even if it is not written down.

To another, independent observer, it might equally be clear that such imprecise verbal agreements are bound to lead to potentially catastrophic confusion, but for now both men are content with the arrangement.

'I shall consider you third officer of the expedition,' Burke tells him, 'subject to the approval of the Committee, from the day of our departure from Menindee, and I hope that they will confirm the appointment.'[72]

What Burke particularly impresses upon Wright is the importance of him getting back to Menindee safely, and then immediately bringing the rest of the men, supplies and animals forward to Cooper's Creek. For it is only once the parties are joined again that their hold on that Depot can be consolidated.

As Burke will state in his next dispatch to the Committee, he has ordered Mr Wright, 'to follow me up with the remainder of the camels to Cooper's Creek to take steps to procure a supply of jerked meat'[73].

Wright is quick to declare himself up to the task.

Mr Burke is satisfied with that, no matter the many caveats Mr Wright has placed on his quick return, nor even the fact the station manager has never been as far as Cooper's Creek, or 'the Barcoo' as some call the area.

Further, in a missive that Burke hands over for Wright to send on to the Committee by regular mail once he gets back to Menindee, the leader is careful to formally advise them of his appointment of Wright, subject to their approval, and to express confidence in his own decision.

> *If Mr Wright is allowed to follow out the instructions I have given him*
> *I am confident that the result will be satisfactory: and if the Committee*
> *think proper to make inquiries with regard to him they will find that he*
> *is well qualified for the post and that he bears the very highest character.*
> *I shall proceed on from here to Cooper's Creek. I may or may not be able*
> *to send back from then until we are followed up. Perhaps it would not*
> *be prudent to divide the party; the natives here have told Mr Wright that*
> *we shall meet with opposition on our way there. Perhaps I might find it*
> *advisable to leave a Depot at Cooper's Creek and to go on with a small*
> *party to examine the country beyond it. Under any circumstances it is*
> *desirable that we should soon be followed up.*[74]

In sum?

With a view to the current situation, the first line in Robert O'Hara Burke's notebook – the one he had purchased after becoming leader – is instructive. For, clearly, he has written it in the manner of advice to himself, the thing he must *most* remember to do, as he has been tripped up on it before.

Think well before giving an answer and never speak except from *strong convictions.*[75]

Sometimes on this trip, he has got it right. Sometimes he has got it wrong.

Right now, it is too early to tell which is the case with Mr Wright.

But, the least that can be said is that, according to what Mr Burke has told his third officer, it is very important, Wright, that you come back immediately, *after* you get approval from the Committee, though it is *fine* that you first see your family off on a paddle steamer, *and* wait until Mr Brahe comes back with some animals for you, but if you leave Menindee *before* the animals arrive and you meet them, then go back and load more goods . . . so I expect to see you back at Cooper's Creek, *straight away*.

And so Mr Burke must reluctantly agree. Mr Wright will head back to the south, to Menindee, in the company of the two blacks and four horses. Before Wright departs, however, on the morning of this last day of October, there is something Burke must do.

With Mr Wright by his side, he has all his men assemble before him to explain the situation. Mr Wright is going back. He, Mr Burke, is going on. What happens from that point is not certain.

'I may have to leave a few men behind in a few days, or perhaps at Cooper's Creek [when we get there]. It all depends on how we find the country. Any man who does not choose to be under those orders might return with Mr Wright to the Darling . . .'[76]

Not too content to just leave the question general, he asks each man in turn – Wills, Brahe, King, Patten, McDonough, Dost Mahomet and Charley Gray – if they are happy to go on? All seven of them insist that they wish to stay the course, to push for the Gulf, notwithstanding that they will now be heading into wilderness never explored before by white men.

So be it.

Burke and Wright shake hands, the two groups say their farewells, and Wright is soon on his way south with his two native guides, leaving Burke with seven men to continue with their preparations to go on to the north, towards Cooper's Creek. This time, to help guide those heading north, they are aided by a man from the Torowoto area, a native man whom they 'can scarcely understand'[77] but who, nevertheless, makes it very clear that he knows the layout of some of the landscape for the 150 odd miles that lie between Torowoto and Cooper's Creek.

30 October '60, Melbourne, press gang

Rumours swirl around the great southern city like a wintry breeze, rustling up the highways and byways, down the back alleys, along the boulevards and . . . chilling no few souls to the marrow as it goes. *The big expedition, have you heard? Some big quarrels! They're fighting like cats in a sack, and the camel fellow, Landells, has already stormed off.* True, the details are sketchy but the theme is consistent – the whole thing is coming apart. Though the rumours are troubling for Dr Macadam and the Committee, it quickly gets worse when the Honorary Secretary is approached by the editor of the Melbourne *Herald*, saying they now have someone with strong credentials and staggering stories about Mr Burke, which they intend to publish soon because they are so salacious.

Dr Macadam, of course, has little doubt that that damned trouble-maker Ferguson is behind the whole thing, spreading the vicious gossip and even briefing the newspapers now!

Well, too bad. In the absence of solid information himself, Dr Macadam simply denies everything. The expedition is in fine shape, and Mr Burke is doing a grand job!

1 November '60, on the banks of a clay pan, shedding shoddy shoes by the shore

On this afternoon Burke and Wills, their six companions and native guide reach an extensive, shallow lake, which is said by the natives to stretch up to the Bulloo[78] River, in Queensland, and they keep tight to its banks, as – happily – the waters narrow and it pushes north. The further they go, the more abundant, and even munificent, does nature seem.

'There was plenty of water in this part of the creek when we passed,' Wills will note, 'but I cannot speak to its permanence. The banks are well lined with box timber, as well as with marshmallows and wild spinach: the land on either side consists of well-grassed sandy rises. At four or five miles above this . . . we found about sixty blacks camped here . . .

'In the creek there is abundance of fish, and the ducks and other waterfowl on it are numberless. From what we have seen of the blacks, I should say the population cannot be far short of 150, and it might be considerably more . . . The blacks have here gone to the trouble of making paths for themselves, along which we turned off from the creek on a N.N.E. course, and at about three miles, coming on earthy plains, with no signs of water ahead, we again turned in to the creek and camped at a small waterhole.'[79]

But, hard going?

Yes. Hot. Exhausting. Sweaty. Dusty. Constantly swarmed by flies. And like a snake shedding its winter skin as the hotter weather comes, Burke's 'camel-cade' continues to shed their wretched excess as they go, on this evening dumping two dozen pairs of the extra camel shoes they'd been carrying all this way. Even dumping them, they still have five extra sets for each camel, and surely that is enough!

5 November '60, Menindee, a question of authority

And here they are!

After six days pushing south from Torowoto, on this afternoon[80] William Wright is still seven miles short of Menindee when, arriving at a spot on the Darling River where it intersects with Pamamaroo Creek, he is surprised to find the camp of the Victorian Exploring Expedition!

In their absence going north to Torowoto, it appears the men left behind under the command of Dr Beckler had been able to make a new base, the 'Pamamaroo Camp', where there is bountiful grazing for their animals, including their nine remaining camels, 'on a spot high and dry and near a cluster of beautiful Gum-trees'[81].

The perfect spot to rest a while!

Wright walks around the camp, eager to share the news that he is the new man in charge, after Mr Burke's promotion of him, but neither Dr Beckler or Mr Hodgkinson are around – having gone on a brief scientific excursion to the Scropes Range, to collect specimens and make sketches – so it is Ludwig Becker who fields the news.[82] And the German is quick to bring up the issue of whether Wright is *officially* recognised as the third officer.

On that subject, Wright indeed would like confirmation from the Committee himself – and most particularly that he will actually receive the pay that he and Burke have agreed on . . . which appears to be a serious question.

For only shortly after returning, it comes to Wright's attention that there is a real issue of the Victorian Exploring Expedition's cheques not being honoured by the Melbourne banks. The Menindee store-keeper, Edward Wecker, described as 'a genial, but somewhat dispirited, Teuton'[83], is even refusing to extend credit, and in a settlement of just 15 Europeans it doesn't take long for the news of the dishonoured cheques to be known by all. At least Tom Paine, who runs the sole pub at Menindee, does allow them to run up a tab, but the whole situation is in a state of flux.

That will have to be resolved.

The key decision for now, of course, is whether to head to Cooper's Creek as quickly as possible.

After all, only a week earlier Wright had faithfully given Mr Burke his word he would 'take the remainder of the party out as soon as I return'[84].

But the thing is . . . now that he is here . . . and exhausted . . . as are the animals . . . Wright decides to stay a while. In fact, he could not turn around right now and head off with his 'Supply Party', even if he wanted to.

With no less than 10 tons of gear to lug some 400 miles, he has just nine camels and seven horses to call on – of whom just one horse is present and ready at the moment. The two horses he'd just returned from Torowoto with are in urgent need of a spell. And the other four horses have departed the day before, with Dr Beckler and William Hodgkinson. Even when those horses return, it won't be enough. It means Wright will have to either buy some, with funding presumably being sent from the Committee, or wait for Burke's men to arrive back from up north with extra beasts – presumably in the care of William Brahe. Either way, it will need time for the situation to become clear.

Beyond the problem of animals, there is the issue of food. They have no jerked meat, and it will take some time to organise.

Another factor is Wright's own family – just 21 miles away at Kinchega – who, as agreed with Mr Burke, he must see off to Adelaide on the next available paddle steamer.

Under such circumstances, Mr Wright is not at *all* inclined to head north, to commit what he estimates will be at least five months of his time to this project, when he is not yet confirmed in his position, nor with an assured salary for his efforts.

'I did not rightly know what to do,'[85] Wright will later acknowledge, a state of mind which, through human history, generally lends itself to deciding to do nothing at all, which certainly describes the station manager's subsequent inaction.

At least, however, write to the Committee, and inform them of the situation, via the regular mail service? Wright will do just that. He takes leave of the camp and rides into town, to see when the next post leaves.

And here now, as it happens, arriving at much the same time, is one Trooper Lyons, bearing a missive from the Committee for Mr Burke, including, apparently, updates on just what the explorer Stuart has discovered in the interior of Australia.

Wright is eager to know what is in the communications himself, realising there is a very real possibility that the missive might recall Burke, reel his authority in, or at least rebuke him.

Which would in turn affect Wright. As one now moving into a position of authority himself, Wright feels a great need to know just what is the attitude of the Committee.

It might even be that a new second officer has been appointed to replace Landells, and is on his way. One typically unnamed sage in the press has recently opined that given the troubled 'progress' of the expedition it might be they do not have 'the right man in the right place'[86].

Perhaps the Committee now agree with them?

All up, it is a very curious Mr Wright indeed, who, the best he can, invokes his authority as third in command, and, um, asks to see the Committee dispatches *immediately* . . . if you don't mind?

Alas, the worthy Trooper Lyons takes a very simple attitude.

'My instructions,' he says dutifully, 'are to deliver these dispatches to Mr Burke himself.'[87]

Very well then. That matter is settled. The next matter is where the good trooper might find the expedition leader, so he can fulfil his duty. Well, it is Mr Wright's best estimate that Burke and his advance party should be somewhere a couple of days north of Torowoto by now, perhaps taking their first rest to allow their animals to graze, before heading on to Cooper's Creek, whereupon Burke said they plan to 'rest . . . for about 14 days'[88] and establish a Depot. If Lyons leaves in the next few days he would probably 'overtake [Burke] at a spot some four hundred miles from here'[89].

To facilitate his journey, Wright at least offers Lyons use of the horses, and two of his best men, the first of whom is Dick, the local guide who has already made the journey to Torowoto Swamp, and just come back with him. And he also offers Alexander MacPherson, the saddler.

The only problem is Trooper Lyons will still have to wait at least a couple of days for Dr Beckler and Mr Hodgkinson to come back from the Scropes Range with the other horses.

Wright now goes to visit Mr Wecker to ensure that Mr Burke's latest dispatch – which includes the news of Mr Wright's appointment as third officer, and seeking their confirmation of the same – is sent on its way to Melbourne, with sundry other post from the party, to the Committee. It will leave with the regular mail next week, and he is hopeful that, if all goes well, he might receive confirmation of his appointment in five weeks.

In the interim, he can make necessary preparations, like jerking meat, sorting the stores, checking the rations are unspoiled and – if the financial problems can just be resolved – purchasing new horses, and saddles to ride them, as well as putting on more men.

An upside of delay for Wright is that waiting a little longer will give him more time with his family at nearby Kinchega station, where, as one of the men notes, he will be able to engage in one of his primary pursuits, which is to do a whole lot of 'knocking about . . .'[90]

6 November '60, Bendigo, the soldier style won't make 200 miles

In the meantime, far to the south, in the settled districts of Victoria, more and more reports continue to come in from the outposts that the Victorian Exploring Expedition has passed through, and an ever firmer view starts to take root, as expressed in this report in the *Bendigo Advertiser* on 6 November 1860:

> The opinion of parties able to judge on the Darling is, that Mr Burke will not make more than two hundred miles beyond the settled district this season, and that he is not the right man for the work he has undertaken. It is stated that instead of making himself agreeable to the men, he harasses them in the soldier style, and on coming to camp at night will not allow a man to dismount until he gives the word, although he may be a mile away.[91]

6 November '60, Bulloo – or, 'Wright's Creek' if you will – the name game

Pushing further and further into the previously 'masterless lands', Burke and Wills are, in fact, such masters of their domain that, with just a few strokes of Wills's pen in his notebook, entire geographical features bear for perpetuity whatever name he decides on. Initially, Wills had kept to Indigenous names when he could, courtesy of the various guides they had had along the way, who knew the name. Between Menindee and Mutawintji, Wills had recorded no fewer than 15 Paakantyi names for various geographical features, including: *Watneyalty, Dorpulka, Toteynya, Yandthoro, Kokriega, Bunnabool, Bilpa* and *Botoja*.

But now he changes tack.

No matter that the watercourse before them has been called Bulloo by the Aboriginal people for millennia now . . . now it is called . . . let's see . . . Wills decides . . . 'Wright's Creek', as it is Wright who had told them of its existence and instructed the native guides to take them there. Oh, and that creek right by where they had set up Camp 54 is now McDonough Creek, after the young 26-year-old, one of four Irishmen in the current party of eight. The waterway upon which they set up Camp 56 will forevermore be Brahe's Creek.

With so many features to come, Burke makes a list of friends and influential people he can name things after.

Names for places[92]

Thackeray	*Wrixon*
Barry	*Cope*
Bindon	*Turner*
Lyons	*Scratchley*
Forbes	*Ligar*
Archer	*Griffith*
Bennet	*Green*
Colles	*Roe*
C.S. Nicholson	*Hamilton*
Wood	*Archer*

Wills has another name in mind, which he is keeping for the right moment. His most dearly cherished friend, Richard Birnie, is someone often on his mind, and he definitely deserves the honour of having something named after him – and it must be something more than a mere creek or stream. William Wills wants to wait until he finds a really *impressive* geographical feature – as impressive as Richard – before enshrining his name in that manner.

7–8 November '60, Melbourne, resigned to bad publicity

In Melbourne, Richard Birnie is one of thousands who devour every day's papers for news of the expedition. Today, for example, the *Argus* is filled with accounts of Mr Landells's resignation, including Burke's dispatches from Menindee heavily criticising his former first officer, the resignation letters of Landells and Beckler, and eyewitness accounts from William Hodgkinson and – yes! – William Wills.

Most gratifying is the *Argus* assurance that 'Mr Wills has been selected by Mr Burke to take the place of Mr Landells, as second'[93], a real feather in the cap of young William.

In the meantime, apart from such resignations in the Victorian Expedition party, the news of the 'race' between Stuart of South Australia and Burke of Victoria is starting to capture the imagination of the public, courtesy of such publications as *Melbourne Punch*, and the wonderful illustrations and verse they publish the next day.

8 November '60, Scropes Range, Beckler's botanical bliss

A man of somewhat melancholic aspect, prone to embracing the negative – the hell of the last three months has been heaven for engaging both dispositions – Dr Hermann Beckler is not easily thrilled. But even he is beside himself with the outstanding success of his just completed collecting trip from the cracked clay beds of Lake Pamamaroo to the 'friendly little mountain range'[94] of the Scropes Range and back.

For four days he had been able to indulge his scientific passions uninterrupted, observing the scenery and the wildlife – drawing, taking notes, collecting and cataloguing specimens – and been stunned by the diversity of discoveries. The Scropes Range had been particularly bountiful, nothing less than the Ballarat of botany – he even finds a new plant that gave off such 'a disagreeable odour'[95] that it had given him a headache, worse than the ones he got listening to Ludwig Becker spout about art for too long!

Even more exciting than his own sketches, however, had been the native art – likely dating back thousands of years – that he, Hodgkinson and their native guide, Peter, had found in a cave on the side of a beautiful red rock gully. On the walls were the earthy coloured outlines of human 'hands, large and small ones with outstretched fingers, the fingers always tending upwards or sideway'[96]. The coloured paints, Peter had explained, were 'obtained from different ochres and made into a paste with water'[97].

And so it is with an unusually joyous disposition that Dr Beckler walks back into camp on this day, beside a horse so laden down with plant specimens it looks more like a four-footed flower display. His bright mood, alas, lasts no longer than being told his position as the man in charge of the Supply Depot has been superseded by Mr Wright. True, Hermann Beckler had already resigned from the party of his own free will, but still the news does not sit easily, particularly when he finds out that not only is Mr Wright absent at the moment, but is usually so – off with his family at Kinchega.

He has been replaced, thus, by an habitual absentee?

Yes, the said absentee, William Wright, blithely informs him the next day, when he returns. With no preamble, Wright simply hands Dr Beckler a letter from Mr Burke, confirming, without apology, the news.

10 November '60, Menindee, super trooper departs

After a few good nights of blessed sleep – not entirely disconnected from several evenings at Tom Paine's pub – Trooper Lyons and his two companions make ready to depart. And yes, Trooper Lyons looks as calm as ever – it is his way – but still the quiet sweat on his brow is not from the heat alone, but from a certain tension. Being a trooper in a far-flung police district had been one thing. But taking two men on exhausted horses into the wilderness, in search of a man long gone, is another, and he knows it. Dick, the native guide, and Mr MacPherson know it too – as they continue to pack the provisions without a word – and it frankly seems as if even the sullen horses have a fair clue that what awaits will be testing. As the saddler MacPherson knows better than any of them, all four horses they are taking – one for each man, and a packhorse – are not remotely recovered from the 400-mile return trip to Torowoto Swamp and are still very 'much knocked up'[98]. Of course it would be best to rest, lest they break down, but they must take that chance. Every day they wait is a day that the Burke party risks getting further away from them, and so they must go. The dispatch must get through!

They carry provisions for one month only, with just 20 pounds of flour, seven pounds of sugar, two pounds of tea and four pounds of meat biscuit – though are hopeful of retrieving some stores that Mr Wright tells Lyons that Mr Burke has buried 'in the sand-hills near the lagoon'[99].

Not to worry, Trooper Lyons, Dick knows exactly where to dig. And so, travelling light, and fast, their job is to take the dispatches that Lyons bears in his saddlebag and get them to Burke. As to where that gentleman might be found, Mr Wright has been clear. Dick will guide them to the place the natives call 'Tooruta', but they have called

Torowoto Swamp, about 200 miles to the north of where they are now, and Mr Burke's party should be about a few days journey on from there.

How many days? Mr Wright doesn't know. Mr Burke, as was his wont, had not been specific. And Mr Wright has never been to Cooper's Creek himself. But, not to worry. He is sure, he tells Trooper Lyons, that they can catch up with Mr Burke and his men if they ride hard.

The way both Wright and Lyons see it, they should be able to get there just before Mr Burke departs for the Gulf of Carpentaria.

The question is, just where is Mr Burke now?

CHAPTER NINE

COOPER'S CREEK CALLING

To give you an idea of Cooper's Creek, fancy extensive flat, sandy plains, covered with herbs dried like hay, and imagine a creek or river, somewhat similar in appearance and size to the Dart above the Weir, winding its way through these flats, having its banks densely clothed with gum trees and other evergreens – so far there appears to be a considerable resemblance, but now for the difference. The water of Cooper's Creek is the colour of flood-water in the Dart; the latter is a continuous running stream; Cooper's Creek is only a number of waterholes. In some places it entirely disappears, the water in flood-time spreading all over the flats and forming no regular channel.[1]

William Wills, letter to his sister Bessie, Cooper's Creek, 6 December 1860

The feed upon the Creek is good and the horses and camels have greatly improved in condition but the flies, mosquitoes and rats which abound here render it a very disagreeable summer residence.[2]

Mr Burke reports to the Committee, 13 December 1860

14 November '60, Melbourne, Landells lands some haymakers

The sun shines, the birds sing, the people of Melbourne have a spring in their step, and . . . Mr George Landells, just arrived in the metropolis this morning, storms along Collins Street like a thunderstorm about to burst.

Barely knocking, he confronts the startled Dr John Macadam in his office, handing him a report that thunders in its own right of the

216

outrages Mr Burke has visited upon him, and demands to know when the Committee is next due to meet.

'I will go and see the members of the Committee and procure a meeting this afternoon,'[3] Macadam replies, and for once is as good as his word. Within hours the Committee is indeed gathered at the Royal Society's Hall, with Dr Richard Eades in the Chair, who quickly takes to the matter in hand.

'There is,' he says in his sonorous voice, looking around at the members, 'a written report from Mr Landells, directed to the Honorary Secretary of the Exploration Committee. The best thing is to read it at once, and then come to a conclusion.'[4]

With which Macadam rises, and begins to read out loud the report which proves to descend into every petty grievance and every major blue of Landells's time with Mr Burke – from the leader not observing the Sabbath right up to challenging his camel overseer to a duel. It is embarrassing, it is unseemly . . . and every word of it will be published on the morrow, as the journalist from the *Argus* who is unfortunately present carefully takes down every sensational word . . .

'Mr Burke's conduct to me has been ungentlemanly, and his constant interference highly prejudicial to the best interests of the party . . . as has led to the conviction in my own mind that, under his leadership, the expedition will be attended by the most disastrous results . . .

'I have on several occasions entertained grave doubts of his sanity. His temper was quite ungovernable. He usually carried loaded fire-arms, and I often was fearful that he would use them injudiciously whilst in a passion.

'I am in a position to state that Hodgkinson was engaged going amongst the men, and running Mr Burke down, so as to enable Mr Burke to know what was going on in the camp. McDonough also was continually occupied in the same mean system of espionage . . .'[5]

Against all that, however, William Wills's letter to Professor Neumayer of 16 October is also produced, reporting that all is going wonderfully well and the Committee, not surprisingly, decides to believe that, and so remain unanimously in support of Robert O'Hara Burke and his new second-in-command, William Wills. Good day, Mr Landells, we said *good day*!

15 November '60, Torowoto, high-stakes hide and seek

Where is the flour?

Where is the cache of stores that Mr Wright had assured them young Dick had personally seen Mr Burke bury a month earlier?

Since leaving Menindee five days ago, they have already made a good dent in their supplies, so Trooper Lyons and Alexander MacPherson, not to mention Dick himself, are more than eager to find the precious cache, now that they have arrived at Torowoto, but . . .

But, alas, upon arrival, it turns out that Dick had not *actually* seen Mr Burke bury the supplies, but only had a vague idea where it was. In fact, now that they are here, 'Dick [is] quite ignorant as to the spot, Mr Burke having wisely resolved not to trust any of the natives with the secret.'[6] Perhaps it is buried under the ever-changing sand, 'the drift . . . so great since they were put there that it would be impossible to find them out'[7]. Dick, MacPherson and Lyons search the ground, all around, with vigour, but to no avail.

All they have been able to gather from Burke's secreted stashes so far has been two dozen sets of camel shoes, which they'd found at the first camp out of Menindee.

For now, there is nothing for it but to get back on the track from early the next morning, determined to make the rations that remain – '7 lb. or 8 lb. of flour, 5 lb. of sugar, 2 lb. of tea, 2 lb. of biscuit, and two tins of preserved mutton'[8] – stretch as far as they can, together with their now filled waterbags. Mr Wright had, after all, assured them that Mr Burke would likely be only two days travel north of where they are now.

Sticking to the cavalcade's tracks, left a month earlier, by noon they arrive at one of Mr Burke's former camps. It is clear Burke's men had had plenty of water then. Not now. There is a certain green slime at the bottom of what had been the waterhole, 'but so bad that neither horses nor men could drink it. Even when made into tea, it was too nauseous for use.'[9]

Pushing on, the men lead their exhausted horses, so as to spare them, and keep walking until well after sundown. From up ahead, Dick suddenly shouts into the night, 'Plenty of water!'[10]

Sure enough, pushing forward, MacPherson and Lyons can soon see it, too, a large sheet of water about half a mile off to the side of the track. Alas, when they get there, it proves to be 'only a half-dried clay pond, containing a very shallow layer of water, so thick that it could scarcely be swallowed'[11].

Making the best of it, they slosh into the middle of the sludge and dig a hole to give the horses a drink, but, strangely, as clearly thirsty as the animals are, they sip only, and do not gulp. Well, Trooper Lyons, MacPherson and Dick are not so fussed. They gulp and gulp, till they get their fill and return to the shore, whereupon they soon begin to vomit violently. It is all they can do to unsaddle the horses before lying down for an exhausted sleep, punctuated by regular vomiting sessions.

18 November '60, Pamamaroo Camp, knockin' about

The men lolling around under the shade of the box trees at Wright's ramshackle Pamamaroo Camp listlessly swatting the myriad flies?

Could be any of the party.

Could be all of the party.

No one is ever quite sure who's where anyway, as there is little structure. Very few have specified roles, as their major role is simply . . . waiting. It is the torpor of the times. Summer is rising. They are the men who've been left behind, judged not worthy of taking on to Cooper's Creek, and there appears to be no move whatsoever for Mr Wright to take them forward. Truth is, Mr Wright is not even here most of the time, as he is staying with his family at their nearby home at Kinchega station, and is often in Menindee on business. Most of the men's needs, meanwhile, are amply catered for. As their camp is by the Darling River, they have plenty of supplies, and the Menindee pub is only an hour or so's walk away. And so they wait. And wait. And wait. And listlessly bicker. Usually it is Becker against Hodgkinson, or Beckler against Hodgkinson, or Becker and Beckler against Hodgkinson, and it must be said that the former journalist is far and away the least popular person in the camp.

'We had an insolent, malicious lad with us,' Dr Beckler would recall, 'the worst legacy Burke left us . . . [he] annoyed, insulted and attacked us without exception and without cause . . . Without him we could have lived together peacefully. He alone was the scorpion, the gnawing worm we carried with us . . . the most evil animal of a person that I have ever encountered.'[12] Ah, yes, 'Fighting Billy', it seems, has lost none of his boyhood love of quarrelling, he delights in provoking and perplexing his comrades.

Sometimes, on a bad day, however, Wright can run him close, as no one can work out what his game is, whether he is genuinely in charge, and what his plans are. He still has their vague confidence, though, including Dr Beckler's.

While allowing that Wright is ill-educated, swears far too much, and is not always the most communicative, Beckler would also later note, 'his manner inspired my confidence. Apart from his customary good humour, Wright had a certain natural equanimity, to my mind an excellent quality in an explorer, and one which in no way hinders the massive and continuous exertion of energy that is demanded at times. If I were to criticise him for anything, it would be that we were somewhat inadequately organised . . .'[13]

True. But does that really matter?

Not particularly, to the scientific and artistic officers who wake every morning feeling blessed that they do not have to face the brutal slog across impossible terrain and can at last engage in the scientific and artistic work that is their passion. None is happier than the oldest man in the party, Ludwig Becker, who had felt the travails of their slog more than most, and is now able to spend his days sketching such things as camels and camps, birds and beetles, while also carefully noting down the words of Aboriginal songs.

18–20 November '60, Cooper's Creek, the green thread of fertility

From a great distance, they look like bobbing heads in the mirage, some heads more grotesque than others. It is, of course, Robert Burke and his caravan of camels, now cresting gentle ridge after gentle ridge of this slowly transforming landscape, followed by the weary men and

Robert O'Hara Burke –
photograph of a portrait
by artist William Strutt

(SLV H29496)

William John Wills
– the photograph
that Wills gave to
Richard Birnie

(Thomas Adams Hills, 'Wm.
J. Wills, 1834–1861', c. 1860,
a128695, MIN 50, State
Library of NSW)

Ludwig Becker, the expedition's official artist and naturalist – a lithograph portrait (SLV H84.273/2)

George Landells, the camel master – a sketch by William Strutt from his sketchbook of the Burke and Wills encampment at Royal Park, Melbourne, 1860 (Reproduced with permission of the Victorian Parliamentary Library)

Julia Matthews – Burke's sweetheart. This photo was likely taken in the mid 1860s by William Bardwell (SLV H10272)

Dr Hermann Beckler, official medical officer and unofficial chronicler of the expedition (From the State Botanical Collection, Royal Botanic Gardens Victoria, photographer M. Biegner)

Part of the Royal Society of Victoria's instructions for the Victorian Exploring Expedition

(Reproduced with permission of the Royal Society of Victoria/SLV MS13071 Box 2082/3d)

Tally of the secret ballot held to elect the leader of the Victorian Exploring Expedition

(Reproduced with permission of the Royal Society of Victoria/SLV MS13071 Box 2075/1c)

One of the sepoys overseeing a camel in Royal Park as the expedition prepares to leave. Sketch by William Strutt (State Library of NSW ZDL PXX4 f.16b)

The expedition commences. 'The first day's order of march', watercolour by William Strutt. Most likely this was the scene heading out of Essendon on the afternoon of 21 August 1860. In the third group from right, the man on a grey horse and leading two other horses could be Wills. At front of centre group on camels is likely Landells, followed by Burke (in blue poncho) then Becker. Behind him is a sepoy then possibly Beckler (with round hat), and King or Drakeford leading pack camels. (SLV H5107)

'Love at first sight' – a cartoon published in *Melbourne Punch*, 21 June 1860, depicting
Burke embracing an expedition camel (SLV)

THE GREAT AUSTRALIAN EXPLORATION RACE.

A race! a race! so great a one
The world ne'er saw before;
A race! a race! across this land,
From south to northern shore!

A race between two colonies!
Each has a stalwart band
Sent out beyond the settled bounds,
Into the unknown land.

The one is captain'd by a man
Already known to fame,
Who with Australian annals has
For ever linked his name.

The other owns a leader, who
Has all his bays to earn;
Let's hope that he, a well-won wreath
May claim on his return!

The horseman hails from Adelaide,
The camel rider's ours:—
Now let the steed maintain his speed,
Against the camel's powers.

No small concealments each from each,
No shuffling knavish ways,
No petty jealousies and strifes,
No paltry peddling traits.

Will find a place in such a race,
But honor, virtue, worth,
And all that can ennoble man
Will brilliantly shine forth.

A cheer then for each member, and
A big one for the lot,
For it is known how all have shown
These virtues.—*Have they not?*

'The Great Australian Exploration Race' – Nicholas Chevalier's cartoon from *Melbourne Punch*, 18 November 1860 (National Library of Australia)

'Portrait of Dick, the brave and gallant native guide', painted by Ludwig Becker on 21 December 1860, just two days after Dick returned from the desert with vital news of Trooper Lyons and MacPherson (SLV H16486)

'Meteor seen by me on Oct. 11t. at 10h 35m p.m. at the River Darling', watercolour from Ludwig Becker's sketchbook

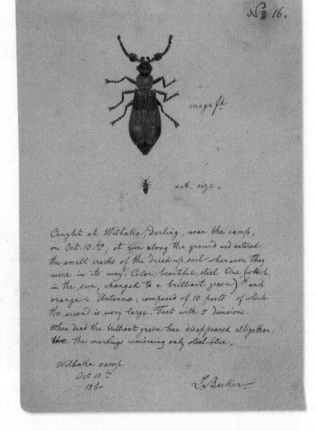

Ludwig Becker's exquisite watercolour and ink drawing of a beetle, from his expedition sketchbook

The steamer *Moolgewanke* – the vessel that transported some of Burke's supplies up the Darling to Menindee (State Library of SA PRG 1258/1/2718)

'Camp on the edge of the earthy or mud plains: 40 miles from Duroadoo [Torowoto]', watercolour by Ludwig Becker from his expedition sketchbook (SLV H16486)

horses, their heads bobbing on a lower plane. Having left the rugged country of the past weeks travel, they have entered the undulating, empty, sunburnt plains that seem to have no end and . . .

And there!

It has been a long haul, including a false start a week earlier, when what they thought was Cooper's Creek proved to be just a tributary that soon got lost in open, cracked plains. But now it is really happening, they are travelling along a good waterway, a promising thread of green in the barren landscape, which *has* to be Cooper's Creek.

Finally, three months after leaving Melbourne, at 10.15 on this hot morning of 20 November, the eight-strong Burke party come upon a spur of blessedly shaded land . . . right by a wonderful waterway! A larger river coming in from the north-east meets the creek along which they have been travelling, and Wills is quick to confirm it: they are now, without a doubt, on Cooper's Creek – first visited by Sturt back in 1845.

'A fine watercourse . . .' Sturt had described it. 'I would gladly have laid this creek down as a river, but as it had no current I did not feel myself justified in doing so . . .'[14]

At this moment Mr Burke has no interest in whether it is a creek or a river, and only cares that it is 'an eligible spot for the Depot'[15], which he quickly gives orders for his men to establish. To a man, they are delighted.

The landscape is magical. Cool, muddy brown water, flanked by towering red gums and majestic coolabah trees. At first glance, it is nothing less than an Antipodean Garden of Eden, a place of bountiful life – of turtles, blue-claw yabbies, bream, yellow-bellies, catfish, perch, kangaroos, dingos, ducks, goannas and, yes, even serpents – where all else leading up to it had felt like the Valley of the Shadow of Death.

That roar?

Well, it could be applause from the public for their significant achievement in making it this far, but it is in fact flocks of white corellas, screeching and wheeling about the red gums, watched over by kites and kestrels, while crows, cockatiels, crested pigeons, budgerigars and galahs perch on every branch and nestle in every nook. There are even pelicans, bickering among themselves as to just who these curiously attired, stunningly *white* strangers might be.

It is an eligible spot, indeed. Sitting as it does next to 'a fine hole about a mile long, and on an average one chain and a half broad'[16], Wills diligently tests the water depth, and is impressed to find 'It exceeds five feet in depth everywhere that I tried it, except within three or four feet of the bank.'[17] This means they shall have a sure supply of water, all through the coming summer.

In short order Burke and his men get down to some hard yakka, establishing Camp 63, their major staging post, halfway from Melbourne to the Gulf – a secure place to store supplies and weaponry, under the care of good men – before a small party of them will launch north to the Gulf of Carpentaria.

(Though Mr Burke makes no announcement, Mr Wills is now more certain than ever. He writes to his sister: 'I hope by the time that this reaches you we shall not only have been entirely across, but back here again, and possibly on our way to Melbourne . . . I expect to be in town again within twelve months from the time of starting.'[18])

As the thrill of arriving to their Depot camp begins to wear off, Wills looks around and notes that, 'the feed in the vicinity of Camp LXIII is unexceptionable, both for horses and camels . . . the grasses are very coarse, and bear a very small proportion to the other plants. By far the chief portion of the herbage consists of chrysanthemums and marshmallows; the former, to judge from their dried-up powdery state, can contain very little nourishment, although some of the horses and camels eat them with great relish; the latter, I need hardly mention, are at this time of the year merely withered sticks.'[19]

From the point of view of the area's potential for pastoral use for future settlers, Wills carefully notes down that 'Wherever there are sand banks or ridges the feed is almost invariably good; the salt bush is healthy and abundant, and there are a variety of plants on which cattle would do well.'[20] Flies, ants and mosquitoes annoy the men, but the worst of it is the bold, hairy native rats that appear that night, trying to get into their stores and too often succeeding.

21 November '60, Lake Bulloo, lost in translation

It is now 11 arduous days since Trooper Lyons and his men left Menindee, and they continue to struggle for food and water. The whole party is weak, the horses badly knocked up, and their rations severely depleted. Still they are following in the path of Burke – starting every morning with strong hopes of meeting up with him that very day – and ever more coming to abandoned camps where water clearly used to be plentiful but has now all but dried up.

On this morning, they start out early and are pushing towards a plume of smoke up ahead – could it possibly be Burke and his party? – when they are suddenly confronted by native men, shouting at them *'Bulloo Bulloo!'*[21] and indicating that they want the whitefellas to follow them.

'They were five in number,' MacPherson would recount, 'fine-looking men, about the middle stature, somewhat fat and muscular.'[22]

It is *extraordinary* how these natives, so primitive, so unsophisticated, can also be so clearly well fed in a land where the white men are all but entirely dependent on what they have brought with them.

'Bulloo Bulloo!'

As the blacks are indicating a direction which is roughly the way Trooper Lyons wants to go anyway, he leads on, following the blacks 'over sand-hills and fine well-grassed flats, shouting at intervals, *"Bulloo! Bulloo!"'*[23] After 16 odd miles, they reach 'a deep creek, containing plenty of good water and splendid feed'[24].

They are saved! Perhaps *'Bulloo! Bulloo!'* means 'water and food this way'? As welcome as the sight is, and as delicious as the water feels running down their parched gullets, the day is too young not to keep moving – and they stopped off that evening at the same spot where Burke and his men had clearly camped. But what is this? Suddenly no fewer than 30 natives appear right in front of their horses. There is more than a hint of violence to them as the natives now even grab at the horses' reins.

'They were a fine stalwart body of men,' MacPherson will chronicle, 'in a state of nudity, and far superior to any natives I had seen in the colonies.'[25]

But dangerous? No doubt.

Trooper Lyons, MacPherson and Dick, panicked, look to each other. MacPherson's view is clear: 'We are now done for.'[26]

Perhaps, however, there might be some hope. They have run out of shot, but at least their shotguns are charged with small stones which could do a lot of damage – and Trooper Lyons's revolver is fully loaded with six bullets, while MacPherson has four. But what if they fire?

'We should be instantly speared,'[27] MacPherson has no doubt.

Never taking their eyes off the natives, Trooper Lyons talks to his men. 'Only fire if they attempt to strike . . .'[28]

And now dismounting, it is time to proceed with the next part of the plan. Taking their horses in hand, they push confidently through the natives, without saying a word – which results in a furious discussion taking place among the blacks.

'From their gestures and actions we expected to be killed,' MacPherson would note, 'but after a short consultation we could see that there was a division of opinion . . .'[29]

The opportunity is too good to miss. Move! Move! Move!

It is all over quickly. So quickly, that they are through the natives within seconds, and the fearful jabbering behind them gets louder . . . but . . . much as their spines tingle . . . no spear, club or boomerang comes their way. Yes, some of the blacks follow them but, the main thing is . . . they are through!

Still, MacPherson can't help but notice what a fine-looking bunch they are.

'These natives are a very fine race of men,' he will note, 'remarkably clean about their persons, their hair cropped close and their whiskers trimmed down regularly.'

Obeying Trooper Lyons's instructions, the blacks following them are ignored and, after a mile or so, they drop off. Trooper Lyons and his men continue walking through the rest of the day, and through much of the night, pushing the horses, trying to place as much distance as possible between themselves and the troublesome blacks, and . . .

And what was *that*?

The men are as skittish as horses walking through long grass with snakes about. Every noise to their rear has them jumping, jerkily peering back into the darkness, positive that there are blacks in the blackness, getting closer. The horses, too, are not only weak but agitated.

After walking some nine miles from Bulloo, Trooper Lyons and his men make camp in the darkness, rather than risk giving away their position by lighting a fire.

Dawn finds them still by a creek bed of sorts, but as MacPherson will recount, 'all the country around us in this part was much burnt up, and there was no vegetation of any kind visible . . .'[30]

Worse, even such water as there is in the creek is undrinkable, meaning they must quickly get underway, re-saddling the animals, in the hope of finding both food and water before the heat of the day comes on.

22 November '60, Cooper's Creek, desert rats and detours

For some among the expedition members, the fact that they have reached Cooper's Creek is a real feather in their cap, an achievement to be proud of, a time to take pause and reflect on how far they have come. Mr Burke is not of their number. He has no interest in merely reaching the same distant destination on the map that other explorers had. He wishes to draw a fresh map of his own. For the leader, Cooper's Creek is the starting point of the journey proper, the one into the unknown.

Hence why the furrows on Mr Burke's oft thunderous brow are now getting deeper, even as his pale blue eyes flash ever more angst. The warming weather means that summer is nearly upon them, which means they must be *on their way*, before it hits in full. No, he doesn't yet tell the others of his intent to quickly get going once more, as he must first resolve a few other things (even beyond the wretched, swarming plague of rats that hit the camp last night) such as, what route, precisely, are they to take?

The instructions of the Exploration Committee are clear: 'The object of the Committee in directing you to Cooper's Creek is, that you should explore the country intervening between it and Leichhardt's track, south of the Gulf of Carpentaria, avoiding as far as practicable, Sturt's route on the west, and Gregory's down the Victoria on the East.'[31]

In the corridor of 'ghastly blank' presented, Burke must find a new route north from Cooper's Creek, across ground never previously crossed by white men. All he knows is that it won't be easy, as he has already explained a few days previously in a letter to his uncle John Burke, 'the difficulties to contend with are want of feed and water and the hostility of the natives'[32]. True, there has been no such hostility as yet, but the experiences of Sturt and Leichhardt, particularly, mean that it is a likelihood.

Against that, should they proceed the way Burke's thinking is turning – to leave half the party at Cooper's Creek, while making a dash for the Gulf and back – they will need only about half as much water and feed. He will see.

In the meantime, so as to fulfil his instructions, Burke continues their newly formed practice of reconnoitring the lie of the land without the full party in tow.

This morning, after less than a day since establishing their new digs on Cooper's Creek, Burke spurs his horse out of camp with young William Brahe by his side.

Off on his first scouting venture to see what lies to their north, he has picked Brahe to come with him for the obvious reason: beyond Wills, Brahe is the only expedition member who can travel using a compass, and he also has some bush skills, a crucial asset, as Burke started with none at Royal Park and has picked up – dot three, carry five, subtract four – zero since. Brahe's own estimation is that Burke is 'such a bad bushman that he could not safely be trusted 300 yards away from the camp'[33]. The division of labour between the two men, thus, is clear: Burke will lead, while Brahe keeps them alive and, most importantly, gets them back to their starting point.

As it happens, he is called on for the second skill within a very short time, as Brahe and Burke return on the following day, informing the rest of the party that the particular route they had taken just 25 or so miles to the north is so dry, so barren, it is out of the question for them to proceed that way.

They shall have to try a different route.

22 November '60, beyond Bulloo, a bloody night-mare in daylight
Oh, the exquisite pleasure!

After walking waterless miles all morning with their animals – all of their tongues as rough as sandstone – in this early afternoon, Trooper Lyons strikes a beautiful waterhole upon which pelicans glide, proud chins held high, unperturbed by the 'large flocks of wild fowl'[34] that hoot and honk and flap about.

The men's mouths salivate at the sight of water. As MacPherson would later note, 'it certainly made us extremely glad when we saw it, as we expected to find Mr Burke not far from here'[35].

True, there is little feed available for the animals – just dried up grasses, mostly – but the water is abundant, and they are happy enough for that!

'This sheet of water,' MacPherson would recall, 'was as wide as the Murray, and we followed it along for about five miles, it still continuing the same in width.'[36]

Alas, as impressive as it is, it does not last long. There is no current, and as they push north along its banks, it is not long before the 'creek' narrows to near nothing again, and they are once more in a relatively barren and certainly sweltering wilderness – a real problem, as they have almost no rations. That night, the best they can do is to camp by a small waterhole in the bed of a dry creek.

Things are grim and getting grimmer, until the worthy black fellow, Dick, says, 'Me think'um crayfish in'um hole.'[37]

Going to look, he soon returns with six small crayfish about the size of a middle finger, and as MacPherson would appreciatively record, 'they were extremely good eating, and after our long fast they were indeed welcome to us'[38].

Waiting for the billy to boil, the exhausted trekkers can barely keep their weary eyes open. Finally, they are able to drink their tea before drifting into their swags and off to sleep – though the crack of dawn, as ever, finds the trio have already got cracking long before, so they can hit the day hard.

Today, as ever, they are filled with the vain hope that it really is the day they will finally catch up with the elusive Robert O'Hara Burke.

This is not just so they can fulfil their mission – but now, even more critically, so they can get feed and water for the horses and themselves.

For all this time, Trooper Lyons has pushed on in the lead, always hopeful that just over the next rise they might sight Mr Burke. But the truth is starting to dawn. At none of the Victorian Expedition's camps that they come across is there *any* sign that Burke and his men have left recently, and every indication that they are weeks ahead. And they certainly wouldn't have stopped in this kind of country as, again, the further Trooper Lyons and his men go, the more the waterholes disappear and they find themselves in cruel country with 'a wild, barren, dreary, black appearance . . .'[39]

Gazing about, they observe the barren ground, covered with purple flint stones and, in the distance, mountains from which huge boulders are bursting forth, 'very sharp, and standing up edgeways'[40].

Still they press forth the best they can – the horses becoming 'quite crippled' – and soon find one of Mr Burke's clearly long abandoned camps, this one marked with Burke's initial, 'B', and the number 'LIV', sitting inside a square cut roughly into a gum tree beside a notably *dry* creek bed. In fact the whole area is scorched, sandy and bare.

Should they turn back, and head for the safety of the waterholes they know to be behind them?

No. Trooper Lyons is made of sterner stuff, and decides they will push on, still hopeful that, by some miracle, Burke and his men might have stopped just a small way ahead. Pushing on through the day, still with no food and water, the horses are getting progressively worse. In the afternoon they come across another of Burke's halting places, and can see 'tracks up and down the bed of the creek, as if some of Mr Burke's party had been seeking for water'[41]. Alas. After another mile and a half, they finally stop once more by a small but propitious patch of grass and shady trees right by where a creek must run, when in season. They turn the horses out for a couple of hours before going again.

Though the sunlight fades, in these parts the moonlight can be so bright it is nearly as good for illuminating your path, and on this night it is so strong that, far to the north, the men can see a mountain which they make towards . . . until the horses, in pains of dehydration and starvation, refuse to go further. The men, too, 'feel very ill and weak'[42].

They make camp for the night, but once again there is no water for them, and they all – man and beast – pass a restless night.

The next day, 24 November, a stinking hot one, all of Trooper Lyons's doubts are starting to come together, weakening his previous resolve to continue, come what may. And that is not the only thing weakening. For the horses start to lie down often, and it is all that the trio can do to make them rise again, and continue, even while bearing almost no load. At two o'clock in the afternoon, at the base of a lofty hill, two of the nags simply lie down and refuse to rise.

'Should we,' Trooper Lyons poses the question, 'cut one horse's throat, and drink the blood?'[43]

Upon discussion, they think better of it.

Trooper Lyons, half-mad with thirst and hunger – they had run out of food and water more than 36 hours earlier, and are embarking on their second straight day without it – realises that he is close to his last chance here. Climbing the hill on his own, ignoring his swollen and blistered feet, his leaden legs, and his general light-headedness, he keeps going, praying for a miracle. Maybe, at the top, he might look to the north and see either Burke's party, or water, or at least . . . greenery?

What he sees instead is endless . . . stony . . . desert. Miles of it. Rocks rule this kingdom, and the only thing vegetation can do is make a few scraggy protest votes in the form of scattered, sad, stunted plants. And the whole thing goes on for dozens of miles, stretching on to a hundred hazy horizons of hellish nothingness.

It is enough to decide Trooper Lyons.

Clambering down to the bottom again, he rasps to MacPherson and Dick that, 'All around is just the same as we have come through during the past two days'[44].

Damn the dispatches, duty has been done, and seared sanity now calls for a retreat.

We must, he tells his men, 'retrace our steps, and relinquish the attempt to overtake Mr Burke'[45]. Unsurprisingly, there is no counter-argument.

Before leaving, Lyons grabs a large stick, sharpens one end, and drives it into the ground, with stones at its base, before affixing a torn piece of rug to its top, to mark their northernmost point of advance. True, it is less a triumphantly planted flag to conquer a kingdom, than a flag

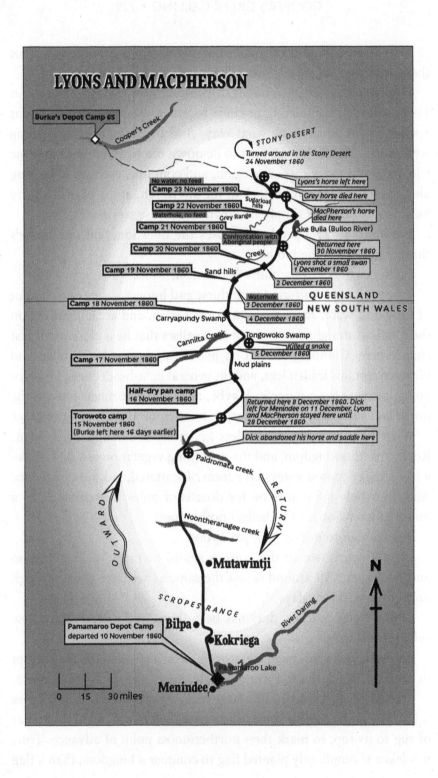

LYONS AND MACPHERSON

Burke's Depot Camp 65

Cooper's Creek

STONY DESERT

*Turned around in the Stony Desert
24 November 1860*

Lyons's horse left here

No water, no feed
Camp 23 November 1860

Grey horse died here

Camp 22 November 1860

Sugarloaf hills

MacPherson's horse died here

Waterhole, no feed
Camp 21 November 1860

Grey Range

Lake Bulla (Bulloo River)

Confrontation with Aboriginal people

Camp 20 November 1860

*Returned here
30 November 1860*

Creek

Camp 19 November 1860

Sand hills

*Lyons shot a small swan
1 December 1860*

2 December 1860

Camp 18 November 1860

Waterhole
3 December 1860

QUEENSLAND
NEW SOUTH WALES

Carryapundy Swamp

4 December 1860

Cannilta Creek

Tongowoko Swamp

Killed a snake

Camp 17 November 1860

5 December 1860

Mud plains

Half-dry pan camp
16 November 1860

*Returned here 8 December 1860. Dick
left for Menindee on 11 December, Lyons
and MacPherson stayed here until
28 December 1860*

Torowoto camp
15 November 1860
(Burke left here 16 days earlier)

Dick abandoned his horse and saddle here

Paldromata creek

R E T U R N

O U T W A R D

Noontheranagee creek

●Mutawintji

N

SCROPES RANGE

River Darling

Pamamaroo Depot Camp
departed 10 November 1860

Bilpa ●

●**Kokriega**

Pamamaroo Lake

Menindee ◆

0   15   30 miles

of surrender to preserve their lives, but it is something – Trooper Lyons simply feels that, given their struggle, the moment requires something more than a swivel of their heels in the dust.

But now, swivel they do, and their flag is soon left behind, hanging dully.

Noticing one of the horses appears to have more strength than the others, Lyons decides to go on with him ahead, with waterbags, in the hope of getting to the last waterhole to bring water back to the others.

The plan is good, bar one thing. After 10 miles, the horse lies down, and will not rise. All Trooper Lyons can do – after removing the saddle and having a short rest to gather himself – is turn back on his turning back and about face for the second time that day. He meets MacPherson and Dick about halfway down the track winding back, still trying to push the three horses along before them.

'You should have waited, and rested, until we came up,'[46] MacPherson rasps.

In reply, Lyons says something entirely incoherent, even as he starts removing his clothing.

'He seemed deranged from want of water,' MacPherson would note, 'and in great pain.'[47]

They are soon all together on their way back to the first horse. At two o'clock, in the searing sun, they arrive to where the stricken animal is . . . not. He's up and gone, no doubt in search of water. Water? Ah yes, water. They cannot search for the horse . . .

Water is more important. The sun falls . . . the sun rises again . . . and they are *still* moving. In a haze. In a fog of their own exhaustion. But the remaining three horses will not move with them. In desperation, Trooper Lyons and MacPherson leave Dick with the horses, while they head off carrying two waterbags, hopeful of following their own tracks back to the waterhole that was here, just a few days ago. If they can find it, they will bring the water back to him and the horses – unless he can muster them to come on themselves.

'If you cannot get the horses to come along,' Trooper Lyons tells him, 'you can take the saddles off and leave them, and come on yourself to the water.'[48]

And now they are off, Dick and the three ailing horses soon disappearing behind them, as they stagger on, walking all through the night.

It is noon the next day before they rest, and then only briefly. On this excessively hot day, now nearing 72 hours since they have had food or water, both men, in their delirium, are in danger of losing the track.

In agonising pain, their tongues begin to swell so badly, they can scarcely speak. What to do?

It is time to take the piss. With no choice but to drink their own urine, or at least rinse out their mouths with it, they do exactly that. Anything to relieve 'such excruciating agony from thirst'[49].

Disgusting, true, but *wet* disgusting, and that makes some difference.

'When we got up we could not see the tracks,' MacPherson would recount, 'we were so giddy, and we were nearly blind . . . I presently looked round and saw Lyons going ahead as if he had found the track, but I could not cry out to ask him, and I felt angry that he did not turn round . . . I followed, staring after him, and I then found the track.'[50]

Finally, at 5 pm, just as the sun mercifully starts to wane, they reach the waterhole, to find actual water!

'Our feelings now I cannot describe,' MacPherson would chronicle. 'I felt as if that waterhole was worth the world. I shall remember that moment while I live. I feel as if I could cry when I think of it.'[51]

Like madmen, not coincidentally, they put their pots in and gulp the blessed water – and gulp and *gulp* and GULP – scarcely daring to believe that this part of their agony is over, at least for the moment. After drinking an entire two pints each, they 'feel very queer'[52], but still drink another pint regardless.

'This brought all the skin right off our mouths, and tongues, and lips, and we felt great pain. We then threw our feet into the water, which relieved us greatly, and we bathed each other's head, which also was a great relief to us.'[53]

Finally sated, they vomit up some of the water before all but instantly falling asleep.

•

Troubling news begins to spread among the people of the Yandruwandha nation, living along Cooper's Creek.

Pirti-pirti, redfellas (for the milky white European complexions turn red indeed under the unrelenting Outback sun), extraordinary-looking men – at least we think they're men, but they might be spirits – have arrived at *Kini-papa*. Yes, there have in recent years been similar visitations by equally strange-looking men, but this is different. These ones are accompanied by strange beasts, one of which is at least four times the height, and 20 times the sheer bulk, of an Old Man Emu. They snort, they sniff, they spit, they chew, they groan, they grunt, they galumph along, they look positively *evil*.

And yet those animals are far from the strangest thing about these new arrivals.

For they do not follow the customs of these parts, which date from the beginning of the Dreamtime, which is to wait on the edges of Yandruwandha territory until approached to find their purpose in these parts, where they are from, where they are going to . . . at which point they will likely be *invited* to venture forth, to share in the bounty of Yandruwandha, to make their camp in a specific invited spot, with the understanding that they are passing through only.

25 November '60, 90 miles north of Cooper's Creek, sand to hand

Over to the north-west of the woe-stricken couriers – they can't be more than 100 miles away – Mr Wills and Tom McDonough are also out in unknown territory. After Burke and Brahe's failed foray, it is Wills's turn to explore directly 'north of Cooper's Creek where they struck it, to see if there is an available route more to the north-east of Mr Sturt's track in 1845'[54].

They need to find points to their north where water may definitely be found. The pair have three of the camels, and, in the belief that they will definitely be making better inroads than Burke and Brahe had managed, they have provisions for a week.

And travel far they do. Over sand-hill after sand-hill. Wills records in his notebook: 'Nothing but sand ridges are visible over the sand-hills.'[55]

So at least there is *some* diversity in the landscape.

25–26 November '60, lost, dead on their feet

In the wee hours of the morning – hours that no Godly man would rightly keep – the native tracker Dick arrives. Lyons and MacPherson rise from their swags, shaken at the sight of their naked, shoeless and horseless Aboriginal companion. The horses, Dick advises, have been left tied up under the shade of some trees. After having had no food or water for the last 60 hours, he too, drinks, and vomits, before wanting to fall asleep . . . but there is *no time*, Dicky!

So urgent is it to get back to the horses and keep them alive that after only three hours, and still in the silent watch of the night, with filled waterbags, the trio set off back to them. But it proves impossible to keep the track in the darkness, so they must await till dawn, before setting off once more and . . .

And there they are now.

At mid-morning, on 26 November, some 15 miles from their waterhole, they find two of the horses – the brown and the grey – both of them lying, dying. The third horse is gone. Can the other two be revived? While Dick goes out in search of the third horse, Trooper Lyons and MacPherson take an oilskin and, holding it by the corners, put some water at the bottom, to make a rough trough, for the brown horse to sip from. And he tries, he really tries. But the brute cannot swallow, with nearly all of the water soon snorted out his nostrils, 'mixed with dirt and skin'[56]. The grey proves to be in even worst shape, so they try the brown once more.

It takes some time, but while the brown is soon back on track, the grey remains on the track itself: unmoving, dying. While Lyons stays with it, MacPherson starts off at noon to lead the stronger brown horse back to the waterhole . . . but does not get far. Only 20 minutes after the two men have parted company, the grey dies and when Trooper Lyons sets off to follow MacPherson he finds him, at six o'clock, just two and a half miles away, with his own dead horse. After passing copious amounts of blood, the beast had given up the ghost.

There proves to be only one bit of good news for the morning, and here it is now. Dick, with the third horse, a black beast, Pussy. Both Dick and the horse, as it turns out, are as weak as kittens, but Pussy can still walk, just, and all three now make their way back to the waterhole, arriving at about 7 pm.

26 November '60, 100 miles north of Cooper's Creek, a recce wrecked

Some 100 miles north of the rat-plagued Depot, Wills and McDonough continue on, and have still found no water source to speak of. It has been three days, and with their own water supply much depleted, and the camels also appearing thoroughly depleted, Wills feels they have no choice but to return. Far to the north-east, perhaps some 20 miles over the range, as they walk at around four o'clock in the afternoon, they can see a thin plume of smoke suddenly rise, which is likely very significant.

'If we find any water . . .' Wills tells McDonough, 'we will go and see what is over there. It appears to me there is permanent water over there . . .'[57]

(Already, Mr Wills has learnt to read the signs. Strong smoke rising at four o'clock in the afternoon like that tends to come from native fires in large encampments, and in country this dry, such a camp could only be from a waterhole that is *always* there.)

Still, however, they keep moving south, looking for more local water to keep them going *now*, as the sun sets out to their right, and so into the evening hours, still picking their way forward.

In the whispering breeze of the twilit evening of 26 November – amid all the sounds of the Australian bush, the cockatoos, the cicadas, the hum of crickets, the creak of the branches of the box trees – there is a new sound.

It is a persistent *nuuuurrrrr . . . nuuuuurrrrr . . . nuuurrrrrr*, a sound not native to these parts.

Wills leads McDonough and the three groaning camels – *nuuuurrrrr . . . nuuuuurrrrr . . . nuuurrrrrr* – into a small clearing in the tangled scrub as they prepare to stop for the night, after completing 10 miles of their return journey. Finally, with the full moon now rising so splendidly, Wills takes the opportunity to walk to some higher ground nearby to take an observation so as to determine their exact latitude, while McDonough is to tend the weakened camels.

Atop his knob of land, Wills is quickly lost in the stars as he begins his 90-minute solitary ritual of working out their position from what the heavens tell him. With his sextant, his watch and his nautical almanac by his side, he is soon taking sightings, marking down notations and crunching calculations.

McDonough, thus, is on his own as he leads the camels to some nearby likely feed, only to find they are so 'done up'[58] they are little inclined. Sometimes they get like this, most particularly when there is no water for them, and the Irishman decides to leave them for a time, so as to return to the camp to cook supper. He can keep an eye on them from there, and proceeds to do so.

Upon Mr Wills's return, McDonough is able to present him with a plate of Johnny cakes, small pancakes of damper, allowing the two to sit quietly by the campfire, eating exhaustedly . . . when McDonough notices the camels going into the scrub.

Nuuuurrrrr . . . nuuuuurrrrr . . . nuuurrrrrr.

Rising, McDonough gathers them in without trouble and brings them to within 30 yards of the camp. Even if the camels go at a hobble, they can go all night long.

Returning, McDonough finishes his supper, only to look up to see the camels no longer . . . there.

Rushing over, even as the moonlight gives way to dark, there is no sign of any of them, nor can he hear them, strain his ears as he might. Fighting a rising panic – for not only are the camels their means of travel, but they also have most of their supplies – McDonough calls for Mr Wills to come quickly, to help with the search. Alas, the darkness presses.

Where are the sperm candles when you need them? Abandoned somewhere, weeks before.

For the next two hours, the two men crash through the brushy bush to no avail – even calling the names of the missing camels ('Cassim!' 'Nano!') hoping for a *nurrr* of response in the darkness – until, at midnight, Mr Wills stops calling their names and instead calls a halt. They need to have a quick rest, and try again.

Typical of him, he does not bother admonishing McDonough, but nor does he hide the gravity of their situation.

'If we do not find the camels . . .' says he grimly, 'we are lost.'[59]

They return to the camp to snatch a couple of hours' sleep, in the hope that the same whimsy which compelled the beasts to wander off might now compel them to wander back.

At two o'clock in the morning the two men rise and begin a tortuous trek to a hill they can see some 15 miles away. And now as the sun starts to rise, so do they once more, this time to the summit, and at daybreak are in position atop the knobbly peak, allowing Wills to take his opera glass and scan in every direction for *any* sign of the wandering beasts.

Alas, there is nothing.

'As we found . . .' Wills will note in his diary, '[the camels] travelled all night showing they were not quite as much done up as they appeared to be.'[60]

At 9 am, the two return to camp to follow the camels' tracks in full daylight, following the distinctive impression their unique feet make in the soil, which is fine while the animals are indeed on dirt.

But once they move over slaggy rock it proves impossible, and the tracking men have no clue. In the absence of the camels, they have no choice but to use 'Shanks's pony'. Things are grim. They have precious little bread and water – just 35 pints and four Johnny cakes – and just one revolver and a compass. On the bright side, Shanks's pony doesn't require a saddle, so they stash away the camels' saddles and their extra goatskin waterbags, to retrieve later.

They might be in danger of being 'lost' in one sense, but not in another. For William Wills has an uncanny sense of direction and a way of solving puzzles of place that baffle most men. At the age of 17 he waltzed through the famously fiendish Hampton Court maze in less than 10 minutes, a feat that astonished his friends and father, and confirmed that here was a boy who knew how to find his way in life no matter what the hazard or predicament.

They set off to the south, sipping a little from the goatskin bag as they go, whenever they can't bear the thirst any longer, soon coming on a dry creek bed, which they follow with rising excitement, reckoning it 'the most likely route for the camels to have taken especially as they were in want of water'[61]. And yet, while their hopes soar with the appearance of 'box trees growing about the creek' and 'cockatoos and several other birds'[62], they continue 'two miles without seeing a drop'[63].

Mercifully, after only eight miles, they come across the remains of a waterhole bearing a kind of putrid green slimy stagnant water in the bottom – now, where are their purifying charcoal filters when they need them? – and are able to refresh themselves for the moment, as well as fill their goatskin bag, which soon weighs all of 45 pounds, for the next push. Yes, heavy and awkward to carry, but with the temperature now risen to 130 degrees Fahrenheit in the sun, and 112 in the shade – with the first figure being the operative one, as that is precisely where they find themselves for the rest of the day – a *lot* of water is *sine qua non*.

They walk on. In every 12-hour cycle, around the clock, they walk for eight hours, rest for four, and just keep going.

27 November '60, Rat's Hole, rats in the ranks

Getting warm now. Nay, *hot*. Still three days before summer is to begin, and on this day at the Cooper's Creek Depot the thermometer stands at 109 degrees in the shade . . .

Alas, it only gets hotter, and is replaced by another, now familiar discomfort, just after the sun goes down.

Rats. First a few, then dozens of them. And now . . . *hundreds*! Ash-grey, with dirty white undersides, and teeth even more prominent than their claws. They race, they hiss, they squeak, they squeal, they bite, they scamper, they clearly *breed*, for now there are THOUSANDS!

'Swarms of migratory bush rats,' William Brahe would note, 'infested the locality and over-ran everything.'[64]

Hanging their supplies from the branches of the trees is working out. It is not a bad temporary measure. But it does nothing to alleviate the situation for the men who, of course, are sleeping on the ground where the rats can still get at them, gnaw at them, hiss at them, look at them, drive them *mad*!

Can nothing stop them? Yes. Snakes. For now, slithering after the rats come taipans and brown snakes, both hideously venomous.

Oh, the horror.

Mr Burke starts to wonder if they might need to move their Depot.

27 November '60, lost, horses for courses

Certainly, there is no use in flogging a dead horse, but what about eating one? MacPherson and Lyons – Dick is not consulted – feel they have no choice, as they have had no food at all since the night of 22 November. On this morning, all they can think to do is for MacPherson to go back, on the slightly restored Pussy, and cut away some of the meat from the dead animals, as their best hope of getting to Torowoto, to search once more for the supplies Mr Burke had left there.

While it is one thing to decide on it, it is quite another to actually do it. MacPherson stares down upon the bloated carcass of the brown horse, trying not to gag from the terrible stench.

Still, so hungry he could 'eat a horse and chase the rider', as the expression goes, he does his best, striking his knife into the hind-quarters and cutting away a bit of rancid meat that he soon has roasting on a fire. Alas, once more, after eating just two pieces, he faints.

'On recovering,' a contemporary chronicle records, 'he cut half a small bagful of the meat, hung it up, and went on to where the grey horse was lying, about two miles further on.'[65]

It is no good. Dazed, weakened, he cannot bring himself to take any meat from the grey, while still conjuring just enough strength to take off its saddle and hoist it over his own slumped shoulders. Even when he gets back to where he has left the meat of the brown horse in the tree, the stench is so strong he knows there is no point in taking it with him, when they would all vomit it up anyway.[66]

Leaving, thus, the bundle of rotting, stinking flesh, twisting in a hot wind made worse by the thousands of flies that swarm all over it, all he can do is retrieve the saddle from the carcass and deposit it next to the other one, lightly covering both with an oilcloth, ready to be retrieved upon his return.

When he gets back to the waterhole, just after sundown, where Lyons and Dick await – the former expressing great disappointment that MacPherson has brought no horsemeat with him – all they can have for tea is a cup of tea itself . . . which they promptly vomit up anyway. MacPherson has had enough and, giving up all hope, simply sinks to the ground. It is with some astonishment he finds he does not die, but is kept alive to suffer more.

'That night,' MacPherson will chronicle, 'I was quite mad with pain and weakness.'[67]

And yet, such is the nature of nature, that there are some compensations. For when he does at last get to sleep, as he would recount, 'I dreamed of magnificent scenes and palaces. On waking I felt a little better.'[68]

28 November '60, Cooper's Creek, boomtown for rats

One hundred miles to their west, at Camp 63, if anything, the rats are getting worse. In just one night William Brahe manages to kill no fewer than 300 of them, through use of traps and his revolver. They are here for the same reason the blacks are here, the same reason the expedition is here, the same reason the birds, reptiles and animals are here – the water of Cooper's Creek, and the grasses and seeds that surround it, is the source of *life*, where all around is arid death. It just so happens that this *particular* spot appears to be the rats' favourite.

More than ever now, Mr Burke is convinced they must move their Depot and so begins to make plans.

29 November '60, Camp 63, Cooper's Creek, back on two legs, in two legs

Mercifully, after walking no less than 80 miles in a total of 50 hours, including stoppages, Wills and McDonough are able to make their way back to camp, arriving this morning – completely spent, as on the last night they had had to make do with no water at all as the wretched goatskin bag had leaked.

But, oh, the sheer *joy* of arriving back in the camp to find people, supplies and water.

'It is astonishing,' Wills writes to his younger sister, Bessie, using a pencil, for it is now so hot that the ink on the pen-nib dries too fast to work, 'how a walk like this gives one a relish for a drink of water. For water such as you would not even taste, one smacks their lips as if it were a glass of sherry or champagne.'[69]

Despite the disaster of losing the three camels, and the narrowly avoided catastrophe of losing Mr Wills and McDonough, their trip to the north has not been in vain. Given the general lack of water found on their 90-mile trip, Burke feels quite sure there is little use in heading in that direction, but will make his final call after a couple more forays.

Meantime, everyone is impressed with Wills, and the sheer resilience he shows, despite having very nearly lost his life. While McDonough remains shattered by the ordeal, within just one day, Wills is again all guts and gusto, heading out once more to retrieve the secreted saddles, this time with Burke and King, before returning to camp empty-handed.

3 December '60, Melbourne, pleasing progress

If you cock your ear just right, the heavy rain thundering down on the roof tiles of the Royal Society of Victoria's new premises sounds very much like thunderous applause, as if the Gods themselves are offering a standing ovation. And why not? For the news coming from Mr Burke's latest dispatches is wonderful.

'We are happy to state they are of a satisfactory character,'[70] announces the chairman Dr Macadam, modestly, but his expression says it all. Things could not be going better. The Victorian Exploring Expedition has been proceeding at 20 miles a day, meaning that by now they must be well established at Cooper's Creek itself. We also know that Trooper Lyons, with missives from us concerning Stuart's explorations, should be there any day, while Mr Wright's party will likely have joined Mr Burke by now too. It is all coming together so perfectly!

6 December '60, northern approaches to Torowoto Swamp, from swans to rats

To the amazement of Trooper Lyons, MacPherson and Dick, they are still alive – as is Pussy, though the most they can load on the poor nag is their woollen blankets, and their hopes for the horse's recovery to strength. In the last week, they have been able to slowly continue to the south, staggering from waterhole to waterhole and living off some mussels, crabs and whatever shellfish they gather at creeks along the way, and a small swan, which Lyons shot. Today, after crossing a large and arid plain, they get to 'a small pool of dirty and clayey water'[71], where they and Pussy are able to drink their fill, before also filling their goatskin bag. Though hefty at 33 pounds that full bag allows them to make it in turn to another waterhole with relative ease – even killing a four-foot-long snake on the road. Best of all? The new waterhole is overrun with rats, and MacPherson is able to kill three of them, which accompany the snake for their evening meal.

Yes, things are grim when the best thing that happens in your day is that you get to eat serpents and rodents, but such is their lot. The men push on through the blistering heat of the day and the cripplingly cold night in the hope they will reach Torowoto Swamp soon. By the time they arrive early the next morning their withered bodies can barely stay standing under their own weight. They need sleep, yes, but more than that they need food, and quickly start searching for the promised stores. To their rising despair, however, there is nothing – or certainly nothing they can find. Mercifully, there are at least some blacks there, who give them some of their 'seed-cake', a curious concoction that they make out of hard-shelled seeds of something they call 'nardoo'. It seems the blacks crush the shells by placing them on a large grinding stone and rhythmically hammering it with a pounder stone, until the seeds become a 'crude flour', which is mixed with water to make a kind of dough. This dough can then be shaped into small cakes, placed on the glowing coals for a few minutes and you have a meal.

'They seemed to pity us very much,' MacPherson will chronicle, 'treating us with great kindness – finding us waterfowls and other native provisions.'[72] Which is wonderful. But what will happen when the blacks, inevitably, move on?

5 December '60, Cooper's Creek, a dash decided

With still no reduction in the rat problem, on this morning, Mr Burke packs up the camp, and while he and five of the men, 10 camels and 14 horses begin moving further down the creek, in search of a spot where they can have relief from the infernal rodents, Mr Wills and John King head off once more on their two exhausted camels to make a second attempt at recovering the three lost camel saddles.

The following day, Burke finds the very spot for the new Depot, a beautiful waterhole beside two imposing coolabah trees, side by side, their enormous green branches reaching out to give the party a shady welcome on the morning of 6 December 1860.

'The feed upon the Creek is good,' Burke will note, after settling into their new Depot at Camp 65, some 20 miles down the creek from Camp 63, 'and the horses and camels have greatly improved in condition but the flies, mosquitoes and rats which abound here render it a very disagreeable summer residence.'[73]

Yes, the insects have found them, and come in droves. Mosquitoes. Moths. Flies. Flies. *Flies*. Nothing pleases flies so much as smelly moisture and, as all of them are providing exactly that by the bucket-load, the bush-flies are soon all over them, getting into their mouths, their nostrils, their armpits, and even their eyes and ears.

'The flies are very numerous,' Wills notes to his sister Bessie about living by the creek, 'so that one can do nothing without having a veil on; and whilst eating the only plan is to wear goggles.'[74]

Burke, for one – even though it is a little better than their last Depot – does not want to stay here for long. He wants to make a dash for the Gulf.

But dare they risk it?

It is the key question he has been wrestling with for the last week. There is no doubt it will be dangerous to push north to the Gulf just as the weather is coming into high summer, particularly when their forays have shown that water to their immediate north is scarce. And there has still been no arrival of Mr Wright with the fresh supplies, which would secure their base, and even open a line of communication between this base and Melbourne as Burke had been ordered to do.

But could they really wait out the summer here at this new Depot? Do nothing in the infernal heat? Go only in the autumn, and delay their arrival back in Melbourne as much as nine months from now? Leave Stuart to complete his own crossing and return the conquering hero as the first man to cross the continent, justifying the vicious barbs of the Burke critics, all while he festered with the flies at Cooper's Creek and Julia Matthews, no doubt, would finish with another man worthier of her love? He couldn't *stand* it!

The only way to break free, he decides, will be to split the party once more, and make a drive for the Gulf with just four of them, leaving the other four behind. Ideally, they will wait for Wright to arrive, so they can be assured that their base is secure and avail themselves of the best of Wright's supplies, but if he does not come, they will go anyway.

Either way, he must wait for Wills to return before making any final decisions.

Meanwhile, the men get to work, setting up the Depot and establishing a routine for the animals. One hot and lazy afternoon, the sepoy Dost Mahomet runs into the camp – having left his post with the animals, just a short way away – all a'fluster, 'trembling all over'[75], saying 'the blackfellows are outside [the camp]'[76].

Seemingly unflustered himself, Mr Burke mildly tells McDonough to go and deal with it.

Yes, Mr Burke.

Taking his revolver and his gun, McDonough soon sees why the sepoy was trembling. Here, now, are no fewer than 50 blacks, many of them with a couple of their front teeth knocked out, the result of a tribal ritual – a lack which somehow contrives to make them even more terrifying. Pressing forward, some reach out to touch his ribs, apparently a native gesture 'to see if I was afraid'[77].

What to do?

McDonough has the answer.

'I caught one and heaved him down and fired my revolver over his head and they ran away about one hundred yards distance.'[78]

Mr Burke is impressed. This is a man they can trust to hold the fort.

8 December '60, Torowoto, let battle commence

Elsewhere, another decision about moving on is being made – with Trooper Lyons and MacPherson in firm agreement. So perilous has their situation now become, they feel they have only one hope left. Dick, who is the strongest of them, must go for help and do his best to get back to Menindee. Trooper Lyons and MacPherson will stay here, where at least the water is plentiful, and survive the best they can.

In the meantime, however, on the afternoon of 8 December, suddenly something is up, something about to happen, something out of the ordinary. It is Dick who tells them what it is.

The following day, he says with a gleam in his eye, there will be a 'big-fellow fight'[79], between the two local tribes. The Wanyiwalku are outraged at the Malyyangapa for something – they can't be sure what – and are intent on punishing them for it.

And, sure enough . . .

'The next morning,' MacPherson would recount, 'we were surprised at hearing a deal of noise and shouting, and looking around us we saw a large number of blacks coming over the sand-hills, armed with all the native implements of war. They halted about 50 yards from the other tribe.'[80]

Dick is simply beside himself with joy, and goes to speak with the tribe that has just arrived, disappearing into their midst before re-emerging, and coming back, his eyes shining, his spirit 'in ecstasies', as MacPherson would put it.

'Good fellow,' he says pointing to the newly arrived tribe, 'that fellow belong my language.'[81]

When he announces he is going to fight with them, however, Trooper Lyons must step in.

No, Dick, you are *not* going to fight with them.

'If you go and are defeated,' the good trooper points out, 'we will meet with our fate . . .'[82]

And then what? It seems quite possible that after killing Dick, the tribe might turn their attention to his two white companions, Lyons and MacPherson.

Dick reluctantly accedes to their request, while between them, Trooper Lyons and MacPherson decide that 'an armed neutrality would suit us in our present untoward circumstances'[83].

Carefully now, and at a safe distance, they watch as the two tribes of men – perhaps 50 in each one – form up in two opposing lines, one man deep, some 50 yards apart. And now two older men, bearing many scars – surely the chiefs of the two tribes – walk to meet each other in the middle, as their men make furious grimaces behind, brandishing their clubs of all descriptions, and their boomerangs.

A brief parley ensues, surely agreeing on some basic rules. This may include no spearing allowed, because neither side is bearing any spears as they start to shuffle closer to each other. And now to the next part of what has clearly been agreed.

For now, the first chief steps forward and hurls a well-aimed boomerang straight towards the opposing tribe. There is no alarm to see him do it. They know that he is aiming high.

And now the second chief steps forward and hurls his own boomerang, for the same result. It goes above the heads of his opponents.

And yet, just as if that second throw is the equivalent of the trumpet sounding 'charge!', a roar goes up from both tribes, and they rush towards each other.

'And then ensued a terrific combat,'[84] MacPherson will recount. Clubs swing, skulls crack, blood flows, bones break, teeth are spat out and badly wounded men on both sides either lie still or try to crawl away, only to be fallen upon once more.

'In this fight,' the white observers will recount, 'the natives used their boomerangs as swords, butting with and not throwing them.'[85]

Hideous, primal shouts fill the air, together with screams, as no quarter is asked for or given. It is a fight of the ages, for the ages, with its roots in ages past, perhaps going back for thousands of years.

As the white men watch, entranced, with Dick jumping from foot to foot beside them, clearly feeling every blow, revelling in every successive successful swing from his own men, who 'belong my language'[86], the battle ebbs and flows, as does the blood from both sides.

It lasts all of 60 minutes and in the end there is a clear victor. Dick's mob has completely thrashed the Malyyangapa mob.

'The casualties on the defeated side were large,' MacPherson records. 'There were broken arms, legs and noses in any quantity, and in several cases broken heads.'[87]

Finally, with Trooper Lyons's blessing, Dick is allowed to go to his people and he soon returns with the victorious tribe, beaming with pride to introduce them to his small party of Europeans.

And now it is the turn of the black men to be entranced.

'They were very much surprised at our appearance,' MacPherson records, 'particularly our white skin, feeling and pulling us, and making gestures that we were the first white men they had ever seen.'[88]

Best of all, Dick tells his tribe just how desperate their situation is, and how it has been decided that he will go back to the Darling for help, leaving the two white men here. In response, the victorious tribe 'seemed to pity them, but did not further interest themselves'[89]. They do, nevertheless, promise to give them food until Dick returns – and the more so on Dick telling them he would 'bring them plenty toma-hawks and shirts with him when he came back'[90].

Trooper Lyons, meanwhile, scrawls off a quick note with a pencil on a stray scrap of paper, for Dick to give to Mr Wright, in the hope the black fellow will indeed get through . . .

11th December: —

> *Mr Wright, Sir.— It is with the greatest regret that I have to inform*
> *you that we are at the lake where you left Mr Burke, placed in a most*
> *miserable position, destitute of the necessaries of human life, which we*
> *have been since 23rd November last. We have been about 380 miles*
> *further than here, but . . . made our way back here in hopes to find the*
> *flour that Mr Burke planted, but all our hopes were blasted . . .*
>
> *The black boy [Dick] will be able to give you all particulars; we are*
> *unable to proceed any further for weakness and want of food; we are two*
> *miserable objects, God pity us! We will remain in hopes of being relieved*
> *by your goodness before many days, but when I say days, two or three*
> *may put an end to our earthly existence, for we cannot last much longer.*
> *We remain, yours in misery,*
> *MYLES A. LYONS, ALEX. MACPHERSON.*[91]

Oh.

And in a quick follow-up note, Trooper Lyons adds:

> *Sir,— Will you have the goodness to send me from the store six tomahawks and six shirts, as there are some blacks here who have promised to procure us some waterhens, which will be our only support until we hear from you.*
> *Your humble servant, in the greatest misery.*
> MYLES LYONS[92]

Dick is soon on his way with Pussy, leaving Trooper Lyons and MacPherson on their own at Torowoto Swamp, languishing in the shade. Yes, they have plenty of water, but the problem is food. Despite the promises of the tribe to look after them, and provide for them, it has not worked out like that. As MacPherson will disgustedly chronicle, 'after Dick left they went away, and we never saw them again, thus showing that they possessed, in common with their countrymen, these distinguishing traits of aboriginal falsehood'[93].

The only exception is two blacks who had helped to guide Burke north from Torowoto six weeks earlier. They stayed for a couple of days and – in return for such things as clothing and the promise of tomahawks – bring Lyons and MacPherson a couple of waterhens they have killed with boomerangs, together with a small collection of iguanas, snakes and 'several large insect larvae'[94].

(Another witchetty grub? No, I couldn't possibly . . .)

But now they have gone, too.

What then, can they live on, beyond hope?

MacPherson has an idea. For, watching the natives closely, he has a rough notion of how they prepare their 'seed cakes' by taking a pile of seeds like dry, dark, split peas, which they then pound 'between two large stones, and mixing it [with water] into cakes like flour or porridge like oatmeal. These cakes they baked in the ashes . . .'[95]

But where does the seed come from?

Befriending a native woman, and giving her small gifts, MacPherson successfully beseeches her – despite the anger of her tribe – to show him where the plant grows. It proves to be a kind of stumpy water-fern with leaves a little like clover that grows on the mudflats, and he is able to gather 'a small tin dish full of the seeds, after which she promptly disappeared'[96].

Imitating the native manner of preparation, MacPherson and Trooper Lyons at least now have *something* to eat, even if it is barely enough to keep body and soul together, while also, strangely, causing their bowels to loosen with extraordinarily large stools. Yes, the preparation is seriously hard work – and not for nothing would the women of one nearby tribe be frequently heard to lament *pita-ru*, as in 'always-pounding . . .'[97] as the relentless 'tap-tap' from their stones can be heard emanating from their camps long into the night – but it dissipates the hunger of Trooper Lyons and MacPherson, and that is no small thing.

CHAPTER TEN
PUSHING NORTH

Burke led his party, very much as he would have led a forlorn hope, into the jaws of death.[1]

The Leader, Melbourne, 1887

I consider myself very fortunate in having Mr Wills as my second in command. He is a capital officer, zealous and untiring in the performance of his duties; and I trust that he will remain my second as long as I am in charge of the expedition.[2]

(Signed) R. O'Hara Burke, Leader, in his final dispatch to the Committee, from Cooper's Creek, 13 December 1860

A most dangerous enemy grew up amongst us in the irresistible impatience to come to the end of our journey.[3]

Ludwig Leichhardt, 1845

Early December '60, Cooper's Creek, Brahe bushwhacked, advance party picked

On a notably hot day at the beginning of this second week of December, Robert Burke and William Brahe are reconnoitring the north section of Cooper's Creek – just seeing what lies that way – when they come across such a fine waterhole that even the ever dutiful Burke cannot resist.

'Let's have a bathe,'[4] says he.

Brahe does not have to be asked twice. A carrier, digger, stockkeeper and horse-handler who has been in Australia since 1851, the German is one who can be counted on to work hard and follow all suggestions of *der* boss-man, including this one.

After living in close quarters with his leader for months now, Brahe knows all too well the signs of Mr Burke's growing, boiling-over impatience. It's the way he stalks around the Depot, fusses over the stores, jerks extra meat (they have killed and stripped two horses since arriving at the Depot) and constantly scans the southern horizon for any sign of Wright with the supplies. It is the way he clearly views every day of staying stationary at the Depot as sapping the glory from his grand expedition. Brahe suspects Burke will head off with a small party very soon, and only hopes that he will be asked to come along.

Stripping down, the two soon dive into the blessed relief of the waterhole, plunging through the tepid, near foetid water on top, to the cool and fresh depths that lie just beneath.

While they are in the water Burke suddenly remarks, 'I want someone to stay here and take the party back to the Darling if we don't return. I will give you the command if you stop. It will be a distinction.'[5]

Brahe does not need long to consider the proposal.

'I don't *vant* *zer* distinction,' he says firmly. 'I *vant* to go *viz* you.'

'So be it!' says Burke.

And yet, for once, the choice of who would stay had not been a solo Burke decision, and it had only been after long discussion with Wills – who had pushed strongly for Brahe – that Burke had decided on him as the one best capable of holding the fort. After all, if the worst comes to the worst and the 'Depot party' have to return to Menindee without the 'Gulf party', it is important that they have a very capable man to do so. And a man who could guide them there; Brahe, unlike the others, has the ability to 'travel by compass and observation'[6].

Not that it *particularly* matters, as Wright should arrive shortly, meaning Brahe's appointment is likely only temporary.

Still, it is judged as important enough by Wills himself that the next day, for the first time, he goes so far as to seek to change Mr Burke's decision. It works. Wills's argument is so compelling that, a short time later, the second officer seeks Brahe out at the camp, invites him into his large tent and says quietly to him, 'We are in a fix. Someone must take charge here. You do it.'[7]

Brahe likes Wills. And he likes Burke. He doesn't want to let either man down when they both seem so keen on him doing it. But he doesn't want to stay. He really does want to go *with* them. Caught betwixt and between, Brahe hems and haws, he says neither yes nor no, *nicht ja noch nein* – he . . .

He is interrupted by Burke, who just on this instant arrives.

'Brahe has offered to stay,' Wills tells the expedition leader.

'That's good,'[8] Burke replies warmly, patting the German on the shoulder.

Brahe simply does not have the strength to tell them otherwise. In any case, as the expedition leaders, it is their right to tell him to do whatever they want. He has, after all, signed a formal contract that allows exactly that. It is polite of Mr Burke to ask, but he and Mr Wills can order if they like.

And so it is settled. Brahe will stay. What's more, his new appointment is far beyond his original post as a worker, for now, he is no less than an officer.

Now, as to who will go forward in the last push to the Gulf, Mr Burke selects himself and Wills, of course, to be accompanied, firstly, by the quiet young Irishman, John King, who has been in charge of the camels for the last two months . . .

'I am taking a party of four to the Gulf of Carpentaria,' he says to King. 'You are to come with the camels.'[9]

Yes, Mr Burke. With a gap this large between them in hierarchy, there is no question of the leader asking the worker if he would like to come. King is simply told what is happening, and that is that.

The fourth man for the Gulf party – and the strongest one among them – will be the runaway sailor from Swan Hill, Charley Gray. Two officers, and two hard workers, the balance is ideal.

An interesting man, Gray. He is very much a jack-of-all-trades – sailor, cook, punt-man, rouseabout and ostler (a handler of horses) – and master of none, and his sheer physical strength is bound to be a great boon.

For his part, King is quietly not sure about the choice of Gray. It is not that the Scot is a bad man, but it has become apparent on the way north that he has a propensity for going on 'sprees'[10], drinking sessions that are so overwhelming he can no longer even stand up, and it is King's view that over time – and despite his massive frame and, yes, obvious strength – they have affected his constitution. There is a certain rheumy air about him (not to mention rummy breath) and a bloodshot dissolution, which makes King wonder if he will be up to it. Against that, there is no doubt that Gray is more of a bushman than any of them, undaunted by this endless, harsh wilderness. At Swan Hill, where he had been hired, he was known as 'a steady hardy man, and an able bushman'[11]. You could send him 'fifteen miles right back into the scrub [for] cattle'[12], without turning a hair, and 'no man at Swan Hill was equal to him'[13].

Burke has ordered that supplies be prepared and all up the party of four are taking '300 lbs. of flour, 110 lbs. of dried meat, 30 lbs. of meat biscuit, 90 lbs. of salt pork, 30 lbs. of oatmeal, 50 lbs. of sugar, 50 lbs. of rice, 12 lbs. of tea, 50 lbs. of salt; a few tins of preserved vegetables, and some butter'[14].

It is enough for just under two pounds of food per man for 90 days. This should be enough to keep them going for at least three months, which is how long Mr Burke estimates the journey will take if all goes well. And yes, ideally, they would take more food. But, as supplies are limited, and Wright has not yet arrived, the more they take the less there will be left for Brahe and his men, making their position at the Depot more precarious. Besides which, taking more will only slow them down. Mr Burke lops even more weight off their cargo by deciding they will proceed without tents, and sleep in the open – and under whatever shelter they can find, when it rains.

To carry the supplies, they will be accompanied by six camels, and just one horse – at least one as yet unjerked horse – Burke's favourite, Billy.

Now, when it comes to what specific direction they will proceed after leaving the Depot, that too has been under strong discussion.

Mr Burke is reluctant to go too directly north, 'unless I can feel confident in a supply of water', which he can't, thanks to Wills's reconnaissance trips, which had turned up little but misery. As he reports to the Committee, 'I am satisfied that a practicable route cannot be established [northward between Gregory's and Sturt's track] except during the rainy season or by sinking wells, as the natives have evidently lately abandoned that part of the country from want of water, which is shown by their having sunk for water in all directions in the beds of the creeks.'[15]

Instead, they will follow Cooper's Creek downstream a few days, before striking out north across the Stony Desert in the hope of hitting Eyre's Creek, the waterway reached by Sturt in 1845, which had saved him, just in the nick of time. It is the only known water beyond Cooper's Creek, so it is their best chance.

What finally persuades Burke to get going is the appearance in the second week of December of ominous clouds on their northern horizon, complete with endless flashes of lightning cracking and crackling, dancing and detonating, which he suspects are coming from enormous storms that are unleashing serious rain.

Which, of course, means, the waterholes and creeks in the region – if they exist – should suddenly be replenished, even for a short time, and that they should strike out *now*.

So it is that he writes to the Committee, advising them of his key plans . . .

> *I have . . . left instructions for the officers in charge of the party, which*
> *I expect will shortly arrive here, to endeavour during my absence to find*
> *a better and shorter route between the Depot (Camp 65) and Wright's*
> *Creek, or between the Depot and the Darling. I proceed on tomorrow*
> *with the party, to Eyre's Creek and from thence I shall endeavour to*
> *explore the country to the north of it in the direction of Carpentaria, and*
> *it is my intention to return here within the next three months at latest.*[16]

All else being equal, they will leave on the morning of 16 December.

'I did not intend to start so soon,' Mr Burke writes, 'but we have had some severe thunderstorms lately, and as I have given the other route a fair trial I do not wish to lose so favourable an opportunity.'[17]

Burke also informs them of his appointment of 'Mr Brahe to the rank of officer . . . I hope the Committee will confirm the appointment.'[18]

Burke does not just outline his possible plans via letter to the Committee, he communicates them directly (and individually) to his men.

'I expect Mr Wright up in a few days,' he says to McDonough on the day before departure, as the latter is taking his *very careful* watch

– *steady, steadyyyyyyy now* – attending the camels. 'A fortnight at farthest. I left him positive instructions to follow me . . .'[19]

McDonough takes the opportunity to ask the boss – for such conversations are not frequent, and the chance may not come again – just how long he and the rest of the Depot party will be here at Cooper's Creek, waiting for the return of the Gulf party.

'You are to stay for three months,' Burke replies, 'or as long after as your provisions last. I'm leaving you sufficient [supplies] to ensure your return to the settled districts.'[20]

In passing, Burke also makes clear to his friend McDonough that he had wanted to take him to the Gulf, too, and would have if he'd been able to keep to his original plan of taking six men, leaving just two here to hold the fort and wait on Mr Wright's arrival. But you must understand, McDonough, that with so many blacks here, I dare not risk it. So you must stay as part of the four.

Very well, Mr Burke.

16 December '60, the Depot, Cooper's Creek, bound for glory

So the time has come, on this sixteenth day of December. Just as the summer is settling in for the duration, the expedition leader is doing the exact opposite. On this hot and steamy morning – which is just what this part of the world seems to specialise in – Burke makes his last preparations before departure.

As McDonough packs up the last of Mr Burke's clothing, he can't help but notice that, due to his repeated gifts to the natives, the leader actually has very few garments left.

Typically, Burke barely blinks when McDonough again brings it to his attention.

'I do not care, McDonough,' says he, using the same curious words he spoke once before at Menindee, 'if I get on board the vessel with only a shirt on me, if I get through.'[21]

Vessel? McDonough does not pursue it, but presumes Mr Burke is once more referring to the possibility of a vessel coming to pick them up in the Gulf of Carpentaria.

Meantime, on the night before departure, Burke reminds Brahe that he can expect Wright to arrive here at Cooper's Creek 'within two days'[22].

At least he hopes so.

'Should [we] put ourselves on short allowance,' Brahe asks, 'as a prudent measure in regard to the uncertainty of your return?'

'There is no reason for so doing,' Burke replies, quite reasonably, 'as it is impossible for me to be longer away than three months with the provisions I have.'[23]

Strangely, Burke also hands Brahe a 'small parcel of pocket books'[24], together with odd instructions.

'These,' he says, 'are of a private nature . . . In the event that I do not return, you must destroy them before you depart.'[25]

Burke is quite serious, even specifying the manner of their destruction.

He watches Brahe seal the parcel closed with a hot blob of wax and piece of yarn, and says, 'Throw them into the water should I not return, when you leave the creek.'

'I shall burn them,' Brahe suggests.

Burke agrees.[26]

Still trying to work out just how long the Gulf party will likely be away, Brahe floats the possibility that, on the return journey, Burke and his men 'might be compelled to make for Queensland?'[27]

That has, after all, been a subject of some conversation between Brahe and Wills and their companions, as just a quick look at the map reveals the clear advantages of 'traversing the shorter distance and known practicable track to Queensland'.[28]

Oddly, the thought seems genuinely not to have struck Burke to this point. Still, now that the leader does consider it, he does not disavow that it is a possibility.

Something that Mr Burke fails to tell Brahe, or McDonough for that matter – despite his promise to do exactly that – is to be sure to go back to Menindee with some horses and camels, where Mr Wright is waiting for the fresh animals so he can bring the supplies languishing at Menindee up to Cooper's Creek. Such an omission means the two parties Mr Burke leaves behind, at Menindee and Cooper's Creek, will both be obliged to sit and wait for the other to ride and arrive, unless something changes.

A stunning omission? Perhaps. But not entirely surprising.

'Mr Burke,' Wright would note, 'used to alter his mind so very often at different times, it was not possible to understand what he really did mean at times.'[29]

Just like his personality, the leader's orders are full of contradictions. And despite his carefully composed self-admonition atop the first page of his notebook to 'Think well before giving an answer and never speak except from strong convictions'[30], it is, like so many of his resolutions, an admirable sentiment not remotely reflected in his subsequent actions. The result, in this case, is that he leaves behind now two pieces of the jigsaw of his expedition, not only not fitting together, but with neither piece having a clue as to how they are *meant* to fit to the other.

Shortly thereafter, at 6.30 am, Burke calls his men to order before him and, in the sticky heat of this rising morning, formalises the situation.

Now, it would be said of Burke that, as a policeman, 'walking about his room he would dictate a dispatch upon occasion that read like the sound of a trumpet . . . there was the tramp of a charge and the ring of a sabre about it – extremely characteristic of the man . . .'[31]

And so too, now. Though his room is now the whole open Outback, his voice still rings forth as he dictates his determined plans, pausing only now and then for the trumpets to crescendo, and to allow for a little sabre-rattling.

The time has come, gentlemen, the time to embark on the great venture for which we have journeyed to this part of the Australian wilderness. We are about to make the unknown, *known*; the unexplored, *explored*; the unconquered, *conquered*.

This very day gentlemen, I, Mr Wills, John King and Charley are heading north, north to the Gulf of Carpentaria. Those of you staying behind will also have a very important duty to fulfil. You will need to build a stockade, and thereafter hold the fort, protect our stores and ensure that the supplies will be at hand for our return. Your leader will be William Brahe, until such time as the third officer, Mr Wright, arrives. Mr Brahe will be coming with the Gulf party for this first day, before returning to his new command, albeit a temporary one.

'I expect Wright [will arrive] tonight or within two days,'[32] Burke says, before pausing.

Almost as an afterthought he now adds: 'But perhaps he might not be able to come at all. I cannot be sure of him . . . He may not come at all, he may be prevented by accident.'[33]

Yes, it is a rare moment of uncertainty from Mr Burke, when he seems so sure of everything else – all as the trumpets sound – but it is important they understand the reality of their situation. This is hostile country, filled with hostile natives who might attack at any time. It is your job to be on your guard, to keep the Depot secure, to keep the stockade stocked. Ideally, Mr Wright will help you to do that when he arrives, but you must also prepare for the possibility that he is delayed. Either way, once we return, we shall head back to Melbourne to honour and glory. Only then shall this expedition be complete, our task at its end, our duty done.

Trumpets!

And now, one by one, Burke goes along the line to shake the hand of each man who is being left behind, to have a few words, to wish him well, finally coming to the expedition's blacksmith and armourer . . . William Patten.

Of them all, it is perhaps the 'Splendidly built, very strong'[34] Irishman who is the greatest loyalist to his countryman, Burke; the one who hangs on the leader's every word, who believes the bushy black beard can do no wrong. And of those left behind, it is Patten who is most affected to be so – left *behind* – now shedding tears, his mighty shoulders heaving in his high emotion at the parting.

Burke warmly shakes hands with him.

'Patten,' says he, not entirely unaffected, 'you must not fret. I shall be back in a short time. If I am not back in a few months, you may go away to the Darling.'[35]

Even beyond Patten, the mood is heavy as these men, deep in the Australian wilderness, must divide up. In these parts, unity is strength, but they all accept Burke's logic. It must be done.

Still, sensing the gloomy mood, and feeling for his men, Mr Burke seeks to salve . . .

'I will not run the *slightest risk* on account of provisions or scarcity of water,' he says. 'If I find any difficulties, I might return in a month's time. I won't go ahead if I have any great difficulties!'[36]

Which are fine words. But William Brahe is not fooled for an instant. He knows Mr Burke's passion for this endeavour, his way of doing things. And while it is fine for him to *say* he will be happy to simply fill the gap in the map – that lies between Mr Sturt's last surveyed land at the Stony Desert and Mr Gregory's trek up in the north – the man that is Mr Burke will not be happy with any such thing. He wishes to get to the Gulf, to be the first white man to cross Australia, and that is that. And now, finally, at 6.40 am, it is time to depart. With a final wave of their hats to the men they leave behind, the Gulf party pushes off, with only Brahe accompanying them as far as their first camp, some 22 miles west down Cooper's Creek.

The men who remain watch closely by the two coolabah trees as they move off, with Burke atop his steed, Billy, followed by Brahe on a horse, then Wills, Gray and King all on camels, the rest of the camels following behind in a long tethered line.

Within minutes, they are lost from view, their bobbing heads disappearing ever deeper and lower into the Australian bush, until they are swallowed whole by the scrub.

16 December '60, Cooper's Creek, black fears and white solutions

For all the high emotion of the parting, things feel better with every step forward on this fine morning. There is a certain contentedness that the final push has begun!

'The stock was in splendid condition,' King would note, 'and we were in high spirits.'[37]

At the first break, the dutiful Mr Wills writes with some satisfaction in his freshly started notebook:

Sunday December 16th, 1860.
The two horses having been shod and our reports finished, we started at six 40 am for Eyres Creek, the party consisting of Mr Burke, myself, King, and Charley, having with us six camels, one horse, and three months provisions.[38]

After passing several waterholes lined with coolabahs, they note off to their right the 'stony rises' of sandstone mesas, with 'plains sprinkled with salt bush, occupying the intervening flat'[39]. Every hundred yards or so, their approach causes flocks of pigeons to take flight, their wings glittering against the pristine sky. They keep to the creek, the banks of which Wills notes carefully, 'are very rugged, and stony, but there is a tolerable supply of grass and salt bush in the vicinity'[40].

The further they push along the creek, the stonier its banks become. They keep riding beside the happy gurgle of the creek when . . .

There!

There is movement in the scrub ahead, flitting black figures, and suddenly, silently the blacks emerge from seemingly out of nowhere, all around them – some bearing shields and large boomerangs, with just one or two bearing long, lethal-looking spears.

But . . . friendly?

Yes. *Too* friendly in Burke's view.

For through sign language, the blacks indicate they would like Burke and his men to come 'to their camp and have a dance'[41].

Burke will have no part of it, and through their own sign language, which includes pointing their rifles straight at the Aboriginal men, indicate they will shoot them DEAD if they do not go away.

Luckily, as Wills loosely notes in his journal, 'They are . . . easily frightened and . . . decidedly not of a warlike disposition.'[42]

But he does not like them, and no mistake. 'They were very troublesome and nothing but the threat to shoot will keep them away.'[43]

In sum, no dancing!

Burke and his troop keep moving, and as they proceed through the day, Brahe soon finds himself up the front with the leader, discussing the obvious – just when it is that the Gulf party will likely be back in these parts, and how long the men should wait at the Depot – while Wills listens in from behind. After a little Mr Burke bluster with blarney thrown in, Brahe is, frankly, not precisely sure what exactly the leader's intentions are, as even his final instructions are oddly vague: 'to remain three months, certainly, or longer, according to circumstances . . .'[44]

Just what those circumstances might be, Burke does not make clear – and certainly does not write down. That is just his way. He is a handshake man, a look-in-the-eye-and-tell man, a lead-by-example man. Formal instructions are simply against his nature.

Remain three months, or consider us perished . . . unless circumstances change. That is clear enough, isn't it?

Not for Wills it isn't, and as one who has a far better appreciation even than Burke of just how far it is to the Gulf and back, and just how long it will likely take, based on how long it has taken them to get this far, he is firm in his view.

For, at the first opportunity, after they make camp on the banks of Cooper's Creek, Wills looks to have a quiet chat with Brahe, just before the German is to head back upstream to the Depot camp, taking advantage of the last few hours of daylight to get back that night.

As it happens, Brahe conveniently opens the subject, noting that the provisions that Mr Burke and his party are taking north with them would go no further than three months . . . ?

Exactly what Wills wants to talk to him about.

Whether or not the provisions last for three months or longer, Wills says softly – as for the first time, likely in his life, he is breaking the chain of command – he would like Brahe and his party 'to remain at least four months'[45].

Brahe broadly agrees.

Ah, but now Mr Burke wishes to speak to Brahe once more, this time about the natives.

'They will be very troublesome,' he says, 'and if they annoy you at all, shoot them at once.'[46]

Yes, Mr Burke.

Oh, and one last thing, Brahe, before you go.

'If Mr Wright's party should arrive at the Depot within two days after my leaving, you are to follow my tracks with the dispatches brought by

Mr Wright, and to join us for the remainder of the journey, in which case Gray is to return.'[47]

Yes, Mr Burke.

'And tell Mr Wright to explore the country between the Darling and Cooper's Creek and find a nearer route if he can.'[48]

Yes, Mr Burke.

After saying his farewells to Mr Burke, Mr Wills and Charley Gray, Brahe sees King tending to the camels a good distance away, and rides over.

'Good-bye, King,' says he, in his light German accent, 'I do not expect to see you for at least four months.'[49]

For his part, King wishes the German well – the two have always got on well together, and respect each other's quiet ways – and with that Brahe turns his horse back towards the Depot, and is soon lost among the trees.

Behind him, the four men of the Gulf party prepare for sleep in a rather novel way. For one thing their group is so small, but for another there is no canvas between them and the stars, as they simply lie out on the camel pads stuffed with horsehair, covered with their blankets, beneath what Burke, Gray and King call 'the stars', and Wills sees as a fascinating array of constellations, planets, meteors and astronomical bodies, moving in patterns that continue to enthral him. There really is something slightly . . . *vulnerable* . . . and uneasy about their once grand expedition now being reduced to just four men around the fire, deep in the Australian wilderness. Alone with their thoughts, they really do feel . . . alone. Just a few yards away, the camels *nurrr* unhappily, also trying to get used to the new way of doing things, as they are hobbled permanently when at rest. There can be no repeat of what happened to Mr Wills and McDonough.

Still, in the common vulnerability of the men comes a companionship, a bond of common purpose far stronger than when they had been with the larger group. John King, for one, notices how close Mr Burke and Mr Wills have become, later recalling of the older man, 'He was usually in the habit of addressing [Mr Wills] as "My dear boy", for although twenty-seven, and wearing a beard, he had such a youthful appearance that few would have taken him for more than twenty when he left Melbourne.'[50]

Gray and King themselves are included in Mr Burke's warmth. Now freed from the burden of managing a large group, the leader is more easily able to be his natural self, which is nothing if not garrulous, and the four of them soon begin to open up, talk more of their lives. None of them is married, all are particularly close to their sisters; in the case of Charley Gray, the only relative he has alive.

•

When Brahe arrives back in the Depot camp it is not long before he is asked by Patten, in front of the others, just how long they are to remain here.

'Mr Burke,' Brahe replies, 'instructed me to remain three months or as long as our provisions would last us.'[51] However, 'Mr Wills asked me to [stay] four [months] . . .'[52]

•

When the Yandruwandha people move along the creek, the cockatoos barely rise. For the native way of moving is *of* nature, and no cause for alarm among the birds who have been here only a bit longer than the blacks.

Not so, the whitefellas. They are noisy. They have strange animals in tow. They sometimes fire sticks in the air, which kill. Clouds of cockatoos rise at their sight, their wings glittering in the sun.

Brahe and his men are building a stockade next to one of the two glorious coolabah trees that give such welcome shade.

It will, Brahe insists, help protect their precious supplies from the thieving attentions of the dastardly Yandruwandha. (Still, the fact that the door of the stockade is made of leather stretched over wood is a fair indication that it is far from impregnable – a single flash of blade could cut through it.) And yes, Mr Burke had instructed him to simply shoot the Aborigines if they even annoyed them, but – obedient as he generally is – he is not so disposed. It is much better to just protect themselves in this manner, and no one will have to be killed.

Apart from that, the Depot party are soon settled into a regular routine of rather stultifying dullness beneath the blazing sun. They rise, they eat, they look after the animals, with one man, usually Patten, taking the horses as far as 10 miles up or down the creek to where they can graze on whatever grass they can find, while another – the sepoy Dost Mahomet – takes the camels to do the same, albeit in another direction. Meanwhile, back at the stockade, the other two, usually led by Brahe, are effectively minding the fort, gathering firewood, getting the evening meal ready . . . wondering just when it is that Mr Wright, his men and his fresh supplies will arrive . . .

17 December '60, Torowoto, much nardoo about nothing

The two wan figures lying listless over yonder, in the diminishing shade of the coolabah trees? That is the worthy Trooper Lyons, with Alexander MacPherson right beside him, and they are both slowly starving. Just two days after Dick had gone south, the tribe he'd asked to look after them had gone north. But, thanks to the kindly woman who'd shown them where the nardoo plant grew, the two men have been daily gathering a pint of such seeds between them, and are just managing to subsist, but it is obvious to both that they will not be able to last long.

Back at the depot on the Darling, Dr Beckler and his men are certainly wondering what has become of Trooper Lyons, MacPherson and Dick, but can do nothing, bar constantly looking to their north, hoping for a sign.

But day after day, nothing happens.

'No one came,' Dr Beckler would faithfully record, 'and we exhausted our imaginations with conjectures about the fate of these men . . . We were . . . forced to conclude that they were perhaps delayed by a shortage of water and that they sat captive somewhere where they had found water.'[53]

19 December '60, Camp 69, the four forge a path

Burke and Wills *et al*, labour long, trudge mightily, and keep going!

By now they are all but exclusively on foot, leading the camels and Billy the horse to spare the animals as much as possible. They are now veering north-west as Cooper's Creek had turned south-west, and though it is hard to leave the reliable water source, they must.

As Burke writes in a rare diary entry: 'We started from Cooper's Creek, Camp 66, with the intention of going through to Eyre's Creek without water. Loaded with 800 pints of water, four riding camels 130 pints each, horse 150, two pack camels 50 each, and five pints each man.'[54]

Soon the rows of coolabahs along the creek's banks had receded out of sight and they now enter lightly timbered plains, with a carpet of saltbush and grass. And the birdlife! With their every approach to a waterhole, huge flocks of gorgeously red-breasted cockatoos take flight, as do lesser flocks of pigeons, crows and hawks; the warm air a cacophony of cackling, screeching and laughing. These flocks have shared the waterholes with the Yandruwandha for millennia, but are not at all sure they wish to do the same with these intruders.

19 December '60, Menindee, return of the native

Nowadays, no sooner does day break than it starts to melt, as the average state of the mercury in the daylight hours is over 90 degrees Fahrenheit. And yet the heat, and its likely depleting effect on the waterholes in the terrain between them and Cooper's Creek, is just one factor that decides Wright that the time is not yet right to move. Above everything else, he has not yet received confirmation that he is indeed now in the employ of the Exploration Committee, on Mr Burke's promised salary of £400 annually. After all, it would be a terrible thing to go to all that effort, take all those risks, and *not* be recompensed for it. For it is now apparent that while it is one thing for Mr Burke to have promised him that salary, it might be something else again for the Committee to actually be able to pay it. With more and more of their cheques being dishonoured in Menindee, it is obvious that the Committee's finances are strained.

And yes, Mr Burke has made it clear that he will be counting on Wright to push north, but, with summer now coming on, there are two possibilities. Mr Burke will have made a dash for the Gulf, in which case he won't be getting back before late February – meaning there is no need to hurry now. Or, Mr Burke is going to sit out the summer at Cooper's Creek and make the push for the Gulf in the cooler months from February on – meaning there is no need to hurry at all. Either way, Burke and his men had headed north from Torowoto Swamp with enough supplies to last until early June, so it is not as if they are relying on the supplies that Wright has to survive.

Yet another factor in delaying Wright's start is the lack of decent animals, both camels and horses. If only MacPherson and Trooper Lyons could soon return, with the extra pack animals that Burke had promised to send so that Wright and the men here could at least start planning their move to Cooper's Creek.

Where are they?

Wait, stop. What's that? Through the trees? Do you see the movement?

It is coming closer, it is stumbling, not paying any mind to silence or stealth . . .

Dr Beckler is out examining the drying meat when he notices the native approaching the camp – and is immediately wary. But there is something different about *this* black fellow. Firstly, he is not simply gliding from bush to bush as so many of them do, moving as smoothly as they do stealthily. Nor is there any aggression in his manner, as some of the blacks have betrayed lately. No, this fellow is, in fact, near staggering, and instead of wearing the knot of grass to cover their privates like most of the men do, this one, extraordinarily, has some clothes and is carrying . . . what? . . . an *India-rubber water-bottle*?

It couldn't be, could it . . . ?

Could it?

It just might be.

For now the native comes to him, and lies wistfully and soulfully at Beckler's feet, looking up.

'Are you [Dick]?' Beckler asks this 'shadow of a man'[55].

The native, 'his previously full face was sunken, his tottering legs could hardly carry him, his feet were raw, his voice hoarse and whispering'[56], replies that it is he.

Dick has only just made it, arriving 'enfeebled by hunger, and almost prostrated by fatigue'[57] – having lived off just a couple of lizards and as many birds in the last week – but it is clearly merciful that he has. For he brings news of Trooper Lyons and MacPherson, in serious trouble up at Torowoto Swamp. They need help, and they need it urgently. (And so does he, having walked nearly all of the 200 miles since leaving eight days earlier – Pussy had knocked up after the first day and had to be abandoned. Their other horses are dead and though he has left the two men in the care of the Wanyiwalku people, it is uncertain how long that will work before they move on.)

Quickly the doctor takes care of Dick, gives him water, and calls for Belooch to fetch Mr Wright from Kinchega. Wright arrives in short order and learns the contents of Lyons's missive.

Mr Wright thinks to go out himself, along with Belooch and Dick, but Dr Beckler – only recently accused by Mr Burke of being too scared to leave the settled areas – not only volunteers to go to Torowoto, but is soon happily on his way in the company of Belooch and the black fellow, Peter.

They take with them three camels and one horse, and provisions enough for not only themselves but for the two men they hope to rescue. Dr Beckler has much to contemplate as he moves off.

19 December '60, Menindee, excuses abound if nothing else

Beyond everything else, the failure of Trooper Lyons to make contact with Mr Burke means that Wright's last hope of getting fresh animals back from Cooper's Creek is now gone. And as he has no money to buy fresh animals from settlers around Menindee, it puts his planned trip north in greater peril than ever. For how can he go, with such men as he has, with so few animals, and no guarantee of money or authority for himself?

Clearly, what he needs now more than ever is both money, and authority, from the Committee, and given that they have not responded so far, all he can think to do is to send an emissary, Hodgkinson, to go south with Wright's dispatch in his hands.

As he cannot write himself, Wright dictates his messages to Hodgkinson, and does so now, forming up his first official dispatch to the Exploration Committee in Melbourne, informing them of the surprising situation and giving reasons for his delay:

'. . . the camels (9) left behind by Mr Burke were too few in number and too inferior in carrying powers to carry out a really serviceable quantity of provisions. Of horses but seven were left at the Depot, and of them four are dead, one just dispatched on urgent business, and the remaining two are too poor to be available.'[58]

Despite his hopes, Trooper Lyons has not overtaken Burke's party and therefore had been unable to return with all the horses, so there had been no relief on that account.

Quite the contrary:

'I regret, however, to have to inform you that the Aboriginal returned to the depot camp yesterday, on foot, greatly exhausted, and that he brought with him a piece of paper, signed by Lyons and MacPherson, and imploring immediate assistance to rescue them from imminent starvation.'

Yes, those in Melbourne must understand just how grim their overall situation is here, that they actually need support.

'. . . In short, it is my duty to point out to the Committee the necessity of the depot stores being at once conveyed to the front.'[59]

Wright also sounds a warning.

'As I have every reason to believe that Mr Burke has pushed on from Cooper's Creek, relying upon finding the Depot stores at that watercourse upon his return, there is room for the most serious apprehensions as to the safety of himself and party, should he find that he has miscalculated.'[60]

19 December '60, Tirrawarra Swamp, lost in the stars

On this night, some 588 million miles above the earth, the path of Jupiter's innermost Galilean moon, Io – slightly bigger than the earth's sole orb – is about to disappear into Jupiter's shadow. It is something that will be closely observed by astronomers, most of them in observatories, who know to look up on this night thanks to their trusty *Nautical Almanac* – the astronomer's Bible – which charts the motion of Jupiter's satellites (and the Earth's Moon, of course), giving the precise mean time for such celestial events. Their number includes one fellow, high in the very heart of Australia, who uses no grand telescope. At

Camp 69, William Wills takes his small Fraunhofer telescope from its leather case, and with the smooth movements of one who is deeply practised at his art, brings the powerful lenses to bear on the planet high above.

There!

A little after 3 am, the 27-year-old is able to observe Jupiter's moon wink out, as it disappears into the planet's shadow.[61] Consulting his *Nautical Almanac*, Wills is able to work out an approximate local time on the golden watches he carries with him – drifting, as they have, from each other and synchronises the watches to the precise time, allowing him accurate calculation of their longitude. All these years on, he still retains a sense of wonder that such things are *possible*, simply by looking to the heavens, just as he did that first time he *saw* a telescope, many moons ago as a small child, in a shop window in Devonport.

•

The following day Wills and his three companions continue their broad push to the north-west, towards Sturt's Stony Desert, and by the following evening make camp at a point where a creek enters a large lagoon, at a spot which 'swarms with wild fowl of every description. It is . . . surrounded by the most pleasing woodland scenery, and everything in the vicinity looks fresh and green . . . There was a large camp of not less than forty or fifty blacks near where we stopped. They brought us presents of fish, for which we gave them some beads, and matches . . .'[62]

For his part, Burke, though typically truncated in his own remarks, can't help but note the blacks being even more hospitable in their approach: '20th Made a creek where we found a great many natives. They presented us with fish, and offered their women. Camp 70.'[63]

Perhaps the blacks are not quite as dangerous as Burke and Wills – who had, of course, studied the travails of previous explorers with the natives – first thought? That certainly appears to be Burke's opinion for, by the following morning, he even tries to persuade one or two of the natives to accompany them, to act as quasi-guides – whatever else, they seem always able to find both plentiful food and water – but it is to no avail. The blacks seem to want to help them, but not be *with* them.

Perhaps they fear the white men will move permanently into this part of the country, just as they have done elsewhere, unstoppable.

Countenancing that precise outcome, Wills continues to make his copious notes, recording the kind of country they are travelling through, much of which will be no doubt pleasing to the Committee as they look for commercially arable land.

'Up to this point the country through which we have passed has been of the finest description for pastoral purposes. The grass and saltbush are everywhere abundant, and water is plentiful with every appearance of permanence.'[64]

Whoever can first settle this country will become very wealthy indeed.

For the most part, despite the enormous effort of pushing so hard every day – day after day – the food that Burke allows them is reasonably plentiful.

'Our daily provisions,' King would recount, 'were one pound of damper, three quarters of a pound of dried meat, and a quarter of a pound of pork, and every other day Mr Burke would allow some pound or pound and a half of rice to be boiled, to be divided among the four.'[65]

They continue their overland thrust to the north-west, and now, just as they expect to find – courtesy of Charles Sturt's previous explorations in the area, and the maps he has formed – the landscape starts to change. The next day, leaving 'one of the most delightful camps we have had in the journey', they push north-west-by-north and bit by bit the fecundity of the soil begins to give way to 'high ridges of loose sand . . . partially clothed with porcupine grass'. The going is tougher, in fact the toughest they have faced on the whole journey to date, 'as the ridges were exceedingly abrupt and steep on their eastern side, and although sloping gradually towards the west, were so honeycombed in some places by the burrows of rats, that the camels were continually in danger of falling'. As they press on, they cross flats and clay-pans which have 'that encrusted surface that cracks under the pressure of the foot'.

Having covered eight miles on the day, 'we camped at the foot of a sand ridge, jutting out on the stony desert . . .'[66]

Sturt's Stony Desert! They are now on its outer rim. Frankly, it does not look as fearsome as they expected. As William Wills gazes upon the infamous desert, he feels strangely let down that it does not match its awesome reputation.

'I was rather disappointed, but not altogether surprised . . . to find the latter nothing more nor less than the stony rises that we had before met with, only on a larger scale and not quite as undulating.'[67]

Tomorrow, they will push out into that terrain.

21 December '60, Scropes Range, an art revealed

Pushing north, in search of Trooper Lyons and MacPherson, hopefully to be found alive at Torowoto Swamp, Dr Beckler is quite stunned at the sheer beauty of the landscape before him. The colours! The contours! The sheer exoticness of the plant life in this extraordinary country, a botanist's wonderland. *Wie wunderschön!*

And now there is something new under the sun, something he knows at first sight to be . . . a mirage.

'Parts of the chain of the hills before us,' he will record, 'seemed to be reflected on expansive surfaces of water whose edges the eye could never determine. Here and there vertical lines cut through the wavelike contours of the chain of hills; once again everything seemed to blur into a bluish haze. To the east, the ghostly shapes of gigantic treetops, towering over sheets of water, appeared to form the entrance to a fairyland. What could be more magical than that this unexpected mirage should intensify the magic of this land, a land we had never seen, that we entered as the first Europeans, a *fata morgana*, the gateway to *terra incognita*!'[68]

But the delights do not stop there. For as they continue north, they presently see a rock overhang and on the vertical face beneath it, an extraordinary thing.

'The walls and the ceilings were covered with the impressions of outstretched human hands in the most varied colours, a decoration which had something ghostly about it at first sight . . . I could not think how the natives could create these painting in which their own hands . . . formed the stencil. Later I was informed by a native that the artist held a solution of colour in his mouth and sprayed it over his or another's hand, which was held spread out over the rock. These people paint with their mouths, and their oral cavity also forms their palette . . .'[69]

23 December '60, Cooper's Creek, routine and rations

It is now a week since the Gulf party left, and Brahe is more than a little surprised to have seen no sign of Wright and his party joining them, but nevertheless is relatively content with his lot. On this day they finish their stockade, measuring 20 feet by 18 feet, and within it they erect Mr Burke's tent, in which they put all their 'ammunition and firearms'[70].

Their daily routine is now set, and is manageable, despite the hot conditions. And though food is plentiful – each day they share a pint of raw rice, boiled for breakfast, with some sugar, some salt pork or beef for lunch with half a pint of tea, and for dinner a couple of biscuits of pemmican mixed with flour, washed down by a pint of tea – they have been able to add to this basic diet by shooting down ducks, which will allow their rations to go further.

23 December '60, the Stony Desert, is that all there is?

Good Lord. Yes, for the Gulf party, this is in one sense just the next of many obstacles that have stood between them and the mighty Gulf of Carpentaria, all the way from Melbourne. But none has been so daunting as this.

It is a desert of endless horizons, stretching on and on before them, a desert covered with a curious covering of purple flint stones. At 5 am, just as the first rays of the sun are appearing, they push off, four men, six camels and a horse. This is the moment that both Burke and Wills have been bracing for, as they are all too aware that the horrific conditions of the gibber plains of the Stony Desert had defeated an explorer as otherwise unstoppable as Charles Sturt. But they cannot stop, if they are to get to the Gulf. They must get through!

In fact, as Wills records, they are in for a surprise . . .

'23 Dec We found the ground not nearly so bad for travelling on as that between Bulloo and Cooper's Creek; in fact, I do not know whether it arose from our exaggerated anticipation of horrors or not, but we thought it far from bad travelling ground and as to pasture, it is only the actually stony ground that is bare, and many a sheep run is in fact, worse grazing than that.'[71]

Still, the further they push out into the desert, the more arid it becomes, and the larger the stones – usually about a foot square with gaps between them, which are difficult for both themselves and their animals to get across. Sturt had reported that the stones had caused his horses to limp, and so it proves on this day for both Billy the horse, and the camels.

It is true, of course, that natives have been in these parts for millennia, and that Sturt has traipsed across it, but still Burke and his men feel like theirs are the first eyes to ever see the unfolding vista before them. Every dune brings an array of saltbushes and other stunted growth. Yes, it is desert, but still it is criss-crossed by creek beds that clearly flow in the wet season – marked by lines of box timber – and in the odd spots there are even watercourses that appear to have had puddles of the precious liquid that have only dried recently. At one such spot they find several 'gunyahs' and 'wurleys' – Aboriginal bush huts, for several people or just one person respectively, constructed from branches and bark, of which they have already seen a few on their journey thus far. The campsite has clearly been abandoned only recently, as they can see lots of grass the people have gathered from the plains, 'from which they had beaten the seeds'[72].

In some spots, it is so barren, so flat and empty – across the shimmering landscape, the air throbbing in the heat – that what can look like a tree growing two miles away, proves . . . oh dear . . . to be no more than a three-foot high shrub just a few hundred yards ahead.

Still, it is a matter of bemusement more than bedevilment.

'Our progress was literally smooth and pleasant,' King would chronicle, 'reminding one of walking over a gravel path, or a hard sea beach sprinkled with water worn pebbles.'[73]

The further they go, however, the more rare even empty waterholes become. Nearing sundown, they find themselves in uninterrupted desert, wondering just what to do. When three flocks of pigeons pass over, heading due north, it seems that their best chance of finding water is to head in that direction, and so they do. By mid-morning the next day, they have found it, a veritable oasis, 'a splendid sheet of water more than a mile long, and averaging nearly three chains broad . . . 2 or 3 feet deep in most parts'[74].

Mr Burke names it 'Gray's Creek', in honour of the party member who is, effectively, their chief cook and bottle-washer, their sailor so far from the sea, who keeps tab on how their supplies are holding out, prepares their meals, and cleans up afterwards. John King, meanwhile, sets up the camp and feeds the animals before hobbling the camels even as Mr Wills attends to his instruments and records his findings – habitually spending 90 minutes making notes, before spending as long as three hours every night making astronomical observations.

Mr Burke? He broods on what to do next.

24 December '60, Melbourne, of plum pudding and dried parrots

Ah, how Melbourne will laugh.

As a Christmas holidays treat, the popular satirical magazine, *Melbourne Punch*, will publish, on the basis of news received so far, together with clever speculation, its version of . . .

LATEST ACCOUNTS FROM BURKE'S PARTY.

[From Melbourne Punch.]

[BY SPECIAL CONVEYANCE.]

Central Australia, December 24, 1860.

We arrived this day at a sort of half-way oasis in the desert . . .

When the camels seemed inclined to flag, it was only to show them a rum-bottle and they shambled along with renewed cheerfulness . . .

Towards night the thermometer fell to about 150°, and we were enabled to sleep pretty well, although the mosquitoes made such a droning noise that a Scotchman of the party was dreaming all night about the bagpipes . . .

December 25. Christmas day went over very agreeably. We dined off plum-pudding and dried parrots, although we generally do without animal food in the very hot weather, excepting the flies, which rush down our throats with every spoonful of food . . .

Just at sundown, we observed in the distance a party of natives, who approached in a pacific attitude, waving something like a dirty white flag. On near approach, these poor ignorant people put their thumbs to their noses, which, from previous observation, we have ascertained to be a sign of profound submission and reverence . . .

Yours,

R. O'H. B.[75]

24–25 December '60, Sturt's Stony Desert, rest ye merry gentlemen

So pleasant is it to be by such a large sheet of water, that on this, the day before Christmas, Mr Burke decides they will all have that rarest and most wonderful of things . . . a day off.

Wills, for one, is thrilled, with their 'delightful oasis in the desert. Our camp was really an agreeable place, for we had all the advantages of food and water, attending a position of a large creek or river, and were at the same time free from the annoyance of the numberless ants, flies, and mosquitoes that are invariably met with amongst timber or heavy scrub.'[76]

By Christmas Day itself, however, Mr Burke's spirit of generosity is so spent that they are up and preparing from first light, and actually pushing off by half past four, as they begin 'to cross the earthy rotten plains in the direction of Eyre's Creek'[77].

They keep pushing, their course guided by two primary needs: to keep heading roughly north to where the Gulf lies, and to keep close to wherever the water lies. Most prized, thus, are small creek channels that proceed roughly on the north/south longitude and, mercifully, there are quite a few.

They keep on keeping on even as the flies buzz, their blisters grow, their throats parch, their skins burn and the sweat runs down their furrowed brows and into their stinging eyes, when . . .

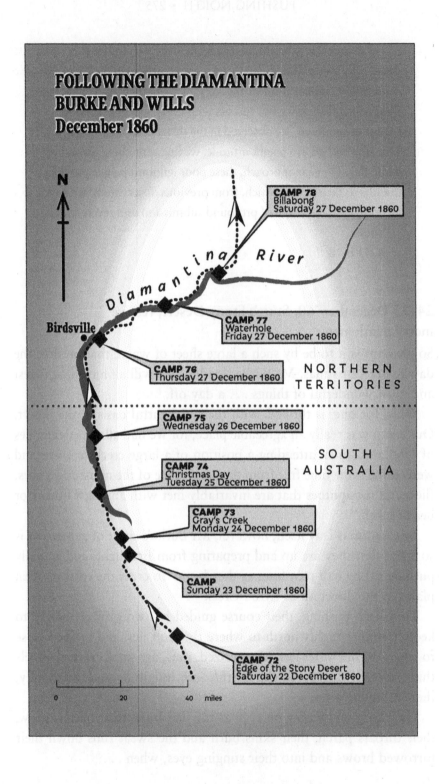

FOLLOWING THE DIAMANTINA
BURKE AND WILLS
December 1860

N

Diamantina River

CAMP 78
Billabong
Saturday 27 December 1860

Birdsville

CAMP 77
Waterhole
Friday 27 December 1860

CAMP 76
Thursday 27 December 1860

NORTHERN
TERRITORIES

CAMP 75
Wednesday 26 December 1860

SOUTH
AUSTRALIA

CAMP 74
Christmas Day
Tuesday 25 December 1860

CAMP 73
Gray's Creek
Monday 24 December 1860

CAMP
Sunday 23 December 1860

CAMP 72
Edge of the Stony Desert
Saturday 22 December 1860

0   20   40   miles

When it happens. A Christmas miracle! Just as they come over the top of one particularly large dune, expecting to see endless more dunes stretched out before them – as has been the case for the last few days – suddenly they see the *vision splendid* of a green floodplain *extended*. There is some kind of river up ahead! Soon reaching its splendid banks, they gaze in stunned amazement at a flowing waterway, every bit as fine as Cooper's Creek and maybe finer!

It is also, for all that, exhausting, and it is not just the men who feel it, as Mr Burke records:

'At two pm, [the camel] Golah Singh gave some very decided hints about stopping and lying down under the trees. Splendid prospect.'[78]

Burke, for once, doesn't mind taking a rest. For it is, in fact, a stroke of colossal good fortune to strike such a waterway just 150 miles north of Cooper's Creek, precisely when they need it most. Much further to the west of their course, they would have struck the Simpson Desert just as Charles Sturt did. Much further to their east, they would have found no water, as had happened to Augustus Gregory. But by pursuing this particular course they have hit directly onto a branch of what will become known as the Diamantina River. With steep clay banks, copious grass on the flats by the river, and tall trees inhabited by pink and suddenly glittering white clouds of Major Mitchell's cockatoos registering their dismay at the intrusion, it is, effectively, an elongated oasis, running south-west to north-east broadly parallel to Cooper's Creek, making it the ideal thoroughfare to pursue, as long as it continues to meander in the rough direction of the Gulf.

27th December '60, Torowoto, the doctor makes a house-call

It has been a long haul for Dr Beckler and his two companions, but one not without its pleasures for a German fascinated by the exotica of Australia. Why, just yesterday, as Beckler had noted in his journal, they 'had the pleasure of seeing six or seven emus hurrying past us at full speed. What grace there was in the bearing of these colossal birds, how elegantly the rounded, hairlike plumage rose and fell at every step; how rapidly they fled past us, these feathered children of the Australian soil.'[79]

But the doctor is not just a delighted tourist, he is a man with a mission, and finally, after a solid week of pushing ever onwards, on this morning the Aboriginal guide, Peter, indicates to them that they are now getting very close to Torowoto Swamp, where Trooper Lyons and MacPherson are thought to be and . . .

There!

Just a couple of hundred yards ahead, the movement of a slow-rising shadow, in the dappled light thrown by the overhang of the coolabah tree, gives an indication of life. It proves to be, indeed, the shadow of the man who once was the robust Alexander MacPherson, now little more than a skeletal wreck. They have arrived just in time. The figure had been stooped in the motion of gathering something from the ground – nardoo, as it happens – but now slowly rises before staggering towards them.

He looks up at them.

They look down on him.

He . . . . simply . . . . cannot . . . . . . *speak.*

It genuinely takes minutes, for speech is quite beyond him, but finally he gets it out.

'Oh doctor!' he cries, the tears streaming down his dusty cheeks. For his part, Beckler can barely believe it is the same robust fellow whom he'd seen such a short time ago.

'This man,' he would recount, 'had left our camp on the Darling some seven weeks before in the most blooming health, well built and with exuberant strength. He was now shrunken to a skeleton and a picture of total despair. His eyes were hollow and it seemed that he could move them only with difficulty. His voice was broken and scarcely audible, his legs tottered and trembled and were hardly capable of carrying him.'[80]

Slowly, and with great care, MacPherson takes them back to their central camp – marked by a sad 'old camel blanket of raw, dark wool'[81] strung between two trees – where the worthy Trooper Lyons is to be found, exhaustedly and exhaustively pounding the nardoo that had been gathered on the previous day. The good trooper, too, is beyond relieved to see them, and can barely believe that his prayers have been answered. In marginally better physical shape than MacPherson, he is in an even worse state of nerves, and even though now saved, 'had to be cheered up constantly by the other so that he did not despair completely'[82].

In short order, Beckler, Belooch and Peter have a fire roaring, and are serving the two skeletal men – both of them covered in angry red welts from the mosquitoes that have been devouring them, and from their own maniacal scratching – the best of their supplies.

The following morning, 28 December, at the insistence of the two invalids, and the hesitant approval of Dr Beckler, they head off south, the invalids riding atop the camels. Progress is slow, so by the next day, Dr Beckler judges it permissible for himself and Peter to make a side-trip out to a nearby mountain range that the natives call *Goningberry*. Now, ordinarily, as Dr Beckler has orders from Wright to bring the men straight back, he should do exactly that. But the German doctor simply cannot bear to miss an opportunity that lies one small detour away – to be 'the only European ever to have . . . the good fortune to see and admire [*Goningberry*], this small paradise which still slumbered in the state in which it had been created'[83].

A scientist at last liberated from having to answer to a taskmaster who sees the landscape not as a botanical and geological wonderland so much as mere miles to be covered, Dr Beckler is determined to *mach das beste daraus*, make the most of it, and so orders Belooch to take Lyons and MacPherson on to the next creek and wait for them there, while he spends another day or two doing some genuine exploring, expanding the frontiers of scientific knowledge.

Late evening, 30 December '60, Melbourne, a missive, a meeting and a mess

The sound of thundering hoofs drawing a rattling cab on city streets is unnerving enough in daylight, but when heard in the dark, on the cobbled streets of Melbourne, it is alarming, a sign that something is wrong. What is going on?

Dr John Macadam is about to find out, as, after 11 days of brutal travel from Menindee, William Hodgkinson at last arrives in Melbourne Town on this Sunday night, and, bearing in mind the importance of the missive he bears, goes straight to Macadam's house, pounding on the knocker.

Macadam wastes no time in opening both the door and then the grubby envelope that Hodgkinson hands him, speaking in whispers to the unexpected visitor for fear of waking Mr Burke's nanny, Ellen Dogherty, who has moved in, and is sleeping upstairs.

He begins to read, with ever more worried thoughts tumbling forth.

Depot Camp, Pamamaroo Creek,
Darling River, N.S.W., Dec. 19, 1860.

To the Gentlemen of the Exploration Committee. Gentlemen, – I have to inform you that, pursuant to a previous understanding with Mr Burke, it was my intention to rejoin that gentleman, with the members of the party and stores at present in this camp.
I delayed starting . . . [84]

Wright STILL has not gone!

Macadam reads on, bristling like an angry echidna at every outrage of Wright's letter . . . and there are many! There aren't enough horses and camels at the supply depot on the Darling to send north . . . the trooper sent from Swan Hill with the dispatches never caught up with Burke and is now in trouble in the wilderness . . . It goes on, getting worse and worse with every word, and, yes, sure enough, here it is, a request for more money.

In short, it is my duty to point out to the Committee the necessity of the depot stores being at once conveyed to the front.
With the carriage at my disposal, it is impossible to effect this . . .
I estimate the expenditure necessary at £250 for ten horses and accoutrements . . . I have to request that the Committee, if disposed to sanction the outlay, will be good enough to forward me, by Mr Hodgkinson an authority for purchasing all I may deem absolutely necessary, with full particulars as to my modes of payment . . .

I have the honour to be, gentlemen, your obedient servant,
W. WRIGHT.[85]

Such a letter contains merely smoke signals of the whole situation – one that Hodgkinson himself is intimately acquainted with, and Macadam now sits with him, to ask him a few questions. By the time the two men part, Macadam is more than ever aware of just how dire things are. Not only has Wright not moved, he is not even close to so doing, meaning if Burke and his party have gone north to the Gulf, as expected, they will be returning to a Depot at Cooper's Creek that, so far, has been entirely unreplenished by the stores at Menindee.

Macadam consequently passes a restless night, spending no little time staring at the cracks in the ceiling before, first thing the following morning, sending out missives to the Exploration Committee, who are told the news.

In response, no matter that New Year's Eve is just hours away, an emergency meeting of the Exploration Committee is called, and just after 1 pm on New Year's Eve, gathered around the table of the Royal Society are such men of distinction as His Excellency the Governor, Sir Henry Barkly; His Honour the Chief Justice, Sir William Stawell; the Drs Eades, Macadam and Wilkie, and Gillbee; Capt. Cadell, and several others. Also present, a little overawed, is William Hodgkinson.

And yet, he need not worry.

While he might have had concerns that he would be hammered with hard questions, in fact, there is very little of that. Mr Hodgkinson is happy to assure members of the Committee that all of the celebrated camels are so fit they're dangerous (no, really, just ask Ludwig Becker), as are the members of the supply party, and all they need is more money.

After due consideration, a motion is indeed passed 'that the sum of £250 be at once placed in the bank at the disposal of Mr Wright, for the purchase of these horses, accoutrements, &c.'[86]

Much discussion follows; this being the Exploration Committee, of course the discussion soon becomes diverted on the topic of whether or not to send a flock of sheep or a herd of bullocks up to the men, *sheep of course have a quick capacity to breed and yet bullocks have more meat* . . .

(Typically, when told that Rome might soon be burning, the Committee's central focus is less on how to get water to the fire and more on whether it be better to cook lamb or beef by its flames.)

His Excellency now ends the dilettante digressions with an important question.

'How long do you think it will be after your return before Mr Wright will be able to start to Cooper's Creek?'

'I think most probably in three days,' Hodgkinson replies firmly, 'and that he will reach it in about a month from starting. Mr Wright is so certain that the Committee will grant his request that I expect he will have the horses looked up, and everything ready, against I get back.'[87]

Which is good to hear!

Ahem.

There is the rather delicate matter of the cheques from the Committee not being honoured up Menindee way? Hodgkinson is skittish to raise it, but feels he must. Choosing his words carefully, he notes, 'there are a few small accounts, amounting to about £30, which were incurred at the Menindee station, but which Mr Wright did not like to discharge, as the ratification by the Committee of his appointment as Third Officer never reached him, the letter containing it having gone on to Mr Burke'[88].

The letter containing it having gone on to Mr Burke? It is an odd statement, particularly given that both Hodgkinson and everyone else on the Committee involved enough to actually understand the nuances of the situation knows it is not true. The Committee has sent no such approval. At least Sir William Stawell notes it.

Sir William – clearly of the view that Wright's appointment has not yet been so ratified – goes on to state the best way forward will be to recognise Mr Wright as 'Third Officer of the Exploring Expedition', in a formal resolution approving of his appointment.

Oh. And one more thing, noting that not long ago, 'a lubra on the Darling had been presented with a brass medal for saving the life of a white man', Captain Cadell says that if the Committee agrees he will commission and send a similar one to the black fellow who had saved Trooper Lyons and MacPherson saying: 'Presented to Dick by the Exploration Committee for being instrumental in succouring trooper

Lyons and saddler MacPherson, 1860.' (*Hear, hear.*)[89] In fact, they even authorise Mr Wright to give Dick whatever financial reward he 'may deem proper (not exceeding five guineas) . . .'[90]

The meeting breaks up, and while the men of the Committee go off to prepare for the festivities of New Year's Eve, William Hodgkinson is soon rushing north – intent on getting back to Menindee as quickly as possible, bearing a dispatch for 'Mr Wright, third in command, indeed' formally confirming his appointment and that he now has up to £400 on credit to spend immediately. As to getting Wright moving, the Committee does get to that, in passing, right at the end of their letter.

> *In conclusion, it is hoped that your endeavours to remove the stores*
> *from your present depot to Cooper's Creek will be early and successfully*
> *accomplished.*
>
> *Sir, I have the honour to be,*
> *Your obedient servant,*
> *(Signed) JOHN MACADAM, M.D., Hon. Sec.*[91]

30 December '60, Cooper's Creek, William Brahe draws the line, and raises them a gun

Blacks. Everywhere. Pressing in from all sides. For William Brahe and his men at Cooper's Creek, these have been particularly worrying days as 1860 comes to a close, and the blacks press ever closer. Just a little under a week ago, after the white men had finished the stockade, some Aboriginal men had managed to get close enough to steal six camel pack-bags, which the Depot party had washed that morning and left out on the turf on the water's edge to dry. The extraordinarily adept thieves had crept along the water's edge, using the high bank for cover, and then simply snatched them. As much as possible, Brahe now insists that everything valuable be kept inside the stockade next to the largest coolabah tree, starting with ammunition and firearms being placed in Burke's tent. But still the worries go on to the point that this afternoon he sees 'some blacks stealing stealthily along the bank of the creek towards the camp, while one of them directed them from behind a big tree'[92].

Brahe allows them to come within 20 paces of the camp, before he and his men first shout at them and then . . . open fire.

Yes, they are still shooting over their heads, and Brahe is not yet ready to follow Mr Burke's advice to just shoot those that annoy him, but he is certainly closer to it than he ever was.

In the end, Brahe meets with the tribe a short distance from the camp. They present an imposing spectacle, 'the men armed, some with spears and some with boomerangs; most of them had painted their faces and bodies'[93].

Taking a stick, he '[marks] a circle round [the camp.] I gave them to understand that they would be fired at if they entered it. On some of them crossing the line, I fired off my gun into the branches of a tree, when they retired, and did not molest us any more.'[94]

You blacks must understand: this is *our* land. You must not trespass on it.

For the moment they are holding them off. But, even with their guns, just how long can three white men and one sepoy hold off an entire tribe of blacks?

30 December '60, Following an unnamed river, gathering momentum

Everything is so much easier now. And faster.

With just four of them, broken free of the caravan, the tents, the two dozen animals, the endless logistics of getting going, of never being able to move faster than the slowest member, all now feel liberated.

No matter how early the sun rises, it never beats them as they are up and moving with the first gleam in the gloom of the new day coming. Charley Gray with his dancing mermaids begins packing, while John King un-hobbles the camels and starts loading, a process that needs the occasional help of Messrs Burke and Wills. Now if Mr Wills is just a little less active in this first crack of dawn, the others are more than understanding, given that he usually gets by on two or three hours sleep less than them – having spent the time making astronomic observations, taking notes, calculating their route and so forth.

The camels are loaded and placed in their correct order, joined by the ropes that go from the saddle of the first camel, to the nose-peg of the second; and from his saddle to the nose-peg of the third . . . and so on. And they are off, usually with Mr Burke in the lead, followed by Mr Wills, Charley Gray leading Billy and John King leading the camels. Only after notching up 10 miles or so in the early morning cool do they stop for a quick breakfast, before they are off again, pushing north, and on into the day, until somewhere near sundown Mr Burke calls a halt. Ideally, this will be at a spot near water, or shelter, or vegetation that the camels can eat – or all three – but it needs to be done with enough light that they can make camp, that King can gather wood for the fire, and Gray can prepare their evening meal with ease. A quick meal, and so to sleep, at least for three of them, in the bedrolls they place around the fire – while Mr Wills busies himself with his notes, the night sky, and all the rest.

And so it goes.

And the going has been grand of late, given they are still roughly following that unnamed but unseasonably generous watercourse. And along the waterway, as well as the occasional deep waterhole, naturally, come natives, but none have brought any bother.

As the as yet unnamed river they have been following for the last five days, over 90 miles, is now starting to head far more east than north, Burke decides they have no choice but to abandon it, and cross over to strike out to the north once more, even away from the water.

(The spot where Burke and his men parted company with the river, as they headed north, and it headed east – *roll, you old man river, roll* – is 40 odd miles east of where the iconic town of Birdsville now lies.)

As there are stony ranges now visible on the northern horizon, there would seem a good chance that there will be some creeks coming out of them, and so this is as good a time as any to leave their river and head due north once more. Before doing so, the four-strong party fill every container they possess, including their own stomachs, with every drop of water they can hold – about 10 days supply in all – and then, and only then, do they strike north-east by north. Burke's idea is to try to skirt the range as it appears, hopefully gathering in some water on its edges, without having to so laboriously climb over that range – most particularly since all of his camels, horses and men, not to mention himself, are showing signs of wear and tear.

'A northeast by north course was first taken for about seven miles . . .' Wills records. 'The whole of this distance was over alluvial earthy plains, the soil of which was firm, but the vegetation scanty.'[95]

Two days later, as Burke and the men walk along, with all the hopes and renewed feelings that one tends to have as the sun rises on the first day of the new year, and despite the weary muscles and joints, they hear a group of blacks 'muttering'[96] at a close range. They keep going and soon run into a group of 50 or so, moving together in the opposite direction.

John King would recall of the blacks: 'They must have saw our fire [from the night before] & were making to the spot. When they saw us they kept going away & point[ing] to where the water was. They seemed very shy and would not come near us.'[97]

Mr Burke, atop Billy, rides over to them and, unable to make much headway with words and signs, hands out handkerchiefs as a gesture. The blacks fight over the small items, before moving off once more.

The Gulf party presses on.

1 January '61, Chambers Creek, South Australia, New Year's resolute . . .

Refreshed, a little – and replenished, a lot – on this first day of the year, John McDouall Stuart leaves the tiny outpost of Chambers Creek once more, heading north. Determined to try again, to achieve this time what he had so narrowly failed to do several months before, he now takes with him a slightly larger party – a dozen men, 49 horses and enough supplies to keep them going for seven months.

CHAPTER ELEVEN

ONCE MORE UNTO THE BREACH, DEAR FRIENDS . . .

Oh, Mr Burke
'Tis risky work
To seek the northern coast,
Then have a care
Or else prepare
To be a desert ghost.

'Mid sand and stones
You'll leave your bones
'Tis said, if all be true.
For says report,
You're not the sort
To take the party through . . .[1]

Poem by 'OLD BUSH', *South Australian Advertiser*, 28 December 1860

30 December '60, Goningberry Range, dingo diviner

It is possible, Dr Beckler realises, that he has made a terrible mistake. At first, his detour to the Goningberry Range with the Aboriginal guide, Peter, had been a great joy, as an unending array of splendid vistas had presented themselves, and he had been able to gather staggeringly diverse scientific data and specimens.

But now the green has been replaced by dusty plains, shade by searing sun, and their water is running ever lower. Through his rising anxiety, wondering if they should perhaps turn back to where they know water can be found, Dr Beckler can't help but notice that his companion, the worthy Peter – who had been raised in the traditional tribal environment before becoming a stockman – does not appear to be remotely worried and . . .

And suddenly Peter reins in his horse, dismounts and points to a spot on the ground.

'You see this?' he says in his thick native accent. 'A dingo has scratched here for water and we will . . . find enough water for us and our horses.'[2]

Dr Beckler is stunned, for he can, frankly, see nothing much about the tiny patch of ground that Peter is pointing to that is any different to the hundreds of thousands of acres they've been traveling through, bar, yes, a few stray scratches in the yellowish soil. He climbs down, and the two men are soon pawing away at the ground, making an indent in the soil, only to find . . . their hands are getting wet! Continuing to dig, they quickly come to several large slabs of rock which they are able to lift and, to their infinite joy, 'we had a little basin before us which quickly filled with water again and again, however often we filled our hats to quench the thirst of our poor animals . . . In less than half an hour we felt as much at home as if we had known the place for years.'[3]

Dr Beckler looks upon Peter with renewed respect.

The next day, on their way back to Trooper Lyons, MacPherson and Belooch, who – all being well – should be camping at the creek awaiting them, the attention of Dr Beckler and Peter is suddenly caught by something or someone, up ahead.

In the light of the setting sun, they can see movement which proves to be . . . hang on . . . *Belooch*, 'with bent body and shuffling gait he was wandering exhausted in little circles'[4]. With the sepoy's very poor grasp of English, and his desperate thirst, it takes some time to work out what has occurred: Belooch, Trooper Lyons and MacPherson had quarrelled as to which was the correct route, and Belooch had been dispatched to investigate. Alas, when he had come back to where Lyons and MacPherson were to wait, they had disappeared and he had been wandering for most of the day looking for them – with no luck – and so is more than usually pleased to see Dr Beckler now. They are soon a trio, thus, who continue south, becoming ever more exhausted and only perk up when they see a fire up ahead just as the twilight of dusk is falling.

Could it be Trooper Lyons and MacPherson?

Coming to a broad creek, they peer into the bush on the other side, when suddenly, almost as if from nowhere, they are surrounded by shouting natives!

'They were no less surprised than we were ourselves,' Dr Beckler records. 'When they recognised one of their own countrymen . . . their interest grew to an excitement which would have worried us had it arisen from different motives. Men, women and children crowded around us in colourful confusion.'[5]

As had happened before, the natives are simply astonished at their white skin, their clothes, their extraordinary animals, and continue talking to them in a language which has as little to do with English as Beckler's German has with Belooch's Hindustani.

'*Balera, Knappa, balera, imba, imba, balera,*'[6] they continue to roar over and over again, while delightedly pointing to the visitors, and then back at themselves.

'The pleasure that they took in us and particularly in Peter seemed endless,' Beckler chronicles. 'One question followed another and their laughing and shouting rang out far into the silent, moonlit night.'[7]

The revelry is such that it is not until past midnight that the white men head off, following three of the tribe, to a spot only a short distance away, where they find Lyons and MacPherson in their own camp. The missing men are pleased to be reunited with Beckler for a second time.

To give gentle indication to their newfound native friends that the time to part has come, as the whitefellas must be on their way with the rising of the sun, Beckler gives them some small gifts of farewell and the delighted blacks soon fade into the night, carrying their booty.

Behind them they leave three exhausted whitefellas, one sepoy and one exhausted blackfella, all relieved to be reunited with each other, if highly irritated that a cloud of mosquitoes appears to have assembled to celebrate the occasion.

But, if Dr Beckler's fascination for the Aborigines has markedly risen in the last 24 hours, it rises still more in the morning after a brief few hours of sleep are snatched. For even before the sun's fiery top has peeked over the lip of the horizon, the blackfellas are back, emerging once more from fading night, full of good cheer, and clearly come to see them off.

'As we still had a large stock of provisions for the few days of our trip to the Darling, we decided to give them everything we could spare. They were overjoyed at this and took pains to show their gratitude in every way.'[8]

As the natives mill around, sometimes letting out cries of delight with their new gifts and showing each other what they have, Dr Beckler suddenly notices that one of his prized tomahawks has gone missing, right by where some of the tribe had been standing!

After a brief discussion with Peter, who in turn talks to the tribe, one of the Aboriginal men quickly, if sheepishly, appears before Becker, proffering the missing tomahawk, 'with words and gestures that looked like apologies'[9].

Beckler is stunned at the humility, the honesty . . . the *humanity*. It is the act of a gracious man with a conscience that Beckler had previously not considered the Aborigines capable of. Just like real people! With fond farewells, the Beckler group and the Aborigines part, when suddenly there are cries from behind. The tribe indicate they wish Peter to return to them for a moment. He does so, and returns a couple of minutes later, bearing a gift.

'He showed us a very pretty waterbag made from the skin of a kangaroo which still retained the shape of the animal. It was sewn very cleanly and carefully and was decidedly the nicest object made by the natives that I had ever seen. There was very little stitching at all on the waterbag, only the severed tail and legs, and an opening, perhaps 4 inches long, made in the stomach. All the hair was retained and the bag held no less than 3 gallons of water . . .'[10]

The sophistication of these people! The generosity!

But really?

The sheer *cleverness*.

Three days later, in the ebbing of the daylight hours of 4 January, Hermann Beckler is relieved to come over a rise and look down to see the unmistakeable dark outline of Lake Pamamaroo lying below.

Turning behind, smiling, he expects to see equal relief in the expressions of Trooper Lyons and MacPherson, only to see instead the 'strain of the last two days'[11], on their stained, gaunt faces. These men are completely spent, all of their vitality sapped by 'their weakness and the agony of riding'[12]. (Beneath them, the camels are clearly the same, stumbling along in their own shattered exhaustion. Their naturally inscrutable expressions are, for once, highly scrutable – they are, all at once, unhappy, totally buggered, and desperate to bite any man who dares come within range.) Of the whole party, however, Belooch, is clearly the worst, fading fast and obviously 'very ill'.[13]

Despite that collective exhaustion – in fact, because of it – Beckler decides to get going once more, tonight, to get to the sustenance and rest that the Pamamaroo Camp offers as soon as possible, rather than sleeping rough, one more time. And so, carefully, the small party descend 'the familiar sand-hills',[14] arriving at the rear party's camp in the silent watch of the night. The camels stumble to their knees, the men tumble to their bed, just barely pausing long enough to get the loads off the camels' backs. Within minutes, all are asleep.

Early January '61, Gipps Land, enter the tall, dark stranger

There are, of course, many interested readers devouring the news that Mr Burke had split his party up at Menindee, but few are more interested than one Alfred Howitt, a tall English bushman who for the last several months has been leading a prospecting party in the wilds of Gipps Land, up near the source of the majestic Mitchell River, looking for gold and following events as closely as he can, when, on occasion, stray newspapers have come his way. For months, he has been reading of the problems the Burke Expedition has been having – the cumbersome loads they are carrying, the dismissals, the resignations, the huge fallout with the departures of Charles Ferguson and Mr Landells, the slow rate of advance.

But this news? The fact that Mr Burke has split his party up at Menindee, 'leaving the greater part of his equipment there and pushing northwards himself with a small party and a slight outfit . . .'[15]

It truly astonishes him.

'I felt a strong foreboding of future misfortune for Burke and his companions,'[16] he would recount. It is one thing to split a party, but quite another to split the forward party from their bulk of supplies, with no certain method of connecting with them again – particularly when even your supply party has an uncertain grip on its position.

Indeed, so concerned is Howitt that, talking with his men about it around the campfire that night, the explorer is frank in his assessment.

'I feel that Burke has no idea of what is before him in Central Australia.'[17]

The others agree and, only half-joking, Howitt follows up, 'Who knows that they may not lose themselves? If so, then I might have to go and look for them.'[18]

Two of his long-time companions, Alexander Aitkin and Weston Phillips, not only agree, but add, 'If you go, take us with you.'[19]

Howitt, a man in the image of the expedition he leads – pared to the bone – nods. If it comes to it they will be the first two he will pick. And maybe the only two at that. Howitt does not believe in large expeditions.

5 January '61, Kings Creek, building a better fish trap

For the most part, on this white man's journey from Menindee to the north, the blacks have been essentially distant, scattered figures, if that. They have flitted in the distance, 'over there', and when they have occasionally approached it has nearly always been in the manner of intruder, pressing themselves into the white man's world.

But this is different.

Three weeks since Burke and Wills with their two companions had headed off on their own, crossing deserts, plains and ranges, they have now, just south of where Wills knows the Tropic of Capricorn lies, come upon 'a creek with a long broad shallow waterhole', with such clear signs of heavy Aboriginal occupation that, for the first time, in as small and vulnerable number as they are, it is hard to escape the impression that they are intruders in the black man's world.

'The well-worn paths, the recent tracks of Natives,' Wills notes, 'and the heaps of shells, on the contents of which the latter had feasted, showed at once that this creek must be connected with some creek of considerable importance.'[20]

Stopping for the day, so as to give the camels and horses both rest and the chance to graze, they are on their way once more the following morning when they see it – an extraordinarily sophisticated set-up for catching fish.

'It consisted,' Wills would describe, 'of a small oval mud paddock about 12 feet by 8 feet, the sides of which were about 9 inches above the bottom of the hole, and the top of the fence covered with long grass, so arranged that the ends of the blades overhung scantily by several inches the sides of the hole.'[21]

The sheer ingenuity of it!

Not for the first time, and certainly not for the last, William Wills must re-examine his previous 'low opinion of their intellectual powers'[22].

They push, push, push ever harder now as time presses, mud sucks, sands burn, creeks dry, animals stumble and the four of them get, with the slower progress, progressively more exhausted.

'I am satisfied,' Burke is prompted to make a diary entry, 'that the frame of man never was more severely taxed.'[23]

By the second week of January they are in country so dry their only way of continuing is to draw heavily on the water they are carrying with them, and the going is tough. And now, suddenly, Mr Wills sees it: 'Sheets of water'[24]. It laps, too, within just a few yards!

The famed inland sea, at last?

No. A mirage, 'sufficiently smooth and glassy to be used for an artificial horizon . . .'[25]

And yet, though the water is not real, the terrain suddenly improves as if it, too, has been fooled into growing greener because of it. As they cross the Tropic of Capricorn now, there is no doubt about it: 'The country improved at every step. Flocks of pigeons rose and flew off to the eastward, and fresh plants met our view on every rise; everything green and luxuriant. The horse licked his lips, and tried all he could to break his nose-string in order to get at the food. We camped at the foot of a sandy rise, where there was a large stony pan with plenty of water, and where the feed was equal in quality and superior as to variety to any that I have seen in Australia . . .'[26]

As they press forth, soon enough they are walking beside actual flowing water, a great waterway that Burke names – if he does say so himself – the Burke River.

White gum trees remain unbowed at their all-conquering passage, though the 'cicadariae', as Wills effortlessly summons the plural, roar their acclaim. In the distance, kangaroos bounce along in excitement at their very appearance. Even grass grows greener than any of them had even thought possible.

Early January '61, Pamamaroo Camp, the return of the scorpion

Dr Beckler *ist Verblüfft*, is flabbergasted.

Looking up this morning at Pamamaroo Camp, he can see a familiar figure limping wide-legged towards them – the mark of a man who has ridden hard on a horse for many days – and the straight dark eyebrows of the German medico shoot upwards, forming a high arch, before narrowing, as his brow furrows with contempt.

It had been his fervent hope, and belief, that the 'insolent, malicious lad'[27] who has caused him 'many unpleasant hours . . .'[28] would succumb to the temptations of Melbourne once arrived there, turn his back on his responsibilities, and remain there permanently. But . . . *nein*. William Hodgkinson has returned, filled with stories of how he had 'done the journey of a thousand miles in eleven days at a total cost of 3s. 6d'[29].

Yes, true, he tells everyone. For no one would charge him anything!

'Even the ferrymen refused the usual toll.'[30]

For all his wonder at his own journey, however, Hodgkinson cannot quite believe how far away his next trip appears to be. For after nearly four weeks, he finds everything . . . exactly as he had left it. There is no flurry of activity, no carefully packed stores, weighed and ready to be loaded on the camel's back, not the slightest sense that they have been waiting his return so at last they can get going – as he had assured the Committee there would be.

Mr Wright himself barely blinks, but for the flies that swarm his face constantly, and makes no recorded comment when Hodgkinson finally hands over a dispatch from the Exploration Committee, the very authorisation he claims to have been waiting for, the last 10 weeks, formally confirming his position as third officer. Slowly, Wright's eyes scan the letter, taking in what he can, word by word. His position is confirmed, he understands, and he does have the requisite money. It is something.

The next morning, as the tidings trickle through camp that the Committee has authorised Mr Wright to spend up to £400 resupplying his party – far more than the £250 he had asked for – his men dribble into their best version of 'action'. Yes, it is as hot as a drover's damper fresh off the coals, and they are exhausted before they start, but it's time to actually move once more.

One way or another, good horses must be procured and secured (the Committee stipulating 'not more than ten'[31]) as well as packsaddles, riding saddles and other accessories for the animals, together with provisions for the men, including sheep ('say 150'[32], the Committee suggests from 500 miles away).

Now, with the advice from Dr Beckler that there is 'hardly one dependable watering place on the first stretch from Menindee to Torowoto (200 miles)'[33], Wright orders that Beckler himself will go ahead some 60 miles, with one of the expedition's new recruits, John Smith, a half-caste – born to an Aboriginal mother and a European father – and drop off a supply of water.

Still, as it is apparent to Wright that MacPherson remains too ill to make another foray into the interior, he asks a noted local bushman with 'many years of dealing with the natives on the Darling'[34], Mr Charles Stone, to join them. It is true that Stone has not long ago received treatment for syphilis – but the fact he fails to raise this with his new leader means it is not an issue, for the moment. Right now, Stone, resisting the urge to scratch the pustules around his groin, professes himself not only up for the challenge, but maintains he actually prefers 'a service of real hardship and danger' to any 'quiet life you are compelled to lead sometimes'[35].

Most importantly, Stone speaks a little of the language of the Darling natives. His inclusion brings the party's number up to eight and, to sustain them in the wilderness, beyond the month Wright estimates it will take them just to get to Cooper's Creek, Wright acquires supplies for six months – meaning they will have plenty for the Gulf party, when they return. All up, the camp turns from its torpor and creaks to tired life, wearily organising, packing and weighing their loads.

By mid-January, Wright has completed his purchase of 10 new horses, most of them from the Menindee publican, Thomas Paine. All that remains is to break the horses in – which should take a week or so – and Mr Wright's supply party can be on their way, only three months later than Mr Burke had envisioned.

•

Clearly, the desert is now far behind the Gulf party and, as Wills confirms, they are now well into the tropics, with the Tropic of Capricorn already some 100 miles behind them.

And yet, in this second week of January, as they continue to place boot-prints where none have ever gone before, their wary eyes begin to see the opposite of a glassy flat horizon emerge. For now, almost like a distant wave of land that comes ever closer and threatens to break over them, they soon cannot help but note they are slowly approaching high ranges . . . After wading the deep creek that lies at the base – 'Patten's Creek', they call it after the expedition's blacksmith they've left back at the Depot – their long, but initially gentle climb up the wave of land begins.

Early in the afternoon of 11 January, as they continue along in 'fine well-watered country'[36], a shadow begins to fall over them. Looking up, Wills notices the suddenly 'reduced temperature and peculiarly gloomy appearance of the sky'[37]. A shadow, perhaps thrown by the range?

No.

In fact, it is from the eclipse of the sun!

Yes, only three weeks earlier Wills had been so immersed in matters of the heavens, he had been impatiently waiting the eclipse of the first moon of Jupiter, but now, he has been near blindsided by this much more significant event.

A single glance skywards confirms it, as the moon continues to move across the face of the sun, even as they move across the face of the earth. The moon is faster, taking just three hours in total, but it does what it can for them: cooling the air well away from the typically unbearable midday heat, allowing them to move faster and more easily, and lifting their spirits, just as the country itself does.

'The country traversed has the most verdant and cheerful aspect,' writes Wills, 'there is an "abundance of feed and water everywhere" ...'[38]

Over the next few days they are into the wave proper, first traversing a 'series of slatey, low, sandstone ranges'[39] that mark the ramparts of the intimidating 'Selwyn Range'. Red cliffs tower over them, jagged peaks magisterially refuse to even blink as these minuscule white ants try to find a way through, around, across the slopes of these endless miles of towering mountains, criss-crossed by deep valleys – with, yes, lots of actual ants' nests, bigger than men – and gargantuan gorges. Even here, however, well beyond the ants, life bursts forth, with extraordinary birdlife – countless flocks of pigeons, parrots, cockatoos and brolgas career, careen and cruise effortlessly above them, often cackling in laughter or cawing in derision at their feeble efforts – all attesting to the fecundity of the area, despite its severity for those seeking to cross it.

John King, for one, is impressed, recounting how 'extensive amphitheatres were richly carpeted with succulent grasses, while the hills which enclosed them were lightly timbered with the mallee scrub, as likewise with the native orange tree'[40].

The further they go, however, the more impenetrable the ranges become, and the slower their progress. Perhaps, if they can get to one of the high peaks they can see a way through?

'Messrs Burke and Wills,' King records of 14 January, 'ascended one of the neighbouring mountains, but could see nothing but a succession of ranges stretching from east to west.'[41] And yet, one geographical feature does rather take the fancy of William Wills – twin hills in yonder ranges, standing as silent sentinels before a striking isolated rock pillar. Just for fun, he decides to give the two hills a single name: Mount Birnie. For of course, dear Richard Birnie will enjoy the joke. A geographical oddity, a one-off on two hills, a paradox, an enigma, and maybe too, a kind of tribute to their deepest of all friendships, two men united, two who are one.

But now, back to it. For while it is one thing to see peaks and mountains, to name them, far more important is to be able to identify the path forwards.

All they can do is continue to try to push through the best they can, the situation sometimes so perilous that even Burke himself feels obliged to make a rare journal entry on 18 January: 'Still on the ranges. The camels sweating profusely from fear.'[42]

At least some sign that they might be nearing the end comes the following day when, crossing a creek, they are suddenly confronted by the image of a black man in a tree with his young son 'cutting out something; and a lubra with a piccaninny'[43].

So absorbed are the blacks that Wills is able to get right up close to them before they become aware . . . at which point 'they were dreadfully frightened; jumping down from the trees, they started off, shouting what sounded to us very like "Joe, Joe"'[44]. The whole family of them are soon running away, over the stones and porcupine grass.

Burke notes:

January 20th
I determined today to go straight at the ranges, and so far the experiment has succeeded well.[45]

Soon after, they see another sign that they are nearly out the other side – clear plains ahead . . . just before they see what is the most frightening part of their trip to date. For they have emerged onto a platform of rock, which is like the last step at the bottom of a large set of stairs. They look down upon what King will describe as 'a precipitous descent of 400 feet, so rugged and abrupt that it made us pause and for a moment recoil from the attempt to clamber down . . .'[46]

'Do you think the camels can do it?'[47] Mr Burke asks John King.

King replies in the manner of a man who knows there is really only one answer – *they'll have to* – but there is a much better, and less presumptuous way of saying that to his leader.

'Yes,'[48] says he, simply.

And now, as good as his word, hauling on the lead of the first camel, he takes them down. They stall, they stagger, they stutter, they stress . . . but they keep moving. Gravity trumps reluctance, and nature does the rest – for all their ungainliness, their sheer awkwardness, it is amazing how sure-footed the camels are with the padded balls of their feet, in stepping over and around the worst obstacles and within 15 minutes the whole lot of them are at the bottom, with an astounded King, Gray and Messrs Burke and Wills! (Amazingly, the only one bruised by the experience is Billy the horse, who had hated every moment of it, just as he seemed to have hit every outcrop of rock on the way down, as his hoofs had inevitably slipped.)

For the first time, and with seemingly no sense of irony, Mr Burke says the only positive words ever recorded against his name about the camels:

'This,' he says sagely, 'is another illustration of their great value.'[49]

Yes, Mr Burke.

He names their route 'The Camel's Path' in their honour and, though the camels are 'bleeding, sweating and groaning'[50], he is pleased that they quickly come to a generous creek which bubbles with a crystal clear water, 'which seemed to relieve them very much'[51].

This creek soon gives way to another grander one.

What to call the grand one?

Well, one of the privileges of the whole expedition into uncharted territory is to name for perpetuity every significant feature they see. In this case, Burke decides to call it after his distant relative in Ireland, Edward Lawless, 3rd Baron of Cloncurry, and that evening, in his journal, as ever, Wills takes his lunars, works out their exact position, draws the ranges and the creek, and writes on the map the name of the creek: Cloncurry. (Such are the times. The minor British aristocrat may leave his mark on little in his life, but the fact that he married Burke's favourite cousin will see his name endure on a part of the planet he has never conceived of, let alone set foot upon.)

•

The tranquil routine of the men at Cooper's Creek Depot is broken this morning. William Patten, astride one of the horses on routine exercise, is surprised when the beast suddenly turns into a bucking brumby that sends him flying. Patten cries out, and goes down *heavily*, badly hurt. Bravely, however, the stoic man gets up, and does his best to carry on ... before being obliged to take to his swag, under the shade of the coolabah trees at the Depot, for he simply cannot stand.

Mr Brahe is not alarmed, but he is reminded how fragile their strength truly is, how quickly things can turn. He keeps his cool, they man the stockade and wait.

26 January '61, Pamamaroo Camp, by the Wright, slow march

It is nigh on 100 days to the day since Burke had asked Wright to get the men moving north, and, at last, they are finally ready. They are a disparate, oft desperate, party of diverse backgrounds. There is Wright, a station manager; Hodgkinson, a journalist; Dr Beckler, medico and botanical expert; Becker, an artist and geologist; Charles Stone, a syphilitic bushman; William Purcell, a cook; Belooch, the sepoy; and John Smith, the 'Australian native half-caste'[52].

All up, it is far from sure if their combined skills will allow them to overcome the obstacles that await, but at least, at last, they are on the point of moving. That is if, on this morning of departure, they can work out just how to squeeze the 'quantity of large articles' that 'still lay around in colourful disorder'[53] into the packs in racks on the backs of these highly reluctant animals. All they can do in the end is to stuff stuff in the best they can, where they can, tying bits down awkwardly using 'makeshift packsaddles'[54], and hope the best that the lashings will last. Some of the things that don't fit anywhere are put on the backs of the horses instead.

Finally, it is done, and it is time for the first of them to leave. It is a staggered and staggering start. Dr Beckler is sent off first, at 11 am, in charge of all 10 camels, headed for a camp on the other side of the lake from which Pamamaroo Creek runs. Next away, at one o'clock, is Smith accompanied by the native lad, Dick, with four of the newly purchased and notably unruly horses – who are not yet quite broken in, and are certainly unhappy about the weight they carry. They are followed at 2 pm by William Hodgkinson and Charles Stone with five horses, and an hour later again by the artist, Ludwig Becker, and Wright himself with the remaining four horses.

And what a time they have of it!

Not long into the journey the horses' loads start to slip from their harnesses, throwing them off balance and into a fit of frustration. With 'nearly every horse throwing off his load'[55], as Wright would recount, most of the afternoon is a stop-start pack-again affair and by the time camp is made that night, they have covered only five miles. Two horses have broken loose with their packs still on their backs – they will have to be searched for on the morrow. For his part, despite the warning from Dr Beckler, Wright is in no small way amazed. When he had come this way in late October with Burke the waterholes had been full, the creeks running, and the pastures so plentiful the animals fattened on the way and the sun had shone benignly on their general well-being.

Not this time.

Now the sun does not shine, it *beats*. The waterholes, such as there are, tend more to the way of sludgy puddles than delicious depths, and the creeks are as dry as Dead Man's Gulch.

To add to Mr Wright's concerns about the heat, some of their animals have wandered so far it takes a full two days to gather them in, with Dick being instrumental in tracking and bringing back the . . . *deserters*.

Which gives Dick an idea.

27 January '61, Camp 106, 170 miles from the Gulf, fly by night

Messrs Burke and Wills and their two companions are also struggling in this notably blazing Australian summer. The weather in previous days has been a frenzied and ferocious furnace – hot and humid with an intensity that none of them had imagined possible. The only way to proceed, Mr Burke has decided, is to do half their travelling at night, at least when the moon is high, as it is now. They started at five minutes past two this morning, and after following the bends of the creek in the moonlight, as it proceeded in a fortuitously north-easterly direction, have been following it ever since. And they are, mind, not by the creek, but *in* it, for there is no flow to speak of, and just a few miserable puddles here and there. The steep earth banks are good evidence of just how hard it must roar when there is rain, but, as Wills notes in his diary, 'there is no appearance of the creek having flowed in this part of the channel for a considerable period'[56].

28 January '61, Menindee, desertion and desperation

On the third day, most of the Wright party are *still* at Pamamaroo Lake, having now made a grand total of six miles since departure. Like Burke, Wright decides that if they are to improve their pace, and actually make some miles, they too must travel at night to escape the heat – starting tonight – but they will have to do so less one valuable man.

'After breakfast,' Wright records in his journal, 'Dick, the native, who had shown on several occasions a disposition to slip away, borrowed a clean shirt and then bolted. His unwillingness to accompany the party arose from his fear of the natives, and was to be regretted, as his absence deprived us of our only interpreter . . .'[57]

Does Dick need to head out once more with the mad whitefellas, to face possibly madder blackfellas? He does not. And he will not.

Wherever Dick is, the one thing they know is that he is *hot*, for they certainly are, and getting hotter all the time, as the thermometer gets to 104 degrees Fahrenheit in the shade at just 10 am. After resting through the day thus, and starting to pack in the early evening, at 9 pm they are on their way once more, the men on horseback taking the lead, followed by those leading the camels.

At last, at 7 am on 29 January '61, after walking through the night – all of them as parched as dry bones – Wright calls a halt 'at the base of a rocky range, 25 miles NW of the Darling' – it is the Scropes Range – where they find 'a large cave adorned with native drawings', which gives them 'an acceptable shelter from the scorching heat'[58].

It is, in fact, so hot that when Dr Beckler arrives two hours later, to go straight to the spot where, a week earlier, he and Smith had secreted two huge leather waterbags it is to find with shock the bags nearly empty . . .

Desperate now, the men fan out, knowing that as the natives clearly come here often there must be a water supply close by, somewhere, and so they start to 'dig under the rocks surrounding the natural reservoir'[59]. Sure enough, just a stone's throw from the mouth of the cave, Hodgkinson and Smith strike liquid gold as 'water commenced to percolate through the sand, and ultimately several buckets of a rather nauseous though desirable fluid were obtained'[60].

No matter, they gulp it down like dogs maddened by thirst, and glory as it washes down their dry throats. All but instantly it works its way into their thirsty flesh and muscles, and revitalises them to the point they can soon start ferrying buckets of it over to the horses and camels, who are equally uncaring about its murky nature, caring only that it *is* water. As bucket after bucket is taken, the well continues to fill 'with water quickly and repeatedly,'[61] until it just as suddenly disappears 'all at once with a gurgling sound before our eyes, never to appear again'[62].

They are bereft, and one look at the horses says they might soon be bereaved. Each of the nags – who generally drink at least 10 gallons a day – had only had a six-gallon bucket when the water had run out, and the camels just half that. As the sun continues to beat down, the horses, particularly, are in pain, staying stubbornly huddled around the dried-up well, and continually snorting and sniffing at the barren sand, hoping, fruitlessly, to find it wet, and 'refusing to feed until near sunset'[63].

No matter that the horses are hobbled, after the men spend a restless night, at dawn the next day, they wake to find NO bloody horses. With no water here, the equines have gone in search of it elsewhere, and this time there is no Dick to fetch them. All up, it will take the entire day and the whole party to gather the horses in once more, to start out for Bilpa, pushing themselves, as to stay here will be to die of thirst.

30 January '61, Camp 108, Golah won't go

Pushing north along a dry creek bed, flanked by steep banks with date trees growing on the banks, at least the Gulf party has some shade. But they now have a serious problem. Every now and then they come to waterholes too deep for the camels to get through, requiring them to climb up the banks. But in these parts the sides are so soft, steep and sandy it is completely exhausting even for the strongest of the camels.

Soon enough, one of the most troublesome of their camels, Golah, has had *enough* and now refuses to move. Despite encouragement – ranging from kind words to harsh words to a severe thrashing with the whip – Golah will not be moved. The only hope is to find an easier bank for Golah to climb and so, while the others clamber out of the creek bed and follow along the grassy plains next to the Cloncurry, King walks the camel along the creek bed. It is difficult to keep contact as the banks are lined with box trees, sometimes extending out onto the plains for several hundred metres.

Only a few miles on, Wills appears on the bank above King, telling him to stop. *Come now*, Wills insists. There are blacks in the trees up ahead, watching them, likely ready to attack. *Come, quickly!* King now has no choice. Poor Golah must be abandoned and left to his fate . . .

31 January '61, Bilpa, ships of the desert run aground

With no little difficulty, Dr Beckler made Bilpa the previous day, and though grateful to find the water cache intact, declines to let the camels drink their fill on the grounds that when the horses arrive they will be in far greater need.

Das ist korrekt, Herr Doktor.

A couple of hours after dawn, Wright arrives with the horses and they are indeed as thirsty as shipwrecked sailors.

The horses are given two gallons each, which they gulp down in seconds, their massive tongues swirling around the bottom of the bucket to get the last drops. It is far from enough to sate their thirst, but it is enough to keep them going for a bit, and the party starts out behind Beckler, 'travelling over 18 miles of uninteresting and arid sand-hills'[64].

Alas, once arrived at their next cache of waterbags, far from finding the copious water they had hoped for, there is in fact 'just enough to make some tea'[65]. As Beckler would sorrowfully recall, 'despite its being carefully hidden and thickly covered over, most of it had evaporated'[66].

Wright's shoulders slump. In six days since leaving Pamamaroo Camp they have managed to make only 56 miles and, while the camels and men have managed to cope, the poor bloody horses are growing mad and unruly from their lack of fluid. Clearly in severe abdominal pain, they are unable to empty their bowels, have no energy and want to do nothing more than roll around on the ground. Gazing upon them, Dr Beckler is shocked how *quickly* these animals deteriorate, just for want of water, even for a short time! Their once shiny coats are dull, their one-time rounded forms are now hollow, their eyes 'lustreless in their sunken sockets', and they barely have the strength to keep their heads off the ground. At the other end, 'the anuses of the poor animals lay deep between the surrounding soft parts and stood wide open. Through the opening one could see into a much larger, dark cavity whose mucous membranes were completely dried out and resembled dark red velvet.'[67]

That night, the men must keep an eye on the horses, lest they stray, and Beckler continues to observe the stricken beasts closely: 'They were not quiet for a moment ... Each time they passed our fireplace they searched anxiously for water in every bucket and every pot. From there they turned to the still-glowing coals. Hoping to find something drinkable they pushed their lips into the embers and scorched them. Some had become so crazed that they slowly and thoughtfully tested the glowing coals, but despite our watchfulness we could not stop them burning their lips again and again.'[68]

Still, most stunning to him is just how different, how furnace-hot *dry* everything is, compared to how it had been when he had first ventured to these parts only a few short weeks earlier.

'I still remember this scene as the saddest of our journey; a water-less land and a quiet, cloudless night in a region where all native life seemed to have died out.'[69]

Wright, whatever else, really is experienced with horses, and knows that it requires urgent action, or the horses will perish. As the nearest known water is 20 miles to the north in the Mutawintji Range, Hodgkinson and Belooch are quickly dispatched with all 10 camels and five pairs of waterbags.

'At 1 a.m.,' Wright would recount, 'they reached the Mutawintji Range, tied up the camels, and worked all night at filling the bags from a small rocky basin situated in a gloomy ravine.'[70]

But will they make it back in time to save the horses at camp? The following morning, after just one look at his bellicose beasts, Wright doubts it and, leaving their packs and saddles behind, starts to drive the animals towards the Mutawintji Range, in the hope of intercepting Hodgkinson and the water on the way back.

'To my great satisfaction,' Wright would recount, 'I met Hodgkinson and Belooch with a supply of water . . . I immediately gave the horses a bucket of water each, which enabled them to go on to Mutawintji, where we arrived in the course of the afternoon, and camped in a valley covered with kangaroo grass, leading to a rocky basin containing an abundance of beautifully clear water.'[71]

The plan is to stop long enough here – at least five days – that the animals can recover enough to go on with strength, and they can recover enough to feel half-human again.

Good God, what a hellish journey! But, whatever they might say about William Wright, he has earned his keep this day.

5 February' 61, Adelaide, tall tale but true

In the dingy little office of the *South Australian Advertiser* on this day, a weather-beaten figure with exhausted eyes is speaking slowly to a reporter who dutifully takes down every word. It is Alexander MacPherson, finally arrived back in civilisation, after a long, slow journey from Menindee to Adelaide on one of Captain Cadell's paddle steamers, *Wakool*.

The story he tells is simply staggering. How three men had left Menindee with seven days of supplies, only to wander through the wilderness, in fruitless search for the Burke party – having any number of extraordinary interactions with the blacks along the way – and had been out there for 47 days, before they had been rescued.

'Fearfully suffering from want of water, Lyons wanted to cut one horse's throat and drink the blood . . .'[72]

Indeed, so extraordinary is it that the paper adds a note at the end of the interview: 'In case any of our readers should feel incredulous, it is but right that we should state that, from the simple manner in which the story was told to us, we have no doubt whatever respecting the truth of it.'[73]

Beyond the wonder, however, of what has happened to the three men, the news of how severe the conditions are, and that Mr Burke's party has disappeared into the middle of it, is very worrying.

6 February '61, Mutawintji Range, paradise found

It's been a troubling five days for Wright and the supply party, despite remaining anchored to their one water-rich camp in the Mutawintji Range. Indeed, worries continue to beset the party like a slow yet relentless rising tide that starts to inundate them, fight as they may.

If a camel hasn't strayed off, then a horse has suddenly bolted. When Becker and William Purcell go missing on their way from their last stopping point, Dr Beckler and Mr Wright search for them all day in one direction, as does Smith, in another direction, neither group finding any trace. Returning to camp that night, desperate, and convinced Becker and Purcell are lost, the missing men are found, sitting by the fire.

'You can see,' Beckler notes in his diary, 'how small accidents and difficulties mounted up after only a few days.'[74]

At least this respite in the Mutawintji Range – nothing less than an oasis – has done wonders for the beasts and the men. Dr Hermann Beckler cannot quite get over the wonder of the place.

'Nature, so sparing over large areas here, had lavishly thrown a wealth of varying beauty and grace over the Mutawintji Ranges ... On the flat floor of the valley the scene was so peaceful and inviting that one thinks of oneself as surrounded by cultivated lands and wants to look for the homes of civilised people. This was Mutawintji ... I do not hesitate to call Mutawintji a small paradise ... [At] the second gorge from the south, the most magnificent of them all and the one which held the largest and loveliest reservoir ... the traveller is overcome with a sense of reverent awe.'[75]

None thrive more than the camels, now standing 'chest-deep in the best feed wherever the gravelly bed of the creeks entered the valley. There was also plenty of grass available so that the horses were equally well provided for.'[76]

The primary relief though is for the men themselves.

If only they could stay here? But no, after so long waiting at Menindee, now that they are on the move they must keep going, and Wright tells them they must depart the following morning.

That evening, while others make preparations and pack what can be packed, Beckler and Wright walk to the good doctor's favourite gorge one last time – 'the most magnificent of them all', the one that the local natives call 'Motuanje' and for which the entire range derives its name. The pair slip into the pool. They make their way through a 'narrow crack in the rock, just wide enough to let us pass, into a second, long pool that was enclosed by vertical, overhanging rocks which almost touched. Between the rock-faces a blue strip of the firmament peered through . . .'[77]

Life here, abounds, buzzes and flourishes all around . . . from the wasp nests that hang precariously from the overhead rock faces, to black leeches and frogs and tadpoles that inhabit the pools themselves, to the colourful and flashy water-beetles and dragonflies that dash and glide over the water's surface. Getting out of the pool, thankful for what will surely be their last bath in a while, they head back to their camp, which is in the usual slovenly disarray, borne of carrying too much and widely varied equipment, not to mention having a leader who is not inclined to act as a strict disciplinarian to demand better order.

By the morning of 7 February, they are at last ready and start off at the break of day.

7 February '61, 60 miles south of the Gulf, promise fulfilled

And now for the Gulf party, the threat of native attack might have gone but the threat of dangerous delay is omnipresent. The country is starting to level out, blacken and suck at their feet as they walk. Thick green growth abounds all around, led by lines of trees that stand silent, spectacular sentinels to the rivers and their tributaries which in this, the wet season, have overflowed, forming boggy swamps that have all but obliterated the usual native paths, which mark where the most solid ground is usually found. Late in the morning, Mr Wills gazes to the horizons in every direction, looks at his maps, and pronounces with some portentousness, 'We are now in the explored country; and so far as I can calculate, upon the "Plains of Promise".'[78]

As Mr Burke knows, Wills is referring to the brief excursion made by Captain John Stokes of HMS *Beagle*, back in 1841. From the Gulf of Carpentaria he sailed 50 miles up the Albert River, then took to walking. He had named this flat, rich, wet country between the Albert and Flinders rivers the 'Plains of Promise' as they were well wooded, flat and he thought they had enormous agricultural potential. Both Ludwig Leichhardt and Augustus Gregory had walked on the Plains of Promise thereafter – both, sensibly, in the dry season – and Burke had read both their accounts.

And from the point of view of the Committee's original instructions, it is significant, as they have now conquered that tract of unexplored land between Gregory's, Leichhardt's and Sturt's previous explorations.

From here, they can walk along the eastern bank of the waterway they are on, which will hopefully lead them all the way up to the Gulf. Which sounds easy enough, but still there is much to worry about. They have supplies for a three-month journey. And here they are, one month and 22 days into it, still some 50 miles from the Gulf, the halfway point. Both men and supplies can only be stretched so far.

If they turn back now – and there is a strong argument that they should – then in no way could their mission be deemed a failure. Their part in filling the 'ghastly blank' on the map is accomplished!

And yet, Mr Burke never even considers it.

'I will not turn my face backwards,' he says to King with some force, 'until I have reached the sea.'[79]

In truth? Mr Burke might be a little bit mad. But rational explorers had never come this far before. Sure, it *is* a gamble, but Mr Burke has always been a gambling man. The further they go, the more lush the country becomes, and never lusher than when, for several miles, the plains are covered with 'a species of wild vine, bearing a red berry, having an acrid and nauseous flavour'[80]. They are still trying to follow the river at this point, but it becomes ever harder as gullies criss-cross it, other creeks join it, and large masses of rock block their passage beside it. The only way forward is to move further out into the plains and try to keep steering broadly north.

By the next day, they are still going and the landscape changes again, and 'herds of kangaroos were disporting on magnificent plains, heavily timbered in places with box'[81]. Again, the timber slows them down somewhat – on this trip everything seems to do that – but by the following day they are hopeful that, perhaps, just perhaps, even through now heavy rain, they might see the sea!

On the evening of 9 February, as they make their way back to the creek, they are elated to find not only does it clearly ebb and flow with the tide, but the water is quite salty!

They are close, very close.

And yet now, after having struggled so hard to get to within coo-ee of the Gulf, the four men come to the hardest country of all. After the heavy rain, the black soil plains they are travelling over are so sticky, so energy-draining, that time and again the heavy camels sink into the mud up to their knobbly knees and have to be laboriously dug out again. The groaning is terrible, and the camels are little better . . .

With every step, their boots sink so easily into the ground, the bog lets out a satisfied, muddy burp . . . followed by a rather more strangled gurgle as you, with great difficulty, pull it out again. It is exhausting, it is debilitating and many times men and beasts lose balance.

Soon enough it is obvious that they simply cannot go on like this, and must come up with a different way. With a heavy heart, Burke decides they must split the group up again – for the fourth time. Yes, that is the way. Gray and King can remain here at Camp 119, with the supplies, camels and horses – and Mr Burke and Mr Wills will push for the Gulf alone, on foot, albeit with Billy the horse to carry provisions enough for three days.

According to Wills's calculations, they are within roughly a day's walk of the Gulf.

They set off after breakfast on 10 February, with the good wishes of Gray and King ringing in their ears, and yet are in trouble within minutes. When they attempt to cross Billy's Creek, just a few hundred yards after leaving, Billy himself – for which the watercourse is of course named – gets so deeply bogged in a quicksand bank that he is all flank, no legs. It takes every ounce of strength they have to extricate him – *neigh, neigh*, nay, nay – digging all the mud out from under him so that he is able to fall back in the creek. They continue on the best they can, but all are exhausted and they have barely begun.

'A great deal of the land,' Wills records, 'was so soft and rotten that the horse, with only a saddle and about 25 pounds on his back, could scarcely walk over it.'[82]

When, just five miles later, Billy again gets badly bogged while crossing a creek, the serious question becomes who will drop first: them or the horse? In the end, the only way is to get away from the river again, and try their luck heading north.

Now, at least, the land is firmer, with sandstone rock bursting through the alluvial soil.

And yet, as ever on this trip, travelling across this extraordinarily diverse land, they have not proceeded far before the landscape changes again – a curious patchwork of gravelly soil on which box trees and swamp gums grow, and a kind of boggy swamp that they must wade through with great difficulty, often up to their knees.

'After floundering through this for several miles,' Wills would recount, 'we came to a path formed by the blacks, and there were distinct signs of a recent migration in a southerly direction. By making use of this path we got on much better, for the ground was well trodden and hard.'[83]

Entering a forest, still following the path of the blacks, they come to what must have been a recent camp made by the natives, for right by the ashes of their recent fires, they find the signs of recent yam diggings. The blacks have clearly only eaten the juiciest of these edible roots, which taste remarkably like sweet potatoes, while leaving the poorer specimens lying on the ground.

'We,' Wills notes, 'were not so particular but ate many of those that they had rejected, and found them very good.'[84]

Slowly, surely, they keep moving to the north and . . .

Just there!

Through the trees, Burke, as ever in the lead, can see a native lying by his typically spare campfire, 'whilst his gin and piccaninny were yabbering alongside'[85].

It is nothing for the explorers to be concerned about, but still Burke follows regular practice. He stops so they can retrieve their pistols from Billy's load, with the intention to then slowly but noisily approach so the natives might see them from a distance, and not be frightened into doing anything rash. (Like hurling a spear.)

In fact, only a short time after they have their pistols in hand, the native stands up, stretches, and looks blankly in their direction . . . before realising that he and his family are not alone.

Still, the native's movements are not sudden. He simply makes a silent signal and the family all drop to their 'haunches, and shuffled off in the quietest manner possible'.[86]

Now moving forward, Burke and Wills discover the family's habitation, just back from the fire, 'a fine hut, the best I have ever seen, built on the same principle as those at Cooper's Creek, but much larger and more complete: I should say a dozen blacks might comfortably coil in it together'[87].

The sophistication of the structure, the obviously advanced skill that has gone into making it, adds to the explorers' growing respect for these people they had previously thought of as tragically primitive.

From having eaten their leftover meal just a few hours before, and been grateful for it, they now look covetously at this delightful abode.

Situated right on the edge of the forest, on firm ground, it looks out over an enormous marsh, over which 'hundreds of wild geese, plover and pelicans, were enjoying themselves in the watercourses'[88].

Beside the hut is a stream of fresh water!

What more could any family want, ever, than what is right here, right now, almost an Antipodean Garden of Eden?

'The neighbourhood of this encampment,' Wills notes, 'is one of the prettiest we have seen during the journey.'[89]

It is with some regret that they must be on their way again, nudging across the marsh – finding the water remains brackish, a sure sign that the sea is close.

Coming to a deep channel, through which seawater clearly courses when the tide is in, the way across is not obvious and they are unsure how to proceed until three natives appear, fine black men, 'who, as is universally their custom, pointed out to us, unasked, the best part down. This assisted us greatly, for the ground we were taking was very boggy.'[90]

•

In the absence of Mr Burke and Mr Wills – they have said they will be away for about three days – King and Gray are able to get some precious rest, while also looking after the camels and trying their luck with a little hunting and fishing.

Unfortunately, while they are able to catch just a few fish, all they can get in the way of game is a few crows and hawks. It is slim pickings, and though some birds in the hand are worth two in the bush, the meat provided by both is barely worth the buckshot.

11 February '61, Camp 120, no cairn, no flag, no footprints

Camping for the night, both Burke and Wills have rising excitement that their goal is near at hand. Rising at daybreak, they decide to push ahead to the Gulf alone, leaving Billy 'short hobbled', in such a way that the beast can move around to feed himself, but not wander far. If all goes well, they will be back within the day.

Alas, the further north they push, and they are now well over a dozen miles from where they have left King and Gray, the more difficult it becomes as the ground becomes ever boggier and the mangroves more impenetrable. Possibly the only thing wetter than the terrain is their armpits and crotches as the perspiration simply *pours* out of them, in the oppressive humidity, so thick it almost has weight.

Still, Burke and Wills are close now, oh so desperately close. As they watch intently, it is clear that water covering the salt flats is actually a tide, which rises by the better part of a foot! *Taste* it. It is salty! They can *smell* the sea, they can feel the sea-breeze lightly wafting from the north. The only thing they lack is to be able to actually see the sea, the open ocean, to capture the vision splendid that has kept them going every dusty step across this extraordinarily large continent. If they could, they would now even jog-trot the last few miles. Alas, far from that, their steps now become still more slow and strained, as their feet sink deeper and deeper into the boggy sand of the salt flats. The best they can, they continue to wade forward, knee-deep in the muddy mess, but the further they go, the more difficult it becomes. It is not the mangroves ahead that trap and block them, it is the gravity that sucks them down,[91] helped by a vicious summer sun that keeps relentlessly pounding upon them, wanting them to drop, sapping their spirit, their energy, their will to keep going, as they sweat and strain onwards, mile after mile, hour after hour.

Until ...

Enough.

Mr Burke calls the halt.

This far and no further.

Yes, they wanted to formally reach the Gulf, but these tidal salty mud flats are confirmation enough that the Gulf has reached them.

For both men, it is enough. True, it is not quite the moment that they had envisaged all these months, of actually wading into the ocean in celebration, but they have no choice. The tangle of muddy, stinking mangrove swamps will simply not allow them to get closer. Yes, they are the first men to have crossed the continent, an enormous achievement – after *six months* of dusty tracks, boggy marshes, towering mountain ranges, debilitating deserts and threatening blacks, withstanding heat, cold, wet, drought, sandstorms, howling winds and humidity to kill a brown dog – but after all that, *after all that*, they are denied the chance to engage in what would be a veritable sacrament of baptism, the chance to throw themselves in the waters of the Gulf.

Instead, it's like getting to within a stone's throw of the summit of a mountain, only to find yourself blocked by a cliff-face, and even then it is shrouded in mist so thick you just can't quite see it.

As Burke would note with some regret in his journal: 'It would be well to say that we reached the sea, but we could not obtain a view of the open ocean, although we made every endeavour to do so . . .'[92]

Wills, too, is deeply disappointed, but accepts Burke's judgement that they have no choice but to turn back. Now, correct form in such matters – long established by explorers – is to leave their 'mark', to leave something of relative permanence at the furthest point of their expedition, to prove that they have got there, which is . . .

A problem.

Building a cairn is out of the question, as handy stones with which to form it are absent. And as to 'blazing' the mangrove trees in the classic manner, they cannot do that either, as they have not brought knives or axes with which to do so.

So now there is nothing for it, they must turn for home.

As is typical of him, there is no record of Burke doing anything other than turning on his heel – a bristling Irish man-o'-war who has hit the

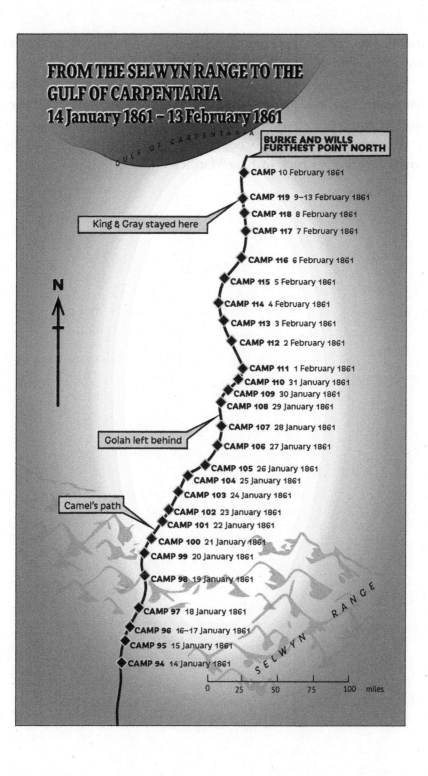

north coast and is now eager to get to the south coast as quickly as possible – with the ever faithful Wills in his powerful wake.

Burke has done what he said he would do – has dreamed of doing, has worked so hard to do – even while overcoming more obstacles than he could have possibly imagined.

And now, first going by Cooper's Creek, some 1000 miles to the south, he must get back to Julia Matthews.

CHAPTER TWELVE

HOMEWARD BOUND

Gray was the best bushman of the party – the strongest and most willing and useful man . . .[1]
Lockhart Morton, Royal Society member and staunch critic of Robert O'Hara Burke, 1 February 1862

Hasty in temper, [Burke's] language was some times scathing, but the unfortunate man who came under his anger had not long to suffer. He quickly forgot anything but a lie; that he never forgave.[2]
Ovens and Murray Advertiser, 9 July 1874

12 February '61, Gulf of Carpentaria, return fare

On this searing hot and sticky afternoon, the two men – having made their way back to the ever faithful, long-suffering Billy – pick their way through the mangrove swamps, crossing the channels, sticking close to their own footprints. They know exactly what an effort it is going to be to return to Melbourne. It has taken them the better part of six months to cover the 2000 miles to get to this point, and there is no doubt the extraordinary journey has weakened them, their party, and their animals.

The once rounded men of bulging muscles are now angular; their bony frames a weak structure on which their tattered and torn, salt-striped clothes sadly hang. Each night now, despite their crushing fatigue, sleep does not come easily over the roar of their aching and overworked muscles, the searing pain of the blisters on their feet, which are themselves little more than traumatised nubs, begging for time to heal. Getting up and about the next morning is not a matter of springing to their feet, so much as creaking upwards, lurching awkwardly, wobbling precariously and waiting for a semblance of normal move- ment to return, as the agony shoots up their calves, bounces off both hips, and careers around their bodies from there, as they waddle from their campsites, often only hitting some semblance of a stride by the late morning. Yes, they remain mentally strong, but there is no doubt they are getting ever more physically weaker, as the meagre rations they take – an inelegant insufficiency – cannot possibly supply them with the nourishment they need to keep going at this pace. The hunger is like a howling beast, yowling for food, insatiable, gulping whatever sustenance is given and then howling some more, *never* satisfied. All they can do is learn to live with this beast and its desperate, angry howl. Ignore it. Keep going. It is only going to get worse, and our only hope is to get to the Depot at Cooper's Creek quickly.

By now, having gone through almost three-quarters of their supplies – notwithstanding the fact that along the way they have been able to live off the land and the kindness of the natives to a certain extent – their need is for haste. Their supplies cannot last, and Burke is well aware that he has told Brahe to stay at Cooper's Creek for just three months – that is just a fortnight from now, and yet they are still at least six weeks away. Burke is convinced, however, that Brahe will not actually leave unless in the case of 'absolute necessity'[3] – and so long as Wright has got his men and supplies forward, there will be no such necessity for Brahe. Fortunately, Burke has no doubt that Wright will already have been there for at least seven weeks.

They slurp and slip and struggle on, through the mangroves whose branches contrive to block them, to hold them back, to claw at them and make them linger longer, though all they want to do is break free of their muddy embrace and push south!

Second week of February, towards Torowoto

This infernal heat! The humidity! Since leaving Pamamaroo Camp, Wright, his seven men, 10 camels and 13 horses have moved just 160 miles, at an average of a dozen miles a day. The problems are myriad, including frequently losing Burke's tracks – as their 'course lay over clay plains, on which Mr Burke's track [marks were] very indistinct, and in some places altogether invisible'[4] – in much the same manner as they frequently lose track of their own camels and horses, which wander off when grazing. Worse still, 'in places where [Burke] had found water there was none when I went out'.[5]

The heat has simply sapped all water and life from the barren earth.

On the approaches to Torowoto Swamp, Wright records in his diary, 'The heat was excessive. The camels were unable to stand in one place more than a few minutes, lifting their feet from the hot sand in quick succession.'[6]

Yes, so hot that even the *camels* – the gift of God for man to travel these very regions – burn their feet. Not even God had planned for such a searing.

Finally, at 5 pm on 12 February, the sun is still high in the sky, effortlessly beaming its hellish inferno down upon the men, when they at last make Torowoto Swamp. The last time Wright had done this journey, with Mr Burke, it'd taken 10 days. This time . . . 18 days. They make camp, on the spot where Mr Burke had established Camp XLV.

Among the natives who greet them are two older women. Dr Hermann Beckler is not impressed and, focusing on their unseemly 'pendulous breasts and . . . unkempt appearance', describes them as 'very ugly'. For what else do you call women like that, 'holding one arm over their breasts to protect them from the flies, while the other was constantly swung to fend away these pests'?[7]

Ludwig Becker has the answer. Transfixed by the way they carry themselves, the natural stateliness in their bearing, his view is that they have 'presented themselves in the attitude of the Venus de Medici'[8], and he soon gets to work sketching them.

Becker and Beckler – countrymen separated by one letter of the alphabet, and an entire world.

12 February '61, below the Gulf, a reunion in the mangroves

At much the same time, almost 1000 miles to the north, King and Gray look up to see the intrepid duo re-entering the camp, *just a little bit later* than expected.

'We have vainly tried to get a glimpse of the sea,' Burke tells the two men rather matter-of-factly, 'but we have accomplished our task for here is the tide. Our rations are running short and it is not worthwhile to incur any further risks for a nominal object when the actual work is achieved.'[9]

On the subject of those rations, it is time for something of a stocktake and, as it is within the province of Charley Gray to oversee their supplies, the one-time sailor reports that as they head for home, they have '83 lbs flour, 3 lbs pork, 35 lbs dried meat, 12 lbs biscuits, 12 lbs rice; and 10 lbs sugar'[10]. The calculus of catastrophe confirms that things are grim. Burke immediately reduces their daily rations by half. And they must do their best along the way to hunt and gather what food they can.

But, as John King would note of their attitude, 'some privation would be endurable, because every step we took would bring us nearer to the bounds of civilization and nearer also to cooler regions than those in which we then were'[11].

On that subject . . .

'Get ready for the return start,'[12] Burke tells them. They must be on their way by early tomorrow morning. Activities now include King blazing a capital B and the Roman numeral CXIX to indicate which camp they have made – on no fewer than 15 trees as proof *positive* they really have made it to the Gulf of Carpentaria.

In the interests of moving as fast as they can on the way back, they also make a 'small plant', burying such things as a 'few camel pads and the camp oven, and a few other small articles, and a . . . considerable quantity of books'[13], together with a note.

This should ease the camels' burden, a little, and after loading them up at first light on this thirteenth day of February, the reunited Gulf party head off in pouring rain, which sometimes sees the camels up to their knees in mud.

No matter. For as King would note, they are buoyed by 'cheerfulness and pride . . . We had fulfilled the work we had undertaken to perform.'[14]

And now they head for home, to reap their rewards. Having left their last camp going north, Camp 119, their next camp heading south shall be 'Camp 1R', with the 'R' standing for 'Return', the camp after that to be 'Camp 2R', and so on. If all goes well, and they can maintain the same speed going south as they did coming north, there will be 54 'R' Camps between them and Mr Brahe waiting at Camp 65, the Depot. Alas, they do not have 54 days of rations left.

Rush, rush, rush, Mr Burke! Push, push, push! Survival and glory depends upon it.

13 February '61, Torowoto Swamp, the shirt off his back

Natives. Coming this way. There are 17 of them, now on the edge of the Wright encampment at Torowoto Swamp. Big men, strong men, gaily attired with a tassel around their loins, but that is not the most arresting thing about their appearance.

'[They were] smeared with fat and paint and had feathers in their hair,' Dr Hermann Beckler would record with no little interest. 'Some had large, reddish dog's tails bound around their heads and over their ears. These gave them a singularly savage appearance . . . Several possessed truly satanic faces . . .'[15]

For Wright, the opportunity is too good to miss. Taking two tomahawks with him, and some broken pieces of biscuits, he hands the items over and tries to make the blacks understand that he would like two of them to act as guides for his party in this unknown country to the north . . . and they appear to agree!

'I selected two, and gave them each a shirt.'[16]

The two men, blessed with shirts, are suddenly the envy of the others, and, more importantly, become instantly co-operative.

To the best of their ability, they try to indicate what the whitefellas will find on their journey to the north – waterholes, ranges, and so forth. 'Our mutual ignorance of each other's language,' Wright would note, 'rendered it impossible to obtain any serviceable information.'[17] But they will manage. He hopes.

In the evening, a surprise, as Wright notes in his own diary: 'They brought their women to the camp, and freely offered them as presents in return for the few things we had given them. Most of the males were circumcised, but the cicatrices in the arms and breasts peculiar to some tribes were not marked in the Torowoto natives.'[18]

The next day is spent getting ready to move north, 'mending saddles, cleaning firearms, and looking over the stores'[19].

As the men move about the campsite, one of them comes upon the hoops of a cask, covered in dirt, surely from the barrel of flour secreted here by Burke back in October. No doubt discovered and devoured by the natives.

Dr Beckler, meanwhile, points out the camel rug under which Lyons and MacPherson had been taking shelter when he had rescued them, presumably still there because the natives thought it too heavy to bother with.

21 February '61, south of the Gulf, rain and reunion

Trudging. Trudging. Trudging along.

A fog of exhaustion.

A slowly changing scene of endless boggy billabongs, melaleuca forests and tussock grass, followed by a muddy mess of more of the same, as they push across the flat, wet, open plains, almost halfway to the Selwyn range and the dreaded Camel's Path.

And though they feel grim, the weather feels grimmer still, storming as it has been for the last 24 hours. In the late afternoon big, billowing black clouds to their south and south-east herald the arrival of yet *more* thunder and lightning. At four o'clock the heavy thunderstorm breaks over them with enormous force.

Sheets of rain!

Buckets of it!

Rain like they have never experienced in their lives. It doesn't merely *fall upon* them, it *sweeps towards* them, a charging wall of water. Within minutes they are sopping and 'the ground [is] so boggy that the animals could scarcely walk over it'[20].

They have no choice but to settle down for the night at Camp 6R – at least the best they can, huddling under a sheet of oilcloth, trying to keep their blanket dry and free of mud during a tropical monsoon – intending to get an early start, and yet the following morning they quickly realise that the ground remains too boggy to continue and it will be better to camp for the day.

'In the afternoon the sky cleared a little,' Wills records, 'and the sun soon dried the ground . . . Shot a pheasant, and much disappointed at finding him all feathers and claws.'[21]

Come evening they are underway once more in the moonlight, only for the thunderstorm to follow them, delivering rain . . . and something more.

'The flashes of lightning,' Wills records, 'were so vivid and incessant as to keep up a continual light for short intervals, overpowering the moonlight . . . the following morning was both sultry and oppressive with the ground so boggy as to be almost impassable.'[22]

But pass they must, the best they can, no matter how long it takes, and no matter how much energy it sucks out of them.

Trudging, trudging, trudging along. Four white men, far from home, and as far as they know, still two months march from the nearest succour.

Together with the difficulty of the mud comes the suffocating nature of the air itself.

Wills records of the following evening, when they are again making a moonlight march, 'the slightest exertion made one feel as if he were in a state of suffocation. The dampness of the atmosphere prevented any evaporation, and gave one a helpless feeling of lassitude that I have never before experienced to such an extent.'[23]

The men grow more and more exhausted . . . and hungry, as want of rations begins to tell.

By the second day of March – as they leave the coastal region and the ground underfoot gets firmer, they speed up – they have covered 135 miles of their return journey, and are now nearing their old 'Saltbush Camp', where the ground is covered with lots of those low bushes with edible red berries . . . when . . . when they see him!

Remarkably close to where John King and William Wills had had to leave him back on 30 January it is . . . Golah!

'He looks thin and miserable,' Wills notes, 'seems to have fretted a great deal, probably at finding himself left behind . . . He began to eat as soon as he saw the other camels.'[24]

Oh, the irony. Not for love nor money, nor food, nor whipping, could they get Golah moving over a month earlier, but now he has had time to rest – mostly grazing back and forth on the same patch of track – he is clearly glad to see them and wants to stay with them. Against that, he is not a well camel, and has no strength. Whether he will actually be of use to them – beyond the meat he carries – is yet to be seen.

Still, they keep going, and the following evening, as they cross a creek in the moonlight, Charley Gray is in the lead, guiding his camel over what first appears to be a small log . . . only . . . only to see it move, and start to slither away!

SNAKE!

In an instant, Charley is off his camel, and swinging a stirrup iron at the snake – as shouts, imprecations and *nurrrrrs* fill the startled night – until the 'log' stops moving. It proves to be the largest serpent any of them have ever seen.

'Eight feet four inches in length and seven inches in girth round the belly,' notes Wills, 'it was nearly the same thickness from the head to within 20 inches of the tail. It then tapered rapidly. The weight was 11½ lbs.'[25]

Despite the fact that the python is obviously not venomous, its massive black head, yellow underside and 'irregular brown transverse bars on a yellowish brown ground'[26], make it look evil incarnate.

That evening, after dining heartily on the snake, Mr Burke decides to call this spot 'Feasting Camp', timing that proves to be fortuitous. For, only shortly after starting off once more at 2 am, Mr Burke falls ill with dysentery – and so filthy are the consequences – well, it's a good thing he didn't name the camp at this point. It is four hours before Burke feels well enough to go on, and even then it would, perhaps, be best if the others stay downwind of him?

Two days later, Burke seems on the mend – at least for those who remain upwind of him – and, like them all, is able to push himself forward through inspiration . . . where perspiration alone might not provide.

But their animals are not inspired and Golah once more is soon 'completely done up', refusing to budge, even when the pack and saddle are taken off.[27] The obvious thing, perhaps, would be to shoot him and jerk him, adding considerably to their stores of dried meat, but Burke is against it, and that is that. Deciding that their major enemy now is time – getting back to the Depot at Cooper's Creek before Brahe and his men leave – they simply let Golah go free.

Now, move! Move! Move!

Next, it's Charley Gray's turn. Poor Charley can *barely* move. As Wills records on 7 March at Camp 20R, 'He caught cold last night through carelessness in covering himself.'[28] It is the occasion to have a real look at this sailor so far from the sea, and it is not a little shocking. Just in the last month his once massive frame has withered to the point that the once voluptuous mermaids on his biceps have suddenly developed wrinkles and appear to be sagging even more than he is. Clearly, he is ailing.

On the reckoning that they can only go as fast as their slowest man, any illness among them is a great worry … and getting more of a worry all the time as the numbers continue to turn against them. The Gulf party is only 200 miles south of their turning point at the Gulf, only a third of the way to the Depot at Cooper's Creek, having averaged just 10 miles a day since turning. The problem is that going north, they had moved at seventeen and a half miles a day, and all of Burke's initial calculations on how many supplies they would need had been predicated on moving at 18 miles a day consistently.

11 March '61, north of Torowoto, though the mercury rises, there is none for Charles

Wright's supply party are having serious problems. Nominally, they have been on the trail north for over six weeks by now, but their effort has been somewhere between a struggle and a straggle at best, a strain always, and a straying most of the time – occasioning endless searches for camels, even as the condition of both the men and their animals fall away with poor feed and unbearable heat. The group is constantly broken up and reformed as 'camel search parties' come and go.

Most draining of all, however, is the battle they face every day to find both sufficient water for man and beast – and to find the track itself. To overcome the first problem, Wright must continually go on ahead, leading a small reconnaissance party to find creeks or a waterhole that has enough water, while sending Beckler and others back to the last good water at Torowoto to bring up a supply.

As to finding Burke's tracks, it seems four months of wind and rain have conspired to obliterate them. Sometimes, as when the men find a blaze on a tree, they know they are right on it, and never more than when Wright sees Burke's tracks 'embedded in the mud'[29], made when everything was sodden and green, now hard-baked when all is brown and dry. Other times, the tracks simply disappear. If they had a navigator like Mr Wills with them, they would at least know where they are, and what direction exactly they must head to get to Cooper's Creek, but in that respect they are rudderless. All they can do when lost is try to keep heading north, and hope they will come across the tracks once more.

Wright gives names to their camps along their way, and it would not take Sherlock Holmes to determine how fares the trip so far. See here, Watson, I think there is a *clue*, in these names on the map! Watson looks, and knows that Holmes has done it once again: 'Desolation Point . . . Mud Plain . . . Rat Point.'

Making things worse still, just 40 miles north of Torowoto Swamp, with still some 280 miles to go before they can get to the Depot – there is now no denying it for Wright and his men.

They are being stalked and stricken by scurvy.

The first to fall ill is Ludwig Becker, closely followed by Charles Stone, with both men quickly complaining of sore gums and lethargy, while displaying ugly splotches on their skin, bleeding noses and terrible dysentery. (Beyond scurvy, Stone's syphilis is also tightening its ghastly grip, like the deadly scourge it is, with pus-ridden sores now multiplying all over his face, torso, groin and down his legs. There is nothing that Dr Beckler can do to help him, no mercury is present to inject into his veins.)

Put together, it makes Becker and Stone no more than invalids who must be cared for and carried – hoisted gingerly onto horses, regularly allowed to halt – rather than contributing members of the party.

And even beyond the woes of those two men – Wright, Smith and Belooch are suffering from diarrhoea, while William Purcell complains of swollen legs and numerous sores.

Of the party the one who seems most well – *physician, heal thyself* – is Dr Beckler.

Mid-March '61, Ballarat, a father's foreboding

Night after night, sleep escapes the middle-aged Englishman, as in his well-appointed home, he tosses and turns, trying to escape the vision horrid that comes of a prodigal son who *doesn't* return.

'As time passed on,' Dr Wills would recount, 'forebodings came upon me that this great expedition, starting with so much display from Melbourne, with a steady, declared, and scientific object, would dwindle down into a flying light corps, making a sudden dash across the continent and back again with no permanent results.'

He couldn't help but notice that although his son, young William, had taken on more responsibilities than ever, no assistant surveyor had been sent up to him, and no successor appointed to Dr Beckler. What is more, when Professor Neumayer had turned up back in Melbourne, he had with him many of the scientific instruments, asserting that, 'If I had not done so, Mr Burke, who is unscientific and impatient of the time lost in making and registering observations, threatened to throw them into the next creek.'[30]

The night drags on, with no sleep for the doctor.

Mid-March '61, towards the Selwyn Range, the land rises, the sun burns

Pushing on now, the exhausted, ragged band might be forgiven for thinking that the exhausted, ragged landscape that confronts and near crushes them goes on like this forever, but now it happens. Like the lone ripple of a wave on an otherwise stagnant pond, followed by a bigger ripple still and then another and another – there is life out there, somewhere! – the men become aware over the course of an hour that the otherwise boggy flatness is giving way to a series of tiny rocky ranges.

And now, after several of the lone ranges fall behind, and the next ranges get closer together and higher, as the men get ever closer to the source of these ripples of land … they can see something, they can really see something!

The Selwyn Range appears up ahead.

Now, while it had been one thing to face the Camel Path heading north, with gravity always pushing you forward and down, it is quite another, now that they are trying to get those same camels *up* the same rocky path – *as round and round the rugged rocks, the raggedy rascals run* – with the combined force of gravity and the camels' extreme reluctance making it hard going indeed.

It is, William Wills records, the 'most dangerous part of our journey'[31], as the jagged orange-red rocks tower over them, tear at them, and continue to glower their resistance, while the camels moan their shuddering, juddering terror with every difficult step upwards. All they can do is keep going, keep climbing, half pulling the camels, half pushing and just managing to make progress, to make it to Camp 24R, another crucial 'R' closer to the Depot.

•

The ranges have eyes. Blackfella eyes. They belong to the warriors of the Kalkadoon nation and – unbeknown to the four whitefellas now struggling south through the Selwyn Range – they watch very closely from all points high as the intruders make their way through Kalkadoon country. Should they attack?

This is their plan, but older, wiser heads have prevailed. No attack. They are too strong … and they don't mean the whitefellas, but the 'giant roaring beasts'[32] which accompany them, seemingly from another world. And so the Kalkadoon hold back. Watching. Waiting. Wanting the intruders to leave.

•

At last emerged from the Selwyn Range, Mr Burke, Mr Wills, King and the still ailing Gray are vastly relieved, not to mention their five remaining camels – their 'giant, roaring beasts' – and blessed Billy.

It is not that the ground is easy from here, as most of the ground is very boggy after the big wet, punctuated now by many stony ridges that they must slowly pass over, but the point is that it is easier. At least, now, they can proceed more or less straight and don't have to constantly make detours to find passes in the high ranges, avoid cruel cul-de-sacs, and cling to the side of passes that actually want to throw them and their animals into the abyss below.

The relative respite allows Mr Burke to fully focus on the next most obvious thing that might kill them – starvation. They have precious little left of the supplies and must make it last for as long as possible. From now, Burke tells the cook and effective quartermaster, Charley Gray, they must go to just one-third rations, with each man given a daily allowance of just a quarter pound of flour and 10 strips of meat.

Mid-March '61, Melbourne, Lockhart unlocks his heart

It is a very pointed letter, appearing in the *Herald,* penned by none other than William Lockhart Morton – more sure than ever that living history will vindicate his criticisms – and he is not long in getting to the point.

> For some time I have felt a good deal of anxiety as to the fate of Mr. Burke and party and I am induced to make public my reasons for feeling anxiety . . . on the hope that everything will be done to prevent any calamity befalling them
>
> What I have to suggest is that no time should, be lost in offering a reward of two or three hundred pounds, or more, to any small vessel that will proceed from Sydney or any port of Queensland, to the head of the Gulf . . . [33]

One who takes particular satisfaction in reading such remarks is Dr Wills, whose own growing disquiet in recent months at the lack of news has moved to outright fear – and anger at the lack of activity.

But with this letter?

Dr Wills has no doubts. It will, surely, 'stir up the Committee to take some steps to ascertain if Mr Wright was moving in his duty'[34].

Good. Because Dr Wills himself has not even had his own letters to the Committee's Dr John Macadam – asking for information, trying to prod the sod into action – acknowledged. He had, though, heard back from a man who always replies: his son's mentor, Professor Neumayer. Dr Wills had sought the answers to the two questions that haunt him every moment: Where is William? And is he safe?

Professor Neumayer had come back to him promptly: 'I think that by this time the party must have reached the Gulf of Carpentaria, supposing them to have proceeded in that direction. In fact, I think they may have recrossed already a great part of the desert country, if everything went on smoothly after leaving Cooper's Creek. I have a thorough confidence in Mr Wills's character and energy, and I am sure they will never fail . . .'[35]

Enormously relieved to hear it, still Dr Wills cannot escape the nagging worry that things are amiss. It is a worry that grows with the passing of every day. It is a father's fear, a feeling that cannot be reassured by reason.

Mid-March '61, Selwyn Range, the heavens weep

While it is the nature of nature to hurl an enormous variety of obstacles in the way of all those who try to suckle from its bosom but avoid its wrath – by walking 2000 miles across an entire continent, for example – still Burke and his men could be forgiven for being shocked at nature's new tactic: giving them too much of a good thing. The men now have but 550 miles to go before they rest beneath the coolabah trees at the Depot. The heavens themselves might weep with gratitude that much of the hardest country is now behind them, and . . . so they do . . .

At the end of this long day, as the men are making camp by a gurgling creek, the black clouds that roll in are not long in drenching them to the bone, as well as their animals, as well as everything they are hauling with them, while the creek itself quickly becomes a roaring torrent. The ground becomes too boggy once more for their poor exhausted and malnourished animals to proceed, the creeks in their path swell and block their passage. 'Our progress was slow,' Wills writes on 14 March, 'as it was necessary to keep on the stony ridge instead of following the flats, the latter being very boggy after the rain.'[36] They are once again forced to go at the pace of a sodden snail.

16 March '61, Cooper's Creek, Brahe frays, as time plays tricks

Just as he does often, the wan figure on horseback makes his way to the top of the conical hill that lies some nine miles north-west from the Depot and gazes mournfully in all directions. William Brahe is looking for a sign, *any* sign, that either Mr Burke and the Gulf party are on their way back from the Gulf or, at long last, Mr Wright and his relief party are on their way from Menindee.

And every time it is for the same result. There is nothing. Absolutely nothing, bar Cooper's Creek ribboning off in two directions, east and west.

Brahe is starting to get more than just slightly worried.

Even a fortnight earlier he had noted in his diary that he had been looking out anxiously for Mr Burke's return.[37] But now that anxiety is beginning to firm into a resolution to do something. To start to think about leaving.

It is three months to the day since Mr Burke had left with the Gulf party, this is the day, by the leader's estimation, that they are due back – the day that, by Mr Burke's orders, Brahe and his men are free to leave. Of course, there is no sign of them, and Brahe intends to do no such thing. Brahe is not surprised at their absence. Three months had always seemed optimistic to him – to go 2000 miles, there and back, when 20 miles a day had been very good going to this point, means they would surely be 100 days as a bare *minimum* – and certainly it had seemed optimistic to Mr Wills, too, for he had told him to wait for four months.

Brahe still intends to do that . . . but is agonisingly aware that they won't be able to wait much longer, as their supplies dwindle, just as they become weaker the longer they stay in these infernal climes. Yes, perhaps they could make their supplies last longer by living like the blacks do, and engaging in such activities as catching fish . . . but such is the general lassitude abroad, Brahe and his men can never garner much enthusiasm for it.

'On two occasions we caught some fish,'[38] McDonough would recall, while Brahe's estimate would be they caught fish 'Only once'[39]. Anyway, it seems to Brahe as he heads back to the Depot 'neath the coolabah trees that, while in their own supplies they have only 'very large hooks . . .' from observing the natives it is clear that what is required is 'fine small hooks'[40], and as he 'had never been in the habit of fishing'[41], it is not something he really focuses on.

Late March, 500 miles north of the Depot, a shamming and a shaming

Miles of mud! For well over a week now, Burke and his party have been squelching their way through it, sapped white with exhaustion, groaning with the effort very nearly as much as their five camels and horse, who are also clearly suffering. As it happens, when one camel is put out of its misery by being shot, the misery of the four men in turn is alleviated as for a short time they gorge on its precious meat at what becomes another aptly named 'Feasting Camp'. True, one less camel means one less shaky ship of the desert to carry cargo, but they can deal with that later. For the moment, feast!

To regroup, and set themselves to go again, Mr Burke decides to call a halt for the day, so they can try a night march beneath the moon. In the meantime, during the day, the four men work at lightening their load, throwing out most bar the essentials – which is everything bar food. All up, they are able to leave behind, in the crook of a tree, a third of the total weight they are carrying – bundles of clothing, some ammunition, gun-smithing tools, beads for the natives, horseshoe nails and shoeing equipment, mending gear, horse furniture, leather buckets and canvas bags. Yes, they will be marginally less comfortable, but comfort no longer matters. *Survival* does, and that will come from moving quicker, which will come from travelling lighter. A virtuous circle.

For all that, though their own packs are commendably lighter when they start off that evening at a quarter to six, more rain has seen the criss-crossing creeks they must cross-criss in turn become impassable and again they must quickly make camp for the night, in what is at least easier country, 'an immense extent of plain . . . of the finest character for pastoral purposes'[42].

It is as well, for by now the fading foursome – hanging ever looser on their shrinking frames – are, if not on their last legs, getting there. And if the country is easier, the conditions are not, as evidenced by the names they give the camps they stop at over the next three days: 'Humid Camp . . . Muddy Camp', and 'Mosquito Camp'.

On 21 March, it becomes clear that a lightening of the load does not lead to a quickening of the road.

'Unable to proceed on account of the slippery and boggy state of the ground. The rain has fallen very heavily here today, and every little depression in the ground is either full of water or covered with slimy mud. Another heavy storm passed over during the night, almost extinguishing the miserable fire we were able to get up with our very limited quantity of waterlogged and green wood . . . We started again at seven o'clock, but the effects of the heavy rain prevented our making a good journey.'[43]

They make Camp 34R, on the thirty-seventh day of this aching return. And the latest rations – *starvation* rations – are taking their toll. Yes, a camel had been slaughtered just days ago, but there had not been a day spare to jerk it, nor weather that would make it possible to do so. So after the feast had come the famine. Their bodies are now consuming themselves more voraciously than ever before, and with any scrap of fat long gone, it is their muscles that now rapidly deteriorate. Every evening, mealtime becomes a practically sacred event, with due ceremony.

Once the food is prepared by Charley – mud being a ubiquitous ingredient thanks to the relentless rain – Mr Burke personally doles it out on to four plates, carefully ensuring that the amount of food on each plate is equal, to the best of his abilities, before asking the three men to turn their backs. And now, like a priest at the altar, he carefully places the plates, side by side before him, and covers them with a towel.

Each man must now call a number, and is given his assigned plate, with Burke himself taking the one plate that remains. It is the perfect system, King will note approvingly, 'so that no person could be favoured with a larger quantity than the others'[44]. Clearly, the man suffering most is Gray, the oldest among them, who has been ailing since they left the Gulf country. He is constantly complaining of general weakness, dizziness, terrible pain in his legs and back – and severe headaches.

True, he had complained a little on the way north of similar weakness, but the other three had thought it of little moment. Now, the complaints are constant and even have a hint of desperation.

Quietly, Mr Burke tells Mr Wills and King, that Gray is very likely 'shamming'[45], feigning illness, so as to justify doing less work, and perhaps to eat more. Mr Wills and King quietly agree. The three of them are weak, certainly, but have no such pain in their legs or backs, nor suffer from the headaches that Gray describes.

Shortly afterwards, Gray says he has dysentery, and asks whether he might have an extra portion of flour – the most highly regarded remedy – to help rid himself of the debilitating condition. And yet, after Wills 'examined his stools – several of [them]'[46] and pronounces them to not have the tell-tale signs of being either watery or bloody, Mr Burke declines the request.

Still, Mr Burke does not openly challenge Gray on it, and even allows the nominally sick man to ride on his horse, Billy, while he walks along beside. For the moment it is something to assess, to see if, hopefully, whatever is ailing Gray – be it in his head or his body – will pass.

Alas, only a few days later, it is John King starting to feel weak, while also suffering shooting pains in his legs and back, rather similar to what the still ailing Charley has been complaining of – at some length. Could he have the same ailment, whatever it is? Or is it that they are walking such long distances on ever shorter provisions?

After a day beginning with a 5.30 am start on 25 March, the four comrades follow a creek, with banks of 'the richest alluvial soil . . . clothed with luxuriant vegetation'[47], halting for breakfast under a pod of large white gums lining the bank. Mr Wills notes some strange familiarities and recognition dawns. They have been here before! Yes, he is sure of it. Wills realises they are very near Camp 89 of their northern journey.

Given that it had taken them 24 days to get to this area from Cooper's Creek, that gives them an approximate arrival date back at the Depot of 17 April, if they can maintain the same pace. And as they are *already* nine days longer than the original three months envisioned, it means it will be well over four months from leaving the Depot, to returning ... but all they can do is hope that Wright, Brahe and the men will be there.

After a grimly sparse breakfast from their dwindling rations, Wills struggles up the steep creek banks to get purchase on the bordering grassy plains with his watch and sextant to check their position. That accomplished, with all his calculations and conclusions pencilled into his field book, Wills heads briefly back upstream to retrieve a ramrod he had previously discarded, but has now decided they will need. Who knows? They are getting close, but an extra ramrod to keep their guns in good nick may make all the difference between life and death.

Halfway between the camps he suddenly comes across, *what* ... ?

Charley Gray, *hiding* behind a tree and eating skilligolee, a type of gruel made from the very precious flour they have been running so short of. It is a question of who is more shocked.

Is it Wills, to discover this perfidy? Or Gray, for having been so unexpectedly found out?

'Do you have permission to take it?' Wills asks, hoping against hope that, perhaps, Mr Burke will have allowed it.

'I have not,' Gray replies miserably. 'But I am suffering from dysentery.'[48]

Both men know this is no excuse for – yes – his *theft* from the limited food supplies that remain. And though Wills is not a man to become particularly enraged himself, he knows he has no choice.

'Please report yourself to Mr Burke,'[49] he says.

Shaking, fearing Mr Burke's rage, Gray cannot bring himself to do that and instead goes first to find King, asking him to tell Mr Burke for him. Wills, though, takes King aside.

'If you possibly can,' he says, 'urge Gray, to make some acknowledgment of it to Mr Burke before I return, as I know that if I have to acquaint Mr Burke with it, he will be much more severe on Gray than if he acknowledges it himself.'[50]

And, as Mr Wills heads off, King tries to do exactly that.

But, lacking both the physical and moral strength to willingly face the fire a second before he has to, Gray refuses, insisting that King must do it for him.

Very well, then . . .

Begging your pardon, Mr Burke, but I regret to inform you of something?

Yes?

'Mr Wills found Gray sitting under a tree, some distance from our camp, eating this porridge.'[51]

Alas, alas, Mr Burke proves to be angry enough for *three* men.

Mr Burke roars out for Gray to come to him instantly.

'What do you mean by stealing the stores?'

Gray has no answer.

'Do you not receive an equal share of the rations?'

Gray cannot deny it, and even acknowledges that he has been helping himself to the stores for some time, in the hope of curing his weakness. The situation is grave, very grave. If Gray has been stealing food since they left the Gulf – and he had every capacity to do so, as the food was in his charge – then they may be as much as a week shorter in rations than they had thought.

There is nothing for it.

As later documented by John King, who is present, Mr Burke proceeds to give Gray 'several slaps on the head as a chastisement . . .'[52] and even, 'several boxes on the ear with his open hand . . .'[53]

(It is equally characterised by Wills as 'a good thrashing'[54], based on Burke telling him afterwards 'I have given Gray a good thrashing, and well he deserved it.'[55] However it is described, it is a measure of Gray's weakened state that Burke dares to do it. Only three months ago, boxing the ears of the sailor twice his size would have been unthinkable. But, now, Gray is powerless to resist.)

A good part of the anger of the other three is that it is not as if this has happened just once. Upon investigation, it seems obvious to King that Gray has stolen 'a considerable quantity of flour'[56].

While it is problematic to so treat an already severely weakened man, it certainly seems unlikely that Gray will dare transgress again.

For one thing, he is to have nothing more to do with the stores, or the cooking, and that job is henceforth the province of King.

And at least, Burke is a man of swift forgiveness, telling Gray not long afterwards, 'not to think of what had passed, for he forgave him all he had done'[57].

(Wills, as it turns out, is slightly less forgiving. To this point, his every reference to the errant sailor in his journal is as 'Charley'. Henceforth he is referred to only as 'Gray'. Wills likewise names their breakfast halt 'Detection Camp', to mark the event.)

Despite it all, they are quickly on the march south once more, with Wills happily able to use a phrase never used on the journey to date: 'the camels in first-rate spirits'[58].

And despite the deep unhappiness of the morning, even the Gulf party – less the sullen, sick and battered Gray – are in better spirits, courtesy of the fact that they are now coming back onto their old path. After three months in the deep wilderness, it really is something to see familiar sights once more, ones that they know are in the same region as the Depot, as gay flocks of pigeons flutter forth on the wisps of winds they generate as they rise in a glittering gala from seemingly every clump of trees on the party's approach and the men are once more among the criss-crossing creeks, which form a lush latticework amid what had been 'the luxuriant growth of fine grasses and small bushes'[59].

True, what had then 'looked so fresh and green, is now very much dried up; and we saw no signs of water anywhere'[60]. As ever, it is remarkable how quickly the Australian landscape can radically change, in just half-a-day's march. Mulga scrub and cruel spinifex soon appear as they approach the desert climes once more.

But still, it is familiar, and that is really something.

Though they are still at least three weeks away from the Depot, and succour, at last there is a genuine sense that the end of the most arduous part of their journey – the dash to the Gulf and back, removed from all support – is nearing an end.

The men press forth, soon realising that the unfamiliar billabongs they start to pass must have been parts of the creek the last time they were here.

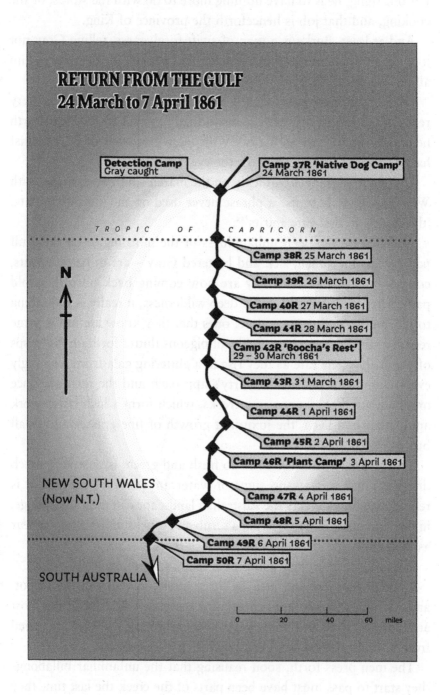

RETURN FROM THE GULF
24 March to 7 April 1861

Detection Camp
Gray caught

Camp 37R 'Native Dog Camp'
24 March 1861

TROPIC OF CAPRICORN

N

Camp 38R 25 March 1861

Camp 39R 26 March 1861

Camp 40R 27 March 1861

Camp 41R 28 March 1861

Camp 42R 'Boocha's Rest'
29 – 30 March 1861

Camp 43R 31 March 1861

Camp 44R 1 April 1861

Camp 45R 2 April 1861

Camp 46R 'Plant Camp' 3 April 1861

NEW SOUTH WALES
(Now N.T.)

Camp 47R 4 April 1861

Camp 48R 5 April 1861

Camp 49R 6 April 1861

Camp 50R 7 April 1861

SOUTH AUSTRALIA

0   20   40   60   miles

Late March '61, Melbourne, love's deception

That fetching young woman, in Melbourne, talking to the old biddy?

Why, it is Miss Julia Matthews herself, the famed and beautiful actress, the one a very select few know is the sweetheart of Mr Burke, who is leading the Expedition to the Gulf!

'I hope to deceive him, certainly,' she is saying.

'But mayhap, Miss . . .' replies the biddy. 'Then he mayn't fancy a young lady who has played him such a trick.'

'Ah, these men are sad plagues,' replies Julia firmly. 'Deceive them before marriage and they are in a fury. Reserve the pleasure till afterwards and then they are not satisfied!'[61]

And now she throws her head back and laughs uproariously.

And so, of course, does the large crowd who have been hanging on every word.

Encore! Encore! ENCORE!

If not the finest performance of Miss Julia Matthews's extraordinary and burgeoning career so far, it must run it close.

The beautiful young actress is not speaking ill of Mr Burke at all, but rather appearing with her fellow actors on stage of Melbourne's fine Theatre Royal in *The Eton Boy*, and at its conclusion the crowd near lifts the roof in their wild acclaim.

Late March '61, 330 miles north of the Depot, desert desertion

Out in the desert once more, the quartet are more likely than ever to feel like ants trekking across a vastness that simply cannot be conquered. No talking now, just the odd grunt, some more frequent groans from their ailing, flailing, failing camels and the occasional whinny from Billy as they keep pushing south. And now on this endless afternoon, what starts as a mere strong breeze, so hot it's like a burst of breath from a dragon's roar, soon turns so cold in the late afternoon that they have to throw extra clothes on, and then turns hot again as they find themselves in a dust storm.

Nature, which has thrown so many barriers up against them during the expedition, has now sent heat, cold, heat, sand and howling wind at them in the space of a few hours. No, it hasn't stopped them, but it has certainly sapped them, *and* their animals, none more than their exhausted camel, Boocha, who must pay the price, within days . . .

Saturday, March 30. Camp 42R. Boocha's rest.
Poor Boocha was killed; employed all day in cutting up and
jerking him: the day turned out as favourable for us as we could have
wished, and a considerable portion of the meat was completely jerked
before sunset. [62]

There are now, in this last week of March, just three camels left, Rajah, Landa and Gotch, and one horse – the ever faithful Billy.

31 March '61, Koorliatto, Ludwig Becker completes his rainbow of illness

'With every passing day,' Dr Beckler writes in his diary, 'our camp came more to resemble a hospital than a resting place for enterprising travellers. Mr Becker and Purcell could only move with great effort, their bodies were bent forward. With stiff legs bent at the knee, they crawled more than they walked. Stone, too had deteriorated greatly and Belooch was ill.' [63]

As Wright searches up and around the Bulloo River for Burke's tracks, Beckler cares for the invalids at a waterhole named Koorliatto, a depot of medical misery.

The man suffering the most is the doctor's German compatriot, Ludwig Becker. By now, Mr Burke's old wish to break the artist has been more than amply achieved by disease. Now in the full terrible grip of scurvy, Becker's once ample girth is reduced to skin and bones, his former healthy red sheen now no more than a dull grey pallor, with green tinges and mottled ghastliness, all of it covered with a sickly sweat.

The most extraordinary thing?

Despite it all, Ludwig Becker still insists on sketching and painting, and is able to escape his appalling circumstances for hours at a time by sitting in his tent and, with extraordinary concentration and exquisite skill, bring to life the things he has seen, such as his current 'Camp on the edge of the earthy or mud plains'.

Such resolution is inspirational, and all the more so because the horror of Becker's situation is not merely because of the weakness of his body alone, but what comes with it – the myriad flies attracted to a figure frequently sitting in its own filth, too weak to shoo them away.

'They helped Becker at his work with his sketches and almost made him despair,' Dr Beckler records, 'they sucked the colours and inks from his quills and brushes and threw themselves recklessly on to every damp spot on his paintings.'[64]

Despite it all, despite it *all*, Ludwig Becker keeps going.

Early April '61, Cooper's Creek Depot, Brahe decides the day

The weather is starting to cool, with the only showers being not enough to 'lay the dust'[65]. William Brahe is now *really* worried. Three and a half months have gone by since Mr Burke had left with the Gulf party, and there is *still* no sign of them returning, or Mr Wright arriving from the south. With veritable vacuums, thus, to both his north and south, it is less a case of Brahe feeling the pressure, than being torn apart. What to do?

Yes, he could send a party ranging to the north to look for signs of the Gulf party returning, or to the south for Mr Wright, but as he only has four men including himself who are able and working here at the Depot, that would leave this place – the main base of the entire expedition – dangerously undermanned should the natives mount an attack.

On the subject of Mr Burke, Brahe is always somewhat inclined to consult McDonough, the leader's personal friend. Of course the Irishman can't speak for Burke but if Brahe can get McDonough's agreement to leave, it would help to cool whatever anger Mr Burke might feel later at the decision that has been made. And so, Brahe asks, what does McDonough think about leaving in the next couple of weeks?

'No,' says McDonough, 'we might be as well to remain until the 1st of May.'[66]

And so Brahe must continue making his deliberations, his calculations. Yet one more thing to consider is the possibility that once the Gulf party get to the Gulf of Carpentaria there will be a ship there waiting to meet them, to whisk them away – meaning Brahe and his party would just be waiting uselessly. Still, there has only been talk of such a ship, and Burke's specific instructions to him had not mentioned it. McDonough, though, seems to believe the ship is a strong possibility, recalling Professor Neumayer saying to Burke before departure, 'I hope to meet you, Burke, in the vessel.'

And, of course, when McDonough himself had twice lightly noted to Mr Burke that he shouldn't be giving away all his clothes, the leader had said, 'I do not care, McDonough, if I get on board the vessel with only a shirt on me, if I get through.'[67]

On reflection, both odd remarks now convince McDonough, as he would later note, that 'there would be probably a vessel to meet him at Carpentaria'[68], so he shares them with Brahe.

For his part, Brahe is confused. He is the man in charge of the Depot, the one Mr Burke had given specific instructions to, and in all their discussions, there had never been any mention of any vessel. Burke had made it clear the Gulf party expected them to wait on at Cooper's Creek, because that is where they intended to return. The only alternative to them heading this way that Brahe can see is that perhaps circumstances have forced Mr Burke's hand and they have changed direction entirely and gone through northern Queensland towards the coast?

No one *knows*. The Gulf party are just as likely to appear anytime in the next hour. And just as, back in December, every rising flock of birds from the south had made Mr Burke think Mr Wright had at last arrived, so, too, does Brahe brighten whenever he sees birds rising in the north. Always, however, it is merely a case of . . . birds rising in the north, the sun and the breeze combining to make them a distant, soaring, scattering of confetti against the impossibly blue sky.

Brahe can't help but alighting on the same thought: they must go sometime soon, for their own safety.

Which begs the next calculation to work out. Just how much of the supplies should be left behind for the Gulf party? The sooner Brahe and the men go, the more they can leave. If they do stay, say, another six weeks, and the Gulf party joined them at that very point, that would mean they would have dwindling supplies, and suddenly another four mouths to feed – for by that time the Gulf party would surely have all but run out of their own supplies. And they may even be starting to run out of *men* . . .

•

For William Patten, it is the queerest thing. Like a rising damp of stiffness that slowly engulfs him, his limbs are becoming overwhelmed by a soreness that just won't let go. Yes, he'd been hurt when thrown from that damn horse back in January, but he had recovered from that. And this pain? Well . . . it's worse than that pain. Perhaps then, some internal injury has occurred, something slow? Perhaps. Or perhaps it is something more insidious still. For this constant aching never varies, no matter how he positions his body. The others can see a certain lameness entering his gait, and worriedly inquire, but Patten plays it down. He is like that. He is a worker. He wants to get on with things. But this . . . thing?

It is . . . troubling him more than ever. After taking over both legs in preceding weeks, and then his left arm, it is now even more apparent in his right arm, his prime working arm. It is enough to . . . panic him. On the morning of 1 April, he approaches the leader of the Depot party.

'I had better shoe the horses now, Mr Brahe,' Patten says as calmly as he can. 'I think I won't be able to do it if I left it any longer. My elbow is getting stiff.'[69]

Without a further word spoken, Brahe knows precisely what Patten is getting at. Horses are shod when they are about to embark upon a journey . . . and in this case there is only one possible journey to undertake . . . The one *back* to Menindee, Mr Brahe.

Well, then, Mr Patten, you may indeed proceed.

Sure enough, once the shoeing is over – in his weakened state it takes just over three days – it is clear that Patten has done it just in time, for, as Brahe notes in his diary, 'Patten, after shoeing two horses, was obliged to take to his bed, suffering acute pain, and was not afterwards able to move about.'[70]

Ja, not only are his arms no longer capable of lifting the hammer to shoe a horse, but his body is now no longer capable of standing.

Something is very, very queer here. And what is worse, Patten is not alone in his ailing, Brahe himself soon notes shooting pains in his own legs, despite his not having been thrown from a horse, which is puzzling. They're not severe pains, but they are constant, and his gums are sore too.

Thomas McDonough is also complaining of much the same thing, a strange tightening in his limbs, a pain in his ankles, a pain in his gums . . .

'Patten is getting worse. I and McDonough begin to feel alarming symptoms of the same disease,' Brahe writes.[71]

Patten makes his own feelings known, and they are as strong as such a weak man can manage. He wants to return to civilisation, he croaks, to get medical help as soon as possible.

'If we don't return [soon],' Patten continues, his once mighty form now starting to waste away before their very eyes, 'I will not have any chance of recovering.'[72]

He is saying they must head south soon, as a matter of life and death – his own – and there is no doubt that his wan visage and wasted figure, lying feebly in his tent, makes exactly that case.

Brahe is further persuaded, when, after more pleading plaints from Patten, Brahe asks McDonough once more. Should they leave?

'Of course,' the Irishman replies, 'if it is a benefit to Patten to do so.'[73]

When even McDonough agrees it is the best thing to do, Brahe is decided. They will leave on, or about, 20 April.

3 April '61, 250 miles north of Cooper's Creek, a plant among the plants

On current calculations, given that they are averaging 15 miles a day on their way back from the Gulf, it seems likely to Wills that they will get back to the Cooper's Creek Depot about 20 April.

A measure of how desperate they are to keep going, to get there in time, is that on this morning, when the camel Gotch refuses to move, he is merely abandoned, while they keep going. Once again, there is no time to kill and jerk him. This leaves just two camels – Rajah and Landa – together with Burke's valiant horse, Billy. But as brave and as valiant as those animals have been, a sad truth beckons.

'[The] two remaining camels are knocked up and only just able to stagger along . . .'[74]

They are no longer strong enough to carry all the supplies they have with them, and it is 'necessary to relieve them of as much as possible of their loads'.[75]

Burke gives the order that they are 'leaving behind everything but the grub and just what we carry on our backs . . .'[76] And of course they keep the guns. Everything else will be 'planted' here in a marked spot by yonder creek bed, and once we have got back to the Depot, Mr Wills can come back here with someone to dig it up and retrieve it.

It is an extreme step, and Wills, for one, is troubled. To leave behind his precious astronomical and meteorological instruments, which tell them just where on the map they are at any given moment – by virtue of the position of the sun, moon and stars – means they will be, effectively, trekking blind. They will be able to manage when retracing their own tracks coming north, but what if they need to go off that beaten track? Yet there really is little choice. The instruments are simply too heavy to carry, and it is as much as they will be able to do to carry what they do have, 'scanty rations in the shape of a small quantity of flour and a strip of dried meat cut from the rump of a camel . . .'[77]

So, as soon as the sun goes down, they begin, working in pairs – though the ill Gray struggles – in short, alternating spells. First they loosen the soil at the designated spot with sticks, before scooping it up with their hands and carefully placing it in a blanket, which, in the moonlight, they carry to the creek and throw the dirt in. There are to be no tell-tale signs. Like ghostly grave-diggers in the night, the work keeps going. A couple of hours before midnight, Wills halts. It is with great regret that he now must take his precious instruments in hand to make one final series of sightings on the stars to find their exact latitude before . . . the moment comes. The first task completed, it is with infinite care that the next task is undertaken.

Carefully now, lovingly, the man who was once a little boy in England staring with adoration through the window at the display of a nautical instrument maker's shop, takes his oh so precious belongings, 'one sextant, one universal circle, one pocket sextant, one artificial horizon with wooden mercury bottle, two prismatic compasses, one aneroid . . .'[78] – and wraps them in cloth, for their better protection in their dark night that awaits. And now they are further wrapped in an old rag and placed in a camel trunk, ready for burial.

The men keep digging.

As the quarter moon starts to wane, the eastern skies lighten just a little as the rising sun approaches the horizon. Just before it gets there, the box is buried, with a good foot of soil over it, and then for good measure they have their morning campfire over it, 'to hide all trace of disturbance'[79], leaving the ashes spread around. This time, they leave no blaze on any nearby tree to mark the spot. It will be for Wills himself to return here and find it.

They are soon on their way again, leaving 'Plant Camp', as Burke names it, Camp 46R, slowly falling behind them.

At least Wills has been able to keep a few light things, including 'my watch, prism compass, pocket compass, and one thermometer'.[80]

As for King, the one-time soldier, he is sure to keep his most valuable instrument: his double-barrel shotgun. Science is dispensable, survival is not. As long as he has breath in his body, he intends to keep the shotgun close.

And yet, while it is one thing to be lighter, *nothing* can make Charley speed up, as he continues to lag behind the others . . .

He is starting to worry them all.

4 April '61, Bulloo watercourse, a dream of rivers, a river of dreams

And that is typical.

On this morning, just over two months since Wright had left Pamamaroo with his now straggling band of sick, exhausted men and animals, they continue to follow the barely perceptible traces of Burke's track over 'a narrow belt of sand-hills . . .' until they arrive at the spot 'where Mr Burke had pitched his 52nd camp'[81] and find . . . no water.

The air buzzes with insect life. The wilderness presses in upon them. Along the menacing horizon they can see the smoke from the signal fires set by the blacks who are, clearly, watching them and quite likely shaping to make an attack.

No water.

With no choice in the matter, Wright gives the order to move on and this time, for once, is rewarded with good fortune. For just eight miles later, in the late afternoon, a river appears before them, and it is flowing!

That's it. At the very point they strike the river, Wright commands that they make camp. Is this, perhaps Cooper's Creek? Without a navigator there is no way of knowing, but Wright's suspicion is that it is not.

'From the absence of any indication that Mr Burke had stopped at this creek,' he will note, 'I felt convinced that Cooper's Creek lay still farther in advance . . .'[82]

Either way, in such dry conditions, the station overseer is little inclined to keep going until they can gather their strength, and that might take a matter of weeks, if at all. Here, they can indulge in the luxury of stopping, and do so. Seeds are even planted by the river, that's how sure Mr Wright is that they will be staying long enough to at least see them grow a little.

7 April '61, 215 miles north of Cooper's Creek, grave concerns

Continuing to follow their tracks south, on this morning the struggling Gulf party come to what, in late December, had been a wonderfully rushing river, with copious feed for the animals on its banks, some 10 days trek north of the Depot, but is now little more than a muddy mess with next to no feed at all, which, as it happens . . . is just like them.

For covered from head to foot in sweaty grime, they have now run out of supplies bar tiny amounts of jerked camel meat.

Compounding their problems, Gray is getting progressively worse, on this morning even stopping outright, meaning that Messrs Burke and Wills must stop for all of 15 minutes while King goes back to get him and lead the rambling, shambling shadow of a man forward.

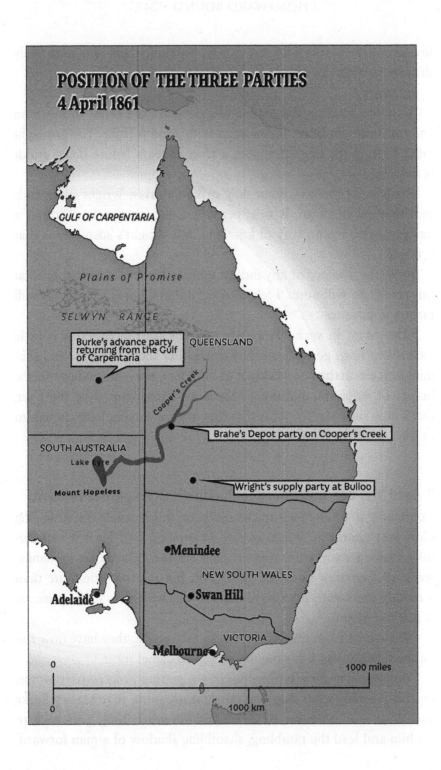

POSITION OF THE THREE PARTIES
4 April 1861

GULF OF CARPENTARIA

Plains of Promise

SELWYN RANGE

QUEENSLAND

Burke's advance party returning from the Gulf of Carpentaria

Cooper's Creek

Brahe's Depot party on Cooper's Creek

SOUTH AUSTRALIA

Lake Eyre

Wright's supply party at Bulloo

Mount Hopeless

Menindee

NEW SOUTH WALES

Adelaide

Swan Hill

VICTORIA

Melbourne

0   1000 miles

0   1000 km

Despite this pathetic sight, more than ever, Messrs Burke and Wills are convinced that Gray is 'shamming', with Mr Wills recording in his journal that this one-time sailor 'pretended that he could not walk'[83].

Wills even tells King he is sure that the *real* problem for Gray is not the critical lack of food in recent times so much as the fact that his 'constitution is gone through drink, as he had lived in a public house at Swan Hill . . .'[84]

After all, if Gray's problems are from food alone, why aren't they all suffering too, given that they are walking exactly the same miles, doing the same work, and living on the same food?

John King knows what Mr Wills means, but still King has sympathy for Gray, due in no small part to the fact that, just in the last few days, he has also been suffering from 'pains and weakness in the limbs . . .'[85]

It has changed his whole attitude.

'It convinced me,' King would later note, 'that Gray was not shamming.'[86]

8 April '61, Melbourne, His Excellency assures the faithful that things are excellent

What a grand occasion. Never have the rich mahogany and plum fittings of the Royal Society of Victoria's meeting hall been so outdone by an even more impressive crowd as on this evening, as for this, the first meeting of the Royal Society this year, so many of the leading figures in Melbourne gather to hear the inaugural address of the Royal Society President, and esteemed Governor of Victoria, Sir Henry Barkly, which is now just beginning . . . so hush!

'Gentlemen of the Royal Society of Victoria,' Governor Barkly begins in his reserved tone, 'it is to the preparations for exploring the interior of Australia that the time and energy of a large number of the members of this Society, who were nominated a Committee for the purpose . . . have been chiefly devoted during the past year.'[87]

It is true, Sir Henry acknowledges, that, a certain explorer from South Australia has been engaged in much the same pursuit as the Royal Society's own Mr Burke. But let Sir Henry go on . . .

'As regards the Victorian competitor – I will not call him rival – in this glorious race, Mr Burke, we might long since have looked to hear of his arrival at the pre-concerted depot on Cooper's Creek, and of his departure thence to skirt the eastern border of the desert, as the shortest route to the Gulf of Carpentaria . . .'

But there have been various, likely inconsequential, problems – including 'the delay which occurred in the transmission of the second portion of his stores from the Darling, which probably deterred him from sending back a messenger with the news of his movements'.

But not to worry. The second portion of the stores is well underway to the north now. Whatever the fate of Mr Burke, we must maintain level heads until we have news, and, 'we must be prepared to act promptly, according to the tenor of the first advices which may reach us'[88].

In short, despite what you might have heard, gentlemen, despite these scattered reports in the press, and a growing unease in the public that no news may indeed mean bad news, everything is fine, and all is in place to ensure that if there is a problem, we can move quickly.

It very much seems as if all the growing anxiety over Mr Burke and his party has been overblown, after all. They are surely all right.

9 April '61, 175 miles north of Cooper's Creek at Camp 52R, a sacrificial steed

It is the nature of nature:

A lull before a storm. A drought before a flood. And a creek that effectively marks the edges of the desert. The saltbush-lined waterway that Burke, Wills, King and Gray are camped by on this night lies on the northern edge of Sturt's Stony Desert.

At least, this time, they will be crossing it in far more moderate temperatures, and they know that if all else goes well, they are just 10 days from the Depot!

The question, however, is whether the poor nag Billy will make it to the other side. No animal in the history of the Australian continent has ever travelled such a great distance, let alone in such a small time, and it shows. Compounding his poor condition, as Wills notes, is that he 'has not had a proper feed for the last week until last night, and is, consequently, nearly knocked up'[89]. At least there is enough grass in the creek bed that he really can graze properly for now, to go with the saltbush, but will that be enough to recover him?

If he can't make it, jerking him for meat is going to be more than problematic in a place where there are no trees from which to suspend the lines and hang the slices.

Burke decides they will wait till morning before making a decision. The result?

It is as far from a shot in the dark as it gets – a gunshot in the daylight of the early morning, with the muzzle of King's gun pointed straight to the brain of the worthy Billy.[90]

A suddenly tearful Burke must look away, but there is no doubt that it has to be done. As the only horse, ever, to cross the continent, there is simply no horsepower left, and, as Wills notes, Billy is 'so reduced and knocked up for want of food that there appeared little chance of his reaching the other side of the [Stony] desert; and as we were running short of food of every description ourselves, we thought it best to secure his flesh at once'[91].

With one shot, thus, the worthy Billy is converted from being a means of locomotion to the expedition, to one of nutrition for its remaining members. The rest of the day is spent with Burke, Wills and King – for Gray is now too ill to help – cutting the meat from his body in thin strips, now left high and dry in the belting sun. Some of the meat, however, is of course cooked on the spot to serve as lunch and dinner.

'We found it healthy and tender,' Wills records, 'but without the slightest trace of fat in any portion of the body.'[92]

Such nourishment that poor Billy provides is more than welcome, most particularly as by now Gray is not the only one ailing, and the other three, too, are starting to feel weak in the legs, while also suffering shooting pains. All of them now are clearly going downhill . . . while moving as if always heading uphill, with the gradient becoming progressively steeper and more exhausting, as the days pass.

And yet, and yet, these be among God's most beautiful things: a diamond in the rough, a bird in the hand, and *rain in the desert* . . .

For after two more days of pushing through the Stony Desert, the rain that starts falling even before dawn on this fifteenth day of April – to continue throughout the day – is more than welcome. At least they are able to refresh themselves, fill their waterbags, and stave off further the fear that they will run out of water before getting to the other side – hopefully only a two-day march away.

The only downside is the difficulty the animals have climbing the wet sand-hills and by 4 pm Landa is so knocked up that Burke calls a halt for the day, as they make camp 'at a clay-pan among the sand-hills'[93].

Yes, they are all exhausted, but there is also a growing excitement among them. After four months and a bit, they are only a little under a week away from getting back to the Depot, where the rest of the party await, with copious supplies!

•

In his journal, back at the Cooper's Creek Depot, on 15 April the exhausted and ever weaker Brahe, with an ever shakier hand, writes: 'Patten is getting worse. I and McDonough began to feel alarming symptoms of the same disease.'[94]

With Patten begging for pity's sake to be taken back to civilisation, back to Menindee, and on to Melbourne, to receive serious medical treatment, what choice does Brahe have? So grave is the situation, but so likely is it that medical help will save Patten, it is Brahe's view that Patten 'had a good right to expect to be removed when that time [of waiting for Burke] expired . . .'[95]

And it *has* expired, every bit as much as Patten is clearly about to if they don't get him to help. By the promise Brahe had given to Mr Burke, it had expired five weeks ago; by the promise he had given Mr Wills, a week ago.

In any case, his impression, as he would later recount, is that once he gets back to Menindee, 'I should hear of Mr Burke's being [in Queensland]'[96], just as they had discussed back in December, before Burke had left. That is, if he had not taken another route entirely, perhaps going westward to Gregory's Track.

Either way, the point remains.

'I had not given up Burke for lost, but had the best reasons in the world for knowing that he was a bad bushman. My impression was that if he found the route a bad one he would come back another way . . . My idea at the moment was that he was out somewhere near Eyre's Creek, in the interior.'[97]

•

As they continue to make their way across the Stony Desert – extraordinarily dry, ferociously flat and sandy, with, yes, stones that measure from pebbles to boulders – it is clear that Gray is getting worse. *Much* worse. For several days now he has been so weak that not only can he not walk, he cannot even ride and must be *strapped* to a camel, for he is simply 'unable to sit alone'[98].

As to his spirits, they are, as might be expected, as low as the Valley of Death, and he and his now haggard tattoo mermaids seem likely to be heading for six feet even lower than that. When Burke finally calls a halt for the day – at a point where they are estimated to be just 15 miles from Cooper's Creek, and 40 miles from the Depot, right by a swamp covered with the tangled bush, *polygonum lignosum* – all they can do is to make the now phonetically eponymous Gray as comfortable as possible by the fire. Clearly, never has Gray himself felt so pessimistic as to his chances of survival.

'I wish,' he rasps, 'in the case of my death, inform Mr Foster [Superintendent of Police, Swan Hill], and ask him to get my effects to my parents.'[99]

Only a short time afterwards, however, Gray has moved from thinking his death a mere probability.

'I will not live till morning,'[100] he rattles, before slumping back.

There is nothing to be done, bar make him as comfortable as possible.

And yet, as good as his word, just before sunrise, as they make ready to leave, and come to gather up Gray . . . the other three look down upon his form to see that he is having some kind of seizure. Oh, poor Charley! He shivers, he shudders, he shakes, he shuffles off this mortal coil, he settles . . . he dies before their eyes.

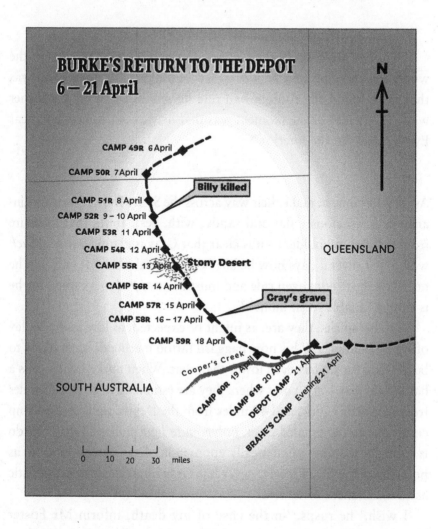

'Both Burke and Wills,' King will later note, 'were sorely distressed by the unexpected and sudden nature of his seizure.'[101]

Mr Wills is bereft at the memory of accusations past, thinking how cruel 'Poor Gray' must have thought him for having accused him of shamming, when he in fact had 'suffered very much'[102].

Truthfully?

The death of Gray is sad, but as unsurprising as it is . . . almost . . . welcome. In these last few days he has been almost an invalid, and without him they will be able to speed up, and hopefully get back to the Depot at Cooper's Creek. And it is far from insignificant that their remaining supplies will now only have to be divided by three, instead of by four.

•

In Melbourne, on this same morning, an editorial in the *Argus* is soon attracting comment.

> It is now eight months since the Victorian Exploring Expedition started from Melbourne, and it is not too early to inquire whether we can be of any further assistance to it. We have first to consider what is the probable position of Mr BURKE and his men at the present moment – where on the map of Australia we are to look for him . . .
>
> If we can . . . ascertain what route Mr BURKE had determined on, we do not see that the *Victoria* could be better engaged than in proceeding to that part of the coast.[103]

Doubts are being raised. Just where are they? What has happened to them?

Despite the governor's assurance at the Royal Society meeting just a week earlier that there is 'no ground for anxiety as to [Burke's] safety'[104], that anxiety nonetheless appears to exist. Reading the articles, Mr Lockhart Morton feels a certain savage vindication. Far from being alone in his worry for the expedition – fraught as it was, from the start – he now finds a public ally in no less than the *Argus*. Swelling with pride in his own prescience, he plucks a pen and begins to write with acerbic flourish . . .

> Sir,
> Having a short time ago suggested that a vessel should be sent to the north coast, I regarded the remarks made by His Excellency as tending to prove that such a step was not considered necessary by the Committee. If I am right in this, I beg to say that I entirely differ from the opinion of the Committee, and I am glad that you have taken the matter into consideration. It is my firm belief that Mr Burke, instead of starting from Cooper's Creek either for

the west or north-west coast, or for the centre of the continent, undoubtedly started from Cooper's Creek with the intention of going direct to the nearest point at the head of the Gulf of Carpentaria ... Professor Neumayer can throw a great deal of light on this matter; but, as he has not taken any notice of what I said before on this subject, I would now beg, most respectfully, to ask the professor, if Mr Burke did not urge upon him the necessity of the Committee sending a vessel to the Gulf? As I said before, and I have seen no reason to change my views, if he is not now at the Gulf he is lost; and I would add, if by forced marches and by throwing away every encumbrance, the party has gained the head of the Gulf, in the hope of finding help there, what state must they be in there now? Even supposing that the party have got through to the north coast, have they with them provisions to enable them to return to Coopers Creek?

I am, Sir, yours respectfully,

W. LOCKHART MORTON.

April 17.[105]

•

The death of Charley Gray hits the others hard and, whatever else, causes no little delay in their journey. To just bury him quickly at Camp 58R and move on would not be ... decent, not respectful, not the gentlemanly thing to do, and so they take their time. True, this might not be a particularly wise decision under the circumstances, but, starved, thirsty, and in a fog of exhaustion – perhaps tempted by having a good reason to stop their infernal trek, if even for a few short hours – it is the one Mr Burke makes.

After closing Gray's eyes, and crossing his arms in the classic manner of a Christian burial, they remove what few personal effects he has on him.[106]

Ordinarily, for such a task, had they been healthy, it would have only taken them under an hour to bury him. But, as weak as they are? It is as exhausting as it is difficult, scratching away at the hard terra-cotta ground to gouge a three-foot deep grave with bleeding hands, and hearts, is no small thing – particularly when it is only John King and William Wills doing it. Mr Burke, either by virtue of rank or exhaustion, does not help. It is equally King and Mr Wills who, once the grave is dug, with great delicacy, wrap the corpse in 'a flannel shirt, trousers and a large piece of oil-cloth'[107]. And now Charley is safely placed in the spot he will rest for all eternity, with his soul to rise to a place where there is no dysentery, no scurvy, and you can eat as much skilligolee as you like, with no repercussions, certainly no thrashings, *and* there are real mermaids.

Under the wide and starry sky, dig the grave and let me lie . . . Home is the sailor, home from the sea, and the hunter home from the hill.[108]

'With this act, my mournful duty to the dead was closed,' King would recount. 'I went then to [look] after the straying camels, during which time Messrs Burke and Wills interred the corpse . . .'[109]

Now, it is Burke himself who leads the service, expressing his hope, in his thick Irish brogue, that the same Good Lord who has steered them to this extraordinary place, and taken Gray's life, will at least have mercy on his eternal soul. And yet, yet, still they are not done. Not satisfied that Gray's body will be able to lie undisturbed from the attentions of wild animals – for his corpse is only a couple of feet deep, rather than the six feet deep they would have liked – Mr Burke insists, now that King is back with the camels, they engage those very beasts to pull heavy logs from a good distance away, for most of the rest of the afternoon, to lie over the grave and protect it. Now, and only now, is he satisfied.

'We remained a day to bury him,' King would recount, 'but were so weak that we could with difficulty accomplish it . . .'[110]

By the time it is all done, the first signs of twilight are already streaking the sky, and Mr Burke decides to take the opportunity to rest, announcing that they may stay here, and leave the following morning. Yes, time is pressing, but a few hours either way is unlikely to make any difference. Besides, they are completely spent, and couldn't walk another mile if they wanted.

At daybreak the next day, however, they are on their way. They pass a lake just two and a half miles from Charley's grave and, soon after, they are back fully on Cooper's Creek, and heading upstream, towards where they know the Depot lies – with the three men rotating between walking and riding on the two camels.

To further speed up these last few days, Burke insists they leave behind the last few things that are not essential, and in short order, some of the horsehair-stuffed camel pads, a tin pot, and a few other bits and pieces are left by the wayside. These are placed in a bag and hung from a high branch of a tree, while even a rifle is put in a hollow trunk, in the hope that, like Mr Wills's instruments, once they have got back to the Depot, they can send out a party to retrieve these things. For now the key is to keep moving, as fast as they can.

Mr Burke is now, however, more confident than ever that they are just days from their own salvation. So much so, in fact, he asks King what he would like to do once he gets back to what Burke is sure is now a 'permanent Depot'.

'Do you wish to remain at the Depot or accompany me to town? I am sure I can get you permission to remain a few weeks in town and then return to the Depot.'[111]

Mr Wills makes King the same promise.

They really could be back in Melbourne, triumphant, by early July!

•

At the Depot, Brahe continues supervising his men as they make the final preparations for their forthcoming departure. Whatever else, he is sure to keep a close eye on the horses, as just in the last few days, as feed has become ever more scarce, five of them had wandered as far as 15 miles away before being gathered in once more. Making the matter even more problematic is that neither Patten or McDonough is now well enough to either search for them if they get away again, or hold the fort back at the Depot if Brahe has to leave to look for them once more. It is yet another factor in Brahe firming in his resolve that they *must* leave, and very soon.

For now, he is more certain than ever that there is no longer any point in staying, as he notes in his journal on 18 April.

'There is no probability of Mr Burke returning this way. Patten is in a deplorable state, and desirous of being removed to the Darling to obtain medical assistance, and our provisions will soon be reduced to a quantity insufficient to take us back to the Darling, if the trip should turn out difficult and tedious. Being also sure that I and McDonough would not much longer escape scurvy, I, after most seriously considering all circumstances, made up my mind to start for the Darling on Sunday next, the 21st.'[112]

•

For Burke, Wills and King, it is a wonderful day in the life of the expedition.

They are not only moving through familiar country, but they know they are close to the camp where Mr Wright and the others will be waiting for them, with, surely, plentiful supplies!

In fact, so confident are they that they will soon be able to eat to their hearts' content that Burke allows them to eat as much of poor Billy as they like – and they avail themselves in full.

It is 11 days now since they have eaten anything *other* than Billy and yet, while his taste is far from succulent, still they would not call the king their uncle as they gorge themselves, getting just a little more energy to move on through the comforts of familiar land.

That tree! That rock with the curious knob! That watercourse!

They are really getting *close* now!

By sunset, they know they are no more than 30 miles away, and though it will be a long haul, they can do it in a single day if they are on their way at first light. Camp 61R is a camp of rich feasting and good cheer, for this will be their last camp before the Depot.

CHAPTER THIRTEEN

A DEPARTURE AND
AN ARRIVAL

*The contrast between the circumstances under which I had
commenced and terminated my labours stood in strong relief
before me. The gay and gallant cavalcade that accompanied me
on my way at starting – the small but enterprising band that I
then commanded, the goodly array of horses and drays, with all
their well-ordered appointments and equipment were conjured up
in all their circumstances of pride and pleasure; and I could not
restrain a tear, as I called to mind the embarrassing difficulties
and sad disasters that had broken up my party, and left myself
and Wylie the two sole wanderers remaining at the close of an
undertaking entered upon under such hopeful auspices.*[1]

Edward Eyre, writing of his ill-fated journey to Central Australia in 1842[2]

*It vexes me . . . that John does not take a top prize, for I see by
his countenance that he understands as much, if not more, than
any boy in my school; yet from want of readiness in answering
he allows very inferior lads to win the tickets from him.*[3]

Mr Porter, one time academic to William Wills in England

21 April '61, Camp 65, Cooper's Creek Depot, timing
is everything

The spring day dawns bright and perfect, with nary a cloud in the
sky. The gnawing nip of the night is soon replaced by the warmth
of the rising sun, summoning the birds, bees and butterflies to come

out in force. William Brahe is up early, as there is much to do on this day ... the day he will finally lead his men away from the Depot to the south, after they have, literally, held the fort for the last four months and four days.

Are they *really* going to do it?

Ja.

Brahe has gone through the arguments for and against too many times in the last weeks – most of them with himself – to go through them all again. He is convinced they have no choice and there is no hesitation in his movements now as he sets about ensuring that all is as it should be before they leave.

Among the many items that Brahe packs up in preparation for departure is a parcel of Mr Wills's clothes, left with him by the man himself. For one thing, as Brahe would note, 'We ourselves were very badly off'[4], as their own clothes are now mere rags, and for another it seems unlikely in the extreme that Mr Wills will ever be back in these parts to claim them himself.

A similar sentiment guides the note he now writes. It is not addressed to Mr Burke or Mr Wills. It is not addressed to anyone. It says only:

Depot, Cooper's Creek,
April 21, 1861.
The Depot party of V.E.E. leaves this camp today to return to the Darling. I intend to go SE from camp 60, to get onto our old track near Bulloo.
 Two of my companions and myself are quite well; the third – Patten – has been unable to walk for the last 18 days, as his leg has been severely hurt when thrown by one of the horses.
 No person has been up here from the Darling.
 We have 6 camels and 12 horses in good working condition.
 William Brahe[5]

(In fact? Brahe has gilded the lily more than a little in describing the condition of both the party and their animals, as they have struggled to survive in this godforsaken hellhole and are departing with no little relief. They actually have one *seriously* ill man in Patten, two fairly ill men in himself and McDonough, and at least two of the camels are in very poor shape. But the Prussian man has written it thus, for a very specific purpose. It is highly unlikely that Burke and the Gulf party will ever read it. No, it is far more likely it will be Wright's supply party, should they ever show up, or, God forbid, a search party sent out by the Committee from Melbourne. And in that case, as he would relate, 'I did not wish to give any uneasiness to any party in coming up on our account. It is very probable if I had stated we were ill that they would have thought we should never reach the Darling.'[6])

The men pack up the goods they need, all other objects being left in a careless clutter – barrels and shovels lie randomly about – they are too weak to leave order where none is required.

The division of the remaining supplies is a key equation that Brahe has had to resolve. Who has priority? His own four men – including a gravely ill one – who most definitely need it now, or the four men who *might* be out there, coming back, but in all likelihood will never arrive to claim it? In the end, Brahe has favoured his own men, setting aside 50 pounds of flour, 50 pounds of oatmeal, 50 pounds of sugar and 30 pounds of rice to be left for the Gulf party. It amounts to one third of all the food he has, and should be enough to sustain Mr Burke and his men for three weeks on full rations – while, most crucially, there is enough for his own four men for six weeks.

'Taking into consideration that we would be obliged to travel slowly on account of Patten,' he would recall, 'and on account of the scarcity of water which I calculated to have to contend with, and would probably be on the road to the Darling at least six or seven weeks, I considered that I could not take less provisions.'[7]

(One thing they won't have to carry back are Mr Burke's 'small parcel of pocket-books'[8] that Brahe had solemnly promised to burn should the leader not come back. For Brahe now indeed gets a good blaze going and then, one by one, throws in each successive 55-page leather-bound notebook that Mr Burke had given him, watching them burn with Tom McDonough as his witness.)

The food left for the Gulf party, he decides, will be buried at the base of a large tree that stands right by the stockade, right by where the horses are usually tied up – where their hoofs already toss the soil around a good deal anyway.

The men put the supplies in a large wooden chest, a 'camel trunk' ideal for the purpose, three feet broad, as many feet long, and 18 inches deep. Brahe rolls the note and puts it through the opening in a bottle, which is now placed at the top of the supplies, and then the lid closed, before the whole thing buried, with a good 18 inches of soil above it. Carefully, he throws horse dung around and over it, so that it looks exactly like all the other earth around the Depot. Taking the rake, he spreads the dung under the coolabah tree, leaving the rake leaning against the stockade. It is a thorough job. Under no circumstances must the natives have a clue that valuable supplies lie beneath.

On the tree, Brahe blazes the word DIG,[9] the blade cutting deep and the sap instantly weeping. On another tree, he marks the initial B for Burke and the camp number LXV, as well as the dates of their arrival and departure, DEC 6-60 and APR 21-61.[10]

•

Still scanning the horizon to the north, hoping against hope the expedition party might suddenly appear, at 10 o'clock in the morning, Brahe gives the order.

Break camp, *meine Herren*.

A long journey awaits, and so off they go, moving at that fair clip always engaged in by men through the ages when they are turned for home. Within 30 minutes their breakfast campfire is no more than a small smudge on the horizon far behind them, and by 40 minutes it has been swallowed entirely.

•

At this very moment, Burke and his party are just 14 miles away. They are so exhausted that, for the first time on the entire journey from Cooper's Creek to the Gulf and back, they stop walking and get on the camels, with Mr Burke climbing aboard the groaning small camel, Landa, while Mr Wills and King cling to the doubly groaning, but at least larger, Rajah.

They push on along the creek.

Nearly there now!

It has been a long, hot, exhausting day. But why not push hard, when the object of their dreams – the Depot at Cooper's Creek – is so near at hand? And it is not just the usually undemonstrative Robert O'Hara Burke who feels it, this rising sense of joy, of relief, it is that he seems to feel it most of all. He takes his natural place in the lead, and sets a fair clip for the last mile into camp. For perhaps even the camels feel it, too, knowing that succour and rest is near at hand if they can just get there.

The sun has just gone down, as Burke gets to within a couple of hundred yards of their camp.

'I think I see their tents ahead,'[11] Burke calls back with uncharacteristic fervour.

And now he calls the names of the men he knows must be waiting.

'Coo-ee . . . Brahe! Coo-ee . . . McDonough! Coo-ee . . . Patten!' (There is no call for Dost Mahomet.)

For the moment, there is no reply, which is a bit odd.

Still, entirely undaunted, Burke continues to charge forth to find . . . no one. Emptiness. Not even an echo to their cries in the wilderness. Just a light breeze . . . blowing wistfully through an abandoned and entirely disinterested camp.

'I suppose they have shifted to some other part of the creek,'[12] Burke offers hopefully.

The cicadas roar ever louder.

Wills concedes it as a possibility.

They roar. Oh, they roar.

Perhaps the men had moved camp in search of better feed?

But no. Now that they look more closely, it is to see there is fresh dung scattered about, and certain things like barrels and shovels tossed aside here and there, and a good rake up against the stockade that would most certainly have been taken with them if they had merely just moved a mile or two up or down the creek. No, this looks distinctly as if they have . . . gone for good, gone on their long journey to the south.

For the moment, the leader simply wanders around in a state of 'bewildered astonishment'[13] that, one more time, he has arrived *just that little bit too late*, and that instead of the succour they had so earnestly hoped for, strived for, they remain . . . all alone . . . in the wilderness, with, yes, their only remaining supplies being 'a pound and a-half of dried meat'[14] – the last of poor Billy.

For his part, John King is equally devastated, but cannot help but notice Mr Wills's strange reaction. For the effect of the whole situation on Mr Wills, he would recount, was 'to excite a feeling of merriment in the mind of Mr Wills, whose philosophy was essentially that of Mark Tapley'[15]. (Tapley being Wills's favourite character in Charles Dickens's *Martin Chuzzlewit*, with a philosophy that 'there's no credit in being jolly' when everything is going well. Therefore, Tapley deliberately sought adversity 'to come out strong under circumstances as would keep other men down'[16]. What greater test of this ambition is the current circumstance of William Wills? Fate has laughed at him, now he laughs at his fate.)

Wills dismounts with difficulty – it is no easy thing for a seriously weakened camel to bend at the knee and lower itself to allow the seriously weakened man atop to dismount gracefully – and is staggering around himself, when he sees it.

Upon a coolabah tree, just above the bank of the creek, is clearly marked the word:

DIG

From the cuts in the tree, fresh sap is weeping.

Wills, observant as ever, looks down at the ground and surrounding trees, in search of more clues.

There! Another weeping inscription on a tree just a few yards off. He walks over to get a closer look. On one side is Brahe's initial and the camp number:

B

LXV

Around the other side of the tree is pure torment:

DEC 6-60
APR 21-61

. . .

. . .

'They have left here today!'[17] he calls to the others.

His words echo in their very souls and it is a moment before the cruel implications of this information can be fully comprehended. It is staggering, extraordinary, impossible to believe . . . but believe it they must, for when King puts his hand down above the ashes of the fire it is to find it still hot. There is even a tiny flame flickering from the end of one log! They must have left just *hours* ago.

Wills falls to his knees, soon joined by King, as they push away the horse dung and scrabble at the loose dirt, beneath where the word DIG has been carved. Within a minute, they find a camel box, and quickly prise off its lid, as the still dazed Burke stares down upon them. Inside, mercifully, they find welcome supplies of flour, rice, oatmeal, sugar and dried meat, 'a few horse-shoes and nails, and some odds and ends'[18], together with a corked bottle.

'Whatever instructions there are,' Mr Burke says quickly, 'will be in that bottle.'[19]

Without a word, King dashes the bottle against a tree trunk, and hands Mr Burke the note inside.

After scanning the contents, which confirm that Brahe's party left mere hours earlier, Mr Burke informs the others there is at least some good news.

'The Depot party is in good condition,' he says, 'except one man, Patten, who is suffering from the kick of a horse . . . The animals are all in good working order . . .'[20]

Handing the note over, Wills and King read it for themselves. The Brahe party really has left *just that morning*, to return to the Darling. Extraordinarily, there has been no sign of Wright in the entire time they've been away. Brahe and his men have got six camels and 12 horses in good working condition, which means . . . that even though they only left hours earlier, they are surely too far away by now. Every hour would be taking Brahe's party three miles further away from the Gulf party at the Depot.

•

In fact, at this moment, given Patten's perilous state, Brahe and his men are no more than 14 miles upstream of the Depot, or three hours hard march. Not too far at all. What's more, the animals are not in the condition Brahe had thought.

'I had not travelled half-a-dozen miles when I found that [the horses and camels] were hardly able to travel,' Brahe would recount. 'I had to lighten the loads the first day, and they were but very lightly packed with water bags.'[21]

A concerted effort by Burke, Wills and King – or even just the strongest of them, King, on foot, following Brahe's fresh tracks – on through the night, 'neath the three-quarter moon, might catch them. It might at least bring him close enough to them that Brahe's party would hear a rifle shot, bearing in mind how far the sound of such a shot can travel at dawn. But that is not the way the note reads to the trio. They are exhausted men, on completely spent animals, who have travelled 30 miles on this day. If they can do that, how far away must the fresh Brahe and his group be, notwithstanding that they would be travelling with many supplies?

The short answer, likely, is *too far*.

For now, Mr Burke individually asks both Wills and King, for once, *their* views.

'Are we,' he rumbles, 'able to proceed up the creek in pursuit of the party?'[22]

Without hesitation, both men reply, 'No.'

'I thought it my duty to ask you,' Burke nods, 'but [even if you could], I myself would be unable to do so.'[23]

With one glance, neither Wills nor King are surprised, for the leader looks just as they feel: not totally at the end of their tether, but they can certainly see the tether's end from where they stand, and would be sure to find it only a short way up the creek.

Burke, clearly feeling the weight of his decision to remain at the Depot, rather than try to chase Brahe's party, reiterates his feeling on the matter.

'It would be madness to attempt to follow them, as the men are in good order and the camels in good order . . .'[24]

It really is unimaginable to set out now.

They have missed them, and there is nothing to be done for it. And in fact, so crushed are they by how close they have come that, as King would note, 'It was as much as any of us [could do] to crawl to the creek for a billy of water.'[25]

That at last done, however, they can help themselves to such supplies as have been left them – to make 'a good supper of some oatmeal porridge and sugar'[26] – an oh so welcome change from the dried horse-meat they have been solely existing on for breakfast, lunch and dinner over the last fortnight. (And in fact, King would even note that, starving as they are, the first sight of the food lifts them a little, recounting, 'we did not mind it very much, as there was plenty to eat'[27]. Their major disappointment in terms of the supplies left is the lack of clothes, as they now wear little more than stinking and shredded rags.)

Upon discussion around their sad campfire that night, Burke determines that their best hope will be to stay here for at least a couple of days. And he has also determined their next course of action.

'I have decided,' he says, 'we should try to make Mount Hopeless. I have been assured by the Committee in Melbourne, that there is a cattle station within 150 miles of Cooper's Creek.'[28]

Mr Wills and King take his words in.

Their best hope, nay *only* hope, is a station in north-east South Australia at a place called . . . 'Mount Hopeless'?

Once more, these are extraordinary times. Never before has Mr Wills ventured an opinion, one way or another, on any pronouncement made by Mr Burke. He has been simply content to follow orders.

But this time he speaks unbidden, albeit in deeply respectful terms.

'I am not inclined to follow this plan,' says he. 'I wish to go down by our old track.'[29]

It seems to Wills that even though Mount Hopeless is the closest settlement, the safest way is to push down Cooper's Creek, before heading to Torowoto Swamp and then to Menindee.

No one asks King his views. But he silently agrees with Mr Wills.

Mr Burke listens to Wills, but then makes his case. The simple fact is that while Menindee is some 500 miles away on the other side of the perilous Grey Range, if they stick to their old track – and they would have no native guides this time, to help them find what little water there might be – Blanchewater station, right by Mount Hopeless, is at the other end of a creek, and is a much shorter distance. Our limited supplies will only last 40 days at most, and so are unlikely to take us through to Menindee, and Augustus Gregory has already demonstrated that survival, *in extremis*, lies in these parts by way of Mount Hopeless, and in 1858 he had managed it in less than a week.

Now, it is not that Mr Burke's case is compelling. But he is the leader, he has decided, and that is that. True, the previous year, in the bright winter sunlight on the greensward of that small church in Essendon, Mr Burke had faithfully promised that he would do as Dr Wills had requested, when it came to William: 'If you ask his advice, take it'[30]. And yet now, when their very lives are at stake, when a course is asked of a born surveyor, the boy who ran through Hampton Court maze as though he had designed it himself, Mr Burke asks, but does not take Wills's advice. That same evening, that same conversation, Dr Wills had said to Mr Burke, 'Should he see you going to destruction, he will follow you without a murmur.'[31]

Sure enough, in the face of this life or death decision, William Wills does not murmur. He simply begins to plot the best route from here to Mount Hopeless . . .

At least, Mr Burke says, they may stay here for a couple of days to gather themselves, and regain some of their strength, before pushing on.

Through it all, Wills remains almost unnaturally calm, with King observing, 'he never once showed the slightest anger or loss of self-command'[32].

In fact, Wills is simply hiding his high emotions well, which is typical of him. As they settle down for the night, Wills takes the opportunity, first, to pen his thoughts in his diary.

Our disappointment at finding the Depot deserted may easily be imagined; returning in an exhausted state, after four months of the severest travelling and privation, our legs almost paralysed, so that each of us found it a most trying task only to walk a few yards. Such a leg-bound feeling I never before experienced, and I hope

never shall again. The exertion required to get up a slight piece
of rising ground, even without any load, induces an indescribable
sensation of pain and helplessness, and the general lassitude makes
one unfit for anything.[33]

As exhausted as he is, Wills's thoughts turn guiltily to poor Gray. How many times had they looked askance at his shambling gait, his constant insistence on resting, his slowness to get going in the mornings and thought him 'shamming'. It is with great shame that he realises Gray was simply suffering, two or three weeks earlier, what they are suffering now. How lucky they are, to have been able to get to at least this point, with some fresh supplies, before the worst of it has come upon them. Already they can feel the beginnings of *some* strength returning to their limbs, some of the stiffening lifting, as their bodies react to taking in something other than dried Billy. It is so sudden and so strong that both Burke and Wills talk of it, how it is 'a most decided relief and a strength in the legs greater than we had had for several days'[34].

•

On this night, a wedge-tailed eagle from its position high in the sky might be able to spot several flickering lights in the night, to go with the impossibly sparkling panorama of stars above.

There directly below are the three tightly placed fires of Burke and Wills, and their faithful trooper, King – a fire for each of them is the best way to keep warm on cold nights, each man lightly curls his body around the small corral of flames. Just 14 miles down the path to Menindee is the rather larger and cheerier fire of Brahe and his companions. Another 125 miles away over the Grey Range, is Wright's party at Bulloo, still stranded there, after several excursions to the north have failed to reveal either Burke's forward track or any supplies of water. Besides, it is anyone's guess where they actually are. 'Wright,' Dr Beckler would note, 'had no way of telling whether we were not already on a part of Cooper's Creek as none of us were able to make astronomical observations – although from all we knew, Cooper's Creek had to be quite distant from Bulloo.'[35]

And those other sparkles across the vast wilderness? They are the Yandruwandha people, who have not only survived, but prospered in these parts for something like the last 18,000 years. To them, it is just another night of the Dreamtime or *Pukudurnanga*. Their bellies are full, in this land where food abounds in this season of plenty. Their families are secure in the gunyahs and among their kin. All is right with the world, as the spirits of the Dreamtime play across the sparkling night sky.

22 April '61, Koorliatto, portrait of a parlay in black and white
Noises in the night! A chanting in the distance. And there, too, comes the sound of the rhythmic tapping together of heavy wood on wood, even as the haunting, pulsing chant rises and falls.

It sounds . . . menacing.

Something is going on, and it is more than enough to put the Wright camp at Bulloo on edge, and perhaps even over it. There are many natives in these parts and there is a growing sense that they are unhappy with the white men's presence. But the white men can no more admit defeat and go back than they can find the tracks of Mr Burke and go forward.

Alas, there is no respite with the dawn, for in the mid-morning, Wright looks up to suddenly see them.

Natives!

Eight of them. Big men. Strong men. *Black* men – so impossibly black their skin more glows in the bright sun than shines. And they are heavily armed 'with new boomerangs, spears and waddies'[36], together with *nulla nullas* – wooden clubs, ingeniously designed to . . . beat in heads.

It is a worry, and a serious one. In his own party now, Wright has seven men, of whom three are ill, one of them – Charles Stone – gravely. (Stone, in fact, blighted by syphilis and scurvy at the one time, seems likely headed straight for a grave. He has lightning-like pains down his legs, seizures and fits. The man is in a medical hell while stuck in hellish desert conditions to boot.) In terms of defending their patch, Wright can really only call on Dr Beckler and their half-caste, John Smith, as Hodgkinson has gone off searching for camels that have strayed, accompanied by the sepoy Belooch. And the odds against the white men are about to be stacked even higher.

'In a few minutes,' Wright would recount, 'a large body of them appeared on the bank of the creek, distant sixty yards from our stores, thronging through the scrub, and occasionally showing in the open, in parties of seven and eight.'[37]

The white men recognise one of the blackfellas from previous interactions. He is the obvious leader of the group, and well known to the men.

'This native conducted himself in an especially friendly and courteous manner and seemed to be very perceptive,' Dr Beckler recalled of their first meeting. '[He] behaved so openly and seemed so friendly and ready to help . . .'[38] He had even indicated that he could guide them along Mr Burke's track.

Wright had rewarded the charismatic native with gifts – a cap and a shirt. Taking the new items in hand, the native man had barely been able to contain his excitement. A shirt! For it is the shirt he loves, never mind the cap, and he dons it proudly, chest puffed out. Indeed, he had been so obviously delighted, so very, very proud of his new shirt that the European men – down on their luck, but not bereft of humour – had dubbed him 'Mr Shirt'.

And he wears the shirt now.

But on this visit, Mr Shirt – wearing his precious shirt, of course – seems changed; less friendly, 'impudent'[39] even, in the eyes of Mr Wright.

With some 30 of his fellow black fellows with him, Mr Shirt is arrogant, insolently walking around their pile of stores, as if he *owns* the very ground the white men are camped on – his swagger helped by the fact that in his every step he is flanked by two remarkably powerful blacks, who almost look as if they are the high officers for this black leader.

'Mr Shirt,' Dr Beckler chronicles, 'now appeared in the foreground and we could immediately recognise the parliamentarian in him.'[40]

That's it! The way he harangues those around him, flourishes his hands in extravagant gestures. The way they look to him for leadership. He is every bit a black parliamentarian, albeit one with weaponry!

And what is he doing now?

Suddenly dropping his aggressive demeanour, Mr Shirt transforms before their eyes, coming forward with no weapons, ignoring the cries of Wright to *'Stay back! Stay back!'* and sits before them, clearly inviting the white men to join him.

Why, why . . . it looks as if he wishes to *talk* with them!

'It was one of the most interesting experiences of our journey,' Dr Beckler will carefully chronicle, 'to see an Australian savage display the same characteristics and the same behaviour that we would normally associate with the concept of a "diplomat" even though he had never seen a European apart from Mr Burke as he quickly passed through.'[41]

There is, yes, even a certain *nobility* to his coal-black features, 'an unshakeable calm . . . in his movements'[42].

And he really does have a message he wishes to impart to them.

'In a sign language which he supported with quiet but flowing speech,' the stunned Dr Beckler records, 'and which seemingly cost him no effort at all, he explained that we must leave this place. The area belonged to his tribe . . .'[43]

Extraordinary!

With not a word of the Queen's English in him, Mr Shirt makes them understand that he found 'especially impudent that Wright had dug up a small piece of ground at the water and had planted various seeds'[44].

This is *not* the white man's land to do any such thing, and they must leave.

'We could do nothing else,' Dr Beckler notes, 'but boldly declare to him that we intended to remain here for the time being.'[45]

This prompts yet more dissertation from Mr Shirt on why that would be a mistake on their part.

And yes, his words, for now, remain quiet, but the fact that the blacks behind him are edging ever closer underlines that, like all of the most successful diplomats, he does have other – shall we say, less *pleasant* – options, if his interlocutors don't listen to reason.

Wright has no doubt as to their intention, noting how the other blacks kept 'drawing nearer to us, violently gesticulating, making signs that they were hungry, and that we were camped upon their ground'[46].

Wright has had enough.

'Stand up!'[47] he shouts at Mr Shirt.

Mr Shirt calmly declines to do so.

Mr Wright now steps forward and, grabbing the black man by the collar of his much-vaunted shirt, lifts him to his feet and shoves him back to the other blacks, where a lissom maiden, as naked as the day she was born, has now appeared. Mr Shirt's woman? Dr Beckler, for one, cannot take his eyes off her.

'From time to time she threw her head back scornfully and with inimitable grace, she let out a ringing, derisive laugh that showed her shining white rows of teeth. Crossing her snakelike legs over each other she held her slim boomerangs between her back and her twisted arms with the most charming lack of self consciousness.'[48]

Wright, too, is impressed by her, recounting how 'one tall, strapping lubra accompanied them, and was exceedingly active, bearing a boomerang with considerable grace, and inciting her companions to attack us'[49].

For his part, though, Mr Shirt barely blinks. Yes, he has angry men behind him, and one angry woman, but he knows they won't make a move until he gives the word. And yes, too, the white man may now be angry and undignified himself, but the black man, this Aboriginal prince, will not so lower himself.

Speaking softly, using hand movements, Mr Shirt continues 'to repeat his demand – our departure. The words which accompanied his gesticulating were eerie; they were spoken quietly but occasionally they were short and disjointed.'[50]

He makes them understand that if they remain here, it is not just the blacks at his back the white men will have problems with. No, they must understand that several large tribes will come together to drive them out, his black hands indicating the direction they will come from, and just how extraordinary their number will be.

'In all, he brought a magnificent army together.'[51]

Despite himself, Dr Beckler continues to be impressed, even going so far as conceding that the whole of this territory in dispute the blacks 'with all justice called their own, and . . .'[52]

And now what?

A preliminary battle, just to test each other out?

Perhaps.

For now, two boys come out of the bush, carrying boomerangs and the like, which they casually throw on the ground before their fathers, uncles and elder brothers.

'This scene too,' Dr Beckler notes, 'was very much reminiscent of those old, aristocratic knights who considered it beneath their dignity to carry their weapons with them before battle and were served by their pages and sword carriers . . .'[53]

Picking the weapons up, the blacks start clapping their boomerangs together. It is the same sound Wright's party had heard in the night!

Are they framing for an outright attack?

Wright has no doubt of it, and as he, Dr Beckler and John Smith bring their weapons to bear on these insolent black men, the former station manager unleashes his entire vocabulary of 'Australian "bush-slang", wishing them to the very depths of hell . . .'[54]

And now another voice is suddenly heard.

It is that of the severely ailing Charles Stone, lying prone in his tent. He speaks something of the language of the Darling natives, 'and in the broken voice of a dying man, [tells the blacks] that they should try our patience no longer for we did not want to hurt them . . .'[55]

Mr Shirt lightens for a moment, allowing Wright to do the same, the latter even going so far as to offer him some dead rats by way of compensation for their land . . . which Mr Shirt condescendingly accepts. It is something of a stand-off, which continues until Ludwig Becker croaks feebly from where he lies, warning Wright that natives coming from another direction are now creeping towards their cooking fire by the creek, where they have most of their utensils and some of their washed clothes.

Taking Smith with him, and their guns, Wright walks towards these natives, their fingers on the trigger in the same spirit as the blackfellas are 'fingering their boomerangs as if impatient for a [fight] . . .'[56] And now the brutes are helping themselves, lifting up the flaps of the tent in which Purcell lies gravely ill, and unpacking the medicine basket, even as one black fellow brings an entire armful of extra boomerangs for his brother warriors, so they can help themselves.

This time Wright really has had enough.

Grabbing Mr Shirt by the shoulder, he brings his revolver to the black man's head 'and threatened to shoot him on the instant if he did not soon clear off willingly'[57].

Mr Shirt, with a *sang-froid* that again simply astonishes Dr Beckler, drops the previously proffered dead rats at Mr Wright's feet and indicates that Wright should pick them up for him.

Mr Wright will do no such thing, DON'T YOU UNDERSTAND?

This time Wright's patience really has gone – the *insolence* of Mr Shirt carrying on like this – and he continues shouting at him, still with his revolver at Mr Shirt's head, marching him backwards.

Following his lead, Dr Beckler, Hodgkinson and Smith also push forward, with their rifles aimed right at the blacks, making it clear that they will shoot if the natives don't clear off, now!

Wright is also aware that the amazingly plucky Charles Stone, though at death's door, groaning, has rolled over on his bed, and is backing them up, aiming his revolver at the natives.

Mercifully, by now the natives have witnessed for themselves the extraordinary power of these noisy sticks the whitefellas have – able to kill birds at a height and distance far beyond the power of their own boomerangs – and, for now, have no desire to face that destructive power at such close quarters.

As quickly and mysteriously as they have appeared, they now melt away once more, taking with them 'every portable article from the fire, throwing away the tea and salt', but 'taking the bags'[58] for they interest them more.

Within a minute there is no sign of them. It is as if the country has swallowed them whole.

'Eventually we got rid of them,' Dr Beckler chronicles with relief, 'and without having to hurt any of these despairing defenders of their motherland.'[59]

Not long after they have gone, however, Wright faces his next crisis. It is Stone, who calls out weakly for him.

'I am going,' he croaks simply, before asking Wright repeatedly to 'throw cold water over me, as I cannot breathe'[60].

Within 10 minutes, Stone has dropped like one, breathing his last, and in the twilight of that evening, Smith and Dr Beckler carry his withered body a short distance from the camp and bury him. Wright fears Stone may not be the last casualty, as William Purcell is now so weak that it is as much as he can do to occasionally, wanly, drink a little water, at which point he faints.

23 April '61, Camp 65, the Depot, departure to destiny

For Burke, Wills and King – now wearing washed clothes that they have patched with pieces of horse-blanket – it is time to depart, to head off west down Cooper's Creek to Mount Hopeless. At least the last 36 hours has helped to restore them a little, and they have gathered together 'all the odds and ends that seemed likely to be of use . . . in addition to provisions left in the plant'[61].

Burke and Wills have, in turn, placed their precious journals in the camel box they had dug up, for safekeeping. Burke has also found strength to pen a note to whomever may find it, detailing their situation.

Depot No. 2, Coopers Cr
Camp No. LXV.
The returned Party from Carpentaria, consisting of myself, Wills and King (Gray dead), arrived here last night and found that the Depot party had only started on the same day. We proceed on tomorrow slowly down the creek towards Adelaide by Mount Hopeless and shall endeavour to follow Gregory's track, but we are very weak. The two camels are done up and we shall not be able to travel faster than four or five miles a day.
Gray died on the road, from exhaustion and fatigue.
We have all suffered much from hunger. The provisions left here will, I think, restore our strength.

We have discovered a practicable route to Carpentaria the chief portion of which lies on the 140th Meridian of East Longitude.

There is some good country between this and the Stony Desert. From there to the Tropic the land is dry and stony. Between the Tropic & Carpentaria a considerable portion is rangy but it is well watered & richly grassed.

We reached the shores of Carpentaria on the 11th of Feby 1861.

Greatly disappointed at finding the party here gone.

R O'Hara Burke

Leader

April 22nd 1861

P.S.

The camels cannot travel and we cannot walk or we should follow the other party. We shall move very slowly down the creek. [62]

Just before closing up the camel box, Burke tears the pages from the spine of his notebook – which he plans on keeping with him – and places them inside, before the lid is lowered. Whatever happens, it is proof that they made it to the Gulf of Carpentaria, and gives an account both of what has happened to them so far, and their intent from this point. Burke had also ensured that Mr Wills and King had put some effort into filling in the hole from which they have taken the supplies, and then covering it with horse and camel dung. Taking the rake, which he finds leaning against the stockade, King makes the whole surface level, with the dung evenly spread, just as it had been when they had found it. Leaning the rake against the tree, he steps back to survey his handiwork, wanting to do all possible to make sure that not the slightest sign of digging is left behind. This is done, King will recount, 'so that the blacks should not find it out'[63].

Perhaps they should carve something new – beside the blaze on the tree – to be seen and understood by the first white men to arrive?

It is the consensus of the weary trio to leave it as it is. For as King would recall, 'We thought the word "dig" would answer our purpose as well as it would theirs.'[64]

Burke is insistent that everything must be left *exactly* as they found it.

King has already been careful to take the broken pieces from the bottle out of sight, and put them atop one of the planks atop the stockade. The exception is that, using a lancet, Mr Wills and King have cut 'a large square out of the hide that formed the door of the stockade'[65] and stuck it on a nail protruding from the stockade. It is a small, subtle sign, should anyone of Brahe's party return this way, but which they think the natives will miss. In the same spirit, King also can't resist scattering some nails around.

At quarter past nine in the morning they move off to the west, keeping to the southern bank of Cooper's Creek.

Shortly after departure, they come across a couple of dozen black-fellas, but Mr Burke has no interest in engaging with them at all.

'There are too many of them,' Burke says, 'and it is no good wasting time.'[66]

Still, it is a measure of Mr Burke's concern for the exhaustion of their two remaining camels – and indeed the growing exhaustion of his own troop of men – that after proceeding for just two hours, when they come to a billabong where the grass grows green and plentiful the leader announces they will make camp here. He said they were going to move very slowly and he means it.

The trio are feeling much better, if colder, as Wills records in his journal that evening. 'We find the change of diet already making a great improvement in our spirits and strength. The weather is delightful, days agreeably warm, but the nights very chilly. The latter is more noticeable from our deficiency in clothing, the Depot party having taken all the reserve things back with them to the Darling.'[67]

They have now taken stock of what Brahe has left them and think it should keep them going for 40 days, or 80 days if they stay on half rations – a reckoning that makes them realise just how grim their situation may become.

Defying William Wills's reckoning that there likely is no God, however, the following morning, just as they are about to start off once more, some blacks appear, bearing freshly caught fish. It takes only a small bit of bartering – giving them a few leather straps and some matches – and they are able to secure 12 pounds of fish! 'This is a great treat for us, as well as a valuable addition to our rations.'[68]

The best thing? As they move down the creek, and the blacks move up it, the trio have some sense that they have successfully fooled their providers, for the men with the matches and straps are 'little thinking that in a few miles they might be able to get lots of pieces for nothing, better than those they had obtained from us'[69].

23 April '61, Bulloo ballyhoo

Where is Charles Ferguson when you need him? Seven years earlier the foreman of the expedition had been one of the men who had helped to build the Eureka Stockade at Ballarat, and, on a much smaller scale, that is exactly what William Wright has decided he needs now at Bulloo. With Hodgkinson and Belooch returned that morning with the camels, Wright gets them all to work building a stockade. After sharpening logs at one end – the logs initially intended for a small hut – they begin partially digging a series of small holes, and start pounding the logs into the ground.

Bit by bit it takes shape, with the logs going as high as about four feet, which is to the good. The bad is that there are not enough, and they can only complete two sides. To make up the difference, the men pile up everything they can get their hands on, from saddles to camel boxes to packs, for the final two walls. Yes, it is rag-tag construction which looks like the stockade that Jack built on a drunken day, but the point remains: the party have protection should the blackfellas come again, while allowing the white men to fire easily over the top.

Now, inside the stockade, they gather every weapon they have, together with their stockpiles of ammunition. Wright also brings the cooking fire within 10 yards of the stockade, so even when they are eating, they will be close enough to instantly defend it. From 8 pm at night, until six o'clock the next morning, they will take their turns doing watch, gazing into the darkness, straining their ears for any sign, any sound of an attack.

23 April '61, Melbourne, whereto the ship of the damned?

In Melbourne, hands are still being wrung about whether a boat should be sent for Burke. Professor Georg Neumayer dutifully tells the *Argus*:

> In compliance with the request of Mr Lockhart Morton . . . I feel great pleasure in stating the following facts . . . Mr Burke informed me that he was determined to proceed towards the southernmost point of the Gulf of Carpentaria, on or near the Albert River; that he intended to propose to the Government of this colony sending a vessel round to that part of the Australian coast . . .
>
> It was the distinct understanding, however, that no direct steps should be taken in the matter, unless it came first from Mr Burke himself . . .
>
> I concluded – in which conclusion the Committee joined – that Mr Burke had abandoned his first idea of a rendezvous at the Gulf, and proceeded, relying upon his own resources.
>
> . . . I remain. Sir, your obedient servant.
> GEORG NEUMAYER.,
> April 22.[70]

Unsatisfied, Lockhart Morton makes reply the next day:

> BURKE'S PROBABLE ROUTE
> TO THE EDITOR OF THE ARGUS
> Sir . . .
> Has the Committee considered what quantity of stores Burke took with him from the Darling. Does it know what Wright took? And

has it met lately to calculate the probable condition of the party, even should it be still in the neighbourhood of Cooper's Creek?

I put these questions with the view of simply urging the Committee to take care that no evil happens through its neglect. Let us hope it will not refuse to be enlightened.

I am, yours obediently,

W. LOCKHART MORTON.[71]

Slowly, but surely, the fate of the Burke Expedition is becoming the talk of Melbourne – what on earth has happened to the man?

24 April '61, Wright's camp at Bulloo, menace and mockery

It is a bad day indeed when the death of one of your party is close to the least of your problems, but so it is for Wright and his men at Bulloo, as poor William Purcell has 'died in the doctor's presence during the night'[72].

The news of Purcell's death is sad, but not shocking.

'For some days past he had been so weak,' Wright will note, 'as to faint after drinking a little water, and we had long been expecting his decease.'[73]

No moment to dally, Wright must get on with the business of the day, and begins by sending Smith and Belooch out to look for the horses, feeding somewhere nearby.

Soon after they leave, Wright is aware that several blacks are approaching. Once again they come heavily armed, this time 'with new boomerangs, spears, and [war clubs]'[74], and once again Mr Shirt is with them.

With Hodgkinson by his side, thus, Wright moves out 'to clear them off'[75]. Of course, the natives do not understand the meaning of any words used, but the sentiment is certainly clear enough as most quickly disperse.

But not Mr Shirt. Belligerently, flanked by his two big men right behind him, and still another dozen behind them, he stands his ground. Wright will have none of it – he grabs him, turns him, and physically pushes him away.

'I thought proper to do this,' Wright would recount, 'as he was evidently only brought to insult us, and at length he retired, with the others, to a short distance.'[76]

Wright is relieved . . .

. . . until he spots that the natives up and down the creek have quickly been joined by another two bands of natives, who had been concealed in the creek timber!

The whole lot of them start to cluster around the freshly dug grave of poor Stone. One of them gathers up a dead rat, yells at it something unknown, before flinging it contemptuously in the general direction of Wright and his men who . . . don't react.

Oh, really?

Try *this* then.

The blacks scoop up dirt from Stone's grave and throw it in the air, before picking up some logs and pretending to build their own stockade.

Now, perhaps something is lost in the translation, in terms of the sign language, but the blacks seem to indicate that it won't be long before Wright and his men are also dead.

'I was very unwilling to fire at them,' Wright will recount, 'and allowed them to throw several sticks at us rather than commence actual hostilities.'[77]

It works. By noon the blacks tire of it and move off to their own camp a little to the north.

The day finishes with Dr Beckler and Hodgkinson quietly going off to begin digging poor Purcell's grave.

•

William Brahe and his men are travelling well, under the circumstances. They travel 28 miles on the third day, reaching Camp 60 – blessed with 'a little water and plenty of good grass'[78] – meaning they are now 50 miles to the south-east of the Depot.

'Finest country in the neighbourhood,'[79] Brahe later reports to the Committee.

But, not to tarry. Within 15 hours, after a good night's rest, they are on their way once more.

Now, they ride into the night, and start again before dawn the next day, covering as much as 34 miles a day for three days straight. McDonough would later report things are so frenetic that, given he had to do his share of watching the horses and camels for the greater part of the night, he 'got no more than two hours' sleep each night'[80].

•

After a sad morning interring their friend Purcell, Wright orders Smith to venture forth with him now and look for the horses, which have strayed overnight . . . only to suddenly feel uncertain . . . and vulnerable with every step that takes them further from camp.

After yesterday's visit from the natives, they are on edge. And here's the thing to tip them over it . . .

Signal fires! To their front. To their right. To their left. Behind them! By now they know what the thin plumes of smoke mean. It is the blacks, indicating to each other, in some ancient system that only they know, exactly where the white men are.

Are they readying for an attack?

Wright thinks it highly likely, and with some speed he and Smith head back to camp.

•

A stirring. A twitching swag in the dawn. It is 5 am, 25 April, and Wills wakes after what would have been a great rest, had he not been awake for most of it, fighting the cold.

It is a benign chill, not yet deep enough to reach into his body and take grasp of his bones, nor even to freeze the dew-drops that cover all by dawn, and the rising sun quickly warms everything and dissipates those dew-drops out of existence by the time the first flock of cockatoos flashes over.

In short order, the others, too, are up and about and they have just finished their breakfast of meagre portions of flour, oatmeal and sugar when suddenly, from all around, 'our friends the blacks'[81] appear once more. They are the same ones from whom they had received fish the day before, and seem inclined to want to travel with them down the creek. This time they are given some sugar, which clearly pleases them, and Wills will carefully note in his journal that 'they are by far the most well-behaved blacks we have seen on Cooper's Creek'[82].

In his early time in Australia, Wills had worked as a station hand at Deniliquin and had not been impressed with the Aborigines. Now, his opinion has risen markedly. For the scientist in him recognises the obvious. The Aboriginal people have adapted superbly to this difficult environment. They are prospering, strong and healthy, while for the white man every day is a daily struggle just to survive.

By 9.30 am, the white men are on their way once more, heading down the most southern branch of the creek, which, happily, pushes generally south-west – precisely the direction they wish to go. The trick will be to turn south at one point, to get from Cooper's Creek to Strzelecki Creek, which, several miles down, should run off Cooper's and head south towards Mount Hopeless.

Precisely, or even roughly, where that junction is, they can't be sure alas. At least it is heartening to see that the water-fowl – the ungainly native birds that abound around the billabongs – are numerous. Proceeding thus, and with another good sleep overnight, the next day, 26 April, they are making their way through 'the most splendid salt-bush country that one could wish to see, bounded on the left by sand-hills, whilst to the right the peculiar-looking flat-topped sandstone ranges form an extensive amphitheatre, through the far side of the arena of which may be traced the dark line of creek timber'[83].

A spring in their step? Not quite, but there is no doubt it is at least joyous to be back on Cooper's Creek, have a sure supply of water, greenery all around, and be a little revived from their near-starvation.

27 April '61, Bulloo, things are quiet, maybe a little too quiet . . .
After a beautifully still morning, with nary a whiff of wind and almost as little movement from the party of William Wright, suddenly, at 11 o'clock, the cry goes up.

'Natives!'[84]

In an instant Wright and his men are on their feet moving everything they can, including themselves, into the stockade.

'On looking out,' Wright will record, 'a body of natives, numbering between forty and fifty, could be seen advancing towards us from the west, not seeking any cover, but marching in good order straight across the open plain.'[85]

This is not merely a visit. This looks suspiciously like an *attack*. The blacks are daubed in a kind of war paint, 'with a deep red band, from the neck down the centre of the chest, crossed by similar bands at right angles to it'.

All are carrying 'more spears than we had seen on any former occasion'[86].

Ah, but there is still worse. Over to the right, another mob of 50 blacks are coming forward, moving down the creek, in what almost looks like a carefully calculated flanking attack.

And as to the blacks in front, though they have been walking fast towards the white men's stockade, once they get to within a couple of hundred yards, suddenly they start running, 'exciting each other with war cries, and placing their arms in position [to throw spears]'[87].

Right at the front is Mr Shirt!

Wright makes every motion for them to stop, but they don't.

'Faster and faster the enemy lines moved towards us,' Dr Beckler will recount. 'We could hear the screeching words of command and communication ... This time we could see they had not come to be driven away with threats. Shirt's voice could be heard above them all. He seemed to speak to all of them.'[88]

Still they advance, and are now just 30 yards away.

'No closer!'[89] Wright roars, pointing to their weapons and indicating they will shoot. It makes no difference. *Still* they keep coming, as Mr Shirt raises his hands and shakes his head in a way that suggests he has done all he can but the matter is now beyond him. To Wright and Dr Beckler it looks more like Mr Shirt is, in fact, the one whipping the others up – and to Beckler's eyes, it seems he is saying 'that nothing could help us anymore, that we were lost'[90].

They keep coming. They keep *coming*!

Now Beckler yells at them. 'Do not come closer! Do not come closer!'[91]

They keep coming. They keep *coming*!

When it seem clear that Wright must shoot or perish, when the blacks are just 20 yards away, Wright gives the order: 'Fire!'[92] and a volley of shots rings out, followed by several more ragged volleys, most of which go over the heads of the blacks.

But not all. One obvious target for William Wright in the mass of blacks is Mr Shirt, and as the aggressive black man surges forward in their lead, just 10 paces away, Wright draws a bead, slowly squeezes the trigger and . . . and now that very shirt suddenly flowers with blooming red splotches. Mr Shirt is hit and goes down hard . . .

'Shirt fell right before us,' Dr Beckler would recount. 'He was a hero from head to toe.'[93]

And in fact, though clearly 'severely wounded'[94], Mr Shirt rises again.

Though more fighting is not in him, still he is able to hurl upon them shouted words that are no doubt that the 'curse of his tribe' will be on them for generations, or the like.

Despite it all, Wright's men are not without sympathy for him.

'It was to our advantage,' Dr Beckler will recount, 'that it was he, the leader, who alone fell, but we all felt sorry for this noble leader and representative of his tribe.'[95]

But it is far from over.

Though in all the confusion, it is clear that the natives have decided against continuing *this* attack – and soon turn and run – they have only gone some 600 yards, before they stop, turn and start to regroup. Clearly, this is a job for one of the long-range guns, the 'excellent Terry rifle . . .'[96]

'I fired . . . at them,' Wright would note proudly, 'and . . . dispersed them.'[97]

Indeed, the shower of sand that a single bullet raises, just behind the blacks, is indication enough that the white's thunder-sticks are powerful even at this distance – 600 yards – and it is further encouragement for them to move further away.

Mr Shirt is last seen 'hobbling slowly [away], pressing his dirty shirt carefully to his abdomen . . .'[98] and soon disappears into the scrub.

Throughout the night thereafter, they can hear the 'distant lament of a native'[99]. Now, whether the wailing is the devastated keening of the lissom maiden who had stood as Mr Shirt's companion and fellow warrior just days before, or Mr Shirt himself, or the others, no man can say. But eventually the haunting sound stops.

So be it.

Vastly relieved, Mr Wright goes to visit the ailing Ludwig Becker in his tent shortly afterwards, to check on his condition, only to find that his condition is so far gone that he had not even been aware of the armed confrontation.

Worried, Dr Beckler tries to tell him in his native German what has happened, 'but he showed no sign that he understood my reports'[100].

The medico is not surprised, having himself become completely exhausted, simply in trying to look after him.

'He was dependent of me in every respect,' Dr Beckler would recount, 'and a major part of the day and night was spent exclusively in tending him. My nightly rest was interrupted so much by this that I slept only very little, and hence all the more heavily as soon as I had peace, hearing neither Becker's quiet calling nor his little bell. Nothing remained but to tie a string around my arm. This ran under the wall of the tent to his bed; by pulling it he could call me to him at any time.'[101]

The following morning, it is apparent that Becker is at least doing just a little better than Mr Shirt. For although through the night they have listened to 'the loud, distant lament of a native, undoubtedly Shirt or the natives who were with him . . . by morning all was quiet'[102].

It is time for Wright to reassess.

'I now resolved to quit Bulloo immediately,' he would recount, 'as such a small party were quite unfit to maintain a long contest against the large tribes around, and any men would be picked off while necessarily absent in search of the camels.'[103]

It will take a day or two to pack and get going, but it is time to retreat to Torowoto Swamp.

28 April '61, easier for a camel to get through the eye of a needle than Cooper's Creek . . .

Yes, some say that Sunday, as the day of the Lord, should be a day of rest, even for explorers. But Burke and Wills are not of that school of thought – the former is still too frantic to keep moving, the latter

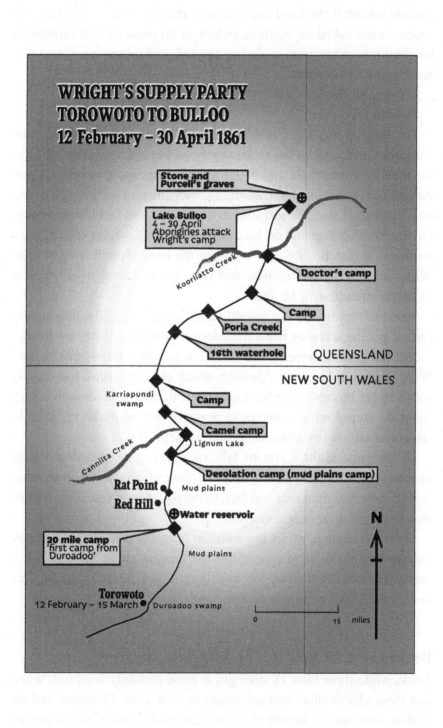

entirely unsure if the Lord even exists in the first place – and King, of course, is not asked his opinion. In fact, at no point on this expedition has Burke ever put time aside for any religious observance, and this Sunday is no exception.

Is the Lord displeased?

Possibly.

For, early on this day, five days after they have begun their trek down Cooper's Creek, one of the remaining two camels, Landa, gets stuck in the mud by a waterhole and is too weak – *nuur, nuur, nuurr* – to pull himself out. Grumbling and snuffling, snorting and sniffing, groaning and moaning, Landa almost sounds like an old and feeble man trying, but unable, to get up and off his deathbed. More worrying still, Landa's weakness is matched by their own, for the newly found strength that Wills had noted with the new diet does not last long when there is anything strenuous to be done.

Strain as they might, dig around Landa's legs as they do, they simply cannot get the scrawny beast free, despite working all day to do so.

'All the ground beneath the surface was a bottomless quicksand,' Wills records in his diary, 'through which the beast sank too rapidly for us to get bushes or timber fairly beneath him, and being of a very sluggish, stupid nature, he could never be got to make sufficiently strenuous efforts towards extricating himself.'[104]

By the time night starts to fall, they have progressed precisely nowhere, and the only result of all of their efforts sees Landa more deeply immersed than ever – in fact, so deeply, there seems some chance that he might disappear entirely!

'As a last chance, we let the water in from the creek, so as to buoy him up and at the same time soften the ground about his legs, but it was of no avail. The brute lay quietly in it as if he quite enjoyed his position.'[105] Like a hippopotamus.

Before dawn, 29 April '61, Brahe returns, Becker departs

Look, while three into 18 does go, it most certainly does not, when just three able-bodied men are trying to look after 12 horses and six camels, who are so thirsty they are half-maddened. Then, it can be very untidy indeed, as witness the situation with Brahe and the Depot party trying to control their animals, particularly when their horses are used to running freely after spending four months doing just that near the Depot, and the 'want of water makes them inclined to ramble'[106].

Overnight, once again, several horses have got away and, once again, it is Brahe himself who takes on the responsibility of going out after them, starting out on his horse, even before first light, following their tracks as they appear to head north-east.

Just as dawn breaks he first hears some whinnying up ahead, and then a few seconds later, he sees them!

Just under a quarter of a mile away, there are the errant horses and . . .

And what is that?

For just beyond the horses, a plume of smoke is rising.

It can only be a native encampment.

Cautiously, Brahe rides closer. If so, he might be able to enquire of them if they have seen hide or hair of 'the Darling party', Wright's mob.

Only a few yards further, Brahe sees him.

A European man, advancing towards him!

A few yards further again, and he recognises him. It is William Hodgkinson! A diminutive Hodgkinson, to be sure, a much thinner, more gaunt figure than he remembers. But Brahe is in no doubt that his own form cuts a much smaller shape these days too.

There in the Australian wilderness, the two men, who have not seen each other for six months, shake hands, each completely stunned by meeting with the other. Hodgkinson, of course, leads Brahe back to Wright's camp.

'I placed myself and party,' Brahe would chronicle, 'under the orders of Mr Wright.'[107]

For his part Wright is delighted to have the two parties meet, but not as stunned as Brahe at the meeting. In the otherwise silent watch of the night, just gone, Wright and his men had heard that most civilised sound, a bell, to their south, and been able to dimly perceive 'dark objects, like cattle . . . through the darkness'[108].

Hodgkinson had been sent out at first light to investigate and returned shortly afterwards with Mr Brahe. The two camp leaders

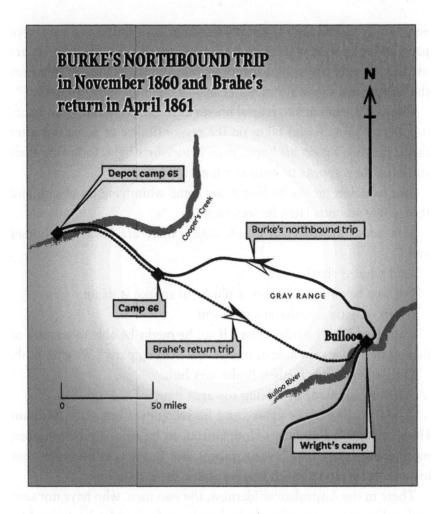

BURKE'S NORTHBOUND TRIP in November 1860 and Brahe's return in April 1861

N

Depot camp 65

Cooper's Creek

Burke's northbound trip

GRAY RANGE

Camp 66

Brahe's return trip

Bulloo

Bulloo River

0   50 miles

Wright's camp

quickly exchange precious news. Brahe explains to Wright that he had not been following the exact course between Bulloo and Cooper's Creek that Burke had pursued, but gone by a more direct course to reach Mr Burke's Camp 52, eight miles south of where they are now. To a certain extent, the plan had worked, in that Brahe's party had covered the ground relatively quickly, with one significant problem.

'My horses,' Brahe tells him, 'have been without water for 100 hours.'[109]

In fact, the likely reason the horses had broken from Brahe's camp is they smelt the very water that Wright is camped beside at Bulloo.

Mr Wright knows Brahe's current camp well, having passed it on their way to Bulloo on 4 April, nearly four weeks earlier.

Since leaving Menindee in late January Wright's party have been beset by widespread illness, by attacks from Aborigines, by constant problems with both horses and camels straying, and by lack of water. They had been right on the point of retreating, this very day, had Brahe not found them.

From here, Wright decides on the obvious, to bring the two camps together, and accompanies Brahe back to Camp 52, where his men are shocked to see Wright – the very man they have been waiting to join them for the last *five months* – and he, in turn, is quite shocked at their condition.

'I found,' the station manager would recount, 'Patten suffering from scurvy to an alarming extent, McDonough almost unable to work, and [Dost Mahomet][110] complaining . . . Of the camels brought down by Mr Brahe I found three – Beer, Rowa and Mustana – suffering severely from scab.'[111]

After Brahe's men pack up, it is noon before they arrive back at Wright's camp and reunite with his party. There is Dr Beckler, Smith, Belooch, Hodgkinson and a gravely ill Ludwig Becker, together with myriad supplies, 10 camels and 10 horses. There is, of course, a fair measure of hail fellow well met. And yet the clear truth is that many of Wright's party are in fact as far from hale and hearty as can be. All of Brahe's party are quite shocked by their appearance.

'They were . . . in the most wretched state,' McDonough would later recount, 'everything thrown about in the greatest disorder.'[112] Just in the last week, Wright's party has lost two men to illness, Charles Stone and William Purcell, and their fresh graves are just 100 yards over yonder, by the water.

There is a pall of gloom over the camp so thick and dirty it is like a funeral shroud covered in flies. And for good reason . . .

'Our sojourn on the lovely waters of [Bulloo] now hung by a single tenuous thread,' Dr Beckler would recount. 'We still had to wait for the passing of Mr Becker, who had been on the verge of death for several days.'[113]

When Beckler takes Brahe to pay his respects to Ludwig Becker, the old man 'no longer even recognised [Brahe] and now he spoke only occasionally in disjointed sentences'[114].

When the sun falls, the ailing Ludwig Becker . . . who has come so far, and done so much . . . clearly approaches the long night ahead, the way he may have looked for succour from his mother's breast as a baby in Germany all those years ago. For that long darkness has a peace that the agonising daylight cannot deliver, and he is only sure he never wants to leave . . .

In the mournful moment Dr Beckler can do nothing bar watch his fellow officer, fellow artist and fellow German . . . slip away. Still, though clearly at death's door, it is so typical of Ludwig that he just manages to jam his foot in the said door, and find a way to poke and provoke his former tent-mate one more time for the road. For as Dr Beckler hovers close, Becker struggles to speak.

Yes? What is it, Ludwig?

'I want your neck,'[115] he says.

Mein neck! He wants me hung? His scurvy ist my fault, he thinks? We have had our differences, but this is . . .

Becker's little, and last, joke. For after a tiny pause Becker gurgles to life once more to complete his sentence: '. . . to take a bold swing to the right.'[116]

Ach, so, quite amazed that Ludwig can still summon humour in so grave a situation, Dr Beckler 'gives his neck', bending a little to offer it to his dying comrade, who . . . reaches up, grips his hands together at the top of Dr Beckler's neck so that, indeed, with a bold swing to the right, he can be moved into a more comfortable position. In fact, the move evolves into something resembling a warm embrace, as they both recognise that the end is near. They have had their differences, and are entirely different kinds of men, but Dr Beckler is filled with pity as he gently lays the old man – for he has never looked older than right now – into a final lying, dying position.

Within minutes, Ludwig Becker breathes his last.

'That night,' Dr Beckler chronicles, 'we dug a third grave and laid Becker with his traveling companions.'[117]

Over breakfast on the morning after poor Ludwig has been buried, it is Brahe's right-hand man, Tom McDonough, who asks the question all in the Brahe party have been thinking: what on earth has delayed you in reaching us?

'I did not think,' Wright replies, 'I had sufficient horses or sufficient provisions to leave the Darling. The horses were knocked up by Lyons and MacPherson. [Also,] what is the good of my living up there with three or four months' provisions?'[118]

Brahe cannot help himself, even though Wright is now his superior in rank, his remark is impertinent.

'You have both camels and horses,' the German remarks, crisply.

'I waited because my appointment was not confirmed,' Wright insists. 'I wanted more money to buy more horses to carry up the provisions. It is no good for me to run on with a few camels and horses.'[119]

On the subject of just where Burke and his party are now, William Wright is firm.

'Lost,' he says flatly. 'Neither gone to Queensland nor gone anywhere else; the man has rushed madly on depending upon surface water, and the man is lost in the desert.'[120]

So what does it matter that Wright is five months late? (Truthfully, Brahe's news that Burke never got there anyway is further vindication for his lack of early action.)

There is really only McDonough to vociferously argue the toss with him, even going so far as to wager 'a bet that [Mr Burke will] be found at Queensland or turn up somewhere'[121].

The Irishman is convinced that his friend Burke is just too strong to die. He *must* be out there somewhere!

1 May '61, Cooper's Creek, another death in the party

A little over 150 miles to the north-west at this moment, Burke, Wills and King are struggling.

Specifically, they are struggling with Landa who is – not surprisingly under the circumstances – in exactly the same position as the previous day. Up to his knees in mud. Once again, they do their best to extricate him, but in the course of another day's struggle it becomes apparent to Burke they have but one option left.

A shot rings out. Now, it may be easier for a camel to pass through the eye of a needle than for a rich man to enter heaven, but it is easier still for a bullet to pass through the eye of a camel and for three men to have a rich feast. Either way, Landa's suffering is no more.

The best they can, over the next two days they strip the stringy flesh from his bones, to cut into small strips, which are soon drying in the sun, even as Rajah, their last remaining camel, watches closely.

This is what happens to camels who can no longer pull their weight; a clear problem for Rajah, as the weight he must now bear is likely greater than ever. The men transfer whatever they can of Landa's load to him – including some of the weight of the dried meat of Landa himself – but soon realise Rajah is not fit to carry much at all. Back when they had left Royal Park eight and a half months earlier, they could have loaded Rajah with as much as 400 pounds, and he would barely blink, but now they are able to load him up with only 40 pounds. The three explorers keep, as Wills recounts, 'a small swag each, of bedding and clothing for our own shoulders'[122].

Inevitably, they must discard much of the rest – 'Camel pads,' King will note, 'and such things as bed clothing we had to leave behind'[123] – before they set off once more, at 8.40 am, on 1 May.

From the first, it is obvious that under the new conditions it is going to be difficult.

'Our load was so much heavier now,' King would recount, 'that we had to travel very slowly, and the other camel was beginning to knock up.'[124]

Pushing further down the creek, they keep to the right bank until they come to a native camp up ahead, at which point they cross to the left.

On they go, trying to find the branch of Cooper's Creek they are looking for, which will lead into Strzelecki Creek, which will take them all the way to Mount Hopeless.

At a point where the creek turns north, they hopefully continue west along a native path, thinking the creek must turn back to them, as it had been on the maps Wills had seen, hoping for . . .

There it is!

Having crossed an open plain, and a few sand ridges, they spy Cooper's Creek again. They push along it, heading west.

•

Among the Yandruwandha people, the word soon spreads up and down Cooper's Creek. There are three *kurrani*, mad white men, wandering all over the creek, 'like ghosts'[125]. They had got back to *pula pula*, the waterhole where the other white men had been, and appear to be sick, or starving, or both. The most devastating thing is what the white men had done to the *yirrbandji*, coolabah tree. They had hacked into it. The sacred home of some of the Yandruwandha's spirit ancestors senselessly attacked!

The Yandruwandha simply cannot fathom why anyone would do such a thing.

1 May '61, Bulloo, the retreat advances

Today is the day. Now two days since the two parties have joined up, Wright, as the officer in charge, has decided that the time has come to move their now expanded cavalcade back south, down to Menindee. Of the nine men, only five of them – Dr Beckler, Mr Hodgkinson, Mr Brahe, Dost Mahomet and Mr Wright himself – are healthy, and, as Wright would explain, 'I did not see the utility of pushing on the Depot to Cooper's Creek for the purpose of remaining there the few weeks our stores would last.'[126]

For some of the men – led by William Brahe – the idea of turning their back on Cooper's Creek, now they have supplies a'plenty, does not sit easily.

Too bad. Wright makes it very clear to Brahe and the rest of the men waiting with him at Bulloo that he has no hope that Burke is still *alive*, let alone relying on them to move forward.

'He is gone to destruction,' he says firmly, 'and will lose all who are with him.'[127]

McDonough is not so sure at all, and the whole thing sits uneasily with him, too. As far as he knows, Mr Burke and all the rest are still relying on them to go forward, and it seems odd that they have not done so. Yes, Mr Wright has been left in charge, and McDonough can do nothing bar follow orders, but still. He *feels* Mr Burke is out there.

Which is as may be. But on this first day of May, Wright has given the order, that they are moving south. Saddling and loading done, at half past ten in the morning, all is set to go, and Wright gives the word.

'Our cavalcade,' William Wright's diary records on this day, 'made quite an imposing appearance, with its twenty-two horses and [16[128]] camels, and the spirits of the whole party were animated by the prospect of regaining the settled districts.'[129]

True, it proves to be slow going, as they must stop many times to re-organise their loads so that the camels will keep going, as well as making their ailing invalids more comfortable – though nothing seems to relieve Patten, who is in a terribly bad way – but they indeed reach their old camp at Koorliatto Creek by mid-afternoon, and stop for the rest of the day. A modest start to the trip south, yes, but a start nevertheless . . .

The problem is, what now?

'McDonough, Patten and [Dost Mahomet] were suffering from scurvy on their arrival at Bulloo,' Wright would note, 'and, with the exception of [Dost Mahomet], became quite unfit for the slightest exertion or movement.'[130]

2 May '61, Cooper's Creek, let them eat cake

After breakfasting by the light of the moon, Burke, Wills and King start at half past six. Heading down the creek, moving west, after six miles they come across an encampment of blacks on the creek bed, who react quickly to the sight of the white men.

Jumping to their feet, they rush forward to . . . offer 'presentations of fish and cake'[131], the latter being like small, circular bits of heavy bread. The white men don't know what it is made from, but it fills their bellies, and that's all that matters. In return, Burke offers them fishhooks and sugar.

A small parenthesis here. Quite why these particular natives need, or would be interested in, fishhooks when they have prospered in these parts for some 40,000 years without them – using cleverly woven nets made from the matted stems of plants – is not clear. Equally odd? Burke, Wills and King have a diminishing supply of rations, in an area where fish abound. They do not have the skills of the blackfellas in catching these fish by traditional methods – mostly using nets – but are so disinterested in using the Western method, with fishhooks, that they are giving them away. Close parenthesis.

The men strike out again, only to find that the creek breaks into, first large waterholes, now small ones, now a few larger ones . . . now smaller still . . . and now nothing.

What had been the creek, King would recount, 'lost itself in the channels of an earthy plain, and accordingly [we] had to retrace [our] steps to the last water left'[132].

Rajah only just makes it, and shows the all too familiar signs of being done up, and is now trembling worse than ever. Is there anything that can be done to save him?

The only thing possible is to lighten his load still further, 'to the amount of a few pounds by the doing away with the sugar, ginger, tea, cocoa and two or three tin plates'[133].

It is unlikely to make much difference, and they all know it. What now?

The whole situation is dispiriting, as they had understood that 'the creek along Gregory's path was continuous'[134], and it surely had been when he had ventured along it in 1858. But it isn't now.[135]

That evening, at their camp, there is little talking, but much quiet, miserable reflection.

'We were all three beginning to feel bad now . . .'[136] King would note. In an effort to give Rajah every chance of some recovery they give him 'balls of sugar and oatmeal', while also consuming 'a considerable quantity of sugar'[137] themselves. After boiling the water, they slowly stir in the oatmeal and sugar.

3 May '61, Koorliatto, but what if they are there?

It has taken a couple of days, but William Brahe has at last made headway in convincing Wright that it is wrong to simply turn their back on the Depot at Cooper's Creek. After all, now that their parties are combined, with supplies, and they are no longer in danger of running out, there really is no risk in returning. And with just the two of them, with three horses, travelling light and fast, without a whole clumping, clumsy, cumbersome caravan on their trail – and Brahe himself knowing where all the water can be found – they could do the whole 300 mile round trip in as little as 10 days. It makes sense.

Beyond that, Brahe, personally, is feeling stronger with the better food; Patten, on the other hand, is now so ill that it is more dangerous than ever to move him. Yes, his spirit remains admirable, and he even manages to rasp to Brahe at one point, 'I will be carrying you on my back yet . . .'[138] but that prophecy appears ever more forlorn. In fact, Brahe is in no doubt that poor Patten really is dying, and his only hope is good food, with complete rest.

Much better that Patten stay still for a fortnight, in the doctor's hands, while Brahe and Wright go back to the Depot?

'Mr Wright not having been to Cooper's Creek,' Brahe would recount his views, 'I thought that we could not be better employed than in going back there as a last chance for Mr Burke.'[139]

Finally, Wright agrees. He and Brahe will go back, starting today.

'I resolved to give the sick a further spell,' he would later recall, 'while I advanced with Mr Brahe to the Depot at Cooper's Creek, for the purpose of ascertaining whether Mr Burke had returned or the provisions left there by Brahe had been discovered by the natives.'[140]

His men, however, fail to get the impression that Wright's own calculations have much to do with the safety of Mr Burke and the Gulf party at all. For one thing, Wright and Brahe are taking practically *no* supplies with them, bar the ones they will need themselves carried on a single pack of their packhorse.

'My opinion,' Tom McDonough will later state, 'was, that his object was to go to see Cooper's Creek, but not to relieve Burke. That is the impression I got from his conversation.'[141]

After all, there is no getting around the fact that Brahe has made it clear that they were all expecting Wright's party at the Cooper's Creek Depot in the middle of December. Wright is in little doubt that when they get back to Melbourne questions will be asked. Getting there six months later is not good, but it is at least better than not getting there at all.

3 May '61, Castlemaine, campaign trails

Gentlemen, I give you, your local member!

In Castlemaine's theatre – 'literally crammed, boxes, pit, and stalls . . . full to overflowing'[142] – the applause for Dr John Macadam – who, by the by, is the newly appointed Post-Master General of Victoria – is warm and sustained. He is now campaigning for his return to the Legislative Assembly in the forthcoming election, and there seems little doubt that he will romp home once again. Still, he can't help but list all the things he has done for this fine electorate while representing their interests down in Melbourne Town. Why, in all humility . . .

'I may fairly take credit for the assistance I rendered to the exploration cause,' he offers, 'at the head of which exhibition is Mr Burke, your fellow townsman.'[143]

He pauses. This time the crowd seem oddly mute.

'I was the proposer of Mr Burke,' he tells the crowd, as if letting them in on a secret, 'And saw, as far as possible, that the vote for exploration causes was properly distributed.'[144]

And now comes a rather awkward interjection from the heart of the crowd, 'What about the I.O.Us?'[145]

(*Damned Burke, and his damned debts!*)

Of course, Dr Macadam ignores the heckling and ignores Mr Burke now too, sensing that self-interest, not explorers, is what will gain him votes. Are the electors aware he personally ensured that six water reservoirs will be erected in this district? No? He will eloquently elucidate at length, as always.

5 May '61, Cooper's Creek, out in the 'wild wastes of this vast continent'[146]

The cockatoos no longer rise at the sight of the white men. For no more is this a noisy camel-cade, so much as three exhausted men, trudging, trudging, trudging along, struggling, as things are grim and getting grimmer. Time and again, Burke, Wills and King pursue offshoots of the creek heading south, hoping it will turn into the blessed Strzelecki Creek which will take them all the way to Mount Hopeless, only to find . . . nothing. Every time, the creek simply shrinks, falters and stops in the earthy plains. If only they had Robert Bowman with them – the man who had so irritated Burke with his constant references to the way Mr Gregory did things – it would surely be easy. Bowman had actually been with Gregory in 1858 when he had made his way from here to Mount Hopeless, via the Strzelecki. But Bowman has long since been sacked and his now suddenly priceless memories are not available.

All they can do is retrace their steps, push further west, and try the next promising tributary . . . only for the same thing to happen again and again and again . . . until it is Mr Burke and King themselves who begin to shrink, falter and stop on the earthy plains.

In desperation, William Wills encourages them to rest, to make camp with their remaining camel beside a billabong, while he proceeds to the south alone, looking for the creek that will save them. As before, however, the soil by the banks of the creek offshoot he is following becomes drier and more cracked, even as the box trees beside it become wearier and smaller the further he goes, until they, too, disappear into nothing . . . just like the creek.

Spying a high sand ridge to the west, which might afford a view, he treks to that – noting, as he gets close, how the bushes on top stand on tip-toes, as the whipping wind has removed so much of the sand around their roots – only to see another, even higher ridge further west. Finally, getting to the top of that, he is able to indeed get a good view of the surrounding country, and searches earnestly for the line of green somewhere to his south which might indicate Strzelecki Creek, but he sees only 'earthy plains, apparently clothed with chrysanthemums'[147].

Exhausted, defeated, he has no choice but to slowly make his way back to where he has left Mr Burke and King.

•

For his companions Wills remains jolly and optimistic, but his journal records his true state of mind.

From Camp No. 10 back to No. 9.

Monday, 6th May, 1861.—
The present state of things is not calculated to raise our spirits
much. The rations are rapidly diminishing. Our clothing, especially
the boots, are all going to pieces, and we have not the materials for
repairing them properly. The camel is completely done up and can
scarcely get along, although he has the best of feed, and is resting half
his time. I suppose this will end in our having to live like the blacks
for a few months.[148]

They should be so lucky. For the next day, heading further down the creek, they come across some blacks fishing, who not only give them half-a-dozen fish each but some more of that 'cake' they had the other day. It is a curious kind of . . . bread, really, that they discover the blacks have made from pounding up the seeds of a vegetation that grows in abundance near here. The blackfellas call it . . . *nardoo*. Wills, the one man of science among them, recognises it as a curious black seedpod that is very edible, and possibly even nutritious. And it is this that the women are grinding and pounding to mix with water and make their small cakes.

At the blacks' invitation, Burke and Wills accompany them back to their camp, where they are given more fish and nardoo than they can eat.

This time, to entertain the blacks, Burke demonstrates how he can light a fire. No, not in the laborious way the blacks do it, by rubbing sticks together, but by striking the large red phosphorous head of the match against any rough surface.

'[The trick] with matches,' Wills records, 'greatly delights them, but they do not care about having them. In the evening, various members of the tribe came down with lumps of nardoo and handfuls of fish, until we were positively unable to eat any more.'[149]

It is wonderful, with only one problem, as Mr Burke reports to John King the next day, when he returns to where they have left the young man nursing Rajah: 'We could not explain that we wished to be shown how to find the seed ourselves.'[150]

John King also has news. Rajah has not remotely improved. (The bitter truth: Rajah is now so weak there is a real question as to whether he can carry his own hump, let alone the lump of another.)

'I don't think he can linger . . . more than four days,'[151] King tells Burke. The significance of Rajah's impending doom escapes none of them. With a healthy camel carrying water for them, they could cross a desert for as far as 100 miles between waterholes. Without one, they are effectively restricted to staying on Cooper's Creek.

CHAPTER FOURTEEN

FULL CIRCLE

It was he who really took Burke across the continent and brought him back to Cooper's Creek. Without Wills, Burke would have been absolutely helpless.[1]

Alfred Howitt, 1907

8 May '61, Cooper's Creek Depot, not always better late than never

Finally, it has come to this.

Five months after Burke had been expecting him, William Wright arrives at the Cooper's Creek Depot. Back then, Mr Burke had been expecting him with an officer and three men, 10 camels and seven horses, all hauling several tons of fresh supplies.

On this day, at 8 am, Wright arrives with just one other man, William Brahe, each on a horse, with one packhorse for their own supplies.

But, beyond that, Mr Wright?

As one contemporary observer, Andrew Jackson, will later archly note, Wright 'did not bring even a morsel of bread or a cup of cold water to help the poor sufferers then pining away for lack of food in the wilderness in the very hour of their victory!'[2]

Both men tie up their horses, near the tree where the cache of supplies is buried, and dismount. In the first instance both men are vastly relieved to see no obvious signs that any Europeans have been there since Brahe left – as it vindicates the actions of both. But they need to be sure.

'Take particular notice,' Wright tells Brahe unnecessarily, 'to see if the place was in the same way you left it . . .'[3]

405

For of course Brahe is soon walking all over . . . to the stockade . . . all around the trees . . . down to the creek . . . looking carefully for any signs, any tracks in the light brown dirt that might tell of recent arrivals.

Now if Peter, the Aboriginal guide, had been with them – the man capable of finding water in the desert by a few scratches of a dingo – he would have been able to tell them, no doubt, the complete story of who had been there, when, with how many and what kind of animals . . . and which way the wind was blowing at the time.

But such expertise is completely beyond Wright and Brahe.

'I saw the old tracks where the camels had been,' Wright would note, 'but even if I had noticed the tracks or taken any notice of the tracks about the camp it was so short a time after Mr Brahe had been there that I should not have noticed any difference in the tracks; after a track is a week old a person does not know whether it is a week old or ten or twelve days old.'[4]

There are no discernible footprints, which is not surprising. The whole place is very dusty, there are the scurry marks of rats everywhere, human footprints would never last long. The cache is exactly as it was when Brahe had left it – yellow sand, now covered by dry camel dung. The easiest way to find out if Burke's Gulf party had been back there would be to dig up the cache and to see if the bottle or supplies have been taken, but Wright rejects that outright.

'I thought if I disturbed the place where the things were buried and took the bottle up,' he would recount, 'the chances were the blacks, as I supposed they had been at the Depot, would discover them . . .'[5]

What Brahe and Wright do notice is the remains of three different fires, which definitely is different from the way they had left things. Clearly, the natives have been here in the interim.

'There was not a stick of wood as large as one of the pens on the table, which was not burned,' Wright would recount, 'just as a black fellow makes a fire, he just brings what is enough to keep a fire and no more.'[6]

(It is a conclusion that Lockhart Morton, for one, will, later, bitterly criticise, proclaiming how this errant assumption conclusively demonstrated 'their want of bush knowledge or bush skill in observing. A black fellow's fire is no more like that of a white man's than a gum tree is like a pine tree.'[7])

Brahe pokes around some more, and concludes that everything does appear exactly the same. There is the tree, just as it was when Brahe had left it 17 days earlier. Certainly there are the dried remains of the weeping sap from the blaze that Brahe had cut upon it, but there is no fresh blaze there. There is a rake leaning against the tree, which Brahe had in fact left leaning against the stockade, but, in the moment, it does not catch the German's attention. Nor does the broken bottle strewn across a plank above the stockade. Nor does he remark, particularly, on the small strip of leather missing from the door and now hanging by a nail from the stockade. Most likely the blacks cut it from the door for some mysterious native reason. Who knows, with them? It doesn't matter. The point is, there is no sign of any civilised man having been here, no sign of occupation, of digging, of empty tins, of anything.

For his part, Wright is interested in the tree with DIG emblazoned upon it, and had he been there without William Brahe, would likely have done exactly that – to inevitably discover the note left by Mr Burke, establishing that they are still alive, just 30 miles down the creek. But with Brahe – who has explained the whole thing, and what they buried – there is no need, and so Mr Burke's note goes undiscovered.

Beyond the tree, Mr Wright betrays little interest in much of anything, bar one thing – he wishes to *absolutely* ensure that no one can know they've been here.

'We will put our horses in here now,' Wright tells Brahe, referring to the spread horse dung, 'and let them walk about on it, and the blacks will never think of digging there if they should happen to be looking about.'[8]

Meanwhile, neither he nor Brahe make any move to leave a fresh blaze on the tree, for what would be the point? The blaze of the twenty-first of April contains all the essential information necessary, and it is not as if anyone is likely to come upon it anyway.

Should they stay the night?

Mr Wright is of a mind to, and suggests it, but Brahe demurs, as their horses are familiar with this area.

'If we stop here to-night,' the German says, 'the horses will certainly go back five miles up the creek, to the place where they used to run, and we shall have to walk up there in the morning for them.'[9]

In sum, no more than 15 minutes after they arrive, they turn, walk away, and are soon on their long ride back to join their party where they have left them at Bulloo Creek.

Now, if Brahe, on this occasion, has a certain lightness of spirit it is fair enough. The decision to leave the Depot before Mr Burke had come back with his party had not come easily to him, and he had retained the haunting fear over the last fortnight that he might have made an error. They might have been just days away? He might have been abandoning them to their fate?

But, no. Here they are, 17 days later, and there is *still* no sign of them. He is more convinced than ever that, if they are still alive, they have either been picked up by a boat at the Gulf of Carpentaria, or, more likely, made their way back via Queensland. They are probably almost 1000 miles away now, and more than likely having a well-earned beer.

10 May '61, Cooper's Creek, the last ship of the desert goes down

Rajah has not improved. He is 'so weak that he couldn't get up off the ground'.[10]

They remove his load.

He won't get up.

They remove his saddle.

He won't get up.

'Shoot him,'[11] Burke orders.

As instructed, John King does the honours and, afterwards, using the only sharp tools they still have – 'two broken knives and a lancet'[12] – jerks the camel's meat in the sun.

William Wills leaves them at work and goes 'out to look for the nardoo seed for making bread. In this I was unsuccessful, not being able to find a single tree of it in the neighbourhood of the camp.'[13]

Wills returns to find that Burke and King have made a good start on the jerking. While eating some of the meat that evening, it is decided that on the morrow, Wills can continue with that task, while Burke

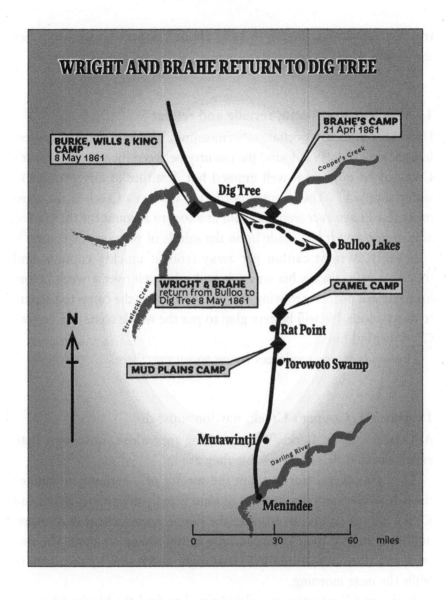

WRIGHT AND BRAHE RETURN TO DIG TREE

BRAHE'S CAMP
21 Apri 1861

BURKE, WILLS & KING
CAMP
8 May 1861

Cooper's Creek

Dig Tree

Bulloo Lakes

WRIGHT & BRAHE
return from Bulloo to
Dig Tree 8 May 1861

CAMEL CAMP

Strzelecki Creek

N

Rat Point

MUD PLAINS CAMP

Torowoto Swamp

Mutawintji

Darling River

Menindee

0   30   60   miles

and King go back to the blackfellas' camp where they had been so
hospitably entertained four days earlier, so they can find out all they
can about how to find the tree with the nardoo seeds.

After they depart the following morning, Wills sets to with a will,
conscious that he must also set his mind to finding 'some means for
trapping the birds and rats. What a pleasant prospect, after our dashing

trip to Carpentaria, having to hang about Cooper's Creek living like the Blacks.'[14]

13 May '61, Koorliatto, reveille and retreat

Upon his return to Koorliatto this morning, Wright is quick to profess himself shocked: 'I . . . found the country between [here] and Cooper's Creek to be in general well grassed but destitute of any permanent water supply . . . The country bordering Cooper's Creek is the most miserable I have ever seen and I am at a loss to account for the favourable impression it has made upon the minds of previous explorers.'[15]

Frankly, Wright cannot get away from it quickly enough, and though – as is always his way – it will take well over a week before his party are properly moving, he gives orders for the camp to prepare to move south. He will be very glad to put the whole scene at Cooper's Creek behind him.

Heaven help any explorers trying to survive there.

17 May '61, Cooper's Creek, nardoo must do

At Cooper's Creek, Burke, Wills and King are realising now, more than ever, just what desperate trouble they are in.

They are not yet starving, but the spectre of it certainly looms for the trio. With their own supplies of food rapidly dwindling, Burke and King head off down the creek to the native encampment once more, hoping to call on their kindness, only to find them . . . gone. The two explorers sleep in their gunyahs that night and return up the creek to Wills the next morning.

Burke and King try again, determined to find the blacks wherever they are . . . this time going upstream, before giving up and turning back, empty-handed.

What now?

Exactly.

'We must do something,' Mr Burke says, 'for if we do not find nardoo, we shall starve. I intend that we put aside enough dried meat and rice to carry us to Mount Hopeless.'[16]

Such is their situation, however, that Mr Burke is beyond *ordering* them to do anything.

First to Mr Wills and then to King, Mr Burke instead asks the question: 'Are you willing to make another attempt to reach the South Australian settlements?'[17]

Both men agree they have no choice, and they prepare for their big push, packing all that remains of their provisions: 'two-and-a-half-pounds of Oatmeal, a small quantity of flour, and the dried meat; this with powder and shot and other small articles made up our swags thirty pounds each, and Mr Burke carried one billy of water and I another.'[18]

On the first day they follow the creek back upstream, making eight miles, and camping at a deserted blackfellas' camp. On the second day of the march to Mount Hopeless, they leave the creek and strike south-east.

They have only gone a short distance from the creek, when, on a flat at the foot of some sand-hills, King, in the lead, spies a strange-looking plant, which he initially takes to be clover. On looking closer, however, he sees it for what it is . . .

Who says there is no God, Mr Wills?

'I have found the nardoo!'[19]

And he really has. A single glance reveals it to be the seed that the natives use to make their cake. It is thrilling. The best thing that has happened since, well, since the last time something good happened, which was a long time ago. Perhaps, when Burke and Wills had more or less reached the Gulf?

Far from a tree, as they had been expecting, the nardoo seeds actually grow on a small, green, fern-like plant a few inches high with leaves like clover.

'This discovery,' Wills records, 'caused somewhat of a revolution in our feelings, for we considered that with the knowledge of this plant we were in a position to support ourselves, even if we were destined to remain on the creek and wait for assistance from town . . .'[20]

Yes! This may indeed be their salvation.

They might be able to stay alive long enough for some kind of rescue mission that must surely be being mounted at this very moment. It just depends how long it will take Brahe and his men to get to Menindee to report that they have disappeared.

For now, they must still do their best to get to Mount Hopeless, and so move on, continuing their slow wander down Cooper's Creek. Sure enough, that very afternoon, they find a promising creek bed heading south! It is a watercourse coming straight off Cooper's Creek, and quite a substantial one. *This must be it, this must be Strzelecki Creek!* True, all these dry creek beds look much the same, and there is no telling which one is going to be the substantial one they are looking for, the one that will lead to still established waterholes, but this one looks promising!

With rising excitement, the three men follow the creek as it heads south, sometimes forming into large rivulets as it cuts its course through the plains, before reforming into just the one creek ... smaller than before. They keep following until finally it stops outright. There is no more creek, just a light indentation in the desert, if that.

Far to their south, across the clay-pans and desert plains they can see sand-hills, perhaps a day's march away. The next day, girding their loins, they stagger towards them, their joints aching, their spirits rising and falling much like the sand-hills themselves. Higher and higher go their hopes, deeper and deeper goes their despair. The only constant is their enduring exhaustion and their pain, as they stumble on, with ever smaller steps, with all of their hips, knees and ankles screaming for relief, making each one of those steps a gruelling labour. Their feet, covered in dirt and blisters, are generally numb, yet still capable of causing agony, as even a small rock, stepped on the wrong way, shoots pains up their leg and causes their knees to buckle, sending them sprawling. At first when one falls, the others help him up. But soon enough, they all understand – it is every man for himself, and the others have no energy to spare.

Still, perhaps on the other side of that mound they should at least be able to see a dozen miles or so to their south, and just the tiniest fleck of green in that direction, or indeed *any* direction, will tell them which way lies Strzelecki Creek, and they will surely be saved.

It is late afternoon before they slowly, agonisingly traipse towards the top of the sand-dune, their tattered boots sinking deep into the shifting sand and exhausting them further with their every step.

At last on top, the light breeze whips off the desert sands, and they peer earnestly to their south to see . . .

More desert. In every direction, all they see is just more desert. Not a flick of green.

Making camp that evening by the dune, the three talk as they slowly, and with great delicacy, eat the evening portion of what daily rations are left to them – 'one small Johnny cake and three sticks of dried meat daily'[21].

What to do now?

All they can do. Shiver. The nights now are cold, and getting colder. Winter is coming, with Mr Wills's notes in his journal at this period telling something of the story 'calm, clear and cold'[22] . . . and 'very cold'[23].

Between them, the next morning, they decide to keep walking south until about two o'clock in the afternoon. If, at that stage, there is still no sign of water, of the creek, of anything giving them any indication where they might be able to sustain their lives – a trail of smoke, indicating the presence of natives would do it – then they will turn back.

And so it goes.

After a long, agonising struggle, their eyes constantly scanning the hazy horizon to their south, they must come face to face with the stark reality. It is two o'clock. And there seems to be nothing ahead of them but more desert.

Turn back?

They can't.

First they sit down for an hour, resting.

'We all felt satisfied that had there been a few days' rain,' King would recount, 'we could have got through: we were then, according to Mr Wills's calculation, forty-five miles from the creek.'[24]

But there is not only no rain, the sky holds no suggestion of any rain coming.

In the space of a fortnight, since taking the decision to go to South Australia, the position of the trio has moved from being on a journey towards their salvation to . . . simply trying to survive. Perhaps there will be a rescue party sent out to look for them. Perhaps not. Either way, their goal this day is to be their goal every day – live, *survive*.

Silently, they turn their backs on their main plan of redemption, and head back through the sand-dunes, towards Cooper's Creek, walking long into the night and all of the next day, before finally making it back to the nearest water on 21 May, and back to the creek the next day.

Gathering some nardoo, starving, they have no grinding stones and no energy to pound it the way Wills had seen the native women do it, but at least they manage to boil them, and try to eat them that way.

That night it is not quite that they 'sleep', for that would connote too peaceful a state. But they certainly collapse in a manner that might resemble sleep to the untutored eye.

Their key hope remains that an alarm will be raised, at which point the Committee in Melbourne will surely send out a rescue party to look for them.

22 May '61, Koorliatto, scurvy dogs

This then, is what has become of William Wright's mighty relief expedition that Robert O'Hara Burke had placed so much faith in. Instead of a fresh force with copious supplies pushing north in mid-November, they are pushing south in late May, a defeated mob of mostly sick cripples, with such limited supplies their own existence is threatened.

Some of the sick men, like William Patten, can only be moved a few minutes at a time by being carried on a stretcher strapped to a camel, before their moans and groans are heeded and they are allowed to rest.

'Patten,' Dr Beckler would recall, 'begged us in heaven's name to travel more slowly even though the column was moving with the speed of a solemn funeral procession.'[25]

Patten knows just whose funeral is intended . . .

'Patten became delirious,' Wright records, 'insisting that we had brought him on to kill him, and begging to be allowed to die where he then was.'[26]

Thomas McDonough would likely be carrying on in much the same manner, bar the fact that he is mercifully unconscious.

'It is well nigh impossible to describe to the reader,' Dr Beckler will chronicle, 'the deeply depressing effect of this futile struggling; the yearning to be delivered on one hand and our helplessness on the other.'[27]

As a doctor of no little experience, Beckler is completely flummoxed as to just why scurvy is so prevalent among his many charges, despite everything he has done to prevent it. The citric acid treatment Beckler relies upon – simply citric acid mixed with sugar and water, given to the men three times a day – does nothing, as unlike the fresh juice from a lemon or a lime, it contains none of the vitamin the men need. Dr Beckler can see his patients slowly heading the way of the late Ludwig, and he is as powerless now to do anything as he had been almost three months earlier when those same debilitating symptoms had first shown up in the German artist.

'Keeping watch in our camp each night was now pure misery,' he would ruefully recount. 'Wild dogs fought close by over the last remains of one of our horses . . . But the wild howling of these beasts was not half as unpleasant to the ear as the moaning and groaning of our invalids . . .'[28]

Desperate, he scrambles to concoct a treatment from the materials he has around him.

He considers how the blacks in these parts are so healthy, so strong. And despite having a diet that is mostly meat-based, just like the explorers, they do not appear to suffer from scurvy. So what is it that they are eating? Dr Beckler takes more interest and finds that, beyond the nardoo, they also eat raw – no cooking, no boiling – a flowering plant he recognises as *Mesembryanthemum*, a succulent, salt-tolerant herb. Why not try it? In short order, Beckler and the men chew 'the thick, juicy, three-sided leaves'[29]. In addition, Beckler boils the leaves and they all, hopefully, gulp down the cooled liquid.

Miraculously, the men – with the dreadful exception of poor Patten – seem to improve and there is sudden hope that these native plants may provide the cure they've been looking for. But for Patten, there is no relief. He spirals ever further down his mortal coil.

24 May '61 Cooper's Creek, Victorians salute Victoria

True, they are three men in the wilderness, lost, starving, fighting for their lives, but there are still some proprieties that must be observed.

Because today, as Wills is very much aware, it is time 'to celebrate the Queen's birthday'[30].

In Melbourne it would occasion a toast to Her Majesty and even a speech to whichever jolly gathering you were a part of. Here . . . Wills and King leave their camp at the gunyahs by the fine waterhole at Cooper's Creek and walk up the dry creek they have named 'Nardoo Creek' to the flat at the foot of the sand-hill to gather nardoo seeds.

It is now the late morning, John King and Mr Wills are bent over at the hip, laboriously picking the nardoo seed from the ground – it is far more draining than they had anticipated, in their weakened state – when, from far to their east, comes the distinct sound 'of an explosion as if of a gun . . . We supposed it to have been a shot fired by Mr Burke . . .'[31]

Strangely though, thrillingly, on returning at two o'clock to Mr Burke at the gunyahs, the leader informs them that he had fired no such shot!

Who then?

True, there is a chance it is some natural phenomenon, but they can at least rule out a crack of lightning on such a sunny day. Some years earlier, Charles Sturt had reported that, in the middle of Australia, the heat could suddenly split rocks with terrible cracks, but this sounded so much like a gunshot they cannot bear to believe it is not.

The trio discuss it, as they prepare their evening meal, pounding the nardoo seeds into flour, before mixing it with water to make a dough and cooking it in the ashes, to make something that roughly resembles the 'cake' the blacks had first presented them with.

Given that the sound had come from the direction of their old Depot, Mr Burke makes a simple request of Wills.

As he is the fittest among them, he must prepare to return to the Depot to investigate the sound, to see if it was indeed the shot of a rifle. If so, they are surely saved. If not, and the Depot is unchanged, Wills must at least open the cache, and put a fresh note in the bottle, advising that they have not gone to Mount Hopeless after all, but are just 40 miles down the creek. He must also bury the field books of the journey to the Gulf, as they are a precious record of what has occurred and – whatever happens – must be preserved and protected.

Three days later, Wills bids his farewell to Mr Burke and King and gets on his way, still filled with hope that redemption might be near at hand.

If not with a rescue party, perhaps . . .

This? Some three hours after starting off, when near the spot where Landa was bogged, he passes a couple of women and their children on a flat picking the greatest abundance of nardoo seed he has ever seen. 'The ground in some parts was quite black with it.'[32]

The women point out the direction to their camp, and shortly afterwards Wills is overtaken by some 20 friendly blacks who insist he comes with them to their camp, where they will give him fish and nardoo. One friendly native carries his shovel, while another one who is even more friendly – Wills take his name to be 'Pitchery'[33] – his swag, and they are as good as their word.

'In the evening they supplied me with abundance of nardoo and fish and one of the old men, Poko Tinnamira, shared his gunyah with me.'[34]

Late May '61, Cooper's Creek, beware of creeks bearing gifts

As it happens, Mr Burke and John King are receiving their own gifts of fish from natives, as a group of them suddenly appear a few days after Wills leaves to fish at the waterholes, and generously give the white men some of their fish over three successive days. It is so kind of them that, for once, on the third day, Mr Burke invites them back to the camp, whereupon he catches one of the natives stealing an oilcloth from the gunyah where they keep their ammunition and remaining supplies.

Mr Burke doesn't hesitate and, taking his revolver, fires it over the native's head, who drops the oilcloth with a start, even as the other natives fall to the ground before running away, taking all their food-gathering and fishing skills with them, not to mention their nardoo and fish.

Still, some others return at a time when Mr Burke and King are separated by a few hundred yards on the creek. When a group of them indicate to King that they would like to take him to a waterhole to eat fish, King declines for fear that the other natives would take all their things while he was away.

Worse, when King calls out for Mr Burke to come, one native takes his boomerang, insolently lays it on King's shoulder and indicates that if King continues to call, he would be hit on the head with the boomerang.

Well.

This time it is King who pulls his gun, lines them all up in front of the gunyah, and now fires it over their heads.

Sure enough, they run away.

Despite everything that has happened on the day, that evening they come back, bearing some cooked fish, calling out 'white fellow'[35].

Mr Burke is having none of it. Taking his revolver with him, he goes out to confront them. There they are, 'a whole tribe coming down, all painted, and with fish in small nets carried by two men'[36].

As King watches closely, he sees that the tribe wish to surround Mr Burke, but the burly Irishman with the big black beard is too fast for them.

First, Mr Burke knocks 'as many of the nets of fish out of their hands as he could', and now he shouts out to King to 'Fire!'[37]

King does exactly that, firing over their heads, as they run off.

'We collected five small nets of cooked fish,' King would recount. 'The reason he would not accept the fish from them was that he was afraid of being too friendly lest they should be always at our camp.'[38]

Hopefully, the Aborigines have learnt their lesson.

There are to be no more gifts of food in this fashion.

In fact, the blacks learn precisely that lesson, and it's not long before Burke and King are in more desperate need than ever of a rescue mission to be organised by someone, *anyone*!

28 May '61, Melbourne, specimens, speculations and sloth

In Melbourne Town, the Royal Society men meet on this day to discuss, well . . . mostly plant specimens, collected by Dr Beckler, which have now been classified and are being proudly displayed by Dr Mueller. The learned gents, impressed with the plants, some of which were previously unknown, appear to have no particular concerns about the fate of Mr Burke and his companions, but the same cannot be said of the press, which is now asking more questions than ever, as evidenced by a small article which appears in the *Age* on the same day:

> We ought now to receive intelligence from the Exploring Expedition; and although any alarm with regard to its safety would be premature and ill-founded, yet anxiety on behalf of Mr Burke and his companions arises naturally from the nature of their situation. Either the purposes of the Expedition have by this time been accomplished, or have for the present been abandoned. The party ... defeated in its object, and obliged to fall back on Cooper's Creek.[39]

30 May '61, Cooper's Creek, Wills makes his way ...

Funny they should say that ... At last approaching the Cooper's Creek Depot late on this notably crisp morning – winter is just two days away – the eyes of William Wills earnestly scan the horizon, looking for the tell-tale smoke of a campfire, his ears strain for the sound of horses, camels, chatter, the shout of a man at a recalcitrant beast. That shot they had heard, *must* have come from somewhere! He is all too aware that their salvation rests upon whether or not Europeans are there. If not ... impending doom.

Alas, the sky is pristine blue, with nary a trail of smoke nor hopeful smudge to be seen, and the only sound is that low hum of the Australian bush, together with the odd bored cry of the billabong birds. But, on the other hand, maybe there is only one or two of them, and they will hopefully appear the instant he gets there ... ?

Maybe Mr Wright at last? Maybe even Professor Neumayer?

Maybe ...

But there is nothing.

Completely deflated, Wills walks around the abandoned Depot, looking for signs that someone has *been* there. But everything is exactly as they had left it over five weeks earlier. The cache is entirely undisturbed, and the horse dung scattered over it, exactly as they had left it. The rake still leans against the 'Dig' tree, just as Mr King left it, too. All is just as it was. 'No traces of any one except blacks having been here since we left.'[40]

Carefully, quietly – looking every which way to establish that he is not being observed – Wills digs up the cache and adds his journals and the note he has prepared:

We have been unable to leave the creek. Both camels are dead, and our provisions are exhausted.

Mr Burke and King are down the lower part of the creek. I am about to return to them, when we shall probably come up this way.

We are trying to live the best way we can, like the blacks, but find it hard work.

Our clothes are going to pieces fast.

Send provisions and clothes as soon as possible.

W J Wills.[41]

In a quick burst of uncharacteristic bitterness, Wills adds a separate page to his original note.

The Depot party having left, contrary to instructions, has put us in this fix.

I have deposited some of my journals here for fear of accidents.

W J W[42]

Carefully now, he reburies the camel box, covers it all back up, and then spreads the dried dung around once more. By mid-afternoon he is on his way back once more, camping at the first waterhole down the creek. He is relieved to see cloud cover as the sun falls below the horizon, as he knows that means the night will not be so bitterly cold as usual.

Perhaps Shakespeare said it best:

> As after sunset fadeth in the west;
> Which by and by black night doth take away,
> Death's second self, that seals up all in rest.[43]

3 June '61, Cooper's Creek, hail fellow well met

Traipsing along the south bank of Cooper's Creek in the early morning light, William Wills walks like a man bearing a 50-pound load. In fact, he is carrying little, and it is not his kit that is the problem. His body has not been receiving proper nourishment for the better part of six months now, and there is only so much more he will be able to sustain before collapsing outright, and he knows it. Just the previous day he had been obliged to stop his trek back to Mr Burke and King, for fear of precisely that.

Wills hears crows ahead, sees a trail of smoke pluming skywards, and hears a long 'Coo-eeeeee!'[44]

It is his new friend, Pitchery, on the other side of the creek, who now, with great delight directs him to keep coming this way and that *malkirri karlukarlu ya ngardu*, an abundance of fish and bread, awaits.

The young Englishman, still feeling faint, is soon being led by Pitchery up the sandy path that leads to the camp where he sees half-a-dozen blacks cooking a large pile of fish in their particular manner.

Has he come just as they are having their morning meal?

No. All those fish, as it turns out, are for *him*.

They have known he has been coming for some time. They also know he is faint with hunger. They are expecting him. They want to look after him. They want him to eat the lot.

And he does – even as a couple of the blacks are kept busy pulling bones out of the fish before they hand them to him. Still not done, they now give him as much nardoo cake as he can possibly stuff in, all of it washed down by as much water as he can hold.

He thinks.

But now Pitchery brings him 'a large bowl of the raw nardoo flour, mixed to a thin paste, a most insinuating article, and one that they appear to esteem a great delicacy. I was then invited to stop the night there . . .'[45]

6 June '61, Rat Point, Brahe and Wright finally dig . . .

It is an odd thing to be digging a sad grave by the light of a cheery fire, all in the silent watch of the night, but so it is on this night at Rat Point, still about 150 miles north of Menindee.

At 4 am, William Brahe had been woken with the sad news: 'Patten is dead.'[46]

Brahe is saddened, but knows Patten's death is a mercy, suffering as he was. Partly out of decency and partly for the fact that they are the two healthiest in the party, Wright and Brahe continue to dig the grave by the twinkling light of the fire. Early the next morning, a quick funeral is held over the grave and shortly thereafter the party is on its way once more. If all goes well they should be back at Menindee well before June is out.

6 June '61, Cooper's Creek, needs must when the devil drives

Mr Wills's news, when he arrives back to the gunyahs by 'Nardoo Creek', where he had left Mr Burke and King, is mixed.

On the one hand, when it comes to the source of what they had thought was a gunshot coming from the Depot, he is firm: 'I have seen nobody.'

On the other hand, he tells the story of his encounter with the nearby natives.

'They were very kind to me,' he says, 'and gave me plenty to eat both on going up and returning.'[47]

The news of Mr Burke and King to Mr Wills is just grim all round. While Mr Wills had been away, the leader had been cooking some fish in their gunyah when a gust of wind had caught the flames, which had in turn caught the gunyah – and in an instant the whole thing had caught fire.

Everything they still possessed – including some clothing, their carry bags, the camel pads they used as bedding, and their store of nardoo – had been turned to ashes, with the sole exception of a revolver and a gun that had been outside the gunyah. Oh, and Mr Burke had lost his temper and fired his revolver over a native's head, causing them to all run away. They'd come back, with more gifts of food, but Mr Burke had fired again. This time they had not come back.

Which . . . is a real problem.

For it is now becoming more clear than ever – their only hope of surviving is by availing themselves of the kindness of the blacks. They must follow the Yandruwandha, in the hope that they will receive enough fish and nardoo to stay alive. (And hope there are no hard feelings about firing their thunder-sticks over their heads.)

On that count, at least, Mr Wills is optimistic, noting that, if it comes to it, they would be easy to live *with*.

Sure enough, by that afternoon Mr Wills has rejoined the Yandruwandha and he determines to stay with them to 'test the practicability of living with them, and to see what I could learn as to their ways and manners'[48].

Sure enough, the natives are indeed 'very hospitable and friendly', keeping him with them two days.[49]

At the conclusion of those two days, however, as Wills is enjoying his breakfast, his otherwise generous hosts wave their arms in a manner whereby their meaning is unmistakable: You . . . whitefella. You go now.

William Wills, suddenly feeling extremely vulnerable, keeps eating his breakfast and pretends not to understand. He just looks back at them with his watery blue eyes, hoping they might take pity on him.

But the blacks will have none of it. First they point at themselves, jabbering all the while, and then they point up the creek. That's where they are going. And now they point at Wills, and wave down the creek.

Clear, whitefella?

Either way, they don't appear to care. After breakfast they simply give Wills some nardoo – this is for you and the other whitefellas, they make clear – before heading up the creek. In no more than a minute, the Australian bush has swallowed them whole.

Wills makes it back to his comrades.

But now the problem is all too apparent.

They are entirely dependent on the blacks. They must go back to them, and *beg* them, if necessary, to be allowed to stay with them. And so, taking what few things they can carry, the next afternoon the three of them head off up the creek once more to the spot where Wills had been with them just the day before.

Another problem is soon apparent, however, as Wills notes: 'We found ourselves all very weak in spite of the abundant supply of fish that we have lately had. I myself could scarcely get along, although carrying the lightest swag – only about thirty pounds.'[50]

But still, the blacks must be just up ahead now! Willing themselves, *forcing* themselves forward, knowing the blacks will be just up ahead around the corner, and will likely give them so much fish they will not be able to eat another bite, they keep going and . . .

They reach Pitchery's camp . . . to find them all gone. They have not returned. And there are no plumes of smoke on the horizon to indicate they are anywhere close.

There is nothing. No blacks. No food supplies. Nothing. Just their gnawing hunger.

After passing a restless night, Mr Burke decides they must head off this day to the next black camp, the one that Wills had come across on his way back to the Depot, a week or so earlier, where he'd found a couple of women and their children picking nardoo in a flat clearing.

Alas, when they arrive it is to find the same thing.

The blacks have gone.

Further pursuing the blacks up the creek, at least with all three of them, is not worthwhile. Firstly, they don't have the strength. Secondly, there is no knowing how far away the blacks are by now. Thirdly, there is no telling that, even if they can find them, they will be willing to help. They had been very firm with Mr Wills that their patience was at an end, and would be even less likely to accommodate all three of the white men.

So they must stay here. They must learn to gather the nardoo themselves, and live off that.

They fall into a daily pattern whereby, in the mornings, Mr Wills and King head out to harvest at least a bag's worth of nardoo seed, leaving Mr Burke pounding away at yesterday's haul, so they will be able to have some nardoo cakes for dinner, with enough left over for breakfast the next day.

As the days go by, however, their general weakness gets worse, with Burke and Wills usually alternating as to who will accompany the stronger, younger man, King, when he goes out to collect and then prepare the nardoo – both arduous tasks, that get more arduous with time. Soon enough, it is King who must go out alone, for neither Burke nor Wills can accompany him – though Mr Burke does gather himself to make one unsuccessful excursion up the creek to look for the blacks, finding not the slightest trace of even recent occupation.

The second-in-command's situation is deteriorating before their eyes.

'Wills . . .' King will note, 'suffered most. The Nardoo passed through him as soon as eating . . .'[51]

7 June '61, Ballarat, the doctor decides to take action, dammit

Finally, in Ballarat, Dr Wills has had enough of impotent waiting, of writing letter after letter to Dr Macadam to which he 'had deigned no reply'[52].

The last straw comes when even Professor Neumayer fails to reply to one of Dr Wills's letters seeking further reassurance. The professor's assistant writes that he is absent and now Dr Wills decides it is time that, he, personally, must be present.

So, taking stick in one hand, his small pack on his shoulder, and his umbrage, on 7 June he leaves his Ballarat abode, and starts on the long walk to Melbourne – along the highways and byways, in this notably cold winter – to accost those who need to be so accosted, to call them to account.

14 June '61, Cooper's Creek, give us our daily bread

None of them can understand it. They have food, they have, it seems, the secret of native bread and yet, as Wills records in his journal, doubts are seeping in as to the worth of their food and labour.

Friday, 14 June 1861.
King out for nardoo; brought in a good supply. Mr Burke and
I at home, pounding and cleaning seed. I feel weaker than ever,
and both Mr B. and King are beginning to feel very unsteady
in the legs.[53]

The most confusing thing for Wills is their continuing debilitation from starvation, *despite* the fact that they are actually eating a fair amount of nardoo.

'I am not a bit stronger. I have determined on beginning to chew tobacco and eat less nardoo, in hopes that it may induce some change in the system.'[54]

•

Now arrived in Melbourne, Dr Wills first calls at the home of Dr Wilkie, a man he knows reasonably well, only to find him issuing circulars for the forthcoming meeting of the Exploration Committee, to 'consider what was to be done'[55].

This is no solace to Dr Wills.

'My heart sank within me when I found that no measures whatever had yet been taken.'[56]

Perhaps the now returned Professor Neumayer will know more, and can at least give him a firm answer about whether or not it 'had been arranged with Mr Burke that a vessel should be dispatched round the coast to the Gulf to meet him there'.

'A conversation on that point did take place between Mr Burke, your son and myself,' Neumayer replies, 'but Mr Burke enjoined me not to move on it.'

It leaves Dr Wills with no choice but to attend the meeting of the Exploration Committee the next day, to press the case for the salvation of his son and fellow expedition members, for he is now deeply worried.[57]

To Dr Wills's stupefaction, there appears to be no alarm at the lack of news, no sense that the expedition might be in trouble in the far north and *no* ship has been sent to the Gulf to meet the expedition.

'One [member] talked of financial affairs, another of science, a third of geography, a fourth of astronomy, and so on,' he would note. 'A chapter in the Circumlocution Office painfully unfolded itself.'[58]

Dr Wills bears it for as long as he can, and then interrupts, noting how long it has been since word has been received, and wondering what the Committee is doing to ensure that all is well, that the expedition is getting the support from Melbourne that it needs? Surely it is time to send out the equivalent of a search party, to see what the situation is, to see if contact can be made with William, last seen heading towards the Gulf, seven months earlier, and *from whom nothing has been heard since.*

'What are you in such alarm about?' The Surveyor-General Mr Charles Ligar dismisses his concerns. 'There is plenty of time. No news is good news. You had better go home and mind your own business.'[59]

Dr Wills will do no such thing. The survival of his son *is* his business and, at last, he is relieved to even get some support from another man at the meeting who he does not recognise.

'Seeing my anxiety,' Dr Wills would recall, 'and feeling that the emergency called for immediate action, [he] appealed to them warmly, and the result was a decision, *neminem contradicente*, that it was time to move, if active and trustworthy agents could be found.'[60]

In fact, so persuasive is the unknown gentleman that Dr John Macadam himself now takes the lead, proposing that one Alfred Howitt – the well-connected and well-heeled Victorian explorer and naturalist of some renown – who has recently arrived in Melbourne after his latest successful sortie up Gipps Land way – be approached to lead a party of four to travel to Swan Hill by train and coach, there purchase 16 horses, and from thence proceed to the Darling, thence to Cooper's.

Dr Embling disagrees and suggests none other than Mr Landells, who is in Melbourne, and understands what is required better than anyone, as the best person to be leader.

Preposterous!

Alfred Howitt is resoundingly endorsed, and Mr Landells thumpingly rejected.

For his part, Professor Neumayer proposes one Edwin Welch – a nautical astronomer and decorated naval veteran from the Crimean War – be appointed as the second to Howitt. Yes, he is only 23. But as one who had been a naval cadet in the Crimean War at just 15, he has seen much, done much, and after coming to Australia to dig for gold, had found work at the observatory in Melbourne this year, courtesy of the astronomy he had learnt in his naval schooling. Professor Neumayer insists he is a first-class man, and the others quickly assent. At this point Dr Wills cannot help himself and, *ahem*, offers his own services . . . ?

It is a proposal that meets with something less than small acclaim though, and is kindly denied.

It is finally determined that while one sub-committee will be established to investigate the advisability of sending a vessel to the Gulf to look for Mr Burke and his men, another overland rescue expedition will definitely be mounted immediately, with Mr Alfred Howitt to be offered the position of leader, and Welch the position of second-in-command. (And, as you'd expect, a sub-committee is quickly appointed to help in organising it.)

On 17 June, the Committee is pleased to announce that Mr Howitt has indeed accepted the post and will immediately set about organising men and supplies, hoping to be on his way within a week. (As to his companions, that is quickly organised. Edwin Welch accepts the Committee's offer to accompany Mr Howitt, who in turn has fulfilled his promise by successfully offering two of the available positions to his two long-time companions, Weston Phillips and Alexander Aitkin – who had first said they wanted to come with him when discussing it around the fire early in the New Year.)

Not to be outdone, the Premier of the Colony of Victoria, Richard Heales, announces Her Majesty's Victorian Ship *Victoria* will be dispatched to the Gulf of Carpentaria.

At last, things are starting to move!

Most gratified is Dr Wills, his only hope being that it all happens in time to save his son.

17 June '61, Menindee, Paine's pub relieves the pain . . .

It is a strange Antipodean echo to Napoleon Bonaparte's march on Moscow, which occurred on the other side of the world some half a century earlier . . .

Back then, in 1812, the mighty city of Paris had cheered on as Napoleon's glorious *Grande Armée*, some 700,000 strong, had marched on the Russian capital. They were confident that *les feroces soldats* would bring Russia to its knees, only to see just 120,000 shattered survivors return to France six months later, a ragged remnant of what they once were, defeated by a crippling winter and Russian soldiers who simply would not give in.

All of Melbourne had farewelled Mr Burke's mighty expedition in August, the largest ever assembled in the land, and yet here the ragged remnant of his men stand in the heat of the Menindee afternoon – the shattered survivors, defeated by the crippling summer and the Australian desert that gave no quarter.

Menindee is agog to hear the news. Burke and the Gulf party are missing, four men in all. Another four men have died, and even of those eight men who have survived and arrived, two are gravely ill. One Menindee resident is shocked just to see them, noting, 'several of them are still invalids, nearly the whole of them having suffered severely from scurvy and low fevers . . . some of them in a dying state . . . But the whole party show symptoms of great suffering, particularly about the eyes, which have grown eager-glanced and careworn.'[61]

This same resident, as it happens, is in no doubt where the blame lies. Not with any of these brave souls, and certainly not with any of the missing heroes who have tried so valiantly to get to the Gulf. No, the villains are rather further afield. 'If Mr Burke and his party have perished, their deaths must forever lie at the doors of those who, in spite of all sorts of remonstrance from men of experience, sent him forth, and sent him, not provided, but encumbered as he was.'[62]

For his part, Wright has two major concerns. Firstly, he wishes to see his family in Adelaide. Hodgkinson will go with him. And secondly, he must write his third dispatch to the Committee explaining his actions and defending himself from the inevitable attacks to come from a body of men who will unavoidably find themselves under heavy fire and can be expected to blame *him* – 'Sir, I have the honour to announce my arrival to Menindee on Monday the 17th inst. and the establishment of my camp in its former position, at the junction of [Pamamaroo] Creek with the Darling . . .'[63]

It is William Brahe who will have to ride on ahead, as soon as he has recuperated just a little, to get out the news of what has happened as quickly as possible to the Committee in Melbourne.

19 June '61, Melbourne, slow exposure to a natural bushman

In Melbourne itself, the news of Mr Howitt's appointment to lead the rescue party is well received by those who know of him and his work, and for good reason. For Howitt is a highly educated and accomplished 31-year-old Englishman, who had first come to Australia 10 years earlier to visit his uncle on the Ballarat goldfields and had stayed on thereafter, working variously as a geologist, gold warden, police magistrate and crown lands commissioner – picking up many skills along the way. As a bushman, Howitt is close to as good as it gets for a white man.

That rarest of breeds, a natural bushman who is also scientifically interested in the nature of the bush, Howitt knows that for this mission he and his three companions must travel light and move fast. As a man who perfectly answers that description himself – he is so thin he appears tall, his nose so long and sharp it could be the point of an arrow – he is now a blur of activity as he makes his arrangements . . .

The Victorian public takes an enormous interest in his mission, and suggestions flood forth like the River Yarra after heavy rain. Howitt rejects all the strange yet well-meaning suggestions . . . bar two.

The first comes from Sir William Stawell himself, and it is that they conduct some photography on their historic mission. At first blush it seems impossible, by reason of sheer weight of taking a portable 'darkroom, and the requisite adjuncts for working the wet plate process', but through consultation with one of Melbourne's leading photographers, a solution is arrived at. They will provide a camera and four dozen dry plates, and the plates could be developed on their *return*. Revolutionary! Edwin Welch is given carriage of 'a dainty little stereoscopic camera, of standard size, fitted with one dark slide only, the usual pattern at that time, and a light tight box, containing 48 dry stereo plates'[64] – it is among the lightest in the world, weighing only 30 pounds – and instructions on how to operate it.

The key, Welch is told, are the plates, which have been in a stronger than usual nitrate of silver bath, before being 'thoroughly dried and placed in a bath of strong coffee, dried, again, and packed in a light, tight box, ready for use'[65]. They produce wonderful results, so long as the subject of the photo remains unmoving for about six minutes. Once the photo is taken, it can only be removed from the camera in the pitch-darkness. Put all the exposures in this special box, and get them all back to us, so we can develop in our darkroom. Any exposure to light will completely destroy them, do you understand?

Welch, an intelligent man, and a quick study, understands completely.[66]

Oh. The second proposal that Howitt likes? It is a cooing coo-ee proposal that will ruffle feathers, many of them, but is too good to resist giving a go . . .

He will see.

20 June '61, Cooper's Creek, Wills and testament
With wavering hand to match his quavering voice, William Wills writes on, with overwhelming exhaustion,

I am completely reduced by the effects of the cold and starvation . . . . I cannot understand this nardoo at all – it certainly will not agree with me in any form. We are now reduced to it alone, and we manage to get from four to five pounds per day between us. The stools it causes are enormous, and seem greatly to exceed the quantity of bread consumed, and is very slightly altered in appearance from what it was when eaten.[67]

The next day, it is even worse, and even one with so forgiving a nature as Wills is beginning to feel embittered.

I feel much weaker than ever, and can scarcely crawl out of the [gunyah]. Unless relief comes in some form or other, I cannot possibly last more than a fortnight. It is a great consolation, at least, in this position of ours, to know that we have done all we could, and that our deaths will rather be the result of the mismanagement of others than of any rash acts of our own. Had we come to grief elsewhere, we could only have blamed ourselves; but here we are, returned to Cooper's Creek, where we had every reason to look for provisions and clothing; and yet we have to die of starvation, in spite of the explicit instructions given by Mr Burke, that the Depot party should await our return, and the strong recommendation to the Committee that we should be followed up by a party from Menindee. [68]

Within two days Wills is too weak even to get to his feet, and the others are not much stronger.

Sunday, June 23rd 1861
All hands at home. I am so weak as to be incapable of crawling out of the [gunyah]. King holds out well, but Mr Burke finds himself weaker every day. [69]

In truth, in this place, it is only the cold and the wind that get stronger as the days pass. That night they combine into a southerly gale that howls through the trio's gunyah and chills all three men to the marrow of their bones. They lie there, agonisingly, caught on the cliff between the cold and their crippling need for rest. If they had had some warm clothing it might have been bearable but they have naught but rags. All that Mr Wills has in total is his 'wide-awake [hat], a merino shirt, a regatta shirt without sleeves, the remains of a pair of flannel trousers, two pairs of socks in rags, and a waistcoat'[70], and the others are scarcely any better. All they have for bedding is 'two small camel-pads, some horsehair, two or three little bits of a rag, and pieces of oilcloth saved from the fire'[71].

Oh, how diminished they are from the grand days of nearly a year ago when they had been equipped with everything from a punt wagon to enema kits to 7100 pounds of flour, 200 pounds of Captain's biscuits and 3000 pounds of sugar.

In the morning, only King is strong enough to go in search of nardoo and returns with a good haul at the end of a long day. He is, as Wills describes it, 'terribly cut up'[72].

'I can no longer keep up the work,'[73] King says simply.

It sets Mr Wills to thinking. A terrible decision is upon them, his strong feeling is that the sooner they make it the better. That night, peering to the east, sleepless, John King sees a curious light with a haze of brightness coming up from it.

'It is quite as large as the moon, and not dim at the edges,' he tells the others who also lie there, sleepless. Now, ordinarily, it is the sort of thing that would immediately have William Wills up and out of his swag and gazing earnestly to the heavens, but on this night, he just can't manage it.

All he can do is have King minutely describe the phenomenon to him, from which he concludes that 'it must have been Venus in the Zodiacal light that he saw, with a corona around her'[74].

The three settle back to their thoughts, waiting for the warmth of the dawn.

William Wills drifts in and out of conscious thought, now unable to even look up at the sky; his boyhood dreamscape, his lifelong passion. No more Venus and her crown of light. No more Jupiter and her many moons, winking in the night. The next eclipse will likely be his own, and already he feels the darkness closing on his soul. This time, even the warmth and light of dawn brings no relief, as that growing stain of darkness continues to spread.

From the fortnight to live that he'd estimated just a few days earlier, it seems likely he has just a few days left, if that, and his thoughts now turn, inevitably, to his cousin Harry who, 14 years before, had perished with 128 others on the Sir John Franklin expedition, trying to find the Northwest Passage to connect the mighty Atlantic and Pacific oceans across the top of the Americas . . .

The next morning, slightly revived with the rising of the sun, Wills pushes a proposal that King – the only one of them still capable – go out and gather as much nardoo as he can over the next three days, and with that supply there would be enough to leave Wills a little here in the wurley, while Mr Burke and King could go out in search of the natives.

'It is our only chance,'[75] Wills says.

Evening 26 June '61, Melbourne, Howitt cuts to the chase

Finally, they are off.

It has taken a little over a week to get organised and provisioned, but on this evening, the 'Victorian Contingent Party' – as far as anyone knows, there is not yet any need for a 'Relief Party' – gets underway. No grand departure from Royal Park, 'this sombre expedition has no fan-fare'[76].

If the Victorian Exploring Expedition was the full set of silver, this contingent party is more a high-quality hunting knife with a blade sharpened to a razor's edge – utilitarian, light, with no view to being showy . . . and thus slowy. The only thing particular about the four men boarding the 5.45 pm train at Spencer Street Station is that they are clearly carrying heavy packs. Alfred Howitt, together with his faithful offsider through the Gipps Land expedition, Alexander Aitkin; the surveyor, Edwin Welch; and ostler William Vining have a simple plan. From here they must travel by train to Digger's Rest, 20 miles to the north, where they will catch a Cobb and Co. coach to Swan Hill and buy 16 horses, before proceeding to Menindee.

They will press forth, press *north*, from there, looking, firstly, for a 'Mr Wright'. From him they hope to add some camels to their retinue.

Mr Alfred Howitt is also taking four carrier pigeons with him, with the intention that, as soon as he has any solid information, the news will be winging its way back to Melbourne. Four birds were selected from those given by Mr Ambrose Kyte – the expedition's original anonymous donor – and the Hon. George Coppin. They are champion 'homers', worth a great deal of money.

Howitt is convinced that, wherever Mr Burke and his party are, they are likely in terrible trouble, and his key hope is to be able to get to them in time.

26 June '61, Cooper's Creek, something will turn up

Some 700 miles to the north, on this same day, 26 June,[77] in their gunyahs on Cooper's Creek, all three men are keenly aware that they are nearing the end, bar a miracle, as Mr Burke now fatalistically writes an entry in his notebook.

26 June:
I hope we shall be done justice because we fulfilled our task but we were ~~aband~~ not followed up as I expected and the Depot party abandoned their post.
R O H Burke, Leader.
For the Committee
Cooper's Creek
26th June 1861[78]

William Wills retains some hope. And all that hope lies in Mr Burke and King heading up the creek on the morrow and finding the blacks. It is their only chance of salvation. Wills is simply too weak to accompany them and knows he must stay in his wurley, shivering, with only the two nearby gunyahs to stand silent sentinel over him.

John King has at least finished his three days of collecting nardoo, so it is not as if they will be leaving Mr Wills without supplies. Still Mr Burke and King feel ghastly about leaving him behind, both showing 'great hesitation and reluctance with regard to leaving me'[79], and constantly asking Wills if he agrees with their decision.

'Do you still wish us [to leave you]?'[80] Mr Burke asks Mr Wills again and again.

But Mr Wills insists, as much as a dying man can ...

'You must go up the creek while you have strength,' he rasps, 'and look for the blacks, as our only chance of life.'[81]

It is the difficulty with which he speaks, and his pale, disintegrating and agonising form that are his most persuasive arguments.

'Wills ...' King would recount, 'was getting worse all the time and suffering great pain.'[82]

'We didn't like the idea of separating, but it seemed to be our only chance.'[83]

At least King thinks so. Mr Burke, however, needs *still* more persuading – and Mr Wills insistence alone will not see him agree to leave his second-in-command.

A year earlier, back in Royal Park, John King would not have dared venture the opinion to Mr Burke that it was a sunny day, let alone make a case that the leader should do one thing or another.

But strength to weakness has an authority all its own, as does health to sickness, and there is no doubt that King is far and away the strongest and healthiest of the trio. And he is able to make the case to Mr Burke strongly enough that Mr Wills is absolutely correct and it is their *only hope*. Finally, the leader agrees.

Wills is relieved, noting in his diary just how perilous the Irishman's own situation is:

'Mr Burke suffers greatly from the cold, and is getting extremely weak; he and King start tomorrow up the creek, to look for the blacks; it is the only chance we have of being saved from starvation. I am weaker than ever ...'[84]

Yes, they have been able to eat nardoo, but somehow the work required to gather and prepare the flour seems to take more from them than it gives them.

'Nothing now but the greatest good luck can now save any of us; and as for myself, I may live four or five days if the weather continues warm. My pulse is at forty-eight, and very weak, and my legs and arms are nearly skin and bone. I can only look out, like Mr Micawber, "for something to turn up" . . .'[85]

Not that it is altogether unpleasant.

Even in such bitter circumstances, the scientist in Wills, the observer, can't help but carefully note down the interesting part of this rare human experience among those equipped to record its features.

Starvation on nardoo is by no means very unpleasant, but for the weakness one feels, and the utter inability to move oneself, for as far as appetite is concerned, it gives the greatest satisfaction. Certainly fat and sugar would be more to one's taste, in fact, those seem to me to be the great stand-by for one in this extraordinary continent; not that I mean to depreciate the farinaceous food, but the want of sugar and fat in all substances obtainable here is so great that they become almost valueless to us as articles of food, without the addition of something else.[86]

In the face of the likely death of Wills – a likelihood that increases with each passing moment – Mr Burke is something beyond devastated. All up, in their whole time together, this once magnificent figure of a man – now a mere shuddering shadow himself – had never had a cross word with the young man who had never delivered to him anything other than unswerving loyalty, devotion and hard work. Face to face with Wills's mortality, the leader is, of course, also confronted with his own likely forthcoming demise . . . which begs the question, *why go on?* Why continue to fight a war he just can't win? Why not lie down here, beside Wills, and let the angels of death alight, to take him away? Beyond all that . . .

'How can I leave him,' he plaintively asks King, gesturing towards his languishing loyal deputy of the last eight months, 'that dear, good fellow?'[87]

In fact, Mr Burke is so 'dreadfully distressed'[88], as King will describe it, that the younger Irishman is once again only able to persuade him with 'great difficulty'[89], that the best chance Mr Wills has is if they do in fact leave him, and go up the creek to find the blacks, to get the food and help they need. Mr Burke at last, very reluctantly, agrees.

Before leaving, however – hanging onto a shred of hope for a miracle – Burke is realistic enough about Wills's low chances of survival to give him some advice about what he should put into a letter the young Englishman is now penning to his father. The advice is to make a claim on the Committee, that his father should be given financial compensation for the loss of his son.

'Wills,' Burke commands, 'be sure to say something to that effect.'[90]

Pale, and with a shaky hand, Wills begins to write, even as Mr Burke and King busy themselves burying the last of the field notes, weather and navigational records from the trip from Cooper's to the Gulf and back in a spot by the gunyah, where they will be secure . . .

Wills's letter slowly takes shape.

Cooper's Creek . . .

My Dear Father,
These are probably the last lines you will ever get from me. We are on the point of starvation not so much from absolute want of food, but from the want of nutriment in what we can get.

Our position, although more provoking, is probably not near so disagreeable as that of poor Harry and his companions.

We have had very good luck, and made a most successful trip to Carpentaria, and back to where we had every right to consider ourselves safe, having left a Depot here consisting of four men, twelve horses, and six camels.

They had provisions enough to have lasted them twelve months with proper economy, and we had also every right to expect that we should have been immediately followed up from Menindee by another party with additional provisions and every necessary for forming a permanent Depot at Cooper's Creek. The party we left here had special instructions not to leave until our return – unless from absolute necessity. We left the creek with nominally three months' supply, but they were reckoned at little over the rate of half rations. We calculated on having to eat some of the camels. By the greatest good luck, at every turn, we crossed to the gulf through a good deal of fine country, almost in a straight line from here.

On the other side the camels suffered considerably from wet; we had to kill and jerk one soon after starting back. We had now been out a little more than two months and found it necessary to reduce the rations considerably; and this began to tell on all hands, but I felt it by far less than any of the others. The great scarcity and shyness of game and our forced marches, prevented our supplying the deficiency from external sources to any great extent. . . . We got back here in four months and four days, and found the party had left the Creek the same day, and we were not in a fit state to follow them.

I find I must close this, that it may be planted; but I will write some more, although it has not so good a chance *of reaching you as this. You have great claims on the committee for their neglect. I leave you in sole charge of what is coming to me. The whole of my money I desire to leave to my sisters; other matters I pass over for the present.*

Adieu, my dear Father. Love to Tom.

W. J. Wills

P.S. I think to live about four or five days. (My religious views are not the least changed and I have the least fear of their being so.)[91]

My spirits are excellent.[92]

When completed, he reads the whole thing out loud to Mr Burke and King, the latter understanding that Mr Wills does so in order that they would know 'that he [did] not say anything to our disadvantage, mine or Mr Burke's . . . that we would see it was the truth and nothing but the truth'[93].

So help him, God . . .

But, no. For now, even if there were a God, He has left them, at least left Wills.

After leaving beside William Wills as much nardoo bread as they can spare – eight days supply – together with a billy of water and a pile of firewood within his reach, the two men know that no more can be done for their dear companion. Both upright men utter their fond and tearful farewells, which Mr Wills is only just strong enough to acknowledge.

One last time Mr Burke asks the question.

'Do you still wish us to leave?' he asks. 'Under no other circumstance will we leave you.'

'It is our only chance,'[94] Mr Wills says once more.

He then gives to Mr Burke the letter he has written, together with his watch.

'If you should survive Mr Burke,' Wills says to John King with quavering voice, 'I hope that you will carry out my last wishes and give the watch and letter to my father.'[95]

There is time for one last look back at the weak figure lying placidly in his wurley, before they are on their way, heading up the creek to look for the blacks.

Burke and King spend the day in search of the natives, but can only move painfully slowly, as Burke is so weak and complains of general weakness, dizziness and terrible pain in his legs and back.

The two settle down for the night, dining – though 'eating miserably' might be closer to the mark – on nardoo. The first rays of dawn seem to find Burke a little better, just a little stronger – seemingly by virtue of having given his body 10 hours respite rather than any sustenance of note. For, alas, as soon as he and King get going again, still pushing up along the creek, still looking for the blacks, Burke weakens so rapidly it is all they can do to make two miles before he announces he can proceed no further.

Ah, but Mr Burke, you can.

King is able to help Mr Burke to his feet and keep him moving, just a little as they proceed to search, and is full of admiration, for, as the younger man will later note, 'every step he took in advance was a chance for Mr Wills, and he never flinched from his duty while power was left him to raise a limb'[96].

Still, by late afternoon, all Mr Burke can do is stagger along, and further carrying his swag, or indeed anything, is out of the question. When Mr Burke throws it away, King has no strength to argue, let alone carry it for him.

28 June '61, Cooper's Creek, the undiscovered country . . .

In his own gunyah, William Wills closes his diary, and lies back, perhaps thinking of the words of that man, William Shakespeare, so beloved by his most cherished friend in the world, dear Richard Birnie . . .

To die: to sleep; No more; and by a sleep to say we end
The heart-ache and the thousand natural shocks
That flesh is heir to,'tis a consummation
Devoutly to be wish'd.[97]

•

As the sun begins to sink, so does Mr Burke, judging it to be time to stop for the night and, once again, it is all King can do to get him to move just a little further to a spot less exposed to the wind where they do indeed 'make camp'[98], as King is pleased to describe it – if simply lying down in a semi-comatose state under a large box tree with a thick canopy can be called that. It is right by the waterhole the blacks call *Yinimingka*.

Mr Burke can go no further, as he at last lays him down to rest, yea though he walks in the shadow of the valley of death.

'He walked till he dropped,'[99] King will note admiringly, but now, drop Mr Burke most certainly does.

Realising his time is likely coming to an end, Robert O'Hara Burke now summons what little energy remains to falteringly take his notebook from his pocket and write a final letter to his dear sister, Hessie.

Cooper's Creek[100] . . .
Good Bye, my dearest Hessie
When leaving Melbourne I foolishly made over what I left behind to a young lady with whom I have only a slight acquaintance. I hope you will not take ill of me. I was wrong and I only meant and mean the bequest to apply to the few money accruing to me in Melbourne and not to anything derived from home.
Good Bye dear Hessie, my thoughts are now fixed upon you . . . I hereby cancel the bequest or will I left in Melbourne, and I leave all I possess to my sister Hessie

Burke, but I wish her to make over any money derived from my Salary or the sale of my things in Melbourne to Miss Julia Matthews.

R O'Hara Burke for Miss Burke.[101]

In the meantime, with no rations left, the only hope for any nourishment whatsoever is to get some nardoo, which King is able to gather from a nearby patch, and grinds enough to make a small bit of cake for them both.

Wills, at this point, is some 12 miles away as the crow flies, and when King is able to bring that bird down with a single shot, he and Mr Burke are able to share its scrawny remains to expand their tiny meal, before entering the long night.

And long for Mr Burke it indeed threatens to be, as the presentiment grows within the leader's breast – lying in their makeshift 'camp' 'neath a large box tree, amid tall plants that give some shelter from the cold winds that blow – that he does not have long to live, perhaps a matter of just hours.

Is it that his body has been so denied, so much, for so long – while engaged in exertions so far beyond its ken – that something inside him must break?

Such appears to be the case to John King as, even from the moment they stop, Burke's weakness only worsens.

'I hope you will remain with me here until I am quite dead,' Mr Burke rasps. 'It is a comfort to know that some one is by, but when I am dying, it is my wish that you should place the pistol in my right hand, and that you leave me unburied as I lie.'[102]

(Yes, perhaps a strange request. But Burke is all too aware if they had not delayed an entire day in the burying of Gray, they would have made it back before Brahe and his party had left. On such a key decision, such an unnecessary pause, had rested the fate of their entire party. If King is to save himself, and maybe even Mr Wills if he is still alive, he must not tarry.)

With the last ounce of energy he has in him, Robert O'Hara Burke now slowly . . . shakily . . . takes his notebook from his pocket and, with quivering quill, jots down what is effectively a post script to his previous final note to his dear sister.

Dearest Hessie King staid with me til the last. He has left me at my request unburied and with my pistol in my hand
Good-bye again dearest Hessie, my heart is with you.[103]

Burke, despite his weakening grip, now writes another note. This time, it is for his loyal companion to the end, John King, in the hope that his words will be read by the society back in Melbourne and King's deeds will be given due reward.

King has behaved nobly and I hope he will be properly cared for.
ROH Burke
And he goes up the creek in accordance with my request.
June 30th 1861[104]

In the same spirit as Mr Wills had read out his final letter to his two companions, Mr Burke now reads with faltering voice the words in his notebook he has just penned.

King bows his head at the kindness of his leader.

'I am convinced,' Mr Burke rasps weakly, 'I cannot last many hours.'[105]

So strongly does this presentiment of his imminent demise weigh upon Mr Burke that he even begins to make his final arrangements, giving his watch to King, and asking that it be given to the Committee, as they had given it to him. He also hands over his pocketbook, asking King to ensure that he gets it to Sir William Stawell.

'Under no circumstances,' he implores, 'are you to deliver it to any other gentleman.'[106]

Perhaps most sacred of all to him, he finally gives to King the watch and last letter of that 'dear fellow', William Wills, entrusting the trust that has been given to him, now to the young Irishman.

•

If Burke is thinking of young Julia, so too is she thinking of him, having already penned a letter that Alfred Howitt has with him, specifically to place in the leader's hands.

In her delicate hand, from her heart, it is clear:

> *Dear Sir,*
> *It is with fear I now address you but I hope my fears will soon be*
> *allayed by hearing of you safe and sound . . . Hoping my dear Sir that*
> *you and all your party are safe, that you met with a pleasant journey*
> *& good feed which is a great thing in travelling, my dear sir I dare say*
> *you almost forget me but if you scrape your various reminiscences of the*
> *past, you will recollect the laughing and joyous & c.*
> *Cupid*
> *PS My sincere regards to you all; all the citizens in Melbourne join in*
> *love to you, bless your little heart . . .* [107, 108]

30 June '61, Cooper's Creek, a journey's end . . .

Robert O'Hara Burke slumps back, his face grey, his breathing laboured, his eyes glazed over, his skin so pale across his sunken cheeks it is almost translucent.

As the darkness falls, and the skies light up, the two souls lie there, side by side. One is only dimly aware of the man beside him, if at all – the other, practically monitoring every breath.

Yes, Burke is holding on the best he can, but they need a miracle, which would most likely come in the form of the blacks he had once advised Brahe to shoot outright rather than engage with . . . now suddenly appearing with food.

But there is no sign of any such miracle, as the light fades, on this nigh moonless night.

'I am dying,' he says simply at one point in the darkness.

It is indeed the voice of a man convinced he has hours to live at best.

And that, certainly, is the impression of John King as, now, in that darkest hour before the dawn, he can hear Burke's muttered prayer, 'Our Father, who art in heaven ... forgive us our trespasses ...'[109]

But can Mr Burke forgive those who have trespassed against him? Perhaps ... and perhaps not. In the fog of his misery, his impending doom, clearly the circumstances of Brahe's departure, such a short time before they had arrived at the Depot, is weighing upon him.

'King,' he rasps in the darkness, 'this is nice treatment after fulfilling our task, to arrive where we left our companions where we had every right to expect them ...'[110]

Where, oh where, had Brahe gone?

•

It is not quite Australia's answer to 'Dr Livingstone, I presume?' and more as if Stanley had run across Dr Livingstone, or one of his party, in a pub just after starting out. For only three days after leaving Melbourne, Alfred Howitt and his three companions have just arrived at the Durham Ox Inn, on the Loddon River 65 miles south of Swan Hill, to slake their thirst – the same pub where an exceptionally worn fellow is drinking in the corner. There is an air about him of both having many miles under his belt in recent times, and *not* wanting to talk about it. Whatever story he has to tell is one he might tell in due course, to the right people, but it will not be told casually – and the man is in fact travelling as hard as he can to get to the closest telegraph station, which is at Bendigo. In fact, this man knows of Alfred Howitt, and his trip to the north looking for Mr Burke and his party, as it has been published in the papers, and is the talk of this outpost.

Inevitably, in such confined circumstances, it is not long before the two are face to face, and, in his native Nottingham accent, Howitt asks the stranger the obvious question.

And you would be, sir?

I am William Brahe.

Of . . . ?

The Victorian Exploring Expedition.

Howitt is as stunned as he is eager to hear Brahe's story and in short order the broad brush-strokes tumble out, as the German, after confirming that this really is Alfred Howitt, tumbles over himself to tell the Englishman everything:

The journey north. The appointment of Wright. The heat. The flies. The rats. The endless trekking. The waiting . . . waiting . . . waiting. Their departure south, and meeting up with Wright. The deaths.

Howitt takes it all in, distressed that the whereabouts of Burke and Wills and their party remains unknown. What seems obvious is that they are likely to still be a *long* way north, and that Howitt's small party will be unlikely to have the wherewithal to reach them. Deciding drastic action is called for he no sooner sends his men on to Swan Hill, before he quickly returns to Bendigo, with William Brahe in tow, and from that town's telegraph office, he sends the news to the person who needs to know first.

> June 29.
> The Hon. John Macadam, M.D.
> Sir.
>
> I met Mr Brahe at the Loddon with dispatches, and received the following message: 'Mr Wright has reached Menindee with eight men, having been joined by Mr Burke's depot party from Cooper's Creek. Messrs Becker, Purcell, Stone, and Patten died on the journey. Mr Burke left Cooper's Creek on the 16th December. Nothing has been heard of him since that date. He was accompanied by Messrs Wills, King, and Gray. The natives proved hostile, and the country for 180 miles was waterless. Two camels and three horses died, and one was lost.
> W. Wright.
>
> I shall be in town with Mr Brahe tomorrow morning.
>
> A. W. Howitt,
> Leader of Contingent Party[111]

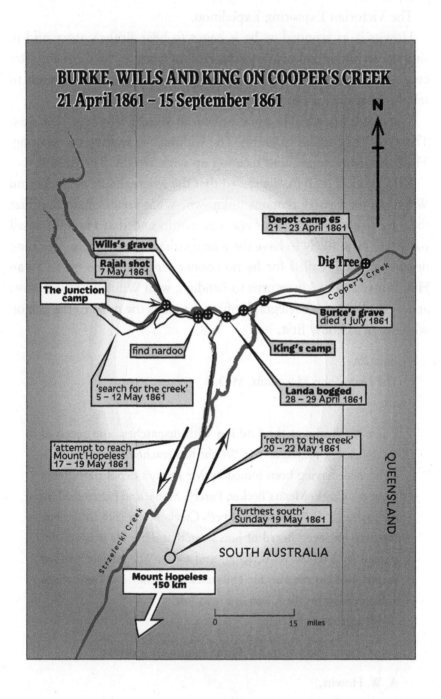

BURKE, WILLS AND KING ON COOPER'S CREEK
21 April 1861 – 15 September 1861

N

Depot camp 65
21 – 23 April 1861

Wills's grave

Rajah shot
7 May 1861

Dig Tree

Cooper's Creek

The Junction
camp

Burke's grave
died 1 July 1861

find nardoo

King's camp

'search for the creek'
5 – 12 May 1861

Landa bogged
28 – 29 April 1861

'return to the creek'
20 – 22 May 1861

'attempt to reach
Mount Hopeless'
17 – 19 May 1861

QUEENSLAND

Strzelecki Creek

'furthest south'
Sunday 19 May 1861

SOUTH AUSTRALIA

Mount Hopeless
150 km

0   15   miles

Howitt now races back to Melbourne in the company of Brahe in order to meet with the Exploration Committee, and gather more men and resources.

It now seems more likely than ever that Messrs Burke and Wills and their Gulf party are in *real* trouble, and that makes their collective action more urgent than ever.

•

To King's surprise, Mr Burke is still alive at the dawn. But somewhere in those early daylight hours of the new day, his murmurings cease entirely and when, at 8 am, King checks once more, there is no movement.

No breathing.

Indeed, no pulse.

The once dominating, domineering, demanding figure of Mr Burke, the man who led the best equipped, most glorious expedition ever to venture out into Australia, the man who was the first to cross the entire continent, south to north . . .

Dead.

Gun in his hand.

All the sting has gone out of him.

King falls to the ground, and weeps.

Strangely, though dead, Mr Burke still provides some company in this wilderness, the dead Irish soldier lying by the bank of *Yinimingka*, and despite the urgency of finding the natives, King stays by the body for the next couple of hours before reluctantly deciding that he must move once more up the creek. Observing Mr Burke's final wishes, King makes no move to bury the fallen leader. Mr Burke had been right. There is no point.

Finally, King rises, bending only to retrieve Mr Wills's gold watch and the last letter the Englishman had written to his father, which he places carefully in a small leather pouch he wears around his neck.

His duty now is to 'try and find help for Wills'[112].

A lonely figure in the wilderness, a scarecrow of a man and the last soul left, King staggers off once more.

Moving up the creek, his exhausted eyes perpetually scan the horizon for a sign of human life.

Oh, what a life he has led! And what strange circumstances have led him to this point, from home sweet home in Ireland, to India, to Melbourne for just six weeks, to a journey across an entire continent and half of the way back to be now the only living white man in hundreds of miles, all alone, just 22 years old with no bush skills, no navigational skills and, let's face it, John . . . precious little hope of surviving. But he must try. Though of the blacks there is no sign, he is at least able to find some nardoo in one of their camps and, courtesy of another crow he is able to shoot, has enough food to keep going, as he makes his slow way back to Mr Wills, hoping against hope that the Englishman is still alive, that he, King, is not actually the only European in hundreds of miles in any direction. All he can do, meantime, is sleep in the natives' deserted wurleys along the way.

'I felt very lonely,'[113] he would note.

CHAPTER FIFTEEN

OFF TO THE RESCUE

The whole expedition appears to have been one prolonged blunder throughout; and it is to be hoped that the rescuing party may not be mismanaged and retarded in the same way as the unfortunate original expedition was. The savants have made a sad mess of the whole affair; let them, if possible, retrieve themselves in this its last sad phase.[1]

The Age, 1 July 1861

Late June '61, to Melbourne, Howitt circles the Circumlocution Office

Mr Howitt, as is his wont, moves quickly.

Talking to Brahe as they catch the train south from Woodend to Melbourne, he quickly establishes that the young German man is willing to return north with him – an enormous boon, given his 'knowledge of the country'[2]. Subject to the approval of the Committee – for everything must be run past them – Howitt promises to take him back to Cooper's Creek to search for Burke.

And now here they are, in front of the Committee in the Royal Society Hall.

The first order of business, of course, is to closely question Brahe on one thing in particular.

'What is your opinion as to where Mr Burke now is?' Sir William Stawell asks him.

'There might be a hundred causes for his absence,' the German replies. 'I could only give a guess. It is my opinion, however, that after Mr Burke left Eyre's Creek, he found large waterholes, which would

451

be dried up on his return. He went too far away from water, and still kept pushing on, hoping to find some, until at last he was unable either to go on or return. I am very much afraid too, after the experience of our party, that Mr Burke's party was attacked by scurvy.'[3]

Sir William agrees, but suggests that 'he might be in some place where it was not advisable to leave until the rainy season set in. Mr Burke has, it appears, acted most prudently, and done just what a wise man would have done.'[4] But perhaps, too, it is offered hopefully to Brahe, Burke might have headed to Queensland?

'During the conversations I had with Mr Burke,' Brahe replies, 'he never spoke to me about his future course. I asked him whether he would make for the settled district upon the east coast, if he did get to the other side, but he never seemed to have heard about it. He asked me, "Where is that?"'[5]

Sir William Stawell is stunned, observing, 'Mr Burke spoke about those districts when in Melbourne.'[6]

Frankly, it makes Mr Burke sound somewhat . . . irrational?

The most obvious thing is that to find Burke, and follow his tracks, Howitt will need a party a little more like Burke's, capable of establishing a Depot on the Cooper and then following his tracks from there. So he urgently needs to recruit more men. For his part, Howitt applies to the Committee for 'a medical man with if possible some bush experience'[7].

Having already closely questioned Brahe about the number, and condition, of horses and camels that await at Pamamaroo Camp – together with Mr Wright and other survivors – Mr Howitt is of the opinion that he need not expand his own number of horses and camels commensurate with the increased size of his own party, as he can use the animals in Menindee that would be rested for a month by the time he reached them.

'With this party,' Howitt states to the Committee in the formal report he now reads to them, 'I should push on for Cooper's Creek as rapidly as I could do in justice to the pack horses, and should then endeavour to find a more favourable spot for a depot than the last.'[8]

From Cooper's Creek the first step would be to explore the country to the north, to look for whatever diaries or documents the Gulf party might have buried, and from there take instruction from the situation they find. If there proves to be water available in the course of the Burke party's tracks, Howitt and his men should be able to follow those tracks all the way. If not, they will need to divert to water when needed, and hopefully pick up the tracks once more.

There is no doubt Howitt will receive the full support of the Victorian public, which has been devastated to read terrible reports of what has occurred, with the tone set by the *Age*.

> The unexpected news of Mr Burke's expedition of discovery, which we publish this morning, is positively disastrous. The entire company of explorers has been dissipated out of being, like dew-drops before the sun.[9]

Once Mr Howitt's formal submission is made to a sub-committee of the Exploration Committee, they are quick to consider it and by late afternoon of 1 July – within the day – come back with their proposals.

It is their belief that Mr Howitt's party 'should be strengthened to about twelve individuals, including one or two aborigines'[10].

As to Mr Howitt's proposal that, perhaps, once they have some basic information, a party of five or so be sent back with dispatches, the short answer is . . . no. 'A separation in Mr Howitt's party should be deemed admissible only under the most urgent circumstances . . .'[11]

Mr Howitt is authorised to purchase however many horses he might need, as well as 'availing himself of any serviceable horses and dromedaries brought back by Messrs Wright and Brahe'[12].

Very well.

Howitt isn't too fussed. He simply wants to get moving with all possible speed.

Early July '61, Melbourne, fatal news and last hopes

People are gathered on street corners around the metropolis passing the *Argus* between them, and the extraordinary news spreads, with the headline telling the most stunning part of the story.

The Exploration Party. The Death of Four Men[13]

Mr Burke's party! One of their number has just turned up on the Loddon River and reports no trace of Mr Burke has been seen by others of the party since *last December*. In Bendigo, the *Advertiser* tells the same grim story, but has one hopeful conjecture:

> Of course there is a chance, though a small one, that Mr Burke has crossed the Continent, and he may now be at Blunder Bay, or the Gulf of Carpentaria, whither, if it be not too late, a steamer must be sent at once, unless the Government wish to be associated in the disgrace which is already attached to the Exploration Committee.[14]

Early July '61, Cooper's Creek, King in his own domain

Still traipsing. Still going. Still the same scarecrow of a man, making his way along the creek bed, the only white man anywhere within 400 miles in any direction. At least, the only white man who's still alive.

John King has been fighting the urge to simply give up, just managing to continue pushing himself forward, sleeping at night 'in deserted [gunyahs] belonging to the natives'[15].

Of those natives in the flesh, so far, there has been no sign, but on this morning, 3 July, two days after Mr Burke died, King finds something almost as precious in one of the empty gunyahs: 'A bag of nardoo, sufficient to last me a fortnight . . . I also shot a crow . . .'[16]

That evening, for the first time in weeks, King is able to eat his fill, still hopeful of finding the natives, though fearful of the chance they will stumble upon him, eating *their* nardoo . . .

4 July, Melbourne, searching for four needles in an outback

Howitt has agreed to everything. What choice did he have? This party is a little too big for his liking, but so be it. On this morning, his enlarged party assemble once more at Spencer Street Station, bound for Woodend, where they will catch a Cobb & Co coach, to rejoin Welch, Aitkin and Vining, who are waiting with the horses in Swan Hill.

The new recruits include none other than William Brahe, now formally appointed as his second officer; Dr William Wheeler; and three other men, Messrs Sampson, Calcutt and Phillips.

Yes, it is something that help is on its way. But is it all too late?

Many around the nation certainly hope not, and from seemingly all points on the compass, Australia is rallying to send out search parties. From Port Phillip Bay, Captain William Norman will soon depart on HMVS *Victoria* to the Gulf, to be accompanied by the sailing-brig *Firefly*, to meet in Brisbane the great explorer Mr William Landsborough – recommended by Mr Gregory himself – who will be leading the Queensland rescue party. Landsborough is a hearty, independent man, and one of his friends would note of him that 'He was an excellent horseman, a most entertaining and, at times, eccentric companion, and he could starve with greater cheerfulness than any man I ever saw or heard of'[17].

Precisely what is required in all good Australian explorers.

South Australia has determined to send its own rescue mission, and there are more, as Australia seemingly becomes a continent explored by search parties, all seeking Robert O'Hara Burke and the three men with him, Wills, King and Gray.

Morning 5 July, Cooper's Creek, a final duty

Two days after being forced to stop, now feeling partially restored, John King sets off once more, carrying as much nardoo as he can and three further dead crows – both for himself and Mr Wills, in the unlikely event the expedition's second officer is still alive. Arduously traipsing his way westward along Cooper's Creek for the entire day, some 10 miles and as many hours later – though King himself measures his journey neither by hours, or miles, but by the three waterholes that lie between Mr Burke and Mr Wills.

Finally, as the twilight hour sets in, John King quietly approaches the gunyah where he had left Mr Wills. The young Irishman is silent and attentive in the hope of sensing, seeing or hearing some movement, *any* movement, but all is uncomfortably . . . still. Flies are buzzing, unpleasantly.

And there is Mr Wills, exactly where King and Mr Burke had left him. Dead.

King is saddened, but not surprised. The body has, to a certain extent, been disturbed as it seems the natives have been there and helped themselves to some of the clothes Wills had been wearing.

Given that Mr Wills had not extracted a promise from him not to bury his corpse, King, the best he can, now digs with his hands a very shallow grave – hardly a depression – for the expedition's second-in-command. And now, with the last of his strength, he drags the body into it – before covering it with sand and the fallen boughs of a tree to give it some protection.

Second week of July '61, congestion at the crossing of the Murrumbidgee

That rather elegant, ascetic-looking man who rides so beautifully in the saddle it almost looks as if he might have been born there? It is Alfred Howitt, up Swan Hill way, riding from station to station, 'scouring the country'[18] for the decent horses he needs to take on to Cooper's Creek so the search proper for the Gulf party can begin. As for his unfortunate surveyor, Mr Edwin Welch, it feels to him like his right eye has been scoured by the thumb of a giant, having been temporarily blinded from looking through a mal-adjusted sextant in the blaring sun. He has 'Congestion of the Retina'[19], according to the local doctor. Still, a new sextant is on its way from Professor Neumayer and once it arrives, and they have the last of the horses they need, they will be on their way, 'ere another week has passed, with Weston Phillips doing the surveying duties for the moment. They can adapt, and keep moving, which is all that counts.

Howitt and all of his men are activated by a sense of urgency, gripped with the feeling that if Burke and his men are still alive, time is likely running out for them.

10 July '61, Cooper's Creek, with the natives

With his stock of nardoo now running short, John King must move once more, and so starts off after the natives again, this time tracking their footprints from where they had been when, he thinks, they had stolen Mr Wills's clothes. (John King is unaware the clothes have not been taken, but buried, out of respect for the dead by the Yandruwandha.) As ever, King uses his gun on whatever crows or hawks fly overhead and it is after bringing down one of the latter that the young man suddenly looks up to find himself near surrounded by natives who have come to investigate the source of this boom of thunder on a sunny day.

He has found them! Or, rather, they have found him.

Though King is fearful, for there are so many of them, and he is so weak, the natives prove to be nothing but friendly and take him back to their nearby camp where he is given as much nardoo and fish as he can eat. As well, they pluck and roast his birds for him, and show him 'a gunyah where I was to sleep with three of the single men'[20].

With his strength again at least marginally improved by the next morning, the natives do their best to converse with him.

Using sign language, one of them puts his finger on the ground, covers it with sand, and points in the direction where King had left Mr Wills, saying something that sounds distinctly like 'whitefella'.

With similar sign language they ask where the third white man is?

Carefully, King puts two fingers on the ground, covers them with sand, and makes them understand, they're *both* up the creek. Dead.

In response, the natives evince the universally expressed emotions of sadness for what has occurred, and compassion for King. The white-fella's friends are dead. He is all alone. His leader lies at *Yinimingka*, he has no place. He is dependent on them. They understand.

Over the next four days, eating and resting, a little bit of basic strength returns to young John King. He is soon strong enough, in fact, that the natives themselves have clearly come to the view that he can cope without them, now making clear signs that while they are now going up the creek, it is time for him to go down, to leave them.

'I saw,' King would note, 'that they were becoming tired of me.'[21]

King knows exactly what to do.

'I pretended not to understand them.'[22] Just as William Wills had done.

Now the blackfellas respond just as they had to Wills. They start packing up, getting ready to move on. The native women gather up their babies, nestle them on their hips, while also slinging dilly bags – made of woven grass – on their hips, filled with food and cooking implements. The men carry their weapons – boomerangs and spears – and themselves, with great purpose.

No one says anything to King, or even tries to communicate anything through hand gestures, but as it is obvious that without them he will not last much longer than Burke or Wills, it is an energy born of desperation which makes King get up and follow them, as soon as they start to move up the creek. It is all he can do to keep contact, but that is precisely what he does.

When they stop, he stops. When they move, he moves.

When they stop at their new encampment in the late afternoon, he is right there with them.

The tribe, which is about 30 adults strong, notes his slightly surprising presence among them, *still*, with passing interest – *who knew the white-fella had that in him?* – but no more than that.

It will take something a little more than his mere presence to ensure any change of heart from them. And yet, when an opportunity suddenly presents itself, King, with his double-barrelled shotgun, is able to rise to the occasion.

It so happens that, just as he arrives, a flock of crows fly overhead at some speed, and it is only the very best of Aboriginal warriors who could bring them down with a boomerang. But the white man barely blinks. He just points his stick in the general direction of the crows, and once again, thunder comes from it! In response, the tribe throws themselves to the ground.

But look now . . .

Into their own midst, miraculously, comes a handful of crows!

The tribe is very pleased. So much so, they make a break-wind shelter for King, so the man with the weird white skin and strangely coloured eyes can pass the night more comfortably – promisingly, it is right in the centre of their own camp – before, as King would recount, they 'came and sat round me until such time as the crows were cooked, when they assisted me to eat them'[23].

This joint display, of the power he holds in his hands and the ability to provide a meal of birds with so little effort, suitably impresses them.

And now one of the older women, Carrawaw – about five foot tall, and in her forties, her breasts and upper arms marked with tribal scars – to whom he has given some crow, gives him a small ball of nardoo, making him understand that she would like to give him more, but because of the large boil she has on her arm, she cannot pound. It gives King an idea.

Boiling some water in the billy, he takes a sponge and carefully washes her whole arm, with particular attention to the boil, as the whole tribe gathers around, watching closely. With the woman's husband sitting beside her as she cries in pain it is a risky operation, but the natives at least clearly sense that he is trying to help, not hurt. And now that the boil is at least cleaned, King uses some of the last of the medical supplies he has with him, some nitrate of silver, to disinfect the wound.

In response, the woman leaps to her feet and runs off, yelling 'Mokow! Mokow!'[24] the same word the natives have used to describe the fire King has built to boil the billy.

But by the following morning when the boil is clearly healing, King's position with the tribe is consolidated, starting with Carrawaw and her *nhipa*, husband, bringing him a small quantity of nardoo every night and morning. From a strange pasty-faced nothing who has somehow wandered into their existence, he is now no less than the tribe's medicine man! And Carrawaw is his – how does she say it? – *ngumbu*, friend.

As a mark of the newfound respect the tribe has for him, he is invited to go on fishing excursions with them – amazing, how easily the fish can be caught! – and begins to learn some of the basics of the Yandruwandha language.

Minha nganha drikana – tell me your name.

Ngapakurna – waterhole.

Karlukarlungadi – going fishing.

Kapanda – come on, let's go.

Walypala – whitefella.

Kakarrili – cockatoos.

Windra – spears.

Dakamirri – pelicans.

Kapada! – come here!

Nhinapandi! – sit down![25]

'I could not learn to talk to them,' King would chronicle, 'but I began slowly to understand what they were saying.'[26]

'*Kapadow Kinganyi! Thawarla ngali karlukarlungadi!*' – Come on, King! Let's go fishing!

The thrust is clear, if not necessarily every word. But King is in no doubt that he must fit in, join in and belonga them.

When the tribe moves to a new encampment, he is helped to make a wurley, and in return, King, who carefully preserves his still ample ammunition, regularly shoots down crows and hawks, which the tribe plucks, cooks and shares. Despite that, every few days the tribe still surrounds him and asks whether he intends to go up or down the creek.

It takes some time, but, as King would chronicle, 'at last I made them understand that if they went up I should go up the creek, and if they went down I should also go down'[27].

John King is a young man, but wise beyond his years.

Second week of July '61, Victoria, Sir Charles Hotham and the busy doctor

After all his letters, all of his pounding on doors, all of his meetings, at long last Dr Wills has succeeded in making at least a little headway in Melbourne's infernal resistance to do something to try to save the expedition they had so gloriously farewelled nearly a year ago, with so many fine speeches and so much flag-waving. And yet, while gratified with the departure of Mr Alfred Howitt and his party to Cooper's Creek, and the forthcoming departure of HMVS *Victoria*, still that is not quite enough for Dr Wills. He wants, and gets, more. Most agreeable is that his dear friend, and host in Melbourne, the businessman James Orkney, has just dispatched – at his own expense – the steamer SS *Sir Charles Hotham* to head towards the Gulf, where it can aid HMVS *Victoria* in searching along the coast of the Gulf of Carpentaria.

The other breakthrough has come from South Australia, which has not only announced it will be mounting a rescue expedition to Cooper's Creek under the leadership of one John McKinlay, but Dr Wills himself has been called upon to take the two strongest of the six camels that Mr Burke had left behind, put them aboard SS *Oscar*, and bring them to

Ludwick Becker's pen and sepia ink sketch, 'Reservoir in Mootwanji Ranges', from his expedition sketchbook (SLV H16486)

Sturt's Stony Desert, showing the area around Burke and Wills's Camp 72 when they left the sandy Strzelecki Desert and first ventured out onto the Stony Desert

(photo © Dave Phoenix 2014)

'First camp from Duroadoo [Torowoto]' by Ludwig Becker. The figure on the camel furthest right is William Wright (SLV H16486)

Photo of the Dig Tree, carved with the legend DEC 6-60 APR 21-61, and showing the remains of the Depot's stockade. This is an enlarged section of a photo taken by John Robert Dick in 1898 (State Library of QLD 42815)

The Selywn Range (photo © Dave Phoenix)

The Gulf country just north of Camp 119. This photo was taken in the wet season, where every footstep is a wade through mud (photo © Dave Phoenix)

Tuesday, June 23rd 1861

Night calm clear & intensely cold especi
towards morning - near daybreak King repor
seeing a moon in the east with a haze of light
stretching up from it, he declared it to be quite
as large as the moon and not dim at the edges
I am so weak that any attempt to get a sight
of it was out of the question; but I think it
must have been Venus in the Zodiacal
light that he saw, with a corona around her
Mr Burke & King remain at home cleaning
& pounding seed, they both getting weaker
every day. the Cold plays, the deuce with us
from the small amount of clothing we have
my wardrobe consists of, a wide awake, a merin
shirt, a regatta shirt without sleeves, the remains
of a pair of flannel trousers, two pairs of socks in
rags, and a waistcoat of which I have managed
to keep the pockets together. the others are
no better off. besides these we have between us for
bedding, two small camel-pads some horse
hair two or three little bits of a rug & pieces of
oil cloth saved from the fire.

The day turned out nice & warm.

One of Wills's last journal entries. His handwriting has deteriorated markedly. The correct date for this Tuesday was 25 June (National Library of Australia MS30/7)

THE LAST HOURS OF Mr WILLS.

'The last hours of Mr Wills' – an engraving by Montagu Scott, published in the preface to Dr Wills's book, *A Successful Exploration through the Interior of Australia, from Melbourne to the Gulf of Carpentaria*, 1863 (courtesy Colin Choat, gutenberg.net.au)

Cooper's Creek near Innamincka. Burke died near here (photo © Dave Phoenix)

Dr John Macadam, Hon. Secretary of the Royal Society of Victoria (From University of Melbourne, *Medical School Journal*, University of Melbourne, 1914)

Sir Francis Murphy, key Commissioner of the Burke and Wills Royal Commission (University of Melbourne, c. 1896, University of Melbourne Archives, BWP/7118)

Burke's Irish nanny, Ellen Dogherty, who arrived in Australia too late for Burke but in time for his funeral (SLV IMP 31/01/63/1)

Alfred Howitt, explorer and leader of the party sent to relieve or rescue Burke and Wills, and charged with the sad task of bringing their remains back to Melbourne. Photo circa 1864

(SLV H37475/26)

Photo of John King, taken in 1863, two years after the tragic end of the expedition
(SLV H90.90/12)

Photo of the Burke and Wills funeral car, taken on 21 January 1863, the day of their funeral in Melbourne. The funeral car is outside the undertaker's office, which was across the road from the Royal Society of Victoria, where the bodies of Burke and Wills were laid in state (courtesy Royal Historical Society of Victoria/Dave Phoenix)

The Dig Tree as it was in 2008 (photo © Dave Phoenix)

Adelaide so Mr McKinlay may have use of them. Dr Wills is only too happy to oblige, pleased to be able to do something beyond merely advocating.

In the meantime, up at Blanchewater station, just short of Mount Hopeless, an extraordinary thing has happened, which will have a bearing on McKinlay's expedition. Opening the door of his hut one morning, a worker had been confronted by . . . two camels! They must, there can surely be no doubt, have come from the Victorian Exploring Expedition! (Those two camels, Cassim and Nano, lost by Tom McDonough eight months earlier, had come a very long way indeed – about 600 miles.)

Perhaps these escapees can be of use for the rescue?

With the cabled blessing of Dr Macadam from Melbourne, McKinlay is quick to claim the camels for his own expedition, to go with the two brought across by Dr Wills.

Late July '61, through New South Wales, following the circus

For the last four weeks now, for Alfred Howitt and his men – heading north across the bottom third of Australia – it has been like following the trail of a careless travelling circus. At nigh on every stop they come across the discarded detritus of an expedition that had been ludicrously overloaded from the first. At places like Balranald and at Tarcoola station, the discarded items had included two whole wagons, one of which actually carried a flat-bottomed punt, 'six sets of wagon harness; a spare wagon axle; and two spare hind wagon wheels', together with 'an assortment of the tools, implements, and general equipment'[28].

He ain't seen nothing yet . . .

For Howitt is never more stunned than when, after crossing the Darling River and trekking to Pamamaroo Camp, he goes through the stores of what Mr Burke and his men had left behind this time.

There are *tons* of it! Here are saddles and stirrups, there are preserved vegetables, tomahawks and hacksaws. Over there, a whole pile of harnesses, hundreds of bottles of medicine and, most surprising, lots of hooks, lines and sinkers. And then there are – as he notes in his careful hand to send back to the Committee, so they can know what has become of their property – such things as 'horse brushes, curry combs, 300 lbs flour, box of tea, 25 lbs biscuits, 400 lbs oats, pepper, mustard, 3 lbs tobacco, 12 packages preserved vegetables, box of rockets, 12 camel pack bags … camel medicines, small chisels, hammer, solder and iron, horse nails, 4 rifles, 5 double fowling pieces, 8 revolvers, 3 powder flasks, 2 flags, gunpowder … bullets, caps, wads, rifle cartridges, looking glasses, martingales, saddles, hobble chains, bells.'[29]

It is not just the sheer amount of it that shocks him, but the illogicality of it.

'Some of [the things] in my opinion,' the Englishman will note, 'need never have been taken, while there were other things left behind which would certainly be required and could not be obtained when wanted beyond the settlements.'[30]

Of all the things he and his men find, it is the fishing gear that surprises Howitt the most. Why leave behind the things that will allow you to live off the land?

In the meantime, he is at least gratified to find that arrangements are sufficiently well advanced – with his collection of men, horses, camels and supplies all building satisfactorily – that he should be able to start for Cooper's Creek within two weeks. The men he will take will not include the two sepoys he finds at Pamamaroo – Dost Mahomet and Belooch Khan. It is Howitt's firm opinion, as he will recount, that 'any man who was good with horses could manage camels'[31].

He will go north without them – something that appears to relieve the sepoys mightily. They are to stay and await instruction at Pamamaroo Camp with six of the camels.

The camels, Howitt would recount, are now placed 'under the charge of Brahe, who did the work to my complete satisfaction'[32].

In the meantime, if while out in the bush Howitt had been a whirlwind – eating up the miles day after day, a trail of swirling dust in his wake – here in Menindee he is more of a willy-willy, hustling around and about the outpost and nearby stations every day, whistling up the supplies he needs, salvaging what he can of the material left at Pamamaroo and getting some of it repaired. Regarding the animals, he writes to Macadam: 'of the thirteen camels now here, seven are considered fit for the journey if only lightly loaded' but good horses are what he prefers to rely on in any case.[33]

Late July '61, Cooper's Creek, loving *kurrakurrari*

It is not that John King is getting strong among the Yandruwandha people. But he is, at least, a little stron*ger*, and surviving, which is something, and bit by bit integrating into their tribe. The fact that this now includes sharing his gunyah with a young and comely Aboriginal woman, Turinyi, who is none other than Carrawaw's daughter, helps immeasurably. For King is every bit as taken with her as she is taken with him. Her brown eyes . . . her flashing brown eyes. Her slim form, shoulder-length black hair, bewitching smile. Around the tribal elders, Turinyi is silent and respectful, for it is both her way and the way to be 'quiet among much older men'[34] but when she is alone with this young man, her laughter and talk are irrepressible. It has been a long journey, which has taken 22-year-old King from the green fields of Ireland, across the seas to India, to the battles of Lucknow and Cawnpore, and across the seas once more to now find himself living with an Aboriginal tribe deep in the heart of Australia, in love with an Aboriginal woman, but it is not without joy on a good night. For she is, she teaches him, his '*Pudupa*' woman, and he is glad of it.

He continues to learn ever more words.

Pirripirri for spirit *and* white man. (John King slowly comes to understand – they think the white men are spirits of their ancestors. But are they *Ngapitjali*, good spirit ancestors, or *Kurnki*, bad spirit ancestors? Mr Wills and John King appear friendly and good. But the heavily bearded Burke . . . well he may be *Kurnki*.)[35]

Kalpurru for a coolabah tree.[36]

Karru – an initiated Aboriginal man.[37]

Kurrakurrari – a madman . . . like you.[38]

Kandrakandra – upstream.[39]

Gow! Gow! – All right![40]

Ngapakurna – waterhole.[41]

Kirrayindri – get too thin.[42]

With his improvement in language, and simply through living with the people, King also comes to understand just how much more sophisticated their system of living is than he had previously imagined – how they move up and down according to where the food is most abundant, how each camp is supplied not only with gunyahs ready to move into, but grinding stones for the nardoo, so they don't have to carry them from camp to camp. He watches closely the clever way the native women and children gather nardoo, and can't help but compare it to the hopelessly time-consuming methods he used to employ with Mr Burke and Mr Wills. For the blacks have it down to a fine art, and sweep brush across the nardoo plants to make the seeds fall to the ground, which are then swept into heaps, crushed and winnowed. So simple yet sophisticated. If only he had known earlier, if only they had made the attempt to learn more from the blacks, how different everything might have been . . .

Slowly, slowly, King's strength continues to return, until the Yandruwandha judge him able enough to provide the answer to the question they want answered. Through sign language, they communicate to King:

Where exactly is the whitefella leader?

King promises to show them and, as the course of their nomadic existence inevitably brings them close once more to where Mr Burke is keeping his eternal rest, one day when King and the Yandruwandha are fishing in the waterholes that lie close by, he decides the time is opportune.

'I took them to the spot,' King would recount. To *Yinimingka*. To his fallen chief.

That sound, an instant afterwards? That curiously communal wailing, that is less a sum of its parts and more the whole body of them weeping at once?

'On seeing his remains,' King would recount, 'the whole party wept bitterly, and covered them with bushes.'[43]

The pathos of the fate of the white men affects the tribe deeply, and it is not a feeling that passes.

'After this, they were much kinder to me than before,'[44] King records.

Yes, his situation remains grim. He is lost in the wilderness, but at least he is alive, at least the tribe is looking after him, and ultimately he has every confidence that some kind of rescue mission will be mounted, that the Committee will not simply allow their Gulf party to disappear without sending out a search party for them.

So confident is King of this point that, time and again, by the fire at night, eating fish and nardoo, he frequently points to the moon, raises two fingers and says '*Walypala*', 'white-fellows', as his way of indicating his belief that the rescue party will be here within two months.

They understand. It becomes part of their own conversation.

'They used to talk about the "white fellows" coming, at the same time pointing to the moon,' King would recount. 'I also told them they would receive many presents, and they constantly asked me for tomahawks, called by them "bomayko" . . . They treated me with uniform kindness, and looked upon me as one of themselves.'[45]

And King will do anything for them in return, bar one thing. He will *not* show them what he has in the leather pouch he has around his neck – *pani, pani, pani, no, no, no* – where he has secreted such things as Mr Wills's last letter and gold watch, together with Mr Burke's notebook. That last, he had specifically promised to give to Sir William Stawell alone, and he intends to do precisely that.

4 August '61, Port Phillip Bay, Victorian departure

Cutting through the 'white horses' of Port Phillip Bay on this fine late afternoon, HMVS *Victoria* makes a proud sight to behold. The colony's first warship, the grand 880-ton sloop had been launched in London just six years earlier and has just returned from seeing service in the New Zealand War – ensuring supply to outlying posts, bombarding the shore, and even unleashing its sailors to fight as infantry at Kairau and Matarikoriko. But now it is off on its most important mission of all. Under the command of Captain William Norman, it is heading to the Gulf of Carpentaria to look for Robert O'Hara Burke and his men!

On current reckoning, it should take them four weeks to get to the Gulf, and on the way they will be joined off Brisbane's Moreton Bay by SS *Firefly* – which had already left Melbourne a week earlier. (Alas, that will be *it*, in terms of help from other vessels. James Orkney's steamer, SS *Sir Charles Hotham*, is aground up Maroochy way, north of Brisbane, with a hole in her keel, and can take no further part in any rescue effort.)

13 August '61, leaving Menindee, with as little delay as possible, just for a change

It is time to leave Menindee, and get on with it.

For the last two weeks, using the camp at Pamamaroo Creek as his base, Alfred Howitt has been refreshing the animals, building supplies, and gathering men; they are now thirteen all up, including two Aboriginal guides. Tomorrow they will set off for Cooper's Creek, meaning the time is right, tonight, for Howitt to dash off a quick missive to Melbourne: 'I have the honour to report to the Exploration Committee that my arrangements are now so far completed that I expect to leave this camp with the contingent party for Cooper's Creek tomorrow morning, taking with me seven camels and thirty-seven horses, and full stores for five months . . . I shall proceed with as little delay as possible, but for the first week I do not expect to make more than sixty or seventy miles, judging from the difficulty we have already experienced in keeping our horses together, on account of the camels.'[46]

●

For John King, life has started to become, if not normal, then at least familiar. This young man is now, if you please, 'John King of the Yandruwandha people'. Both he and his tribe understand it; his tribal name *Kinganyi*, is now used by all. With his gun he brings down crows and hawks for them all to feast upon. And they teach him to make such things as a wurley – at least as well as a whitefella can – while also bringing him nardoo and fish. Most importantly, of course, in the biggest sign of their acceptance of him, he can enjoy the love of Turinyi with their blessing. And so the days pass. John King learns to live like a black, among the blacks, while always keeping an eye to the horizon for what he truly wants to see – whitefellas. Surely, by now, Melbourne must have sent out a rescue expedition to search for survivors? Where can they be?

•

And now the cockatoos rise once more. This time, not because Mr Howitt and his men are an enormous group, but simply because they are moving *fast*. This is no plod, this is a trot, eating up mile after mile, from sun-up to sundown and even into the semi-darkness. No time is lost to desertions, to duels declined, to quelling mutinies, to searching for lost camels, to trying to find water. Even Edwin Welch, a man who delights in recording every anecdote he comes across, can find very little to say bar rather dry annotations concerning the country they pass through, with the exception of something that occurs on the nineteenth of August: 'At the Bengora Creek, saw the first Warrigle Blackfellows one of whom run after us talking and gesticulating considerably but when spoken to could give no intelligible information.'[47] Ah well, onward. Torowoto Swamp comes and goes, with Welch noting, surprised, how 'perfectly dry'[48] it is. Things would be grim, if they were reliant on such water, but Mr Howitt and his men are carrying so much water with them – and there are so few of them to drink it and they are moving so fast between waterholes – it is not a problem. Onward, gentlemen. Cooper's Creek is now in our sights and will soon be beneath our feet.

Early September '61, approaching Cooper's Creek, Howitt fishes for an answer

After eight weeks of hard travelling, Howitt and his party of 12 men are at last closing in on Cooper's Creek. From Menindee, they had faithfully followed the path of Mr Burke until 2 September. Then, drawing on William Brahe's knowledge, they had declined to take Burke's long loop out to the north-east, to Bulloo, and had gone straight across to the north-west, with their navigator and surveyor, Edwin Welch – still one-eyed – steering them towards Mr Burke's Camp 60. Welch uses the co-ordinates from Mr Wills's early field books, the most precious cargo that returned with Brahe from Cooper's Creek.

Among the many questions Alfred Howitt puts to William Brahe along the way – as they cross red soiled ranges, vast open plains, hard sandy ridges and patches of scrub – some of his most persistent concern fishing.

Surely, he asks, Cooper's Creek had plenty of fish, like all major waterways in Australia? Brahe's answer had quite stunned him.

'Although I saw the blacks with fish,' Brahe had told him, 'none of my party had caught any, excepting when they bailed out a small hole and caught a few small ones . . .'[49]

This seems extraordinary to Howitt. Brahe and his party had left the Depot essentially because they were running out of supplies, and yet they had not pursued fishing as a sure source of fresh food.

Howitt and his men keep riding hard, and after crossing through some high red sand-hills, on this eighth day of September, they come to earthy plains where, sure enough, on the distant horizon they see a smudge which, as they get closer, is seen to have, first, flecks of green, and then billowing clouds of it, from trees a'plenty.

Trotting forth, they cross another set of sand-hills to . . . suddenly come upon a native camp with four wurleys and just one blackfella playing with a dog. The man gives 'a succession of yells and then ran off as if electrified'[50].

(Edwin Welch would note, 'He gave a series of yells and bounded away like a kangaroo.'[51])

The next day they come across a blazed tree indicating Camp 61, demonstrating that they are once again on the right track – Burke's – a track they soon note is progressively more littered with discarded cans, empty boxes and the like. Seriously, on their way north, the Burke party appears to have lost everything, bar their will to live.

The Howitt party keeps going until they come to a particularly large branch of Cooper's Creek, where they make camp for the night, only to find five blackfellas appearing the next morning, on the opposite side of the creek, shouting and waving their arms. Howitt – following the advice of their two native guides, Sandy and Frank – now breaks a branch, to indicate they may approach, if they come in peace.

One of them wades across the creek towards them, soon followed by the others, all of them leaving their weapons on the opposite bank.

'They were all fine well-built young men with open intelligent faces,' Howitt chronicles. 'They wore nets wrapped round their waist and one, apparently the headman, had his front-teeth knocked out.'[52]

The best he can, Howitt – calling on Sandy to interpret – tries to question them as to whether they have seen any white men, or at least stray camels about, and Sandy does his best, but the language problems are insurmountable.

The next day, as they head west along the creek – Brahe guiding them towards the old Depot – there are more interactions with black-fellas, including with one who Brahe recognises 'as one of the party who tried to surprise the Depot last season'[53]. That fellow had been nothing less than the 'ringleader'[54] of those who had so threatened them. Lifting their sense of unease further is that all the natives they come across seem to be very excited, are 'eternally hovering about us, and shouting "Gow!" and waving their hands'[55].

It is like they either want the whitefellas to go away, immediately, or are pointing them in a particular direction, like there is something up ahead they should see, but Howitt and his men tend to the view that the blacks are very unhappy about their presence.

Still, now in terrain familiar to William Brahe, the party pushes forward for the next three days, and have almost reached the Depot, when Howitt calls a stop at a deep waterhole, where they make camp. Desiring to satisfy his growing curiosity on one issue, Howitt takes one look at the waterhole, and is *sure*, with just one look, that it must have fish in it – and cannot wait to find out. As soon as he has unsaddled his horse, thus, to let him graze, the bushman takes his fishing line, baits it with a sliver of jerked meat, and drops it in the water. Immediately, he feels a tug on the line and hauls ashore a good-sized fish. And then another and another!

'Caught five silver perch, weighing from 1½ lbs to 3 lbs, and several others . . .' he will recount. 'The fish . . . of a fine flavour.'[56]

He and his men dine like royalty that evening, including Brahe, who might be forgiven for looking a little green around the gills himself at this demonstration of just how bountiful the food here is for anyone who cares to use basic bush techniques.

By mid-morning the next day, they reach the old Depot. Brahe affirms that everything is just about exactly as they had left it. Clearly, the Burke party has not been here meantime, which relieves him no end. And though it has clearly been visited by the natives, just one glance at where Brahe and his party had buried the cache, reveals, as Edwin Welch records, 'the plants of buried provisions [remain] undiscovered'[57].

But, surely, they should dig it up anyway, just to be sure?

No. Howitt is certain it is unnecessary, as he would later explain.

'There was no trace of any one having been there and as I had plenty of provisions, if I had opened this plant, I must either have carried the provisions with me . . . or I must have buried it again with an increased risk of being found by natives . . . If the stores were spoiled they would be useless to me, and if they were not spoiled they would in all probability keep in the same state until I required them for my return.'[58]

As it is, the Howitt party remains there no longer than an hour as there is no point. What Mr Howitt wishes to do first is search along Cooper's Creek – near which they camp several miles west of the Depot – before likely heading further west along the creek from there. The following day, 14 September, acting on Brahe's advice, they camp further west, a quarter-mile from Burke's first camp after he left the Depot at Cooper's Creek, heading to the Gulf.

The strange thing? They can see a spot where camels have been tied to a tree – all the lower branches have been denuded of leaves, and there are camel droppings all around – but there is no tree with a blaze on it to show this was a formal camp. What is more, Brahe tells Howitt, 'I am certain our camels [from the Depot days] have never been [here], as they were watched every day near the Depot and tied up at night.'[59]

(Yes, Brahe had come this way nine months before, when accompanying the Gulf party on their first day, but that had been on the north bank of the Cooper, and today they are on the south bank.)

Strange. The whole thing, Howitt records, 'puzzled me extremely, and led me into a hundred conjectures'[60].

Stranger still is that the camel tracks seem to go every which way, without staying together and going in a common direction. The only explanation Howitt can come to is that 'stray camels [must have] been about during the last four months'[61].

That evening, by the light of the fire a dark theory takes hold. The Gulf party under Burke must have returned, and been killed by the blacks! Yes, that's it. That would explain the wandering camels! Helping them along these lines of thinking is William Brahe, who tells Mr Howitt that, 'the blacks were troublesome while we were at the Depot. I was once obliged to fire my revolver over their heads to frighten them away'[62]. The ringleader of that attack, who they had seen just a few days ago, is still around, *still* in this area. Brahe and his men had been able to beat off the attack because they had had plenty of provisions, were well-armed, and had a lot of ammunition. But could the weakened Gulf party, in a depleted state, perhaps without weaponry and ammunition, have been able to beat off a similar attack?

Probably not!

Those *bastard* blacks!

'The general opinion in the party seemed to be that Burke and his companions had probably been killed by the natives before leaving the creek, or immediately on their return to it,' Howitt would note. 'I felt extremely puzzled, and certainly inclined to the belief that such a theory might prove correct.'[63]

It all makes sense, I tell you!

'Dire were the threats of vengeance among the men should it turn out that the blacks had murdered Burke.'[64]

•

Across much of the continent on this day, and the surrounding waters, other rescue parties are gearing up to look for traces of Burke and Wills, and gather information on everything they see in the meantime.

From Rockhampton, since the second week of September, Frederick Walker, a famously experienced if ruthless bushman – he has killed many Aborigines, mostly in his time as Commandant of the NSW Native Police from 1847 to 1854 – is leading a dozen mounted men to the Gulf, in search of Burke's party. Having left from Rockhampton, they are pushing west towards the Albert River, and are now 150 miles inland, on the Nogoa River, about to head for the Flinders River. Unless

Walker encounters Burke's tracks, he intends to follow the Nogoa all the way to Cooper's Creek.

On this evening, HMVS *Victoria*, now accompanied by the 188-ton brig SS *Firefly* – the latter of which has been sent by the Victorian Government and bears the noted bushman and explorer William Landsborough and the Queensland Relief Expedition – are more or less off the east coast of Cape York consumed with a problem. That is, *Firefly* is more *on* the coast than *off* it, run aground, and Commander William Norman and his men are doing their best to re-float it. Aboard *Firefly*, Landsborough and his eight men are chafing at the bit to be on their way once more, to make a landing at the Gulf of Carpentaria so they can head south along the line they think Burke and his men have likely taken, while Norman is to stay right there on the coast and establish a base.

The South Australian Burke Expedition led by John McKinlay, the six-foot four-inch Scot, experienced bushman and crack shot, left Adelaide on 14 August with nine men, including two Aboriginal guides, 26 horses, four camels and one cart. It is now up near the Flinders Ranges, getting ready to head north, and going from there via Mount Hopeless before making a stop at the last outpost of civilisation, Blanchewater station, then steering east of Lake Eyre to Cooper's Creek. They will be driving 70 sheep and a dozen cattle with them, as a food supply. Accompanying McKinlay as his first officer, and also 'in charge of the camels'[65], is none other than William Hodgkinson, who had just arrived in Adelaide from Menindee when the Burke Relief Expedition was assembling, and agreed to head back up as an experienced guide.

Alas, their numbers do not include Dr Wills, who had brought two of the camels over from Melbourne. Though the good doctor is personally impressed with the explorer and his group – 'Mr McKinlay was a fine fellow, well adapted to the work,' he would recount, 'his companions strong and lively, and of a proper age, neither too old nor too young'[66] – it had soon become apparent to both of them that they were all too strong and lively for the 51-year-old medico to be able to make a worthwhile contribution. All he would have done would have been to slow them down, and there was no time to spare.

15 September '61, Cooper's Creek, in the name of wonder . . .

With every hour now, it is more obvious to Howitt that they are in an area where Messrs Burke and Wills and their party have passed, if not passed away.

This morning he and the Aboriginal guide Sandy have left the others behind to look for more tracks, any signs of the party that they can follow. Sure enough, right by the lower end of a large waterhole, they find many such tracks – old ones of horses with horseshoes, and somewhat fresher ones of men with boots. And here is the handle of a clasp-knife!

Even more promising is 'a distinct camel's track and droppings on a native path'[67]. Howitt judges the track to be about four months old, and starts to follow it with rising excitement, even though it quickly fades in drier ground. Scouring back and forth, looking for further signs, Howitt instructs the 'black boy', Sandy,[68] to follow the winding creek, while he strikes across some sandy country, much as Burke and Wills likely did, to join up with where he can see a creek bend well up ahead.

The relief party's surveyor, Edwin Welch, meanwhile, has been hanging back on this morning, taking no shortcuts, but carefully, slowly, winding and wending his way along, interested in the way the creek turns, and marking it down accordingly on his nascent map.

Looking up from his notebook, Welch notices something that is more than passing odd.

Atop the opposite bank, a large group of black men appear to be jumping up and down, waving their arms, and 'gesticulating violently' before running off, leaving . . .

Leaving . . . *what is that?*

Atop his horse, Piggy, Welch gallops through the shallow creek to the other side, leans forward to look closer . . .

The blacks appear to have left one of their number behind and, extraordinarily, the figure even seems to be wearing some 'scarecrow rags and part of a hat . . .'[69] which is stunning. Yes, you sometimes saw natives near towns in such attire, but never this far out.

Before he can pull up, Welch has passed the figure, which is on its knees, and now turns back. As he does so, the figure throws up

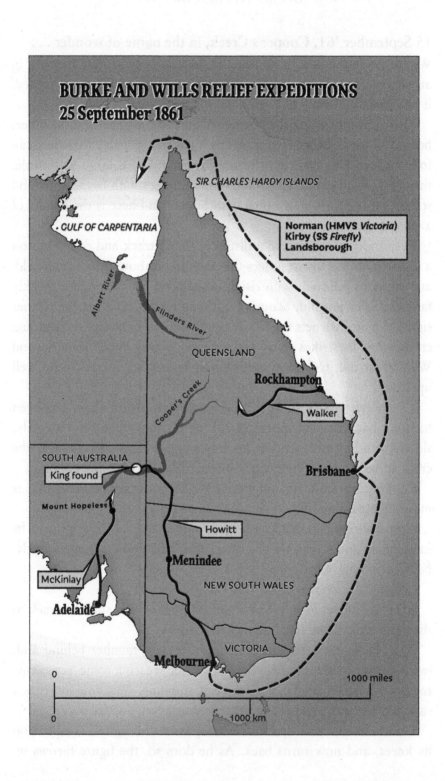

its hands, almost in the manner of a European supplicant for prayer throwing his hands in the air to thank the Lord . . . before it falls over, face flat in the sand.

Whoa, Piggy, whoaaaa!

The horse now under control, Welch dismounts rapidly, by which time the extraordinary figure has partially risen. With just a few bounds, Welch is beside it, excitedly asking: 'Who in the name of wonder are you?'

'I am King, sir,' the figure croaks back in reply. In *English*!

Welch, dazed, uncomprehending, still trying to take it all in – and completely clueless, as he would later recount, 'that the object of our search was attained, for King being only one of the undistinguished members of the party, his name was unfamiliar to me' – ploughs on.

'King . . .' Welch says.

'Yes,' says the figure, 'the last man of the exploring expedition.'

'What! Burke's?'

'Yes,' he croaks.

'Where is he – and Wills?'

'Dead, both dead, long ago . . .'[70]

The effort of saying the last seems to finish him, for again he falls to the ground.

While Welch gives him immediate care, the Aboriginal guide Frank – summoned by way of Welch's booming revolver sending shots into the sky – races along Howitt's tracks in search of the leader.

•

An hour later, Alfred Howitt has come to a bend in the creek, and is still trying to pick up tracks, but in the meantime is following a promising native path – exactly the kind that Burke and Wills would likely have followed. Some four miles later he comes to a large body of water, on the opposite side of which he can see a number of native wurleys. Crossing at a neck of sand, he again comes upon a track going up the creek.

And here is something strange . . . ?

It is a native, an excited black man, gesticulating wildly, and definitely pointing down the creek whence Howitt has come, bawling out, '*Gow! Gow!*'[71] at the top of his lungs.

It is almost as if the native wants him to head back to the camp where Welch and co had been left? When Howitt approaches, the native runs away. Still, turning back broadly in the direction the native has indicated, albeit via a different path, following this time a camel track, Howitt soon finds horse tracks as well, and now three pounds of tobacco. For all that, he is at a loss to piece it all together. There seems no coherent movement in one direction by Burke and Wills, just relatively aimless wanderings. Still, he keeps heading back and soon comes across the two black boys, Sandy and Frank, looking for him. They have extraordinary news.

'Find 'im whitefella!' they cry. 'Two fella dead boy and one fella live.'[72]

•

The immediate concern for Welch over the last hour or so has been to try, as quickly as possible, to get some basic strength back into the heart and soul of John King. For, upon examination, it is obvious that he is so depleted physically and spiritually, so very much on his last legs, literally and figuratively, that Welch has the very real fear that, with the added shock of now being found, he might soon expire.

Yes, looking closely, the surveyor finds King 'more like an animated skeleton than a living man'[73].

Carefully, King is placed for the moment back in the wurley the natives have built for him, so that Howitt's medico, Dr William Wheeler, can spoon-feed him a special combination of rice drenched with ghee, to try to get some basic nourishment into him as quickly as possible. This is a man who has been through an ordeal that has near finished him.

It is here that William Brahe, aghast, sees King for the first time. It's been nearly a year since Brahe had wished King well on his journey, saying, 'Good-bye King, I do not expect to see you for at least four months.'[74]

Brahe can barely believe that the ruined figure before him is the same robust and confident young man of last December.

He can't help but feel partially responsible. And certainly can't help asking the question that has *haunted* him since he had given the orders to leave the Cooper's Creek Depot.

'When did you get back?'

'On the 21st of April,' the scarecrow croaks.

One day apart! It is close to his worst fear.

'And I . . . left . . . on the 20th . . .' says Brahe, dazed, confounded.

'No,' King says, 'it must have been the 21st, because your fire was burning when we got there in the evening.'[75]

It *is* Brahe's worst fear. They have missed each other by hours. The colour drains from his face.

A small commotion outside.

It is Howitt, arriving with a rush, desperate to see King with his own eyes.

'He presented a melancholy appearance,' Howitt would recount, 'wasted to a shadow, and hardly to be distinguished as a civilised being but by the remnants of clothes upon him. He seemed exceedingly weak . . .'[76]

Yes, they are able to converse a little, but Howitt finds it, 'occasionally difficult to follow what he said'[77].

Howitt is as hungry as a ravenous dingo for more detail about just what has happened to the whole Gulf party – how it all went so terribly wrong – but now is obviously not the time to press King. Anything that touches on it reduces him to tears. Most urgent now is that he rest, and Howitt quickly leaves him be – even giving orders that rather than take him back to their own camp, eight miles away, that camp will move here to spare him the effort. The way it looks now, they might need to stay here for as long as 10 days, until King can muster the health, and strength, to be safely moved.

At least King's immobility helps with one thing on this day – taking a photo.

First the camera is retrieved from the tent where it has been placed, after having been brought all the way from Swan Hill on a quiet mare, and it is set up. Edwin Welch looks down the barrel of the camera, just as he was shown, and takes the first historic photo:

Here is John King, on the day of his discovery. Later he will take all of the Howitt relief party, standing still for the six to seven minutes it takes for the plates to be fully exposed. And here are the Aborigines, trying to stay as still as they can, the very people who have so sensationally looked after King. In fact, it is not difficult to keep them still, as 'the natives were all gathered round, seated on the ground, looking with a most gratified and delighted expression'[78].

Those delighted expressions do not change.

It has been an extraordinary day. For King. For the Yandruwandha tribe. For the Howitt party.

•

Softly, softly.

Now installed in his own tent, John King is getting stronger, day by day, but it is a laborious, exhausting process for all concerned.

'His constant craving,' Edwin Welch records, 'was for food – more food, and this was generously supplied in the shape of boiled rice, mixed with ghee, for which he had acquired a taste during his life in India, and of it there was, fortunately, a plentiful supply in the camp for the use of the camels.'[79]

To make the ghee even more nourishing, sugar is stirred into it and one or other of the party is always close at hand to spoon-feed him until he can take no more, at which point 'he would roll over and sleep for an hour or two and wake to ask for more'[80].

Bit by bit, he is able to talk more of his experiences, even though 'his talk was constantly interrupted by floods of tears and moans'[81].

As King speaks, occasionally and gently interrupted by the two Englishmen, Howitt and Welch scribble down every rambling word they can grasp, every staggering revelation, as they try to sort out, in inevitably slightly differing accounts, just what on earth has led to this pitiful figure being the last man left standing of this once grand expedition. With enough hay in him now, the scarecrow speaks, and reluctantly tells them how one of the party became a thief, Welch's flying pen trying to capture it in his own manner:

'Gray was getting knocked up worse and worse every day, and then he got to taking more than his share of the flour and sugar when he got a chance. Mr Burke threatened him and boxed his ears for this, and when he turned in one night, about two days before we expected to reach the depot, he said he felt he would not live till morning, and, sure enough, he didn't. When we turned out at daylight, Gray was dead . . .'[82]

In all, King is stunned at being alive himself, while still grieving for the deaths of his companions, with Edwin Welch later noting how, 'King spoke freely at all times on all matters connected with the Expedition and the causes of its failure, but with pronounced respect and devotion to the memory of his lost leaders.'[83]

Still, it is possible, just possible, that Alfred Howitt and his men have misjudged just how fragile the physical health of John King is. For while they have judged him against their own robust forms, he judges himself against the wreck of a man he had been when Mr Burke and Mr Wills had died.

'I think I could have lived for a long time with [the blacks],' King recounts, 'for I was all the while getting a little bit stronger.'[84]

In fact, just three days after his discovery, King informs Howitt and Welch that he is feeling strong enough to accompany them as they head down the creek to look for the earthly remains of Burke and Wills.

Howitt, judging that King can now safely be put on a horse, agrees and on the morning of 18 September '61, they set off. With King occasionally nodding in this direction or that – mixed with various moans and groans – the party of Howitt, King, Brahe, Welch and Dr Wheeler slowly make their way down Cooper's Creek, first looking for 'the two gunyahs erected on the sand in the bed of the main creek between two waterholes'[85], that King has previously described and . . .

And there is one that, from a distance, answers the description. King stiffens in his saddle the moment he sees it. They are just a mile from the flat where Burke, Wills and King procured nardoo seed, on which they managed to exist for so long.

Slowly all the fit men dismount, and, after helping King to do the same, they all approach the site with some trepidation, treading softly, as startled lizards, beetles and ants do the best they can to scurry out of their way.

It does not take long. One look at King confirms this is the very spot where he had left Mr Wills's body 10 weeks earlier – inside the gunyah, covered with branches and sand, the best he could do.

'But I am sorry to say,' Welch will recount, 'we found it much disturbed, the gunyah being partly pulled down, and the bones of the arms and legs scattered widely round. The skull was nowhere to be found, but the greater portion of the hair was matted together amongst the horse hair from the camels' cushions, on which he had died. The body itself being enclosed in two shirts, and the sand not yet removed, was not altogether destroyed.'[86]

The fact that any of the body remains is surprising, for all around it are the paw prints of dingoes. All that is left above the broken pieces of skeleton is a lower jaw, and upon that jaw can be seen pieces of a tawny beard, which both Brahe and King instantly identify as belonging to Mr Wills. There is something about beards on even desiccated corpses that helps instantly identify them. Beside the remains of Mr Wills are the nardoo grinding stones, together with some remaining nardoo. Clearly by the time Mr Burke and King had left him, he was so far gone he could barely feed himself, if at all.

Now, no matter Wills's own disinclination towards faith in the Almighty, it is the religious belief of the man still alive and presiding over his burial that counts. For Howitt has no hesitation in first burying Wills, before reading, with sombre feeling, the most hallowed words of I Corinthians Chapter XV over his windswept grave.

'Now this I say, brethren, that flesh and blood cannot inherit the kingdom of God; neither doth corruption inherit incorruption. Behold, I shew you a mystery; We shall not all sleep, but we shall all be changed. In a moment, in the twinkling of an eye, at the last trumpet: for the trumpet shall sound, and the dead shall be raised incorruptible, and we shall be changed. For this corruptible must put on incorruption, and this mortal *must* put on immortality. So when this corruptible shall have put on incorruption, and this mortal shall have put on immortality, then shall be brought to pass the saying that is written, Death is swallowed up in victory. O death, where *is* thy sting? O grave, where *is* thy victory?'[87]

As Howitt intones the sacred words, the others huddle close, profoundly moved by the pathos of it all.

'I here feel no shame,' Welch will later relate, 'in acknowledging that the first tears which I had shed for years, forced themselves into my eyes, when I reflected on the fateful and melancholy death of this fine young man. These reflections were still further embittered by the knowledge that a similar task was yet to be performed for another.'[88]

Finally, it is done, and the only sound to be heard is the lightly whistling wind, as they all pause to reflect before rousing themselves to action once more.

Putting a cross above Wills's grave is out of the question for the simple reason that there are neither planks handy, nor straight branches with which they can fashion a cross.

But Howitt at least takes his axe and blazes a tree to mark the spot, 45 yards to the north-north-west, where the final resting place of the deceased can be found.

W J WILLS

NNW XLV Yds

A.H.[89]

Sadly, the men ride away, Howitt at least now having securely in his possession, 'the field-books, a note-book belonging to Mr Burke, various small articles lying about, of no value in themselves but now invested with a deep interest from the circumstances connected with them, and some of the nardoo seed on which they had subsisted, with the small wooden trough in which it had been cleaned'[90].

'We returned home with saddened feelings,' Howitt writes in his diary that evening, 'but I must confess that I felt a sense of relief that this painful ordeal had been gone through. King was very tired when we returned; and I must, most unwillingly, defer my visit to the spot where Mr Burke's remains are lying until he is better able to bear the fatigue.'[91]

19 September '61, Adelaide, news from strange quarters

Dr Wills has been in Adelaide for a month on his mission of reinforcement, when out of the blue, after answering a knock on the door, he receives a note from a policeman.

September 19th.

MY DEAR SIR,
Would you kindly call in at my office? I have important news which
must interest you.
Yours very truly,
[MAJOR] WARBURTON.[92]

Good Lord! The policeman at the door was merely a messenger for the commissioner himself! Mr Burke's old rival to lead the expedition in the first place!

Dr Wills is on his way within minutes, heading straight to the address provided. Major Warburton has no sooner answered the door than he is confronted by the good doctor who asks, almost breathlessly:

'What news – good or bad?'

'Not so bad,'[93] Major Warburton replies.

He is cautious, true, but quickly fills Dr Wills in with the news.

'It was stated that a police trooper in the North had sent down information, derived through a black, that at a long distance beyond the settled districts some white men were living, and that the black had obtained a portion of their hair. The white men were described as being entirely naked, and as living upon a raft on a lake, supporting themselves by catching fish: that they had no firearms nor horses, but some great animals, which, from the description given by the native, were evidently camels. There could, therefore, be but little doubt as to this being Burke's party, or a portion of it . . .'[94]

The best that can be worked out, the mysterious whitefellas and their lumpy animals – 'gobble gobbles' the black informant calls them – are somewhere up on the newly discovered waters between Cooper's Creek and Eyre's Creek . . .

All up, the news raises Dr Wills's 'sinking hopes to a high pitch'[95]. He is *convinced* that this must be them.

Of course, the good doctor and Commissioner Warburton are quick to contact Police Inspector George Hamilton – who can send a man out immediately to convey the urgent news – pointing out that John McKinlay and his group are right now, 'on the spot indicated by the black'![96] – and urging action to contact McKinlay as fast as humanly possible.

Afternoon 19 September, '61, Cooper's Creek, free as a bird

Up on Cooper's Creek, the task now is to get the devastating news back to Melbourne, and Howitt intends to do it in the quickest manner possible, thanks to the ongoing generosity of Ambrose Kyte and Mr George Coppin, down in Melbourne.

All this way, Howitt and his men have been transporting those carrier pigeons in a cane coop by camel. Now he can put them to use, by attaching a note to the well-trained pigeons' legs and letting them fly straight south, unbothered by terrestrial concerns.

After writing his note detailing the fact that Burke and Wills are dead – as is Gray, but King lives, and they have already found and buried the corpse of Wills – the 30-year-old Englishman opens the cage. Alas, the first thing he notices is that after so long bouncing around, over so many miles aboard, all of the carrier pigeons have had their tail feathers rubbed right off.

What to do?

Some shots ring out, and seconds later some passing crested pigeons plummet earthwards.

A can-do man of the sort they just don't make anymore, Howitt – it later being noted of him by Welch that 'among his many other gifts, [he was] a skilful taxidermist'[97] – plucks their tail feathers, and, as he would describe it, 'inserted [the] feathers in the stumps of our carriers, fastening the splices with waxed threads'[98].

Now, let's see how they go! The first signs are good, as the pigeons seem to flutter around their makeshift aviary – the largest of the tents – better than ever.

It is time.

The next morning at daybreak, with a flutter in his heart to go with the fluttering pigeons' wings, Howitt releases them to the heavens, each one bearing the same note.

Alas, alas . . .

While the first bird is immediately knocked from the skies, attacked by black birds of prey and savaged before his eyes, the next two simply disappear into the scrub – but they are clearly not flying south. Things are looking grim. Still, on the reckoning that a bird in the hand is worth two in the bush, there seems no reason not to pin their hopes on the fourth pigeon. Let's see . . .

'The fourth, after making a large circle, pitched in a tree about a mile off. After breakfast he was found under a bush, with a kite watching him: and the feathers of one of the other pigeons was found not far off, having been killed.'[99]

In the afternoon, they find one of the missing pigeons has turned its back on Melbourne entirely, and instead has taken up residence in a gum tree by their camp. Nothing will possess it to fly.

This is, as Howitt records, 'not a proper proceeding for a carrier-pigeon, according to my ideas'[100].

The news will have to reach Melbourne by rather more traditional methods.

The man dreading it most is William Brahe. For just what will the world say when it finds out that the Gulf party had arrived at the Depot on the same day that he had left with his party? Will they understand that he had to go, that he had no choice, or will he be blamed?

•

King appears completely shaken – more physically than mentally – by the process of finding Mr Wills, and it seems out of the question to strain him any further. Howitt, after waiting three days, decides he can 'no longer defer making a search for the spot where Mr Burke died . . .'[101] and so embarks on an alternative plan. Garnering as precise directions and descriptions from King as the sick man can muster on the whereabouts of Mr Burke, Howitt leaves the weak but rallying young man in the care of William Vining and five others while he and Messrs Brahe, Welch, Wheeler and Aitkin head off up the creek, led by the two blacks, Sandy and Frank.

Now, to get from here to where Burke died is no easy matter. They proceed for some 10 miles over the course of the morning, before deciding they must have gone too far and so turn back.

It takes some doing, scouring to the left and right of their previous path, but late in the day, having covered two miles back towards camp, sure enough, Howitt senses they are close. For, just over there – now apparent in a way they hadn't noticed going up the creek – is indeed a collection of 'tall plants under a clump of box-trees'[102], much as King has described. This *must* be it. Most extraordinarily, it is a place they have seen before and are familiar with, as it is within 200 yards of the last camp they had made before finding Mr Wills – the night they had discussed killing the blacks – and just 30 paces from their previous course. But now they know what they are looking for, this is it all right, they are more sure than ever as they mournfully approach the spot.

The heat beats and the flies buzz, as their eyes scan the ground ahead.

And suddenly there he is, or rather, there *it* is, the mostly skeletal remains of Robert O'Hara Burke, partially obscured by some branches that the natives had placed over it – the whole thing being some 10 feet from his original resting place, likely having been dragged by dingoes, their tracks visible in the dirt all around. They've also been at his extremities as both his hands and feet are missing. Next to where his right hand should have been, however . . .

'I found the revolver, which Mr Burke held in his hand when he expired, partly covered with leaves and earth, and corroded with rust. It was loaded and capped.'[103]

After Welch sets up his camera once more, another historic photo is taken of exactly how the skeleton looked upon discovery, 'partially hidden by undergrowth among the huge marshmallow [flowers]'[104]. This time, there is no issue with restricting movement for the long exposure.

It is done, but the hardest part remains.

Gently now, and with elaborate respect, the men gather together the earthly remains of Robert O'Hara Burke, and wrap them in the one Union Jack they have brought with them – 'the most fitting covering in which the bones of a brave but unfortunate man could take their last rest'[105].

Under the blazing sun, insects swarming, it is William Brahe who digs the grave of the leader – right by where his remains lie, at the base of a 'gnarled old Box Tree'[106] – knowing all too well that when the news gets out in Melbourne of what had happened, there will be many who will say that it was Brahe himself who killed Australia's hero.

No one speaks as the men shovel and the pile of yellow sand, falling from the hour-glass of eternity, continues to grow. And now, carefully, what is left of the leader is gently placed at the bottom of the hole.

'It is impossible,' Howitt would recount, 'to describe the feelings of sadness and awe that filled our minds as we gazed on this sad spectacle. It was lying down to die on the very threshold of success and home, after the heat and burden of the day were passed.'[107]

As they gather closely around, Howitt takes the bible he always has with him, and with great feeling reads from the Gospel according to John, Chapter XI, Verse XXV.

'I am the resurrection, and the life,' he intones solemnly, over the chatter of the gaily singing birds. 'He that believeth in me, though he were dead, yet shall he live: And whosoever liveth and believeth in me shall never die . . .'[108]

Welch's eyes well with tears for the second time in mere days.

It is done, bar one last thing, as on the tree that must pass as Mr Burke's gravestone, Howitt carves the blaze:

R. O'H. B.
21/9/61.
A. H.[109]

Riding away, Howitt is near overcome with an overwhelming sense of horror, of what might have been, what he might have done. After all, when they had camped by that billabong just a week ago, 'it only needed that we should have found the skeleton of a white man, who Brahe would probably have recognised as Burke, lying unburied in the bush with his revolver beside him, to have fully confirmed the theory current among the men that Burke had been killed by the natives'.

In that case?

They would have, mistakenly, likely killed them all.

For one of those they would have killed would have been a white man, skinny as a scarecrow in his ragged clothes.

Hence the horror.

It is hard to put into words, but Alfred would do his best, years later, in a public lecture.

'I think that I should have believed it, and . . . that, burning with vengeance, we should have burst into the camp of friendly blacks with whom King was living and he might himself have fallen a victim. The possibility of such a mischance is terrible to contemplate.'[110]

CHAPTER SIXTEEN

LONG LIVE THE KING!

*My wonderful deliverance and ultimate preservation from death,
is such that I am a wonder to myself. The Almighty has been
so gracious to me, and I feel humble at His great mercy, that I
cannot believe that it would be right for me to present myself
under Mr Coppin's direction for any pecuniary advantage ...
I beg therefore, to leave myself in the hands of a paternal and just
Government, to be rewarded by it as it may deem proper for my
services as one of the members of the late ill-fated expedition.*[1]

John King, declining the £1000 offer to appear as the star turn of a Burke
& Wills panorama, organised by the theatrical impresario George Coppin,
intended to tour Australia, telling the story of the expedition

24 September '61, Cooper's Creek, baubles, bangles and beads
Now well over a week since the discovery of John King, Alfred Howitt
is preparing to move his men south. But first, he must properly thank
the blacks, who have looked after King so well. At the saved Irishman's
behest, they have on this morning lined up in what Howitt describes
as, 'a long procession. Men, women and children, or, as they here
also call them, piccaninnies – and at a mile distance they commenced
bawling at the top of their voices as usual.'[2]

By now, some of the blacks, particularly the men, are known
to Howitt and his party. For here, among them are some of their
leading figures, with once strange names now familiar like 'Pitchery',
'Tchukulow' and 'Borokow'.

Some of the men wear a 'net girdle' around their nether regions, while
the women wear a mix of leaves and feathers. These wild accoutrements
protect the blackfellas, not from the sun, but from the strange attitudes

that the white men have towards nudity. For the most part however, as Edwin Welch would document, they 'appeared in a perfect state of nudity, as they exist. The generality of the men are circumcised, in addition to the loss of the front teeth . . .'[3]

There are around 40 of them in all, soon gathered on a little flat just below their camp. With the help of John King – whose calls of '*Dunka!*' and '*Nhinapandi!*'[4] instruct the tribe to come over and sit down – Howitt is able to hand out the gifts he has for them.

Moving lightly among them, he distributes 'tomahawks, knives, looking glasses, beads, [and] coloured ribbon'[5].

Clearly, the Yandruwandha people are absolutely delighted, Howitt recording, 'I think no people were ever so happy before, and it was very interesting to see how they pointed out one, or another whom they thought might be overlooked.'[6]

Just like white people, displaying generosity and politeness! Howitt is quite amazed.

The piccaninnies are brought forward by their parents so they can have a 'red ribbon tied round their dirty little heads'[7].

At the behest of John King, it is the old woman, Carrawaw, who is most loaded down with presents, but still Mr Howitt has not got to his *pièce de résistance*.

For their kindness in looking after John King, each and every one of them is to be given, yes, a pocket-handkerchief-sized Union Jack, a token from a grateful Empire.

'They were very proud . . .'[8] Howitt records. 'I think they understood that these [presents] were given to them for their kindness to the white men, and especially to King.'[9]

Better still, wrapped inside each piece of Union Jack cloth is a rough pound of sugar, which they are soon eating, and they are also given a pound of flour, which 'they at once called "white-fellow nardoo"'[10].

After the blacks are finally given whatever clothes Howitt and his men can spare – many of them immediately worn – they show their appreciation in the best manner they know.

For, as Howitt documents, 'the affair ended in several of our party and several of the black fellows having an impromptu corroboree, to the intense delight of the natives, and I must say very much to our amusement'[11].

They keep going until all must stand to rest, to breathe, as Edwin Welch sets up his camera, one more time for the road. Oh what a photo that will be when it is developed! That accomplished, the photographic task is now completed, all 48 plates on all 'subjects of vital interest'[12] are carefully packed away in the box they came in, shielded from the light, and put back on the quiet mare they have been brought north on.

The blacks, meantime, wander back to their camp, repeating the only word in English they know, over and over again: 'Whitefellow, whitefellow, whitefellow . . .'[13]

•

The next morning, early, on this auspicious day, 25 September 1861, Howitt and his men prepare to head off on their long journey to the south.

Gathered to see them off are the Yandruwandha people, with their eyes all fixed on just one thing. Of course, it is John King – now perched atop his camel. He mournfully, if dazedly, gazes back at them. In the time since he has been rescued he has had no time alone with the people who have taken him in, least of all with the young native woman who has become his consort, Turinyi. But now they are all together once more, for what all recognise will likely be the last time . . .

The *last time*!

What starts as a few cries, and then strangled sobs, quickly turns into a kind of collective keening, above which the piercing howls of one woman can be heard. It is Carrawaw, mother of Turinyi, who has come to regard King as her deceased third son, a great man who has come back to life as a 'jumped up white fellah'[14]. She simply cannot bear it. She wails and wails. King ails and ails. She even slashes her breasts 'with the razor-like edge of a mussel shell'[15].

The whitefellas – including the dazed King – ride on.

Slowly, slowly, the sound of the wailing lessens.

Not because Carrawaw has stopped.

But because they have moved on . . .

Such is the route back to Menindee that Howitt must pass by the Depot camp again, and, knowing what he does now, when his party arrives there three days later – the journey has been slow because of King – the leader calls a halt by the coolabah tree. For months now, this gracious tree has been asking for one thing. The blackfellas, the whitefellas, the kangaroos, the cockatoos . . . none have paid it any heed. But finally its demands are met, and Alfred Howitt and his party begin to do what it has begged for so long and 'DIG'.

And here it is! It is a camel box, and when it is opened, they find a whole series of documents, including Burke's note of 22 April and Wills's additional note deposited on 30 May, along with his journals and also the maps that he has so laboriously formed up to mark their route to the Gulf and back. While John King is perhaps distantly interested to see what they have found, he is too frail to care much. They have only been able to get him this far by taking him down off the swaying camel – always threatening to throw him to the ground from a great height, and in the meantime making him sea-sick – and putting him on a rather sedate horse, and even then it has been touch and go . . . slowly.

With that in mind, they only move another three miles before Alfred Howitt calls a halt at their former camp at the enormous billabong they call 'the Fishpond', known to the locals as *Ngapa Merri*. So exhausted and frail does King prove to be, Howitt decides to stay here the next day, too, so King can rest. It is a great opportunity to see just how munificent such waters might be when it comes to fish, and they don't have to wait long . . .

Many fish are caught that evening, some as big as three pounds and a quarter. The next day, just two men alone manage to catch an extraordinary 72 pounds of fish in the few hours from three o'clock in the afternoon to sundown! Perch, bream and yellow-belly abound, first flopping on the bank and soon sizzling on the fire.

'They are the most excellent eating,' Howitt records in his diary, 'I do not know any fish of as fine a flavour.'[16]

Sitting around the campfire that evening, they feast on fish just a few miles from the very spot that William Brahe had felt obliged to abandon for want of food.

•

Dr Wills is devastated.

A trooper had indeed been sent out after John McKinlay with the news of the naked white men living on the lake, but the same trooper had equally come back with news of his own: McKinlay does not believe it for a moment.

'[I] did not give the report much credit,' McKinlay would explain, 'knowing how easy a person may be misled from the statement he hears from natives, and the probability of putting a wrong construction upon what he hears.'[17]

But Dr Wills never stops believing it.

'The white men alluded to,' he would later avow, 'were, unquestionably, Burke, my son, and King with exaggeration as to their being without clothes, and living on a raft.'[18]

Either way, John McKinlay and his men push on, heading towards Cooper's Creek.

10 October '61, Poria Creek, Brahe's dispatches of death, the sequel

For William Brahe, the territory is as familiar as the situation. The last time he had pushed south from Cooper's Creek and had reached this large waterhole just 20 miles south of Koorliatto – 'Poria Creek' – William Wright planned to send him on ahead from Menindee to break the news that Mr Burke and the Gulf party were missing. Back then, however, he had borne bad news that nevertheless vindicated his decision to leave the Depot on 21 April – Mr Burke and the Gulf party had simply gone missing into the vast gaping maw of the Australian wilderness.

This time?

This time, Howitt is sending him on ahead to break the news, which is devastating on two counts – Messrs Burke and Wills, and Charley Gray are dead; and the decision taken by him, William Brahe, to leave the Depot on 21 April had been responsible for the deaths of the first two, as they had arrived there just hours later.

It is with a heavy heart, thus, that – in the company of Weston Phillips until Menindee – Brahe takes leave of Alfred Howitt and the rest of them camped at the waterhole on Poria Creek, and races on ahead, bearing not just the diary and papers of William Wills but also a missive from Howitt for the Committee that breaks the news in relatively neutral terms.

'I have . . . found John King, the only survivor of Mr Burke's party, living with the Cooper's Creek natives. Mr Burke and Mr Wills had died some time previous to my arrival, from hunger and exhaustion, and Gray died before reaching Cooper's Creek on their return journey from the Gulf. King is in very weak, exhausted state . . .'[19]

21 October '61, 40 miles from Cooper's Creek, the trouble with scorpions

Somewhere north-west of Cooper's Creek, William Hodgkinson is engaging in an activity which he has long demonstrated he has a special talent for: annoying everyone. In this case, his capacity for causing trouble is directed at a higher than usual target: none less than the leader of the South Australian Burke Relief Expedition, John McKinlay, a fellow 'to whom a sextant and artificial horizon were dark and inscrutable instruments'[20].

As Hodgkinson has recently learnt how to use such navigational instruments, it now gives the former journalist a chance for mischief as he works out their location for his ignorant master.

'Where are we, Hodgkinson?' McKinlay asks while sitting on a log, waiting for the reply.

'Ten miles east of Bangkok,' Hodgkinson replies solemnly, 'the capital of Siam!'

'Am I a lunatic or are you?' says McKinlay.

'Am I the scientist of this party or are you?'[21] replies Hodgkinson with a straight face.

Alas, when the tired McKinlay goes to the third member of the party, a camel-keeper by the name of Thomas Middleton, and asks him to take the bearings instead, it is to find that he, too, has been infected by Hodgkinson's humour.

For Middleton comes back with the answer that they are 'twenty miles west of Christchurch, in New Zealand!'[22]

The tired McKinlay curses 'the evil fate that sent a man at his time of life meandering across the Australian continent in the company of a pair of hopeless lunatics'[23], but, despite the tomfoolery, the main thing is they are actually getting closer to the search area now.

Despite McKinlay's initial dismissive response to reports of naked white men living on a lake up near Cooper's, they hear further rumours from an Aboriginal man named Bulingani, who they meet on their way. True or not, the rumours are persistent, making McKinlay feel obliged to investigate further. After establishing a Depot camp at Wantula waterhole for most of the South Australian Burke Relief Party, he, the infernal Hodgkinson, Middleton and their Aboriginal informant, Bulingani, had gone ahead, journeying for three days to a lake which lies just over 65 miles west-nor'west of Burke's Depot at Cooper's Creek.

Having seen a fire the previous night on a relatively near horizon, on this fine morning the four men head out, suspecting to find a native encampment . . . only to find something far more interesting. Instead of a native camp they find, yes, the remains of a European encampment from some time ago! Right by a small lake, here are ashes left over from a large fire, and inside one of the wurleys, Hodgkinson finds nothing less than 'a square canteen . . . similar to those supplied to the Burke Expedition'[24].

Most stunning of all, however, is that right by the lake, and just a short distance from the wurleys, they find a grave, with a 'few boughs'[25] thrown over a clearly dug-up section of earth, and the heap of ashes nearby. This, right out here in the middle of the wilderness, is clearly a European grave, 'far more rudely constructed than those used for the interment of the natives'[26].

It is a ghoulish exercise, but there is no choice. They are on a mission to find trace of Mr Burke and his party and here in the wilderness, in the area they have passed through or near, is a grave that is surely for one of them. After returning to the camp to enlist the aid of two other members of McKinlay's party, they return to the gravesite and, using 'a native sword' – 'an Instrument of semicircular form, five to eight feet long, and very formidable'[27] – they carefully begin to dig, unsure just how deep the body will lie.

'We found,' Hodgkinson will recount, 'a European corpse buried about six inches beneath the surface, a mound of sand some two feet in height being heaped above. The face lay downwards the body on its back, the head being dislocated. A flannel undershirt, with short sleeves, was on the body. The skull still retained a tuft of straight dark hair, much decomposed and short.'[28] Nearly all of the flesh has gone, bar 'a soft substance in the socket of the eyes and the cavity of the chest . . .'[29]

Most stunning to them, however, is the violent manner in which this person died. For there, they can see it clearly, 'the skull . . . marked with apparent sabre-cuts, two in number, one over the left eyebrow, another on the right temple, inclining towards the ear'[30].

With a cursory glance McKinlay can tell that it really is a European, and not just from the clothing. The shape of the skull is distinctly that of a white man, and the fact that the two front teeth on the upper jaw are intact makes it all but certain. And now all eyes and ears turn to Hodgkinson, who obviously knew Mr Burke, Mr Wills, King and Gray. Could this corpse be one of them? Well, he can be sure of only a couple of things: 'I know the body was not that of either Wills or Gray, from the texture and colour of the tuft of hair . . .'[31]

Burke or King, then? Perhaps. But both had very black hair, and Burke a fierce, bushy black beard. This corpse has absolutely no trace of a beard at all.

'I am of the opinion,' Hodgkinson will faithfully chronicle, 'from the facial angle of the skull, and the absence of hair from a beard, that the remains are those of King . . .'[32]

Completely unaware that John King is alive and recovering not far from their current location, McKinlay, too, is convinced with a dreadful certainty that he is staring at his corpse. Though, unfortunately there are no identifying papers or clues accompanying the corpse, McKinlay carefully takes a piece of the flannel shirt for possible later investigative purposes, together with some bones, and then they all bury the body once more, this time deeper – covering it with heavy branches and lots of earth, to better preserve its sanctity – before blazing on a nearby tree: 'MK. October 21, 1861.'[33]

The mystery deepens even further a short time later when Bulingani, their Aboriginal guide who had participated in the grave-digging with great reluctance, now leads them to a creek just 200 yards to the east, where 'the traces of a European encampment, occupied some time, became visible. Close to an overhanging box-tree, with broken boughs, a quantity of horse-dung lay; and at the foot of other trees the dung of camels marked where those animals had been tied up, and indisputably identified the party as Burke's.'[34] (At least it is indisputable to Hodgkinson.) The fact that the two large fireplaces are filled with both ashes and the bones of fish are testament to the fact that the Europeans had been here for some time, and there are yet more points of interest.

'A piece of a cabbage-tree hat, a fragment of a light blue shirt of fine wool, the remnant of an Eley cartridge, and a portion of a nautical almanac, with the date of 1858, and seemingly used for wadding, led to the most dismal conjectures, rapidly hastening to horrid certainties . . .'[35]

For yes, Bulingani now informs Messrs McKinlay and Hodgkinson that 'the natives had eaten their victims'[36].

Stunned, the two European men examine the ashes more closely, and to their eyes it seems they are 'partly composed of [bleached] bone, a small portion of which Mr McKinlay picked up and retained'[37].

Nearby again are what appear to be open graves dug with a spade, with locks of European hair strewn about – 'one light sandy, inclining to golden, the other dark curly brown; the third black and straight. The holes were dug up but no remains found, except one small foot bone.'

The explanation?

'The natives dug up and ate the bodies!'[38] Bulingani tells them.

For Hodgkinson it is now an open and shut case.

'Mr Wills had light sandy hair, inclining to golden. Gray had curling brown hair. The third dark hair must have belonged to King or Burke. At any rate, four individuals were accounted for.'[39]

McKinlay agrees, noting in his official report to the government, 'From information, all Burke's party were killed and eaten.'[40]

In short order, McKinlay sends – *good riddance* – William Hodgkinson south with news of the grisly discovery, meaning that for the second time in under a year, the former journalist for the *Age* is the bearer of bad tidings about the fate of the Burke expedition.

•

Alfred Howitt has been proceeding slowly and carefully, with their prize of John King growing just a little stronger, and they arrive back at Menindee in early November, to find the town joyous at their safe return! One resident, however, is noted to be happier than most, albeit for different reasons. It is Mr Wecker, the Menindee storekeeper.

'On our return to Menindee,' Welch would recount, 'Wecker was jubilant. He had succeeded in trading off the braces and candle moulds with a hawker for a lame horse . . .'[41]

Wecker is careful and quick to entrust the box with all 48 negatives to the next steamer heading south from Menindee, with the instruction that the Royal Society send them to Batchelder & O'Neill, the only studio in Australia capable of developing them into actual prints.

Howitt, meantime, works out how best to get King back to Melbourne as soon and safely as possible. The rivers and creeks around Menindee are flooded and Howitt is wary about the best way to transport his most precious human cargo. Idly, he wonders how William Brahe is going, and how the news he bears will be received in the Victorian capital.

•

The last time William Brahe had headed south from Swan Hill, in late June, he had been intercepted at the Durham Ox Inn by Alfred Howitt and everything had turned topsy-turvy within minutes. This time, the inn passes by without incident, other than the regular changing of the horses, and Brahe is no more than an anonymous passenger alighting from the coach when it arrives outside the Shamrock Hotel on the corner of Pall Mall and Williamson Street, Bendigo, late on the afternoon of 2 November 1861. Quickly asking directions, he heads to Bendigo's telegraph station, and dictates his telegram, addressed to Dr Macadam . . .

BENDIGO, NOV 2 1861

BURKE CROSSED CONTINENT.

RETURNED TO COOPERS CREEK WITH WILLS & KING &
TWO CAMELS.

ATTEMPTED TO GET INTO SOUTH AUSTRALIA. CAMELS
KNOCKED UP. COMPELLED TO FALL BACK UPON THE CREEK.
BURKE + WILLS DIED ON OR ABOUT TWENTY EIGHTH JUNE.
KING FOUND IN A TRIBE OF NATIVES IN GOOD HEALTH.
LEFT HOWITT ON HIS WAY TO MENINDEE.

WILLIAM BRAHE[42]

Evening 2 November '61, death at the door

It is a slightly odd thing to be in someone's wonderfully gracious home
when your hosts themselves are not there – almost like it is disrespectful
to them to sit down and really make yourself at home – but so it is for
Dr Wills on this quiet Saturday evening. His dear friends Mr and Mrs
James Orkney have given him the run of their large apartment, which
lies within the highly esteemed Sir Charles Hotham Hotel, while they
go off to the opera, to see the hit of the season, *The Bohemian Girl*.
Outside there is the sound of many other hotel guests going to and
fro – as so many out-of-towners have flooded into Victoria's fairest
town for the inaugural running of the biggest horserace in the history
of the colony, the Melbourne Cup, due to run in a few days time – but
inside, all is quiet and likely to stay that way. Dr Wills is not expecting
the Orkneys back before midnight. Hence his surprise to hear by the
sudden opening and closing of doors that they have returned early.

Perhaps, Dr Wills thinks, 'something unpleasant must have
happened'[43].

Suddenly, an ashen-faced servant appears, asking could he speak
to Dr Wills privately?

Fearing the worst, Dr Wills is taken aside, and quietly told it.

The worst.

The seemingly confirmed deaths of Burke and Wills have been announced from the stage by the manager of the theatre, at the interval of the opera, and Mr and Mrs Orkney rush home to tell the doctor.

Dr Wills reels.

His son is dead.

The only good news is that one of the party, a John King, has been found alive.

But both Burke and Wills have perished, and their bodies, after confirmed identification, buried.

Dr Wills, to be sure, is soon floundering in the deepest condolences of the devastated Orkneys, but is certainly not prepared to leave it there.

No. Once sufficiently recovered from the shock, he and Mr Orkney are soon in the latter's buggy, proceeding at a fair clip to the home of Dr David Wilkie, the treasurer of the Exploration Committee, who is known to Mr Orkney.

Roused from his bed, Dr Wilkie is asked by Dr Wills if *he* has received confirmation?

No, comes the answer, no more than the same report others have heard. But the Committee has heard nothing official whatsoever.

At this moment, Dr Macadam, the Honorary Secretary, comes in from a night carousing with friends.

He, too, professes himself completely bewildered and believes none of it. He has certainly received no telegram – an important point, given that any official confirmation would be sent to him first.

It is all enough to give Dr Wills some hope – perhaps the whole thing is a dreadful misunderstanding – until a horrifying thought strikes.

'But,' says he to Dr Macadam, 'when were you at your own house last?'

'At seven o'clock,' comes the reply.

'Good God!' exclaims Dr Wills, 'jump into the [carriage].'[44]

The four men head back to Dr Macadam's house, hoping against hope there will be nothing . . . only to spy it, the instant the front door is opened.

The blue stock writing on the white paper of the telegram glares back at the Drs Wills and Macadam as they jointly read Brahe's words.

Bendigo, Nov 2 1861

Burke crossed continent.

... Burke + Wills died on or about twenty eighth June. King found ...

William Brahe[45]

It is all so flat, so final, so incontrovertible. It is shattering.

•

Only hours later, in the dim light of pre-dawn, the restless, stricken figure hovering at Spencer Street Station on this sad Sunday morning with the bloodshot eyes of one who has either been weeping or staring sleepless at the ceiling – and likely both – is, you can be sure, Dr Wills.

After a wretched night, still trying to comprehend the catastrophic news, the misery-struck medico is here in the hope of intercepting and interrogating William Brahe, who he is certain will soon be arriving. Around and about as he mournfully waits, people all over the station are gazing at the stunning one-page flyer put out by the *Argus* on a day there are normally no papers at all.

THE CONTINENT CROSSED.
DEATH OF BURKE AND TWO OF HIS PARTY.
Their remains found.

The Argus Office,
Sunday Morning.
The following dispatch has been received from our Sandhurst correspondent:-
SANDHURST, Nov. 2.
Mr Brahe, of the Exploration Contingent, arrived here this afternoon, from Cooper's Creek.
The remains of Burke and Wills, who both died on the same day from starvation [supposed on or about the 28th of June], near Cooper's Creek, have been found.
Gray, another of the party, also perished.
King is the only survivor.
They had crossed the continent to the Gulf of Carpentaria.
All Burke's books, &c., have been saved.[46]

Perhaps, Dr Wills thinks, in among, 'All Burke's books &C.', Brahe might have with him something from his son?

To Dr Wills's distress, Dr Macadam – a man he has come to detest, and never more than since last night – is also here, and what is even more appalling is that he has clearly been drinking heavily, likely through the whole night.

Only a minute after the train pulls in, a subdued figure with haunted eyes emerges, who proves indeed to be William Brahe. He is clearly shattered by his experience, but does indeed have the journals and letters, and it is with some relief, as the burden of that responsibility at least is lifted, that he hands them over to Dr Macadam. For his part, Dr Wills refuses to let the journals out of his sight – fearing Dr Macadam excising anything in the documentation that might be critical of himself or the Committee – and tightly follows the carriage of Macadam and Brahe as they make their way to Government House in Toorak. His reward is to be there as the governor himself, Sir Henry Barkly, entrusts the valuable documents to the safe 'hands of Dr Wilkie'[47].

Dr Wills takes his leave – Dr Macadam, Dr Wilkie, Governor Sir Henry Barkly and young Brahe have a lot of talking to do. 'I have nothing more to say of Dr Macadam,' Dr Wills would later recount, 'except that I sincerely trust it may never be my fortune to come in contact with him again, in any official business whatever.'[48]

•

Things move quickly.

So widespread is the public grief, so high is the veneration for the dearly departed that within two days the Exploration Committee has agreed to the suggestion of Governor Sir Henry Barkly that henceforth the ill-fated venture north will be officially known as 'the Burke and Wills Exploring Expedition'[49]. It is also proposed that before coming back from Menindee, Mr Howitt and his group should ensure that 'the remains of the unfortunate men who had died in the cause of exploration would be brought into Melbourne'[50].

For its part, it is in turn proposed within the Victorian Parliament that they fund the return of Howitt to retrieve the bodies, but also that the Colony of Victoria will hold its first 'State Funeral' should the remains of Burke and Wills be returned; that a monument will be erected to their memory, and that, as hurriedly announced by the outgoing Premier Richard Heales, and approved by the governor himself, a full and independent Royal Commission of Inquiry[51] will be held, 'into the causes that led to Burke and Wills being left without succour at Cooper's Creek'[52]. In the Legislative Assembly, Premier Heales notes that while he had initially 'requested the Royal Society to take steps in the matter, upon further consideration, I resolved upon the appointment of a board, who would not only institute inquiries into that particular incident, but also into the general management of the expedition'[53]. What he most wants is a board 'not connected with the Royal Society'[54].

Another small parenthesis here. The Commission is, in fact, to be 'independent' only after a fashion, as despite the fact that Sir Henry has himself been intimately involved in the whole saga, his own father-in-law, Sir Thomas Pratt, the Commander of the British Armed Forces in Australia, is installed as chairman, while a personal friend, Sir Francis Murphy, Speaker of the Legislative Assembly, is the key Commissioner. He will be flanked by four other Commissioners, who will act as judge, jury and prosecutor all in one, trying to get to the bottom of who is at fault for the whole catastrophe. Those appearing before the Royal Commission are not allowed lawyers, and must answer all questions, with no right to silence . . . Close parenthesis.

•

The day after the dreadful news breaks, Julia Matthews is walking in Melbourne's magnificent Botanical Gardens, when – wearing the locket Burke has given her as a bracelet – she loses it. Of course, she places a classified ad in the *Argus*, noting that she, the well-known actress, has lost a locket given to her by Victoria's lost hero.

> Lost and Found
> Five Pounds Reward
> Lost in the Botanical Gardens, yesterday afternoon, a gold bracelet with carbuncle in centre, and miniature. On returning same to Miss Julia Matthews, 21 Napier Street Collingwood, the finder will be handsomely rewarded.[55]

Yes, the news consequently gets out that she was the lost hero's sweet-heart, but, what can a girl *do*? After a suitable period of expected publicity, the 'lost' locket is announced as found by Miss Matthews.

6 November '61, Menindee, the king across the water . . .

It is true. It is not simply in the realms of physics, astronomy, chem-istry, mathematics and the like that genius strikes. Sometimes, it can even strike among rough men, 'neath the searing sun, in the parched plains of the Australian continent.

On this day, specifically, Alfred Howitt's key lieutenant, Weston Phillips, described by Edwin Welch as a 'good all-round bushman and capital traveling companion'[56], indeed displays a curious stroke of genius.

The problem that presents itself is how to get a seriously weakened, panic-stricken John King across the surging floodwaters of the Darling River at Menindee, when he cannot swim, they have no punt and what is more, he has a 'great dread of immersion, fearing that he might be drowned'[57]. He is so weak he cannot sit upright on a horse, even though the horses can swim through the water to Menindee on the other side. Yet, hemmed in by floodwaters on all sides, they must get across, and soon, for fear of the waters rising further.

As Phillips is the strongest swimmer it is he who crosses first – pushing before him a sheet of bark on which they have placed their swags and clothes, before swimming back. Now for the act of genius . . .

With the others agreeing to his plan – less King, who is too weak to agree or disagree with anything – a rope is taken and one end of it is tied around King's torso, beneath his arms. The other end is attached to the tail of the quietest horse they have. The horse is led into the water and slowly pulls King along behind him, while Phillips on one side and Welch on the other swim alongside, cheering him up, calming him down, and assuring him from first to last that they are *nearly there, not long to go now, just a few more yards*! (Thank goodness they have sent the oh so precious photos safely by steamer, or they would have been destroyed crossing this river, among others.)

The surviving hero of the crossing of the Australian continent, on foot, on horseback, on camels, now makes his way towards Melbourne – shivering, sodden, moaning, lightly lashed by a swishing tail, and right behind a horse's arse . . .

'Arrived on the other side,' Welch would recount, 'he was well rubbed down, given some of his favourite rice and ghee, a little weak brandy and water and the march resumed after a short spell.'[58]

Infinitely relieved that King has made it safely to the other side, Howitt, from the Pamamaroo side, yells across the rushing waters his farewell, wishing Godspeed to the three drenched souls for their forthcoming trip to Melbourne.

Waiting till they are swallowed whole by the Australian bush – *onward Christian soldiers!* – Howitt rides back to the Menindee township, where he and the others will wait for the waters to recede.

•

The terrible news hangs over Melbourne like a pall of gloom, getting deeper as more details emerge of the horror of what has happened, the deterioration, the dilemmas, the decisions taken . . . the deaths. In few places, however – and likely nowhere – is that gloom darker or deeper than in a certain boarding house in Fitzroy, where Richard Birnie is quickly 'prostrated by the fearful news of [William Wills's] lingering death . . .'[59]

Later, one thing alone will console the bereaved barrister and that is 'the simple endurance and calm resignation depicted in the last words of the diary — "Starvation by nardoo, father, is not so painful . . ."'[60]

And of course, he will meet many times with Dr Wills himself.

'You perhaps have heard,' says precious William's father, 'that the dear fellow has named a mountain after you. Do you not picture him, with his eye and smile, noting some characteristic of the mountain that recalled you, and laughing as he made a memo of it? Would you not like to see the mount?'[61]

Richard Birnie would like, indeed, nothing better than that, a feeling that would never leave him for the rest of his life.

'I should joy to meet the morning sun up the mount that bears my name,' he would record, 'conscious of a genial and enlivening influence.'[62]

In the meantime, Richard Birnie can do no more than 'lay my laurel wreath on the bust of him, whom living I taught, cheered, and honoured'[63].

Whatever else, neither Burke nor Wills will lack for plaudits from either people or the press, with the *Argus* once again setting the tone, elevating the leader, particularly, to the pantheon of the Gods.

> The name of Robert O'Hara Burke, is henceforth of the people of Victoria. The glory of his deed, and the sorrow of his death, will each render that name memorable in the annals of our country. And well may Victoria be proud of this, her first hero . . .
>
> The sufferings and death of the first white men who crossed the Australian continent will be household words in Australia, when the iron horse has extended from the southernmost point of Australia to the shores of Carpentaria; a country large enough to absorb the surplus population of the world has been discovered. In years to come cities will arise where the explorers rested, and plenty will be found where the explorers perished. All honour then to the gallant four, of whom three died and one survives. The story of his great achievement, if it is the saddest, is also one of the highest in the history of manhood. No fiction was ever half so romantic – no hero more valiant, bold or loyal.
>
> The age of chivalry is restored in an achievement equal to all that war has shown us of hardihood, courage, and devotion.
>
> For this our hero was a soldier, in all the highest points of soldiership. No conqueror dying on the field of battle could earn a fame more pure or glorious. No warrior could go forth more cheerfully to the death struggle. If 'peace hath her victories as well as war', this is a victory in the highest sense, that BURKE and his fellow-heroes have won for us a victory in the cause of knowledge and for the good of humanity – a victory which will live while Australia lasts, to her and our eternal glory. For the hero himself, there could be no cause more noble nor fame more precious. To him it has been given to earn by a deed of the highest order the martyr's dearest crown of glory . . . [64]

Ah yes, Robert O'Hara Burke, it has taken some doing, but you now really do have the eulogistic equivalent of the paeans of praise published after your brother's glorious death in the Crimea.

The same newspapers which in recent times had insinuated and even thundered that you were the wrong leader from the first, now would not dare. The *Argus*, for one, is already certain that the problem lay not with you dead heroes, but with those men rather closer to home.

> Nothing is clearer, than that they need not have perished . . . No one can read the story, with a knowledge of all that has been done and left undone in the past, without feeling that BURKE and WILLS have perished victims to gross negligence and mismanagement . . . [and] might have returned to us in safety, to enjoy the well-earned fame of their success – but for the managers of the enterprise. Upon the Exploration Committee more especially, rests a heavy responsibility in connexion with this enterprise. As the managers of the undertaking, from first to last, with almost absolute power and with ample funds, it is impossible to acquit them of the primary blame attached to BURKE'S melancholy fate . . . Let us ask what Dr MACADAM and his associates have done to ensure the success of the enterprise? . . . From the day BURKE started with his three devoted companions into the far interior, they seem to have been given up altogether by the Exploration Committee . . . sitting idly in Melbourne, with Dr MACADAM as Honorary Secretary . . . Why did they not provide for his return at one or other point – at Cooper's Creek, if not at the Gulf of Carpentaria? Why was there no standing depot at Cooper's Creek, to meet any eventuality . . . ?
>
> Next to the Committee, the blame for BURKE'S desertion and death undoubtedly lies at the door of Messrs BRAHE and WRIGHT . . .[65, 66]

There is more, much more, but the tenor remains the same: someone is going to have to pay heavily for the heroes' death, and all that remains is to find out who it is. The papers have a strong list of suspects, led by William Wright and William Brahe, with George Landells and Dr John Macadam perhaps vying for the lead as they hit the final turn, while the entire Royal Society of part-time amateurs makes up the rest of the field.

And what of John King? Well, he is deserving of enormous accolades, for he has lived!

No, he is neither an officer, nor a gentleman, like Burke and Wills, but the *Age* will at least point out that his pedigree is stronger than it might first appear, noting that he is: 'the son of a man who served in the regular army of Great Britain, and . . . he himself followed for a time in his father's footsteps in the career of arms.'

Fear not, this man is an exemplar of the best of British pluck, and ere little time has passed, the *Age* will anoint him with ink of bubbling purple prose, as it goes on:

> The history of human suffering has preserved for the admiration
> of mankind many glorious examples of self abnegation in the
> cause of humanity, but in no record of disaster by land or sea
> do we read of a more splendid instance of self-sacrifice than in
> the case of John King . . .[67]

The public could not agree more and, if anything, is even far ahead of the newspapers in what it feels for the slender young Irishman, now on his way back to Melbourne. The city of Melbourne bubbles with excitement at the thought of his return.

Still, there is a nasty edge to some of the coverage too, most particularly when Wills's diary, with extraordinary details of a theft by Charles Gray and a 'thrashing' administered by Mr Burke, becomes public on 7 November.

Such a report leads to rumours spreading around the country like a bushfire with a hot westerly behind it that Burke was a murderous brute who beat one of his starving men into the grave. Eyebrows are raised too at William Wills's seemingly callous accounts of Gray's 'shamming' when he was genuinely *sick*. One letter in the *Age* typified the tone and insinuations:

> The symptoms of poor Gray's illness were certainly plainly
> apparent the whole of the return journey, yet an act of the most
> unwarranted cruelty was exercised towards him by giving him

'a good thrashing.' It would be a satisfaction to know how far this act was warranted in the man's weak state, and whether it tended to hasten poor Gray's death or not.[68]

•

Another who is saddened to hear of the death of Mr Burke – if in some ways energised by it – is none other than John McDouall Stuart, now convalescing in Adelaide after his second failed attempt to forge a path through the centre of Australia all the way to the north coast. Yes, Mr Burke has crossed the continent first. But his route had placed him to the east of 'Stuart's country', meaning the £2000 prize for crossing the continent in the manner originally prescribed by the South Australian Government is still on offer. Even now, Stuart is further girding his loins, to make a third attempt.

•

Rest in peace? Not quite.

Even in death, the fallen heroes cause controversy, every bit as much as they did while alive. For even though the government grandly announces that the sacred bodies of Burke and Wills shall be retrieved and returned to Melbourne for a state funeral – on 13 November Howitt is sent instructions in Menindee to that effect – already there is a growing view that they should be allowed to rest in peace, to lie for all eternity undisturbed in their noble desert graves.

20 November '61, Swan Hill, all hail the conquering hero

The word passes around the tiny hamlet of Swan Hill in nothing flat. John King is not far away, and he is coming in our direction! You know, the *sole* survivor from the Burke expedition!

'Almost the whole population of the place,' the *Argus* will chronicle, 'started off in vehicles and on horseback to welcome his arrival.'[69]

It begins.

No matter that Swan Hill is at this time practically 'Swan Island', given the rising floodwaters after recent heavy rain. And certainly no matter that the last time John King had been in their fair town he had been more anonymous than a lost dog. The good burghers of Swan Hill happily splash their way towards the approaching horsemen and before the stunned King – that's him, that's HIM! – quite knows what is happening, he has been transferred from his horse, to the shoulders of Swan Hill's finest, to the best buggy they have, and within minutes is standing atop the courthouse steps, as the town magistrate, Captain Crawford Atchison Denman Pasco, is about to welcome him on behalf of the citizenry, reading from a screed that all 48 inhabitants of the tiny town have previously signed.

And finally he is here!

'To John King,' Captain Pasco intones portentously, 'the only survivor of the advanced portion of the Victorian Exploring Expedition, under the lamented Burke.

'We, the inhabitants of Swan Hill, greeting you on your return to Victoria, while we acknowledge with gratitude the hand of Divine Providence, to which alone we would attribute your wonderful deliverance from the perils you have sustained, desire to offer you our heartfelt congratulations at the success achieved by the gallant little band which you now alone represent . . .'[70]

In response, John King barely blinks, and so Captain Pasco goes on without pause.

'In the early days of the Australian colony the name of King was renowned for the intrepidity and skill of our naval explorer; but you have added fresh lustre to the name by being amongst the first to cross the continent of Australia from the shore of Port Phillip to that of Carpentaria.

'We trust you may, by the blessing of God, who has restored you to us, have many years of health to enjoy, and much grace to adorn, the honours you have won.'[71]

Once finished, with great ceremony, Magistrate Pasco hands over the screed to the rather shrunken figure on the steps beside him – next to Edwin Welch, who hovers nervously, as does Superintendent Henry Foster, who is of course there for the occasion – as all eyes turn to the man of the moment.

What will he say?

. . .

Speak to us, oh great one!

King no doubt would if he could, but words will simply not come to him. From near death, to salvation, to survival, to rescue, to this, all in the space of a few months, is just too much to cope with.

Finally, however, as the *Argus* reports, he is able to get out a few words and, 'begged to postpone his reply till the following morning'[72].

Hurrah! Hurrah!

At least he has spoken, and we have heard him, and seen him with our own eyes, even if Mr Welch now hustles him away, even as Superintendent Foster assures us that Mr King will be back the following morning to make proper reply and . . .

Sure enough, the next morning, he is here as promised, as are we – to read from something he has written, or has had written, overnight.

'Ladies and Gentlemen,' he begins falteringly, 'I return you my sincere thanks for the mark of respect shown me on my arrival here. It is the first public welcome I have received since my return to civilization, and one I shall never forget, and which will always be dear to me.'

Hurrah!

'The name of Swan Hill has often been repeated by my noble and lamented leader, Mr Burke. Often has it been our conversation. The kind reception the members of our party received when passing through here has never been forgotten . . . Charles Gray, one of the inhabitants of Swan Hill, and one of the little band that crossed the continent, was the first who suffered and the first that fell. I, as the only survivor of that little band, consider it my duty to give a true and just statement of his conduct.'

There is a stirring in the crowd at the mention of Charley Gray's name. The crowd had first burst with pride at the news that one of their own had been selected to accompany Mr Burke to the Gulf, and in more recent times suffered at the news that he had been guilty of bad behaviour. But now, magnificently, John King starts to set the record straight!

'He proved himself a very useful man on many occasions,' Mr King says, 'but it seems he is condemned for misconduct. The fact was, he had charge of the stores . . . and on one occasion was found thieving, for which Mr Burke chastised him by giving him several slaps on the head, and not a sound thrashing, as Mr Wills states. I was present at the time of his being chastised, and Mr Wills was not.'[73]

There you have it! From the mouth of the man, himself. Gray, innocent, or so near it doesn't matter.

King says a few more words, but his principal task has been done. Swan Hill's finest, Charley Gray, has been vindicated. A further warm dinner is given to Mr King that evening at the Royal Hotel, where the health of their honoured guest is drunk with all the honours, as the trio wait to catch Cobb's Coach which will be leaving for Melbourne on the morrow.

That night, it takes three quarters of an hour for Mr Welch to get to sleep for the raucous renditions of '"He's a jolly good fellow" without the slightest variation'[74], which keep floating into the air, but it matters naught.

By the following morning, they are indeed in the coach and on their way to Melbourne, getting fresh horses at the Durham Ox Inn where they stay a night, before pushing on to Bendigo where . . . madness, sheer *madness* awaits!

'Crowds of diggers rushed our coach from all quarters,' Welch records, 'blowing horns, firing guns and pistols, cheering and waving flags . . . as much as if it were a triumphal entry of blood Royal.'[75]

Making matters worse for Welch is that he cannot, 'torture King out of his passive dead-and-alive manner to acknowledge himself, so that I was myself taken for King by nearly all', even as, two miles out of Bendigo they are engulfed by 'an enormous procession headed by the "Marsh Troupe" of theatricals in an enormous coach with a brass band on top playing "See the conquering hero comes".'[76]

As it happens, the conquering hero in question is little more than a shuddering wreck by this time, near incapable of functioning at all. While the procession builds into a full-blown cavalcade of revellers, King and Welch are transferred to the open carriage of the Mayor of Bendigo, who has come out to greet them until, finally, mercifully they all arrive at the Shamrock Hotel, where . . . after a reporter notes that, 'He appeared to be still suffering from the effects of the fatigue and hardships he had undergone'[77] . . . a civic reception, complete with 'a profusion of choice treats, and an unlimited quantity of champagne'[78], awaits!

Loyal toasts. Speeches. Endless verses of 'For He's a Jolly Good Fellow'. Welch fears that King will outright collapse, most particularly when, in his few remarks, 'he had occasion to refer to the deaths of his companions in the desert'[79].

On the specific subject of the controversy over Mr Burke, and those who had dared to call into question his behaviour, John King again points out that he was a witness to the episode, the story of a fit punishment reluctantly given has become exaggerated.

'A better leader than Burke [I] never wished to have,' he assures his audience in a shaky voice. 'He proved himself equal to all the difficulties of the task, and was cheerful and had an encouraging word for them all to the very last.'[80]

The Shamrock shakes with cheers as John King sits down. Most of the gathering seems to think that he has simply finished his speech where he intended, but Edwin Welch knows better.

'He returned thanks much better than I expected he would,' he records, 'but became overpowered in alluding to Burke and Wills and fell back into his chair in tears, greatly attributable, I think, to bodily weakness.'[81]

Still, in what is likely a first for Bendigo, there is a new toast, this one to the '"Health of the Aborigines" (who had so kindly treated the explorers)'[82] before there is a commotion from downstairs, a crashing of the door and the landlord of the hotel, Billy Hefferman, bursts through, begging Welch to take Mr King downstairs, 'So that the crowd might see him, as they are tearing down the stairs and balustrades in endeavouring to fight their way up into the room.'[83]

From the sounds coming from downstairs, Mr Welch feels he has no choice, and soon enough, ushers the near catatonic King downstairs, which, far from quelling the crowd makes them roar even louder at the mere sight of him! But at least they have stopped destroying the hotel. There remains only to take King back upstairs and out onto the balcony of the hotel to have the same effect on those thousands in the street who had not been able to fight their way into the hotel, and at last, at *last*, Welch is able to get King back to his room, alone, even if there is continual pounding on the door as a person or people unknown beg to be allowed in. Exhausted, exasperated, stunned at the reception for this fellow who, only two months ago, had been a shattered scarecrow in the wilderness when he found him, still Welch has one more task for the day. Waiting until the pounding on the door finally subsides, he leaves King strict instructions not to leave the room, nor answer to anyone, 'although as he was so weak I had not much fear of him', before slipping out to the telegraph office to send a telegram to Dr Macadam informing him of their time of arrival in Melbourne. Relieved, he returns to King's room to find him . . . *gone*!

(It is a long story, but, essentially, Bendigo has two cemeteries and as a dispute had broken out between them over which should have the right to build a monument to Burke and Wills, the sexton of the Back Creek Cemetery, an Irishman by the name of Paddy Bernard, had more or less abducted King – claiming to be an intimate friend of Burke's – in the hope that the young Irishman would honour their cemetery by picking out the spot where the monument could be built. And *that* would fix the uppity folk of the White Hills Cemetery and their extra-uppity presumption that *they* could build the said monument.)

When Welch finally locates King it is to discover him in a 'state of stupidity . . . neither knowing or caring about anything', in a buggy with Paddy Bernard, who is 'disgustingly drunk, [falling] over King and calling him his lost son, whom he said he closer and closer resembled'[84].

Once Welch gets King back to the Shamrock, he *locks* him inside their private dining room, till they can both think straight, and keeps the only key in his pocket. The only thing that happens for the rest of the evening is that it turns out one of the waiters had taken a bribe to secrete a Mr Marsh of the travelling Marsh Troupe *under their dining table* and – likely exhausted beyond all redemption – Mr Welch agrees to Marsh's request to take Mr King to a specially reserved box for that night's performance downstairs, only to find that they are the star turns! For no sooner have they taken their seats than – forewarned by the cunning Mr Marsh of their presence – the crowd cries out 'King on the stage!'[85] and 'Welch . . . take him on!'[86] An apoplectic Welch – oh, the TREACHERY – point-blank refuses. The crowd in turn point-blank refuses to let King and Welch go anywhere, until they have had satisfaction. The only way out is for Welch to indeed lead King to another box, where the crowd can get a better look at this wonder of Australia, but even now there is trouble as cries of 'Speech!' continue to ring out. Now, both men are overwhelmed, unable to make headway against the throng, verbally or physically, and it is finally the mayor, Mr Strickland, who restores order, insisting that while the show will go on, neither Mr Welch nor Mr King will speak, and everyone must settle down.

It is the first night of John King's life spent in a theatre and a highly uncomfortable one it is, as the players strut their stuff on the stage, while all eyes remain upon his stunted, blinking form – perhaps perceiving, for the first time, that his life will never be the same again.

The next day, there is no respite, as, at last extricated from Bendigo, Welch and King, in their horse-drawn carriage, find themselves on the approaches to Castlemaine.

Having come as far as he has, and seen what he has seen, it takes a great deal to shock Edwin Welch. But . . . he . . . is . . . shocked.

'Every man or woman and child in the township along the road turned out as we passed through,' he will recount, 'throwing bouquets, firing guns, and perpetrating every conceivable stupidity, displaying an intensity of hero worship, little short of mania.'[87]

When their carriage arrives at Woodend, where they are to catch the train to Melbourne, it is even worse. Though they make it to the station's waiting room before the people of that town properly appreciate they are here, it does not take long. For now, so many flood in so quickly and *surround* them, it is only by dint of Welch's liberally flying fists that they are able to break free, and the flabbergasted explorer is able to, by his account, 'drag King along the platform, in front of the station master's house, in which we at length found refuge until the train was ready to start . . .'[88]

This is madness, and they haven't even reached Melbourne yet!

What on earth will it be like there?

At each station along the way, Welch and the frightened King must duck down, as the roaring crowds on each platform look for them, throwing scarves and bouquets into each carriage. Lord knows what might have happened had they been spotted, when . . .

When suddenly, just as the train stops at North Melbourne station the carriage door bursts open, and in walks a man well known to Mr Welch, none other than Dr Wills, the still grieving father of the late, great explorer.

Welch is about to greet him warmly, for the two know each other, only for Dr Wills to completely ignore him, and boisterously welcome King, and tell him that he is to get off the carriage 'for I have a cab all ready for you outside'[89].

Wait! Welch makes strong objection to any such move, noting that King is in his care, not that of Dr Wills, only to receive for his trouble 'a volley of abuse', followed by rather more formal and even officious notification that, 'I am acting according to the instructions of Sir Henry Barkly.'[90]

Welch rises to the moment.

Having beaten off with his own fists an entire crowd at Woodend, he is more than capable of dealing with the good Dr Wills.

'I have not received any instructions, either from the Governor or the Exploration Committee to give King up, before reaching Melbourne,' says he. 'I do not acknowledge your authority, and neither will I suffer King to get out.'[91]

At this point Welch looks up to see, as fate would have it, Mr Richard Nash, the former government storekeeper and close friend of Robert Burke, now the secretary for railways, standing at the door of the compartment.

'Do you intend to persist in this line of conduct?' Nash asks simply.

'I do,' replies Welch.

In that case, Secretary Nash replies, the train must proceed.

Thirty seconds later a lurch on the carriage signals they are underway once more.

'Old Dr Wills amused himself as the train proceeded,' Welch would chronicle, 'by abusing me in the latest and most approved style but my sympathy for the poor old gentleman's loss, kept me quiet under the infliction . . .'[92]

Besides all that, Welch knows, he must brace himself for whatever awaits them at Spencer Street Station . . .

•

In the hall of the Royal Society at this very time, a quick meeting of the Exploration Committee is just concluding, under rather difficult circumstances. For the word of King's impending arrival is out, meaning that people have been congregating outside, and even inside – as well as on all the avenues around – all on the reckoning that King, the companion of the great Burke and Wills and 'the only living human being who has crossed the continent of Australia'[93] will likely be brought here, fresh from the station. Which, as it happens, brings them to their first order of business. How will they get King from the station to here, where he can hopefully address them and give them answers to the many questions they have? Mr Welch has sent them *two* telegrams advising both the time of their arrival, and his view that special provisions will need to be put into place to get King safely through the crowds, but they can't imagine it will be anything too bad.

It is, in fact, a matter quickly resolved as one of the Committee members, Dr William Gillbee, offers to take his own carriage to the station to pick Welch and King up. All those in favour say 'Aye'.

Aye. Aye. Aye.

I'll be on my way, then, says Dr Gillbee, and now departs to traverse the short distance to Spencer Street Station, accompanied by Dr Macadam.

'As it will be seen by the sequel,' the *Argus* will note archly, 'the Royal Society never more miscalculated its arrangements.'[94]

Which, under the circumstances, is saying something.

25 November '61, King of Melbourne

Once again, the word has spread.

He is coming, he is coming! The great man, John King – the only man to have crossed the Australian continent, *and* come back, is to be on the six o'clock train from Woodend.

At Spencer Street Station, all is in a state of high excitement from half past five onwards as the crowd swells, and nary a small dog could have found space on the platform. It is enormously hot, and uncomfortable, but oh, my goodness . . . it is worth it.

For here it comes!

At 6 pm, right on time, a distant cheery whistle presages the arrival of our conquering hero, and shortly thereafter the steam engine – draped with two Union Jacks in honour of their distinguished passenger – thunders into view.

'As soon as it stopped,' the *Argus* would report the next day, 'all was utter confusion. No one appeared to know King when they saw him; and the crowd so surged to and fro in its excitement that all persons having regard for their safety wisely cleared out before they were crushed or torn to pieces.'[95]

So too, would King himself have been lost in the crush, anonymous – for most are looking for a *great* man, a *distinguished* figure, a man who could stand astride an entire continent.

'A very dark and very nervous little man,' one Victorian would later recount, 'carrying a black bag in his left hand, dropped to the platform at my feet; and from photographs I had seen, I recognised King immediately.'[96]

And so do many others! With a triumphant roar, the crowd surges forward to seize him. But again Welch is too big, too strong and too fast for them. Already deeply annoyed that his cables to the Exploration Committee have seen no provisions put into place, and realising it will be up to him, Welch simply puts his arms around King's waist, and *drives* him through the throbbing throng, sending people flying as they go. People grab, cry out, tear at their clothing, but Welch will stop for no one and nothing and keeps driving through with the terrified King until they get to the nearest carriage. He pushes King inside and as quick as he is to close the door, he is still not quick enough to get it shut before Dr Wills and Mr Nash also burst inside.

Again, Welch forbears to allow it under the circumstances.

What now, as the crowd closes?

'Drive to Government House!' Welch roars to the cab driver. It is the closest place he can think of that might provide refuge, for that is exactly what they need right now. Yes, Welch knows the Royal Society are expecting them at their premises, and those are indeed his instructions, but in all the madness, the key is to get *away* from the crowd for safety's sake. Sure enough, as they proceed up Collins Street, the enormous mob lining both sides of the grand thoroughfare outdo themselves 'cheering lustily in their wake'[97].

Ah, but some do not stop at mere cheering.

'There was quite a procession but one without order or decorum,' the *Argus* describes. 'It consisted of the car containing King, which was followed by about thirty others, well crowded, and a hundred or so of people running at full speed.'[98]

Faster! Faster!

Drive! yells Mr Welch. *Push, push!*

The man himself? King has no say. Sitting there dazed, he gazes at the cheering crowds with eyes that are struggling to comprehend.

And yet the cab is not *quite* fast enough.

For no sooner do Dr Wills, Nash, Welch and King arrive at Government House, to be hustled straight inside, than the maddened crowd 'rush' the whole place. Bowling aside the guards and the remonstrating officials alike, the people have a mind of their own. They must see King, touch him, venerate him, elevate him onto their shoulders. Anything!

'Hall, staircase, and landing were in a moment filled by an assemblage which, although numbering a few decent people, was to a large extent composed of persons and dirty boys who did not in the least know what was due to the vice-regal office.'[99]

In extremis, Welch manages to leave Dr Wills behind and push King up the stairs, and into the Executive Council Chambers. Welch is right behind him and quick to slam the door shut and lock it . . . but still not quick enough to shut the other door into the chamber, through which 'Old Wills' now bursts, who locks it in turn.

It is all greatly to the disgust of the mob outside 'who loudly expressed their dissatisfaction, alternating their complaints with cheers for King, that must have made everyone in the house nearly deaf.'[100]

All is chaos, excitement, exultation, anger, wonder, confusion, all together.

But he's here! He's here, in this very building, right now, and so are we!

So is John King's sister, Elizabeth, who has just arrived and, with the help of friends, she is at last ushered to the locked door behind which her brother has fled.

But those inside daren't open it, despite the shouts back and forth for them to do so. They can't risk it.

The original intent of the Exploration Committee at this point had been to interview King to get some answers to their myriad questions. But it is soon apparent that is out of the question. This ragged figure can barely speak, let alone answer intensive questioning.

Meanwhile, the shouts back and forth between those at the door and those with King's sister outside go on.

At last, with the firm assurance that the mob will behave, the door does indeed open for an instant and Miss King is whisked inside, before it is slammed shut once more. Coming through the other internal doorway is the governor himself, Sir Henry Barkly, who shakes hands with King. 'I congratulate you on your safe return to Melbourne,' he says warmly in his well-clipped tones, but he notices at once that the hand he shook is weak and still shaking now on its own. Sir Henry smoothly guides King to a seat. 'Do not stand to receive me, for you are rather weak. Has your health quite recovered?'

'Yes, sir,' quavers King in a voice that belies the truth.

'I suppose you were in a very reduced state when you were at Cooper's Creek with the blacks?'

'Yes, sir . . .'

'You were in India, I believe?'

'Yes, sir.'

'What were you there, may I ask?'

'A soldier, sir.'

'I wish you a good afternoon. I am glad to see you safe back, and in a few days I have no doubt you will be able to face all the receptions awaiting you.'[101]

Indeed . . .

But . . .

Your Excellency . . . ?

Yes . . . ?

There is something that I have long been desirous of doing, and now is the moment.

Taking the leather pouch from around his neck for the first time in five months, John King opens it and removes from it William Wills's gold watch and last letter to his father which, in the presence of His Excellency – who can ever after apply his vice-regal imprimatur to the fact that King has fulfilled his duty in this regard – he hands to Dr Wills.

Sir Henry is kind enough to cut the interview short, advising the poor young fellow to accompany his sister to her friend's house in the quiet suburb of St Kilda, 'to have a few days' perfect rest before you venture to face the public . . .'[102]

If only it could be that simple.

We have a problem.

The crowd will not disperse.

They *insist* on seeing King.

There is only one thing for it, and Dr Macadam, who has now arrived, arranges it.

Venturing onto the balcony of Government House, to the thrill of the crowd who nevertheless fall silent just to hear his words, he tells the people that King will 'show himself at the balcony for a few minutes, but is totally unable to speak'[103].

And he is as good as his word!

For, after some delay, the doors open, and there he is!

King! *King!* KING!

Still completely bewildered, King remains there 'for a few moments, faintly waving his hat, in reply to the cheers that rent the air, and the hats, caps, and handkerchiefs that were flourished in his honour'[104].

But it is enough. At least they can *see* him, get some impression of what he is like, be able to tell their grandchildren they were *there*, they looked into his *eyes*!

'He is not a striking-looking man,' the *Argus* would report, 'but possesses a well-knit muscular frame, to which military discipline (for he has been a soldier) has given a peculiar development. His face and neck are deeply bronzed by the weather, but every action and look showed the extreme debility to which his suffering had reduced him.'[105]

But it really is enough, and once he has been ushered back inside, the crowd slowly disperses, and later that night King is smuggled out of Government House in a carriage provided by a Knight of the Realm and, in the company of the Mayor of Melbourne and two other distinguished personages, taken to St Kilda with his sister.

Not that there is much respite, even there. For as the *Argus* would report, 'we learn that King appeared much worse, and even wandering in his brain, when he returned to St. Kilda'[106].

It is so bad that the mayor calls for his predecessor in the post, Dr Richard Eades, who comes at once. Finally, King calms, and is put to bed, left in the care of his sister.

Back at Government House, Welch is now making his way anonymously through the still milling crowd when he comes face to face with a man *praying* that he will remain anonymous, William Brahe. For hours, he has watched, stunned, at the hysterical reception, the veneration, for the man *he* left behind. Welch and Brahe have much to talk about, and so repair to the only safe haven Brahe knows – his brother's house in Richmond, where the two men converse late into the night before retiring.

•

Back at his sister's house, King lies awake, silently ruminating.

Truly, he is having trouble taking it all in, as the reaction has just been so overwhelming. How is it that, *he*, of all members of the expedition, has been saved? The young man can only put it down to 'the interposition of a merciful Providence'[107].

Yes, the Good Lord must have made him 'the instrument of preserving from destruction the invaluable notes and their memoranda, for the use of the Government and the Victorian public'[108]. He feels himself 'utterly unworthy' of such a role, and that is not even counting the adoration shown him by the endless crowds of people! Just to hear himself mentioned in the same breath as Mr Burke, to read of himself as 'a "devoted follower" and a "true and faithful friend", of so great and generous a man as the lamented Burke will be a source of satisfaction to me as long as I live'[109], he will later recount.

And yet . . . ?

And yet while supremely grateful for such honours, 'at the same time the "honour and fame" which appear to attach to my name are so interwoven with the "misery" and melancholy death of my late leader, Mr Burke, and those of his friend Mr Wills, and attendant Mr Gray, as to cause a feeling of depression rather than that of exultation on receiving the congratulation of my fellow colonists'[110].

•

In the wake of John King's arrival, the veneration for his dead comrades has never been at a higher pitch, creating an acutely delicate problem for the Exploration Committee. What to do about the bodies of the likes of Charlie Gray and Ludwig Becker that have been left out in the desert?

Should Howitt be dispatched to find their bones, too, and bring them back? This time, there is bitter debate.

On this day, in the hall of the Royal Society, Dr Gillbee rises to express his opinion that, 'I believe that it would be more satisfactory to the friends and relatives of the parties deceased, that no distinction should be made, and that all who had died in the cause of exploration should have honour done to them.'[111]

Really? You wish Mr Howitt to go out there and exhume five more corpses?

Yes, really.

Dr Gillbee is most insistent. It is his desire that 'supplementary instructions'[112] are immediately sent to Howitt, and the motion he proposes to that effect is quickly seconded by Captain Cadell. For his part, and not surprisingly, Dr Wills can barely believe it. The Committee really wants his son to be an equal part of a procession of corpses? His *son*, one of the two heroes of the day, to be placed in a giant bag of bones to bounce back to Melbourne on the back of a camel?

'I hope,' says Dr Wills delicately, 'that in the matter of interment, the remains of my son would not be mixed up with those of any other person save Mr Burke.'[113]

And yet, after Dr Wills receives assurance that Mr Howitt will, 'of course take proper precautions to keep the remains separate'[114], the motion is agreed to, and the matter settled.

Or is it? In this Committee any decision that is made can be unmade, and on a matter as emotionally powerful as this, it is obvious that even the corpses of former employees cannot regard their position as settled.

To be resolved . . .

•

Now here is something interesting.

It is a box delivered to the Royal Society building, and it is apparently filled with plates that show images of the most sensational story of the day, the discovery of John King alive among the savages, and the finding of the skeletons. And yes it is marked:

'Not to be opened by anyone except Messrs BATCHELDER & O'NEILL, photographers, Collins Street, Melbourne,'

But the temporary clerk who takes receipt of them has another idea. Taking the box on this bright beautiful morning to one of the Royal Society's many rooms – with sunny daylight flooding in from outside – he just can't wait, as he would later explain to 'see the pictures!'[115]

The result?

All 48 frames, all images of these extraordinary moments, are completely destroyed.

The Royal Society, when they find out, are not well pleased.

'Dismissal was the only punishment possible.'[116]

CHAPTER SEVENTEEN

ROYAL COMMISSION

Third-rate amateurs in science, of no special knowledge or experience in exploration, and having small natural capacity for the work ... We have had meeting after meeting in Melbourne, involving much waste of words and many dispatches to and from the explorers and the committee; but the plain, direct and obvious duty before the committee has been entirely and grossly neglected and to this cause mainly must be attributed the disaster.[1]

The *Argus* gives its take on the proceedings of the Royal Commission, and where the blame properly lies, 1862

Late November '61, Melbourne, responsibility and recrimination

Every proper Victorian saga needs heroes and villains, and, in Burke and Wills, we have titans.

Magnificent, classic men, who make us proud to be British. In John King we have a romantic hero, a wonderful example of how even one not born a gentleman *can* rise to the occasion and accomplish extraordinary things, doing through hard work and British blood what class alone has not provided.

The true question before the Royal Commission – starting this bright morning in this last gasp of November – is, thus, clear.

We, the people, need to know: who are to be the villains in the piece?

The terms of reference give the first clue.

For, among other things, the Commission is 'especially to investigate the circumstances under which the Depot at Cooper's Creek was abandoned by WILLIAM BRAHE'[2].

Yes, William Brahe is one obvious candidate to have marked on his CV the key descriptor: Chief Villain.

The Commission is also 'to determine upon whom rests the grave responsibility of there not having been sufficient supply of provisions and clothing secured for the recruiting of the Explorers on their return, and for their support until they could reach the settlements'[3].

Enter, William Wright, who will also clearly have his every action scrutinised.

Gentlemen gather in the crowded committee room of the Victorian Parliament. Sir Thomas Pratt, the Commander of British Forces in Australia, takes the chair, flanked by an august panel of Commissioners: Sir Francis Murphy, the Speaker of the Legislative Assembly; Mr James Sullivan and Mr Matthew Hervey, distinguished parliamentarians both; and Mr Evelyn Sturt, a respected police magistrate and also the younger brother of distinguished explorer, Charles Sturt.

Over to you, Sir Thomas.

Very well then, let us proceed. Dr Macadam, please step forward, place your hand on the bible and give your oath, followed by your testimony, to be prompted by our enquiries.

In fact, rather than mere evidence, the good doctor unleashes something closer to a *flood*. Consulting the thick folder of documents before him, he reads out dispatches, instructions, letters and lists, and seems intent on drowning the Commissioners in so much information they simply will not be able to draw breath, let alone ask difficult questions. From the first, so help us all, God, he seems less like a witness and more as if he is a Commissioner himself, anxious to direct proceedings from the witness box, and for all the world it seems as though he is running a meeting of the Exploration Committee.

At last, it is only the Chair himself, Sir Thomas Pratt, who is able to momentarily stem the flood by asking Dr Macadam, 'From these instructions it would appear that Mr Burke was left in a great measure free to exercise his own discretion?'[4]

Dr Macadam beams. His point entirely!

'Yes,' he nods his head vigorously, luxuriant flowing red mane bouncing happily, 'and at a subsequent meeting of the Committee, it was decided to leave Mr Burke entirely to his own discretion after leaving Cooper's Creek.'[5]

You see? The Exploration Committee in general, and Dr Macadam in particular, must be entirely free from blame for any of the disastrous errors that might have occurred *after* that point – most particularly the selection of William Wright.

Keen to press this point, nay labour it, Dr Macadam just happens to have, right to hand, one of Mr Burke's last communications with the Committee, and if it please the Commission, he will be more than happy – no, really – to quote from it.

Macadam quotes Mr Burke's words from Torowoto on 29 October, the previous year, '"Mr Wright returns from here to Menindee. I have appointed him as third officer of the expedition, subject to the approval of the Committee, from the day of our departure from Menindee, and I hope they will confirm the appointment. In the meantime I have instructed him to follow me up with the remainder of the camels," and so on . . .'[6]

And so on? Dr Macadam's sudden lack of specificity is privately noted by Sir Francis Murphy. But Dr Macadam continues.

'It will be seen by this quotation that Mr Wright was an officer selected entirely by Mr Burke, that he had every confidence in him, and the Committee afterwards ratified his appointment.'[7]

What is seen by Sir Francis Murphy, in fact, is that, even unbidden, Dr Macadam is desperate to serve up, sliced and diced, the precise thing he thinks they most need – someone – who does *not* have the initials 'DrJM' – to blame for the catastrophe.

But enough.

'I think,' says Sir Francis firmly, 'that the commission would be proceeding more regularly with the business before us if Dr Macadam would at this stage hand in the list of the supplies given to Burke's party, together with the correspondence.'[8]

Particularly the correspondence. Sir Francis is most interested indeed to see what Dr Macadam has *not* been reading out. That correspondence is duly handed over, together with the lists of supplies, and Dr Macadam is quickly away again, telling the Commission, before even being asked, that 'all the articles necessary for the expedition were first of all mainly suggested by Mr Burke'[9] and that Mr Burke's expedition started with provisions 'capable of supporting the whole party for eighteen months'[10].

Eighteen months? Sir Francis finds this a remarkable estimate. Does that include the 'whole party, men, horses, and cattle of all kinds?'[11]

'Yes,' replies Dr Macadam.[12]

As a matter of fact, Dr Macadam comments, 'I may state that though the provisions were calculated to last 18 months yet it was supposed that by care they might last for two years.'[13]

So it is two years now? The preparation for this expedition just keeps getting better and better!

Never let it be said that the Committee scrimped when it came to supplying everything possible for their safety.

'The total expenditure,' Dr Macadam says, 'for stores, and sundry, was £4,585/2s/10d; that included wagons and equipment generally.'[14]

Very well, that is all for today, gentlemen. We shall resume in five days time . . .

•

On 27 November, in the five days since Macadam's appearance, the Commissioners have been going over the many dispatches, diaries and letters the Hon. Secretary had tabled, and Mr Sturt now wants to know:

'Did it ever strike the Committee,' the great explorer's brother asks with the hint of a glint of genuine prosecutorial purpose, 'that Mr Wright's having left Mr Burke at Torowoto on the 29th or 30th of October, and arriving at the Darling on the 5th of November, an immense deal of valuable time had been lost between the 5th of November and the 19th of December, when Mr Wright's dispatch was dated?'[15]

In short, did no alarm bells ring for you, that 'such a long strange silence was unexplained?'

This time, in the face of the long detailed question, Dr Macadam surprises everyone by giving a remarkably short answer.

'It was never made matter of comment,' he says dismissively.

Still, Sturt presses. It was the fifth of November Mr Wright arrived back in Menindee, yes? Mr Wright knew the task and requirements ahead of him, 'and yet he does not appear to have taken any steps to let the Committee know what he was doing until the 19th of December?'[16]

How can six weeks with no word from the man you know Mr Burke is counting on not worry you?

This time Dr Macadam knows he must find the answer.

'Afterwards, upon looking into this matter personally, as one of the Committee, I noticed this great interval of time,' he allows, cautiously. 'But when the dispatches were brought down as they urged great promptitude in our movements this question of delay was overlooked and it was not mentioned at the time. I have no doubt from the excitement of the moment this interval of time was overlooked.'[17]

The 'excitement of the moment'? Well, on the reckoning that such excitement has passed, Mr Sullivan has a question.

'Has there been any explanation obtained *since* by the Committee with regard to this long delay?'

'None whatever,'[18] replies Dr Macadam.

Really? Sir Francis Murphy finds that more than passing curious.

Very well, then. Let us, Commissioner, move on to the painful subject of Mr Landells and . . . his curious claims of a special understanding he had with the Committee regarding the control of the camels?

'Is it,' Sir Thomas asks, 'that he had private instructions from the Committee of which Mr Burke knew nothing. Is that the case?'

'We gave Mr Landells no private instructions whatever,' Dr Macadam flatly denies. 'That has been answered over and over again.'[19]

Thank you Dr Macadam, you are excused. At least for the moment. It is time for the next witness, William Brahe.

The young German has clearly been having a tough time of it in recent months, battered as much emotionally as he had been physically in the early months of this year. For it is he, all of Melbourne knows, who had taken the key decision to leave Cooper's Creek, even as the Gulf party, boasting those magnificent heroes, Burke and Wills, not to mention John King, had been about to arrive. It is he who is pointed out on the streets, in the pubs: that is the man who *abandoned* Burke and Wills, don't you know?

He is a softly spoken, respectful and helpful witness. The key question the Commission wants answered is the obvious one: *why did you abandon your post?* Brahe does his best to explain. The struggles he had. How Mr Burke had clearly said to stay only three months, and yet, at the behest of Mr Wills he had not only stayed four months, but four days longer still!

'You went down with Mr Burke a portion of the way, did you not?' asks Sir Thomas.

'Yes, to his first camp about 22 miles upon the creek,'[20] replies Brahe.

'And on his finally leaving you, did he make any observation to you as his last words?'[21]

'That I was to follow him with dispatches if Wright should arrive within two days of his departure,'[22] says Brahe.

'Then he expected Mr Wright to arrive *within two days?*' asks Sir Francis.

'He did.'

'Were you cognizant of any instructions he gave Mr Wright?'

'No.'[23]

Mr Brahe had been left trapped, practically *marooned* in the desert, a man hired as a worker, suddenly with the responsibility of holding the fort, with the fate of the expedition depending on it. And all of it waiting for a man who had given entirely conflicting signals about his intentions. 'He said,' Brahe tells the Commission, '"If I am not back in three months' time you may consider me perished," and I told him, "Or on your way to Queensland?" and he said "Just so . . ."'[24]

Brahe had taken the leader at his word, and was sure, after Mr Burke did not appear, that he had pursued the other course. Yes, Brahe was sure, he insists, that once they got to Menindee, he would hear news of the triumphant Mr Burke in Queensland. Thus they had left, first leaving a cache of supplies buried, with an explanatory note, and the word 'DIG' blazed on a tree.

'You deposited a note in case Mr Burke should come back?'[25] asks Sir Francis, pointedly.

'No,' replies Brahe. 'If I had expected Mr Burke to have come back I would have given him an explanation, or told him my reasons for leaving, and have addressed the letter to him, but I did not consider that necessary. I left the note only for any party that should come up

– that was most likely to come up from the Darling – to know what had become of us.'[26]

'You placed that there *not* with the expectation that Mr Burke would get it?'[27] presses Sir Francis.

'Certainly not,' replies Mr Brahe, going on to describe how he had carefully buried the cache and the note, covered it with lots of dirt and 'strewed some horse-dung over it'[28], to ensure that the blacks would be fooled, and never think that fresh dirt and signs of digging had been caused by spades, not horses' hoofs. You see? The blacks would never think to dig! Quite. But the Commissioners are all too aware that none of the rescuers had thought to, either, not even Mr Brahe himself, when he returned to this very spot. On that subject, the Commissioners must ask. How is it that, on his return, he missed the fact that the Gulf party had in fact returned to the Depot? Surely, some object had been moved from the last time he had been there?

'Did you leave any things on the surface?'[29] asks Mr Sturt.

'I left a rake, I believe, against the tree, and I found it there when I returned, with Mr Wright, still against the tree,' replies Mr Brahe. 'I do believe that I put it there when I left the creek, but I am not sure.'[30]

A rake! Can it be? On the basis of one sole rake still being against the tree, Mr Brahe had concluded that Burke and Wills had not returned to the Depot? Because of that he made no other investigations? The Commissioners are underwhelmed. We shall adjourn for the day, and the witness is excused for the day, if not excused for that extraordinary admission, while . . .

While to Brahe it seems like only an hour has passed before he is back being grilled. Sir Francis Murphy takes the lead, with a very clear line of questioning – he wants to illustrate Mr Brahe's outright deception, in terms of the note he left buried beneath the 'Dig' tree. Now, Mr Brahe, listen if you would, to your own crucial words!

'*"Two of my companions and myself are quite well; the third (Patten) has been unable to walk for the last eighteen days, as his leg has been severely hurt when thrown by one of the horses; no person has been up here from the Darling. We have six camels and twelve horses in good working condition."* Does that accurately describe the state of the party then?'[31] asks Sir Francis.

'It does in a very careless way,' replies Mr Brahe cautiously. 'I stated yesterday I did not expect Mr Burke would see that note. I left it for any party that would probably be coming up from the Darling, who would be sent up in search of us, and by that note it would appear what had become of the Depot party. I did not think it of any consequence to tell them the exact state of our health.'[32]

'Then it was *not* the exact state of the party?'[33] presses Sir Francis.

'McDonough, [Dost Mahomet] the sepoy and myself were well able to work,' admits Brahe, 'and I said about the camels "that the camels were in good working condition", but I had not travelled half-a-dozen miles when I found that they were hardly able to travel. I had to lighten the loads the first day, and they were but very lightly packed with water bags. I had to throw some of those water bags away that night. I should have told an untruth when I came down here if I had said the camels were in good condition.'[34]

'Then the fact is that the paper you left with the provisions did *not* accurately describe the state of the party?'[35] continues Sir Francis.

'No, it did not,' admits Brahe. 'The doctor's statement of Wright's party must show that. McDonough was laid up shortly after our arrival at Wright's camp, and he was ill for weeks, and the same with Patten. I myself was very poorly when I returned with Wright to Cooper's Creek, and I suffered a great deal from pains in the legs, and had sore gums. I had sore gums for three or four weeks before we left Cooper's Creek, but not knowing what it was I did not state that in the paper.'[36]

'Then your statement *"two of my companions and myself are quite well"* was not the fact?'[37] asks Sir Francis.

'No,'[38] responds Brahe reluctantly.

'Neither was it a fact that you had "six camels and twelve horses in good working condition?"'[39] presses Sir Francis.

'No,'[40] replies Brahe, a little uncertainly. And now he is quick to give his reason for not writing the truth that they were really in quite a bad way.

'I did not wish to give any uneasiness to any party in coming up on our account.' he says. 'It is very probable if I had stated we *were* ill that they would have thought we should never reach the Darling.'[41]

In other words, I had to lie, a little, so that any rescuer might think we were still alive ourselves and worth pursuing.

Sir Francis will have none of it.

'Do you not *see*, if you had reflected for *a moment*, you would have seen the difficulty in which Mr Burke would be placed, if he had known you were ill, and not very well able to make long journeys; he might have been induced to follow you, but seeing you state you were quite well *he did not do so?*'[42]

In short, do you see how your lies practically caused their tragic deaths?

There is a dramatic pause, perhaps only seconds, but it seems so much longer as all the Commissioners, the press and the public gallery lean forward to take in the German man's key response.

'I made so confident that Mr Burke would not return,'[43] says Mr Brahe plaintively. True, Mr Brahe's grasp of the English language is not all that it might be, but everyone understands his meaning and the way he says it connotes sincerity, for he is clearly so genuinely aggrieved. His point is, he was *so sure* Mr Burke would never return, it never even crossed his mind that the note might have fatally misled his leader.

And yet, Mr Brahe is still not free to go. For now Sir Francis produces yet *another* damning document he wishes to quote.

It is a copy of yesterday's *Argus*, which contains a copy of Mr Wills's final letter to his father.

'It is stated . . . in this letter, "the party we left here had *special instructions* not to leave until our return, *unless from absolute necessity?*"'[44]

'I never received such instructions,' says Brahe with aghast force. 'And I do not believe that Mr Wills at the time he left expected that I would receive such instructions, for on our way down he asked me to remain at least four months if possible.'[45]

So, continues Sir Francis, we may then conclude that no 'absolute necessity' arose for your departure?

Mr Brahe considers the words.

'Not exactly an absolute necessity. The time Mr Burke gave me was three months; he said after three months time I had no reason to expect him back, nor did I.'[46]

Very well. 'When you returned to Cooper's Creek with Wright how long did you remain there?'[47] asks Mr Sullivan.

Brahe thinks for a moment.

'I suppose . . . I could not exactly tell,' he says. 'Not more than a quarter of an hour at the Depot.'[48]

A quarter of an hour? Mr Wright took over three months to reach Cooper's Creek, men of his party died on the way to this goal and he and you, Mr Brahe, stayed there for just 15 minutes!

This is hardly the diligence the Commissioners expect in such a potentially life and death situation.

'Did you make any examination about to see who had been there?'[49] asks Mr Sullivan.

'Yes,' replies Brahe. 'I tied my horse up, and so I believe did Wright, near the cache, and went into the stockade and round it and examined all the trees.'[50] *For 15 minutes.*

'Could you not discover any tracks?'[51]

'I saw camel tracks, but supposed them to be our own,'[52] answers Mr Brahe, defensive once more. He knows it looks bad, and is, in fact, bad. They had obviously made a terrible error. But, against that, it is quite reasonable for Mr Brahe to point out, and he does so, that he was under Mr Wright's command at this time. Mr Wright gave the orders for them to go after just 15 minutes, and they did so.

'Did you see any impression of human feet?'[53] asks Mr Sullivan.

'No impression,'[54] says Brahe flatly.

'Why?'[55]

'From the number of rats and the place being dusty.'[56]

The rats. The dust. Really! If not for them, the painstaking 15-minute search of Mr Wright and Mr Brahe would have found the truth: that Burke and his party were still alive, and very close.

'At whose instigation did you return after meeting Wright – yours or his?'[57] asks Commissioner Matthew Hervey.

'Mine.'[58]

'What was the object of that?'[59]

'I had got right,' Brahe explains, 'and Patten was in the doctor's hands. I thought he required rest there, and would get all right in a fortnight's time. Mr Wright not having been to Cooper's Creek I thought that we could not be better employed than in going back there as a last chance for Mr Burke.'[60]

A last chance? Mr Hervey now has Brahe right where he wants him.

'Had you a lingering suspicion that he *might be there*?'[61]

'Yes,' replies Brahe softly. 'There was still a chance.'[62]

And this, my learned friends, is the exact point all along of Brahe's critics – including those who sit in judgement of him on the Royal Commission. There was still a chance, but you left. And if you had made the effort to dig up the cache, to find Mr Burke's note, there was more than a chance that he and Mr Wills would still be alive!

All William Brahe can do now is to sit sorrowfully, and wait for his ordeal to be over. He had come on the expedition as a mere assistant, only to rise to the post of 'officer' and had done his best – only to find himself now accused as one of the prime causes of the disaster. Can nothing save him?

If it please the Commission!

Yes?

A letter has just arrived from Dr Hermann Beckler, right now making his way back from the north and still at the junction of the Murray and Darling rivers. Dr Beckler wishes to advise that he has read a report in the *Argus* criticising the actions of William Brahe, and it will be instructive for the Commission, if the secretary, Mr Robert Haverfield, reads his words to the Commissioners. Go ahead.

'I fully believe that if Mr Brahe had not left Cooper's Creek at the time he did, or a very few days after, he would have been unable to proceed with this small and weak party towards Bulla. With regard to Brahe's service during the expedition I am sure that I only state what everyone of us would corroborate unhesitatingly, that nobody could be more zealous, active and contentious than he was, and that no one could have a stronger attachment to Mr Burke, or a more strict adherence to his orders. The instructions given to him by Mr Burke he repeated to us so often that there could not have been the slightest misunderstanding or want of arrangement.'[63]

It is a strong endorsement from a surviving officer of the expedition, a gentleman, even if a German one, and carries a great deal of weight.

Mr Brahe is excused and relieved. The testimony of the next witness, Thomas McDonough, boosts Brahe further.

'About twelve o'clock the day before [Mr Burke] left,' McDonough says, 'he came out, that was my watch with the camels, and had an hour's private conversation about the matter. I referred to our stay on the creek and he told me we were to stay for three months or as long after as our provisions would last, leaving us sufficient to ensure our own return to the settled districts; he did not say what were his instructions but I just asked him how it was and he told me that.'[64]

He also recalls what Mr Burke said, 'with regard to Mr Wright; he said, "I expect Mr Wright up in a few days, a fortnight at furthest."'[65]

Expect? Mr Hervey wishes to be clearer on this.

'Mr Burke must have been then somewhat doubtful as to Mr Wright getting to you?'[66] he asks.

'No,' replies McDonough. 'I do not think he could have been then, because he said he *would* be there in a few days, or a fortnight at furthest.'[67]

And now Mr Brahe pipes up from the back of the room.

'I recollect well what Mr Burke said. On the morning he left he called us round him and said he expected Wright up that night or within two days, but perhaps he might not be able to come at all. He said, "I cannot be sure of him; I cannot be sure of him; he may not come at all; he may be prevented by accident".'[68]

Mr Burke leaves the Depot without being sure that his third officer will even arrive? It is a curious thing for a leader to do.

Sir Francis Murphy is curious himself about the provisions at the Depot.

'You did not try to make the provisions last out by shooting or fishing, or getting other provisions?'[69] he asks.

'For five weeks we had plenty of ducks and during that time we used very little salt meat,'[70] replies McDonough.

'Could you not continue getting them?'[71] asks a mystified Sir Francis.

'We tried,' answers McDonough, 'but with the constant firing on those two water holes the ducks became shy.'[72]

Shy ducks. Really.

'Did you fish?'[73] asks Sir Francis.

'On two occasions we caught some fish.'[74]

Two occasions?

'Did not the necessity of trying to make the provisions go as far as you could strike you?'[75]

'I did not think there was any fish at the time in the hole,' McDonough replies. 'We only got a few very small fish.'[76]

There is not really a whole lot more to say on the subject of fishing. Thank you, Mr McDonough.

Mr Edmund Wecker now takes the stand, no little stunned that he, the keeper of a fly-blown store in a flyspeck of a settlement in New South Wales, should be the man of the moment in such an important gathering in Australia's grandest city of Melbourne.

The issue at hand is whether, in his role as Menindee's postmaster, he sent a dispatch from Mr Wright to Dr Macadam, for the latter claims he had heard nothing until Mr Hodgkinson arrived in person with a dispatch from Mr Wright in Melbourne.

Sir Thomas Pratt quickly gets to it.

'Mr Wecker. Do you know that there was a dispatch forwarded by the mail?'[77]

'I am pretty certain there was a dispatch forwarded by the mail from Mr Wright,'[78] Wecker replies.

'How soon after his arrival would that be?'[79] asks the Chair.

'A few days after his arrival he would post it; it was by the next mail after his arrival at Menindee,'[80] Mr Wecker states. 'Mr Wright told me many times after he did not intend to start out till his appointment was confirmed by the Committee in Melbourne.'[81]

Indeed? And now Mr Wecker follows up with another interesting comment, entirely unaware of its significance.

'Dr Beckler told me at different times that he would not recognise Mr Wright as third in command until his appointment was confirmed.'[82]

Really? The officer that Mr Burke had left in charge of the camp had declined to acknowledge the authority of the new officer Mr Burke had appointed?

'He was astonished that the command was not confirmed,'[83] says Mr Wecker. 'He expressed it, not only to me but to different parties there, because every party was astonished at Mr Wright's conduct in staying so long at the Darling.'[84]

'That was the general remark?'[85] asks the chairman. *This remarkable impasse was actually general knowledge?*

'That was the general remark,' replies Mr Wecker. 'That it was a piece of folly of Mr Wright's to stop and let the season pass and go out in the summer, and Mr Wright on every occasion said he was waiting for his appointment to be confirmed by the Committee in Melbourne.'[86]

Thank you, Mr Wecker. Most illuminating.

But the dispatch from Mr Wright to Dr Macadam, if we can return to that. Just to be clear, contrary to what Dr Macadam has said, 'that was a dispatch previous to Mr Hodgkinson's being sent down?'[87]

'Yes,' replies Mr Wecker unequivocally. 'Mr Wright said he wished to have the appointment confirmed by the Committee so that he should have somebody to fall back upon for his pay, because the name of the Committee at the time was in great discredit in consequence of small cheques that had been given, being dishonoured.'[88]

What? Another stirring. The testimony is devastating. Rather than a bull in a china shop, this man Wecker is like a happy rat with the bubonic plague, unconsciously devastating everything he touches.

Sir Thomas follows up in amazement.

'Cheques on the Committee?'[89]

'On the National Bank,' replies Mr Wecker, blithely. 'Amounts so small as £1 and 30s., which were in circulation on the Darling, were dishonoured.'[90]

'Whom were they drawn by?'[91] asks Sir Thomas.

'By Mr Burke; and Mr Wright was very anxious to get a document in his hand which would give him a hold on the Committee to get his pay.'[92]

The mighty Royal Society, that holds the regal letters patent, a millennial-old honour most rarely given, granted by Queen Victoria herself, had its cheques *dishonoured*? And Mr Wright so uncertain of the Royal Society's good credit he wants a letter in his hand before he acts? Extraordinary!

All eyes turn to Dr John Macadam, who, unsurprisingly, ashen-faced, rushes to the front to try to limit the damage done. The Commission must understand, he says, that this was a 'transitional' matter of accounts being changed by the Treasurer, Dr Wilkie. Yes, it is possible that two or three cheques *may* have been affected but certainly no more than that.

Well, that is not the way Mr Wecker remembers it. He says many cheques as high as £10 had been dishonoured after being presented to the National Bank!

'I think it interfered so much with Mr Wright,' says Mr Wecker, 'that he would not go out until he had actually his appointment confirmed, so that he would have a hold upon the Committee.'[93]

The Commission thanks Mr Wecker for his evidence. Dr Macadam does not. What is more, in a rather cruel twist, Macadam now has to announce to the Commission that, 'I have just received a telegram from Mr Wright, in which that gentleman offered to come to Melbourne, and give evidence before the commission, for £100, which would pay his expenses and compensate him for loss of employment in taking a quantity of sheep a long way up the country.'[94]

Could the Commission ever have better evidence that Mr Wright was particular about being certain of money before he got going? Dr Macadam's thunderous expression would suggest not. Thank *you*, Dr Macadam. We shall adjourn for today, gentlemen.

•

It is the moment that John King has been waiting for, all this time. Back when Mr Burke had been nearing his last breaths, he had entrusted to the young Irishman his notebook, to give to Sir William Stawell.

'Under no circumstances,' he had rasped, 'are you to deliver it to any other gentleman.'[95]

It has been on King's mind ever since. Through all his time with the tribe, all through the rescue, the trip back to Melbourne and subsequent time staying with his sister, he had kept the notebook with him, conscious that he still needed to fulfil his duty to Mr Burke.

And now, on this very morning that he is to begin his testimony to the Royal Commission, here is Sir William Stawell before him – attending the day's proceedings himself – and King hands the precious 'private pocket book'[96] to him.

Stunned to receive it, the Chief Justice reads to King some of the entries, which the young Irishman finds fascinating, for, despite having it in his possession for all of the last five months, the only thing he had known of its contents had been what Mr Burke had read out to him and Wills, concerning themselves. It had not seemed right to read it after Mr Burke had died. What Sir William does not read out, but recognises its importance, is Burke's last letter to his sister, apologising for leaving everything to Julia, and making it clear that Hessie – his only unmarried sister – is now to get the bulk of the estate. (As Sir William will later tactfully note, 'A portion of the contents were obviously for the Committee, and the remainder for Mr Burke's sister.'[97])

But with this last task for Burke completed, King must now face a dreaded task, speaking in public about his desert ordeal at the Royal Commission. For here, like everywhere else in Australia, King is the star of the show, his appearance only delayed by the fact he has been ill.

Goodness! Horribly ill, it would seem. True, he is no longer the scarecrow in rags found three months earlier up on Cooper's Creek. He wears a sober suit, his face is tanned and his dark hair sports curls from a fashionable barber; but despite this fine surface it is obvious to all, from the moment he stands before the Commission, that Mr King is far from being a well man. Not well in body, nor in mind, as once he starts to speak – stating his name for the record – his weakness in both is apparent. Mindful of his delicate state, the Commission has decided on a singularly delicate questioner. Unlike all other witnesses, Mr King will not be subjected to all five Commissioners flinging questions at him. Instead, Sir Francis Murphy, alone, will gently probe him about what he knows. If you please then, Sir Francis, let us proceed . . . delicately.

'You were one of the original party that started with Mr Burke and Mr Wills from Melbourne?'[98] asks Sir Francis.

'Yes,'[99] says Mr King.

'You went the whole way with them to the Darling?'[100]

'Yes.'[101]

'Were you in any particular charge of any portion of the expedition?'[102]

'Not until Mr Landells resigned,'[103] replies King.

'Where did he resign?'[104]

'At the Darling.'[105]

'You were in no charge till then?'[106]

'No,'[107] says King.

'Merely an ordinary working man with the rest?'[108] Sir Francis posits.

'Yes, just so.'[109]

Gently, Sir Francis leads King through his account of what happened, focusing first on his journey beyond the Darling, and then most particularly what happened after the Gulf party left Cooper's Creek.

'Mr Burke did not intend to take more than three months' provisions?'[110] asks Sir Francis.

'Just so,'[111] replies King.

'And he could have taken more if he had liked?'[112]

'Yes,'[113] answers King unequivocally.

'On the same beasts of burden?'[114] Sir Francis asks, wishing for the point to be clear.

'Yes. The average they will carry is 250 pounds each, I believe.'[115]

The curious point, thus, is made clear for all to see. For the trip north from Cooper's Creek, the leader, let us call him Captain Burke, had sole charge of the fabled ships of the desert, before they headed out into the unknown seas of the interior. And, instead of erring on the side of over-supply, he had given them just a fraction of what they could carry, in what proved to be a fatally light load.

Moving on. For now, painfully, painstakingly, King takes the Commissioners through the story of the Gulf party's daily progress, with Mr Burke and Mr Wills mostly walking in the lead, King following with the six camels, and Charley Gray leading Billy the horse, until, as they were nearing the Gulf, he more often rode, 'for he often complained'[116] of being ill. As King continues to talk, a sad portrait of the doomed party is drawn with ever more detail. Yes, Charley Gray's headaches became a growing problem, but they had kept moving well regardless, getting near to the Gulf in early February. He and Charley had waited at a camp by the river as Mr Burke and Mr Wills had headed off alone.

And now, the young man with the old face talks of the return from the Gulf, as mishap and misadventures deepen to calamity and chaos. Yes, all of it filled with bad luck, bad choices and bad pains in their bodies, mysterious and constant, even as the spectre of catastrophe starts to loom ever larger.

'Where was it that you began to suffer first?'[117]

'Shortly after starting back,'[118] replies King.

After some more back and forth, Sir Francis comes to, perhaps, the most difficult subject of all.

'There is a remark in one of the journals that have been brought back, of Gray taking some of the stores without leave,' notes Sir Francis. 'Do you know anything of that?'[119]

Yes, Mr King most *certainly* does. As it happens, there is a lot he wishes to say on the subject, most particularly to counter the scurrilous rumours of Mr Burke practically beating Charley to death.

That is simply not how it was. He, John King, was there when it was discovered that Charley had been thieving rations:

'Mr Burke then gave him several boxes on the ear with his open hand, and not a sound thrashing, as Mr Wills states,'[120] King says grimly. 'Mr Wills was at the other camp at the time, and it was all over when he returned. Mr Burke may have given him six or seven slaps on the ear.'[121]

'Mr Burke was not in the habit of striking the men?'[122]

'No; it was the first time I ever knew him to do so,'[123] replies King.

'The whole party were on very good terms, were they not?'[124] continues Sir Francis.

'On very good terms . . . very social.'[125]

'Even after that?'[126] Sir Francis asks.

'Even after that, though he abused him at the time,'[127] says King.

'Scolded him?'[128] Sir Francis suggests.

'Yes, scolded him,'[129] replies King.

'When it was over no more was said about it?'[130] says Sir Francis.

'Just so,'[131] finishes King. And so the whispered story about Mr Burke thrashing a man to death has become a mild scolding among a very social party.

'In that journey coming back did you hear what Mr Burke's expectations were on reaching the creek, and whom he would be likely to meet there?'[132]

Oh yes. Mr King remembers that clearly.

'We expected to find those we had left there and also the party from town,'[133] Kings says plainly and firmly. 'I heard Mr Burke speak continually about the party coming up to survey the country convenient to Cooper's Creek; he said he was sure of assistance coming up from town on account of his repeating it so often to the Committee that, *under any circumstances*, we should be followed up, and he had *no doubt*, until we saw our disappointment at the creek, but that there would be a party there.'[134]

'Wright's party?'[135] asks Sir Francis, careful that there should be no ambiguity here.

'Yes, he expected Mr Wright,'[136] King says flatly, almost bemused that there should be any question as to that matter.

And so to the most difficult of all subjects – death. Sir Francis treads lightly, but he asks the questions that must be asked.

'Poor Gray at last became too bad to travel further, did he not?'[137] John King struggles but he answers nonetheless.

'He travelled the evening before his death some seven miles, tied on a camel. Then we camped at Polygonum Swamp, and he got very bad that night, and could scarcely speak. We covered him up, and made him as comfortable as possible, and remained there with him, and the following morning we found him dead.'[138]

'And you buried him?'[139]

'We remained that day to bury him . . . We were extremely weak. It was as much as we could do to dig the grave.'[140]

Though it is a grim business indeed, Mr King is pressed on what the corpse was wearing, for there still remains this strange instance of the corpse and the remains of two other men that Mr McKinlay found buried when searching for Mr Burke. Is one of those bodies Charley Gray?

'I cannot account for it in any other way,' replies King.

Commissioner Matthew Hervey presses, still uncertain as to the identity of this corpse. The remains, he notes, 'were discovered 45 miles to the west, north-west of Mr Wills's grave. Do you think it was that distance from where Mr Wills died?'

'It was full that distance from where Mr Wills died,'[141] replies King.

A puzzle solved it seems, yet still . . .

What of the deep sabre cuts – one just over the left eyebrow according to Hodgkinson's detailed diary notes taken on the day they found the corpse? Did Charley Gray have a scar there, do you recall?

'None that I know of, but being a sailor he might have had some scars.'[142]

How peculiar. How could he possibly have such a deep cut to the skull, that left no visible mark on the skin? And what of the diary account of Mr Hodgkinson, who knew Gray well, noting: 'I know the body was not that of either Wills or Gray from the texture and colour of the tuft of hair.'[143]

The mystery, in sum, remains just that, even after testimony from the sole surviving man who buried poor Charley.

Moving on, then. 'Had you not stopped to bury Gray,' Sir Francis asks, 'you would have been there before Brahe left?'[144]

'We should have been there, all right,'[145] says John King.

They would have been there all right.

Again, there is a pause as all attending this Royal Commission contemplate the horror of it. Mr Wills and King spend an entire day digging a grave for Gray, and, as it turns out, for Mr Burke and Mr Wills as well. But could they have done anything else? Could they have not behaved like civilised Christian men?

Of course not. They had to do it. Still, there is just a touch of the clammy coldness of death in the room, just to reflect on the sheer awfulness of it.

At last Sir Francis rouses himself.

'You arrived at the Depot on the twenty-first?'

'Yes.'[146]

'And you had no difficulty in finding the provisions there?'[147]

'No difficulty. We arrived there about half-past seven in the evening. It was moonlight. We pushed . . . 30 miles that day.'[148]

Again, the extraordinary saga plays out, the deserted Depot, the blazed message saying 'Dig' and the note from Brahe telling them they had missed their own salvation by mere hours. Just hours.

They would have made it all right.

And then Mr Burke's decision not to follow Brahe and his men, but to head for Mount Hopeless and towards Adelaide. Followed by the extraordinary decision not to leave any sign that they had been, for fear of alerting the natives.

'It did not occur to Mr Burke or any one to leave any mark on the tree?'[149] asks Sir Francis, not bothering to hide his own incredulity.

'No,' replies King. 'We did not expect the party would return; we thought the word "Dig" would answer our purpose as well as it would theirs.'[150]

King's own face as he says this once again shows that he remains haunted by how close they had come to salvation . . . only to miss out. Just one more word carved on the tree, and they would have been saved!

Now comes the most tragic part of the tale. The exhausted, starving trio, dressed in rags, getting colder, slower and more desperate, trying to find the way to Mount Hopeless only to become ever more hopeless themselves. The struggle then to simply survive by relying on the natives and their nardoo, only for Mr Burke and Mr Wills to grow ever weaker by the day and then by the hour until . . .

His voice now a raspy whisper, the sounds of a broken man, King tells of Mr Wills's heroism, his selfless request that the two stronger ones leave him, to go for help.

And now Sir Francis returns to the question of responsibility, of how it is that the leader of the expedition is left in such a state and by whom.

'During any part of your return journey to the creek are you aware if you had exceeded three months, or even four months, before you reached the Depot; or from what you heard do you know whether in Mr Burke's mind there was an idea of the party leaving the Depot?'[151] he asks.

'None,'[152] replies King, firmly and definitively. *None*. And now the witness is shaking with emotion, anger not nerves fuelling him.

'Suppose he had been away five months he would *still* have expected to find them there?'[153] asks Sir Francis.

'Yes, we should still have expected to find the party there,' answers King. 'Mr Burke said they should have remained at *any risk*'.[154]

There is a stir in the gallery. This comes, after all, from the mouth of one who was there at the time, from no less than the hero of Melbourne, about the greatest hero of all, Mr Burke. He affirms that the hardy group of heroes had all been expecting the Brahe party to be there, at any risk, and they *weren't*.

Likely sensing just how well his evidence is being received, nay, seized upon, King goes further, to tell the spellbound chamber, recounting the words the great man had said, not long before he died: 'King, this is nice treatment after fulfilling our task, to arrive where we left our companions where we had every right to expect them.'[155]

'Mr Burke, it is to be presumed, was exceedingly weak when you finally parted with him?'[156] asks Sir Francis.

'Yes, he walked till he dropped,'[157] says King, his body shaking and quaking now like his voice, before he suddenly bursts into tears, clearly undone by the horror of the memories he will spend the rest of his life trying to escape. From simple decency, Sir Thomas Pratt does now what clearly needs to be done.

'The Commission will not trouble you any further today,' he says quietly, his words echoing around the silent room over King's sobs, 'and they are exceedingly obliged for the clear statement you have made.'[158]

John King exits the witness box, his shoulders still heaving with emotion, the entire room half-expecting he will fall to the ground at any moment from the pain of it all.

•

In the stand now is the leader of the party that found John King and the bodies of Burke and Wills, Mr Alfred Howitt, who has just arrived from Menindee this morning – come to Melbourne to both testify, and to seek further instruction from the Committee about the retrieval of the bodies of Messrs Burke and Wills. Howitt's testimony is like his exploring: clear and concise, with no frills, and not a word wasted. He has little to add to the journals he has already published concerning the course of his rescue expedition. As for the Commissioners, they are most respectful of Mr Howitt's answers and his sadly belated rescue efforts, but there is one point Sir Thomas Pratt is particularly curious about.

'Do you believe it would have been possible for Mr Burke and Mr Wills to have followed down the route to Menindee at that time, in the state they were in?'[159] he asks.

Howitt pauses. Say the truth? That it was madness from the first, and so slur the name of the venerated leader? No. Much better to be diplomatic.

'It would depend entirely upon the state they were in,'[160] he answers carefully.

But Sir Thomas will not let him escape this easily.

'You have *heard* what state they were in?'[161] he asks again.

'If they had strength enough,' Howitt replies, declining once more to be disrespectful, 'they could have followed it down.'[162]

'Do you think with 40 days' provisions they might have made Menindee from Cooper's Creek, if in the ordinary state of health?'[163]

'With horses in good order?'[164]

'No,' says Sir Thomas firmly. 'Just as they were – on foot?'[165]

'They could not,' replies Howitt firmly, 'because they could not carry 40 days' provisions on foot.'[166]

'Supposing they started [for Menindee] in that condition . . . *with one camel*?'[167] asks Sir Thomas.

Howitt pauses before replying. Ultimately however, Sir Thomas has given him only two options now. He must tell the truth, or lie . . . and he cannot do the latter.

'I think it is very possible they might have,' answers the Englishman finally. 'Or at any rate they would have got very near the Darling.'[168]

Sir Thomas has what he wants. Had Mr Burke chosen more wisely, and headed to Menindee instead of Mount Hopeless, even with just one camel, the strong impression is given, they would have likely survived.[169]

Thank you, Mr Howitt. Let us adjourn for the day. We will reconvene in five days time, on 10 December.

•

Four days later, Alfred Howitt is again the centre of attention as the Exploration Committee invites him and Edwin Welch to attend their meeting in the Royal Society hall. They are to be farewelled, as they are about to return north to Cooper's Creek this evening.

Sir William Stawell presides at the head of the table.

The first item to be discussed is a little delicate, an application to join Howitt's expedition, and if you will permit, Sir William, Dr Macadam would like to read it to the gathering.

Go ahead.

It is from Mr John King . . .

> St. Kilda,
> 6 December 1861.
>
> Sir,
> *As it is the intention of the Government to have the remains of my respected leaders, Messrs Burke and Wills conveyed to town, I therefore offer my services for the occasion. Also that I may be able to ascertain if it was the remains of Charles Gray that Mr McKinlay has discovered.*
> *I am, Sir, your obedient servant,*
>
> *John King.*[170]

In response, all eyes turn to Alfred Howitt.

'I would be most happy to have Mr King with me,' the ascetic Englishman replies, 'but I am afraid that at this season of the year, and under all circumstances, it would scarcely be fair towards Mr King to accept his offer. In his present condition, it would hardly be right to ask him to go as far as Menindee.'[171]

A murmur of approbation moves through the room. (*Hear, hear.*)

Sir William, as ever, perfectly encapsulates the mood of the meeting by noting that, 'The letter from Mr King is just what might have been expected from him, but, at the same time, it would be positive cruelty to let him go.'[172] (*Hear, hear.*)

With that, the matter is resolved, Mr Howitt and Mr Welch take their leave, readying to catch the train north to Woodend this evening – both, however, cognisant that a few other matters will be resolved by the Committee this afternoon, and the decisions communicated to them before they go.

Which brings us, gentlemen, to the even more delicate matter before us, the real reason this meeting has been called – the *bodies*, just what do we want the Howitt expedition to achieve this time? Which corpses, exactly, should they bring back?

While the Legislative Assembly had passed a resolution calling for the remains of Burke and Wills to be brought back, the Exploration Committee later passed a motion calling for *all* the deceased to be found, dug up and reburied in Melbourne. Aware of the great cost of such a venture and the fact that parliament will not foot the bill for a motion in direct opposition to their own, the Treasurer of the Committee now hopes to nip this mass body retrieval in the bud.

Dr Wilkie is insistent, and moves: 'That the resolution of the Committee to bring down the remains of Dr Becker and others who perished in the late Expedition, be rescinded before Mr Howitt's departure.'[173]

After all, as he speaks in favour of his own motion, 'I look upon the remains of Burke and Wills as public property, but the remains of the others are private property only.'[174]

For his part, Royal Society member and long-time editor of *Melbourne Punch*, James Smith, supported by Messrs Elliott and Gillbee, is equally firm that no bones at all should be retrieved, as if they are brought back they will inevitably be displayed in some fashion, and that 'would do away with all the solemnity of a funeral'.

Captain Cadell speaks in favour of Dr Becker's remains, at least, being retrieved along with those of Messrs Burke and Wills, as he was an officer and a gentleman, not to mention a member of the Royal Society, and anything less would be a slight on Melbourne's strong German community.

Sir William Stawell, however, is firm in his own views, which carry a lot of weight in this forum.

'I cannot see,' he says, 'that because honour is shown to the leaders, dishonour would be shown to those under their command.'[175]

Besides which, as he notes, the parliament has already decided on this matter, and generously agreed to fund the retrieval of the bodies of Burke and Wills. The Exploration Committee can hardly override parliament.

So it proceeds, as the argument courses back and forth across the table. In the end it is put to a vote, with five men coming down, for and against the motion, leaving the deciding vote to Sir William who ... gives a nod to a yes, and the resolution is carried.

Only the remains of Burke and Wills will be retrieved.

(Lockhart Morton, naturally, rages against the motion as it stands.

'The last sad act in this tragedy has yet to be performed,' he writes in one of a series of accusatory articles for the *Yeoman and Australian Acclimatiser* on the subject. 'The remains of the two unfortunate brave men are not to be allowed to rest in peace in the graves that best become them; their bones are to be shaken in canvas-bags, on horseback, over a thousand miles. Every part of the tragedy will then be complete, and the dark curtain may fall.'[176])

That evening, Howitt and Welch leave Melbourne Town with firm instructions to retrieve the bodies of Messrs Burke and Wills. Even if the Committee does change its mind, it may well be no easy matter to get the message to them in time, as one Trooper Myles Archibald Lyons might very well attest.

10 December '61, Melbourne, Royal Commission, a present witness, a missing letter

When the Royal Commission reconvenes the next day, 10 December, there is particular interest, as the bushman thought by most to be the true villain of the whole disaster, William Wright, is finally to appear. His £100 has been paid and, for once, he is here on time, as expected, and not five months late!

Sir Francis Murphy quickly gets to the nub of the issue – the position Mr Burke conferred on him.

'What was that appointment?'[177]

'Third in command, if the Committee in Melbourne approved . . .'[178] Wright replies.

'Subject to *their approval*?'[179] queries Sir Francis.

'Yes,'[180] Wright replies firmly, not remotely fussed at his interlocutor's rather badgering tone.

Sir Francis begins to understand. This is no backward bushman. It is true that he is not an educated man, but he speaks with a confident authority, and he will remain firm that he could not head back north until he had formally received *the approval of the Committee*. It is his perfect shield against the slings and arrows of any attack, because it not only protects him, but also deflects those attacks right to where he thinks they should go, right at Dr Macadam and the grandees of the Royal Society.

Why, Mr Burke had made that clear from the first, in the dispatch Wright had been given to take back to Menindee, informing the Committee of his appointment subject to the *approval of the Committee*.

'What did you do when you got that dispatch?'[181]

'I came back to Menindee.'[182]

'There were no other writings?'[183]

'No.'[184]

'No other dispatches brought *back*?'[185] Sir Francis presses.

'I believe there was a dispatch from Mr Wills too, as far as I can recollect, but the dispatches were enclosed in one envelope, if I recollect rightly. I also sent down a letter to the Committee myself at the same time.'[186]

What? Another letter? One written by Wright himself? This has not been mentioned before. It is a potentially explosive revelation, and Sir Thomas Pratt follows up hard.

'Did you ask in your letter to the Committee to have your appointment confirmed?'[187] he asks.

'I just merely stated what Mr Burke had mentioned to me.'[188]

Will Dr Macadam please retake the stand, to . . .

Oh.

He is already there.

No, Dr Macadam booms, his face now as red as his beard and mane, burning with scorn and anger, as he glowers at Wright. Not only did he receive no such letter, he has never heard of it, and nor has anyone else on the Committee.

Thank you, Dr Macadam.

Perhaps, Mr Wright, Sir Thomas asks, you have a copy of that letter?

'I have not,'[189] replies Wright.

An acknowledgement by the Royal Society?

'No, it never was answered at all . . .'[190]

But Wright is resolute. It *was* posted at the same time as Mr Burke's dispatch.

'It was a distinct letter by itself.'[191]

Let us leave that for a moment, then, and get to the real heart of the issue before us. Your delay, Mr Wright. The fact that you arrived back in Menindee at the beginning of November, with instructions to quickly return, and yet didn't get going until the end of January!

'From the 5th of November until then seems an enormous time to remain inactive,'[192] notes Sir Francis, a trifle acidly. 'Did you keep any journal?'

'No, I did not,' replies Wright.

'Now remember what I am saying,' Sir Francis presses. 'From the 6th November to the 19th December we have no record of what took place. What was the party doing during the whole of that long time?'[193]

'Merely looking after the stock, either the camels or the horses,' answers Wright. 'In fact, I did not know what to do, not having had any instructions from the Committee.'[194]

'You *knew* the nature of the country and that it was a bad season,' responds Sir Francis. 'And you *knew* that Mr Burke had gone out at an unfavourable time of the year, and yet *nothing was done*.'[195]

Perhaps it is not quite a direct accusation that Wright's actions are responsible for all the deaths, but only a legalistic split hair from the wig of my learned friend separates it from being exactly that.

Mr Wright is not fussed.

'I was waiting for orders according to Mr Burke's arrangements with me,' Wright replies stoutly.

'But it appears from his letters,' Sir Thomas intones gravely, 'that Mr Burke expected you to follow him so closely as to reach Cooper's Creek some *two or three days* after he started from it. Can you account for that?'[196]

'I do not know how he could have supposed so,' says Wright.

Sir Thomas Pratt, clearly frustrated to distraction at this witness's obstinate refusal to head into the legal corral he has opened the gate to, reads out Mr Burke's dispatch once more, emphasising his desire to be 'followed up' as soon as possible. Now as I read Mr Burke's very words to you, is it not clear what he wanted?

No, not to Mr Wright, it is not.

'Indeed,' the bushman says, entirely unmoved, 'Mr Burke used to alter his mind so very often that it was not possible, at times, to understand what he really did mean.'[197]

Examples? Oh, yes, Wright has quite a few.

'There was a distinct understanding that Mr Burke would send back the camels, and most likely the whole of the horses, after reaching Cooper's Creek. He took *fifteen horses*! I told him that if I did not catch the mail at Menindee it would make a fortnight's difference. Mr Burke made me understand that he would remain at Cooper's Creek, and not attempt the larger journey until I joined him.'[198]

So many assertions of who said what to whom when, and most of them contradictory! It is a muddle, a mess, a mass of allegations and accounts, none of which slot with each other.

Seeking to make one last attempt to at least establish that Mr Wright is untruthful, Mr Hervey now draws Wright's attention to the fact that while his account today depicts the reunited parties of Mr Brahe and himself as being in a quite pathetic state, his impressions recorded in his written journal are the opposite. 'There is some allusion in your journal, after you were joined by Mr Brahe, to the spectacle being an imposing one,' he states.[199]

Sir Thomas Pratt has noted this contradiction too.

'You say that "the cavalcade made quite an imposing appearance."'[200]

Well, Mr Wright? Your answer?

His response is as simple as it is staggering.

I wrote no such thing in the journal.

I did not write any journal.

Mr Hodgkinson wrote the journal.

'That was only an extravagant expression on the part of Mr Hodgkinson,'[201] Wright explains. 'There were two camels which, at the time, could hardly put one leg before the other.'[202]

Thank you, Mr Wright, that will be all for today.

And so the £100 witness steps down from the stand, having presented something that was less testimony and more a wall, an impregnable barrier entirely resistant to the probes of the Commissioners to work out what happened. It is a wall that is still entirely intact, as he grudging submits to further questioning at the next sitting on 12 December.

•

So let us resume, Mr Wright, with your assertion that Mr Hodgkinson did most of the writing, so it was his embellishments that explain your inconsistencies. Now, Sir Francis wishes to know, did Mr Hodgkinson also write the dispatch then, the one finally sent by Mr Wright on the nineteenth?

'Hodgkinson did all the writing,'[203] says Mr Wright.

'Did he write the one that is stated to be missing?'[204] asks Sir Francis.

'No, he did not,'[205] replies Wright.

'*You* wrote that one?'[206] asks Sir Francis.

Mr Wright begins to understand what Sir Francis is getting at. How does an illiterate man write a letter?

'I wrote that with my own hand,' Wright says firmly. 'I just wrote a few words.'[207]

So, *not* illiterate then. Interesting.

'Could your memory serve you sufficiently,' asks Sir Francis, as if he is in fact only mildly interested, 'to write the purport of that letter that is missing?'[208]

'It would not,'[209] replies Wright. Oddly, Sir Francis looks pleased with the response, but goes on.

'Have you no recollection of the general purport of it?'[210]

'I just mentioned that Mr Burke had appointed me to take the party out and take the command. That is about the heads of it.'[211]

At last, Sir Francis asks his real question, 'Have you any objection to write a letter similar to that one, as nearly as you can remember it?'[212]

In other words, can you write a letter for us, Mr Wright? Just a short one? Just a line to show you can write at all, Mr Wright? Would you care to demonstrate your claimed literacy?

'No. I write a very indifferent hand,'[213] answers Mr Wright lamely.

A very indifferent hand? A non-existent hand, that is the implication Sir Francis is making.

Thank you, Mr Wright. You may step down, for the moment.

•

Now, for something completely different, the next witness is not a bushman, nor even a member of the expedition. The next witness is . . . a man of the law. In fact, it is none other than 'His Honour Sir William Foster Stawell, Knight, Chief Justice of the Colony', who was also the Chairman of the Exploration Committee. Oddly, this judge, the most eminent jurist in the land, is about to be examined by a doctor, Sir Francis Murphy – the rough equivalent of having an appendectomy performed by a lawyer, without a scalpel.

And yet, there is no doubt that Sir Francis is probing enough, soon getting to one of the key questions.

'Were the correspondence and dispatches that came down from Mr Burke,' Sir Francis begins, 'always laid before the Committee and attended to?'[214]

'Yes,' replies Sir William. 'They were always read, commented on, and discussed.'[215]

'And generally they were published in the newspapers the next day?'[216]

'They were invariably published,' Sir William corrects him. 'And generally the next day.'[217]

Understood.

'Directing your attention to the first dispatch which arrived from Mr Burke after he left Menindee, the dispatch which he wrote at Torowoto and sent back by Mr Wright to Menindee. That was forwarded by post, and it appears from the documents of the Committee that that arrived here upon the 3rd of December?'[218]

'Yes, early in December,'[219] replies Sir William, a little shorter now, knowing that his fellow Knight has to ask a slightly trickier question, so that justice may not only be done, but be seen to be done, and the key question for him to answer is coming.

'In looking over the newspapers at the reports of the proceedings of the Committee,' says Sir Francis, 'it does not appear that anything was done with respect to that dispatch. There seems to have been no notice taken of it?'[220]

There it is. *Nothing was done. No notice was given*, Sir William, by the Committee which you chaired.

'The dispatch was read and considered,' replies Sir William smoothly. 'I have a distinct recollection of that dispatch being laid before the Committee soon after its receipt, and that, so far as my memory serves me, was as soon as it could be. A meeting was called, the dispatch was read, and the Committee discussed it. There was no formal resolution proposed or passed, simply because, in the opinion of the Committee, any answer whatever to it, would be too late.'[221]

Sir Francis goes on to quote Mr Burke's dispatch at length, focusing particularly on the following two sentences: 'Perhaps I might find it advisable to leave a depot at Cooper's Creek, and go on with a small party to examine the country beyond it. *Under any circumstances it is desirable that we should be soon followed up.*'[222]

Sir Francis now makes his point as clear as crystal: 'There is a very strong expression there about being soon followed up, but it does *not* appear that *any letter* was forwarded from the Committee to Mr Wright or the party at Menindee on the receipt of this letter. The Committee were aware that Mr Burke had gone on, but it does *not appear* that *any* dispatch was forwarded to Mr Wright or the party at Menindee with respect to Mr Burke being followed up?'[223]

Well, Sir William?

'The omission to do so, if omission it was,' Sir William cautiously concedes, 'arose from the construction the Committee put upon the letter received from Mr Burke, and from Mr Wright's silence: no communication was received from him.'[224]

'You considered,' Sir Francis suggests, rather in the manner of an expert angler baiting his hook, 'that it would be idle to attempt to communicate with Mr Wright, when, in fact, he would have started long before?'[225]

Sir William's 100-word reply of careful legal language, boils down to: more or less, yes, but also a bit of no. He is not biting today.

The salient fact he wishes the Royal Commission to focus on is that, as no official communications had been received from Mr Wright, the Exploration Committee's assumption had been that he had already departed with all speed.

But Sir Francis now has some further questions about letters received.

'The Committee also had, 10 December, *another letter* which was received from Dr Becker, dated Menindee, November the 27th,' he says. 'So that the Committee *must have been aware of the delay* taking place at the Darling at this time but nothing was done in fact until the 30th December, when Mr Wright's dispatch of December the 19th was brought down by Mr Hodgkinson?'[226]

Sir William prevaricates, but Sir Francis, with the greatest respect to the Chief Justice, will have none of it.

'Still the Commission wish to ascertain this point – the Committee were *aware* that the party were remaining at Menindee up to the date of Dr Beckler's letter of November 27th?'[227] asks Sir Francis.

Yes, well. After yet more prevarication, Sir William replies, carefully: 'According to my recollection they were not aware of it.'[228]

Ah, but while Sir Francis is not a lawyer, he knows that when legal people start using phrases like 'according to my recollection', you have them on the run.

Do you recall, Sir William, the meeting of the Exploration Committee you attended on 10 December, as reported by the *Argus*, which noted your presence?

Yes, Sir William does recall it.

Do you recall that the Committee received a letter from Ludwig Becker?

Yes, well, now that his memory is refreshed, Sir William *does*, perhaps, recall some sketches being sent by Dr Becker, but that 'letter', if letter it can be called, contained no information of weight.

Oh, yes it did, Sir William. The most damning information of all . . .

'But it was dated a full month after Mr Burke had left Torowoto,' says Sir Francis incredulously. 'Surely the Committee must have known that the party were at Menindee still, and yet they appear to have done nothing on that knowledge, or on the remark in Burke's letter that he was to be immediately followed up?'[229]

I mean, Sir William, not even any *discussion* of making reply, *no resolution* passed to that effect?

'The formality of passing a resolution that nothing should be done was not deemed necessary,'[230] Sir William quips acidly. If you wish to take him on, Sir Francis, be it known that the Chief Justice of Victoria will *not* be cowed.

Very well then. Nor is Sir Francis, who now demonstrates that mastering his brief has included trawling through old newspaper reports with a very beady eye indeed. Let us go to the account in the *Argus* of Mr Hodgkinson's dramatic meeting with the Committee on 31 December 1860. There is one part of the report that may interest you, Sir William.

'In the discussion which took place at the society's meeting when Mr Hodgkinson arrived in Melbourne,' Sir Francis proceeds, 'it was stated that a letter *confirming Mr Wright's appointment* had gone on to Mr Burke. Was there any truth in that?'[231]

'I never heard of it,'[232] replies a startled Sir William.

Oh yes you did, Sir William, because you were there! (Along with the Governor of Victoria! The *Argus* not only confirms it, but records Mr Hodgkinson saying in your presence: 'Mr Hodgkinson observed there were a few small accounts, amounting to about £30, which were incurred at the Menindee station, but which Mr Wright did not like to discharge, *as the ratification by the Committee of his appointment as third officer never reached him, the letter containing it having gone on to Mr Burke.*'

'You do not know anything about that . . . ?'[233] Sir Francis asks, quizzically. The way he says the words, it is almost as if *he*, Sir Francis, is the one who might be confused. But no one in the room can escape his elaborately respectful meaning. Surely, Sir William, *you* can't really be claiming that?

'I have no recollection of anything of the kind ever having passed,'[234] replies Sir William, a little wanly, his bravura gone, and though he is not beaten, he is certainly badly bruised. After a few more questions, he is excused, and clearly relieved to be so.

All watching know that they have seen a masterful examination of the Chief Justice, who has probably escaped with his good name intact, just, but only because the prestige of his office gives him an enormous benefit of the doubt. It is possible, for him, that the salient facts passed him by in the meeting.

Few think that the same can be said for the Committee and especially Dr Macadam, who surely *did* know of the delay; that Wright was not moving, that Mr Burke was not being supported. And yet they still did nothing!

A stir takes over the courtroom as the next witness is called. Why, it is none other than one of the most controversial figures in the entire saga, the former horse-trader, camel master and the first second officer of the expedition, Mr George James Landells.

From the outset, Mr Landells makes it clear he has a much different concept of what this Royal Commission is about than the Commissioners. He is not here to answer questions. He is here to ask them.

No sooner asked the simple question about how far he went on the journey, Landells sighs and replies: 'I shall be happy to give any information that lies in my power if the members [of the party] originally composing the expedition are here. Until [they are here] I cannot exonerate myself.'[235]

A bemused Sir Thomas Pratt is the first to answer this unorthodox demand.

'But it is impossible to have them here. There is no question of exonerating yourself or anyone else before the commission. We simply ask that you should supply any missing links of evidence.'[236]

But Mr Landells is not listening.

'I consider myself extremely ill-used,' he says with fire, 'and require to have evidence to prove that the statements brought against me by different gentlemen can[237] be cleared up. My character has been traduced . . .'[238]

Sir Francis Murphy cuts him off.

'You must understand that the question before the commission, is not . . .'[239]

'I should be very happy to give information,' says Mr Landells, interrupting his interrupter. 'But unless the gentlemen originally composing the Expedition are present I can't do it.'[240]

'Some of them are dead,'[241] responds Sir Francis drolly.

'I am to understand that justice is not to be had,'[242] says Mr Landells with an odd mixture of anger and self-pity. 'The doors of the Royal

Society have been shut against me and I have not been able to get justice from them . . .'[243]

'How could they all be here?' Mr Hervey says. 'We can't send all round the country for those who are alive.[244] We cannot order the persons to attend that you require.'[245]

'Mr Wright is *present*,'[246] Mr Landells replies, pointing the man in question out, and clearly still insistent that he, the King of the Camels, conduct his own Royal Commission into how he could possibly have been so ill-treated by the ingrates so unworthy to have him on their expedition.

Mr Sullivan explains: Mr Wright is here, as you are, to give evidence.

'The object of the commission is to obtain information from those persons who can throw some light on the subject. Further than that we are not disposed to go.'[247]

And they mean it. With Mr Landells's continued refusal to give testimony in a manner appropriate, he is ordered to retire, less than 10 minutes after appearing. Whatever else, at least the Commission can see, better than ever, how difficult it must have been to have such a man as second officer of the expedition, let alone share a tent with him.

At least the next witness, Mr Thomas Dick, is more co-operative, likely because he has not come to defend his own reputation, but that of another dear to him – Charley Gray.

For having read the evidence of Mr John King pertaining to Charley having had his health ruined by drinking too much in the public house where he worked at Swan Hill, Mr Dick is not happy. For that pub, you see, is owned and run by himself, Thomas Dick, and he has come here specifically to restore Charley's unfairly sullied reputation.

'When any of my servants get the worse for drink, I make it a point to sack them at once,'[248] says Mr Dick. 'Gray was the only man I could fall back on.'

Do tell? Then maybe apologies should be made for having doubted Mr Gray's general sobriety. And yet, Mr Dick's character reference has a short way to go, as he continues . . .

'He has, of course, been repeatedly the worse for liquor, when I gave him his wage. I make it a point to pay all my men once a month. He would go on the spree for an afternoon. A general tippler, he was not.'[249]

Mr Dick earnestly continues, entirely oblivious to the grins breaking out around the courtroom, like blooming daisies in the spring, after a long winter.

'In fact, being in a public-house,' he says, 'one might be led to suppose that Charley was continually on the drink, and he wasn't. He only had some six or seven sprees in 18 months.'[250]

The Hon. Mr Hervey cannot resist.

'That is *very* good,'[251] says he, as the whole court explodes into laughter, and for a few moments it is not a gathering of Commissioners, press and witnesses trying to get to the bottom of a serious matter, so much as fellow citizens enjoying Mr Dick's uniquely Australian standard of sobriety.

Thomas Dick, however, is stung. This is *important*. Charley's reputation has to be defended and he is the one to defend it.

'Charley was a steady, hardy man, and an able bushman,'[252] he insists. 'I have no hesitation in saying a better bushman was not to be found.'[253]

Fair enough, then. No employee ever had a more stalwart defender of his reputation than the worthy Thomas Dick. You are excused, sir, so we may examine Mr Wright one last time.

Let us get straight to it. For what we all want to know is: How is it that you received confirmation of your appointment and the requisite money on the 9th of January, and yet it still took you 17 days before you *got going*?

Well, Mr Wright explains, it was not an easy matter to obtain horses of sufficient quality and at a fair price.

Mr Wright, you sent a dispatch, on the nineteenth of December 1861, saying to the Committee that you *could not move* because you had too few camels and horses. But now, to the Commission, you persistently say this was *not* the reason at all, the reason was that you wanted your appointment confirmed. So which of these two statements is true? They cannot both be true?

'In fact there were two reasons,' replies Wright. 'That we had not sufficient carrying power was one thing, and another thing was . . .'[254]

'We simply want you to reconcile the two statements,' interrupts Mr Hervey. 'Because in the first statement you make no allusion whatever to the second.'[255]

'The letter is not worded in the way I intended at all,'[256] explains Wright. But Mr Hervey is not satisfied with the explanation. He wants the question answered. *'Can you reconcile the two statements?'*[257]

'I can give no answer further than the one I have given already,' replies an irritable Wright. 'The dispatch in question was written by Mr Hodgkinson, and was worded very differently from what I intended.'[258]

'It is signed by your name?' asks Mr Hervey.

'Yes, it is. It was read over to me,'[259] agrees Wright.

'Do you suppose Burke anticipated the detention of your party at the Darling for two months? Had he any idea of the kind?'[260] continues Mr Hervey.

'Certainly he had, because he questioned me about the mail, and how long it would take to send a dispatch to the Darling,'[261] responds Wright.

'You don't mention it in the dispatch,'[262] notes Sir Thomas Pratt.

'There were a good many things I did not mention in the dispatch,'[263] Wright replies tartly.

'But in the dispatch . . .' continues Mr Hervey, now near the point of losing his temper, 'I mean, you evidently did not intend to lose a moment?'[264]

'I intended to stop at Menindee till I got my appointment confirmed,' replies Mr Wright as he has so many times before, 'and another reason was that I was waiting for Lyons and MacPherson.'[265]

And now Mr Hervey does lose his temper, and his angry sarcasm is let loose: 'Then, *under any circumstances*, you would *not* have started till your appointment was confirmed, even if you had had *fifty* horses and camels?'[266]

'No, I should not,'[267] replies Mr Wright, getting angry himself. And again he lists his reasons, adding that, 'Letters were sent down by every mail and never answered' and that, 'Mr Burke knew I should not start till I had sent my wife and family home; and I did not know how long the steamer would be.'[268]

On top of that, Burke had told him that Mr Brahe would come down with the horses, some of the 15 horses standing doing nothing at Cooper's Creek, to help to move supplies, and, 'Mr Brahe told me several times that he was to be one of the persons sent back'[269].

Mr Wright's long listing and complaining has finished but Mr Hervey has not, barking: '*Do you consider you have answered the question, and reconciled the two statements?*'[270]

But Mr Wright makes no reply. He has tired of this charade and, from his side, is putting a stop to it. Mr Wright now considers the £100 fee has been more than earned, and he simply refuses to answer any more questions.

Mr Hervey can scarcely believe it.

'I wish to point out to you that *if you do not answer* that question properly, you stand in a very awkward position before the Committee.'[271]

So be it. Call Mr Wright awkward, he still will not speak further, and sits in silent contempt of the Commissioners.

Very well then. You are excused from this gathering, Mr Wright, but the expressions of the Commissioners make it clear that he is unlikely to be excused in their report for his role in this disaster.

And now, unusually, Mr Brahe is called back to give further testimony – not because any Commissioner desires it, but because it is the earnest request of Dr Wills that the German answer some questions concerning his son's clothes. The Commission has agreed, only insisting that his questions, are put 'through the Chairman'.

'I wish to know,' asks Dr Wills, 'whether a portmanteau was left with you belonging to Mr Wills, my son?'[272]

'Yes,' replies Brahe. 'A bag, a calico bag containing clothes.'[273]

'You were aware it was his own property?'[274] says Dr Wills, his voice steady though his face shows his anger clearly.

'I was,'[275] answers Brahe.

'What made you take those clothes back to Menindee, and not leave them in the cache?'[276] presses Dr Wills, his mind filled with the image of his poor boy shivering and dying in rags.

'Mr Wills was as well supplied with clothes as any other member of that party, and I did certainly not think they would be in want of clothes,'[277] replies Brahe.

'Are you not aware that those clothes might have saved his life?'[278]

Mr Brahe looks straight at the father of the dead man, and answers with a voice equally full of emotion, albeit a different one.

'I know a great many things now, that I could not know then,'[279] he says, his voice breaking. 'If I had known then what I know now, I would rather have perished than have left Cooper's Creek.'[280]

The whole room falls silent, under the heady weight of William Brahe's regret.

There is but one more witness for the Commission today and it is Dr Macadam, seeking to clear up Mr Wright's slanderous contention that because he had received no replies to the letters he had sent, the Committee in general and he, Dr Macadam, in particular, was somehow negligent. The Hon. Secretary wishes to note the formal instructions to officers, wherein it is made clear that all such dispatches are to be sent through the leader, and *only* through the leader. No matter that the leader in question had disappeared into the gaping maw of northern Australia, the fact that officers' letters did not come through Mr Burke meant that, although they had been received, they had not been *officially* received, and so there was no need for Dr Macadam to make an official reply.

I beg your pardon?

Sir Francis Murphy, incredulous, can bear it no more.

'That does not affect the question of the statement made by Mr Wright,' Sir Francis interrupts sharply. 'His object was to show the fact that the Committee were in possession of the fact that they were at Menindee?'[281]

Suddenly there is a stirring from behind, of someone jumping to their feet.

'That was the *only* reason!'[282] William Wright bellows from the gallery.

A blow has been struck at Dr Macadam. There is no way around it: it matters not whether the Hon. Secretary of the Exploration Committee knew officially or unofficially, the point is he knew!

He knew that Mr Burke was relying on Mr Wright to head north, that Wright had not moved at all, and still he did nothing!

On the afternoon of 30 December 1861, the Commission into the Burke and Wills saga is brought to a close. The Commissioners have elicited a mass of contradictory and extraordinary evidence, which they must consider, before assembling their report.

In the meantime, all the people of Melbourne and Australia can do is wait, none more keenly than the furious Dr William Wills, the concerned Dr John Macadam and the desperately worried Mr William Brahe – while William Wright, wherever he is, does not appear much fussed either way.

CHAPTER EIGHTEEN

THE VERDICT, THE FUNERAL

The curse of SHAKESPEARE be on him who suggested the removal of the bones! They could not have lain better, in a fitter or more solemn tomb, than under the canopy of heaven, in the desert where the betrayed heroes lay down and died. A simple mound of stones was all the monument they required ... It is a poor honour we do by disturbing those in death whom in life we abandoned. And the most miserable mockery of all is surely to make the Exploration Committee the managers of the funeral – to permit the betrayers of the dead to superintend their obsequies – to handle their bones and befoul their coffins, 'And vex the unhappy dust they would not save.'[1]

> The Argus, 5 January 1863

When the sculptured marble, soon to be reared, has passed away, the story of the heroism of Burke and Wills will yet live. The thousands who crowded the streets came not only to witness a spectacle, they tendered willing homage to those who had died in the service of their country. They were instinct with those emotions which form a people into a nation.[2]

> The Argus, 22 January 1863

If ever a story could excite a people to lasting admiration of the dead, it was the plain unvarnished tale of the sufferings and death of those gallant men, and, when the tale was told, the heart of the colony beat high with admiration of the lost leaders of its first exploring party, and resolved to do them national honour[3]

> The Argus, October 1862

21 February '62, Victorian Parliament, a verdict returned

And so to the day that all of Victoria has been waiting for, the day that the Royal Commission finally hands down its findings. Unlike other worthy but dull government reports that are equally handed down, to so often sit on a table in the legislature to moulder for months, this one has no sooner landed than it is grasped by the members present, who just as quickly flick through the pages, their eyes moving back and forth, looking for the key names, and working out who has been condemned, criticised and exonerated. Well, gentlemen . . . *what does it say?*

'May it please your Excellency,' the report begins in that ruthlessly neutral legal tone that gives the rest of its assertions so much force, 'in conformity with the terms of Her Majesty's commission, we have made enquiry into the circumstances connected with the suffering and death of Robert O'Hara Burke and William John Wills, the Victorian explorers. We have endeavoured to ascertain the true causes of this lamentable result of the expedition . . .'4

And here it comes . . .

'The expedition, having been provided and equipped in the most ample and liberal manner, and having reached Menindee, on the Darling, without experiencing any difficulties, was most injudiciously divided at that point by Mr Burke. It was an error of judgment on the part of Mr Burke to appoint Mr Wright to an important command in the expedition, without a previous personal knowledge of him . . .'5

Here, then, is the first apportioned blame, with Mr Burke himself – surprisingly, for many observers – being already found wanting on two counts, while it is clear that there will be more grief to come for Mr Wright.

'Mr Burke evinced a far greater amount of zeal than prudence in finally departing from Cooper's Creek before the depot party had arrived from Menindee, and without having secured communication with the settled districts as he had been instructed to do; and, in undertaking so extended a journey with an insufficient supply of provisions, Mr Burke was forced into the necessity of overtaxing the powers of his party, whose continuous and unremitting exertions resulted in the destruction of his animals, and the prostration of himself and his companions from fatigue and severe privation.'6

Again, blame for Burke! Ah, but here is the blame that will be most popular with the press and public alike.

'The conduct of Mr Wright appears to have been reprehensible in the highest degree ... It seems extremely improbable that Mr Wright could have misconstrued the intentions of his leader so far, as to suppose that he ever calculated for a moment on his remaining for any length of time on the Darling, Mr Wright has failed to give any satisfactory explanation of the causes of his delay; and to that delay are mainly attributable the whole of the disasters of the expedition, with the exception of the death of Gray. The grave responsibility of not having left a larger supply of provisions, together with some clothing, in the cache, at Cooper's Creek, rests with Mr Wright.'[7]

As to those who had first organised the expedition, and were then charged with sustaining them from afar?

'The Exploration Committee, in overlooking the importance of the contents of Mr Burke's dispatch from Torowoto, and in not urging Mr Wright's departure from the Darling, committed errors of a serious nature. A means of knowledge of the delay of the party at Menindee was in the possession of the Committee, not indeed by direct communication to that effect, but through the receipt of letters from Drs Becker and Beckler at various dates up to the end of November – without, however, awakening the Committee to a sense of the vital importance of Mr Burke's request in that dispatch that he should "be soon followed up" – or to a consideration of the disastrous consequences which would be likely to result and did unfortunately result, from the fatal inactivity and idling of Mr Wright and his party on the Darling.'[8]

And what of William Brahe's culpability?

'We are of opinion,' the Commissioners' report continues, 'that a responsibility far beyond his expectations devolved upon him; and it must be borne in mind, that, with the assurance of his leader, and his own conviction, he might each day expect to be relieved by Mr Wright, he still held his post for four months and five days, and that only when pressed by the appeals of a comrade sickening even to death, as was subsequently proved, his powers of endurance gave way ...'[9]

In sum, Mr Brahe's decision to leave the Depot was a 'most unfortunate'[10] one, yes, and perhaps worthy of censure, but his actions were borne of a 'conscientious desire to discharge his duty'[11], and the tragic outcome of his decision must be cause for his own 'painful reflection' and 'agonising thought', punishment enough for a young man whose initial terms of employment were one of a worker.

Back, then, to the leaders, and one in particular who was not always so conscientious in discharging his duty, especially in his record-keeping.

'It does not appear that Mr Burke kept any regular journal,' the Commissioners point out, 'or that he gave written instructions to his officers. Had he performed [any of] these essential portions of the duties of a leader, many of the calamities of the expedition might have been averted, and little or no room would have been left for doubt in judging the conduct of those subordinates who pleaded unsatisfactory and contradictory verbal orders and statements.'[12]

And there you have it, gentlemen. Mr Wright stands condemned, Mr Brahe receives some deserved criticism but is partially exonerated, the Exploration Committee receives a sharp slap on the wrist, while the gallant and daring but nevertheless mercurial and too often erratic Mr Burke suffers no more than having some of his hasty and unwise decisions placed in a stern light.

Is that all then? The sensation passed? The carnival moves on? The *Ovens and Murray Advertiser* thinks so, reflecting the general feeling that, 'The opinions of the Commissioners will be generally concurred in by those who will carefully and calmly look through the evidence . . .'[13]

Perhaps Dr Macadam is the counter that proves the point? For he does not look through the verdict calmly at all – but with some distress – and does *not* concur with the opinions of the Commissioners, most particularly when it comes to his own actions. Stung by the criticism, by the whispers and sly pointing that his mere presence now attracts on the streets of Melbourne, by the snubs daily delivered by the likes of the infuriating Dr Wills, by his dimming political prospects, he is more determined than ever that a glorious funeral for Burke and Wills, once their bodies at last arrive, will allow him to remove the stain of blame from his name.

And, of course, Dr Wills himself is furious at the report. How could the Commissioners come to such benign conclusions, on the evidence presented?

'The apathy, stupidity, and carelessness of Wright and Brahe are really beyond comprehension,' he writes. 'The effect of their miserably evasive and contradictory evidence, when under examination, can never be forgotten by those who were present.'[14]

It is the official absolution delivered to Brahe that particularly gets his goat; Brahe – the very man who had abandoned his post sooner than he needed to, had left insufficient provisions and had taken William Wills's warm clothes with him! As Dr Wills later writes, the Commissioners have 'an unaccountable tendency to feel sympathy for Brahe, whose evidence left it difficult to decide whether stupidity, selfishness, or utter disregard of truth was his leading deficiency'.[15]

Now, when it comes to the Commissioners' official view of Mr Burke, Dr Wills finds their 'judgment most severe on the leader who sacrificed his life, and whose mistakes would have been less serious and fatal had his orders been obeyed. There is also a disposition to deal leniently with the far heavier errors and omissions of the Exploration Committee.'

So Mr Brahe is excused, Mr Wright vanishes off to the bush without any charge recommended, Dr Macadam suffers mere embarrassment, while poor Dr Wills suffers a daily torment at the loss of his son? It cannot be tolerated.

In response, Dr Wills resolves to write his own, truthful, account of what happened on the expedition, to set both the record straight, and a fox loose in the henhouse of the guilty.

Lockhart Morton has also taken a very dim view of proceedings, and, having taken careful note of every half truth, every evasion, every outright lie uttered by such as the perfidious Dr Macadam, now embarks on writing a whole series of missives for the newspapers that will not only give a straight account, but, more importantly, call to account those responsible for the whole catastrophe. Of course Mr Burke was brave. But he was also foolhardy, surpassed only by the damn fools who had picked him in the first place.

9 December '62, Adelaide, 'Do not repine, my friends, do not weep for me'[16]

It has been almost a year but at last, after having waited for so long to hear from Alfred Howitt, word has come to Dr John Macadam:

> Arrived in Adelaide last night.
> The remains will be brought in on December 11 and are to be met by the Mayor and others on their way through Adelaide.
> They will remain at the Mounted Police Barracks until removed for Melbourne.
> We shall not be able to leave until after the 17th.
> A W Howitt,
> Leader, Victorian Exploring party.[17]

Howitt's trip from Melbourne to Cooper's Creek and back down to Adelaide has gone smoothly, even if its duration was longer than planned, as he took the opportunity to do some more explorations while out there. Coming back, the trek from the Depot to the first cattle station past Mount Hopeless – the very journey on which Mr Burke had bet the lives of the Gulf party – had taken Howitt and his men just 14 days. In contemplating Burke's bet, Howitt would maintain that, 'in the state in which Burke, Wills and King were it would have required at least twice that time for them to get there, even if they had no hindrance on the way'[18].

15 December '62, Royal Society Hall, funeral finagling

As ever with a meeting of the Exploration Committee – and never moreso since their grand public venture had turned to an excruciating public disaster – the discussion around the table on this day is robust.

At issue is the coming funeral for Burke and Wills. How big should it be?

From the beginning, Dr John Macadam leads the charge against the strong view elsewhere around the table that it should be held at St James' Cathedral with as much pageantry as Melbourne can turn for the occasion.

In fact, he believes there is no necessity for *any* funeral service. Just let it be done at the graveside. St James' Cathedral, then? No. It would be a matter of impossibility to stop a procession of such magnitude, in order that the funeral service might be performed.

By contrast, he says, 'If the funeral service is entirely performed at the grave, and the priest sufficiently elevated to enable the audience to see him, it would have an imposing and solemn effect.'[19]

Not at all. The response from the Chair, Dr Wilkie, is insistent. The public will demand nothing less than the full funeral at St James, with a long cortege proceeding through the streets, and he is robustly supported by other Committee members. The Church of England can decide the exact content of the funeral itself.

Now to the details of the procession . . .

For after some two years of the Committee arguing over everything to do with the expedition that Burke and Wills were on, it seems fitting they now argue over what, effectively, has resulted from their arguments: the corpses of Burke and Wills. Should the bodies of the explorers lie in state when they arrive in Melbourne, and if so, for how long? Who will receive special invitations and be allowed to join the official mourning group? In what order will they go in the procession? Will we have coaches to go with the funeral carriage, or is it better we walk? The deliberations go on and, despite oft furious argument, the decisions are made. Let us, for example, at least agree with one member, who insists that 'the clergy ought to walk, and before the body, as they open the gates of heaven. The Protestants might precede, and the Roman Catholics immediately follow.'[20] No, says another, quite the reverse, with the Roman Catholics first! And so it goes as, bit by bit, the structure of the funeral is resolved.

Yet there remains one more thing to do before the meeting closes.

Opening a telegram that has just arrived, Dr Macadam reads it out to the gathering: it comes from the Commissioner of Crown Lands in South Australia, Henry Strangways, and it informs Dr Macadam that Stuart and his party 'have returned safely'[21] to Chambers Creek, near Lake Torrens, and Stuart is expected to arrive in Adelaide soon.

Dawn, 28 December '62, Hobson's Bay, a final arrival

Oh, how different it had been with the landing of the camels, two and a half years earlier. Then, the world had been young, filled with hope, the sun had been shining and the gay crowds had flocked forth.

Alas, at 5 am on this sombre Sunday it is a small graveyard group standing on the quay of Sandridge Pier, as SS *Havilah* – her flags at half-mast – docks, and a gangplank is lowered from the ship to the wharf, to unload, at last, her most precious cargo.

Not a breath of wind stirs, the waters of Port Phillip Bay betray not a ripple. All is quiet, and there is a deathly calm as much with the elements, as with the people who wait.

'It was,' the *Leader* would note, 'as if the elements were hushed into mournful stillness by the presence of the dead.'[22]

It is Alfred Howitt himself who comes down the gangplank first, with four of his men behind carrying the wooden case that contains the two canvas bags that contain the separate earthly remains of Messrs Burke and Wills. The box is covered by the Union Jack, and borne on Howitt's men's strong shoulders. There to receive these tragic remains of the once glorious expedition are several members of the Committee – including the Drs Macadam, Eades, Wilkie, and that elusive sponsor, Mr John Bruce himself – all of whom have been waiting since late the previous evening, when the ship was due to arrive.

As the four men bearing the box make their mournful way to the hearse, the graveyard group falls in tightly behind, their heads bowed. They are led by Dr Eades, who just two and a half years earlier, as the mayor, in the name of the citizens of Melbourne, 'bade a hearty God speed to Burke as he started on his great enterprise as the leader of one of the finest and most complete parties ever engaged for land exploration service ... Now, instead of grasping with cordiality the hand of a returning hero, he follows in mournful silence, a few bones, all that remains of Australia's ill-fated explorers.'[23]

Oh, the pathos. While all feel it, clearly none feels it more than another who is part of this group, one they all pay elaborate deference to. It is a singularly old yet statuesque woman, who quietly weeps in the company of the men as the end of the pier is reached and the boxes are placed in the black hearse that will take them to the Royal Society Hall.

For yes, it is her, Ellen Dogherty, Mr Burke's beloved nanny, who at his request had arrived in Melbourne only four weeks after his departure, and had been waiting for him ever since, at the home of Dr Macadam. And now here young Mr Burke is, in the company of Wills.

The graveyard group climbs into two mourning coaches that follow the black hearse as it slowly makes its way into Melbourne, following the same route of the once victorious camel procession of that marvellous day in June, back in 1860. At last arriving at the Royal Society's hall, the case is deposited, and the sole key to open it handed to a visibly affected Dr Macadam – of the men, it is he who appears most emotional – in his role as Honorary Secretary of the Exploration Committee.

Somehow, the finality of the key being handed over, the remains having reached their immediate destination, relieves Ellen Dogherty of her last needs to show restraint and she now howls uncontrollably, only managing to get out between sobs her desire 'to be left alone with the remains . . .'[24]

Of course, madam.

With heads lowered, the men retreat, close the door behind them, and wait outside as the sound of the elderly woman's wails drift hauntingly through the hall.

•

Just three days later, on New Year's Eve, the same group – less one member, but plus many more – are gathered again at the Royal Society's hall to conduct a sacred ceremony. The remains of our heroes are to be placed in coffins. By 8 pm, no fewer than 50 people – members of the Exploration Committee, politicians, councillors, journalists, gentlemen, all with just one lady – have gathered to oversee the delicate, sombre operation.

Who do you suppose is missing?

No, not the devastated Dr Wills, who is already on his way to England, while his surviving son, Tom, has not been invited.

No, the person being desperately missed is the one man they actively *need*. The one with the key.

That is . . . Dr John Macadam. Where *can* he be?

What starts as a light rumbling of discontent, by 8.15 pm grows to outright dissent, and by 8.30 pm has risen still further to the point of trying other keys with no success. At 8.45 pm, in exasperation, a locksmith is sent for, and they are even contemplating using crowbars to jemmy it open, when just on 9 pm, Dr Macadam arrives, clearly drunk, while claiming to have been merely indisposed. At last proceedings can get underway.

'We are met together for the purpose of performing an extremely painful duty,' Dr Eades begins, 'but the fact is that Dr Macadam had been so overcome that he could not arrive sooner.'[25]

Now, as to the painful duty they are about to perform . . .

'The best way will be to open the case in silence,' Dr Eades says, 'and to take out the bones, and deposit them in the shells prepared to receive them, and then to leave the hall at once, and lock the doors.'[26]

There is a grave nodding of heads. Dr Eades nods gravely in return and says, 'I would ask Dr. Wilkie to open the case.'[27]

And yet, as Dr Wilkie steps forward, Alfred Howitt holds up his hand for a moment, and begs permission to say a few words, 'to prevent any misconception on the part of those present'[28].

The purpose of the 32-year-old's words on this occasion, clearly, is to lower expectations of the gathering as to what they are about to see. These, he says, in his thick Nottingham accent, are not desiccated corpses, these are skeletal remains only. They will be just as I found them on my arrival at Cooper's Creek last year. Do bear in mind, they've been buried for more or less a year, and then have had another six months knocking about on the way back.

Howitt's words are heard in deep silence, and with profound respect. This is the man who has been *out there*, to Cooper's Creek itself – twice! – and had lived on the banks of Cooper's Creek without trouble for eight months, and had explored the surrounding country without raising a sweat, let alone losing a man – and there is such a weathered look of competence about him, such an aura of the Outback itself, that all, even the most eminent, are bound to defer.

Dr Wilkie steps forward once more, removes the black velvet covering and opens the thick wooden case with heavy metal fittings. Once the creaking lid has been lifted and they all peer forward, it is to see inside a Union Jack which, once pulled off, reveals two small canvas packages, each marked with a name.

So small! So unprepossessing. This is all that remains of the once healthy heroes, whose names somehow shimmer above Melbourne Town? *This?*

As planned, Dr James Murray – who had been right by Howitt's side on his second trip, when the remains had been exhumed at Cooper's Creek, and had personally placed them in the canvas bags – carefully takes the scissors he has brought for the purpose and cuts open the bag marked 'Mr Burke', whereupon a skull and bones are revealed, wrapped in a piece of black alpaca wool.

The deathly silence is broken by a cry, as all eyes turn to Ellen Dogherty. Forty years earlier she had nursed 'dear Master Robert'[29], bathed him, laid him in his crib with infinite care. And now, this is all that is left of that once dear boy. A skull, and a set of bones, less the hands and feet that have been taken by the savaging, ravaging wild dogs they call dingoes.

Dear . . . *God.*

Now, she does something that is quietly reminiscent of how she once nursed Robert as an infant. Taking a clean sheet that had long been part of the Burke family linen in Ireland, she lays it inside the open iron shell that will soon contain the remains, before placing at the top of the shell, a small frilled pillow to accommodate the skull.

Two decades earlier, and then one decade earlier, respectively, she had laid out the remains of Burke's parents. Now, though clearly moved, she is at least composed, as 'she awaited in solemn silence the remainder of the ceremony'[30].

While Mrs Dogherty smooths the linen to the state of a sepulchral symphony of perfection – fit for eternity – the key men in the room pass the skull of Robert O'Hara Burke around, for inspection.

Alas, poor Yorick, I knew him well . . .

Solemnly, cupping the skull in their hands, they gaze back at the hollowed eyes, the death's head grin, passing it from hand to outstretched hand to outstretched ha–

A tinkle rings out, tiny, but enough to shatter the otherwise deathly silence.

As one, all eyes go to the floor, looking for the source of this jarring interruption.

Oh, dear.

Oh dear, oh dear!

The death's head grin is now a little fractured as four or five of Mr Burke's teeth have fallen out, free to bounce around on the shining wooden floor, before coming to rest. In an instant, one James Smith, the Parliamentary Librarian, stoops and swoops, picking up the teeth and carefully laying them down in the iron shell next to the rest of the bones, while also slipping a couple in his pocket.

Carefully, Dr Murray now takes the skull and lays it on the pillow, before Dr William Wheeler – who had been with Mr Howitt when the bones had been buried – arranges 'the collar bones, shoulder blades, vertebrae, and the remainder of the skeleton . . . in the shell in conformity with their proper positions. These bones were remarkably perfect, a few of the smaller ones only being missing.'[31]

Ellen Dogherty now presses forward once more and bending over the coffin, 'devoutly kissed the skull, sobbing bitterly the while'[32].

All in the room are overcome by the shattering sadness of it all, including the journalist from the *Age*.

'The scene was a most affecting one,' he would report, 'and the funereal aspect of the hall lent much towards the effect. Not one present but was deeply moved by the affection of the kind old lady.'[33]

Finally, she steps back, and the sheet she has provided is wrapped over the rest of the remains, and the lid of both the shell, and the coffin closed, as attention turns to the remaining bag, containing Wills. For many, including the journalist from the *Age*, the contrast between the two ceremonies, is 'remarkable and affecting'[34].

For, alas . . .

'No pitying female hand waited to perform the last sad offices towards the remains . . . and all that remained of the head which dictated it was the lower jaw.'[35]

So too, with the rest of the skeleton, with many bones missing, and only 'the vertebrae and skeleton . . . kept together by the remains of the shirt in which the poor fellow died'[36].

Still, among all the bones can be identified, 'a small portion of sandy-coloured beard'[37], which some of those present note is exactly as they remember Wills boasting.

Again the bones are laid out with due respect to anatomical order. 'This being done, a sheet was called for, but this the undertaker had neglected to supply, and a strip of glazed calico was torn from a roll, and used for the purpose of a winding sheet. The shell was then closed, and the melancholy ceremony concluded.'[38]

As solemnly as the affair has been concluded however, the *Argus* will be merciless in its report, particularly when it comes to Dr Macadam:

> The wretched farce, which has for the last few days been enacted in the hall of the Royal Society over the bones of Burke and Wills, is a fitting *denouement* to the tragic history of the Victorian Exploration. The unhappy Exploration Committee seem utterly unable to leave their victims alone, even in their coffins. The same spirit which furnished the Expedition, and which left it to perish in the desert, appears to preside over the funeral arrangements. The spirit of Macadam, 'overcome with emotion,' . . . is of a piece with the decency, which defiles his [Burke's] unhappy bones with the filthy emotions of a speechless drunkard. The climax was worthy of a career, which is unmatched for stupendous impudence and imbecility . . . What curse is this, which afflicts this colony, of having Macadam for the perpetual manager of all its enterprises? What have we done to be eternally haunted by this one name? Is there no escape from the inevitable, the universal, the inexorable Macadam – even at the coffins of those whom their country has chosen to honour?[39]

•

Melbourne is agog at the attacks. Dr Macadam is not. He quickly visits his lawyer, and an action for libel is launched against the paper within days, which still does not prevent the *Ovens and Murray Advertiser* having a shot of its own:

> The conduct of the Secretary of the Exploration Committee, on the occasion referred to, is described as being of the most revolting kind ... The weeping Doctor, overcome by emotions which he had imbibed, staggering over the bones of poor Burke, and slobbering drunken kisses upon those sacred remains, must certainly have presented a spectacle ...
>
> There is a stage of inebriety which we have heard variously spoken of as 'stupid drunk,' 'crying drunk,' 'mad drunk;' but we propose that in future when we desire to describe one suffering from the combined effects of drunken madness, lugubriousness, and imbecility, to say in one word that he has been – 'Macadamised.'[40]

•

In the meantime?

In the meantime, we must allow Melburnians to pay their respects to our heroic dead. On this morning, 6 January, the doors of the Royal Society are gently and sombrely opened, and the pressing public allowed in to see the coffins for themselves, notwithstanding that the *Argus* has also taken a very dim view of this, too: 'The whole scene of the lying-in-state ... is indescribably disgusting to every man who pretends to hold in respect the memory of our dead heroes.'[41]

No matter. Ignoring that, over this first day alone, no fewer than 7000 Melburnians file in, and bow their heads before the elevated catafalque. Softly now, quietly, and with great respect, they climb four steps covered with black cloth and crimson bands to gaze down upon the black-draped coffins. The only sound, though considerable it is, comes from an old grey-haired lady, sitting by one of the coffins, intermittently bursting out, 'with bouts of loud and persistent wailing'[42].

The coffins themselves are displayed beneath large white Maltese crosses, while a massive plume of white ostrich feathers hangs directly above them, all of it only just illuminated by the candles of three silver candelabra throwing off 'a subdued light, which considerably enhances the effect of the spectacle'[43].

Over there on the wall, a large Union Jack makes one proud to be British, and on it is a large shield bearing the glorious names of the members of the Exploration Committee, while 'smaller shields on the pillars round the room exhibit the names of the devoted party, Burke, Wills, King, and Gray . . .'[44]

At the head of the coffin of Wills is a large laurel wreath, sent by Professor Neumayer, admiring his protégé to the bitter end.

So it continues for the next fortnight, from 10 am to 8 pm, as a minimum of 6000 people attend every day. Their numbers include His Excellency Sir Henry Barkly, accompanied by Lady Barkly, a quietly weeping Julia Matthews, a noisily weeping John King, who must be led away after one glance, and a deeply sombre Tom Wills.

By the time the funeral approaches, there are precious few able-bodied people in Melbourne who have *not* seen the remains, and even the *Argus* warms to it in the end: 'The hall has been visited by 102,000 people. The orderly behaviour of this vast gathering is worthy of special mention.'[45]

Ah yes . . .

'The Committee has outdone itself in the undertaker line of business. Resolved to prove that, if it cannot manage an exploration, it can bury an explorer . . .'[46]

But it has seen nothing yet, as the funeral proper now beckons . . .

•

What an occasion!

It seems as though the population of the entire metropolis has gathered downtown to pay homage to a great man, a great leader, a great explorer who had so courageously crossed rivers, deserts and swamps; climbed dunes, ranges and hills; and withstood thirst and starvation to successfully lead his expedition across an entire continent. No less than a public holiday has been declared so that all may bow at his passing, and while schoolchildren roam free, spectators peer from every window, from every rooftop, and are perched at every branch along the way. Impatiently, the crowds wait in the hot sun until finally . . . the cheering begins! For there he is, John McDouall Stuart!

A conservative town, Adelaide is not easily given to raucousness, but on this day gives full throat to its joy, as their conquering hero rides slowly through the streets, lauded and applauded, on his way to be given the keys to the city, to humbly accept the great glory that is his. And yet, as Stuart rides, lifting an exhausted hand of acknowledgement to their acclamation, still there is a sadness to him. For as he knows better than anyone, even as he is living his finest hour in the streets of Adelaide, 600 miles to the south-east, two other men who crossed the continent are to be carried through their own streets, as thousands gather to watch, albeit in coffins 'neath wreaths, not crowned with laurels like him.

There is no way around the tragic irony of it all.

After all their rivalry, all the trudging, the drudging, the sludging, the heat, the blistered feet, the fractured feats . . . their race to be the first to cross the continent and back is finishing, in fact, a dead heat . . .

•

In Melbourne, meantime, just as the public had come out two years earlier for the opening page of the Burke and Wills saga – the departure from Royal Park – so too do they come now for the final page, in even greater numbers, streaming down the boulevards, up the avenues, coming in from towns near and far and streaming forth from both Spencer Street and Flinders Street stations.

It is the first state funeral in the history of Victoria and the order of the Premier John O'Shanassy that all public buildings be closed for the occasion has been so strictly observed, the feeling has spread to private concerns, too.

'Many of the shops were closed from the first,' the *Argus* will faithfully report, 'and only a few did more than partially open. As the day progressed, the city became more thronged, and a general closing of places of business took place. This expression of feeling was of the greater value, inasmuch as it was spontaneous, no invitation having been issued by the Mayor . . .'[47]

Melbourne, and indeed the entire continent of Australia, has never seen the like.

For on this gloriously warm day, the birds sing and the people of the metropolis gather, 100,000 strong – more than half the population of Melbourne – as the mortal remains of Robert O'Hara Burke and William John Wills are to be laid to rest for eternity.

•

'Each minute added to the concourse of spectators,' the *Argus* will breathlessly record, 'and when, at a quarter to one o'clock, the coffins were conveyed from the hall and placed upon the funeral car, the assemblage had become enormous. Burke's coffin is borne out first', which instantly sees the crowd remove their hats out of respect, 'and simultaneously a battery of the Royal Artillery, stationed near Carlton-gardens, commenced firing minute guns. Never was there seen so great a concourse in Melbourne as had now assembled. The hall was literally besieged.'[48]

The crowd extends down streets of Melbourne as far as the eye can see, west to the crest of Russell Street, east to Carlton Gardens. Every window is filled with people watching. Every roof has people sitting upon it, the branch of every sturdy tree is occupied, with nary room for a tired sparrow.

'Even the tower of St Peter's Church had its occupants, and high above all, a numerous party of ladies as well as gentlemen, had taken their position on the top of the Houses of Parliament.'[49]

And now, at precisely a quarter past one, the boom of a cannon fired by the Victorian Volunteer Artillery rolls over the hatless, head-bowed streets. It is the signal for the funeral procession, all of four blocks long, to move off, through a crowd so thick that the police have allowed them to step from the footpath and line the streets themselves, with a passage just wide enough to let the cortege through. All of those on foot, and seemingly even the horses, are moving in rough rhythm with the 'solemn, yet martial strains of the *Dead March* floating over the crowd'[50], played by the 'fine brass band' of the Castlemaine Rifle Company.

Off it goes, first along Nicholson Street, now past the Houses of Parliament – with all of its steps holding more hatless mourners – and now into the city proper.

At the head of the cortege come the gaily attired Castlemaine Volunteers – absolutely shining in their blue coats with red collars and cuffs, their white trousers and white 'kepi' hats – dragoons with rifles, leading the way in honour of both Burke's last posting and the fact that he was once an officer, a soldier, who has given service both for the British Empire and for the Hungarian service. With such troops in the lead, the whole pageant has something of a military flavour.

Now come the Castlemaine Police Force, Burke's second calling, his second stint of notable service.

'During Burke's connexion with the police force,' the *Argus* will note approvingly, 'the men became much attached to him, and his brother officers held him in high esteem. Consequently, there was a large muster of both officers and men, anxious to do honour to his memory. Fourteen officers were present, and, including the firing party, 192 men.'[51]

And now here is the open carriage itself, the one bearing the remains of the noble Burke and Wills in mahogany coffins. And what a carriage it is! Appropriately, it has been especially constructed for the funeral procession, following the model of the one that had been used for the Duke of Wellington in London in 1852 – with extraordinary proportions, being 15 feet long, 18 feet wide, and an amazing 21 feet high – all of it pulled along by six magnificent black horses.

As the carriage makes its way through the pressing throng – 'Bourke Street, at first sight, seemed a mass of heads'[52] – the people all lean forward to soak up every detail they can, most particularly of the funeral carriage, with its ornate bronzed wheels.

'The upper portion is divided into four panels. On that on the right was inscribed in gilt letters Burke's initials, "R. O'H. B.", and on that on the left the initials of Wills, "W. J. W." The front panel bears the Royal arms, and the back the inscription, "Carpentaria".'[53]

Way up high, are the two coffins, each some eight feet off the ground, resting on silver-gilt columns rising from the carriage floor, and sheltered once more beneath plumes of white ostrich feathers. Both coffins are covered in wreaths.

Oh, just to see them is to weep!

Into Elizabeth Street, where the roofs have sprouted heads as thick as mushrooms in autumn, and beyond the pressing crowds in the streets, every window is filled with, seemingly, a face to every pane of glass. Even when the cortege leaves the city proper, to make its way through the suburb of Carlton, along the Sydney Road all the way to Melbourne General Cemetery, there is no diminution of the crowd.

'Children, women, and men, were here alike assembled,' the *Argus* reports, 'waiting patiently during the many hours which elapsed before the cortege came into view . . .'[54]

Like a slow wand of silence, at the sight of the cortege all chat falls away, all movement stops, as 'a reverential silence was the homage paid by the people to the memory of the explorers'[55], with the only exception being the sound of sobbing.

Tightly behind the magnificent funeral carriage come the members of the Exploration Committee in solemn pedestrian procession, Dr John Macadam most prominent among them, and the members of Mr Howitt's relief party tread after the bodies now, just as they did across half the country. Here come the six mourning carriages for the nearest and dearest of the dearly departed led by, appropriately, the weeping nurse, Mrs Ellen Dogherty, all dressed in black, while the clearly downcast Victorian Governor, Sir Henry Barkly, rides in the splendid carriage that brings up the rear in stately splendour. Behind comes an endless cavalcade of the great and good of the day, including parliamentarians, consul-generals and Melburnians of distinction.

A notable absentee to proceedings, however, is none other than Professor Georg Neumayer, who had been appalled, *nein*, simply *outraged* that no one from the Melbourne Observatory had been invited to be in the official funeral procession. Also missing is William Wills's dearest friend in the world, a man most precious to him . . . Richard Birnie, even though, geographically, he is not that far away. How could that possibly be? Yes, well, the sad fact is that without young William's steadying influence on him, Birnie's wild flights of fancy had become a little more erratic, his legal performance a little more abysmal, his debts and despair compounded by the grief he felt at news of William's death. One failure has led to another and on this day of all days, he is marooned in Ballarat, trying to stay out of debtor's prison. He had given a public lecture in that town on Shakespeare's *Macbeth* a fortnight earlier but very few of the public paid to see it, leading to immediate large debts to a printer and promoter that Birnie cannot pay. This very day, he has been reduced to having a begging letter published in the *Age,* explaining his circumstances, in the hope that it will 'excite some compassion in the breasts of my kind friends . . . for I am walking through mud and misery'[56]. If they don't send money to him soon, he warns he will soon be sleeping 'sub Jove, after dining with Duke Humphrey'[57] – meaning in the open air, after dining on earth. His sad jokes illustrate a bitter reality: he cannot leave town without being arrested for unpaid debts. So yes, as young William is being farewelled in the most glittering, expensive, pomp-ridden funeral in the history of the continent, his dearest friend is broke, hungry and about to be homeless or in jail. How strangely and quickly life's cycles can turn, even upon two such intimates as this.

A final significant absentee, at least for those handful of people who know where she fits into the saga, is Julia Matthews. But we'll get to her . . .

At last – it is nigh on four o'clock. There is a soft boom as, this time, the Volunteer Artillery in Royal Park announces to everyone within five miles that the cortege is now approaching Melbourne General Cemetery, where the awaiting crowd is biggest of all.

To think that they will actually be here, to witness the coffins being lowered into the vault, is nothing less than *thrilling.* The rhythm of their rising excitement is provided by the cannons of the Volunteer Artillery, which fire every minute, on the minute, until the marchers arrive at the cemetery.

See now, as the pallbearers, slowly, carefully, remove the coffins from the carriage. That little one there, just behind Sir William Stawell, the one sagging under the weight, is, I think, none other than John King!

Another remarkable pallbearer of Mr Burke is Ambrose Kyte – who had first borne the financial weight of the expedition, and is now bearing its results. Sir Francis Murphy tucks in right behind him, and also bears the weight.

As to the remains of William Wills, his pallbearers are led by his weeping brother, Tom Wills, followed by the likes of Dr Mueller, the Mayor of Melbourne, Richard Eades, and Alfred Howitt, who had done so much to first find the remains, and then retrieve them and bring them back to Melbourne.

As the boom of a cannon rolls like a ball of black thunder over the crowd, the procession moves off. In solemn march now, they approach the massive vault that has been prepared for the sacred bones, lying right beneath a large gum tree, its branches spread wide in sad welcome.

With infinite care, the two coffins are placed, side by side, atop the vault in which they will shortly lie, side by side, for eternity – even as the Dean of Melbourne, the Very Reverend Hussey Burgh Macartney, climbs a specially constructed platform to conduct the final obsequies.

A final cannon blast rings out above the crowd . . .

Beside the reverend stands His Excellency the Governor, Sir Henry Barkly, with Sir William Stawell to his right in turn. For this final scene there is to be no music, nor any great oration. Nothing is to distract from the word of the Lord.

'O death, where is thy sting?' Mr Macartney begins the familiar refrain, over the bones of the man who had been hoping to have that thing taken for him, for decades. 'O grave, where is thy victory?'

And so it goes . . .

Finally when the last sacred words are intoned, '*earth to earth, ashes to ashes, dust to dust*', the coffins are lowered into the vault, aligned strictly on the east-west axis, with their feet to the east, so they may be in perfect position to see the Second Coming of Christ on Judgement Day, and then rise again.

'Many pressed forward to obtain a last view of the coffins,' the *Herald* will note, 'and some little confusion was the result.'[58]

Amid that confusion, and in no small way adding to it, is the weeping, shaking, Ellen Dogherty, who has climbed down the steps of the vault, and for some time refuses to ascend. Finally, however, 'she was with difficulty persuaded to remove'[59].

Others now throng 'around the grave in a rather unseemly manner'[60], and it takes no little effort to restore both order and decorum. And now the police contingent execute the last scheduled part of the service, firing three rifle volleys over the grave.

'They fired,' the *Age* would note with approval, 'with a precision which would have done credit to a regiment of Guards.'[61]

Fare thee well, Burke and Wills. Yours is an extraordinary story, as the words on your magnificent tomb attest:

In memory of
Robert O'Hara Burke
and
William John Wills

The first to cross the continent of Australia
Comrades in a Great Achievement
Companions in Death
And Associates in Renown

Robert O'Hara Burke,
Died 30th June, 1861,
Aged 40.

—

William John Wills,
Died 30th June, 1861,
Aged 27.[62]

As the cracks of the three volleys roll over the enormous crowd, the *Argus* notes, 'the last chapter of the mournful history of the Victorian Exploring Expedition was closed'[63].

•

Truly?

Such is the power of this saga that the drama surrounding the fate of Burke and Wills is far from over, with many compelling scenes to come, beginning *this very evening* . . .

For yes, say it again, William Shakespeare:

All the world's a stage, And all the men and women merely players; They have their exits and their entrances, And one man in his time plays many parts . . .[64]

And herein is a case in point, as, after the funeral of Burke and Wills, a public meeting takes place, bringing together many of the surviving key players.

For gather one, gather all, for a public meeting tonight at 8 pm at St George's Hall, owned by none other than Mr Ambrose Kyte – who is to be honoured for his contribution to the expedition on this night. Beyond that, nominally, the crowd is also gathered here to hear an address by Dr Macadam on the history of the Victorian Expedition, as well as listen to a speech by Mr Alfred Howitt on the part he played in its aftermath.

In truth, so grand an occasion has the funeral been, so energised was the crowd by the pageantry, by the sense of history, by the sheer grandeur of the whole thing that for those who don't want the day to end, this is the obvious place to come, and so they do in droves, 2000 people strong.

Yet, despite all the dignitaries assembling, the *Argus* notes, they are 'treated by the audience with as little consideration as is usually shown by university undergraduates towards illustrious personages on a Commemoration Day'[65].

Ah yes, so extraordinary is the occasion, so charged the atmosphere, that one attendee would recall of it clearly, well over six decades later: 'The audience was not an ordinary or an orderly one. The press had inflamed the public mind, and the public intended to expend its wrath on the Committee. Long before the proceeding started the excitement was intense, and public indignation at boiling point.'[66]

There are exceptions, with, most notably, the Governor, Sir Henry Barkly, and Chief Justice Stawell, being warmly cheered as they take the stage. Dr John Macadam, however, is roundly jeered, as is the Mayor of Melbourne, Richard Eades, though he at least gets *some* cheers. Indeed, nearly all of the surviving major players in the saga are present, bar the shattered John King and the ever absent Mr William

Wright, who the last we heard was in Adelaide. (No one has sent him £100, so that is presumably where he remains.)

'At five minutes past eight o'clock,' the *Argus* reporter records, 'the audience began to manifest some impatience, and sounds not unlike those which occasionally proceed from the gallery of a theatre when the green curtain is down too long made themselves audible.'[67]

But hush now, for we are at last about to begin.

It is His Excellency the Governor, Sir Henry Barkly, who has the honour of addressing the meeting first, and he is quick to get to the nub of it.

'We have celebrated today, citizens of Melbourne,' he begins, 'the funeral obsequies decreed by Parliament to Victoria's dead explorers. We have borne them through the streets of Melbourne to their long [way] home, and we have left them there "alone in their glory".'[68] (*Cheers.*)

But to his real thrust . . .

'You are all aware . . . that it has become the fashion to ridicule, if not to abuse, the Committee.' (*Hear, hear.*) 'Of course, as public men, the members of that Committee must be prepared to have their acts exposed to fair criticism. It is quite possible that they have made mistakes – that they have even committed faults . . . But I do not know what other means of managing the exploration could have been adopted which would have been free from mistakes, because it was a most difficult and most arduous service.'

It is for Sir William Stawell, who has been intimately involved with the Committee from the first, to back Sir Henry up, beginning with congratulations to the crowd for their exemplary behaviour on this day of mourning.

'I confess I saw with delight thousands, and I may say tens of thousands, assemble, and behave as well as men could behave under the most trying circumstances. The heat was not to be easily borne, the dust was unpleasant, the crush was overwhelming, and yet not one angry word, throughout the whole proceedings, fell from the lips of any one individual.'[69] (*Cheers.*) 'All seemed animated by one common feeling . . .'

''Tis a lie!'[70] a voice cries out.

'Turn him out!'[71] cry others.

The heckler is quelled, and Sir William continues, warming to the theme of what a glorious event the funeral had been.

'And yet,' he says, starting to narrow in on his target, the leading paper of the day, 'all these proceedings were to be stopped because some persons seemed to hold the singular opinion that they were "a solemn mockery." My friends, in what did the mockery consist? Is it because the Committee – and I am one of them – are supposed to have been guilty of some sins of omission or commission that this great country is to be debarred the opportunity of expressing its sympathy thus publicly?

'Or is it to be supposed that if a country of this kind, which I might almost call a nation, chooses to hold a national funeral, that it is not necessarily to be conducted with a certain amount of pomp? It could not be otherwise. We must be great on great occasions.'[72] (*Hear, hear.*) 'I don't like to see an attempt made to stop a public funeral by calling it a solemn mockery. I think the expression unseemly – quite as unseemly, indeed, as that interruption which was made just now.'[73] (*Loud cheers.*)

Getting ever stronger, with ever greater support, Sir William moves towards accomplishing the key purpose of this meeting, by telling the tale of the anonymous donor, three years ago, being so kind as to give him a cheque for £1000 ...

'That munificent gift was the nucleus around which other contributions gathered, and which ultimately led to the fitting out of the Victorian expedition, and the important discoveries made by the explorers. The man who made that gift was one of yourselves – a man who, by honest industry, had gone on and prospered ...' (*Cheers.*) 'For years I desired to make this public. I kept the secret religiously, but I assure you it weighed heavily on my conscience ... And one of the principal objects of our meeting here this evening is to [honour] that individual – Ambrose Kyte.'

(*Loud cheers, as all eyes turn to the small, slim, serious, clean-shaven and remarkably unremarkable-looking man on stage, the one now lifting a wan hand of acknowledgement to the roars of the crowd.*)

'It might be asked what could induce him, an unscientific man ... to give £1,000 to further the cause of exploration? Were he to strive to find an answer for one thousand years, he could only say in all serious solemnity, that the idea was given to him from above – that it was the Almighty, alone, who put it into his heart.' (*Sensation.*) 'He believed that he had been an instrument in God's hand.'[74]

And there you have it!

With the Lord Himself instrumental in getting the expedition underway, who would dare criticise the way the expedition was organised?

Certainly no one could criticise the manner in which the Committee had organised the rescue of the one surviving member of the party conducted by Mr Alfred Howitt who now (*loud cheers*) takes the podium.

(In fact, as the *Argus* reporter notes, 'The Committee hoped that the address would have been presented to him by Mr John King, the survivor of the expedition, whose life he was instrumental, under Divine Providence, of saving, but the fatigue of the day, and the excitement of feeling, have been such as to prevent Mr King from attending.')[75]

After detailing something of the journey that had in fact saved King, Mr Howitt, in turn, gets to the thing he most wishes to say.

It concerns . . . Charley Gray. There has been much hostile comment over the fact that while no expense has been spared to bring back the bodies of the officers, Burke and Wills, the body of Gray – who had walked every step of the way with them, and most of the steps of the way back – lies a'mouldering in his grave! Adding to the ill-will on the subject is the ongoing stories about what had actually killed Gray, including sensational allegations that it had been by sabre cuts to the head from Mr Burke's own blade, and even stories of *cannibalism*. Now, ever a man to push in the bush, in this situation Mr Howitt slows down and proceeds cautiously, approaching the subject with typical caution and tact.

'There appears,' he says delicately, 'to be considerable misunder-standing as to the place where Gray's remains were found.' (*Hear, hear.*)

He wishes to make clear in this public forum, on this grand occa-sion, that, comparing the position given by McKinlay as to where he found the body, with the position detailed by Burke and Wills, it is clear, 'they were so very nearly the same place, that I have no doubt whatever my own mind as to their being the same'[76].

He is happy to tell this gathering, also, that on returning to South Australia, he had met Mr McKinlay, and that gentleman, too, 'had no doubt whatever that the remains which he found were the remains of Gray . . .'[77]

And what is more?

'The place where I believed Gray to have been buried,' he notes, 'was sixty or seventy miles from Cooper's Creek and at the time I was there, there was no water in that direction.'[78]

'That is no excuse . . .' a voice rings out.

But Mr Howitt insists.

'I took particular care to make inquiries of the natives about the remains of Gray, my instructions not authorizing me to bring the remains back.'[79]

'That is no excuse!'

'My instructions,' Mr Howitt continues, keeping his dignity, 'were to bring in the remains of Burke and Wills, and I have always made it a fundamental rule to carry out my instructions whatever they are.'[80]

(*Cheers, mingled with cries of 'That is no excuse!' and other expressions of disapprobation.*)

Mr Alfred Howitt rises above such cries and will not dignify them with a response. He simply thanks the Exploration Committee for the honour they have done him, and the assistance they have rendered him, 'which had materially contributed to the final success of the expedition which I had had the honour to command'. (*Loud cheers.*)

There are two more minor speakers, one of whom, Justice Henry Samuel Chapman – yes, an esteemed judge to some, but a nobody from nowhere as far as the mob is concerned, simply delaying proceedings – is so poorly received, that, as 'the hissing grew louder and more determined . . . he, therefore, resumed his seat'[81].

No more preliminaries! The crowd is hungry for the main event, the obvious climax to this tragically tumultuous day, the address to be given by the man who stands at the centre of the extensive criticism extended to the Committee, none other than Dr John Macadam, who now steps forward to a mix of loud 'cheers and hisses'. In fact, the hisses continue for so long that it is His Excellency himself who must intervene, stepping back to the podium, and appealing to the meeting 'to give the speaker a fair and impartial hearing'[82].

However noble the sentiment, the truth is that one man in the front row would later note he couldn't hear at all, as Dr Macadam starts speaking.

Dr Macadam – all flowing red hair and billowing red beard – persists as if there is no noise at all. Though he has come with a prepared speech, he is now seen to throw his notes away and is quick to fire his opening salvo in his own defence, and that of the Committee.

'The Exploration Committee,' he insists in strident tones, 'has been grossly misrepresented, and this is a fitting opportunity for the truth to be made plain. The Committee has been continually held up to public indignation, on no grounds whatever.'[83] (*Cries of 'Oh'.*)

This, after all the work he had done for the last four and a half years, after so much labour by night and by day, after doing so much to keep the public informed.

'It is most discouraging,' he avows, genuinely *wounded*, as the hissing fades just a little, 'to be subjected to all the scandals which had been heaped upon me, to have lies circulated with respect to me, and to have to appeal to a jury of my country for redress.'[84] (*Cheers, and again the cat-calls start to fade.*)

'It had been asked, "Why did the Royal Society, and why, under heaven, did Dr Macadam, have anything to do with the Expedition?"'

As it happens, at this point someone has yet another question, as a voice rings out, 'Who starved Burke?'

'Turn him out!' the cry is taken up, towards the heckler, who is swiftly silenced. Nothing should be allowed to interrupt the spectacle of Dr John Macadam in full cry, as he now moves on to the process they had gone through to choose a leader.

'This was no easy matter,' he notes carefully, before going through all the other candidates they had approached, and how they had each knocked the Committee back.

'At all events, the Committee had not any known explorer at their command, and they actually had to resort to public advertisements. Some 14 candidates came forward. Among them was one gentleman who had written against the Committee, and denounced Mr Burke from first to last.' (*Cries of 'No!' and 'Yes!'*)

'Instead of feeling as a man should when displaced by one of superior power and ability, that unsuccessful candidate assumed the position of a coward.'

(*Somewhere, perhaps, as the crowd roars in approval, 'Scientia' or 'Justitia' or Lockhart Morton – or all three in one – shift uncomfortably.*)

Another gentleman, Macadam notes, 'considered that he was entitled to precedence on the ground that he could obviate the want of water in the interior of the colony. His plan for doing this was to erect a tank, support it on saplings at the edge of the Murray, and by means of a hose and a machine carry the water right away across the whole continent.' (*Great laughter.*) 'That gentleman must have had a very curious notion of the rotundity of the earth.' (*Renewed laughter.*)

Dr Macadam is going well, and he knows it. More than anything, he is being entertaining, and has the crowd so entirely with him that the cat-calling has fallen away. Whatever else, they want to *hear* him.

'Ultimately, the Committee found that no candidate was sufficiently grounded in astronomical knowledge, and it was decided to select Burke to be the leader, for his courage, his bravery, and his powers of leadership, (*cheers*) and to supplement him by sending an astronomer with him. This led to the appointment of Wills.'

(*Renewed cheering . . .*)

'Mr Burke was therefore appointed as the leader . . . Now I am prepared to take my full share of any blame which might attach to the Exploration Committee in the management of the expedition but, looking back upon all that had transpired, there was nothing which is a source of disquietude to my conscience.' (*Hear, hear.*)

When it comes to the attacks made on the late, great Mr Burke, 'immediately after his appointment as leader of the expedition, I especially defended him from the charge of being illiterate and ignorant'[85].

Concerning those who accompanied Mr Burke, 'it was necessary that he should appoint a second in command, and that post was given to Mr. Landells.' (*Hear, hear.*) 'I should be ashamed if I make this meeting the medium of attacking any man; but out of all the correspondence which has taken place relative to the conduct of Landells, I believe that the gentleman who stated that he showed "the white-feather" spoke the truth.' (*Applause, and expressions of disapprobation.*)

'I shall be glad,' Dr Macadam continues, upping the ante even a notch further, 'if Mr Landells is present, that he may have an opportunity of hearing what I state.'[86]

There a stirring. A small commotion.

From the back of the room, a man stands up, and approaches the stage.

Sensation! *Sensation!*

Why, look there. It is none other than Mr Landells himself, now calling out to Dr Macadam, and in fact calling *on* him, to, in the name of *God*, cease his 'assassin like remarks . . . !'[87]

What is more, the bluff Englishman now asks His Excellency, 'not to permit Dr Macadam to make any personal reference to me'[88].

When His Excellency rules that, 'Dr Macadam might use his own discretion, and if his speech contained any personal references, Mr Landells might afterwards reply to them'[89], all Mr Landells can do is to ask Dr Macadam to read the whole of the report he had submitted about what had gone wrong on the expedition, and not just select parts of it, as he had been wont to do in recent times.

Uproar! Cries of 'Hear, hear!' ring out, and 'Read it all!'[90]

So great is the uproar in fact, that it once again takes His Excellency himself to restore order, suggesting that Dr Macadam conclude his remarks, and that Mr Landells should have the opportunity of addressing the meeting afterwards.

Dr Macadam agrees, and indeed reads portions of Mr Landells's report – though certainly not the whole – focusing on the fact that the essence of the quarrel between Mr Landells and Mr Burke was over the treatment of the camels. On this issue he has no doubt that Mr Burke was quite right, and Mr Landells quite wrong – most particularly as the last had then resigned.

The result, friends?

'Poor Burke was left at the Darling with a supposed desert staring him in the face, and two of his best men having abandoned him. In this extremity, Mr. Burke placed confidence in a man who afterwards betrayed him – Mr. Wright.'[91] (*Applause, mingled with some expressions of disapprobation.*)

For yes, friends, this was the same Mr Wright who got halfway to Cooper's Creek with Mr Burke, before returning, with the instructions of the leader ringing in his ears, 'Go back for stores, and follow me up at once.'

But he manifestly failed to carry out these instructions and we can all see the result.

'Wright went back to the Darling, and, for reasons which he could not explain to the Royal Commission appointed to investigate the matter, he did not move from there to follow up the instructions of his leader for three months.' (*'Oh, oh,' and applause.*)

What was he doing meantime?

'The Committee had evidence to prove that Wright left his camp and his party on the Darling day after day to look out for land for squatters, instead of doing his duty to the man whose life was in his hands.' (*'Hear, hear' and applause.*)

Dr Macadam, clearly now *enjoying* his time on the stage, goes on to detail the Committee's 'great surprise'[92] to discover on New Year's Eve, two years earlier, that Wright had not moved. Of course Macadam had 'at once summoned the Exploration Committee, and Mr Hodgkinson was despatched back again next morning', with strict instructions to get Mr Wright moving, but still that man, 'actually remained for seventeen days at rest within a few days' journey of Cooper's Creek, although he had every kind of provision and clothing for the poor men who were starving.' (*'Hear, hear' and 'Oh, oh!'*)

Why, he, personally, had been told by Mr King that just as 'Mr Burke was about to leave Cooper's Creek, he said – "I will ask Brahe, if Mr Wright comes up to-night or to-morrow, to follow us on." Was it not evident from this that Burke expected Wright daily?'

The question hangs in the air for just long enough for Tom McDonough, who is also on the stage, to exclaim loudly, 'I heard him say the words.'[93]

Friends, it was in good faith that Wright would follow those instructions that Mr Burke and his companions then departed north. But Wright had disobeyed those instructions, and what is more, Brahe had deserted his post at Cooper's Creek, just hours before Burke and Wills had returned.

And so Dr Macadam now lays before the gathering his key question.

'Can the Exploration Committee, or any body of men sitting 800 miles away, be held responsible for those disasters? Yet the press would not allow the truth to be revealed. It was sufficient for them to say that the Exploration Committee were the murderers of these men and that Dr Macadam was the chief murderer of the lot.'[94] (*Cries of 'Shame'.*)

On a roll now, the Honorary Secretary of the Exploration Committee finishes, saying that, 'the portion of Central Australia which had been thoroughly investigated by Victoria, at so great an expenditure of money, and so frightful a sacrifice of life, should be annexed to the colony with a view to its future colonisation'[95]. (*Hurrah! Hurrah!*)

'Dr Macadam,' the *Argus* would faithfully report, 'then resumed his seat amidst much cheering.'[96]

Is Mr Landells, with his messy mane and unruly moustache, really to follow such a masterful performance, such a *tour de force, tour d'horizon*, of Dr Macadam's carefully crafted defence? He does his best. But, again as documented by the *Argus*, as soon as he rises to speak, 'he was received with such loud hooting, that he was soon compelled to desist'[97].

All Landells can do, over the outcry, is to deny his cowardice and defend the honesty of his own report to the Committee. He also charges that the Exploration Committee has kept some of his letters from the public, a fact proved by the report he is holding in his hand, of the *Argus* of 15 November 1860 . . . but . . . but . . . it is no good.

Dr Macadam has turned the crowd against Landells even before he had a chance to speak.

'The meeting refused to hear him, and he was obliged to sit down, one man calling out, amidst loud laughter, "Take it to the gorilla".'[98]

Oh, the fun of it, as Mr Landells has no choice but to slink away, amid derisive hooting.

It is for the mayor to close the meeting.

Gentlemen, you have heard full accounts from many quarters.

'I appeal to your honour and candour as to whether, after hearing the explanation of Dr Macadam, you could fairly lay a tittle of blame to the Exploration Committee?'

(*Loud cries of 'No, no' . . .*)

'Twenty months ago, the play began, and now the curtain falls. His Excellency Sir Henry Barkly was the Governor when the cavalcade proceeded from the Royal Park. He is the Governor now, and long might he remain so.' (*Loud and repeated cheers.*)

'Three cheers for the Governor!'

(*The call was responded to with great enthusiasm, the whole meeting rising and cheering for some moments.*)

Now His Excellency, whose first remarks of the evening had been begging for order, over the tumultuous uproar, now – seemingly with no sense of irony – concludes the evening by 'thanking the meeting for the orderly way in which they had behaved, under very exciting circumstances, and after the exciting events of the day'[99].

(*Cheers*)

•

Was it indeed the final curtain?

Yes, very nearly.

But in Castlemaine on this evening, at a musical 'Tableau in Memory of Burke and Wills'[100], held at the Theatre Royal, before a full-house audience of 400, Julia Matthews knows she has the perfect song to bring the evening to a close, as she stands on stage beside a pedestal with the glorious inscriptions of 'BURKE AND WILLS'[101] upon it, and effigies of each man beside her.

Ladies and Gentlemen, she would like to conclude with a particular favourite of Robert O'Hara Burke's, and she will sing it now with special feeling for that great man whose image lies on the locket that hangs from her neck.

Quiet now, as she begins to sing in her rich, resonant tones.

Listen now . . .

> *Oh! thou, to whom this heart ne'er yet*
> *Turned in anguish or regret,*

> *The past forgive, the future spare –*
> *Sweet spirit, hear my prayer.*
> *Oh! leave me not alone in grief,*
> *Send this blighted heart relief . . .*

And again, and again, and again . . .

> *Oh! thou to whom my thoughts are known,*
> *Calm, oh, calm these trembling fears!*
> *Ah! turn away the world's cold frown,*
> *And dry these falling tears.*
> *Oh! leave me not alone in grief,*
> *Send this blighted heart relief . . .*[102]

The curtain falls.

EPILOGUE

Burke's best friends will all admit that ... his courage, kindly qualities and generous disposition [aside], he possessed very few qualifications which are essential to an explorer. It is, therefore, much to his credit that in the absence of such qualifications he smartly performed the task he had undertaken, and but for a delay of 24 hours would have returned to Melbourne to be received with triumphal ovations, to be knighted and pensioned for life and pronounced the greatest and smartest of explorers since the days when Alexander the Great made his way to the Persian Gulf. Such is fate ...[1]

The Leader, 18 June 1887

'I will do it or die,' exclaimed Burke when starting on his expedition, and as it was remarked afterwards, 'He did it and died'.[2]

Ovens and Murray Advertiser, 1880

Three years after Burke and Wills were laid to rest, a settler moving in to the back country around the Darling was returning from a trip into the bush with his 'blackfellow', when they were obliged to make camp – hungry and thirsty – in a dry, exposed spot among the mulga. That night, a fierce, haunting wind swept through the trees, making a terrible moaning sound to wake the dead.

The settler slept terribly, dehydrated and worried his horses would break free in search of water. Even so, he was getting better rest than the blackfella, who kept muttering in his sleep as if he were having a long-running nightmare. Sure enough, as dawn neared, the blackfella suddenly woke, and instantly appeared relieved, as if he realised it was just a night-terror after all.

'Methink,' the settler would chronicle his words, 'devil been walk about to-night – not devil belonging to blackfellow, but white-man devil. Methink Burke and Wills cry out to-night, "What for whitefellow no send horse and grub?" You hear wind? That come up from Cooper Creek. My word, master, Mr Burke, Wills too, big one walk about on that creek. Never them leave Cooper Creek. Always, always, always, walk about there, and cry out "long a Menindee, where white man? Why another one white man no come?"'[3]

•

In fact, it was not just in that bit of back country that the spectre of the lost Burke and Wills would loom large for many years to come, as the rights and wrongs of what had happened would be debated for decades, with the reputations of the key players often rising and falling. But we'll get to that . . .

In the meantime, the most real of spectres were the many monuments raised to the dead explorers, and therein lay some sagas all their own . . .

The most famous of these monuments was the likeness in bronze unveiled by Governor Sir Charles Henry Darling, at the intersection of Melbourne's Collins and Russell streets before 1000 attendees on 21 April 1865. Costing the Victorian government £4000, it showed the heroic two atop a granite pedestal 15 feet high, purportedly peering at the Gulf of Carpentaria. In art, as in life, they are giants among men, with the likeness of Burke not an inch under 12 feet high, gazing to the Gulf of his dreams, his right hand resting on the left shoulder of Wills, who sits at his feet. For the record, Dr Wills had campaigned vigorously against such a design, maintaining that an alternative design by another sculptor which showed them standing side by side, as equals, would have been more appropriate. John King was not present in either version, but, as it happens, he was there on the day of the unveiling. In fact, in his speech to mark the occasion, His Excellency, the Governor, singled out King, noting that four years to the day since 'Burke and Wills returned from the Carpentaria shore to the Depot upon Cooper's Creek . . . accompanied only by John King, who I rejoice to say is present here to-day, to hear from my lips the assurance, that we offer to him that full share of the honour we are rendering to his

lamented chiefs, which is due to his distinguished courage and fidelity.'
(*Loud cheers.*)

'He may well take for his motto now, and for his epitaph hereafter, these words, among the last written by the hand of Burke, "King has behaved nobly".'[4] (*Cheers.*)

In February 1886, the statue was moved to the small triangle of land bounded by Spring and Nicholson streets near Parliament House and the Princess Theatre to allow the cable tram to go through at the spot it had been positioned. 'Romance must give way,' thundered one journalist. 'Poor Burke and Wills must be flung on the rubbish heap, or stowed out of sight, round the corner, in some out of the way place, where nobody will ever see them . . . We will still think of Burke dying on the Desert Waste, under the Red Sunset, while the gaunt Wills and King knelt, beside him.'[5]

(Of course, Wills probably died first, alone beside a billabong teeming with fish – albeit at a different billabong – but a quarter of a century later the popular perception of Wills and King kneeling loyally beside their dying leader had taken deep root and would not be swayed.) Still romance would continue to give right of way to progress, as the statue has been moved three times since, and has recently been moved again from the corner of Swanston and Collins streets to be placed in storage for five years, to allow the construction of Melbourne Metro CBD South station.

When it came to the monument above the vault of Burke and Wills in Melbourne General Cemetery, after endless debate and no little exertion, a granite block, 12 feet high and six feet square, weighing 36 tons, was finally installed in 1870, at a cost of £1500.

Oddly, it would be a good three decades after their departure that a curious monument, a large obelisk, would be erected in Royal Park, 'to mark the spot from whence the Burke and Wills Expedition started on 20 August 1860'.

When the Boy Scouts held a parade there in 1910 to mark the fiftieth anniversary since the departure of the expedition, they received a short telegram from England: 'Many sad memories from Robert O'Hara Burke's sister; Mrs Maxwell.'[6] (By the by, the next year, this last surviving sister, *nee* Anne Celestine Burke, would see her granddaughter marry the future British Prime Minister Neville Chamberlain, another sign of just how well-connected was the family of Robert O'Hara Burke.)

•

Beyond Melbourne, monuments to Burke and Wills became something of an industry in Victoria from the early 1860s on, springing up everywhere from Castlemaine to Ballarat, in Bendigo and Beechworth. There would have been a very imposing one at Swan Hill, too, bar the fact that, after taking up a collection for it, Superintendent Henry Foster absconded with the money. The small monument Swan Hill could afford in its stead soon collapsed, and it wasn't until 1914 that a replacement 'Explorers Memorial' was unveiled, which honoured, beyond Burke and Wills who had passed through the picturesque town, other pioneers, such as Captain Francis Cadell and Major Thomas Mitchell.

The dispute in Bendigo concerning which cemetery should boast the monument to Burke and Wills? That was won, of course, by the Back Creek Cemetery, over the claims of the White Hills Cemetery. You must take one more bow for the road, Paddy Bernard – you, the drunken sexton who had abducted John King to have him personally select where the monument should go. It proved to be the winning argument with Bendigo's town fathers.

In Beechworth, the townsfolk rallied enthusiastically to honour their former police inspector who had gone on to such glory, quickly adding The Robert O'Hara Burke Memorial Museum to the Beechworth Athenaeum, with its primary exhibits Burke's bible and the saddlebags from the expedition's camels – both of which were found on Cooper's Creek in 1873. In recent years, in a great coup for the museum, they have also been able to add one of the two engraved pistols Burke was given by his officers when he was transferred from Castlemaine.

Beyond such large monuments, across the broad path that the expedition travelled, headstones and plaques soon sprouted, most of them on the gravesites of the seven men who died – including the spots where Burke and Wills died – lost and lonely relics in the desert winds of the most famed fatal exploration in Australia's history. A final monument worth noting is far across the seas, in William Wills's hometown of

Totnes, Devon, where, I suspect with his father as the driving force, a monument to the young explorer was erected by public subscription in 1866.

•

As to the survivors, although he wasn't included on the main memorial statue in Melbourne, **John King** was at least well provided for, being granted an annual £180 pension by the Victorian government – 10 times his old soldier's wage – which allowed him to buy a house in St Kilda, and two other houses as investments, riches beyond his wildest imaginings. But the mental trauma never left, with one writer recalling an occasion well after the funeral had faded, 'when the mention of Burke's name by a visitor caused King to rush from the room, and when he was followed to see the cause of his hasty retreat, he was found sitting on a chair crying bitterly over the ill fate which had attended the career of the man he had loved so well'[7]. Ever afterwards, he would feel so blessed to have been rescued himself that he and his family would celebrate his birthday not in December when it fell, but on 15 September, when Edwin Welch had found him, the date of his effective 'rebirth'[8]. A decade after his return to Melbourne he married his cousin, Mary, a widow with a young child – and one of three relatives who had been looking after him all that time. Alas, just four months later, on 15 January 1872, King died of pulmonary tuberculosis, aged only 33. What an extraordinary, if short, life he had led! From the green hills of Ireland, to the teeming shores of India, to the desert wastes of Australia, to life as a member of an Aboriginal tribe, to Melbourne's favourite conquering hero . . .

He, too, is buried in Melbourne General Cemetery, albeit in a much more modest grave.

•

William Brahe would be required to defend his reputation for the rest of his days, and managed it well. After the Royal Commission, Brahe moved to Queensland, then New Zealand and on to Fiji, where he married in 1874, before moving back to Victoria to become the Crown

Lands bailiff at Macedon. In 1904, the *Age* interviewed Brahe, then 69 years old. Of Robert O'Hara Burke he was nothing if not candid.

'He was such a bad bushman,' Brahe told the *Age*, 'that he could not safely be trusted 300 yards away from the camp . . . Burke was a splendidly proportioned man, but he was ignorant of bush life, even to the management of a compass, and kept to himself a great deal.'[9]

When it came to William Wills, the German was much kinder, with the newspaper noting, 'Mr Brahe states that any of the men would have followed Wills anywhere, as he was most pleasant and exercised a wonderful influence over them.'[10]

The last man left standing of the Depot party, Brahe died at his home in Elwood, Melbourne on 16 September 1912 – over 50 years after the whole Burke and Wills saga played out – aged 77. He is buried in Brighton Cemetery.

•

After appearing at the Royal Commission, **William Wright** disappeared into relative obscurity . . . with but one flare rising in the gloom of the subsequent decades to give a clue where he lay. In 1913, a small item appeared in the Perth edition of *Truth*, with a reminiscence by one entitled 'Old Chum', recalling: 'I met Wright in Sydney some years ago. He was a frequent visitor to the wine cellar under Temple Court in King Street, where he passed his time in playing dominoes. He was in easy circumstances apparently. He was introduced to me as Mr Wright, third-in-command of the Burke and Wills expedition . . .'[11]

•

George Landells disappeared into obscurity shortly after the Burke and Wills saga was over. He returned to India and died in Rawalpindi in December 1871, aged 46, with the news reaching Melbourne just a few days after the funeral of John King.

•

Despite all of Burke's efforts to thwart him, **Dr Hermann Beckler**'s scientific legacy in Australia was significant. All those hundreds of indigenous flora specimens that he so carefully collected were not pressed, preserved and sent back to Melbourne in vain, but were gathered in by Ferdinand Mueller and classified – expanding the frontiers of science. Many of those specimens, including nardoo, can be found in the Australian collection of the Herbarium at Melbourne's Royal Botanic Gardens to this day. The admiring Mueller would note of his countryman that the expedition's botanist 'did more than hundred others in his place could and would have done'[12].

Hermann Beckler returned to Germany in 1862, and wrote an account of the expedition two years later. It was not published, however, and after his death it was given to a small German museum where it remained, unnoticed for many years, before finally being translated into English and published in 1993. He continued his career as a doctor in Bavaria, right up to his death in 1914, aged 86.

•

The sketches of **Ludwig Becker** – which can now be seen in the State Library of Victoria – are highly regarded to this day, and are also regarded as having a great deal of scientific worth, just as his reports and collated meteorological data are a significant scientific record. Perhaps most highly regarded are his sketches and notes on the Aboriginal people, such as 'a corroboree song and tune which a Murray black had dictated in English . . . [and] the words and music of a love song', which are considered as 'significant contributions to social history and anthropology'[13]. Together they stand as one of the first serious efforts by a European to record Indigenous customs, languages and even stories.

•

The pity of **William Hodgkinson** is that a man who witnessed so much, who, whatever else, was a more than competent chronicler of his times, not only never gave a substantial interview to other journalists on the subject, but never committed to paper his own version of events. He never even testified at the Royal Commission, as he was up at Cooper's Creek with McKinlay's expedition.

Hodgkinson soon returned to journalism, and yet after only a short stint as editor of the Rockhampton *Morning Bulletin*, his restless spirit saw him move on to try his luck with several Queensland mining ventures, none of which occasioned particular success. In 1888 he tried his luck at yet one more career, being elected Member for Burke in the Queensland Parliament, a seat named for none other than Robert O'Hara Burke. Sure enough, it was in this political arena where what Dr Beckler perceived as Hodgkinson's capacity for manipulation and scheming – 'insolent, malicious . . . the scorpion, the gnawing worm we carried with us . . . . the most evil animal of a person that I have ever encountered . . .'[14] – was able to flourish as never before! In 1900, he died of influenza in Brisbane, aged 65.

•

Thomas McDonough, one of the four members of the Depot party under Brahe, moved to New Zealand in 1862 to prospect for gold, having so little luck he quickly became an insurance salesman . . . for less luck still. Slowly moving to impoverishment and poor mental health, by 1904 he had become an inmate of the Melbourne Benevolent Asylum, a charitable institution to house the homeless, destitute and sick. He died there on 13 July 1904, aged 70.

•

Dost Mahomet was awarded no less than £200 for arm injuries caused by a rogue camel named Nero at Menindee. The profitable bite occurred in January 1862, while Mr Howitt was preparing his expedition to retrieve the bodies of Burke and Wills. However, despite the camel mauling, Dost Mahomet became attached to Menindee, working in Ah Chung's Bakehouse and was eventually buried in the spot where he performed his daily prayers for 20 years. His nameless plot was known for decades as 'the Afghan's grave'. But was it Dost's grave? Dave Phoenix's excellent book, *Following Burke and Wills Across Australia*, has a letter from a correspondent to the *Barrier Miner* in 1893 saying, 'It is a pity to spoil the romance, but that is the grave of an Arab gardener who died here 25 years ago.' Romance or not, since 1952 the grave has borne a headstone with the name Dost Mahomet, the last member of Mr Burke's expedition to remain at Menindee.[15]

In 1862, **Belooch** appeared onstage in a Ballarat theatre as . . . himself, in a memorial fundraising theatrical recreation of the journey and death of Burke and Wills, receiving a good review from the Ballarat *Star* for his commanding presence. Just eight weeks later, he married an Australian woman and, after convincing her to return to his native India, the pair boarded a ship . . . only for her to die just 10 days into the voyage. The devastated Belooch returned to Melbourne and in 1865 departed on another expedition, this one in search for Ludwig Leichhardt, using the very camels that had survived the Burke and Wills expedition. The rest of his life was spent on remote Queensland stations.

•

And what of one of my favourite characters of the whole saga, the inestimable **Dick**? At least one more time, he went on an expedition, but thought better of it, with the *Argus* reporting in April 1862 that another explorer, Mr Curlewis, was being guided by Dick ('who, it will be remembered so gallantly saved the lives of McPherson and Lyons') but that he 'has now deserted his party and made the river [Darling]'[16]. Given that Mr Curlewis was murdered only a short time after Dick left, his desertion may well have been a marker of his uncanny survival instincts, rather than any general lack of resolution.

•

For all the palaver over whose body McKinlay's expedition found, there is now no doubt they did find the remains of another expedition member.

On 14 February 1862, on the Diamantina River in South Australia following the path of Mr Burke and his party, they came across the bones of a horse, still in its saddle, surrounded by camel droppings, other detritus and the remains of Burke's Camp 52R. Hello, **Billy the horse**! The only horse to this day to have crossed the continent, as far as it is known. As a memento, McKinlay cut off one of Billy's hooves and it is now in the History Trust of South Australia's Historical Relics Collection.

•

Trooper **Myles Archibald Lyons** resumed his duties at Swan Hill and in 1862 married local woman Flora McDonald, with the two going on to have 13 children – surely a fair sign that, after his extraordinary exertions in pursuit of Mr Burke, he did not suffer any prolonged bouts of ill-health. A decade later he took over Eltham police station, being promoted to the rank of constable, and died in that same town on 19 August 1899, aged 75.

•

Chief Justice Sir William Stawell was wrong in his advice that **Charles Ferguson** had no grounds for his action on wrongful dismissal. Ferguson was determined, and after the case was 'bandied about from court to court'[17], the Victorian Supreme Court eventually ruled in Ferguson's favour, awarding him damages of £183, 6 shillings and 8 pence. From here, Ferguson did a little horse-breaking and cattle-trading, and even started and failed building a career as a restaurateur, before returning to the United States, where among other things he penned an auto-biography, covering such events as his time at the Eureka Stockade and his experience with the Burke and Wills Expedition. Alas, his last reflection on the latter is patently false: 'At the end of sixteen months in the interior, I was the only survivor to return to Melbourne, all the rest, including horses and camels, either had died from exhaustion, scurvy or other illness.'[18] In the end, however, he who laughs last . . .

Ferguson was the longest-lived of the expedition members, passing away in Chico, California, in 1925 at the age of 92.

•

Alfred Howitt's skills as an explorer became rightly legendary. On his return to Cooper's Creek to retrieve the bodies and set up a base for further explorations, he established a vegetable garden that quickly grew like Topsy, soon boasting radishes, melons, potatoes and pumpkins. Thus, right by where Burke and Wills starved to death, Howitt was soon dining on copious meals of fish with all the trimmings, pass the pumpkins. He returned to Gipps Land after his heroic ventures in the north of Australia, becoming, for a quarter of a century from 1863 onwards, a police magistrate and goldfields warden, before becoming the Secretary for Mines in 1889, living in Melbourne. Throughout that time he continued to talk on his own involvement in the Burke and Wills saga – including a seminal lecture he delivered in 1907, where he listed his own views for the failure of the expedition. The reasons were many and varied, but he concluded:

'Burke . . . did not possess that kind of knowledge which is absolutely necessary to enable even the bravest and most determined man to be the successful leader of such an expedition as was committed to his charge . . . It was [Wills] who really took Burke across the continent and brought him back to Cooper's Creek. Without Wills, Burke would have been absolutely helpless.'[19]

In the meantime, lest Alfred Howitt's seeming lack of concern for the fate of the Yandruwandha people at the time of discovering King unfairly define the gentleman bushman, it should be noted that he was able to use his experiences with the Yandruwandha to begin a formidable effort to systematically study Indigenous Australian tribes, becoming widely regarded in the nascent science of anthropology, publishing on the social organisation and customs of several tribal groups. Despite seeing the Aboriginal people of Gipps Land as 'a people doomed to extinction by an extraordinary primitivity'[20], he in fact did a great deal for Gipps Land's Kurnai tribe, including conducting and publishing a study of their culture, regarded as seminal in the field of Indigenous study. He was awarded the Mueller medal (named for Ferdinand Mueller) by the Australasian Association for the Advancement of Science in 1903, and in 1904 he completed his work, *The Native Tribes of South-East Australia*. Howitt was awarded a Companion of the Distinguished Order of St Michael and St George for services to the Commonwealth in 1906. After an extraordinary life, he died in the Victorian town of Bairnsdale on 7 March 1908, aged 77.

•

Julia Matthews went on to prosper on the stage. She moved to New Zealand in 1864, where she married her manager, William Mumford – having three children to him – and continued performing. In 1867, however, George Coppin – him again! – brought her back to Sydney's Prince of Wales Theatre for her farewell Australian season, before she departed for the Old Country, where she became the first Australian-trained singer to sing at Covent Garden Opera House, when she played the principal role of Offenbach's *La Grande-Duchesse de Gerolstein*.

Her professional success was not matched by marital bliss, and it would be said that Mumford regarded his wife as no more than 'a machine for grinding out golden sovereigns for him to waste in drink and debauchery'[21]. (Ah yes, Robert O'Hara Burke, if only *you* had been there to save her, what might have been?) After they separated in 1870, it fell to her to support her three children with the aid of her parents, and she continued to tour 'Europe and America under various managers mostly in [that form of French comic opera known as] *opéra bouffe*'[22]. Sadly, while touring through St Louis, Missouri, in 1876, she contracted malaria and died on 19 May of that year, aged just 36.

•

Ellen Dogherty? One of my researchers, Angus, has an interesting theory. Was she sent for because, Burke, as a high-born Irishman, from a culture of long-term nannies looking after several generations, could want nothing better than his own nanny to look after a child that he and Julia Matthews might produce? I know, I know, pure speculation, but it's hard to resist floating it. She was certainly well looked after by both Dr Macadam – who hosted her in his home for two years – and the Victorian government, which awarded her a pension of £60 a year for life, the result of interest on the £1015 of debentures purchased for her security. She died in Melbourne in February 1871 and is buried in an unmarked grave in Melbourne General Cemetery not far from the grave of Dr John Macadam, and a stone's throw from her beloved Master Robert O'Hara Burke.

•

Despite the fact that Robert O'Hara Burke had died with just 7 shillings and 8 pence in his account, by use of money owing on his salary, Burke's great friend, **Richard Nash**, the executor of his estate, was just able to pay off all of the lost leader's debts – of £452 and 3 shillings. Even then, after Burke's death, the Melbourne Club came forward with an unpaid House Account bill for £18, 5 shillings. This, too, was finally settled, meaning his portrait, with its startling eyes, can to this day gaze down upon the exclusive club's current members, with honour. A running joke among the well-to-do who are habitués of many late nights there, I am reliably informed, is that 'Burke is the only member of the Melbourne Club who ever died of thirst.'

Nash went on to become Secretary for Railways before moving to the Otago goldfields, New Zealand.

•

Dr William Wills Snr grieved for his son for the rest of his life, though drew some comfort from the many 'letters of condolence and sympathy [that] poured in upon me from many quarters'[23], including from Major Peter Egerton Warburton. In part driven by the desire to settle accounts with those whose wilfully careless actions had caused his son's death, Dr Wills wrote a moving memoir of his son's life, based on young Wills's letters and diaries, all the while feeling 'the natural anguish of a father for the loss of a son of whom he was justly proud, and who fell a victim to incapacity and negligence not his own'[24].

•

Richard Birnie, despite his brilliance, also finished his days in the Melbourne Benevolent Asylum. Of the erudite, supremely well-connected barrister, a friend would pithily note, 'Birnie . . . was skilled in all other subjects on earth save the law'[25]. At least, by 1870, Birnie was able to put some of his considerable skills to use by writing for the *Australasian*, and later published essays on gambling and other social issues. He mourned William Wills for the rest of his days and died on 16 September 1888, aged 80. The framed photograph of Wills given to him at Royal Park on the day of departure is now in possession of Sydney's Mitchell Library, having been donated by a dear friend of Birnie's.

•

Carrawaw was later known to the white settlers as 'old Maggie', and to her family as 'Flourbag', because she carried around the empty flour bag that Alfred Howitt had given her – the one containing more flour than the others given to her tribe – for the rest of her life. So enamoured was she of that flour, her great-great-great-great-great-grandson, Aaron Paterson, affirms she was 'known to wet her face and chuck flour on it to represent white people, and the occasion that it was given to her'[26].

Some months after John King was rescued and taken from her and the rest of the tribe, Carrawaw's daughter Turinyi bore a daughter, the first 'half-caste' child in the tribe's history. She was known as a *'padlaka pirti-pirti'* or 'red body' by her tribe – not quite sure what to make of her – while to white settlers she was known as 'Yellow Alice' or 'Miss King'. She married a Yandruwandha man and they had a child named Annie, who was also raised at Nappamerrie and had two children to a white stockman, Robert Parker. Annie King's great-great-grandson, Aaron Paterson, wrote the introduction to *The Aboriginal Story of Burke and Wills*, published by the CSIRO in 2013, and was a great source of advice on the Aboriginal perspective for this book.

•

The prediction of the *Argus* back in June 1860 that 'Years hence, Australia will boast of its race of camels as England does now of her horse'[27], more or less came true. Today, well, perhaps we don't quite boast, but we do export some of our finest camels, most particularly including racing camels, to the Middle East – the animal equivalent of *exporting sands to Arabia?* Beyond that, Australia now has the largest feral camel population in the world, with an estimated 750,000 roaming the interior.

•

Beyond the effect that the crossings of Australia by John McDouall Stuart and Burke and Wills had on land ownership, they also helped redraw the internal map of Australia, when it came to which colonies controlled which land. In recognition of Stuart's expedition, the Colony of South Australia was extended straight up, all the way to the north coast of Australia. (What we know as the Northern Territory did not come into being until 1911.) South Australia also triumphed when it came to securing the contract and mapping the route for the Overland Telegraph Line, as it indeed followed the rough path forged by John McDouall Stuart, starting in Adelaide, and proceeding along 36,000 telegraph poles via Port Augusta, Alice Springs, Newcastle Waters, all the way to Darwin. The first telegram to arrive from London to the South Australian capital arrived in November 1872, after a seven-hour journey via many repeater stations along the way. (A huge leap forward from three months by sea.) For many decades to come, South Australia would be the key Australian communications centre.

South Australia owed a great debt to the efforts of **John McDouall Stuart,** and certainly part of that debt was repaid when he did indeed receive the £2000 prize for being the first to cross the continent. He would need it. He was so shattered by his sixth excursion to Northern Australia that he was never able to mount another major expedition, and returned to Scotland in 1864, dying in London on 5 June 1866, aged 50.

●

With the publication of its ninth and final Progress Report in 1873, the Exploration Committee disbanded – after having been in existence for 15 years and meeting 206 times.

Yet the body which gave birth to the Exploration Committee, the **Royal Society,** survived and thrived and is still prospering in 2017, one of Melbourne's many prestigious professional societies, devoted to promoting science in the wider community, and its meetings are still held in the grand old building which stands on a small triangle of land surrounded by Victoria, Exhibition and La Trobe streets. The hall in which the Committee made all its disastrous deliberations all those years ago, the same room in which the memorandum of agreement was signed by all the men on the expedition prior to their departure, the same room in which the remains of Burke and Wills were placed on display prior to the funeral, and the bones were keened and held vigil over by Ellen Dogherty, who sat in the corner of the room for two weeks . . . is substantially unchanged.

That said, despite Dr Macadam's masterful manoeuvring to escape personal responsibility for what had occurred, the Royal Society itself was severely damaged by the debacle. Of 335 members in 1860, there were just 37 left in 1863.[28] At least they were spared the colossal cost of the expedition, as all of the £57,840 final bill – bar the £1000 donation from Kyte and £2199 from public subscription – ended up being borne by the colonists of Victoria.

An attempt would be made, at least, to garner such scientific information as had been gathered into a book which would help to salvage the society's reputation in that field, but it would be . . . 150 years before *Burke and Wills – The Scientific Legacy of the Victorian Exploring Expedition* was published, in 2011 by none other than the Royal Society of Victoria.

•

Dr John Macadam was never quite called to account for his own part in the disaster, but was certainly obliged to spend a lot of his energies defending it thereafter. Beyond that, he is chiefly remembered for two things. Firstly, and despite the suggestion from the papers that his name become synonymous with suffering 'from the combined effects of drunken madness, lugubriousness, and imbecility, to say in one word that he has been – "Macadamised"'[29], his name actually did enter the English language, specifically for having the 'Macadamia nut' named after him by his good friend and fellow member of the Royal Society of Victoria and the Exploration Committee, the botanist Ferdinand Mueller. (True, some had said he was a nut all along, but still.) Secondly, he is remembered for having been one of two men who umpired the first game of Aussie Rules ever played, back in 1858. In my own wild erratic fancy, with apologies to A. B. Paterson, visions come to me of Dr Macadam bouncing the first ball, as mayhem breaks out all around, before inventing that extraordinary sporting theatre of flag waving every time a goal is scored.

In 1865, aged just 38, Macadam died at sea of a broken rib and exhaustion while on his way to New Zealand to give expert medical testimony on poisoning in a murder trial. One of the attendees at his funeral was John King.

•

Professor Georg Neumayer published his book, *Results of the Magnetic Survey of the Colony of Victoria Executed During the Years 1858–1864*, in 1864, the same year he tried to organise an expedition to search for Ludwig Leichhardt. In 1868 he tried once again to organise a scientific expedition to Australia's interior, but there was insufficient enthusiasm, given the previous disaster of the Burke and Wills expedition. He returned to Germany in 1872 with his reputation enhanced by his work in Australia, and became head of the Hamburg Oceanic Observatory in 1876, a position he would hold for the next quarter century. He went on to chair the International Polar Commission in 1879, was appointed hydrographer to the German navy, and was instrumental in establishing the first German Antarctica Expedition in 1901. The notably successful Norwegian explorer Roald Amundsen, leader of the first expedition to reach the South Pole, studied under Neumayer in 1900. Professor Neumayer died in 1909 in Neustadt, aged 74, and the Neumayer Station III in Antarctica, named in his honour, is still in use to this day.

•

Sir William Stawell remained a highly respected Chief Justice of the Victorian Supreme Court for another quarter century, only retiring in 1886, and appointed a Knight Commander the same year. He died in 1889 on holiday in Naples, en route back to England, aged 73. Stawell in western Victoria is named after him, as is the iconic Stawell Gift foot race, held annually from 1878.

•

For his part, **William Lockhart Morton** remained a persistent critic of the whole exercise, and continued to write on it extensively, including for the *Age* and the *Victorian Review* before – perhaps deciding neither paper was carrying the number of pieces he wanted to write about the folly of Burke and Wills – he established his own newspaper, the *Yeoman and Australian Acclimatiser*, where he could be particularly firm and voluminous in his remarks. Burke, he would maintain for the rest of his days, was, 'a highly excitable, irascible, changeable, and eccentric individual, who could never sit down calmly and devise a definite plan of operations, and who could never execute, to the letter, such plans as he devised . . .'[30]

In 1880, Morton tried to establish a station just 40 miles beyond the Torowoto Swamp, only to go bankrupt in 1882, costing him the lives of two of his sons in the whole ghastly process. He died in Adelaide in 1898, aged 78, survived by one son and his wife of 50 years, Mary Anne.

•

As to other vestiges of the Burke and Wills expedition, in 1908, **Edwin Welch**, still going strong nearly 50 years after being the European to find John King alive, posed an interesting question concerning the cache of instruments buried by Wills at Plant Camp on 3 April 1861, as indicated by the headline in the Sydney newspaper, *World's News*:

An Explorer's Plant.

WILL IT EVER BE DISCOVERED?

(By EDWIN J. WELCH.)

TIME alone can provide the answer to the above query. Under existing conditions it seems highly improbable that the present generation will have the opportunity of inspecting the valuable collection of scientific instruments buried by the explorer Wills . . .[31]

Welch's generation did not discover the plant, but it may be that a modern generation, using modern techniques and technology, has. In August 2007 the former Victorian Government Surveyor-General, Ray Holmes, located Wills's spirit level, followed the next year by Melbourne University's Professor Frank Leahy claiming – after 20 years research – to have found the remains of Burke's Camp 46R, Plant Camp, the spot where, on 3 April 1861, Burke and Wills had left behind the very things that Leahy turned up in 2008, including, 'bullets, buckles, pieces of what could be instrument cases, a sewing kit and a paperweight . . . within two kilometres of a blaze tree from the ill-fated expedition'[32].

(For all that, the Burke and Wills Historical Society remain to be convinced that the find is authentic, with the then society president,

David Corke, quoted as saying that until such times as a sextant or astronomical survey instrument is found, the society would keep an open mind about the finds. 'It is still up in the air as far as most of us are concerned,' Mr Corke said. 'We are sitting on the fence a bit.'[33]) The site, wherever it is, is now protected under the *Queensland Heritage Act 1992*, though at the time of writing, a new dig, carefully controlled, is about to get underway. The Plant Camp remains the Holy Grail of Burke and Wills devotees.

•

The 'Dig Tree', as it has become known, remains the focus of attention for all those who become enamoured of the ballad of Burke and Wills – and though it is now on the Nappa Merrie cattle station, there is public access. For those visiting from a capital city, it is a HELL of a drive to get there, but worth it. When Libby Effeney and I journeyed there in January 2017, in a four-wheel drive from Melbourne, following the expedition's path, we were more acutely aware than ever of just what an extraordinary thing the expedition had accomplished to get even that far. Our respect deepened further as we approached the Queensland border and the country became ever drier, rougher and more difficult to navigate. How they managed it, day after day, week after week, for months, I will never know. Arriving at Cooper's Creek it was impressive to note how well the old coolabahs have survived droughts, floods and termite infestations for an estimated 350 years. In late March, I travelled the final section of Burke and Wills's path, from Birdsville to the Gulf of Carpentaria with Kylie Scott of Desert Edge Tours, and came away even more impressed. The country! The diversity! The obstacles!

•

As to the memory of the explorers in literature, it was within a year of the burial of Burke and Wills that the first slew of what would be dozens of books on the expedition emerged, with Andrew Jackson's *Robert O'Hara Burke and the Australian Exploring Expedition of 1860*, and Dr Wills's *A Successful Exploration through the Interior of Australia from Melbourne to the Gulf of Carpentaria* being the most prominent.

For at least the better part of the next half-century, Burke and Wills was right up there with Eureka and Ned Kelly as one of the key Australian stories, until Gallipoli came along and submerged them all . . . And just as Ned Kelly was one of the first stories to be made into a feature film, so too did the Burke and Wills saga make an appearance early in the history of cinema when, in 1918, the silent movie *A Romance of Burke and Wills Expedition of 1860* was released, quickly becoming a great hit in primary school classrooms across the country.

In 1937, Frank Clune's seminal book, *Dig*, was published to wide acclaim, its popularity lending iconic status to the 'Dig Tree'. A quarter of a century later, the great Alan Moorehead, whose work I have enjoyed across many subjects, published his own effort, *Cooper's Creek: Tragedy and Adventure in the Australian Outback*. The foundation stones for the modern corpus were laid, with works by Thomas Bergin, Tim Bonyhady and Sarah Murgatroyd following, as well as the latest transcription and digitisation efforts of Dave Phoenix, historian and current president of the Burke and Wills Historical Society, which have made everything so much easier for the rest of us, for now and forevermore, trying to work out exactly what happened.

•

In the end, who really was most to blame for the debacle? As you might have gathered, debates on the rights and wrongs of the expedition, and who did what to whom, would go on, as they do to this day. A frequent point of discussion has been whether Mr Wright was actually wrong in not heading back up to Cooper's Creek soon after arriving back at Menindee on 5 November 1860. Alan Moorehead was one who tackled it in 1963, writing: 'There was no basis here for criminal proceedings against Wright, but he had been publicly condemned as the man on whom the guilt chiefly lay, and that was a reputation that he was unlikely ever to live down. He retired to obscurity in Adelaide, leaving behind him still a slight, persistent mystery: why had he really delayed? Was it only because he wanted to make sure of his salary? Was it because he did not want to leave his wife and family and the comforts of the settled districts? Was it merely that he was stupid, lazy and indifferent: a man too mean-spirited to think of anyone but himself? Or was it just possible that he was the victim of that same fated chain of errors that had bedevilled the expedition from the beginning? These were questions that would never be fully answered.'[34]

What he said! But, against that, when you look at it closely, Wright was never going to be in a position to turn around quickly at Menindee and head back – and Burke should have known that. And when he did get going – at the height of summer, with a sick crew – it was a measure of his ability that he got as far as he did.

In 1982, Tom Bergin of New England University would do his best in a Master's thesis devoted to the subject, where he broadly came down on the side of Wright being correct in not turning around immediately. With contradictory verbal instructions from Burke, a skeleton crew of exhausted animals, no money to get the fresh animals he needed, no formal authority from the Committee, and no guaranteed pay for his time and effort, Bergin's conclusion was that it would indeed have been folly, and perhaps dangerous folly at that, for Wright to turn around and head straight back to Cooper's Creek. The real case Wright had to answer, in my view, was why he delayed from 9 January 1861 when Hodgkinson got back to Menindee with money and authorisation, until 26 January – a crucial delay, which made their conditions harder, and made his men suffer even more from the malnutrition which took the lives of three of the party: Becker, Stone and Purcell.

On the subject of that malnutrition, Bergin pushed an interesting theory that what finally killed Burke and Wills was that they prepared their nardoo in a manner different to the natives. This theory held that while the method of preparation the Aboriginal people used involved cooking nardoo, eliminating toxins in the process, Wills and Burke ate their nardoo raw, more or less as porridge, and so were slowly poisoned. Two modern scientists who examined the claim, biochemist Dr John Earl and agricultural scientist Dr Barry McLeary, later argued the opposite, pointing out that heat does little to counteract toxins in a plant that is adapted to the desert. Dave Phoenix, however, the person most expert on the Burke and Wills saga in the country, points out the inconsistency here, noting, 'It is clear from Wills's diary that he observed the Yandruwandha using both methods of preparation, and the explorers used both methods of preparation in their own camp.'[35]

•

Ever stranger stories would continue to circulate about what *really* happened to Burke and Wills, most of dubious veracity but too good not to repeat . . . In 1875, for example, an old Aboriginal woman would tell a Cooper's Creek squatter that while roasting a duck by the fire Burke was killed by "nother one white fellow'[36]. (Anyone truly familiar with the saga might ask the obvious question: 'Roasting a duck by the fire? Sounds very unlikely.') The Aboriginal woman said she had witnessed it herself. The whitefella murderer – whom the squatter took to be King – had come up behind Burke and shot him in the side, and then covered the corpse with bushes. There was enough credible detail that the squatter described the story to the *Town and Country Journal* as more than 'just another blackfellow's yarn'[37]. Once the story made the major newspapers, it generated an enormously sceptical response, letter writers pointing out that the woman could only have belonged to the tribe that had taken King in, in which case all of them would have known it. King, having died three years earlier, was unable to defend his good name. Mr Alfred Howitt, called upon to give his views, denied the story's substance: 'the commander of the search expedition, gleaned nothing that could excite his suspicions of foul play'. In the years after the rumour started, 'Many white men have visited Cooper's Creek and conversed with the blacks since Mr Howitt's time, and yet not one of them has picked up such a tale as that which has just been published in Sydney.'[38]

It is all the more surprising that such an accusation could be repeated against that 'faithful man, of whose conduct his master recorded in his dying moments, "King has behaved nobly to the last"'[39].

Other, ever more outlandish, stories would emerge, including that, while they were all starving at Cooper's Creek – can you believe it? – Burke shot and wounded Wills with a revolver! Yet others said Wills and Burke had faced off in a duel. None of the stories had any credibility.

There is one story, however, that has an intriguing rough plausibility.

In the early 1880s, drover George McIver heard from a Yandruwandha man 'that a quarrel took place between Burke and Wills; that Burke assaulted the latter, striking him several times with his hands and in the end knocked him down'[40].

Again, there was some credible detail, with the location of the assault being pinpointed as 'about fifteen miles below where Strzelecki Creek emerges from the great lagoon, near Innamincka, and not far from where Wills died soon afterwards'[41]. That makes it very likely to be Burke's camp at 'Nardoo Creek', where they spent a considerable amount of time in early June – and where there was ample cause for Wills to be angry. For it was at this time that Wills had stayed with the hospitable natives on his way back from the Depot, and then returned to the starving Burke and King to find that . . . Burke had fired his gun over the natives' heads and scared them off.

The story has it that Wills, by now recognising that their only hope of survival was living off the kindness of the Yandruwandha people, and that Burke's ludicrous hot-headedness had wiped out his own efforts to befriend them and imperilled them all, was LIVID, and didn't hold back – whereupon Burke assaulted him. Shortly thereafter, Wills heads off once more to try his luck living among the natives, only to find them gone. Did it happen? We will, of course, never know, but of all the strange stories, this is the one that most intrigues me. And if Wills wasn't livid, he *should* have been!

The most enduring mystery from the whole saga, of course, is whose body did McKinlay and his men discover?

Dave Phoenix is adamant: 'The body was not Charley Gray's.'

So what of the coincidence that the body was found in much the same place where Gray was buried? That there was a *Nautical Almanac* from 1858? The camel droppings? What on earth is the explanation for that?

I have no clue.

•

Another mystery that fascinates me is what on earth *did* happen to **Ludwig Leichhardt** and his men? Now 170-odd years on since their disappearance, no solid trace of the German explorer and his party of six companions, seven horses, 20 mules and 50 bullocks has ever been found. In 1863, Victorian pastoralist Duncan McIntyre claimed that, being impressed by Landsborough's account of what he'd seen while looking for Burke, he'd departed on a sortie looking for good land, and had not only come across trees blazed with a large 'L' right by the Flinders River, clearly carved many years before, but also found two very old horses nearby.

Even more intriguing, though, in 2006 scientists authenticated a brass plate marked 'Ludwig Leichhardt 1848' – attached to a partially burnt shotgun which was engraved with the initial 'L' – that had been discovered around 1900 by an Aboriginal stockman just inside Western Australia, near the border with the Northern Territory. Very likely, in my view, this is at least an indication that Leichhardt's expedition actually made it two thirds of the way across Australia before meeting its ends. Against that, it is also possible that the plate and gun was found by an Aboriginal tribe hundreds of kilometres away, or even more, and the novelty was traded between tribes from there. It is now appreciated more than ever just how sophisticated such trading routes were.

•

And on that score, there is one thing that is not up for dispute. Back in 1845, Charles Sturt observed of the Indigenous people that 'While I have the consolation to know that no European will follow my track into the Desert without experiencing kindness from its tenants, I have to regret that the progress of civilized man into an uncivilized region, is almost invariably attended with misfortune to its original inhabitants.'[42]

So did it prove for the Yandruwandha people. Having noted their kindness to John King, the Very Reverend Hussey Burgh Macartney, Dean of Melbourne, came to the conclusion that their 'noble conduct gave us strong call upon the members of the Church to endeavour to return their kindness'[43]. Surely, the best thing would be to establish a Christian mission to help the 'poor blacks of Cooper's Creek'[44]. Several attempts to do exactly that were made, all defeated by the harsh conditions of the outback. But the pastoralists, impressed by the water and the adjacent land, were more persistent and by 1873 the first cattle stations along Cooper's Creek had been established, inevitably squeezing the Yandruwandha from their traditional lands. This was followed in 1882 by the establishment of the first police camp, whereupon yet more white settlement came in scattered fashion, variously killing and displacing the locals. Two famous Banjo Paterson poems give a hint of what kind of settlement took place.

In 1889, as Banjo recounted it, a letter was written,

> *Just 'on spec', addressed as follows, 'Clancy of the Overflow'*
> *And an answer came directed in a writing unexpected,*
> *(And I think the same was written with a thumb-nail dipped in tar)[. . .]*
> *'Clancy's gone to Queensland droving, and we don't know where he are.'*
>
> *In my wild erratic fancy visions come to me of Clancy*
> *Gone a-droving '**down the Cooper**' where the Western drovers go;*
> *As the stock are slowly stringing, Clancy rides behind them singing,*
> *For the drover's life has pleasures that the townsfolk never know.*[45]

Four years later, Paterson's famed 'Bush Christening' began . . .

> *On the **outer Barcoo** where the churches are few,*
> *And men of religion are scanty,*
> *On a road never cross'd 'cept by folk that are lost,*
> *One Michael Magee had a shanty*[46]

The settlement continued of course, all through the twentieth century, with still more whites coming to claim and live on what had been Aboriginal land. Still, in 1997, a group of Yandruwandha people began the process of making a Yandruwandha-Yawarrawarrka Native Title claim, which was eventually settled in their favour in December 2015.

ENDNOTES

Prologue

1 *Ovens and Murray Advertiser*, 3 August 1880, p. 2.
2 *Ovens and Murray Advertiser*, 9 July 1874, p. 2.
3 *The Australasian*, 28 May 1898, p. 27.
4 *The Australasian*, 28 May 1898, p. 27.
5 *The Australasian*, 28 May 1898, p. 27.
6 Joseph Carpenter, *The New British Song Book*, G. Routledge and Sons, London, 1866. p. 95.
7 *Table Talk*, 5 February 1886, p. 1.

Chapter One

1 Philosophical Institute of Victoria, *Transactions of the Philosophical Institute of Victoria*, Vol. II, p. 168. https://archive.org/stream/transactionsofph02phil#page/168
2 *The Argus*, 1 September 1858, p. 4.
3 Philosophical Institute of Victoria, *Transactions of the Philosophical Institute of Victoria*, Vol. II p. xlvi. [Reported speech]
4 Philosophical Institute of Victoria, *Transactions of the Philosophical Institute of Victoria*, Vol. II p. xliv.
5 Philosophical Institute of Victoria, *Transactions of the Philosophical Institute of Victoria*, Vol. II, p. xlvi.
6 Philosophical Institute of Victoria, *Transactions of the Philosophical Institute of Victoria*, Vol. II, pp. xlvi–xlvii. [Reported speech]
7 Philosophical Institute of Victoria, *Transactions of the Philosophical Institute of Victoria*, Vol. II, pp. xliii–xliv.
8 F.J. Leahy, *100 Years of National Topographic Mapping*, Canberra, 2011, p. 1. http://www.xnatmap.org/adnm/conf_06_11/c11/Paper%2001.pdf
9 *Geelong Advertiser*, 1 November 1860, p. 2.
10 Royal Society of Victoria, Meeting minutes, 30 November 1857 [no page numbers] (Image 2). http://handle.slv.vic.gov.au/10381/158458
11 *The Argus*, 26 December 1857, p. 6. [Reported speech]
12 *The Argus*, 1 September 1858, p. 4.
13 *The Argus*, 22 January 1863, p. 6. [Reported speech]
14 *The Age*, 31 August 1858, p. 1.
15 John Macadam, Fund Raising Circular, 15 September 1858, p. 1 (Image 1). http://handle.slv.vic.gov.au/10381/158695
16 *The Argus*, 7 March 1854, p. 4.
17 *The Argus*, 30 March 1858, p. 6.
18 *The Argus*, 5 August 1858, p. 5.
19 *The Argus*, 31 August 1858, p. 5.
20 Philosophical Institute of Victoria, *Transactions of the Philosophical Institute of Victoria*, Vol. IV, p. ix

21 Author's note: In this letter he advises they set up their Depot where Cooper's Creek (he calls it Cooper River) meets Strzelecki, which is the earliest seed I have found for the Depot ending up there.

22 Philosophical Institute of Victoria, *Transactions of the Philosophical Institute of Victoria*, Vol. IV, p. viii.

23 *The Argus*, 6 May 1859, p. 5. [Reported speech]

24 *The South Australian Advertiser*, 20 July 1859, p. 3.

25 *The Argus*, 26 July 1859, p. 4.

26 *The Australasian*, 13 March 1886, p. 1.

27 Charles Dickens, *David Copperfield*, Vol. II, Sheldon, New York, 1863, p. 66. [Reported speech]

28 Charles Dickens, *The Life and Adventures of Martin Chuzzlewit*, Chapman and Hall, London, 1844, p. 174.

29 *The Australasian*, 13 March 1886, p. 1.

30 *The Australasian*, 13 March 1886, p. 1.

31 *The Age*, 13 November 1861, p. 5. Author's note: Although the article does not name the 'friends' that recalled hearing Wills say this, I have attributed it to the memory of his dearest friend in Melbourne, Richard Birnie.

32 William John Wills, *A Successful Exploration*, Richard Bentley, London, 1863, pp. 60–62.

33 *The Argus*, 15 October 1859, p. 4.

34 William John Wills, *A Successful Exploration*, pp. 64–65.

35 *The Age*, 31 January 1860, p. 4. [Tense changed]

36 *The Argus*, 26 January 1860, p. 5.

37 *Adelaide Observer*, 25 December 1858, p. 7.

38 *Adelaide Observer*, 25 December 1858, p. 7.

39 *The Argus*, 26 January 1860, p. 5.

40 Author's note: Although Bendigo officially changed its name to 'Sandhurst' in 1854 and then back to Bendigo in 1891, I have used the name Bendigo throughout this book. So many contemporaries and newspapers of the day ignored the official change and still used the name Bendigo throughout this period, that to do otherwise would create confusion.

41 Author's note: Although the records of Bruce's backdoor dealings to secure the leadership for Robert Burke are scant, there is no doubt a meeting must have occurred between Macadam and Bruce, in which the latter successfully insisted Macadam support Robert Burke for the leadership. Author Tim Bonyhady says that Bruce introduced Burke to members of the Committee, including Macadam and Reverend John Bleasdale, at a dinner party at the St Kilda home of John Watson, publican of the Albion Hotel. He gives no date for the dinner, but suggests it happened in January of 1860. If so, my presumption is that it was held in late January, right after the meeting to discuss possible leaders, when Macadam had been in the Warburton camp. My reckoning is that Bruce, in addition to said dinner party, would have appealed to John Macadam personally, given their business and political ties, and Macadam's powerful role within the Exploration Committee.

42 Tim Bonyhady, *Burke & Wills*, David Ell Press, NSW, 1991, p. 28.

43 Tim Bonyhady, *Burke & Wills*, p. 28.

44 *Mount Alexander Mail*, 4 July 1862, p. 5.

45 *The Yeoman and Australian Acclimatiser*, 28 December 1861, p. 8.

46 *Leader* (Melbourne), 18 June 1887, p. 7.

47 *Leader* (Melbourne), 18 June 1887, p. 7.

48 *Leader* (Melbourne), 18 June 1887, p. 7.

49 Royal Society of Victoria, Exploration Committee, Minutes, 30 January 1860, SLV, MS13071, Box 2088B/1, p. 37 (Image 27). [Reported speech] http://handle.slv.vic.gov.au/10381/163008

50 Royal Society of Victoria, Exploration Committee, Minutes, 30 January 1860, SLV, MS13071, Box 2088B/1, p. 37 (Image 27). [Reported speech] http://handle.slv.vic.gov.au/10381/163008

51 *The Yeoman and Australian Acclimatiser*, 28 December 1861, p. 8.

52 Royal Society of Victoria, Exploration Committee, Minutes, undated, SLV, MS13071, Box 2075/2c (3) [no page numbers] (Image 1). http://handle.slv.vic.gov.au/10381/162676

53 Royal Society of Victoria, Exploration Committee, Minutes, undated, SLV, MS13071, Box 2075/2c (3) [no page numbers] (Image 1). http://handle.slv.vic.gov.au/10381/162676
54 *The Argus*, 26 January 1860, p. 5.
55 *The Age*, 1 February 1860, p. 5.
56 *The Herald* (Melbourne), 9 March 1860, p. 4.
57 *The Yeoman and Australian Acclimatiser*, 28 December 1861, p. 8.

Chapter Two

1 *Mount Alexander Mail*, 8 November 1861, p. 4.
2 Charles Sturt, *Narrative of an Expedition into Central Australia*, Vol. 2, T. and W. Boone, London, 1849, pp. 1–2.
3 *Advocate* (Melbourne), 9 April 1904, p. 13.
4 Frank Clune, *Dig: The Burke and Wills Saga*, Angus & Robertson, London, 1976, p. 14.
5 *Mount Alexander Mail*, 24 November 1854, p. 3.
6 *Ovens and Murray Advertiser*, 3 August 1880, p. 2.
7 *Leader* (Melbourne), 18 June 1887, p. 7.
8 *Ovens and Murray Advertiser*, 3 August 1880, p. 2.
9 *Leader* (Melbourne), 18 June 1887, p. 6.
10 *Ovens and Murray Advertiser*, 3 August 1880, p. 2.
11 *Ovens and Murray Advertiser*, 9 July 1874, p. 2. [Reported speech]
12 *Ovens and Murray Advertiser*, 9 July 1874, p. 2.
13 *Ovens and Murray Advertiser*, 9 July 1874, p. 2.
14 *Ovens and Murray Advertiser*, 9 July 1874, p. 2.
15 *Mount Alexander Mail*, 4 July 1862, p. 5. [Reported speech]
16 *The Truth* (Perth), 3 January 1914, p. 3. [Reported speech]
17 P.N. Smithe, Letter to John Macadam, 7 February 1860, SLV, MS13071, Box 2076/2, pp. 1–4 (Images 1–3). http://handle.slv.vic.gov.au/10381/164469
18 *The Argus*, 8 March 1860, p. 4.
19 John Frizzell, Letter to Exploration Committee, 20 January 1860, SLV, MS13071, Box 2076/3, ex1004-191 [no page numbers].
20 John Frizzell, Letter to Exploration Committee, 20 January 1860, SLV, MS13071, Box 2076/3, ex1004-191 [no page numbers].
21 *Mount Alexander Mail*, 4 July 1862, p. 5.
22 *The World's News*, 4 February 1911, p. 10.
23 *Bendigo Advertiser*, 16 February 1860, p. 2.
24 William Denison, *Varieties of Vice-Regal Life*, Longmans, Green & Co., London, 1870, pp. 170–71.
25 Ludwig Becker, Letter to Mueller, 9 March 1860, NLA, MS 1236, pp. 1–4.
26 *The Argus*, 14 March 1860, p. 5.
27 *Ovens and Murray Advertiser*, 3 August 1880, p. 2.
28 William John Wills, *A Successful Exploration*, pp. 68–69.
29 William John Wills, *A Successful Exploration*, p. 69.
30 *The Age*, 11 April 1860, pp. 5–6.
31 *The South Australian Advertiser*, 18 June 1860, p. 2.
32 *The Argus*, 15 June 1860, p. 5.
33 *The Argus*, 15 June 1860, p. 5.
34 George Landells, Letter to Chief Secretary, 21 May 1859, Public Record Office Victoria, VPRS1189/P0000 Unit 757: Inward Registered Correspondence: Letter to the Chief Secretary regarding camels for the Burke and Wills expedition of 1860–61, p. 2. http://www.cv.vic.gov.au/stories/burke-and-wills-have-camels-will-travel/
35 John McKellar, 'John King (explorer): Sole survivor of the Burke and Wills' expedition to the Gulf of Carpentaria, 1860–61', *Victorian Historical Magazine*, Vol XX, No 4, December 1944, p. 108.
36 *The Argus*, 15 June 1860, p. 5.
37 *Sydney Sportsman*, 5 October 1910, p. 3.

38 *The Yeoman and Australian Acclimatiser*, 4 January 1862, pp. 8–9.

39 *Mount Alexander Mail*, 22 June 1860, p. 5.

40 *Leader* (Melbourne), 18 June 1887, p. 6.

41 Falconer Larkworthy, *Ninety-one Years Being the Reminiscences of Falconer Larkworthy*, Mills & Boon Ltd., London, 1924, pp. 245–46.

42 *The Argus*, 20 June 1908, p. 8.

43 *Leader* (Melbourne), 18 June 1887, p. 6.

44 *The Australasian*, 28 May 1898, p. 27.

45 *The Herald* (Melbourne), 21 June 1860, p. 4.

46 *The Argus*, 20 June 1908, p. 8.

47 *The Argus*, 20 June 1908, p. 8.

48 Joseph Carpenter, *The New British Song Book*, G. Routledge and Sons, London, 1866, p. 95.

49 *The Yeoman and Australian Acclimatiser*, 4 January 1862, p. 8.

50 *The Age*, 26 June 1860, p. 5.

51 *The Age*, 26 June 1860, p. 5.

52 *South Australian Register*, 8 October 1860, p. 2.

Chapter Three

1 Ludwig Becker, Letter to Mueller, 9 March 1860, p. 1.

2 William John Wills, *A Successful Exploration*, p. 32.

3 *Ovens and Murray Advertiser*, 3 August 1880, p. 2.

4 *Leader* (Melbourne), 18 June 1887, p. 7.

5 *Leader* (Melbourne), 18 June 1887, p. 7.

6 *The Age*, 25 June 1860, p. 6.

7 *The Argus*, 30 June 1860, p. 7.

8 William Brahe, Letter to Exploration Committee, 2 July 1860, SLV, MS13071, Box 2076/2, pp. 1–2 (Images 1 and 2). http://handle.slv.vic.gov.au/10381/164467

9 Andrew Jackson, *Robert O'Hara Burke and the Australian Exploring Expedition of 1860*, Smith, Elder and Co, London, 1862, pp. 8–9.

10 Alan Moorehead, *Cooper's Creek*, Sun Books, South Melbourne, 1985, p. 11.

11 Charles Sturt, *Narrative of an Expedition into Central Australia*, p. 126.

12 Alan Moorehead, *Cooper's Creek*, p. 14.

13 Alan Moorehead, *Cooper's Creek*, p. 14.

14 Charles Sturt, *Narrative of an Expedition into Central Australia*, Vol. II, p. 93.

15 Webster, Letter to Burke, 11 July 1860, SLNSW, ML D179, Item 7, p. 2.

16 Edward Eyre, *Journals of Expeditions of Discovery into Central Australia*, Vol. 1, T. and W. Boone, London, 1845 pp. 127–28.

17 Charles Ferguson, *Experiences of a Forty-Niner*, The Williams Publishing Company, Cleveland, 1888, p. 380.

18 Charles Ferguson, *Experiences of a Forty-Niner*, p. 60.

19 Charles Ferguson, *Experiences of a Forty-Niner*, p. 380.

20 Charles Ferguson, *Experiences of a Forty-Niner*, p. 380. [Reported speech]

21 Burke and Wills Commission, p. 20, Q453.

22 *The Australasian*, 28 May 1898, p. 27.

23 *The Age*, 5 July 1860, p. 4.

24 Sarah Murgatroyd, *The Dig Tree*, Text Publishing, Victoria, 2012, p. 69.

25 *The Age*, 5 July 1860, p. 5.

26 *Mount Alexander Mail*, 9 July 1860, p. 2.

27 *Mount Alexander Mail*, 9 July 1860, p. 2.

28 *Mount Alexander Mail*, 9 July 1860, p. 2. [Reported speech]

29 *Mount Alexander Mail*, 9 July 1860, p. 2. [Reported speech]

30 *Mount Alexander Mail*, 9 July 1860, p. 2. [Reported speech]

31 *Mount Alexander Mail*, 9 July 1860, p. 2. [Reported speech]

32 *Mount Alexander Mail*, 9 July 1860, p. 2. [Reported speech]

33 *Mount Alexander Mail*, 9 July 1860, p. 2. [Reported speech]

34 *Mount Alexander Mail*, 9 July 1860, p. 2.

35 *Mount Alexander Mail*, 9 July 1860, p. 3. [Reported speech]

36 *Mount Alexander Mail*, 9 July 1860, p. 3.

37 Royal Society of Victoria, Exploration Committee, Meeting, 9 July 1860, Minute Book, SLV, MS13071, Box 2075/1c, [no page number] (Image 33). http://handle.slv.vic.gov.au/10381/162914

38 Royal Society of Victoria, Exploration Committee, Meeting, 9 July 1860, Minute Book, SLV, MS13071, Box 2075/1c, [no page number] (Image 34). http://handle.slv.vic.gov.au/10381/162914

39 Royal Society of Victoria, Exploration Committee, Meeting, 9 July 1860, Minute Book, SLV, MS13071, Box 2075/1c, [no page number] (Image 34). http://handle.slv.vic.gov.au/10381/162914

40 *The South Australian Advertiser*, 3 August 1860, p. 2.

41 *The Sydney Morning Herald*, 28 June 1860, p. 2.

42 *Ovens and Murray Advertiser*, 9 July 1874, p. 2.

43 Andrew Jackson, *Robert O'Hara Burke*, p. 9.

44 *The Age*, 13 November 1861, p. 5.

45 Charles Ferguson, *Experiences of a Forty-Niner*, p. 383.

46 John Macadam, Instructions to Surveyor, Meteorologist and Astronomical Observer; 3 September 1860, p. 2 (Image 3). http://handle.slv.vic.gov.au/10381/212904

47 John Macadam, Instructions to Surveyor, Meteorologist and Astronomical Observer; 3 September 1860, p. 4 (Image 5). http://handle.slv.vic.gov.au/10381/212904

48 John Macadam, Instructions to Surveyor, Meteorologist and Astronomical Observer; 3 September 1860, pp. 4–5 (Images 5 and 6). http://handle.slv.vic.gov.au/10381/212904

49 John Macadam, Instructions to Surveyor, Meteorologist and Astronomical Observer; 3 September 1860, pp. 6–8 (Images 8 and 9). http://handle.slv.vic.gov.au/10381/212904

50 John Macadam, Instructions to Surveyor, Meteorologist and Astronomical Observer; 3 September 1860, pp. 8–9 (Images 9 and 10). http://handle.slv.vic.gov.au/10381/212904

51 William Denison, *Varieties of Vice-Regal Life*, Vol. I, pp. 170–71. https://archive.org/stream/cu31924087994202#page/n191

52 *The Australasian*, 13 March 1886, p. 1.

53 *The Australasian*, 13 March 1886, p. 1.

54 *The Australasian*, 13 March 1886, p. 1.

55 *The Australasian*, 13 March 1886, p. 2.

56 Mary Stawell, *My Recollections*, R. Clay, London, 1911, p. 133.

57 John Frizzell, Letter to Exploration Committee, 20 January 1860 SLV MS13071, Box 2076/2 [no page numbers].

58 *The Argus*, 6 February 1926, p. 7.

59 Royal Society of Victoria, Exploration Committee, Meeting, 17 July 1860, Minute Book, SLV, MS13071, Box 2088B/1, p. 59 (Image 41). http://handle.slv.vic.gov.au/10381/163008

60 Royal Society of Victoria, Exploration Committee, Meeting, 17 July 1860, Minute Book, SLV, MS13071, Box 2088B/1, p. 58 (Image 40). http://handle.slv.vic.gov.au/10381/163008

61 Royal Society of Victoria, Exploration Committee, Meeting, 17 July 1860, Minute Book, SLV, MS13071, Box 2088B/1, p. 58 (Image 40). http://handle.slv.vic.gov.au/10381/163008

62 Royal Society of Victoria, Exploration Committee, Meeting, 17 July 1860, Minute Book, SLV, MS13071, Box 2088B/1, p. 58 (Image 40). [Reported speech] http://handle.slv.vic.gov.au/10381/163008

63 Royal Society of Victoria, Exploration Committee, Meeting Minutes, 17 July 1860, SLV, MS13071, Box 2088B/1, p. 58 (Image 41). http://handle.slv.vic.gov.au/10381/163008

64 George Landells, Letter (Application), 18 July 1860, p. 1 (Image 2). http://handle.slv.vic.gov.au/10381/306915

65 *Geelong Advertiser*, 29 November 1861, p. 3.

66 Royal Society of Victoria, Exploration Committee, Meeting, 10 August 1860, Minute Book, SLV, MS13071, Box 2075/1c, [no page number] (Image 54). http://handle.slv.vic.gov.au/10381/162914

67 *The Age*, 24 July 1860, p. 5.
68 *The Argus*, 20 July 1860, p. 4.
69 *The Argus*, 20 July 1860, p. 7.
70 *The Argus*, 28 July 1860, p. 4.

Chapter Four

1 *Geelong Advertiser*, 24 July 1860, p. 2.
2 William John Wills, *A Successful Exploration*, pp. 76–77.
3 Burke and Wills Commission, pp. 4–5, Q44–46.
4 William John Wills, *A Successful Exploration*, p. 3.
5 Royal Society of Victoria, Exploration Committee, Account Book, p. 3 (Image 3). http://handle. slv.vic.gov.au/10381/162911
6 Royal Society of Victoria, Exploration Committee, Account Book, p. 6 (Image 4). http://handle. slv.vic.gov.au/10381/162911
7 Royal Society of Victoria, Exploration Committee, Account Book, p. 6 (Image 4). http://handle. slv.vic.gov.au/10381/162911
8 Royal Society of Victoria, Exploration Committee, Account Book, p. 6 (Image 4). http://handle. slv.vic.gov.au/10381/162911
9 Royal Society of Victoria, Exploration Committee, Account Book, p. 6 (Image 4). http://handle. slv.vic.gov.au/10381/162911
10 Royal Society of Victoria, Exploration Committee, Account Book, p. 7 (Image 5). http://handle. slv.vic.gov.au/10381/162911
11 Royal Society of Victoria, Exploration Committee, Account Book, p. 7 (Image 5). http://handle. slv.vic.gov.au/10381/162911
12 Royal Society of Victoria, Exploration Committee, Account Book, p. 3 (Image 3). http://handle. slv.vic.gov.au/10381/162911
13 *Mount Alexander Mail*, 4 July 1862, p. 5.
14 Royal Society of Victoria, Exploration Committee, Account Book 1858–1873, p. 9 (Image 6). http://handle.slv.vic.gov.au/10381/162911
15 *South Australian Advertiser*, 27 August 1860. p. 2.
16 Royal Society of Victoria, Exploration Committee, Account Book 1858–1873, p. 2. http:// handle.slv.vic.gov.au/10381/162911
17 *The Argus*, 21 August 1860, p. 5.
18 *The Argus*, 21 August 1860, p. 5.
19 *The Herald* (Melbourne), 21 August 1860, p. 5.
20 Hermann Beckler, *A Journey to Cooper's Creek*, translated by Stephen Jeffries and Michael Kertesz, Melbourne University Press, Carlton, 1993, p. 10. Extracts from Beckler's diary are reproduced with permission from Melbourne University Publishing.
21 *The Argus*, 21 August 1860, p. 5.
22 Hermann Beckler, *A Journey to Cooper's Creek*, pp. 9–10.
23 Hermann Beckler, *A Journey to Cooper's Creek*, p. 10.
24 Alfred William Howitt, Inaugural Address, 7 January 1907, p. 13. http://handle.slv.vic.gov. au/10381/245539
25 Hermann Beckler, *A Journey to Cooper's Creek*, p. 8.
26 Royal Society of Victoria, Exploration Committee, Meeting, 27 July 1860, Minute Book, SLV, MS13071, Box 2075/1c, [no page number] (Image 48). http://handle.slv.vic.gov. au/10381/162914
27 *The Argus*, 28 July 1860, p. 4.
28 *The Australasian*, 13 March 1866, p. 2.
29 *The Australasian*, 13 March 1866, p. 2. [Reported speech]
30 William Shakespeare, *Twelfth Night*, Hackett Publishing, Indiana, 2012, p. 44.
31 *The Argus*, 2 August 1860, p. 4.
32 *Mount Alexander Mail*, 4 July 1862, p. 5.
33 Royal Society of Victoria, Exploration Committee and VEE members, Memorandum of Agreement, 18 August 1860, pp. 1–2 (Images 1 and 2). http://handle.slv.vic.gov.au/10381/188521

34 *The Yeoman and Australian Acclimatiser*, 4 January 1862, p. 8.

35 Charles Ferguson, *Experiences of a Forty-Niner*, p. 386. [Tense changed]

36 *The Argus*, 6 February 1926, p. 7.

37 *The Argus*, 6 February 1926, p. 7.

38 Hermann Beckler, *A Journey to Cooper's Creek*, p. xxvi.

39 *The Age*, 14 August 1860, p. 4.

40 Royal Society of Victoria, Exploration Committee, Meeting, 10 August 1860, Minute Book, SLV, MS13071, Box 2075/1c, [no page number] (Image 53). http://handle.slv.vic.gov.au/10381/162914

41 *The Age*, 31 August 1860, p. 5.

42 *The Age*, 31 August 1860, p. 5.

43 *The Age*, 31 August 1860, p. 5.

44 *The Argus*, 15 November 1860, p. 5. [Reported speech]

45 *The Argus*, 15 November 1860, p. 5.

46 Sarah Murgatroyd, *The Dig Tree*, p. 86

47 *The Argus*, 20 August 1860, p. 5.

48 *The Age*, 10 August 1860, p. 4.

49 *The Argus*, 20 August 1860, p. 5.

50 *The Argus*, 20 August 1860, p. 5.

51 *The Argus*, 20 August 1860, p. 5.

52 *The Argus*, 20 August 1860, p. 5.

53 *The Argus*, 20 August 1860, p. 5.

54 Royal Society of Victoria, Exploration Committee and VEE members, Memorandum of Agreement, 18 August 1860, pp. 1–2 (Images 1 and 2). http://handle.slv.vic.gov.au/10381/188521

55 Royal Society of Victoria, *Transactions of the Royal Society of Victoria, from January to December 1860, inclusive. Vol. V*, p. xvi. http://handle.slv.vic.gov.au/10381/147083

56 Royal Society of Victoria, *Transactions of the Royal Society of Victoria, from January to December 1860, inclusive. Vol. V*, p. xvi. http://handle.slv.vic.gov.au/10381/147083

57 John Macadam, Instructions to Robert O'Hara Burke, 18 August 1860, pp. 1–2 and 4–6. http://handle.slv.vic.gov.au/10381/212493

58 *The Argus*, 22 April 1861, p. 5.

59 Hermann Beckler, *A Journey to Cooper's Creek*, p. 9. [Reported speech]

60 Author's note: This is an estimated figure, deduced from the overall cost of cartage form Melbourne to the Darling River.

61 Royal Society of Victoria, Exploration Committee [unsigned], Instructions to Scientific Observers [no date], p. 4 (Image 6). http://handle.slv.vic.gov.au/10381/212799

62 Royal Society of Victoria, Exploration Committee [unsigned], Instructions to Scientific Observers [no date], p. 7 (Image 9). http://handle.slv.vic.gov.au/10381/212799

63 Royal Society of Victoria, Exploration Committee, Instructions to Scientific Observers [no date], p. 8 (Image 10). http://handle.slv.vic.gov.au/10381/212799

64 John Macadam, Instructions to the Geologist, Zoologist and Botanist, 3 September 1860 [no page numbers] (Images 7 and 8). http://handle.slv.vic.gov.au/10381/212986

65 John Macadam, Instructions to the Geologist, Zoologist and Botanist, 3 September 1860 [no page number] (Image 8). http://handle.slv.vic.gov.au/10381/212986

66 John Macadam, Instructions to the Geologist, Zoologist and Botanist, 3 September 1860 [no page number] (Images 9–10). http://handle.slv.vic.gov.au/10381/212986

67 John Macadam, Instructions to the Geologist, Zoologist and Botanist, 3 September 1860 [no page number] (Image 10). http://handle.slv.vic.gov.au/10381/212986

68 *The Age*, 29 August 1860, p. 5. [Reported speech]

69 *The Age*, 29 August 1860, p. 5.

70 *The Age*, 29 August 1860, p. 5.

71 *The Age*, 29 August 1860, p. 5.

72 *The Age*, 29 August 1860, p. 5.

73 *The Age*, 29 August 1860, p. 5.

74 *The Age*, 29 August 1860, p. 5.
75 *The Age*, 29 August 1860, p. 5.
76 *The Age*, 29 August 1860, p. 5.
77 *The Age*, 29 August 1860, p. 5.
78 *The Age*, 29 August 1860, p. 5.
79 *The Age*, 29 August 1860, p. 5.
80 *The Age*, 29 August 1860, p. 5.
81 *The Age*, 29 August 1860, p. 5.
82 *The Age*, 29 August 1860, p. 5.
83 *The Age*, 29 August 1860, p. 5.
84 *The Age*, 29 August 1860, p. 5.
85 *The Age*, 29 August 1860, p. 5.
86 *The Age*, 31 August 1860, p. 5.

Chapter Five

1 *Ovens and Murray Advertiser*, 28 May 1898, p. 2.
2 *The Queenslander*, 24 January 1891, p. 162.
3 *The Star* (Ballarat), 22 August 1860, p. 2.
4 *The Star* (Ballarat), 22 August 1860, p. 2.
5 *The Herald* (Melbourne), 21 August 1860, p. 5.
6 *The Star* (Ballarat), 22 August 1860, p. 2.
7 *The Australasian*, 13 March 1886, p. 2.
8 Hermann Beckler, *A Journey to Cooper's Creek*, p. 11.
9 *The Argus*, 21 August 1860, p. 5. [Tense changed]
10 Charles Ferguson, *Experiences of a Forty-Niner*, p. 388. [Reported speech]
11 Charles Ferguson, *Experiences of a Forty-Niner*, p. 105.
12 *The Argus*, 21 August 1860, p. 5.
13 *The Herald* (Melbourne), 21 August 1860, p. 5.
14 *The Herald* (Melbourne), 21 August 1860, p. 5.
15 *The Herald* (Melbourne), 21 August 1860, p. 5.
16 *Mount Alexander Mail*, 22 August 1860, p. 3.
17 *The Sydney Morning Herald*, 24 November 1924, p. 10.
18 *The Argus*, 6 February 1926, p. 7.
19 Mary Stawell, *My Recollections*, p. 144.
20 *Geelong Advertiser*, 5 May 1864, p. 3.
21 *Williamstown Chronicle*, 17 February 1934, p. 2.
22 E. Lawrence Abel, 'Cheer, Boys Cheer', *Singing the New Nation*, Stackpole, Mechanicsburg, 2000, p. 35.
23 *The Herald* (Melbourne), 21 August 1860, p. 4.
24 *The Age*, 21 August 1860, p. 5.
25 *The Australasian*, 13 March 1886, p. 2.
26 E. Lawrence Abel, *Singing the New Nation*, p. 35.
27 *The Herald* (Melbourne), 21 August 1860, p. 5.
28 *The Age*, 22 August 1860, p. 6.
29 William John Wills, *A Successful Exploration*, p. 101.
30 *The Australasian*, 13 March 1886, p. 2.
31 Ludwig Becker, First Report, 8 September 1860, SLV, MS13071, Box 2082/4c, p. 2.
32 Ludwig Becker, First Report, 8 September 1860, p. 2.
33 *The Argus*, 31 August 1858, p. 5.
34 Hermann Beckler, *A Journey to Cooper's Creek*, p. 16.
35 Ludwig Becker, First Report, 8 September 1860, SLV, MS13071, Box 2082/4c, p. 2.
36 Charles Ferguson, *Experience of a Forty-niner*, pp. 390–91.
37 *Bendigo Advertiser*, 30 August 1860, p. 2.
38 *Bendigo Advertiser*, 30 August 1860, p. 2.
39 *Bendigo Advertiser*, 30 August 1860, p. 2.

40 *Bendigo Advertiser*, 30 August 1860, p. 2.

41 *Bendigo Advertiser*, 30 August 1860, p. 2.

42 *Bendigo Advertiser*, 30 August 1860, p. 2.

43 *Bendigo Advertiser*, 30 August 1860, p. 2.

44 *Bendigo Advertiser*, 30 August 1860, p. 2.

45 Hermann Beckler, *A Journey to Cooper's Creek*, p. 19.

46 Hermann Beckler, *A Journey to Cooper's Creek*, pp. 20–21.

47 Robert O'Hara Burke, Telegram to John Macadam, 28 August 1860, p. 1 (Image 1). http:// handle.slv.vic.gov.au/10381/212920

48 Robert O'Hara Burke, Telegram to John Macadam, 30 August 1860, p. 2 (Image 2). http:// handle.slv.vic.gov.au/10381/212458

49 *Brisbane Courier*, 11 August 1900, p. 9.

50 *Brisbane Courier*, 11 August 1900, p. 9.

51 Georg Neumayer, *Results of the Magnetic Survey*, J. Schneider, Mannheim, 1869, p. 10.

52 Ludwig Becker, First Report, 8 September 1860, SLV, MS13071, Box 2082/4c, p. 6.

53 Hermann Beckler, *A Journey to Cooper's Creek*, p. 22.

54 Ludwig Becker, Diary, 31 August 1860, State Library of Victoria, SLV MS13071, Box 2082/4c.

55 William John Wills, *A Successful Exploration*, p. 102.

Chapter Six

1 *Leader* (Melbourne), 18 June 1887, p.7.

2 *The Argus*, 18 September 1860, p. 5.

3 *The Argus*, 6 February 1926, p. 7.

4 *The Argus*, 6 February 1926, p. 7.

5 *The Argus*, 6 February 1926, p. 7.

6 *The Australasian*, 13 March 1886, p. 2.

7 Robert O'Hara Burke, Third Dispatch, 10 September 1860 [no page numbers] (Images 1–3). http://handle.slv.vic.gov.au/10381/282264

8 *The Age*, 26 September 1860, p. 6. [Reported speech]

9 *The Age*, 26 September 1860, p. 6. [Reported speech]

10 *The Age*, 26 September 1860, p. 6. [Reported speech]

11 Author's note: I have gone with this spelling of Charley throughout, used by Wills, for the sake of consistency.

12 *The Advertiser* (Adelaide), Saturday, 12 October 1889, p. 6.

13 *Bendigo Advertiser*, 19 November 1860, p. 3.

14 Hermann Beckler, *A Journey to Cooper's Creek*, p. 25.

15 Robert O'Hara Burke, Dispatch to John Macadam, 12 September 1860 [no page number] (Image 3). http://handle.slv.vic.gov.au/10381/282266

16 *Bendigo Advertiser*, 17 September 1860, p. 3.

17 *Swan Hill Guardian*, 20 June 1918, p. 4.

18 Ludwig Becker, Second Report, 30 September 1860, SLV MS13071, Box 2082/4d, p. 2.

19 *Mount Alexander Mail*, 19 October 1860, p. 3.

20 Hermann Beckler, *A Journey to Cooper's Creek*, p. 29.

21 Ludwig Becker, Second Report, 30 September 1860, p. 4.

22 *The Queenslander*, 24 January 1891, p. 162.

23 *The Queenslander*, 24 January 1891, p. 162. [Reported speech]

24 George Landells, Report to Exploration Committee, 14 November 1860, p. 12 (Image 12). [Reported speech] http://handle.slv.vic.gov.au/10381/212896

25 George Landells, Report to Exploration Committee, 14 November 1860, p. 12 (Image 12). [Reported speech] http://handle.slv.vic.gov.au/10381/212896

26 George Landells, Report to Exploration Committee, 14 November 1860, p. 12 (Image 12). [Reported speech] http://handle.slv.vic.gov.au/10381/212896

27 Charles Ferguson, *Experiences of a Forty-niner*, p. 391.

28 Charles Ferguson, *Experiences of a Forty-niner*, p. 391.

29 Charles Ferguson, *Experiences of a Forty-niner*, p. 391. [Reported speech]

30 Charles Ferguson, *Experiences of a Forty-niner*, p. 391.

31 Charles Ferguson, *Experiences of a Forty-Niner*, p. 391. [Reported speech.]

32 Charles Ferguson, *Experiences of a Forty-Niner*, p. 392.

33 Charles Ferguson, *Experiences of a Forty-niner*, p. 392. [Reported speech]

34 Charles Ferguson, *Experiences of a Forty-niner*, p. 392.

35 Charles Ferguson, *Experiences of a Forty-Niner*, p. 392.

36 Charles Ferguson, *Experiences of a Forty-Niner*, p. 390.

37 *The Age*, 26 September 1860, p. 6. [Reported speech]

38 *The Age*, 26 September 1860, p. 6. [Reported speech]

39 *The Age*, 26 September 1860, p. 6. [Reported speech]

40 *The Age*, 26 September 1860, p. 6. [Reported speech]

41 *The Age*, 26 September 1860, p. 6. [Reported speech]

42 *The Age*, 26 September 1860, p. 6.

43 *The Age*, 26 September 1860, p. 6. [Reported speech]

44 *The Age*, 26 September 1860, p. 6.

45 *The Age*, 26 September 1860, p. 6.

46 *Geelong Advertiser*, 26 September 1860, p. 2.

47 *Geelong Advertiser*, 26 September 1860, p. 2. [Reported speech]

48 *Geelong Advertiser*, 26 September 1860, p. 2. [Reported speech]

49 *The Age*, 26 September 1860, p. 6.

50 *Geelong Advertiser*, 26 September 1860, p. 2. [Reported speech]

51 *Geelong Advertiser*, 26 September 1860, p. 2. [Reported speech]

52 *The Age*, 26 September 1860, p. 6.

53 *The Age*, 26 September 1860, p. 6. [Reported speech]

54 Hermann Beckler, *A Journey to Cooper's Creek*, p. 29.

55 William John Wills, *A Successful Exploration*, p. 104.

56 *The Age*, 2 September 1904, p. 9.

57 *The Argus*, 22 April 1861, p. 5.

58 Ludwig Becker, Third Report, 12 November 1860, SLV, MS13071, Box 2082/4e, p. 3.

59 Ludwig Becker, Sketch Book, 'Women in Mourning', 20 September 1860, SLV, MS13071, MS Safe 1, Accession No. H16486, p. 8.

60 Ludwig Becker, Third Report, 12 November 1860, SLV, MS13071, Box 2082/4e, p. 4.

61 Ludwig Becker, Third Report, 12 November 1860, SLV, MS13071, Box 2082/4e, p. 4.

62 Hermann Beckler, *A Journey to Cooper's Creek*, p. 33.

63 Hermann Beckler, *A Journey to Cooper's Creek*, p. 33.

64 Hermann Beckler, *A Journey to Cooper's Creek*, p. 30.

65 George Landells, Report to Exploration Committee, 14 November 1860, p. 8 (Image 18). http://handle.slv.vic.gov.au/10381/212896

66 Hermann Beckler, *A Journey to Cooper's Creek*, p. 34.

67 Hermann Beckler, *A Journey to Cooper's Creek*, pp. 34–35.

68 Australian National Botanic Gardens, 'Mallee plants – surviving harsh conditions', Australian Government, ACT, 2004, p. 16. https://www.anbg.gov.au/gardens/education/programs/mallee.pdf

69 Hermann Beckler, *A Journey to Cooper's Creek*, p. 35.

70 Hermann Beckler, *A Journey to Cooper's Creek*, p. 34.

71 Ludwig Becker, Fourth Report, 26 November 1860, SLV, MS13071, Box 2082/4f, pp. 1–2.

72 William Wills, Surveyor's field notes, 24 September 1860, SLV, MS13071, Box 2082/6b, no page numbers, (Image 4). http://handle.slv.vic.gov.au/10381/195919

73 Ludwig Becker, Fourth Report, 26 November 1860, SLV, MS13071, Box 2082/4f, p. 4.

74 Ludwig Becker, Fourth Report, 26 November 1860, SLV, MS13071, Box 2082/4f, p. 4.

Chapter Seven

1 Robert O'Hara Burke, Letter to John Burke, 30 October 1860, pp. 1–2.

2 Hermann Beckler, *A Journey to Cooper's Creek*, pp. 40–41.

3 *Melbourne Punch*, 8 November 1860, p. 4.

4 *The Argus*, 23 April 1861, p. 5. [Reported speech]
5 *The Argus*, 23 April 1861, p. 5. [Reported speech]
6 Burke and Wills Commission, p. 19, Q430.
7 *The Argus*, 23 April 1861, p. 5. [Reported speech]
8 Georg Neumayer, *Results of the Magnetic Survey*, p. 13.
9 Ludwig Becker, Fifth Report, 22 January 1861, p. 2.
10 Georg Neumayer, *Results of the Magnetic Survey*, p. 13. [Reported speech]
11 Georg Neumayer, *Results of the Magnetic Survey*, pp. 13–14. [Reported speech]
12 Ludwig Becker, Fifth Report, 22 January 1861, SLV, MS13071, Box 2082/4, Item g, p. 2.
13 Ludwig Becker, Fifth Report, 22 January 1861, p. 3.
14 Ludwig Becker, Fifth Report, 22 January 1861, p. 4.
15 Ludwig Becker, Fifth Report, 22 January 1861, p. 4.
16 Ludwig Becker, Fifth Report, 22 January 1861, p. 4. [Reported speech]
17 *The Argus*, 27 August 1910, p. 9.
18 *The Argus*, 27 August 1910, p. 9.
19 *The Argus*, 27 August 1910, p. 9.
20 Ludwig Becker, Fifth Report, 22 January 1861, p. 5. [Reported speech]
21 Ludwig Becker, Fifth Report, 22 January 1861, p. 5.
22 Ludwig Becker, Fifth Report, 22 January 1861, p. 6.
23 Hermann Beckler, *A Journey to Cooper's Creek*, pp. 36–37.
24 Ludwig Becker, Fifth Report, 22 January 1861, p. 6.
25 Hermann Beckler, *A Journey to Cooper's Creek*, p. 38.
26 *The Age*, 13 November 1861, p. 5.
27 *The Age*, 13 November 1861, p. 5.
28 William Wills, Letter to Professor Georg Neumayer, 16 October 1860, p. 3 (Image 3). [Reported speech] http://handle.slv.vic.gov.au/10381/212576
29 William Wills, Letter to Professor Georg Neumayer, 16 October 1860, p. 3 (Image 3). [Reported speech] http://handle.slv.vic.gov.au/10381/212576
30 *The Argus,* 15 November 1860, p. 5.
31 Andrew Jackson, *Robert O'Hara Burke*, p. 19.
32 *The Argus,* 15 November 1860, p. 5. [Reported speech]
33 *The Argus,* 15 November 1860, p. 5. [Reported speech]
34 Ludwig Becker, Fifth Report, 22 January 1861, p. 10.
35 Hermann Beckler, *A Journey to Cooper's Creek*, p. 38.
36 Ludwig Becker, Fifth Report, 22 January 1861, p. 10.
37 Ludwig Becker, Fifth Report, 22 January 1861, p. 11. [Reported speech]
38 Ludwig Becker, Fifth Report, 22 January 1861, p. 11.
39 *The Argus,* 15 November 1860, p. 5.
40 George Landells, Report to Exploration Committee, 14 November 1860, p. 5 (Image 12). http://handle.slv.vic.gov.au/10381/212896
41 George Landells, Report to Exploration Committee, 14 November 1860, p. 5 (Image 12). http://handle.slv.vic.gov.au/10381/212896
42 George Landells, Report to Exploration Committee, 14 November 1860, p. 5 (Image 12). http://handle.slv.vic.gov.au/10381/212896
43 George Landells, Report to Exploration Committee, 14 November 1860, p. 5 (Image 12). http://handle.slv.vic.gov.au/10381/212896
44 George Landells, Report to Exploration Committee, 14 November 1860, p. 5 [and its back page] (Images 12 and 13). http://handle.slv.vic.gov.au/10381/212896
45 George Landells, Report to Exploration Committee, 14 November 1860 [no page number] (Image 13). [Reported Speech] http://handle.slv.vic.gov.au/10381/212896
46 George Landells, Report to Exploration Committee, 14 November 1860 [no page number] (Image 13). http://handle.slv.vic.gov.au/10381/212896
47 George Landells, Report to Exploration Committee, 14 November 1860 [no page number] (Image 13). http://handle.slv.vic.gov.au/10381/212896

48 George Landells, Report to Exploration Committee, 14 November 1860 [no page number] (Image 13). http://handle.slv.vic.gov.au/10381/212896

49 George Landells, Report to Exploration Committee, 14 November 1860 [no page number] (Image 13). http://handle.slv.vic.gov.au/10381/212896

50 George Landells, Report to Exploration Committee, 14 November 1860 [no page number] (Image 13). [Reported Speech] http://handle.slv.vic.gov.au/10381/212896

51 George Landells, Report to Exploration Committee, 14 November 1860 [no page number] (Image 13). http://handle.slv.vic.gov.au/10381/212896 Author's note: There are conflicting reports about the actual dialogue used in these exchanges. I have drawn this particular dialogue from the testimonies of George Landells and William Wills, which roughly corroborate each other. Wills reported that in this particular exchange Landells said, 'Mr B. was mad, and he was frightened to stay in the tent with him.'

52 William Wills, Letter to Professor Georg Neumayer, 16 October 1860, p. 6 (Image 6). [Reported speech] http://handle.slv.vic.gov.au/10381/212576

53 *The Age*, 7 November 1860, p. 6. [Reported speech]

54 *The Age*, 7 November 1860, p. 6.

55 *The Age*, 7 November 1860, p. 6. [Reported speech]

56 George Landells, Report to Exploration Committee, 14 November 1860 [no page numbers] (Image 14). http://handle.slv.vic.gov.au/10381/212896

57 Ludwig Becker, Fifth Report, 22 January 1861, p. 12.

58 *The Age*, 7 November 1860, p. 6. Author's note: Although this letter has been dated '16th October' by George Landells, the articles that surround its publication that day in *The Age* indicate that it was in fact written and left undated on the 7th of October 1860.

59 *The Age*, 7 November 1860, p. 6.

60 *The Age*, 27 November 1861, p. 5.

61 *The Age*, 7 November 1860, p. 6. [Reported speech]

62 *The Age*, 7 November 1860, p. 6. [Reported speech]

63 William Wills, Letter to Professor Georg Neumayer, 16 October 1860, p. 6 (Image 6). [Reported speech] http://handle.slv.vic.gov.au/10381/212576

64 William Wills, Letter to Professor Georg Neumayer, 16 October 1860, p. 6 (Image 6). [Reported speech] http://handle.slv.vic.gov.au/10381/212576

65 William Wills, Letter to Professor Georg Neumayer, 16 October 1860, p. 6 (Image 6). [Reported speech] http://handle.slv.vic.gov.au/10381/212576

66 William Wills, Letter to Professor Georg Neumayer, 16 October 1860, p. 6 (Image 6). [Reported speech] http://handle.slv.vic.gov.au/10381/212576

67 Hermann Beckler, *A Journey to Cooper's Creek*, p. 41.

68 William Wills, Third Dispatch from the Darling, 7 October 1860 [no page numbers] (Image 2). [Reported speech] http://handle.slv.vic.gov.au/10381/212464

69 William Wills, Third Dispatch from the Darling, 7 October 1860 [no page numbers] (Image 3). [Reported speech] http://handle.slv.vic.gov.au/10381/212464

70 William Wills, Third Dispatch from the Darling, 7 October 1860 [no page numbers] (Image 3). [Reported speech] http://handle.slv.vic.gov.au/10381/212464

71 William Wills, Third Dispatch from the Darling, 7 October 1860 [no page numbers] (Image 3). [Reported speech] http://handle.slv.vic.gov.au/10381/212464 Author's note: In the original script, Landells used the word 'burthen', the now archaic word for 'burden'. To avoid confusions, I have modernised.

72 Ludwig Becker, Sketch Book, 'Small Predatory Beetle', Sketch No. 16, p. 12A.

73 Robert O'Hara Burke, Dispatch, 16 October 1860 [no page number] (Image 2). [Reported speech] http://handle.slv.vic.gov.au/10381/282261

74 Robert O'Hara Burke, Dispatch, 16 October 1860 [no page numbers] (Images 2–3). [Reported speech] http://handle.slv.vic.gov.au/10381/282261

75 George Landells, Report to Exploration Committee, 14 November 1860, p. 6 (Image 14). http://handle.slv.vic.gov.au/10381/212896

76 George Landells, Report to Exploration Committee, 14 November 1860, p. 6 (Image 14). http://handle.slv.vic.gov.au/10381/212896

77 George Landells, Report to Exploration Committee, 14 November 1860, p. 6 (Image 14). http://handle.slv.vic.gov.au/10381/212896

78 *The Age*, 7 November 1860, p. 6.

79 Ludwig Becker, Fifth Report, 22 January 1861, p. 12.

80 *Adelaide Observer*, 10 November 1860, p. 6.

81 Ludwig Becker, Fifth Report, 22 January 1861, p. 13.

82 *The Argus*, 26 October 1860, p. 5. [Reported speech]

83 Ludwig Becker, Fifth Report, 22 January 1861, pp. 13–14.

84 *The Argus*, 27 August 1910, p. 9.

85 Ludwig Becker, Fifth Report, 22 January 1861, p. 14.

86 Burke and Wills Commission, p. 77, Appendix A (Instructions to Leader).

87 Hermann Beckler, *A Journey to Cooper's Creek*, p. 41.

88 Hermann Beckler, *A Journey to Cooper's Creek*, p. 41.

89 Ludwig Becker, Fifth Report, 22 January 1861, p. 15.

90 Ludwig Becker, Sketch Book, 'Meteor seen by me', Sketch No. 26, Manuscripts Safe 1, H16486, p. 21.

91 Ludwig Becker, Fifth Report, 22 January 1861, p. 15.

92 Ludwig Becker, Fifth Report, 22 January 1861, pp. 15–16.

93 Ludwig Becker, Fifth Report, 22 January 1861, p. 16.

94 Hermann Beckler, *A Journey to Cooper's Creek*, p. 37.

95 William Wills, Letter to Professor Georg Neumayer, 16 October 1860, p. 5 (Image 6). http://handle.slv.vic.gov.au/10381/212576

96 William John Wills, *A Successful Exploration*, p. 106.

97 William Wills, Letter to Professor Georg Neumayer, 16 October 1860, p. 6 (Image 6). http://handle.slv.vic.gov.au/10381/212576

98 William John Wills, *A Successful Exploration*, p. 112.

99 Royal Society of Victoria, Exploration Committee, Meeting, 13 October 1860, Minute Book, SLV, MS13071, Box 2075/1c, [no page number] (Image 71). http://handle.slv.vic.gov.au/10381/162914

100 Royal Society of Victoria, Exploration Committee, Meeting, 13 October 1860, Minute Book, SLV, MS13071, Box 2075/1c, [no page number] (Image 71). http://handle.slv.vic.gov.au/10381/162914

101 John Macadam, Letter to Robert Burke, 17 September 1860, SLV, MS13071, Box 2083/5, No. 43, p. 2, (Image 2). http://handle.slv.vic.gov.au/10381/212919

102 *The Age*, 15 October 1860, p. 6.

103 *The Age*, 15 October 1860, p. 6.

104 *The Age*, 15 October 1860, p. 6.

105 *The Age*, 15 October 1860, p. 6. [Tense changed.]

106 Author's note: Sources show that there existed many variations in the spelling of 'Torowoto', such as Torowotto, Duroodoo and Duroadoo. I have decided to use 'Torowoto' throughout my account.

107 Burke and Wills Commission, Q1225.

108 Burke and Wills Commission, Q1225, p. 44. [Tenses changed]

Chapter Eight

1 *The Age*, 16 November 1860, p. 6.

2 *The Age*, 7 November 1860, p.4.

3 Ludwig Becker, Sketch Book, 'Menindee', Sketch No. 18, p. 14. http://victoria.slv.vic.gov.au/burkeandwills/archives/views/beckers_sketchbook/becker3.html

4 *The World's News*, 4 February 1911, p. 10.

5 George Landells, Report, 14 November 1860, p. 6 (Image 14). http://handle.slv.vic.gov.au/10381/212896

6 George Landells, Report, 14 November 1860 [no page number, back page of p. 6] (Image 15). http://handle.slv.vic.gov.au/10381/212896

7 George Landells, Report, 14 November 1860 [no page number, back page of p. 6] (Image 15). http://handle.slv.vic.gov.au/10381/212896

8 George Landells, Report, 14 November 1860 [no page number, back page of p. 6] (Image 15). http://handle.slv.vic.gov.au/10381/212896

9 George Landells, Report, 14 November 1860 [no page number, back page of p. 6] (Image 15). http://handle.slv.vic.gov.au/10381/212896

10 George Landells, Report, 14 November 1860 [no page number, back page of p. 6] (Image 15). http://handle.slv.vic.gov.au/10381/212896

11 Hermann Beckler, *A Journey to Cooper's Creek*, p. 41.

12 Hermann Beckler, *A Journey to Cooper's Creek*, p. 41.

13 George Landells, Report, 14 November 1860 [no page number, back page of p. 6] (Image 15). http://handle.slv.vic.gov.au/10381/212896

14 William Wills, Letter to Professor Georg Neumayer, 16 October 1860, p. 10 (Image 11). [Reported speech] http://handle.slv.vic.gov.au/10381/212576

15 William Wills, Letter to Professor Georg Neumayer, 16 October 1860, p. 10 (Image 11). [Reported speech] http://handle.slv.vic.gov.au/10381/212576

16 William Wills, Letter to Professor Georg Neumayer, 16 October 1860, p. 10 (Image 11). [Reported speech] http://handle.slv.vic.gov.au/10381/212576

17 William Wills, Letter to Professor Georg Neumayer, 16 October 1860, p. 11 (Image 12). [Reported speech] http://handle.slv.vic.gov.au/10381/212576

18 William Wills, Letter to Professor Georg Neumayer, 16 October 1860, p. 11 (Image 12). [Reported speech] http://handle.slv.vic.gov.au/10381/212576

19 William Wills, Letter to Professor Georg Neumayer, 16 October 1860, p. 11 (Image 12). [Reported speech] http://handle.slv.vic.gov.au/10381/212576

20 George Landells, Report to Exploration Committee, 14 November 1860, p. 15 (Image 15). [Reported speech] http://handle.slv.vic.gov.au/10381/212896

21 George Landells, Report to Exploration Committee, 14 November 1860, p. 15 (Image 15). http://handle.slv.vic.gov.au/10381/212896

22 George Landells, Report to Exploration Committee, 14 November 1860, p. 15 (Image 15). http://handle.slv.vic.gov.au/10381/212896

23 William Wills, Letter to Professor Georg Neumayer, October 1860, pp. 12–13 (Images 12–13). [Reported speech] http://handle.slv.vic.gov.au/10381/212576

24 George Landells, Report to Exploration Committee, 14 November 1860, p. 15 (Image 15). http://handle.slv.vic.gov.au/10381/212896

25 *Mount Alexander Mail*, 16 November 1860, p. 5.

26 George Landells, Report to Exploration Committee, 14 November 1860, p. 15 (Image 15). [Reported speech] http://handle.slv.vic.gov.au/10381/212896

27 *The Argus*, 26 January 1863, p. 5.

28 Hermann Beckler, *A Journey to Cooper's Creek*, pp. 41–42.

29 William John Wills, *A Successful Exploration*, p. 114.

30 Hermann Beckler, Letter to Robert O'Hara Burke, 16 October 1860, p. 1.

31 *The Age*, 7 November 1860, p. 6. [Reported speech]

32 Burke and Wills Commission, p. 17, Q389. [Reported speech]

33 *The Yeoman and Australian Acclimatiser*, 11 January 1862 (Part IV).

34 *The Age*, 17 October 1860, p. 5.

35 *The Age*, 17 October 1860, p. 5.

36 *The Age*, 17 October 1860, p. 5. [Reported speech]

37 *The Age*, 17 October 1860, p. 5. [Tense changed]

38 *The Age*, 17 October 1860, p. 5. [Reported speech]

39 *The Age*, 17 October 1860, p. 5.

40 *The Age*, 17 October 1860, p. 6.

41 *The Age*, 17 October 1860, p. 6.

42 John Macadam, Letter to Robert O'Hara Burke, 18 October 1860, pp. 2–3 (Images 2–3). http://handle.slv.vic.gov.au/10381/188388

43 Alan Moorehead, *Cooper's Creek*, p. 41.

44 Alan Moorehead, *Cooper's Creek*, pp. 41–43.

45 Ludwig Becker, Fifth Report, 22 January 1861, pp. 19–20.

46 *Bendigo Advertiser*, 19 November 1860, p. 3.

47 *Bendigo Advertiser*, 19 November 1860, p. 3.

48 *Bendigo Advertiser*, 19 November 1860, p. 3.

49 *The Age*, 7 March 1863, p. 7. [Reported speech]

50 Robert O'Hara Burke, Dispatch, 16 October 1860, [no page number] (Image 1). http://handle. slv.vic.gov.au/10381/282261

51 Robert O'Hara Burke, Dispatch, 16 October 1860, [no page number] (Image 2). http://handle. slv.vic.gov.au/10381/282261

52 Robert O'Hara Burke, Dispatch, 16 October 1860, [no page numbers] (Image 2–3). http:// handle.slv.vic.gov.au/10381/282261

53 Burke and Wills Commission, p. 19, Q430.

54 Ludwig Becker, Letter to John Macadam, 30 October 1860, p. 1 (Image 1). http://handle.slv.vic. gov.au/10381/212855

55 Robert O'Hara Burke, Dispatch, 29 October 1860, [no page number] (Image 1). http://handle. slv.vic.gov.au/10381/282222

56 William Wills, Second Surveyor's Report, 30 October 1860, [no page numbers] (Images 3–4). http://handle.slv.vic.gov.au/10381/212551

57 William Wills, Field Book (No. 2), 21 October 1860, SLV, MS13071, Box 2082/6d, [no page numbers] [Image 6]. [http://handle.slv.vic.gov.au/10381/196219]

58 William Wills, Second Surveyor's Report, 30 October 1860, [no page numbers] (Image 4). http:// handle.slv.vic.gov.au/10381/212551

59 William Wills, Second Surveyor's Report, 30 October 1860, [no page numbers] (Image 8). http:// handle.slv.vic.gov.au/10381/212551

60 Author's note: As with many Aboriginal place names written down for the first time by Europeans, the spelling of 'Mutawintji' varies in differing accounts, everything from 'Mutanie' to 'Mootwingee'. To prevent confusion I have used Mutawintji throughout this book.

61 William Wills, Field Book No. 2, 24 October 1860, SLV, Box 2082/6d, [no page numbers] (Image 15). http://handle.slv.vic.gov.au/10381/196219

62 William Wills, Second Surveyor's Report, 30 October 1860, [no page number] (Image 2). http:// handle.slv.vic.gov.au/10381/212551

63 *Bendigo Advertiser*, 19 November 1860, p. 3.

64 *Bendigo Advertiser*, 19 November 1860, p. 3.

65 William Wills, *Correspondence and press cuttings, 1839–1861* [manuscript], 1839, SLV, MS 9504, p. 6.

66 William Wills, Field Book No. 3, 28 October 1860, SLV, MS13071, Box 2082/6e [no page numbers].

67 Burke and Wills Commission, p. 44, Q1235.

68 *South Australian Advertiser*, 6 February 1861, p. 3.

69 Burke and Wills Commission, pp.108-109, Q1235. [Reported speech]

70 Burke and Wills Commission, p. 44, Q1235. [Reported speech]

71 Burke and Wills Commission, p. 109, Q1247.

72 Robert O'Hara Burke, Dispatch, 29 October 1860, [no page number] (Image 2). [Reported speech] http://handle.slv.vic.gov.au/10381/282222

73 Robert O'Hara Burke, Dispatch, 29 October 1860, [no page number] (Image 2). http://handle. slv.vic.gov.au/10381/282222

74 Robert O'Hara Burke, Dispatch, 29 October 1860, [no page numbers] (Images 2 and 3). http:// handle.slv.vic.gov.au/10381/282222

75 Robert O'Hara Burke, Notebook, National Library of Australia, NLA MS 30/1.

76 Burke and Wills Commission, p. 27, Q649.

77 William Wills, Field Book (No. 3), 30 October 1860, SLV, MS13071, Box 2082/6e, [no page number].

78 Author's note: Bulla and Bulloo are both names that the explorers and their contemporaries recorded as the name of the Bulloo River. For consistency and clarity I have chosen to use the spelling Bulloo throughout.

79 William Wills, Third Surveyor's Report, 15 December 1860, pp. 3–5.

80 Author's note: The account of MacPherson is that Lyons arrived on the 9th October, but as he is relating that four months later, with no notes, to a journalist, my conclusion is that Beckler's dates are more reliable.

81 Ludwig Becker, Fifth Report, 22 January 1861, p. 20.

82 Author's note: There is some question as to whether Becker or Beckler first questioned Wright's authority. Beckler denied this at the Commission of Enquiry, but there was conflicting testimony from the local storekeeper Edward Wecker, who maintained that Wright's authority was rejected by *both* Dr Beckler and Ludwig Becker, the dispute leading to Wright not actually staying with the Pamamaroo Depot, something Wecker had been told directly by one or more of the parties involved. I have gone with Wecker's testimony in naming Becker here.

83 *The World's News*, 4 February 1911 p. 10.

84 Burke and Wills Commission, p. 44, Q1235. [Tense changed]

85 Burke and Wills Commission, p. 58, Q1281.

86 *Ovens and Murray Advertiser*, 21 November 1860, p. 2.

87 Burke and Wills Commission, p. 45, Q1265. [Reported speech] http://www.parliament.vic.gov.au/papers/govpub/VPARL1861-62No97.pdf

88 *The South Australian Advertiser*, 6 February 1861, p. 3.

89 William Wright, Dispatch to Exploration Committee, 19 December 1860, p. 2.

90 Burke and Wills Commission, p. 54, Q1484.

91 *Bendigo Advertiser*, 6 November 1860, p. 2.

92 Robert O'Hara Burke, Portion of diary kept by Robert O'Hara Burke on the expedition, 16 December 1860 – 20 January 1861, Undated, National Library of Australia, MS 30/1, p. 41.

93 *The Argus*, 7 November 1860, p. 5.

94 Hermann Beckler, *A Journey to Cooper's Creek*, p. 51.

95 Hermann Beckler, Report, 13 November 1860, [no page numbers] (Image 9). http://handle.slv.vic.gov.au/10381/212524

96 Hermann Beckler, Report, 13 November 1860, [no page numbers] (Image 6). http://handle.slv.vic.gov.au/10381/212524

97 Hermann Beckler, Report, 13 November 1860, [no page numbers] (Image 6). http://handle.slv.vic.gov.au/10381/212524

98 *The South Australian Advertiser*, 6 February 1861, p. 3.

99 *The South Australian Advertiser*, 6 February 1861, p. 3.

Chapter Nine

1 William John Wills, *A Successful Exploration*, p. 147.

2 Robert O'Hara Burke, Dispatch to Exploration Committee, 13 December 1860, p. 1 (Image 1). http://handle.slv.vic.gov.au/10381/282243

3 *The Argus*, 15 November 1860, p. 5. [Reported speech]

4 *The Argus*, 15 November 1860, p. 5.

5 *The Argus*, 15 November 1860, p. 5. [Reported speech]

6 *Empire* (Sydney), 12 February 1861, p. 2.

7 *The South Australian Advertiser*, 6 February 1861, p. 3.

8 *Empire* (Sydney), 12 February 1861, p. 2.

9 *Empire* (Sydney), 12 February 1861, p. 2.

10 *Empire* (Sydney), 12 February 1861, p. 2.

11 *Empire* (Sydney), 12 February 1861, p. 2.

12 Hermann Beckler, *A Journey to Cooper's Creek*, p. 91.

13 Hermann Beckler, *A Journey to Cooper's Creek*, p. 93.

14 Alan Moorehead, *Cooper's Creek*, p. 16.

15 Robert O'Hara Burke, Dispatch, 13 December 1860, p. 1 (Image 1). http://handle.slv.vic.gov.au/10381/282243

16 William Wills, Third Surveyor's Report, 15 December 1860.

17 William Wills, Third Surveyor's Report, 15 December 1860, p. 5.

18 William John Wills, *A Successful Exploration*, p. 146.

19 William Wills, Third Surveyor's Report, 15 December 1860, pp. 9–10.

20 William John Wills, *A Successful Exploration*, p. 165.

21 *Empire* (Sydney), 12 February 1861, p. 2.

22 *The South Australian Advertiser*, 6 February 1861, p. 3.

23 *Empire* (Sydney), 12 February 1861, p. 2.

24 *Empire* (Sydney), 12 February 1861, p. 2.

25 *The Star*, 16 March 1861, p. 1.

26 *The South Australian Advertiser*, 6 February 1861, p. 3. [Tense changed]

27 *The South Australian Advertiser*, 6 February 1861, p. 3.

28 *The South Australian Advertiser*, 6 February 1861, p. 3. [Reported speech]

29 *The Star*, 16 March 1861, p. 1.

30 *The South Australian Advertiser*, 6 February 1861, p. 3. [Reported speech]

31 John Macadam, Instructions issued to Robert O'Hara Burke, 18 August 1860, p. 3 (Image 3). http://handle.slv.vic.gov.au/10381/212493

32 Robert O'Hara Burke, Letter to John Burke, 30 October 1860, NLA MS30/3, p. 2.

33 *The Age*, 2 September 1904, p. 9.

34 *The South Australian Advertiser*, 6 February 1861, p. 3.

35 *The South Australian Advertiser*, 6 February 1861, p. 3.

36 *The South Australian Advertiser*, 6 February 1861, p. 3.

37 *The South Australian Advertiser*, 6 February 1861, p. 3.

38 *The South Australian Advertiser*, 6 February 1861, p. 3.

39 *The South Australian Advertiser*, 6 February 1861, p. 3.

40 *The South Australian Advertiser*, 6 February 1861, p. 3.

41 *The Age*, 6 February 1861, p. 6.

42 Hermann Beckler, *A Journey to Cooper's Creek*, p. 70.

43 *The South Australian Advertiser*, 6 February 1861, p. 3. [Reported speech]

44 *The South Australian Advertiser*, 6 February 1861, p. 3. [Reported speech]

45 *Empire* (Sydney), 12 February 1861, p. 2. [Reported speech]

46 *The South Australian Advertiser*, 6 February 1861, p. 3. [Reported speech]

47 *The South Australian Advertiser*, 6 February 1861, p. 3.

48 *The South Australian Advertiser*, 6 February 1861, p. 3. [Reported speech]

49 *Empire* (Sydney), 12 February 1861, p. 2.

50 *The South Australian Advertiser*, 6 February 1861, p. 3.

51 *The South Australian Advertiser*, 6 February 1861, p. 3.

52 *The South Australian Advertiser*, 6 February 1861, p. 3.

53 *The South Australian Advertiser*, 6 February 1861, p. 3.

54 Burke and Wills Commission, p. 21, Q499. [Tense changed]

55 William Wills, Field Notes (No. 5), 24 November 1860, [no page numbers] (Image 3). http://handle.slv.vic.gov.au/10381/195879

56 *The South Australian Advertiser*, 6 February 1861, p. 3.

57 Burke and Wills Commission, p. 21, Q499.

58 William Wills, Field Notes (No. 5), 26 November 1860, [no page numbers] (Image 6). http://handle.slv.vic.gov.au/10381/195879

59 Burke and Wills Commission, p. 22, Q501.

60 William Wills, Field Notes (No. 5), 26 November 1860, [no page numbers] (Image 6). http://handle.slv.vic.gov.au/10381/195879

61 William Wills, Field Notes (No. 5), 27 November 1860, [no page numbers] (Image 9). http://handle.slv.vic.gov.au/10381/195879

62 William Wills, Field Notes (No. 5), 27 November 1860, [no page numbers] (Image 9). http://handle.slv.vic.gov.au/10381/195879

63 William Wills, Field Notes (No. 5), 27 November 1860, [no page numbers] (Image 9). http://handle.slv.vic.gov.au/10381/195879

64 *The Argus*, 27 August 1910, p. 9.

65 *Empire* (Sydney), 12 February 1861, p. 2.

66 Hermann Beckler, *A Journey to Cooper's Creek*, p. 72.

67 *The South Australian Advertiser*, 6 February 1861, p. 3.

68 Hermann Beckler, *A Journey to Cooper's Creek*, p. 72.

69 Andrew Jackson, *Robert O'Hara Burke*, p. 33.

70 *Ovens and Murray Advertiser*, 8 December 1860, p. 5. http://trove.nla.gov.au/newspaper/article/112915982

71 *Empire* (Sydney), 12 February 1861, p. 3.

72 *The South Australian Advertiser*, 6 February 1861, p. 3.

73 Robert O'Hara Burke, Dispatch to Exploration Committee, 13 December 1860, p. 1 (Image 1). http://handle.slv.vic.gov.au/10381/282243

74 William John Wills, *A Successful Exploration*, p. 147.

75 Burke and Wills Commission, p. 19, Q442. [Tense changed]

76 Burke and Wills Commission, p. 19, Q442. [Tense changed]

77 Burke and Wills Commission, p. 19, Q442.

78 Burke and Wills Commission, p. 19, Q442.

79 *The Star* (Ballarat), 16 March 1861, p. 1.

80 *The Star* (Ballarat), 16 March 1861, p. 1.

81 *The Star* (Ballarat), 16 March 1861, p. 1.

82 *The Star* (Ballarat), 16 March 1861, p. 1. [Reported speech]

83 *The Star* (Ballarat), 16 March 1861, p. 1. [Reported speech]

84 *The Star* (Ballarat), 16 March 1861, p. 1.

85 *Empire* (Sydney), 12 February 1861, p. 3.

86 *The Star* (Ballarat), 16 March 1861, p. 1.

87 *The Star* (Ballarat), 16 March 1861, p. 1.

88 *The Star* (Ballarat), 16 March 1861, p. 1.

89 *The Age*, 6 February 1861, p. 7.

90 *The South Australian Advertiser*, 6 February 1861, p. 3.

91 *Bendigo Advertiser*, 22 January 1861, p. 3.

92 *Bendigo Advertiser*, 22 January 1861, p. 3.

93 *The Star* (Ballarat), 16 March 1861, p. 1.

94 Hermann Beckler, *A Journey to Cooper's Creek*, p. 74.

95 *Empire* (Sydney), 12 February 1861, p. 3.

96 Hermann Beckler, *A Journey to Cooper's Creek*, p. 75.

97 Ian Clarke and Fred Cahir (eds), *The Aboriginal Story of Burke and Wills*, CSIRO, Collingwood, 2016, p. 66.

Chapter Ten

1 *Leader* (Melbourne), 18 June 1887, p. 7.

2 Andrew Jackson, *Robert O'Hara Burke*, pp. 26–27.

3 Ludwig Leichhardt, *Journal of an Overland Expedition in Australia*, Cambridge University Press, Cambridge, UK, 2011, p. 517.

4 *The Argus*, 27 August 1910, p. 9.

5 *The Argus*, 27 August 1910, p. 9.

6 William John Wills, *A Successful Exploration*, p. 178.

7 *The Argus*, 27 August 1910, p. 9.

8 *The Argus*, 27 August 1910, p. 9.

9 Burke and Wills Commission, p. 72, Q692. [Reported speech]

10 Burke and Wills Commission, p. 63, Q1653.

11 *The Argus*, 13 December 1861, p. 6.

12 *The Argus*, 13 December 1861, p. 6.

13 Burke and Wills Commission, p. 63, Q1656.

14 Andrew Jackson, *Robert O'Hara Burke*, p. 63.

15 Robert O'Hara Burke, Dispatch to Exploration Committee, 13 December 1860, p. 1.

16 Robert O'Hara Burke, Dispatch to Exploration Committee, 13 December 1860, p. 3 (Image 3). http://handle.slv.vic.gov.au/10381/282243

17 Robert O'Hara Burke, Dispatch to Exploration Committee, 13 December 1860, pp. 3–4 (Images 3–4). http://handle.slv.vic.gov.au/10381/282243

18 Robert O'Hara Burke, Dispatch to Exploration Committee, 13 December 1860, p. 4 (Image 4). http://handle.slv.vic.gov.au/10381/282243

19 Burke and Wills Commission, p. 18, Q403.

20 Burke and Wills Commission, p. 18, Q402. [Reported speech]

21 Burke and Wills Commission, p. 19, Q430.

22 Burke and Wills Commission, p. 10, Q197.

23 *The Argus*, 14 November 1861, p. 5. [Reported speech. Tense changed.]

24 Burke and Wills Commission, p. 9, Q173.

25 *The Argus*, 14 November 1861, p. 5. [Reported speech]

26 Burke and Wills Commission, p. 9, Q173.

27 *The Argus*, 14 November 1861, p. 5.

28 Burke and Wills Commission, p. 53, Q1447.

29 William Brahe, letter, *The Argus*, 14 November 1861.

30 Robert O'Hara Burke, Notebook, National Library of Australia, NLA MS 30/1

31 *Ovens and Murray Advertiser*, 9 July 1874, p. 2.

32 Burke and Wills Commission, p. 18, Q407. [Reported speech]

33 Burke and Wills Commission, p. 18, Q407.

34 *The Argus*, 27 August 1910, p. 9.

35 Burke and Wills Commission, p. 29, Q697.

36 Burke and Wills Commission, p. 10, Q175.

37 *Bathurst Free Press and Mining Journal*, 28 January 1890, p. 4.

38 William Wills, 'Journey from Cooper's Creek to Carpentaria and return to Cooper's Creek', 16 December 1860, p. 1 (Image 2). http://handle.slv.vic.gov.au/10381/197341

39 *The Australasian*, 7 May 1870, p. 6.

40 William Wills, 'Journey from Cooper's Creek to Carpentaria and return to Cooper's Creek', 16 December 1860, p. 1 (Image 2). http://handle.slv.vic.gov.au/10381/197341

41 William Wills, 'Journey from Cooper's Creek to Carpentaria and return to Cooper's Creek', 16 December 1860, p. 1 (Image 2). http://handle.slv.vic.gov.au/10381/197341

42 William Wills, 'Journey from Cooper's Creek to Carpentaria and return to Cooper's Creek', 16 December 1860, p. 1 (Image 2). http://handle.slv.vic.gov.au/10381/197341

43 William Wills, 'Journey from Cooper's Creek to Carpentaria and return to Cooper's Creek', 16 December 1860, pp. 1–2 (Images 2–3). http://handle.slv.vic.gov.au/10381/197341

44 *The Argus*, 14 November 1861, p. 5.

45 Burke and Wills Commission, p. 17, Q381.

46 Burke and Wills Commission, p. 11, Q218. [Reported speech]

47 *The Argus*, 14 November 1861, p. 5. [Reported speech]

48 Burke and Wills Commission, p. 10, Q200. [Reported speech]

49 Burke and Wills Commission, p. 29, Q726.

50 William John Wills, *A Successful Exploration*, p. 337.

51 Burke and Wills Commission, p. 18, Q405.

52 Burke and Wills Commission, p. 18, Q406. [Reported speech]

53 Hermann Beckler, *A Journey to Cooper's Creek*, p. 48.

54 Robert O'Hara Burke, Notebook, 24 December 1860, NLA, MS 30/1, pp. 7–8.

55 Hermann Beckler, *A Journey to Cooper's Creek*, p. 48.

56 Hermann Beckler, *A Journey to Cooper's Creek*, p. 48.

57 *The Star* (Ballarat), 16 March 1861, p. 1.

58 William Wright, Dispatch to Exploration Committee, 19 December 1860, pp. 1–2.

59 William Wright, Dispatch to Exploration Committee, 19 December 1860, p. 5.

60 William Wright, Dispatch to Exploration Committee, 19 December 1860, pp. 4–5.

61 Author's note: There are no surviving astronomical observations of the expedition's trip from Cooper's Creek to the Gulf, apart from a note in Wills's diary from this night that says he made

'an observation of the eclipse of Jupiter's (I) satellite, as well as some latitude observations'. (William Wills, 'Journey from Cooper's Creek to Carpentaria and return to Cooper's Creek', SLV, MS13071, Box 2083/1a, p. 5, (Image 6). http://handle.slv.vic.gov.au/10381/197341). We cannot know for certain why Wills observed this event, but it is my presumption that he used his observations of the eclipse to fix his watches to local time, and check the drift between them.

62 William Wills, 'Journey from Cooper's Creek to Carpentaria and return to Cooper's Creek', 20 December 1861, p. 6 (Image 7). http://handle.slv.vic.gov.au/10381/197341

63 Robert O'Hara Burke, Notebook, 20 December 1860, NLA, MS 30/1, p. 3.

64 William Wills, 'Journey from Cooper's Creek to Carpentaria and return to Cooper's Creek', 21 December 1861, pp. 8–9 (Images 8–9). http://handle.slv.vic.gov.au/10381/197341

65 Burke and Wills Commission, pp. 29–30, Q736.

66 William Wills, Field Book No. 2, SLV MS13071, Box 2083/1a.

67 William Wills, 'Journey from Cooper's Creek to Carpentaria and return to Cooper's Creek', 22 December 1861, p. 9 (Image 10). http://handle.slv.vic.gov.au/10381/197341

68 Hermann Beckler, *A Journey to Cooper's Creek*, p. 51.

69 Hermann Beckler, *A Journey to Cooper's Creek*, p. 52.

70 William Brahe, Report, 30 June 1861, p. 2.

71 *Empire* (Sydney), 14 November 1861, p. 2.

72 William Wills, 'Journey from Cooper's Creek to Carpentaria and return to Cooper's Creek', 23 December 1861, p. 10 (Image 11). http://handle.slv.vic.gov.au/10381/197341

73 *The Australasian*, 7 May 1870, p. 6.

74 William Wills, 'Journey from Cooper's Creek to Carpentaria and return to Cooper's Creek', 23 December 1861, p. 11 (Image 12). http://handle.slv.vic.gov.au/10381/197341

75 *Melbourne Punch*, 3 January 1861, p. 2.

76 William Wills, 'Journey from Cooper's Creek to Carpentaria and return to Cooper's Creek', 24 December 1861, p. 11 (Image 12). http://handle.slv.vic.gov.au/10381/197341

77 William Wills, 'Journey from Cooper's Creek to Carpentaria and return to Cooper's Creek', 25 December 1861, p. 11 (Images 12). http://handle.slv.vic.gov.au/10381/197341

78 Robert O'Hara Burke, Notebook, NLA, MS 30/1, pp. 9–10.

79 Hermann Beckler, *A Journey to Cooper's Creek*, p. 61.

80 Hermann Beckler, *A Journey to Cooper's Creek*, p. 64.

81 Hermann Beckler, *A Journey to Cooper's Creek*, p. 65.

82 Hermann Beckler, *A Journey to Cooper's Creek*, p. 65.

83 Hermann Beckler, *A Journey to Cooper's Creek*, pp. 76–77.

84 William Wright, Dispatch to Exploration Committee, 19 December 1860, SLV, MS13071, Box 2082/1f, Item 1, p. 1.

85 William Wright, Dispatch to Exploration Committee, 19 December 1860, pp. 5–6.

86 *The Argus*, 1 January 1861, p. 5.

87 *The Argus*, 1 January 1861, p. 5.

88 *The Argus*, 1 January 1861, p. 5.

89 *The Argus*, 1 January 1861, p. 5.

90 John Macadam, Letter to William Wright, 31 December 1860, p. 2 (Image 2). http://handle.slv. vic.gov.au/10381/212698

91 John Macadam, Letter to William Wright, 31 December 1860, p. 2 (Image 2). http://handle.slv. vic.gov.au/10381/212698

92 William Brahe, Report, 30 June 1861, p. 2.

93 William Brahe, Report, 30 June 1861, p. 2.

94 William Brahe, Report, 30 June 1861, p. 2.

95 William Wills, 'Journey from Cooper's Creek to Carpentaria and return to Cooper's Creek', 30 December 1860, State Library of Victoria, SLV MS13071, Box 2083/1a, p. 16 (Image 18). http://handle.slv.vic.gov.au/10381/197341

96 John King, Diary, NLA, MS 30/11, p. 7a.

97 John King, Diary, NLA, MS 30/11, p. 6b.

Chapter Eleven

1 *South Australian Advertiser*, 28 December 1860, p. 3.
2 Hermann Beckler, *A Journey to Cooper's Creek*, p. 78.
3 Hermann Beckler, *A Journey to Cooper's Creek*, p. 78.
4 Hermann Beckler, *A Journey to Cooper's Creek*, p. 80.
5 Hermann Beckler, *A Journey to Cooper's Creek*, p. 81.
6 Hermann Beckler, *A Journey to Cooper's Creek*, pp. 81–82.
7 Hermann Beckler, *A Journey to Cooper's Creek*, p. 82.
8 Hermann Beckler, *A Journey to Cooper's Creek*, p. 82.
9 Hermann Beckler, *A Journey to Cooper's Creek*, p. 82.
10 Hermann Beckler, *A Journey to Cooper's Creek*, pp. 82–3.
11 Hermann Beckler, *A Journey to Cooper's Creek*, p. 85.
12 Hermann Beckler, *A Journey to Cooper's Creek*, p. 85.
13 Hermann Beckler, *A Journey to Cooper's Creek*, p. 85.
14 Hermann Beckler, *A Journey to Cooper's Creek*, p. 85.
15 Alfred William Howitt, Inaugural Address, 7 January 1907, p. 12. http://handle.slv.vic.gov.au/10381/245539
16 Alfred William Howitt, Inaugural Address, 7 January 1907, p. 12. http://handle.slv.vic.gov.au/10381/245539
17 Alfred William Howitt, Inaugural Address, 7 January 1907, p. 12. [Reported speech] http://handle.slv.vic.gov.au/10381/245539
18 Alfred William Howitt, Inaugural Address, 7 January 1907, p. 12. http://handle.slv.vic.gov.au/10381/245539
19 Alfred William Howitt, Inaugural Address, 7 January 1907, p. 12. http://handle.slv.vic.gov.au/10381/245539
20 William Wills, 'Journey from Cooper's Creek to Carpentaria and return to Cooper's Creek', 5 January 1861, p. 17 (Image 19). http://handle.slv.vic.gov.au/10381/197341
21 William John Wills, 'Journey from Cooper's Creek to Carpentaria and return to Cooper's Creek', 6 January 1861, pp. 17–18 (Image 19–20). http://handle.slv.vic.gov.au/10381/197341
22 William Wills, *A Successful Exploration*, p. 22.
23 Robert O'Hara Burke, Notebook, 5 January 1861, NLA, MS 30/1, p. 13.
24 William Wills, 'Journey from Cooper's Creek to Carpentaria and return to Cooper's Creek', 8 January 1861, p. 20 (Image 22). http://handle.slv.vic.gov.au/10381/197341
25 William Wills, 'Journey from Cooper's Creek to Carpentaria and return to Cooper's Creek', 8 January 1861, p. 20 (Image 22). http://handle.slv.vic.gov.au/10381/197341
26 William Wills, 'Journey from Cooper's Creek to Carpentaria and return to Cooper's Creek', 8 January 1861, p. 21 (Image 23). http://handle.slv.vic.gov.au/10381/197341
27 Hermann Beckler, *A Journey to Cooper's Creek*, p. 91.
28 Hermann Beckler, *A Journey to Cooper's Creek*, p. 190.
29 *Brisbane Courier*, 11 August 1900, p. 9.
30 *Brisbane Courier*, 11 August 1900, p. 9.
31 Exploration Committee, Letter to William Wright, 31 December 1860, p. 27 (Image 48). http://handle.slv.vic.gov.au/10381/194756
32 Exploration Committee, Letter to William Wright, 31 December 1860, p. 27 (Image 48). http://handle.slv.vic.gov.au/10381/194756
33 Hermann Beckler, *A Journey to Cooper's Creek*, p. 94.
34 Ian Clarke and Fred Cahir (eds), *The Aboriginal Story of Burke and Wills*, p. 23.
35 Charles Stone, Letter to his brother, 17 January 1861, p. 1 (Image 1). http://handle.slv.vic.gov.au/10381/189732
36 William Wills, 'Journey from Cooper's Creek to Carpentaria and return to Cooper's Creek', 11 January 1861, p. 25 (Image 27). http://handle.slv.vic.gov.au/10381/197341
37 William Wills, 'Journey from Cooper's Creek to Carpentaria and return to Cooper's Creek', 11 January 1861, p. 25 (Image 27). http://handle.slv.vic.gov.au/10381/197341
38 William Wills, 'Journey from Cooper's Creek to Carpentaria and return to Cooper's Creek', 11 January 1861, p. 25 (Image 27). http://handle.slv.vic.gov.au/10381/197341

39 William Wills, 'Journey from Cooper's Creek to Carpentaria and return to Cooper's Creek', 12 January 1861, p. 26 (Image 28). http://handle.slv.vic.gov.au/10381/197341

40 *The Australasian*, 14 May 1870, p. 6.

41 *The Australasian*, 14 May 1870, p. 6.

42 Robert O'Hara Burke, Notebook, 18 January 1861, NLA, MS 30/1, p. 40a.

43 William Wills, 'Journey from Cooper's Creek to Carpentaria and return to Cooper's Creek', 19 January 1861, p. 29 (Image 30). http://handle.slv.vic.gov.au/10381/197341

44 William Wills, 'Journey from Cooper's Creek to Carpentaria and return to Cooper's Creek', 19 January 1861, p. 29 (Image 30). http://handle.slv.vic.gov.au/10381/197341

45 Robert O'Hara Burke, Notebook, 20 January 1861 [no page numbers] (Image 7). http://handle.slv.vic.gov.au/10381/196753

46 *The Australasian*, 14 May 1870, p. 614.

47 *The Australasian*, 14 May 1870, p. 614. [Reported speech]

48 *The Australasian*, 14 May 1870, p. 614. [Reported speech]

49 *The Australasian*, 14 May 1870, p. 614. [Reported speech]

50 Robert O'Hara Burke, Notebook, 20 January 1861, NLA, MS 30/1, p. 40.

51 Robert O'Hara Burke, Notebook, 20 January 1861, NLA, MS 30/1, p. 40.

52 Hermann Beckler, *A Journey to Cooper's Creek*, p. 94.

53 Hermann Beckler, *A Journey to Cooper's Creek*, p. 94.

54 Hermann Beckler, *A Journey to Cooper's Creek*, p. 97.

55 William Wright, Diary, 26 January 1861, p. 1 (Image 2). http://handle.slv.vic.gov.au/10381/197331

56 William Wills, 'Journey from Cooper's Creek to Carpentaria and return to Cooper's Creek', 27 January 1861, p. 31 (Image 32). http://handle.slv.vic.gov.au/10381/197341

57 William Wright, Diary, 28 January 1861, p. 4 (Image 4). http://handle.slv.vic.gov.au/10381/197331

58 William Wright, Diary, 29 January 1861, p. 5 (Image 5). http://handle.slv.vic.gov.au/10381/197331

59 Hermann Beckler, *A Journey to Cooper's Creek*, p. 98.

60 William Wright, Diary, 29 January 1861, p. 5 (Image 5). http://handle.slv.vic.gov.au/10381/197331

61 Hermann Beckler, *A Journey to Cooper's Creek*, p. 98.

62 Hermann Beckler, *A Journey to Cooper's Creek*, p. 98.

63 William Wright, Diary, 29 January 1861, pp. 4–5 (Images 5–6). http://handle.slv.vic.gov.au/10381/197331

64 William Wright, Diary, 31 January 1861, p. 7 (Image 8). http://handle.slv.vic.gov.au/10381/197331

65 Hermann Beckler, *A Journey to Cooper's Creek*, p. 99.

66 Hermann Beckler, *A Journey to Cooper's Creek*, p. 98.

67 Hermann Beckler, *A Journey to Cooper's Creek*, p. 99.

68 Hermann Beckler, *A Journey to Cooper's Creek*, p. 100.

69 Hermann Beckler, *A Journey to Cooper's Creek*, p. 100.

70 William Wright, Diary, 31 January 1861, p. 8 (Image 9). http://handle.slv.vic.gov.au/10381/197331

71 William Wright, Diary, 1 February 1861, p. 9 (Image 10). http://handle.slv.vic.gov.au/10381/197331

72 *The South Australian Advertiser*, 6 February 1861, p. 3.

73 *The South Australian Advertiser*, 6 February 1861, p. 3.

74 Hermann Beckler, *A Journey to Cooper's Creek*, p. 102.

75 Hermann Beckler, *A Journey to Cooper's Creek*, pp. 106–107.

76 Hermann Beckler, *A Journey to Cooper's Creek*, p. 107.

77 Hermann Beckler, *A Journey to Cooper's Creek*, p. 107–108.

78 *The Australasian*, 14 May 1870, p. 6. Author's note: Although there is no contemporary record showing that Wills recognised his location as 'the plains of promise' – this quotation coming from an 1870 account of John King's retrospective narrative – it is my presumption that Wills

indeed had a good idea of where he was, thanks to his proficiency and diligence as a surveyor, as well as his study of previous explorations.

79 Alfred William Howitt, *Personal Reminiscences of Central Austraia and the Burke and Wills Expedition*, Australasian Association for the Advancement of Science, Adelaide, 1908, p. 16.

80 *Empire* (Sydney), 3 June 1870, p. 4.

81 *The Australasian*, 14 May 1870, p. 6.

82 William Wills, 'Journey from Cooper's Creek to Carpentaria and return to Cooper's Creek', 10 February 1861, pp. 34–35 (Images 35–36). http://handle.slv.vic.gov.au/10381/197341
Author's note: The date of Wills's entry at this point simply reads 'Sunday, February 1861'. The fact that it is undated has led to some confusion as to what day Burke and Wills reached the farthest point of their journey. King at the Commission of Enquiry stated that he believed it was the ninth of February, but the relevant Sunday falls on the tenth of February 1861 and as such the tenth is used as the date here and throughout the manuscript for this source.

83 William Wills, 'Journey from Cooper's Creek to Carpentaria and return to Cooper's Creek', 10 February 1861, p. 35 (Image 36). http://handle.slv.vic.gov.au/10381/197341

84 William Wills, 'Journey from Cooper's Creek to Carpentaria and return to Cooper's Creek', 10 February 1861, p. 36 (Image 37). http://handle.slv.vic.gov.au/10381/197341

85 William Wills, 'Journey from Cooper's Creek to Carpentaria and return to Cooper's Creek', 10 February 1861, p. 36 (Image 37). http://handle.slv.vic.gov.au/10381/197341

86 William Wills, 'Journey from Cooper's Creek to Carpentaria and return to Cooper's Creek', 10 February 1861, p. 36 (Image 37). http://handle.slv.vic.gov.au/10381/197341

87 *The Argus*, 7 November 1861, p. 5.

88 *The Argus*, 7 November 1861, p. 5.

89 *The Argus*, 7 November 1861, p. 5.

90 *The Argus*, 7 November 1861, p. 5.

91 Author's note: Dave Phoenix, a man who has walked Australia following Burke and Wills's route himself, made this observation: that the prevailing idea that mangroves stopped Burke and Wills is a myth. It was the mud. The salt flats are flanked by mangroves, but the path ahead was clear but impossible. Aching miles of boggy mud in incredibly taxing heat were what actually prevented Burke and Wills from sighting the ocean.

92 Andrew Jackson, *Robert O'Hara Burke*, p. 223.

Chapter Twelve

1 *The Yeoman and Australian Advertiser*, 1 February 1862, pp. 8–9.

2 *Ovens and Murray Advertiser*, 9 July 1874, p. 2.

3 William John Wills, *A Successful Exploration*, p. 333

4 William Wright, Diary, 11 February 1861, SLV, MS13071, Box 2083/3b, p. 15 (Image 16). http://handle.slv.vic.gov.au/10381/197331

5 Burke and Wills Commission, p. 48, Q1340.

6 William Wright, Diary, 11 February 1861, SLV, MS13071, Box 2083/3b, p. 15 (Image 16). http://handle.slv.vic.gov.au/10381/197331

7 Hermann Beckler, *A Journey to Cooper's Creek*, p.112.

8 Hermann Beckler, *A Journey to Cooper's Creek*, p.112.

9 *The Australasian*, 21 May 1870, p. 648.

10 *The Australasian*, 21 May 1870, p. 648.

11 *The Australasian*, 21 May 1870, p. 648.

12 Burke and Wills Commission, p. 32, Q854.

13 Burke and Wills Commission, p. 33, Q816. Author's note: Some evidence suggests this plant was not dug at Gray and King's camp, but at Burke and Wills's northernmost point. I find the account given in the *Australasian*, (21 May 1870) is more convincing, so I have opted for the former.

14 *The Australasian*, 21 May 1870, p. 648.

15 Hermann Beckler, *A Journey to Cooper's Creek*, p. 166.

16 William Wright, Diary, 13 February 1861, p. 19 (Image 20). http://handle.slv.vic.gov.au/10381/197331

17 William Wright, Diary, 13 February 1861, p. 19 (Image 20). http://handle.slv.vic.gov.au/10381/197331

18 William Wright, Diary, 13 February 1861, pp. 19–20 (Images 20–1). http://handle.slv.vic.gov.au/10381/197331

19 William Wright, Diary, 14 February 1861, p. 20 (Image 21).

20 William Wills, 'Journey from Cooper's Creek to Carpentaria and return to Cooper's Creek', 21 February 1861, SLV, MS13071, Box 2083/1a, p. 38 (Image 38). http://handle.slv.vic.gov.au/10381/197341

21 William Wills, 'Journey from Cooper's Creek to Carpentaria and return to Cooper's Creek', 21 February 1861, SLV, MS13071, Box 2083/1a, p. 38 (Image 38). http://handle.slv.vic.gov.au/10381/197341

22 William Wills, 'Journey from Cooper's Creek to Carpentaria and return to Cooper's Creek', 22 February 1861, SLV, MS13071, Box 2083/1a, p. 38 (Image 38). http://handle.slv.vic.gov.au/10381/197341

23 William Wills, 'Journey from Cooper's Creek to Carpentaria and return to Cooper's Creek', 23 February 1861, p. 38 (Image 38). http://handle.slv.vic.gov.au/10381/197341

24 William Wills, 'Journey from Cooper's Creek to Carpentaria and return to Cooper's Creek', 2 March 1861, SLV, MS13071, Box 2083/1a, p. 39 (Image 39). http://handle.slv.vic.gov.au/10381/197341

25 William Wills, 'Journey from Cooper's Creek to Carpentaria and return to Cooper's Creek', 3 March 1861, SLV, MS13071, Box 2083/1a, p. 39 (Image 39). http://handle.slv.vic.gov.au/10381/197341

26 William Wills, 'Journey from Cooper's Creek to Carpentaria and return to Cooper's Creek', 3 March 1861, SLV, MS13071, Box 2083/1a, p. 39 (Image 39). http://handle.slv.vic.gov.au/10381/197341

27 William Wills, 'Journey from Cooper's Creek to Carpentaria and return to Cooper's Creek', 6 March 1861, SLV, MS13071, Box 2083/1a, p. 40 (Image 40). http://handle.slv.vic.gov.au/10381/197341

28 William Wills, 'Journey from Cooper's Creek to Carpentaria and return to Cooper's Creek', 7 March 1861, SLV, MS13071, Box 2083/1a, p. 40 (Image 40). http://handle.slv.vic.gov.au/10381/197341

29 Author's note: He actually wrote 'imbedded', but I have corrected.

30 William John Wills, A Successful Exploration, p. 241. [Reported speech]

31 William Wills, 'Journey from Cooper's Creek to Carpentaria and return to Cooper's Creek', 11 March 1861, p. 40 (Image 41). [Personal pronoun changed] http://handle.slv.vic.gov.au/10381/197341

32 Sarah Murgatroyd, The Dig Tree, p. 203.

33 The Herald, 22 March 1861, p. 5

34 William John Wills, A Successful Exploration, p. 243.

35 William John Wills, A Successful Exploration, pp. 239–40.

36 William Wills, 'Journey from Cooper's Creek to Carpentaria and return to Cooper's Creek', 14 March 1861, p. 41 (Image 41). http://handle.slv.vic.gov.au/10381/197341

37 Burke and Wills Commission, Appendix I (William Brahe's Report), p. 89.

38 Burke and Wills Commission, p. 18, Q421.

39 Burke and Wills Commission, p. 12, Q236.

40 Burke and Wills Commission, p. 12, Q238.

41 Burke and Wills Commission, p. 12, Q239.

42 William Wills, 'Journey from Cooper's Creek to Carpentaria and return to Cooper's Creek', 21 March 1861, p. 42 (Image 42). http://handle.slv.vic.gov.au/10381/197341

43 William Wills, 'Journey from Cooper's Creek to Carpentaria and return to Cooper's Creek', 21 March 1861, pp. 41–2 (Images 41–2). http://handle.slv.vic.gov.au/10381/197341

44 Burke and Wills Commission, p. 35, Q952.

45 Burke and Wills Commission, p. 35, Q944.

46 Burke and Wills Commission, p. 34, Q934.

47 William Wills, 'Journey from Cooper's Creek to Carpentaria and return to Cooper's Creek', 21 March 1861, p. 42 (Image 42). http://handle.slv.vic.gov.au/10381/197341

48 Burke and Wills Commission, p. 34, Q936. [Reported speech]

49 William Wills, 'Journey from Cooper's Creek to Carpentaria and return to Cooper's Creek', 25 March 1861, p. 42 (Image 42). [Reported speech] http://handle.slv.vic.gov.au/10381/197341

50 Burke and Wills Commission, p. 34, Q936. [Reported speech]

51 Burke and Wills Commission, p. 34, Q937. [Reported speech]

52 *The Argus*, 26 November 1861, p. 6.

53 Burke and Wills Commission, p. 34, Q938.

54 William Wills, 'Journey from Cooper's Creek to Carpentaria and return to Cooper's Creek', 25 March 1861, p. 42 (Image 42). http://handle.slv.vic.gov.au/10381/197341

55 William John Wills, *A Successful Exploration*, p. 229.

56 Burke and Wills Commission, p. 35, Q947.

57 *The Argus*, 26 November 1861, p. 6.

58 William Wills, 'Journey from Cooper's Creek to Carpentaria and return to Cooper's Creek', 25 March 1861, [no page number] (Image 43). [Reported speech] http://handle.slv.vic.gov.au/10381/197341

59 William Wills, 'Journey from Cooper's Creek to Carpentaria and return to Cooper's Creek', 8 January 1861, p. 21 (Image 23). http://handle.slv.vic.gov.au/10381/197341

60 William Wills, 'Journey from Cooper's Creek to Carpentaria and return to Cooper's Creek', 25 March 1861, [no page number] (Image 43). http://handle.slv.vic.gov.au/10381/197341

61 Edward Morton, *The Eton Boy*, Lacy, London, 1842, p. 4. https://babel.hathitrust.org/cgi/pt?id=uc1.31175035136780;view=1up;seq=2

62 William Wills, 'Journey from Cooper's Creek to Carpentaria and return to Cooper's Creek', 30 March 1861.

63 Hermann Beckler, *A Journey to Cooper's Creek*, p. 148.

64 Hermann Beckler, *A Journey to Cooper's Creek*, p. 145.

65 Burke and Wills Commission, Appendix I (William Brahe's Report), p. 89.

66 Burke and Wills Commission, p. 19, Q423.

67 Burke and Wills Commission, p. 19, Q430.

68 Burke and Wills Commission, p. 19, Q430.

69 Burke and Wills Commission, p. 11, Q229. [Reported speech]

70 William Brahe, Report, 30 June 1861, SLV, MS 13071, Box 2082/4h, p. 6.

71 William Brahe, Report, 30 June 1861, SLV, MS13071, Box 2082/4h. p. 5.

72 Burke and Wills Commission, p. 19, Q423. [Reported speech]

73 Burke and Wills Commission, p. 19, Q426. [Tense changed]

74 *The World's News*, 5 March 1910, p. 11.

75 *The World's News*, 5 March 1910, p. 11.

76 William John Wills, 'Wills' astronomical observations made on the return journey from the north, 1861', 3 April 1861, SLV, MS13071, Box 2083/1d, [no page number]

77 *The World's News*, 5 March 1910, p. 11.

78 *The World's News*, 5 March 1910, p. 11.

79 *The World's News*, 5 March 1910, p. 11.

80 Michael Cathcart, *Starvation in a Land of Plenty*, National Library of Australia, Canberra, 2013, p. 112.

81 William Wright, Diary, 4 April 1861, p. 51 (Image 54). http://handle.slv.vic.gov.au/10381/197331

82 William Wright, Diary, 5 April 1861, pp. 52–53 (Images 55–56). http://handle.slv.vic.gov.au/10381/197331

83 William John Wills, *A Successful Exploration*, p. 231.

84 Burke and Wills Commission, p. 34, Q911. [Tense changed]

85 *North Australian, Ipswich and General Advertiser*, 17 December 1861, p. 4.

86 *North Australian, Ipswich and General Advertiser*, 17 December 1861, p. 4.

87 *The Argus*, 9 April 1861, p. 5.

88 *The Argus*, 9 April 1861, p. 5.

89 William John Wills, *A Successful Exploration*, p. 231.

90 Author's note: While there is no account confirming that it is King who shot Billy, it is precisely in his province of operations and later, when Rajah must be shot, it is certainly King who is given the order by Burke.

91 William John Wills, *A Successful Exploration*, p. 231.

92 William John Wills, *A Successful Exploration*, p. 231.

93 William John Wills, *A Successful Exploration*, p. 232.

94 Burke and Wills Commission, Appendix I (William Brahe's Report), p. 89.

95 *The Argus*, 5 November 1861, p. 5.

96 Burke and Wills Commission, p. 11, Q222. [Reported speech]

97 *The Argus*, 27 August 1910, p. 9.

98 *The North Australian, Ipswich and General Advertiser*, 17 December 1861, p. 4.

99 Burke and Wills Commission, p. 36, Q976. [Reported speech]

100 *Bathurst Free Press and Mining Journal*, 29 January 1890, p.4., Edwin James Welch, Diary, SLNSW, ML C332, D179.

101 Edwin James Welch, 'The Tragedy of Cooper's Creek', State Library of New South Wales, A1928, p. 15

102 William John Wills, *A Successful Exploration*, p. 234.

103 *The Argus*, 17 April 1861, p. 5.

104 *The Argus*, 9 April 1861, p. 5.

105 *The Argus*, 22 April 1861, p. 5.

106 *Adelaide Observer*, 17 January 1863, p. 7.

107 *The Argus*, 22 April 1861, p. 5.

108 From Robert Louis Stevenson's poem 'Requiem'.

109 *The Argus*, 22 April 1861, p. 5.

110 *The Australasian*, 21 May 1870, p. 648.

111 Burke and Wills Commission, p. 37, Q1034. [Reported speech]

112 Burke and Wills Commission, Appendix I (William Brahe's Report), p. 89.

Chapter Thirteen

1 Edward Eyre, *Journals of expeditions of discovery into Central Australia*, Vol. 2, T. and W. Boone, London, 18??, pp. 108–109.

2 *The Argus*, 7 July 1934, p.20.

3 William John Wills, *A Successful Exploration*, p. 7.

4 Burke and Wills Commission, p. 15, Q323.

5 William Brahe, Dispatch, 21 April 1861, SLV, MS13071, Box 2082/1d (1), [no page number] (Image 4). http://handle.slv.vic.gov.au/10381/212729

6 Burke and Wills Commission, p. 14, Q311.

7 Burke and Wills Commission, Appendix I (William Brahe's Report), p. 89.

8 Burke and Wills Commission, p. 10, Q173.

9 Burke and Wills Commission, p. 12, Q260.

10 Burke and Wills Commission, p. 12, Q261. Author's note: It is one of the strange twists of this tale that the famous 'DIG' tree that thousands of tourists visit and take photos of each year is not in fact the actual tree that Brahe carved 'DIG' into. That tree still stands just a few feet away, but the bark has grown back over the legendary inscription. There were two trees Brahe marked, one with the dates of his stay, one with the instruction 'DIG'. But a year or so later, a member of another expedition, that of Mr Alfred Howitt, carved 'DIG' on the 'date' tree to indicate a new cache that had been buried there and as the years went by this was mistakenly thought to be the Burke and Wills 'DIG' tree. The instruction and written dates were carefully preserved and can still be seen today. So, the 'DIG' tree visited today was the centre of the stockade, 'Fort Wills', but not the tree that would be so crucial to the fate of Burke and Wills.

11 Burke and Wills Commission, p. 36, Q1010.

12 Burke and Wills Commission, p. 37, Q1010.

13 Andrew Jackson, *Robert O'Hara Burke*, p. 109.

14 John King, Narrative to Howitt, SLV, MS13071, Box 2083/1f, [no page number] (Image 2). http://handle.slv.vic.gov.au/10381/196866

15 *The Australasian*, 21 May 1870, p. 648.

16 Charles Dickens, *The Life and Adventures of Martin Chuzzlewit*, p. 174.

17 Burke and Wills Commission, p. 37, Q1010.

18 William John Wills, *A Successful Exploration*, p. 234.

19 Burke and Wills Commission, p. 37, Q1011. [Reported speech]

20 Burke and Wills Commission, p. 37, Q1011. [Tenses changed]

21 Burke and Wills Commission, p. 14, Q302.

22 John King, Narrative to Howitt (Transcript), SLV, MS13071, Box 2083/1f, [no page number] (Image 2). [Reported Speech] http://handle.slv.vic.gov.au/10381/196866

23 John King, Narrative to Howitt (Transcript), SLV, MS13071, Box 2083/1f, [no page number] (Image 2). [Reported Speech] http://handle.slv.vic.gov.au/10381/196866

24 Burke and Wills Commission, p. 37, Q1011. [Tense changed]

25 Burke and Wills Commission, p. 36, Q999.

26 William John Wills, *A Successful Exploration*, p. 234. https://archive.org/stream/successfulexplor00willrich#page/234

27 *Bathurst Free Press and Mining Journal*, 29 January 1890, p. 4.

28 John King, Narrative to Howitt (Transcript), SLV, MS13071, Box 2083/1f, [no page number] (Image 2). [Reported speech] http://handle.slv.vic.gov.au/10381/196866

29 John King, Narrative to Howitt (Transcript), SLV, MS13071, Box 2083/1f, [no page number] (Image 2). [Reported speech] http://handle.slv.vic.gov.au/10381/196866

30 William John Wills, *A Successful Exploration*, p. 270.

31 William John Wills, *A Successful Exploration*, p. 270.

32 William John Wills, *A Successful Exploration*, p. 335.

33 William John Wills, *A Successful Exploration*, p. 234.

34 William John Wills, *A Successful Exploration*, p. 235.

35 Hermann Beckler, *A Journey to Cooper's Creek*, p. 170.

36 William Wright, Diary, 24 April 1861, p. 62 (Image 65). http://handle.slv.vic.gov.au/10381/197331

37 William Wright, Diary, 22 April 1861, p. 58 (Image 61). http://handle.slv.vic.gov.au/10381/197331

38 Hermann Beckler, *A Journey to Cooper's Creek*, p. 165.

39 William Wright, Diary, 24 April 1861, p. 62 (Image 65). http://handle.slv.vic.gov.au/10381/197331

40 Hermann Beckler, *A Journey to Cooper's Creek*, p. 167.

41 Hermann Beckler, *A Journey to Cooper's Creek*, p. 167.

42 Hermann Beckler, *A Journey to Cooper's Creek*, p. 167.

43 Hermann Beckler, *A Journey to Cooper's Creek*, p. 167.

44 Hermann Beckler, *A Journey to Cooper's Creek*, p. 167.

45 Hermann Beckler, *A Journey to Cooper's Creek*, p. 167.

46 William Wright, Diary, 22 April 1861, p. 58 (Image 61). http://handle.slv.vic.gov.au/10381/197331

47 Hermann Beckler, *A Journey to Cooper's Creek*, p. 168. [Reported speech]

48 Hermann Beckler, *A Journey to Cooper's Creek*, p. 168.

49 William Wright, Diary, 22 April 1861, p. 58 (Image 61). http://handle.slv.vic.gov.au/10381/197331

50 Hermann Beckler, *A Journey to Cooper's Creek*, p. 168.

51 Hermann Beckler, *A Journey to Cooper's Creek*, p. 168.

52 Hermann Beckler, *A Journey to Cooper's Creek*, p. 168.

53 Hermann Beckler, *A Journey to Cooper's Creek*, p. 168.

54 Hermann Beckler, *A Journey to Cooper's Creek*, p. 169.

55 Hermann Beckler, *A Journey to Cooper's Creek*, p. 169.

56 William Wright, Diary, 22 April 1861, p. 59 (Image 62). http://handle.slv.vic.gov.au/10381/197331

57 Hermann Beckler, *A Journey to Cooper's Creek*, p. 170.

58 *The Age*, 19 July 1861, p. 6.

59 Hermann Beckler, *A Journey to Cooper's Creek*, p. 170.

60 William Wright, Diary, 22 April 1861.

61 William Wills, Journal, 23 April 1861, NLA, MS 30/7, [no page number] (Part 134). http://www.nla.gov.au/apps/cdview/?pi=nla.ms-ms30-7-s134-v

62 Robert O'Hara Burke, Note, 22 April 1861, pp. 1–5 (Images 1, 3–6). http://handle.slv.vic.gov.au/10381/251633

63 *Bathurst Free Press and Mining Journal*, 29 January 1890, p. 4.

64 Burke and Wills Commission, p. 37, Q1032.

65 Burke and Wills Commission, p.66, Q1704.

66 *Bathurst Free Press and Mining Journal*, 29 January 1890, p. 4.

67 William Wills, Journal, 25 April 1861, NLA, MS 30/7, [no page number] (Part 134). http://www.nla.gov.au/apps/cdview/?pi=nla.ms-ms30-7-s134-v

68 William Wills, Journal, 24 April 1861, NLA, [no page number] (Part 132). http://www.nla.gov.au/apps/cdview/?pi=nla.ms-ms30-7-s132-v

69 William Wills, Journal, 24 April 1861, NLA, MS 30/7, [no page number] (Part 132). http://www.nla.gov.au/apps/cdview/?pi=nla.ms-ms30-7-s132-v

70 *The Argus*, 23 April 1861, p. 5.

71 *The Argus*, 24 April 1861, p. 5.

72 William Wright, Dairy, 24 April 1861, p. 62 (Image 65). http://handle.slv.vic.gov.au/10381/197331

73 William Wright, Dairy, 24 April 1861, p. 62 (Image 65). http://handle.slv.vic.gov.au/10381/197331

74 William Wright, Diary, 24 April 1861, p. 62 (Image 65). http://handle.slv.vic.gov.au/10381/197331

75 William Wright, Diary, 24 April 1861, p. 62 (Image 65). http://handle.slv.vic.gov.au/10381/197331

76 William Wright, Diary, 24 April 1861, p. 63 (Image 66). http://handle.slv.vic.gov.au/10381/197331

77 William Wright, Diary, 24 April 1861, pp. 63–4 (Images 66–7). http://handle.slv.vic.gov.au/10381/197331

78 Burke and Wills Commission, Appendix I (William Brahe's Report), p. 89.

79 William Brahe, Report 30 June 1861, SLV, MS13071, Box 2082/4h, p. 7.

80 Burke and Wills Commission, p. 20, Q454.

81 William Wills, Journal, 25 April 1861, NLA, [no page number] (Part 130). http://www.nla.gov.au/apps/cdview/?pi=nla.ms-ms30-7-s130-v

82 William Wills, Journal, 25 April 1861, NLA, [no page number] (Part 130). http://www.nla.gov.au/apps/cdview/?pi=nla.ms-ms30-7-s130-v

83 William Wills, Journal, 26 April 1861, NLA, [no page number] (Parts 128-129). http://www.nla.gov.au/apps/cdview/?pi=nla.ms-ms30-7-s128-v

84 William Wright, Diary, 27 April 1861, p. 65 (Image 68). http://handle.slv.vic.gov.au/10381/197331

85 William Wright, Dairy, 27 April 1861, p. 66 (Image 69). http://handle.slv.vic.gov.au/10381/197331

86 William Wright, Dairy, 27 April 1861, p. 66 (Image 69). http://handle.slv.vic.gov.au/10381/197331

87 William Wright, Dairy, 27 April 1861, p. 66 (Image 69). http://handle.slv.vic.gov.au/10381/197331

88 Hermann Beckler, *A Journey to Cooper's Creek*, p. 172.

89 Hermann Beckler, *A Journey to Cooper's Creek*, p. 172. [Reported speech]

90 Hermann Beckler, *A Journey to Cooper's Creek*, p. 172–73.

91 Hermann Beckler, *A Journey to Cooper's Creek*, p. 173. [Reported speech]

92 Hermann Beckler, *A Journey to Cooper's Creek*, p. 173.

93 Hermann Beckler, *A Journey to Cooper's Creek*, p. 173.

94 Hermann Beckler, *A Journey to Cooper's Creek*, p. 173.

95 Hermann Beckler, *A Journey to Cooper's Creek*, p. 173.

96 Hermann Beckler, *A Journey to Cooper's Creek*, p. 173.

97 William Wright, Dairy, 27 April 1861, p. 66 (Image 69). http://handle.slv.vic.gov.au/10381/197331

98 Hermann Beckler, *A Journey to Cooper's Creek*, p. 173.

99 Hermann Beckler, *A Journey to Cooper's Creek*, p. 173

100 Hermann Beckler, *A Journey to Cooper's Creek*, p. 175.

101 Hermann Beckler, *A Journey to Cooper's Creek*, p. 153.

102 Hermann Beckler, *A Journey to Cooper's Creek*, p. 173.

103 William Wright, Diary, 27 April 1861, p. 67 (Image 70). http://handle.slv.vic.gov.au/10381/197331

104 William Wills, Journal, 28 April 1861, NLA, MS 30/7, [no page number] (Part 124). http://www.nla.gov.au/apps/cdview/?pi=nla.ms-ms30-7-s124-v

105 William Wills, Journal, 28 April 1861, NLA, MS 30/7, [no page number] (Part 124). http://www.nla.gov.au/apps/cdview/?pi=nla.ms-ms30-7-s124-v

106 William Brahe, Report 30 June 1861, SLV, MS13071, Box 2082/4h, p. 8.

107 Burke and Wills Commission, Appendix I (William Brahe's Report), p. 90.

108 Andrew Jackson, *Robert O'Hara Burke*, p. 156. https://archive.org/stream/robertoharaburk00jackgoog#page/n173

109 William Wright, Dairy, 29 April 1861, p. 69 (Image 72). [Reported speech] http://handle.slv.vic.gov.au/10381/197331

110 Author's note: Dost Mahomet was sometimes known as Botan. I have used the name he was most often known by.

111 William Wright, Diary, 29 April 1861, p. 69 (Image 72). http://handle.slv.vic.gov.au/10381/197331

112 Burke and Wills Commission, Q458, 28 November 1861.

113 Hermann Beckler, *A Journey to Cooper's Creek*, p 175.

114 Hermann Beckler, *A Journey to Cooper's Creek*, p 175.

115 Hermann Beckler, *A Journey to Cooper's Creek*, p. 175.

116 Hermann Beckler, *A Journey to Cooper's Creek*, p. 175.

117 Hermann Beckler, *A Journey to Cooper's Creek*, p. 175.

118 Burke and Wills Commission, p. 18, Q412.

119 Burke and Wills Commission, p. 21, Q497.

120 Burke and Wills Commission, p. 19, Q436.

121 Burke and Wills Commission, p. 19, Q436.

122 William Wills, Journal, 1 May 1861, NLA, MS30/7, [no page number] (Part 118). http://www.nla.gov.au/apps/cdview/?pi=nla.ms-ms30-7-s118-v

123 Burke and Wills Commission, p. 38, Q1051.

124 *Bathurst Free Press and Mining Journal*, 29 January 1890, p. 4.

125 Ian Clark and Fred Cahir (eds), *The Aboriginal Story of Burke and Wills*, p.xiv.

126 William Wright, Diary, 1 May 1861, p. 70 (Image 73). http://handle.slv.vic.gov.au/10381/197331

127 William John Wills, *A Successful Exploration*, p. 135. [Tense changed] Author's note: In the Burke and Wills Commission, Wright denied saying words to this effect until after he had visited the Depot. But on balance of evidence – most particularly Tom McDonough's testimony at the Royal Commission – I believe it more likely that he said it at this point.

128 Author's note: Although Wright says 15 camels, they in fact have 16, as is corroborated in Beckler's account.

129 William Wright, Diary, 1 May 1861, pp. 70–71 (Images 73–74). http://handle.slv.vic.gov.au/10381/197331

130 William Wright, Third Dispatch, 20 June 1861, p. 12 (Image 13). http://handle.slv.vic.gov.au/10381/212818

131 William Wills, Journal, 2 May 1861, NLA, [no page number] (Part 116). http://www.nla.gov.au/apps/cdview/?pi=nla.ms-ms30-7-s116-v

132 Edwin James Welch, 'Diary of Howitt Expedition, 26 June – 6 Dec 1861', SLNSW, ML C332, D179, [no page numbers].

133 William Wills, Journal, 2 May 1861, NLA, [no page number] (Part 116). http://www.nla.gov.au/apps/cdview/?pi=nla.ms-ms30-7-s117-v

134 John King, Narrative to Howitt (Transcript), [no page number] (Image 2). http://handle.slv.vic.gov.au/10381/196866

135 Author's note: In hunting for Strzelecki Creek, Wills was looking for what he supposed was Gregory's route to Mount Hopeless. However, Gregory didn't go this way. It seems then that by far the most likely explanation for Wills's obsession with finding the Strzelecki as opposed to other possible routes, and his assumption that it joined Cooper's Creek, is that Wills did not have a map.

136 *Bathurst Free Press and Mining Journal*, 29 January 1890, p. 4.

137 Burke and Wills Commission, p. 38, Q1052.

138 *The Argus*, 27 August 1910, p. 9.

139 Burke and Wills Commission, p. 15, Q340.

140 William Wright, Third Dispatch, 20 June 1861, p. 13 (Image 14). http://handle.slv.vic.gov.au/10381/212818

141 *The Argus*, 29 November 1861, p. 6.

142 *Mount Alexander Mail*, 6 May 1861, p. 2.

143 *Mount Alexander Mail*, 6 May 1861, p. 2. [Reported speech]

144 *Mount Alexander Mail*, 6 May 1861, p. 2. [Reported speech]

145 *Mount Alexander Mail*, 6 May 1861, p. 2.

146 *Mount Alexander Mail*, 3 May 1861, p. 4.

147 William Wills, Journal, 5 May 1861, NLA, MS 30/7, [no page number] (Part 110). http://www.nla.gov.au/apps/cdview/?pi=nla.ms-ms30-7-s110-v

148 William Wills, Journal, 6 May 1861, NLA, MS 30/7, [no page number] (Part 108). http://www.nla.gov.au/apps/cdview/?pi=nla.ms-ms30-7-s108-v

149 William Wills, Journal, 7 May 1861, NLA, MS 30/7, [no page numbers] (Part 107). http://www.nla.gov.au/apps/cdview/?pi=nla.ms-ms30-7-s107-e

150 John King, Narrative to Howitt (Transcript), SLV, MS13071, Box 2083/1f, [no page number] (Image 2). [Reported speech] http://handle.slv.vic.gov.au/10381/196866

151 Burke and Wills Commission, p. 102 (Appendix L, John King's Narrative). [Reported speech]

Chapter Fourteen

1 Alfred William Howitt, Inaugural Address, 7 January 1907, SLV, p. 19. http://handle.slv.vic.gov.au/10381/245539

2 Andrew Jackson, *Robert O'Hara Burke*, p. 61.

3 Burke and Wills Commission, p. 50, Q1393. [Reported speech]

4 Burke and Wills Commission, p. 51, Q1410.

5 Burke and Wills Commission, p. 50, Q 1394.

6 Burke and Wills Commission, Q1393, William Wright, 10 December 1861.

7 *The Argus*, 6 November 1861, p. 7.

8 Burke and Wills Commission, p. 51, Q1411.

9 Burke and Wills Commission, p. 50, Q1399.

10 *Bathurst Free Press and Mining Journal*, 29 January 1890, p. 4.

11 John King, Narrative to Howitt (Transcript), SLV, MS13071, Box 2083/1f, [no page number] (Image 2). http://handle.slv.vic.gov.au/10381/196866

12 John King, Narrative to Howitt (Transcript), SLV, MS13071, Box 2083/1f, [no page number] (Image 2). http://handle.slv.vic.gov.au/10381/196866

13 William Wills, Journal, 10 May 1861, NLA, MS30/7, [no page number] (Part 100). http://www.nla.gov.au/apps/cdview/?pi=nla.ms-ms30-7-s100-v

14 William Wills, Journal, 11 May 1861, NLA, MS30/7, [no page numbers] (Part 98). http://www.nla.gov.au/apps/cdview/?pi=nla.ms-ms30-7-s98-v

15 William Wright, Diary, 13 May 1861, SLV, MS13071, Box 2083/3b, p. 74 (Image 77). http://handle.slv.vic.gov.au/10381/197331

16 John King, Narrative to Howitt (Transcript), SLV, MS13071, Box 2083/1f, [no page number] (Image 3). [Reported speech.] http://handle.slv.vic.gov.au/10381/196866

17 John King, Narrative to Howitt (Transcript), SLV, MS13071, Box 2083/1f, [no page number] (Image 3). http://handle.slv.vic.gov.au/10381/196866

18 John King, Narrative to Howitt (Transcript), SLV, MS13071, Box 2083/1f, [no page number] (Image 3). http://handle.slv.vic.gov.au/10381/196866

19 John King, Narrative to Howitt (Transcript), SLV, MS13071, Box 2083/1f, [no page number] (Image 3). [Reported speech] http://handle.slv.vic.gov.au/10381/196866

20 William Wills, Journal, 17 May 1861, NLA, MS30/7, [no page number] (Part 86). http://www.nla.gov.au/apps/cdview/?pi=nla.ms-ms30-7-s86-v

21 John King, Narrative to Howitt (Transcript), SLV, MS13071, Box 2083/1f, [no page number] (Image 3). http://handle.slv.vic.gov.au/10381/196866

22 William Wills, Journal, 14 May 186, NLA, MS30/7, [no page numbers] (Part 93). http://www.nla.gov.au/apps/cdview/?pi=nla.ms-ms30-7-s93-v

23 William Wills, Journal, 17 May 1861, NLA, MS30/7, [no page numbers] (Part 87). http://www.nla.gov.au/apps/cdview/?pi=nla.ms-ms30-7-s87-v

24 John King, Narrative to Howitt (Transcript), SLV, MS13071, Box 2083/1f, [no page number] (Image 3). http://handle.slv.vic.gov.au/10381/196866

25 Hermann Beckler, *A Journey to Cooper's Creek*, p. 179.

26 William Wright, Diary, 3 June 1861, SLV, MS13071, Box 2083/3b, p. 81 (Image 84), http://handle.slv.vic.gov.au/10381/197331

27 Hermann Beckler, *A Journey to Cooper's Creek*, p. 179.

28 Hermann Beckler, *A Journey to Cooper's Creek*, p. 180.

29 Hermann Beckler, *A Journey to Cooper's Creek*, p. 180.

30 William Wills, Journal, 24 May 1861, NLA, MS30/7, [no page number] (Part 72). http://www.nla.gov.au/apps/cdview/?pi=nla.ms-ms30-7-s72-v

31 William Wills, Journal, 24 May 1861, NLA, MS30/7, [no page number] (Part 72). http://www.nla.gov.au/apps/cdview/?pi=nla.ms-ms30-7-s72-v

32 William Wills, Journal, 27 May 1861, NLA, MS 30/7 [no page number] (Part 66). http://www.nla.gov.au/apps/cdview/?pi=nla.ms-ms30-7-s66-v

33 Author's note: The way that Wills refers to 'Pitchery' later, on 3 June, it is clear the two are already acquainted, and it is my judgement that it this native who is the most likely to be him.

34 William Wills, Journal, 27 May 1861, NLA MS 30/7, [no page number] (Part 67). http://www.nla.gov.au/apps/cdview/?pi=nla.ms-ms30-7-s67-v

35 John King, Narrative to Howitt (Transcript), [no page number] (Image 4). http://handle.slv.vic.gov.au/10381/196866

36 John King, Narrative to Howitt (Transcript), [no page number] (Image 4). http://handle.slv.vic.gov.au/10381/196866

37 John King, Narrative to Howitt (Transcript), [no page number] (Image 4). http://handle.slv.vic.gov.au/10381/196866

38 John King, Narrative to Howitt (Transcript), [no page number] (Image 4). http://handle.slv.vic.gov.au/10381/196866

39 *The Age*, 28 May 1861, p. 5.

40 *The Age*, 7 November 1861, p. 6.

41 William Wills, Dig Tree Note, 30 May 1861, SLV, MS13071, Manuscripts Safe 1 [no page numbers].

42 William Wills, Dig Tree Note, 30 May 1861, SLV, MS13071, Manuscripts Safe 1 [no page numbers].

43 William Shakespeare, Sonnet 73, *The Works of William Shakespeare*, Universal Classics, New York, 1980, p. 1234.

44 William Wills, Journal, 3 June 1861, NLA, MS30/7, [no page number] (Part 52). http://www.nla.gov.au/apps/cdview/?pi=nla.ms-ms30-7-s52-v

45 William Wills, Journal, 3 June 186, NLA, MS30/7, [no page number] (Part 53). http://www.nla.gov.au/apps/cdview/?pi=nla.ms-ms30-7-s53-v

46 *The Argus*, 27 August 1910, p. 9.

47 John King, Narrative to Howitt (Transcript), [no page numbers] (Images 4–5). http://handle.slv.vic.gov.au/10381/196866

48 William Wills, Journal, 4 June 1861, NLA, MS 30/7, [no page numbers] (Part 50). http://www.nla.gov.au/apps/cdview/?pi=nla.ms-ms30-7-s50-v

49 Burke and Wills Commission, Appendix K (Mr Wills's Journal), p. 103.

50 William Wills, Journal, 7 June 1861, NLA, [no page number] (Part 44). http://www.nla.gov.au/apps/cdview/?pi=nla.ms-ms30-7-s44-v

51 Edwin James Welch, 'Diary of Howitt Expedition, 26 June – 6 Dec 1861', SLNSW, ML C332, D179, 15 September 1861, [no page numbers].

52 William John Wills, A Successful Exploration, p. 243.

53 William Wills, Journal, 14 June 1861, NLA, MS30/7, [no page number] (Part 30). http://www.nla.gov.au/apps/cdview/?pi=nla.ms-ms30-7-s30-v

54 William Wills, Journal, 14 June 1861, NLA, MS30/7, [no page number] (Part 30). http://www.nla.gov.au/apps/cdview/?pi=nla.ms-ms30-7-s30-v

55 William John Wills, A Successful Exploration, p. 243.

56 William John Wills, A Successful Exploration, p. 243.

57 Author's note: The Minutes of the Exploration Committee confirm that the relevant meeting was held on 13 June 1861, not five days later, as Dr Wills claims.

58 William John Wills, A Successful Exploration, p. 244.

59 William John Wills, A Successful Exploration, p. 244. [Reported speech]

60 William John Wills, A Successful Exploration, p. 244.

61 Mount Alexander Mail, 5 July 1861, p. 3.

62 Mount Alexander Mail, 5 July 1861, p. 3.

63 William Wright, Third Dispatch, 20 June 1861, p. 1 (Image 2). http://handle.slv.vic.gov.au/10381/212818

64 The Australasian, 8 January 1910, p. 51.

65 The Australasian, 8 January 1910, p. 52.

66 Author's note: Although Edwin Welch wrote two newspaper articles in great detail about the preparations, difficulties and photographs eventually taken on this expedition, there is a question as to whether the camera equipment was taken on Howitt's first or second trip to Cooper's Creek. I have chosen to accept the vivid recall and memories of the man who operated the camera and was there at Howitt's side, but note that Dave Phoenix, the foremost authority on Burke and Wills, holds that the contemporary documentation can only prove a camera being taken on the second trip.

67 William Wills, Journal, 20 June 1861, NLA, MS30/7, [no page number] (Part 18). http://www.nla.gov.au/apps/cdview/?pi=nla.ms-ms30-7-s18-v

68 William Wills, Journal, 21 June 1861, NLA, MS30/7, [no page number] (Part 16). http://www.nla.gov.au/apps/cdview/?pi=nla.ms-ms30-7-s16-v

69 William Wills, Journal, 23 June 1861, NLA, (sic; the correct date for this Tuesday is 25 June 1861), MS30/7, [no page number] (Part 12). http://www.nla.gov.au/apps/cdview/?pi=nla.ms-ms30-7-s12-v

70 William Wills, Journal, 23 June 1861, NLA, (sic; the correct date for this Tuesday is 25 June 1861), [no page number] (Part 8). http://www.nla.gov.au/apps/cdview/?pi=nla.ms-ms30-7-s8-v

71 William Wills, Journal, 23 June 1861, NLA, (sic; the correct date for this Tuesday is 25 June 1861), [no page number] (Part 8). http://www.nla.gov.au/apps/cdview/?pi=nla.ms-ms30-7-s8-v

72 William Wills, Journal, 24 June 1861, NLA, MS30/7, [no page number] (Part 10). http://www.nla.gov.au/apps/cdview/?pi=nla.ms-ms30-7-s10-v

73 William Wills, Journal, 24 June 1861, NLA, MS30/7, [no page number] (Part 10). [Reported speech, pronoun changed] http://www.nla.gov.au/apps/cdview/?pi=nla.ms-ms30-7-s10-v

74 William Wills, Journal, 23 June 1861, NLA, (sic; the correct date for this Tuesday is 25 June 1861), NLA, MS30/7, [no page number] (Part 8). http://www.nla.gov.au/apps/cdview/?pi=nla.ms-ms30-7-s8-v

75 John King, Narrative to Howitt (Transcript), [no page number] (Image 5). http://handle.slv.vic.gov.au/10381/196866

76 The Age, 27 June 1861, p. 3.

77 Author's note: From Tuesday the 25th of June 1861 and for the remainder of his days alive, the self-recorded dates of William Wills's journal entries are inaccurate as Wills mistakenly entered this Tuesday as being the 23rd of June (a date he had already correctly entered two days earlier in the same journal). As such, these final days have been given their correct calendar dates.

78 Robert O'Hara Burke, Note, 26 June 1861, pp. 5–7 (Images 6–8). http://handle.slv.vic.gov.au/10381/251633

79 Alfred William Howitt, Diary (13 August–7 October 1861), SLV, MS13071, FB33 (7), p. 5. [Reported speech]

80 William Wills, Journal, 26 June 1861 (sic; the correct date for this Friday is 28 June 1861), NLA MS 30/7

81 *Bathurst Free Press and Mining Journal*, 29 January 1890, p. 4.

82 *Bathurst Free Press and Mining Journal*, 29 January 1890, p. 4.

83 *Bathurst Free Press and Mining Journal*, 30 January 1890, p. 4.

84 William Wills, Journal, 26 June 1861, NLA, (sic; the correct date for this Friday is 28 June 1861), [no page number] (Part 2). http://www.nla.gov.au/apps/cdview/?pi=nla.ms-ms30-7-s2-v

85 William Wills, Journal, 26 June 1861, NLA, (sic; the correct date for this Friday is 28 June 1861), [no page number] (Part 2). http://www.nla.gov.au/apps/cdview/?pi=nla.ms-ms30-7-s2-v

86 William Wills, Journal, 26 June 1861, NLA, (sic; the correct date for this Friday is 28 June 1861), [no page number] (Part 2). http://www.nla.gov.au/apps/cdview/?pi=nla.ms-ms30-7-s2-v

87 William John Wills, *A Successful Exploration*, p. 337.

88 William John Wills, *A Successful Exploration*, p. 337.

89 William John Wills, *A Successful Exploration*, p. 337.

90 William John Wills, *A Successful Exploration*, p. 335.

91 William Wills, Letter to his father (Dr Wills), 27 June 1861, *Correspondence and press cuttings, 1839–1861*, 1839, SLV, MS 9594, [no page number].

92 William John Wills, *A Successful Exploration*, pp. 333–34.

93 Burke and Wills Commission, p. 39, Q1069.

94 John King, Narrative to Howitt (Transcript), [no page number] (Image 6). http://handle.slv.vic.gov.au/10381/196866

95 John King, Narrative to Howitt (Transcript), [no page number] (Image 6). http://handle.slv.vic.gov.au/10381/196866

96 Andrew Jackson, *Robert O'Hara Burke*, p. 151.

97 William Shakespeare, *Hamlet*, Act III, Scene 1, William Heinemann, London, 1904, p. 65.

98 John King, Narrative to Howitt (Transcript), [no page number] (Image 6). http://handle.slv.vic.gov.au/10381/196866

99 Burke and Wills Commission, p. 39, Q1066.

100 Author's note: I have omitted the date that Burke put upon this letter, as though he marked it 26 June it appears likely this was wrong, and confuses the narrative.

101 Robert O'Hara Burke, Letter to Sister, 28 June 1861, SLV, MS13867/20, p. 1 (Image 1). http://handle.slv.vic.gov.au/10381/169989

102 *The Register*, 18 August 1915, p. 8.

103 Robert O'Hara Burke, Letter to Sister, 28 June 1861, SLV, MS13867/20, p. 1, (Image 1). http://handle.slv.vic.gov.au/10381/169989

104 Robert O'Hara Burke, Note, 30 June 1861, pp. 8–9 (Images 9–10). http://handle.slv.vic.gov.au/10381/251633

105 John King, Narrative to Howitt (Transcript), [no page number] (Image 6). http://handle.slv.vic.gov.au/10381/196866

106 Burke and Wills Commission, p. 39, Q1070.

107 'Cupid', Letter to Robert O'Hara Burke, 26 June 1861, pp. 1–2 (Image 2–3). http://handle.slv.vic.gov.au/10381/212820

108 Author's note: I am satisfied that 'Cupid' is Julia Matthews, as are Phoenix, Murgatroyd and Bonyhady. An important piece of evidence is that, at the time, Cupid was Matthews's role in a play called *Cupid and Zephyr*.

109 Author's note: King says of Burke's final hours, 'He prayed to God for forgiveness for the past, and died happy, a sincere Christian ...' (Burke and Wills Commission, p. 66, Q1714.) This is

the most likely form of words a man with Burke's religious tradition, a Protestant, would say – particularly one like Burke. It is the one prayer most Protestants of that era know.

110 Burke and Wills Commission, p. 39, Q1067.

111 *The Argus,* 1 July 1861, p. 6.

112 *Bathurst Free Press and Mining Journal,* 30 January 1890, p. 4.

113 John King, Narrative to Howitt (Transcript), [no page number] (Image 6). http://handle.slv.vic.gov.au/10381/196866

Chapter Fifteen

1 *The Age,* 1 July 1861, p. 4.

2 Alfred William Howitt, Letter to Exploration Committee [no date, ca. 29–30 June 1861], SLV, MS13071, Box 2085/5a, Item 3, [no page numbers] (Image 2). http://handle.slv.vic.gov.au/10381/196758

3 *The Age,* 1 July 1861, p. 6.

4 *The Age,* 1 July 1861, p. 6. [Reported speech]

5 *The Age,* 1 July 1861, p. 6. [Reported speech]

6 *The Age,* 1 July 1861, p. 6. [Reported speech]

7 Alfred William Howitt, Letter to Exploration Committee [no date, ca. 29–30 June 1861], SLV, MS13071, Box 2085/5a, Item 3, [no page numbers] (Image 2). http://handle.slv.vic.gov.au/10381/196758

8 Alfred William Howitt, Letter to Exploration Committee [no date, ca. 29–30 June 1861], SLV, MS13071, Box 2085/5a, Item 3, [no page numbers] (Image 2). http://handle.slv.vic.gov.au/10381/196758

9 *The Age,* 1 July 1861, p. 4.

10 *The Argus,* 2 July 1861, p. 5.

11 *The Argus,* 2 July 1861, p. 5.

12 Royal Society of Victoria, Exploration Committee, Sub-Committee (to aid Victorian Relief Expedition), Report [no date, ca. late June 1861], SLV, MS13071, Box 2075/3a, p. 3 (Image 3). http://handle.slv.vic.gov.au/10381/162817

13 *The Argus,* 1 July 1861, p. 6.

14 *Bendigo Advertiser,* 1 July 1861, p. 2.

15 John King, Narrative to Howitt (Transcript), [no page number] (Image 6). http://handle.slv.vic.gov.au/10381/196866

16 John King, Narrative to Howitt (Transcript), [no page number] (Images 6–7). http://handle.slv.vic.gov.au/10381/196866

17 *The Sun,* 11 April 1911, p. 2.

18 Edwin James Welch, 'Diary of Howitt Expedition, 26 June – 6 Dec 1861', 6 July 1861, SLNSW, ML C332, D179, [no page numbers].

19 Edwin James Welch, 'Diary of Howitt Expedition, 26 June – 6 Dec 1861', 2 July 1861, SLNSW, ML C332, D179, [no page numbers].

20 John King, Narrative to Howitt (Transcript), [no page number] (Image 7). http://handle.slv.vic.gov.au/10381/196866

21 Andrew Jackson, *Robert O'Hara Burke,* p. 170.

22 Andrew Jackson, *Robert O'Hara Burke,* p. 170.

23 John King, Narrative to Howitt (Transcript), [no page number] (Image 7). http://handle.slv.vic.gov.au/10381/196866

24 Andrew Jackson, *Robert O'Hara Burke,* p. 171.

25 Gavan Breen, *Innamincka Words: Yandruwandha Dictionary and Stories,* ANU Press, Canberra, 2015.

26 *Bathurst Free Press and Mining Journal,* 30 January 1890, p. 4.

27 John King, Narrative to Howitt (Transcript), [no page number] (Image 8). http://handle.slv.vic.gov.au/10381/196866

28 Alfred William Howitt, Inaugural Address, 7 January 1907, p. 14. http://handle.slv.vic.gov.au/10381/245539

29 Royal Society of Victoria, Exploration Committee, Account Book 1858–1873, pp. 68–70 (Images 29–30). http://handle.slv.vic.gov.au/10381/162911

30 Alfred William Howitt, Inaugural Address, 7 January 1907, p. 14. http://handle.slv.vic.gov. au/10381/245539

31 Alfred William Howitt, Inaugural Address, 7 January 1907, p. 14. http://handle.slv.vic.gov. au/10381/245539

32 Alfred William Howitt, Inaugural Address, 7 January 1907, p. 14. http://handle.slv.vic.gov. au/10381/245539

33 Alfred William Howitt, Dispatch, 3 August 1861, [no page numbers] (Image 1). http://handle. slv.vic.gov.au/10381/197381

34 Author's note: Familial oral history supplied to the author by Aaron Paterson. Interview 23/12/16.

35 Gavan Breen, *Innamincka Words*, p. 89.

36 Gavan Breen, *Innamincka Words*, p. 21.

37 Gavan Breen, *Innamincka Words*, p. 27.

38 Gavan Breen, *Innamincka Words*, p. 19.

39 Gavan Breen, *Innamincka Words*, p. 22.

40 'Explorations in Central Australia', *Gippsland Times*, 15 March 1870, page 1S.

41 Gavan Breen, *Innamincka Words*, p. 61.

42 Gavan Breen, *Innamincka Words*, p. 31.

43 Andrew Jackson, *Robert O'Hara Burke*, p. 171.

44 Andrew Jackson, *Robert O'Hara Burke*, p. 171.

45 Andrew Jackson, *Robert O'Hara Burke*, p. 172.

46 Alfred Howitt, Dispatch, 13 August 1861, SLV, MS13071, Box 2085/5a, Item 10, [no page numbers, only one page] (Image 7). http://handle.slv.vic.gov.au/10381/197141

47 Edwin James Welch, 'Diary of Howitt Expedition, 26 June – 6 Dec 1861', 19 August 1861, State Library of New South Wales, ML C332 D179, [no page numbers].

48 Edwin James Welch, 'Diary of Howitt Expedition, 26 June – 6 Dec 1861', 27 August 1861, State Library of New South Wales, ML C332 D179, [no page numbers].

49 Alfred William Howitt, Inaugural Address, 7 January 1907, p. 24. [Reported speech] http:// handle.slv.vic.gov.au/10381/245539

50 Alfred William Howitt, Diary, 8 September 1861, [no page number] (Image 4). http://handle.slv. vic.gov.au/10381/201679

51 Edwin James Welch, 'Diary of Howitt Expedition, 26 June – 6 Dec 1861', 8 September 1861, [no page numbers].

52 Alfred William Howitt, Diary, 9 September 1861, [no page numbers] (Image 4). http://handle. slv.vic.gov.au/10381/201679

53 Alfred William Howitt, Diary, 10 September 1861, p. 3 (Image 5). http://handle.slv.vic.gov. au/10381/201679

54 *Ovens and Murray Advertiser*, 11 July 1874, p. 3.

55 *Ovens and Murray Advertiser*, 11 July 1874, p. 3.

56 Alfred William Howitt, Diary, 12 September 1861, p. 4 (Image 6). http://handle.slv.vic.gov. au/10381/201679

57 Edwin James Welch, 'Diary of Howitt Expedition, 26 June – 6 Dec 1861', 13 September 1861, SLNSW, ML C332, D179, [no page numbers].

58 Burke and Wills Commission, p. 54, Q1171.

59 Alfred William Howitt, Diary, 14 September 1861, p. 4 (Image 7). [Reported speech] http:// handle.slv.vic.gov.au/10381/201679

60 Alfred William Howitt, Diary, 15 September 1861, p. 4 (Image 7). http://handle.slv.vic.gov. au/10381/201679

61 Alfred William Howitt, Diary, 14 September 1861, p. 4 (Image 7). http://handle.slv.vic.gov. au/10381/201679

62 *Ovens and Murray Advertiser*, 11 July 1874, p. 3. [Reported speech]

63 *Ovens and Murray Advertiser*, 11 July 1874, pp. 2–3.

64 *Ovens and Murray Advertiser*, 11 July 1874, p. 3.

65 *South Australian Advertiser*, 15 August 1862, p. 2.

66 William John Wills, *A Successful Exploration*, p. 259.

67 Alfred William Howitt, Diary, 15 September 1861, p. 4 (Image 7). http://handle.slv.vic.gov.au/10381/201679

68 *Queensland Times*, 19 November 1861, p. 4.

69 *The Australian Star* (Sydney), 21 June 1881, p. 3.

70 Ernest Favenc, *The Explorers of Australia and their Live-work*, Whitecome and Tombs, Christchurch, 1908, pp. 197–98. https://archive.org/stream/explorersaustra00favegoog#page/n213

71 Alfred William Howitt, Diary, 15 September 1861, p. 4 (Image 7). http://handle.slv.vic.gov.au/10381/201679

72 Alfred William Howitt, Inaugural Address, 7 January 1907, p. 1. http://handle.slv.vic.gov.au/10381/245539

73 Edwin James Welch, 'Diary of Howitt Expedition, 26 June – 6 Dec 1861', 15 September 1861, [no page numbers].

74 Burke and Wills Commission, p. 41, Q727.

75 *The Argus*, 27 August 1910, p. 9.

76 *The Argus*, 4 November 1861, p. 6.

77 *The Argus*, 4 November 1861, p. 6.

78 *The Argus*, 4 November 1861, p. 6.

79 Edwin James Welch, 'The Tragedy of Cooper's Creek', State Library of New South Wales, A1928, p. 23.

80 Edwin James Welch, 'The Tragedy of Cooper's Creek', State Library of New South Wales, A1928, p. 23.

81 Edwin James Welch, 'The Tragedy of Cooper's Creek', State Library of New South Wales, A1928, p. 23.

82 *Bathurst Free Press and Mining Journal*, 29 January 1890, p. 4.

83 *World's News*, 18 September 1915, p. 10.

84 *Bathurst Free Press and Mining Journal*, 30 January 1890, p. 4. http://handle.slv.vic.gov.au/10381/197922

85 Edwin James Welch, 'Diary of Howitt Expedition, 26 June – 6 Dec 1861', 18 September 1861, SLNSW, ML C332, D179, [no page numbers].

86 Edwin James Welch, 'Diary of Howitt Expedition, 26 June – 6 Dec 1861', 18 September 1861, [no page numbers].

87 1st Corinthians, XV, v50–55, King James Bible.

88 Edwin James Welch, 'Diary of Howitt Expedition, 26 June – 6 Dec 1861', 18 September 1861, [no page numbers].

89 Edwin James Welch, 'Diary of Howitt Expedition, 26 June – 6 Dec 1861', 18 September 1861, SLNSW, ML C332, D179, [no page numbers].

90 *The Argus*, 4 November 1861, p. 6.

91 *The Argus*, 4 November 1861, p. 6.

92 William John Wills, *A Successful Exploration*, p. 261.

93 William John Wills, *A Successful Exploration*, p. 261.

94 *The South Australian Advertiser*, 26 September 1861, p. 4.

95 William John Wills, *A Successful Exploration*, p. 265.

96 William John Wills, *A Successful Exploration*, p. 264.

97 Edwin James Welch, 'The Tragedy of Cooper's Creek' (manuscript), p. 33.

98 Alfred William Howitt, Diary, 19 September 1861, p. 5 (Image 8). http://handle.slv.vic.gov.au/10381/201679

99 Alfred William Howitt, Diary, 20 September 1861, p. 5 (Image 8). http://handle.slv.vic.gov.au/10381/201679

100 Alfred William Howitt, Diary, 20 September 1861, p. 5 (Image 8). http://handle.slv.vic.gov.au/10381/201679

101 Alfred William Howitt, Diary, 21 September 1861, p. 5 (Image 8). http://handle.slv.vic.gov.au/10381/201679

102 Alfred William Howitt, Diary, 21 September 1861, p. 5 (Image 8). http://handle.slv.vic.gov. au/10381/201679

103 *The Argus,* 4 November 1861, p. 6.

104 *The World's News,* 1 October 1910, p. 10.

105 Alfred William Howitt, Diary, 21 September 1861, p. 5 (Image 8). http://handle.slv.vic.gov. au/10381/201679

106 Edwin James Welch, 'Diary of Howitt Expedition, 26 June – 6 Dec 1861', 21 September 1861, SLNSW, ML C332, D179 [no page numbers].

107 *The Gippsland Times,* 15 March 1870, p. 2.

108 Henry Ironside, *John,* Kregel Academic, USA, 2006, pp. 261–262

109 Alfred William Howitt, Diary, 21 September 1861, p. 5 (Image 8). http://handle.slv.vic.gov. au/10381/201679

110 *Ovens and Murray Advertiser,* 11 July 1874, p. 3.

Chapter Sixteen

1 *The Argus,* 10 December 1861, p. 7.

2 Alfred William Howitt, Diary, 24 September 1861, SLV, MS13071, Box 2085/6a(1), p. 6 (Image 9). http://handle.slv.vic.gov.au/10381/201679

3 Edwin James Welch, 'Diary of Howitt Expedition, 26 June – 6 Dec 1861', 24 September 1861, SLNSW, ML C332, D179, [no page numbers].

4 Author's note: It is my presumption that King learnt a few Yandruwandha words during his stay with the tribe.

5 Edwin James Welch, 'Diary of Howitt Expedition, 26 June – 6 Dec 1861', 24 September 1861, SLNSW, ML C332, D179 [no page numbers].

6 Alfred William Howitt, Diary, 24 September 1861, p. 6 (Image 10). http://handle.slv.vic.gov. au/10381/201679

7 Alfred William Howitt, Diary, 24 September 1861, p. 6 (Image 10). http://handle.slv.vic.gov. au/10381/201679

8 Alfred William Howitt, Diary, 24 September 1861, p. 6 (Image 10). http://handle.slv.vic.gov. au/10381/201679

9 Alfred William Howitt, Inaugural Address, 7 January 1907, p. 28. http://handle.slv.vic.gov. au/10381/245539

10 Alfred William Howitt, Diary, 24 September 1861, p. 6 (Image 10). http://handle.slv.vic.gov. au/10381/201679

11 Alfred William Howitt, Diary, 24 September 1861, p. 6 (Image 10). http://handle.slv.vic.gov. au/10381/201679

12 *The Australasian,* 8 January 1910, p. 52.

13 Edwin James Welch, 'Diary of Howitt Expedition, 26 June – 6 Dec 1861', 24 September 1861, SLNSW, ML C332, D179, [no page numbers].

14 Edwin James Welch, 'The Tragedy of Cooper's Creek', State Library of New South Wales, A1928, p. 33.

15 Edwin James Welch, 'The Tragedy of Cooper's Creek', State Library of New South Wales, A1928, p. 34.

16 *Geelong Advertiser,* 5 November 1861, p. 3.

17 John McKinlay, *McKinlay's Journal of Exploration into the interior of Australia (Burke Relief Expedition),* Melbourne: F. F. Bailliere, Melbourne, 1863, p. 1.

18 William John Wills, *A Successful Exploration,* p. 266.

19 Alfred Howitt, Dispatch, 10 October 1861, SLV, MS13071, Box 2085/5a, Item 14, [no page number] (Image 2). http://handle.slv.vic.gov.au/10381/198782

20 *Brisbane Courier,* 11 August 1900, p. 9.

21 *Brisbane Courier,* 11 August 1900, p. 9.

22 *Brisbane Courier,* 11 August 1900, p. 9. [Reported Speech]

23 *Brisbane Courier,* 11 August 1900, p. 9.

24 *Sydney Mail,* 1 February 1862, p. 8.

25 *The South Australian Advertiser,* 26 November 1861, p. 7.

26 *The South Australian Advertiser*, 26 November 1861, p. 7.

27 *Sydney Mail*, 21 December 1861, p. 3.

28 *Sydney Mail*, 1 February 1862, p. 8.

29 *The South Australian Advertiser*, 23 November 1861, p. 2.

30 *Sydney Mail*, 1 February 1862, p. 8.

31 *Sydney Mail*, 1 February 1862, p. 8.

32 *Sydney Mail*, 1 February 1862, p. 8.

33 *Sydney Mail*, 1 February 1862, p. 8.

34 *Sydney Mail*, 1 February 1862, p. 8.

35 *Sydney Mail*, 1 February 1862, p. 8.

36 *Sydney Mail*, 1 February 1862, p. 8.

37 *Sydney Mail*, 1 February 1862, p. 8.

38 *Sydney Mail*, 1 February 1862, p. 8. [Reported speech]

39 *Sydney Mail*, 1 February 1862, p. 8.

40 *Sydney Mail*, 21 December 1861, p. 3.

41 *The World's News*, 4 February 1911, p. 10.

42 William Brahe, Telegram to Macadam, 2 November 1861, State Library of Victoria, MS 13071, Box 2080/5b, p. 1 [Image 1]. http://handle.slv.vic.gov.au/10381/198258

43 William John Wills, *A Successful Exploration*, p. 266.

44 William John Wills, *A Successful Exploration*, pp. 266–67.

45 William Brahe, Telegram, 2 November 1861, State Library of Victoria, MS 13071, Box 2080/5b, p. 1 [Image 1]. http://handle.slv.vic.gov.au/10381/198258

46 'Copy of dispatch from an Argus correspondent,' 2 November 1861, SLV, MS 13071, Box 2082/1d (2), p. 1.

47 William John Wills, *Successful Exploration*, p. 267.

48 William John Wills, *Successful Exploration*, p. 267.

49 *The Argus*, 5 November 1861, p.5.

50 *The Argus*, 5 November 1861, p.5.

51 Author's note: I have chosen to use the term 'Royal Commission' to refer to the Commission of Inquiry into the deaths of Burke and Wills. Technically, as the initiating instruction was issued by the Victorian Premier rather than the Governor of Victoria, the Commission was not in point of fact a Royal Commission. But as so many contemporary newspapers, correspondents and witnesses referred to it as the Royal Commission (including Dr Wills and the Commissioners themselves in their final report!) I have invoked the term throughout as to do otherwise would lead to confusion.

52 *The Age*, 9 November 1861, p. 5.

53 *The Age*, 9 November 1861, p. 5.

54 *The Age*, 9 November 1861, p. 5.

55 *The Argus*, 4 November 1861, p. 8.

56 Edwin James Welch, 'The Tragedy of Cooper's Creek', State Library of New South Wales, A1928, p. 36.

57 Edwin James Welch, 'The Tragedy of Cooper's Creek', State Library of New South Wales, A1928, p. 37.

58 Edwin James Welch, 'The Tragedy of Cooper's Creek', State Library of New South Wales, A1928, p. 37.

59 *The Australasian*, 13 March 1886, p. 2.

60 *The Australasian*, 13 March 1886, p. 2.

61 *The Australasian*, 13 March 1886, p. 2.

62 *The Australasian*, 13 March 1886, p. 2.

63 *The Australasian*, 13 March 1886, p. 2.

64 *The Argus*, 5 November 1861, p. 4.

65 *Queensland Times*, 19 November 1861, p. 4.

66 *The Argus*, 5 November 1861, p. 4

67 *The Star*, 28 November 1861, p. 2.

68 *The Age*, 12 November 1861, p. 6.

69 *The Argus*, 26 November 1861, p. 6.
70 *The Argus*, 26 November 1861, p. 6.
71 *The Argus*, 26 November 1861, p. 6.
72 *The Argus*, 26 November 1861, p. 6.
73 *The Argus*, 26 November 1861, p. 6.
74 Edwin James Welch, 'Diary of Howitt Expedition, 26 June – 6 Dec 1861', 21 November 1861, SLNSW, ML C332, D179, [no page numbers].
75 Edwin James Welch, 'Diary of Howitt Expedition, 26 June – 6 Dec 1861', 23 November 1861 SLNSW, ML C332, D179, [no page numbers].
76 Edwin James Welch, 'Diary of Howitt Expedition, 26 June – 6 Dec 1861', 23 November 1861 SLNSW, ML C332, D179, [no page numbers].
77 *Bendigo Advertiser*, 25 November 1861, p. 2.
78 Edwin James Welch, 'Diary of Howitt Expedition, 26 June – 6 Dec 1861', 23 November 1861 SLNSW, ML C332, D179, [no page numbers].
79 *The Argus*, 26 November 1861, p. 6.
80 *The Argus*, 26 November 1861, p. 6.
81 Edwin James Welch, 'Diary of Howitt Expedition, 26 June – 6 Dec 1861', 23 November 1861 SLNSW, ML C332, D179, [no page numbers].
82 *The Argus*, 26 November 1861, p. 6.
83 Edwin James Welch, 'Diary of Howitt Expedition, 26 June – 6 Dec 1861', 23 November 1861, [no page numbers].
84 Edwin James Welch, 'Diary of Howitt Expedition, 26 June – 6 Dec 1861', 23 November 1861, SLNSW, ML C332, D179, [no page numbers].
85 Edwin James Welch, 'Diary of Howitt Expedition, 26 June – 6 Dec 1861', 23 November 1861, SLNSW, ML C332, D179, [no page numbers].
86 Edwin James Welch, 'Diary of Howitt Expedition, 26 June – 6 Dec 1861', 23 November 1861, SLNSW, ML C332, D179, [no page numbers].
87 Edwin James Welch, 'Diary of Howitt Expedition, 26 June – 6 Dec 1861', 25 November 1861, SLNSW, ML C332, D179, [no page numbers].
88 Edwin James Welch, 'Diary of Howitt Expedition, 26 June – 6 Dec 1861', 25 November 1861, SLNSW, ML C332, D179, [no page numbers].
89 Edwin James Welch, 'Diary of Howitt Expedition, 26 June – 6 Dec 1861', 25 November 1861, SLNSW, ML C332, D179, [no page numbers].
90 Edwin James Welch, 'Diary of Howitt Expedition, 26 June – 6 Dec 1861', 25 November 1861, SLNSW, ML C332, D179, [no page numbers].
91 Edwin James Welch, 'Diary of Howitt Expedition, 26 June – 6 Dec 1861', 25 November 1861, SLNSW, ML C332, D179, [no page numbers].
92 Edwin James Welch, 'Diary of Howitt Expedition, 26 June – 6 Dec 1861', 25 November 1861, SLNSW, ML C332, D179, [no page numbers].
93 *The Argus*, 26 November 1861, p. 6.
94 *The Argus*, 26 November 1861, p. 6.
95 *The Argus*, 26 November 1861, p. 6.
96 *Adelaide Chronicle*, 8 January 1916, p. 8.
97 *The Argus*, 26 November 1861, p. 6.
98 *The Argus*, 26 November 1861, p. 6.
99 *The Argus*, 26 November 1861, p. 6.
100 *The Argus*, 26 November 1861, p. 6.
101 *The Age*, 26 November 1861, p. 5.
102 *The Argus*, 26 November 1861, p. 6. [Reported speech]
103 *The Argus*, 26 November 1861, p. 6. [Tense changed]
104 *The Argus*, 26 November 1861, p. 6.
105 *The Argus*, 26 November 1861, p. 6.
106 *The Argus*, 26 November 1861, p. 6.
107 *Leader* (Melbourne), 28 December 1861, p. 11. [Reported speech]
108 *Leader* (Melbourne), 28 December 1861, p. 11. [Reported speech]

109 *Leader* (Melbourne), 28 December 1861, p. 11. [Reported speech]
110 *Leader* (Melbourne), 28 December 1861, p. 11. [Reported speech]
111 *The Argus*, 14 November 1861, p. 5. [Reported speech]
112 *The Argus*, 14 November 1861, p. 5.
113 *The Argus*, 14 November 1861, p. 5. [Reported speech]
114 *The Argus*, 14 November 1861, p. 5. [Reported speech]
115 *The Australasian*, 8 January 1910, p. 52.
116 *The Australasian*, 8 January 1910, p. 52.

Chapter Seventeen

1 *The Inquirer and Commercial News*, 1 January 1862, p. 3.
2 Burke and Wills Commission, p. iii.
3 Burke and Wills Commission, p. iii.
4 *The Argus*, 23 November 1861, p. 6.
5 *The Argus*, 23 November 1861, p. 6.
6 Burke and Wills Commission, pp. 1–2, Q9.
7 Burke and Wills Commission, p. 2, Q9.
8 *The Argus*, 23 November 1861, p. 6.
9 Burke and Wills Commission, p. 2, Q10.
10 Burke and Wills Commission, p. 2, Q12.
11 Burke and Wills Commission, p. 2, Q13.
12 Burke and Wills Commission, p. 2, Q13.
13 Burke and Wills Commission, p. 2, Q14.
14 Burke and Wills Commission, p. 2, Q16.
15 Burke and Wills Commission, p. 6, Q88.
16 Burke and Wills Commission, p. 6, Q89.
17 Burke and Wills Commission, p. 6, Q89.
18 Burke and Wills Commission, p. 6, Q90.
19 Burke and Wills Commission, p. 8, Q110.
20 Burke and Wills Commission, p. 10, Q195.
21 Burke and Wills Commission, p. 10, Q196.
22 Burke and Wills Commission, p. 10, Q196.
23 Burke and Wills Commission, p. 10, Q198.
24 Burke and Wills Commission, p. 11, Q224.
25 Burke and Wills Commission, p. 12, Q253.
26 Burke and Wills Commission, p. 12, Q253.
27 Burke and Wills Commission, p. 12, Q254.
28 Burke and Wills Commission, p. 12, Q262.
29 Burke and Wills Commission, p. 12, Q263.
30 Burke and Wills Commission, p. 12, Q263.
31 Burke and Wills Commission, p. 14, Q301.
32 Burke and Wills Commission, p. 14, Q301.
33 Burke and Wills Commission, p. 14, Q302.
34 Burke and Wills Commission, p. 14, Q302.
35 Burke and Wills Commission, p. 14, Q303.
36 Burke and Wills Commission, p. 14, Q303.
37 Burke and Wills Commission, p. 14, Q304.
38 Burke and Wills Commission, p. 14, Q304.
39 Burke and Wills Commission, p. 14, Q305.
40 Burke and Wills Commission, p. 14, Q305.
41 Burke and Wills Commission, p. 14, Q311.
42 Burke and Wills Commission, p. 14, Q312. [Italics added]
43 Burke and Wills Commission, p. 14, Q312.
44 Burke and Wills Commission, p. 15, Q318.
45 Burke and Wills Commission, p. 15, Q318.

46 Burke and Wills Commission, p. 15, Q320.
47 Burke and Wills Commission, p. 15, Q328.
48 Burke and Wills Commission, p. 15, Q328.
49 Burke and Wills Commission, p. 15, Q329.
50 Burke and Wills Commission, p. 15, Q329.
51 Burke and Wills Commission, p. 15, Q330.
52 Burke and Wills Commission, p. 15, Q330.
53 Burke and Wills Commission, p. 15, Q331.
54 Burke and Wills Commission, p. 15, Q331.
55 Burke and Wills Commission, p. 15, Q332.
56 Burke and Wills Commission, p. 15, Q332.
57 Burke and Wills Commission, p. 15, Q339.
58 Burke and Wills Commission, p. 15, Q339.
59 Burke and Wills Commission, p. 15, Q340.
60 Burke and Wills Commission, p. 15, Q340.
61 Burke and Wills Commission, p. 15, Q341. [Italics added]
62 Burke and Wills Commission, p. 15, Q341.
63 *The Argus*, 29 November 1861, p. 6.
64 Burke and Wills Commission, p. 18, Q402.
65 Burke and Wills Commission, p. 18, Q403.
66 Burke and Wills Commission, p. 18, Q407.
67 Burke and Wills Commission, p. 18, Q407.
68 Burke and Wills Commission, p. 18, Q407.
69 Burke and Wills Commission, p. 18, Q419.
70 Burke and Wills Commission, p. 18, Q419.
71 Burke and Wills Commission, p. 18, Q420.
72 Burke and Wills Commission, p. 18, Q420.
73 Burke and Wills Commission, p. 18, Q421.
74 Burke and Wills Commission, p. 18, Q421.
75 Burke and Wills Commission, p. 18, Q422.
76 Burke and Wills Commission, p. 18, Q422.
77 Burke and Wills Commission, p. 23, Q542.
78 Burke and Wills Commission, p. 23, Q542.
79 Burke and Wills Commission, p. 23, Q543.
80 Burke and Wills Commission, p. 23, Q543.
81 Burke and Wills Commission, p. 23, Q543.
82 Burke and Wills Commission, p. 23, Q543. Author's note: The official Commission transcript only says 'Becker' at this point, but I believe this is a mistake. The reporter recording these proceedings for *The Age* notes that Wecker said that *both* Dr Beckler and Dr Becker did not acknowledge Wright's authority. (*The Age*, 29 November 1861, p. 6.) It is my conclusion that the close similarity of the names led to confusion at this point by the Commission's own short-hand recorder.
83 Burke and Wills Commission, p. 24, Q548.
84 Burke and Wills Commission, p. 24, Q548.
85 Burke and Wills Commission, p. 24, Q549.
86 Burke and Wills Commission, p. 24, Q549.
87 Burke and Wills Commission, p. 24, Q560.
88 Burke and Wills Commission, p. 24, Q560.
89 Burke and Wills Commission, p. 24, Q561.
90 Burke and Wills Commission, p. 24, Q561.
91 Burke and Wills Commission, p. 24, Q562.
92 Burke and Wills Commission, p. 24, Q562.
93 Burke and Wills Commission, p. 25, Q583.
94 *The Argus*, 29 November 1861, p. 6. Author's note: As a point of interest, this exchange was removed from the official transcript, and was only recorded in *The Argus*.

95 Burke and Wills Commission, p. 39, Q1070.
96 The *Age*, 6 December 1861, p. 5.
97 The *Age*, 6 December 1861, p. 5.
98 Burke and Wills Commission, p. 27, Q620.
99 Burke and Wills Commission, p. 27, Q620.
100 Burke and Wills Commission, p. 27, Q621.
101 Burke and Wills Commission, p. 27, Q621.
102 Burke and Wills Commission, p. 27, Q622.
103 Burke and Wills Commission, p. 27, Q622.
104 Burke and Wills Commission, p. 27, Q623.
105 Burke and Wills Commission, p. 27, Q623.
106 Burke and Wills Commission, p. 27, Q624.
107 Burke and Wills Commission, p. 27, Q624.
108 Burke and Wills Commission, p. 27, Q625.
109 Burke and Wills Commission, p. 27, Q625.
110 Burke and Wills Commission, p. 29, Q722.
111 Burke and Wills Commission, p. 29, Q722.
112 Burke and Wills Commission, p. 29, Q723.
113 Burke and Wills Commission, p. 29, Q723.
114 Burke and Wills Commission, p. 29, Q724.
115 Burke and Wills Commission, p. 29, Q724.
116 Burke and Wills Commission, p. 30, Q740.
117 Burke and Wills Commission, p. 33, Q904.
118 Burke and Wills Commission, p. 33, Q904.
119 Burke and Wills Commission, p. 34, Q936.
120 Burke and Wills Commission, p. 34, Q938.
121 Burke and Wills Commission, p. 34, Q938.
122 Burke and Wills Commission, p. 35, Q939.
123 Burke and Wills Commission, p. 35, Q939.
124 Burke and Wills Commission, p. 35, Q940.
125 Burke and Wills Commission, p. 35, Q940.
126 Burke and Wills Commission, p. 35, Q941.
127 Burke and Wills Commission, p. 35, Q941.
128 Burke and Wills Commission, p. 35, Q942.
129 Burke and Wills Commission, p. 35, Q942.
130 Burke and Wills Commission, p. 35, Q943.
131 Burke and Wills Commission, p. 35, Q943.
132 Burke and Wills Commission, p. 35, Q970.
133 Burke and Wills Commission, p. 35, Q971.
134 Burke and Wills Commission, p. 35, Q971. [Italics added]
135 Burke and Wills Commission, p. 35, Q972.
136 Burke and Wills Commission, p. 35, Q972.
137 Burke and Wills Commission, p. 35, Q975.
138 Burke and Wills Commission, pp. 35–36, Q975.
139 Burke and Wills Commission, p. 36, Q980.
140 Burke and Wills Commission, p. 36, Q981.
141 Burke and Wills Commission, p. 36, Q991.
142 Burke and Wills Commission p. 36, Q989.
143 *South Australian Advertiser*, 23 November 1861, p. 2.
144 Burke and Wills Commission, p. 36, Q996.
145 Burke and Wills Commission, p. 36, Q996.
146 Burke and Wills Commission, p. 36, Q1004.
147 Burke and Wills Commission, p. 36, Q1005.
148 Burke and Wills Commission, p. 36, Q1005.
149 Burke and Wills Commission, p. 37, Q1032.

150 Burke and Wills Commission, p. 37, Q1032.
151 Burke and Wills Commission, p. 39, Q1064.
152 Burke and Wills Commission, p. 39, Q1064.
153 Burke and Wills Commission, p. 39, Q1065. [Italics added]
154 Burke and Wills Commission, p. 39, Q1065.
155 Burke and Wills Commission, p. 39, Q1067.
156 Burke and Wills Commission, p. 39, Q1066.
157 Burke and Wills Commission, p. 39, Q1066.
158 Burke and Wills Commission, p. 39, Q1086.
159 Burke and Wills Commission, p. 42, Q1172.
160 Burke and Wills Commission, p. 42, Q1172.
161 Burke and Wills Commission, p. 42, Q1173. [Italics added]
162 Burke and Wills Commission, p. 42, Q1173.
163 Burke and Wills Commission, p. 42, Q1174.
164 Burke and Wills Commission, p. 42, Q1174.
165 Burke and Wills Commission, p. 42, Q1175.
166 Burke and Wills Commission, p. 42, Q1175.
167 Burke and Wills Commission, p. 42, Q1176. [Italics added]
168 Burke and Wills Commission, p. 42, Q1176.
169 Author's note: But would they? In fact, it is no less than 500 miles from the Depot, along Burke's old track to Menindee and Burke's note had said they would only be able to travel four or five miles a day. With their 40 days provisions left for them by Brahe, they would have made just 200 miles at best, before running out, meaning they would not have even reached Torowoto.
170 John King, Letter to Exploration Committee, 6 December 1861, Box 2078/2, p. 1, http://handle.slv.vic.gov.au/10381/193394
171 *The Argus*, 10 December 1861, p. 7. [Reported speech]
172 *The Argus*, 10 December 1861, p. 7.
173 *The Argus*, 10 December 1861, p. 7.
174 *The Argus*, 10 December 1861, p. 7.
175 *The Argus*, 10 December 1861, p. 7.
176 *The Yeoman and Australian Acclimatiser*, 1 February 1862, p. 9.
177 Burke and Wills Commission, p. 44, Q1219.
178 Burke and Wills Commission, p. 44, Q1219.
179 Burke and Wills Commission, p. 44, Q1220. [Italics added]
180 Burke and Wills Commission, p. 44, Q1220.
181 Burke and Wills Commission, p. 45, Q1253.
182 Burke and Wills Commission, p. 45, Q1253.
183 Burke and Wills Commission, p. 45, Q1254.
184 Burke and Wills Commission, p. 45, Q1254.
185 Burke and Wills Commission, p. 45, Q1255. [Italics added]
186 Burke and Wills Commission, p. 45, Q1255.
187 Burke and Wills Commission, p. 45, Q1257.
188 Burke and Wills Commission, p. 45, Q1257.
189 Burke and Wills Commission, p. 45, Q1260.
190 Burke and Wills Commission, p. 45, Q1261.
191 Burke and Wills Commission, p. 45, Q1271.
192 *The Age*, 11 December 1861, p. 5.
193 *The Age*, 11 December 1861, p. 5.
194 *The Age*, 11 December 1861, p. 5.
195 *The Age*, 11 December 1861, p. 5. [Italics added]
196 *The Age*, 11 December 1861, p. 5. [Italics added]
197 *The Argus*, 11 December 1861, p. 5.
198 *The Argus*, 11 December 1861, p. 5. [Italics added]
199 *The Argus*, 11 December 1861, p. 5.

200 *The Argus*, 11 December 1861, p. 5.
201 *The Argus*, 11 December 1861, p. 5.
202 *The Argus*, 11 December 1861, p. 5.
203 Burke and Wills Commission, p. 56, Q1567.
204 Burke and Wills Commission, p. 56, Q1568.
205 Burke and Wills Commission, p. 56, Q1568.
206 Burke and Wills Commission, p. 56, Q1569. [Italics added]
207 Burke and Wills Commission, p. 56, Q1569.
208 Burke and Wills Commission, p. 56, Q1570.
209 Burke and Wills Commission, p. 56, Q1570.
210 Burke and Wills Commission, p. 56, Q1572.
211 Burke and Wills Commission, p. 56, Q1572.
212 Burke and Wills Commission, p. 56, Q1573.
213 Burke and Wills Commission, p. 56, Q1573.
214 Burke and Wills Commission, p. 58, Q1597.
215 Burke and Wills Commission, p. 58, Q1597.
216 Burke and Wills Commission, p. 58, Q1598.
217 Burke and Wills Commission, p. 58, Q1598.
218 Burke and Wills Commission, p. 58, Q1599.
219 Burke and Wills Commission, p. 58, Q1599.
220 Burke and Wills Commission, p. 58, Q1600.
221 Burke and Wills Commission, p. 58, Q1600.
222 Burke and Wills Commission, p. 59, Q1602. [Italics added]
223 Burke and Wills Commission, p. 59, Q1602. [Italics added]
224 Burke and Wills Commission, p. 59, Q1602.
225 Burke and Wills Commission, p. 59, Q1603.
226 Burke and Wills Commission, p. 59, Q1604. [Italics added]
227 Burke and Wills Commission, p. 59, Q1605.
228 Burke and Wills Commission, p. 59, Q1605.
229 *The Argus*, 13 December 1861, p. 6.
230 Burke and Wills Commission, p. 60, Q1610.
231 Burke and Wills Commission, p. 60, Q1612. [Italics added]
232 Burke and Wills Commission, p. 60, Q1612.
233 Burke and Wills Commission, p. 60, Q1616. [Italics added]
234 Burke and Wills Commission, p. 60, Q1616.
235 Burke and Wills Commission, p. 62, Q1643. [Reported speech]
236 *The Argus*, 13 December 1861, p. 6.
237 *The Argus*, 13 December 1861, p. 6.
238 Burke and Wills Commission, p. 62, Q1644.
239 *The Argus*, 13 December 1861, p. 6.
240 *The Argus*, 13 December 1861, p. 6.
241 *The Argus*, 13 December 1861, p. 6.
242 Burke and Wills Commission, p. 62, Q1646.
243 Burke and Wills Commission, p. 62, Q1646.
244 *The Argus*, 13 December 1861, p. 6.
245 *The Age*, 13 December 1861, p. 6.
246 *The Age*, 13 December 1861, p. 6.
247 *The Argus*, 13 December 1861, p. 6.
248 *The Argus*, 13 December 1861, p. 6.
249 *The Argus*, 13 December 1861, p. 6.
250 *The Argus*, 13 December 1861, p. 6.
251 *The Argus*, 13 December 1861, p. 6. [Italics added]
252 *The Argus*, 13 December 1861, p. 6.
253 Burke and Wills Commission, p. 63, Q1656.
254 *The Argus*, 13 December 1861, p. 6.

255 *The Argus*, 13 December 1861, p. 6.
256 *The Argus*, 13 December 1861, p. 6.
257 *The Argus*, 13 December 1861, p. 6. [Italics added]
258 *The Argus*, 13 December 1861, p. 6.
259 *The Argus*, 13 December 1861, p. 6.
260 *The Argus*, 13 December 1861, p. 6.
261 *The Argus*, 13 December 1861, p. 6.
262 *The Argus*, 13 December 1861, p. 6.
263 *The Argus*, 13 December 1861, p. 6.
264 *The Argus*, 13 December 1861, p. 6.
265 *The Argus*, 13 December 1861, p. 6.
266 *The Argus*, 13 December 1861, p. 6. [Italics added]
267 *The Argus*, 13 December 1861, p. 6.
268 *The Argus*, 13 December 1861, p. 6.
269 *The Argus*, 13 December 1861, p. 6.
270 *The Argus*, 13 December 1861, p. 6. [Italics added]
271 *The Argus*, 13 December 1861, p. 6. [Italics added]
272 Burke and Wills Commission, p. 67, Q1729.
273 Burke and Wills Commission, p. 67, Q1729.
274 Burke and Wills Commission, p. 67, Q1730.
275 Burke and Wills Commission, p. 67, Q1730.
276 Burke and Wills Commission, p. 67, Q1731.
277 Burke and Wills Commission, p. 67, Q1731.
278 Burke and Wills Commission, p. 67, Q1732.
279 Burke and Wills Commission, p. 67, Q1732.
280 *The Argus*, 13 December 1861, p. 6.
281 Burke and Wills Commission, p. 68, Q1739.
282 Burke and Wills Commission, p. 68, Q1739.

Chapter Eighteen

1 *The Argus*, 5 January 1863, p. 5.
2 *The Sydney Mail*, 31 January 1863, p.6.
3 *The Argus*, 10 October 1862, p. 5.
4 Burke and Wills Commission, p. v.
5 Burke and Wills Commission, p. v.
6 Burke and Wills Commission, p. vi.
7 Burke and Wills Commission, p. vi.
8 Burke and Wills Commission, p. vi.
9 Burke and Wills Commission, p. vi.
10 Burke and Wills Commission, p. vi.
11 Burke and Wills Commission, p. vii.
12 Burke and Wills Commission, p. vii.
13 *Ovens and Murray Advertiser*, 27 February 1862, p. 2.
14 William John Wills, *A Successful Exploration*, p. 319.
15 William John Wills, *A Successful Exploration*, p. 379.
16 Charles Dickens, *The Complete Works of Charles Dickens: Martin Chuzzlewit, Vol. I*, Cosimo Inc. New York, 2009, p. 160.
17 Alfred William Howitt, Dispatch, 9 December 1862, SLV, MS13071, Box 2085/5a, Item 31, p. 1.
18 *Ovens and Murray Advertiser*, 11 July 1874, p. 3.
19 *Geelong Advertiser*, 16 December 1862, p. 3. [Changed tense]
20 *Geelong Advertiser*, 16 December 1862, p. 3. [Changed tense]
21 Henry Strangways, Telegram to John Macadam, 15 December 1862, SLV, MS13071, Box 2080/5e, p. 1. [Image 1]. [http://handle.slv.vic.gov.au/10381/212371]
22 *Leader* (Melbourne), 3 January 1863, p. 7.

23 *Leader* (Melbourne), 3 January 1863, p. 7.
24 *The Star* (Ballarat), 30 December 1862, p. 2.
25 *The Age*, 1 January 1863, p. 5.
26 *The Age*, 1 January 1863, p. 5.
27 *The Age*, 1 January 1863, p. 5.
28 *The Age*, 1 January 1863, p. 5.
29 Andrew Jackson, *Robert O'Hara Burke*, p. 7.
30 *The Age*, 1 January 1863, p. 5.
31 *The Age*, 1 January 1863, p. 5.
32 *The Age*, 1 January 1863, p. 5.
33 *The Age*, 1 January 1863, p. 5.
34 *The Age*, 1 January 1863, p. 5.
35 *The Age*, 1 January 1863, p. 5.
36 *The Age*, 1 January 1863, p. 5.
37 *The Age*, 1 January 1863, p. 5.
38 *The Age*, 1 January 1863, p. 5.
39 *The Argus*, 5 January 1863, p. 4.
40 *Ovens and Murray Advertiser*, 8 January 1863, p. 2.
41 *The Argus*, 5 January 1863, p. 4.
42 Sara Murgatroyd, *The Dig Tree*, p. 334.
43 *Bendigo Advertiser*, 6 January 1863, p. 2.
44 *Bendigo Advertiser*, 6 January 1863, p. 2.
45 *The Argus*, 21 January 1863, p. 5
46 *The Argus*, 21 January 1863, p. 4.
47 *The Argus*, 22 January 1863, p. 5.
48 *The Argus*, 22 January 1863, p. 5.
49 *The Argus*, 22 January 1863, p. 5.
50 *The Argus*, 22 January 1863, p. 5.
51 *The Argus*, 22 January 1863, p. 5.
52 *The Argus*, 22 January 1863, p. 5.
53 *The Argus*, 22 January 1863, p. 5.
54 *The Argus*, 22 January 1863, p. 5.
55 *The Argus*, 22 January 1863, p. 5.
56 *The Age*, 21 January 1863, p. 5.
57 *The Age*, 21 January 1863, p. 5.
58 *The Herald* (Melbourne), 22 January 1863, p. 5.
59 *The Herald* (Melbourne), 22 January 1863, p. 5.
60 *The Age*, 22 January 1863, p. 4.
61 *The Age*, 22 January 1863, p. 4.
62 *The Argus*, 22 January 1863, p. 5.
63 *The Argus*, 22 January 1863, p. 5.
64 William Shakespeare, *As You Like It*, Simon and Schuster, London, 2011, p. 83
65 *The Argus*, 22 January 1863, p. 5.
66 *The Truth* (Perth), 7 February 1914, p. 10.
67 *The Argus*, 22 January 1863, p. 5.
68 *The Argus*, 22 January 1863, p. 5.
69 *The Argus*, 22 January 1863, p. 5.
70 *The Argus*, 22 January 1863, p. 5.
71 *The Argus*, 22 January 1863, p. 5.
72 *The Argus*, 22 January 1863, p. 5.
73 *The Argus*, 22 January 1863, p. 5.
74 *The Argus*, 22 January 1863, p. 6.
75 *The Argus*, 22 January 1863, p. 6.
76 *The Age*, 22 January 1863, p. 6. [Reported speech. Tenses and pronouns changed]
77 *The Age*, 22 January 1863, p. 6.

78 [Reported speech]
79 [Reported speech]
80 [Tenses changed]
81 *The Argus*, 22 January 1863, p. 5.
82 *The Argus*, 22 January 1863, p. 6. [Tenses changed]
83 *The Argus*, 22 January 1863, p. 6. [Tenses changed]
84 *The Argus*, 22 January 1863, p. 6. [Reported speech]
85 [Reported speech]
86 *The Age*, 22 January 1863, p. 6.
87 *The Argus*, 26 January 1863, p. 5.
88 *The Age*, 22 January 1863, p. 6.
89 *The Age*, 22 January 1863, p. 6.
90 *The Age*, 22 January 1863, p. 6.
91 [Reported speech]
92 *The Argus*, 22 January 1863, p. 6.
93 *The Argus*, 22 January 1863, p. 6.
94 [Reported speech]
95 *The Argus*, 22 January 1863, p. 6.
96 *The Argus*, 22 January 1863, p. 6.
97 *The Argus*, 22 January 1863, p. 6.
98 *The Argus*, 22 January 1863, p. 6.
99 *The Argus*, 22 January 1863, p. 6.
100 *Mount Alexander Mail*, 22 January 1863, p. 2.
101 *Mount Alexander Mail*, 22 January 1863, p. 2.
102 Edward Fitzball, (lyrics), William Vincent Wallace, (music), 'Sweet Spirit, Hear My Prayer', in Joseph Carpenter (ed) *The New British Song Book*, p. 95.

Epilogue

1 *Leader* (Melbourne), 18 June 1887, p.7.
2 *Ovens and Murray Advertiser*, 1880, p. 2.
3 *The Argus*, 8 June 1865, p. 5.
4 *The Age*, 22 April 1865, p. 6.
5 *Table Talk*, 5 February 1886, p. 2.
6 *The Argus*, 22 August 1910, p. 8.
7 *Ovens and Murray Advertiser*, 27 January 1872, p. 2.
8 *The Argus*, 16 January 1872, p. 5.
9 *The Age*, 2 September 1904, p. 9. [Reported speech]
10 *The Age*, 2 September 1904, p. 9.
11 *The Truth* (Perth), 25 October 1913, p. 3.
12 Ferdinand Mueller, Letter to Wilkie, 26 January 1862, SLV, MS13071, Box 2078/3, p. 2, (Image 2). http://handle.slv.vic.gov.au/10381/193353
13 Marjorie Tipping, (ed), *Ludwig Becker: artist & naturalist with the Burke & Wills expedition*, Melbourne University Press, Melbourne, 1979, p. 35.
14 Hermann Beckler, *A Journey to Cooper's Creek*, p. 91.
15 Dave Phoenix, *Following Burke and Wills Across Australia*, pp. 152–153.
16 *The Argus*, 29 April 1862, p. 5.
17 *The Otago Witness*, 15 February 1862, p. 7.
18 Charles Ferguson, *A Third of A Century in the Goldfields*, p. 137.
19 Alfred William Howitt, Inaugural Address, 7 January 1907, pp. 18–19. http://handle.slv.vic.gov.au/10381/245539
20 W. E. H. Stanner, 'Alfred William Howitt', *Australian Dictionary of Biography*, Australian Dictionary of Biography, National Centre of Biography, Australian National University, http://adb.anu.edu.au/biography/howitt-alfred-william-510
21 *Times-Picayune*, 24 May 1876, p. 2.
22 *Australia Town and Country Journal*, 5 August 1876, p. 27.

23 William John Wills, *A Successful Exploration*, p. 351.
24 William John Wills, *A Successful Exploration*, p. 378.
25 Edward Vaughan Kenealy, *Memoirs of Edward Vaughan Kenealy*, John Long, London, 1908, p. 126.
26 Interview with Aaron Paterson, descendant of Carrawaw, oral history, 23/12/2016.
27 *The Argus*, 15 June 1860, p. 5.
28 'Science and the Making of Victoria,' Australian Science and Technology Heritage Centre, Melbourne, 2001. http://www.austehc.unimelb.edu.au/smv/title.html
29 *Ovens and Murray Advertiser*, 8 January 1863, p. 2.
30 *The Yeoman and Australian Acclimatiser*, 1 February 1862, p. 8.
31 *The World's News*, 5 March 1910, p. 11.
32 ABC (Online), 'Burke and Wills tools discovered', 12 June 2008, http://www.abc.net.au/news/2008-06-12/burke-and-wills-tools-discovered/2468740 (accessed: 23.11.2016)
33 *The Sydney Morning Herald*, 12 June 2008, [no page number]. http://www.smh.com.au/national/signs-said-dig-here-for-burke-and-wills-tools-says-researcher-20080611-2p4m.html
34 Alan Moorehead, *Cooper's Creek*, p. 157.
35 Dave Phoenix, 'Did Burke and Wills die because they ate nardoo?', SLV, DIG: The Burke and Wills Research Gateway, 2011. http://burkeandwills.slv.vic.gov.au/ask-an-expert/did-burke-and-wills-die-because-they-ate-nardoo.
36 Ian Clarke and Fred Cahir (eds), *The Aboriginal Story of Burke and Wills*, p. 170.
37 Ian Clarke and Fred Cahir (eds), *The Aboriginal Story of Burke and Wills*, p. 170.
38 *Gippsland Times*, 6 May 1875, p. 3.
39 *Gippsland Times*, 6 May 1875, p. 3.
40 George McIver, *A Drover's Odyssey*, Angus & Robertson, Sydney, 1935, pp. 150–151.
41 George McIver, *A Drover's Odyssey*, pp. 150–151.
42 Charles Sturt, *Narrative of an Expedition into Central Australia*, Vol II, p. 87
43 *The Argus*, 10 December 1861, p 7.
44 *The Argus*, 10 December 1861, p 7.
45 Banjo Paterson, *The Collected Verse of A.B. Paterson*, Angus & Robertson, Sydney, 1921, p. 10.
46 Banjo Paterson, *The Collected Verse of A.B. Paterson*, p. 83.

BIBLIOGRAPHY

Abbreviations

SLV – State Library Victoria
ML – Mitchell Library (part of SLNSW)
SLNSW – State Library of New South Wales
NLA – National Library of Australia
PROV – Public Record Office Victoria
EC – Expedition Committee
RSV – Royal Society of Victoria

Books

Abel, E. Lawrence, *Singing the New Nation: How Music Shaped the Confederacy 1861–1865*, Stackpole, Mechanicsburg, 2000.
Beckler, Hermann, *A Journey to Cooper's Creek*, translated by Stephen Jeffries and Michael Kertesz, Melbourne University Press, Carlton, 1993.
Bonyhady, Tim, *Burke and Wills: From Melbourne to Myth*, David Ell Press, NSW, 1991.
Breen, Gavan, *Innamincka Words: Yandruwandha Dictionary and Stories*, ANU Press, Canberra, 2015.
Carpenter, Joseph Edwards (ed.), The New British Song Book, G. Routledge and Sons, London, 1866.
Cathcart, Michael, *Starvation in a Land of Plenty*, NLA, Canberra, 2013.
Clark, Ian D., Cahir, Fred (eds), *The Aboriginal Story of Burke and Wills: Forgotten Narratives*, CSIRO, Collingwood (Victoria), 2016.
Clune, Frank, *Dig: The Burke and Wills Saga*, Angus & Robertson, London, 1976.
Denison, William, *Varieties of Vice-Regal Life*, Vol. I, Longmans, Green & Co., London, 1870.
Dickens, Charles, *David Copperfield*, Vol. II, Sheldon, New York, 1863.
Dickens, Charles, *Great Expectations*, Vol. I, Chapman and Hall, London, 1861.
Dickens, Charles, *Little Dorrit*, Bradbury and Evans, London, 1857.
Dickens, Charles, *The Life and Adventures of Martin Chuzzlewit*, Chapman and Hall, London, 1844.
Dickens, Charles, *The Old Curiosity Shop*, Chapman and Hall, London, 1841.
Dickens, Charles, *The Complete Works of Charles Dickens: Martin Chuzzlewit, Vol. I*, Cosimo Inc. New York, 2009.
Eyre, Edward John, *Journals of Expeditions of Discovery into Central Australia*, Vol. I, T. and W. Boone, London, 1845.
Eyre, Edward John, *Journals of Expeditions of Discovery into Central Australia, and Overland from Adelaide to King George's Sound, in the Years 1840–1*, Vol. II, T. and W. Boone, London, 1845.
Favenc, Ernest, *The Explorers of Australia and Their Live-work*, Whitcombe and Tombs, Christchurch (New Zealand), 1908.
Ferguson, Charles, *The Experiences of a Forty-niner during Thirty-four Years' Residence in California and Australia*, The Williams Publishing Company, Cleveland, 1888, https://archive.org/details/experiencesoffor00ferg

Howitt, Alfred William, *Personal Reminiscences of Central Australia and the Burke and Wills Expedition*, Australasian Association for the Advancement of Science, Adelaide, 1908.

Ironside, Henry, *John*, Kregel Academic, USA, 2006.

Jackson, Andrew, *Robert O'Hara Burke and the Australian Exploring Expedition of 1860*, Smith, Elder and Co, London, 1862.

Joyce, E. B. and McCann, D. A., *Burke and Wills: The Scientific Legacy of the Victorian Exploring Expedition*, CSIRO Publishing, Melbourne, 2011.

Kenealy, Edward Vaughan, *Memoirs of Edward Vaughan Kenealy*, John Long, London, 1908.

Landsborough, William, *Journal of Landsborough's Expedition from Carpentaria*, Bailliere, Melbourne, 1862.

Larkworthy, Falconer, *Ninety-one Years Being the Reminiscences of Falconer Larkworthy*, Mills & Boon Ltd., London, 1924.

Leahy, F. J., *100 Years of National Topographic Mapping (Nineteenth Century Exploration Mapping: William Wills' Mapping of the Ghastly Blank)*, Canberra, 2011, http://www.xnatmap.org/adnm/conf_06_11/c11/Paper%2001.pdf

Leichhardt, Ludwig, *Journal of an Overland Expedition in Australia, from Moreton Bay to Port Essington: A Distance of Upwards of 3000 Miles, During the Years 1844–1845*, Cambridge University Press, Cambridge, UK, 2011.

McIver, George, *A Drover's Odyssey*, Angus & Robertson, Sydney, 1935.

McKinlay, John, *McKinlay's Journal of Exploration into the interior of Australia (Burke Relief Expedition)* Melbourne: F F Bailliere, Melbourne, 1863.

Moorehead, Alan, *Cooper's Creek: Tragedy and Adventure in the Australian Outback*, Sun Books, South Melbourne, 1985.

Morton, Edward, *The Eton Boy*, Lacy, London, 1842.

Murgatroyd, Sarah, *The Dig Tree*, Text Publishing, Victoria, 2012.

Neumayer, Georg Balthasar von, *Results of the Magnetic Survey of the Colony of Victoria Executed During the Years 1858–1864*, J. Schneider, Mannheim, 1869.

Paterson, Banjo, *The Collected Verse of A.B. Paterson*, Angus and Robertson, Sydney, 1921.

Philosophical Institute of Victoria, *Transactions of the Philosophical Institute of Victoria: From January to December 1857, inclusive* Vol. II, Royal Society of Victoria, Melbourne, ca. 1858. https://archive.org/stream/transactionsofph02phil#page/168

Philosophical Institute of Victoria, *Transactions of the Philosophical Institute of Victoria: From January to December 1859, inclusive* Vol. IV, Royal Society of Victoria, Melbourne, 1860, https://archive.org/details/transactionsofph04phil

Phoenix, Dave, *Following Burke and Wills across Australia: A Touring Guide*, CSIRO Publishing, Clayton (Victoria), 2015.

Pike, Douglas (ed.), *Australian Dictionary of Biography*, Vol. 6, Melbourne University Press, Carlton (Victoria), 1976.

Serle, Percival, *Dictionary of Australian Biography*, Vol. 1, Angus & Robertson, Sydney, 1959.

Shakespeare, William, *Twelfth Night*, Hackett Publishing, Indiana, 2012.

Shakespeare, William, *Hamlet*, William Heinemann, London, 1904.

Shakespeare, William, *The Works of William Shakespeare* (incl. Sonnet LXXIII), Universal Classics, New York, 1980.

Shakespeare, William, *As You Like It*, Simon and Schuster, London, 2011.

Stawell, Mary, *My Recollections*, R. Clay, London, 1911.

Sturt, Charles, *Narrative of an Expedition into Central Australia*, Vol. II, T. and W. Boone, London, 1849.

Tipping, Marjorie (Ed), *Ludwig Becker : artist & naturalist with the Burke & Wills expedition*, Melbourne Universtiy Press, Melbourne, 1979.

Wills, William John, *A Successful Exploration through the Interior of Australia from Melbourne to the Gulf of Carpentaria*, Richard Bentley, London, 1863. https://archive.org/stream/successfulexplor00willrich#page/n9/mode/2up

Manuscripts

Australian Science and Technology Heritage Centre, "Science and the Making of Victoria," Australian Science and Technology Heritage Centre, Melbourne, 2001, http://www.austehc.unimelb.edu.au/smv/title.html

Becker, Ludwig, First Report, 8 September 1860, SLV, MS13071, Box 2082/4c.

Becker, Ludwig, Second Report, 30 September 1860, SLV, MS13071, Box 2082/4d.

Becker, Ludwig, Third Report, 12 November 1860, SLV, MS13071, Box 2082/4e.

Becker, Ludwig, Fourth Report, 26 November 1860, SLV, MS13071, Box 2082/4f.

Becker, Ludwig, Fifth Report, 22 January 1861, SLV, MS13071, Box 2082/4g.

Becker, Ludwig, Letter to von Mueller, 9 March 1860, NLA, MS 1236.

Becker, Ludwig, Letter to John Macadam (Exploration Committee), 30 October 1860, SLV, MS13071, Box 2083/4. http://handle.slv.vic.gov.au/10381/212855

Becker, Ludwig, Letter, 27 November 1860, SLV, MS13071, Box 2083/4, Item 7. http://handle.slv.vic.gov.au/10381/212732

Becker, Ludwig, Sketch Book, "Menindee", Sketch No. 18, SLV, MS13071, MS Safe 1, Accession No. H16486.

Becker, Ludwig, Sketch Book, "Meteor seen by me", Sketch No. 26, SLV, MS13071, Manuscripts Safe 1, Accession No. H16486.

Becker, Ludwig, Sketch Book, "Small Predatory Beetle", SLV, MS13071, MS Safe 1, Accession No. H16486, p. 12A.

Becker, Ludwig, Sketch Book, "Women in Mourning", 20 September 1860, SLV, MS13071, MS Safe 1, Accession No. H16486, p. 8

Beckler, Hermann, Letter to Robert O'Hara Burke, 16 October 1860, SLV, MS13071, Box 2082/2e (2).

Beckler, Hermann, Report, 13 November 1860, SLV, MS13017, Box 2082/4(a). http://handle.slv.vic.gov.au/10381/212524

Beilby, John Wood, Letter (Application), 27 February 1860, SLV, MS13071, Box 2076/1. http://handle.slv.vic.gov.au/10381/304091

Belt, Thomas, Letter to Exploration Committee, 1 March 1860, SLV, MS13071, Box 2076/1, ex1004-035.

Brahe, William, Dispatch, 21 April 1861, SLV, MS13071, Box 2082/1d (1). http://handle.slv.vic.gov.au/10381/212729

Brahe, William, Letter to Exploration Committee, 2 July 1860, SLV, MS13071, Box 2076/2. http://handle.slv.vic.gov.au/10381/164467

Brahe, William, Report, 30 June 1861, SLV, MS13071, Box 2082/4h.

Brahe, William, Telegram, 2 November 1861, SLV, MS 13071, Box 2080/5b. http://handle.slv.vic.gov.au/10381/198258

Burke, Robert O'Hara, Dispatch to Exploration Committee, 29 October 1860, SLV, MS13071, Box 2082/1a, Item 12. http://handle.slv.vic.gov.au/10381/282222

Burke, Robert O'Hara, Dispatch to Exploration Committee, 13 December 1860, SLV, MS13071, Box 2082/1a, Item 13. http://handle.slv.vic.gov.au/10381/282243

Burke, Robert O'Hara, Dispatch to John Macadam, Swan Hill, 12 September 1860, SLV, MS13071, Box 2082/1a, Item 7. http://handle.slv.vic.gov.au/10381/282266

Burke, Robert O'Hara, Letter to Frederick Standish, 18 June 1860, SLNSW, 'Papers relating to Robert O'Hara Burke, 1860, 1917,' Ab 61.

Burke, Robert O'Hara, Dispatch to John Macadam, Menindee, 16 October 1860, SLV, MS13071, Box 2082/1a, Item 10. http://handle.slv.vic.gov.au/10381/282261

Burke, Robert O'Hara, Letter to John Burke, 30 October 1860, NLA, MS30/3.

Burke, Robert O'Hara, Letter to Sister, 28 June 1861, SLV, MS13867/20. http://handle.slv.vic.gov.au/10381/169989

Burke, Robert O'Hara, Note, 22 April 1861, SLV, MS13071, Manuscripts Safe 1. http://handle.slv.vic.gov.au/10381/251633

Burke, Robert O'Hara, Note, 26 June 1861, SLV, MS13071, Manuscripts Safe 1. http://handle.slv.vic.gov.au/10381/251633

Burke, Robert O'Hara, Note, 30 June 1861, SLV, MS13071, Manuscripts Safe 1. http://handle.slv.vic.gov.au/10381/251633

Burke, Robert O'Hara, Notebook, SLV, MS13071, Box 2083/2b. http://handle.slv.vic.gov.au/10381/196753

Burke, Robert O'Hara Portion of diary kept by Robert O'Hara Burke on the expedition, 16 December 1860 – 20 January 1861, NLA, MS 30/1.

Burke, Robert O'Hara, Third Dispatch (Letter to John Macadam), 10 September 1860, SLV, MS13071, Box 2082/1a, Item 6. http://handle.slv.vic.gov.au/10381/282264

Burr, Thomas, Letter to Exploration Committee, [no date], SLV, MS13071, Box 2076/2. http://handle.slv.vic.gov.au/10381/164262

'Copy of dispatch from an Argus correspondent', 2 November 1861, SLV, MS 13071, Box 2082/1d (2).

'Cupid', Letter to Robert O'Hara Burke, 26 June 1861, SLV, MS13071, Box 2083/4. http://handle.slv.vic.gov.au/10381/212820

Frizzell, John, Letter to Exploration Committee, 20 January 1860, SLV, MS13071, Box 2076/3, ex1004-191.

Gregory, Augustus Charles, Letter to the Exploration Committee, 25 November 1857, SLV, MS 13071 Box 2077/5. http://handle.slv.vic.gov.au/10381/188933

Howitt, Alfred William, Diary (13 August – 7 October 1861), SLV, MS13071, Box 2085/6a, Item 1. http://handle.slv.vic.gov.au/10381/201679

Howitt, Alfred William, Dispatch to Exploration Committee (no date, ca. 29–30 June 1861), SLV, MS13071, Box 2085/5a, Item 3. http://handle.slv.vic.gov.au/10381/196758

Howitt, Alfred William, Dispatch, 3 August 1861, SLV, MS13071, Box 2085/5a, Item 9. http://handle.slv.vic.gov.au/10381/197381

Howitt, Alfred William, Dispatch, 13 August 1861, SLV, MS13071, Box 2085/5a, Item 10. http://handle.slv.vic.gov.au/10381/197141

Howitt, Alfred William, Dispatch, 9 December 1862, SLV, MS13071, Box 2085/5a, Item 31.

King, John, Diary, NLA, MS 30/11.

King, John, Letter to Exploration Committee, 6 December 1861, Box 2078/2, p. 1. http://handle.slv.vic.gov.au/10381/193394

King, John, Narrative to Howitt (Transcript, 7 pages), SLV, MS13071, Box 2083/1f. http://handle.slv.vic.gov.au/10381/196866

Landells, George, Letter to Chief Secretary, 21 May 1859, Public Record Office Victoria, VPRS1189/P0000 Unit 757: Inward Registered Correspondence: Letter to the Chief Secretary regarding camels for the Burke and Wills expedition of 1860–61, p. 2. http://www.cv.vic.gov.au/stories/burke-and-wills-have-camels-will-travel/

Landells, George, Letter to Exploration Committee, 18 July 1860, SLV, MS13071, Box 2076/5. http://handle.slv.vic.gov.au/10381/306915

Landells, George James, Report to Exploration Committee, 14 November 1860, SLV, MS13071, Box 2082/4j. http://handle.slv.vic.gov.au/10381/212896

Macadam, John, Fund Raising Circular (Typescript), 15 September 1858, SLV, MS13071, Box 2075/1(a). http://handle.slv.vic.gov.au/10381/158695

Macadam, John, Instructions to the Geologist, Zoologist and Botanist, 3 September 1860, SLV, MS13071, Box 2082/3b. http://handle.slv.vic.gov.au/10381/212986

Macadam, John, Instructions to Robert O'Hara Burke, 18 August 1860, SLV, MS13071, Box 2082/3a (1). http://handle.slv.vic.gov.au/10381/212493

Macadam, John, Instructions to Surveyor, Meteorologist and Astronomical Observer (9 pages), 3 September 1860, SLV, MS13071, Box 2082/3c. http://handle.slv.vic.gov.au/10381/212904

Macadam, John, Letter to Robert Burke, 17 September 1860, SLV, MS13071, Box 2083/5, No. 43. http://handle.slv.vic.gov.au/10381/212919

Macadam, John, Letter to Robert O'Hara Burke, 18 October 1860, SLV, MS 13071, Box 2082/2b (1). http://handle.slv.vic.gov.au/10381/188388

Macadam, John, Letter to William Wright, 31 December 1860, SLV, MS 13071, Box 2083/5, Item 46. http://handle.slv.vic.gov.au/10381/212698

Mueller, Ferdinand, Letter to Wilkie, 26 January 1862, SLV, MS13071, Box 2078/3. http://handle.slv.vic.gov.au/10381/193353

Parry, Samuel, Letter to Exploration Committee, 29 February 1860, SLV, MS13071, Box 2077/2, pp. 2–3. http://handle.slv.vic.gov.au/10381/186209

Royal Society of Victoria, Exploration Committee, Account Book, 1858–1873, SLV, MS13071, Box 2088B/2. http://handle.slv.vic.gov.au/10381/162911

Royal Society of Victoria, Exploration Committee [unsigned], Instructions to Scientific Observers [no date], SLV, MS13071, Box 2082/3d. http://handle.slv.vic.gov.au/10381/212799

Royal Society of Victoria, Exploration Committee, Letter to William Wright, 31 December 1860, SLV, MS13071, Box 2088B/5. http://handle.slv.vic.gov.au/10381/194756

Royal Society of Victoria, Exploration Committee, Meeting Minutes, 30 November 1857, SLV, MS13071, Box 2075/1 (a). http://handle.slv.vic.gov.au/10381/158458

Royal Society of Victoria, Exploration Fund Committee, Meeting Minutes, SLV, MS13071, Box 2088B/1. http://handle.slv.vic.gov.au/10381/163008

Royal Society of Victoria, Exploration Committee, Meeting Minutes, undated, SLV, MS13071, Box 2075/2c (3). http://handle.slv.vic.gov.au/10381/162676

Royal Society of Victoria, Exploration Committee and VEE members, Memorandum of Agreement for the VEE, 18 August 1860, SLV, MS13071, Map case 5, Drawer 6a. http://handle.slv.vic.gov.au/10381/188521

Royal Society of Victoria, Exploration Committee, Minute Book (1858–1861), SLV, MS13071, Box 2075/1c. http://handle.slv.vic.gov.au/10381/162914

Royal Society of Victoria, Exploration Committee, Sub-Committee (to aid Victorian Relief Expedition), Report (no date, ca. late June 1861, adopted at EC meeting on 1 July 1861), SLV, MS13071, Box 2075/3a. http://handle.slv.vic.gov.au/10381/162817

Royal Society of Victoria, *Transactions of the Royal Society of Victoria, from January to December 1860, inclusive. Vol. V.* http://handle.slv.vic.gov.au/10381/147083

Smithe, P. N., Letter to John Macadam, 7 February 1860, SLV, MS13071, Box 2076/2. http://handle.slv.vic.gov.au/10381/164469

Stone, Charles, Letter to his brother, 17 January 1861, SLV, MS13071, Box 2078/1. http://handle.slv.vic.gov.au/10381/189732

Strangways, Henry, Telegram to John Macadam, 15 December 1862, SLV, MS13071, Box 2080/5e. http://handle.slv.vic.gov.au/10381/212371

Tempsky, Gustav Ferdinand von, Letter to Exploration Committee, 11 February 1860, SLV, MS13071, Box 2076/2, ex1004-558.

Webster, Letter to Robert O'Hara Burke, 11 July 1860, SLNSW, ML D179, Item 7. (No first name available.)

Welch, Edwin James, 'Diary of Howitt Expedition, 26 June – 6 December 1861', SLNSW, ML C332, D179.

Welch, Edwin James, 'The Tragedy of Cooper's Creek' (manuscript, undated), SLNSW, ML (Angus & Robertson Collection), A1928.

Wills, William, 'Correspondence and press cuttings, 1839–1861' (Manuscript), SLV, MS 9504.

Wills, William, Dig Tree Note, 30 May 1861, SLV, MS13071, Manuscripts Safe 1.

Wills, William, Field Book (No. 2), Bilbarka to Torowoto, 20–26 October 1860, SLV, MS 13071, Box 2082/6d. http://handle.slv.vic.gov.au/10381/196219

Wills, William, Field Book (No. 3), Torowoto to Cooper's Creek, 27 October–2 November 1860, SLV, MS13071, Box 2082/6e.

Wills, William, Field Notes (No. 5), 24–27 November 1860, SLV, MS13071, Box 2082/6i. http://handle.slv.vic.gov.au/10381/195879

Wills, William, Journal, Trip from Cooper Creek towards Adelaide, 23 April 1861 – 26 June 1861, NLA, MS 30/7, Papers of Burke and Wills Expedition. http://nla.gov.au/nla.ms-ms30-7

Wills, William, 'Journey from Cooper's Creek to Carpentaria and return to Cooper's Creek', SLV, MS13071, Box 2083/1a. http://handle.slv.vic.gov.au/10381/197341

Wills, William, Letter to his Father (Dr. William Wills), 27 June 1861, SLV, La Trobe Library, Australian Manuscripts Collection (Correspondence and Press Cuttings, 1839–1861), 1839, MS 9594.

Wills, William, Letter to Professor Georg Neumayer, 16 October 1860, SLV, MS 13071, Box 2083/4. http://handle.slv.vic.gov.au/10381/212576

Wills, William, Second Surveyor's Report, 30 October 1860, SLV, MS13071, Box 2082/5a. http://handle.slv.vic.gov.au/10381/212551

Wills, William, Third Dispatch from the Darling, 7 October 1860, SLV, MS13071, Box 2082/1b, Item 3. http://handle.slv.vic.gov.au/10381/212464

Wills, William, Third Surveyor's Report, 15 December 1860, SLV, MS13071, Box 2082/5b.

Wills, William, 'Wills' astronomical observations made on the return journey from the North, 1861', SLV, MS13071, Box 2083/1d.

Wright, William, Diary, SLV, MS 13071, Box 2083/3b. http://handle.slv.vic.gov.au/10381/197331

Wright, William, Dispatch to Exploration Committee, 19 December 1860, SLV, MS13071, Box 2082/1f, Item 1.

Wright, William, Third Dispatch, 20 June 1861, SLV, MS13071, Box 2082/1f, Item 3. http://handle.slv.vic.gov.au/10381/212818

Journals/Reports

Australian National Botanic Gardens, *Mallee plants -surviving harsh conditions*, Australian Government, ACT, 2004.

McKellar, John, 'John King (explorer): Sole survivor of the Burke and Wills' expedition to the Gulf of Carpentaria, 1860-61', *Victorian Historical Magazine*, Vol XX, No 4, December 1944, pp. 107–137.

Links

ABC, 'Burke and Wills tools discovered', 12 June 2008, http://www.abc.net.au/news/2008-06-12/burke-and-wills-tools-discovered/2468740 (accessed: 23.11.2016)

Newspapers

Adelaide Chronicle
Adelaide Observer
Advocate (Melbourne)
Australia Town and Country Journal
Bathurst Free Press and Mining Journal
Bendigo Advertiser
Brisbane Courier
Empire (Sydney)
Geelong Advertiser
Gippsland Times
Leader (Melbourne)
Melbourne Punch
Mount Alexander Mail
North Australian, Ipswich and General Advertiser
Ovens and Murray Advertiser
South Australian Register
South Australian Weekly Chronicle
Swan Hill Guardian and Lake Boga Advocate
Sydney Mail
Sydney Sportsman
Table Talk
The Advertiser (Adelaide)
The Age
The Argus
The Australasian
The Australian Star (Sydney)
The Bulletin
The Herald (Melbourne)
The Inquirer and Commercial News
The North Australian, Ipswich and General Advertiser
The Otago Witness
The Queenslander
The Register
The South Australian Advertiser
The Star (Ballarat)
The Sun (Sydney)
The Sydney Morning Herald
The Truth (Perth)

The World's News
The Yeoman and Australian Acclimatiser
Times-Picayune (New Orleans)
Williamstown Chronicle

Other

COMMISSION:

Burke and Wills Commission, 'Report of the Commissioners appointed to enquire into the circumstances connected with the sufferings and death of Robert O'Hara Burke and William John Wills, the Victorian explorers', Victoria (Burke and Wills Commission), Melbourne, ca. 1862. http://www.parliament.vic.gov.au/papers/govpub/VPARLI861-62No.97.

SPEECH:

Howitt, Alfred William, 'Inaugural Address: Personal Reminiscences of Central Australia and the Burke and Wills Expedition', President's inaugural address to the Australasian Association of the Advancement of Science, 7 January 1907, Town Hall, Adelaide, published by Australasian Association for the Advancement of Science. http://handle.slv.vic.gov.au/10381/245539

INDEX

Please note: the subentries for the Burke and Wills expedition,
the Dig Tree and William Wright supply party are grouped chronologically.

A

Aboriginal Story of Burke and Wills (Annie King) 612
Afghani camel-handlers *see* camel handlers (sepoys)
Age (editorial stance) 506
Aitkin, Alexander 292, 428, 434, 454, 484
Albert River 308–309
Antarctica 615
anthropology 609
Argus (editorial stance) 453–454, 499, 504–505, 564, 576–577, 578
Arumpo 147
astronomy 36, 268–269
Attack Creek 48, 171–172, 191
Australian ballot 41
Australian explorers 3, 314 *see also under individual names*
Australian Rules 614

B

Babbage, Benjamin 20, 47
Ballarat (Vic) 5, 582–583, 607
Balranald 131–134, 166, 190
    Burke leaves supplies in 132–134
Barcoo 204, 623 *see also* Cooper's Creek
Barkindji people 52, 188, 289–290 *see also* Dick (Barkindji man); Peter (Barkindji man); Smith, John
    Becker records words of songs at Pamamaroo 220
    Paakantyi language 295
    Paakantyi names 211
Barkly, Lady 578
Barkly, Sir Henry 37–38, 41, 281, 349–350, 500, 578, 582, 584, 586, 587, 596
    King and 514, 518–519
    Royal Commission of Inquiry 501

Barnadown 114–117
Batchelder & O'Neill photographers 496, 522
Becker, Dr Ludwig
    appearance 116
    as artist, naturalist and geologist 92
    background xi, 65
    Balranald, in charge of supplies in 136, 139
    Beckler and 388, 393–394
    at Bilbarka 160–161
    Brahe and 394
    Burke and 82, 158
    Burke orders to give up scientific studies 152
    Burke orders to load camels 151–152, 153
    Burke orders to walk 150, 152, 154–155
    Burke orders to walk to Gulf 155–156
    Burke splits the party at Menindee 141–143, 145–146, 147, 150
    death and burial 393–394
    expedition members ceremony 88–90
    Exploration Committee: proposes examination of candidates 35–36, 41
    Exploration Committee's instructions 94–95, 96
    Ferguson puts to work 134–136
    injured foot 192–193
    journal entries 112–113, 170
    Menindee camp 192–193
    meteor 174
    Mourara Station 175
    Mueller and 49
    repairs and reloads wagons 108–109
    retrieval of remains 521, 547
    Royal Commission of Inquiry mentions 555
    Royal Park departure 108
    Samla (Hindu sepoy) 112
    scurvy 326, 340–341
    sketches *see* Becker, Dr Ludwig: sketches
    supplies 73, 77
    Terrick-Terrick Plains 119

Becker, Dr Ludwig *continued*
  Wright and 207
  Wright's supply party 300, 307
Becker, Dr Ludwig: sketches
  at Arumpo 147
  of beetles 168
  at Koorliatto 340–341
  of native guides from Terekencom 143
  of native women at Terekencom 140–141
  of native women at Torowoto 319
  at Pamamaroo Creek camp 220
  in State Library of Victoria 605
  of Terrick-Terrick Plains 120
Beckler, Dr Hermann
  appearance 116–117
  appointed as medical officer and botanist
      61–62, 92
  background xi, 65
  at Bilbarka 160–161
  botanical specimens from Arumpo 147
  Brahe and 533
  Burke and 82–83
  Burke and camels 167
  Burke orders to give up scientific studies 152
  Burke orders to load camels 151–152, 153
  Burke orders to walk 150, 152, 154–155
  Burke restricts personal luggage 150
  Burke splits the party at Menindee 141–143,
      145–146, 147, 150
  camels 148
  in charge of supplies 77, 78, 94, 102
  Darling River 156
  Exploration Committee's instructions 95
  Goningberry Range 279, 287–288
  Hodgkinson and 220, 294, 606
  journal entries 117, 131
  Koorliatto Creek natives 372, 374, 375,
      376–377, 386
  Lake Pamamaroo 290–291
  Landells and 175, 185, 187–188
  Lyons and MacPherson 264, 267, 278–279
  Menindee camp, remains behind to oversee
      188, 192, 207
  Mutawintji 307–308
  natives 289
  Patten and 414
  plant specimens 213, 418, 604–605
  resigns from expedition 187–188, 195
  Scropes Range 207–210, 213–214, 271–272
  scurvy cure 414
  scurvy treatment 414–415
  supplies 73
  Terrick-Terrick Plains 119
  Wright and 213–214, 220, 370

Wright's supply party 295, 300, 302, 304,
    375, 383
Beechworth (Vic) xvii–xix, 26–27, 602
Beechworth Police 29–30, 36, 56, 106
Belooch Khan (sepoy)
  with Beckler 192, 267, 279, 288, 291
  with Burke 69, 136, 139–140, 161–162, 171,
      172
  later life 607
  Pamamaroo Creek camp 462
  with Wright's supply party 300, 305–306,
      327, 340, 382
Benalla police magistrate 22
Bendigo
  Burke and Wills expedition 114–117,
      210–211
  cemeteries 512, 602
  Howitt relief expedition 447, 496–497
  King: public reception 510–513
  Yandruwandha, toasts health of 511
Bengora Creek 467
Bennett, Richard 100, 132
Bergin, Tom 619
Bernard, Paddy 512, 602
Bilbarka
  Burke, Beckler and Becker 160–161
  Burke dismisses Bowman 146–147
  Burke orders blazing of trees 173
  Camp 30 149–156, 157
  steamer takes stores up to Mendindee from
      170–171
Billy's Creek 310
Bilpa Creek 197, 304
birdlife 277
Birdsville 285
Birnie, Richard
  background xii, 15
  debtor's prison 582–583
  expedition departure 108
  later life 611
  Wills, farewells 106
  Wills, friendship with 14–16, 65–66, 72, 79,
      212
  Wills's death 503–504
  Wills's funeral 582–583
Black, Neil 51
Blanchewater station 369, 461, 569
Bleasdale, Mr 67
Blunder Bay (Northern Australia) 67–68, 70–71
Bolinda 113
Bookey, Inspector 64
Borokow (Yandruwandha man) 487
Bowman, Robert 57, 121–122, 141, 146–147,
    402
Box, R 51

Brahe, William
    application to join expedition 50–51, 57
    as assistant to expedition 92
    background xii, 51, 250
    Balranald 136
    Bilbarka 171, 173
    blame 505
    Burke and 61, 140, 154, 251, 256, 362–363,
        604
    Burke splits the party at Menindee 143
    bush rats 238, 240
    bush skills 226
    Cooper's Creek Depot departure to Bulloo
        River 367, 370, 383–384, 390–391,
        476–477
    Cooper's Creek Depot party command
        251–252, 254, 257, 331–332, 341–343
    Cooper's Creek Depot, returns to with Wright
        405–408, 409
    Cooper's Creek party 192, 196, 205
    Cooper's Creek scouting parties 226, 250
    Exploration Committee question 451–452
    Gulf party, joins for first day 258, 259,
        260–262
    Howitt and 446–449
    Howitt's despatches to Exploration Committee
        491–492, 496–497, 499–500
    Howitt's relief expedition 451, 455, 462, 467,
        469, 484, 485
    King and 262, 476–477
    Koorliatto Creek to Cooper's Creek 399–400
    later life 603–604
    Macadam and 594–595
    Melbourne 430
    Patten and 422
    scurvy 352–353
    testimony to Royal Commission see under
        Royal Commission of Inquiry
    Wills and 261, 361, 604
    Wright and 397, 399–400
    Wright's supply party 391–393
    Yandruwandha, fires on 283–284, 471
British Empire
    claims on Australian continent 48, 75,
        229–230
    Crimean War 27–28
    Indian Mutiny 84, 166
Bruce, John Vans Agnew 13, 20–22, 23–25, 31,
    41, 47, 571
Buckland riots 29–30
Bulingani (native guide) 493, 495
Bulloo River see also Koorliatto Creek
    Burke and Wills expedition 211–212
    Lyons and MacPherson 223–225
    Wright's supply party 340, 346–347

Bulwer-Lytton, Edward 72
Burke, Anne Celestine 601–602
Burke, Hessie 442–443
Burke, James 27–28
Burke, Robert O'Hara
    ambition 26
    appearance 43–44, 66–69, 117
    background xi, xviii, 87
    in Beechworth 26–32
    clothing 105
    Crimean War 28
    expedition, application to join 31–32, 34
    gambling debts 45, 88, 610–611
    horse 107
    leader, Bruce approaches Burke as 31
    leader, Bruce–Macadam clique to support as
        21–25
    leader, Exploration Committee votes on
        41–42
    leader, response to election as 44–45, 49–50
    leadership qualities 28–29
    in Melbourne 78, 106
    Melbourne farewell 105
    power of attorney 88
    remains 573–576
    sabre wound 43
    salary 45
    views of character xvii, xix, 22, 42–44
    warrant for arrest 124–125, 127
    will 87–88
Burke, Robert O'Hara: criticisms of as leader
    by Beckler 82–83
    by Beechworth friend 123
    by Bendigo Advertiser 210–211
    by Bowman 146
    Burke's response 59–61
    by Fletcher 99
    by Landells 216–217
    by Sadleir 100
    by Warburton and Morton 45–47, 88
Burke, Robert O'Hara: eulogies for 504–505
Burke & Wills panorama 487
Burke and Wills – The Scientific Legacy of the
        Victorian Exploring Expedition (Royal
        Society of Victoria) 614
Burke and Wills expedition: funding
    approval process 73
    Burke requests chequebook from Exploration
        Committee 117–118, 127
    Burke's salary 45, 80
    camels supplied 9–10, 39–40
    cost of provisions 77
    cost of wagon-drivers 143
    Exploration Committee budget 80, 127–128

Burke and Wills expedition: funding *continued*
    Exploration Committee funding for Wright's
      supply party 281–283, 295
    Exploration Committee's right of veto 69
    horses supplied 83
    public subscription *see* Exploration Fund
      Committee
    Victorian Legislative Assembly approves 6000
      pounds 19
Burke and Wills expedition: organisation
    Burke improves personal fitness 62–63
    Burke interviews applicants 57–58
    Burke overwhelmed by amount of supplies
      77–78
    Burke studies previous expeditions 52–55
    cattle dropped 74
    equipment put on display at Royal Park 102
    lack of bush skills 57, 81–82
    lack of exploration skills 57–58
    officers appointed by Exploration Committee
      50
    provisions 74–75
    rations 86
    responsibility for supplies 77
    starting date 78–79
    supplies 72–78
    tents 116
    weapons and ammunition 74, 78
    workers appointed by Burke 50, 55, 56, 61
Burke and Wills expedition: route
    Blunder Bay route 67–68, 70–71
    Burke proposal for vessel to meet him in Gulf
      149–150, 196, 255
    Cooper's Creek to Gulf of Carpentaria
      253–255
    Exploration Committee's instructions to Burke
      92–93, 225, 309
    Exploration Committee's instructions to mark
      route 173
    map x, 89
    map: first week 115
    maps left behind in Melbourne 116
    proposals 2, 6, 11, 38
    proposal to start from Northern Australia 33
    Queensland return 255, 342, 452
    supplies: Cadell's proposal to transport up
      Murray 84–85
    supplies: possible alternative route (map) 89
Burke and Wills expedition: transport
    additional horses and wagon-drivers hired
      103, 127–128
    additional wagons hired 94, 103
    by camel *see* camels
    criticisms of transport 109, 132
    horses 83, 131, 146

horse medication 77
horse-drawn wagons 76, 94, 113, 116
loading of wagons 102–103
punt wagon 77–78
Burke and Wills expedition: departure
    delayed 103–106
    Royal Park to Essendon 106–109
    Essendon camp 110–112
    Barnadown 114–117
    Burke requests chequebook 117–118
    Terrick-Terrick Plains 119–121
    wagons become bogged and break down
      108–109
Burke and Wills expedition: Tragowel to
    Balranald
    Tragowel 121–122
    Swan Hill 123–132
    chequebook arrives from Exploration
      Committee 125–126
    men dismissed 129
    Balranald 131–134, 166, 190
    map 126
Burke and Wills expedition: Balranald to
    Menindee
    Burke leaves tracks and pushes across country
      140
    Burke splits the party and leaves the wagons
      behind 141–143, 291–292
    Burke splits the party at Menindee 145–146
    Burke turns back to meet wagon party
      150–151
    Burke transfers some load from wagons to
      camels 150
    Burke orders officers and men to walk 150
    Burke transfers some load to horses 150
Burke and Wills expedition: Menindee to
    Cooper's Creek
    complement of horses and camels 196
    Cooper's Creek party 196
    expedition leaves Menindee 194, 196–197
    supplies 196
    Mutawintji 198–199
    Torowoto 199–202
    Torowoto: Burke asks men if they are happy to
      go on 205
    Torowoto: Burke buries cache of supplies 201
    Torowoto: Burke's instructions to Wright
      203–205
    Torowoto native guide to Cooper's Creek 205
    clay pan below Bulloo River 206–207
    Bulloo 211–212
    arrive in Cooper's Creek 220–222
Burke and Wills expedition: Cooper's Creek
    Depot

Exploration Committee instructions to Burke 92–93, 225

Burke informs Exploration Committee of Cooper's Creek party 194–195

Burke advises Exploration Committee he might go on from 204

Wright as guide to 179

Burke's party arrives 220–222

Camp 63 [LXIII] 222

Burke instructed to find new route 225–226

dash for the Gulf 226, 243–244

scouting parties 226, 233, 235–238, 240–241, 243–244, 250–255

Yandruwandha people 225, 244

bush rats 238–239, 240

Camp 65 [LXV] 243

insects 243

Burke and Wills expedition: Gulf party

camels and horses 253, 277, 303–304, 310

members 252

route 253–255

supplies 253, 270, 309, 310

type of crossing envisaged by Burke 49–50, 139

departure 255–259

Cooper's Creek to Eyre's Creek 259–263, 264–265

Tirrawarra Swamp 268–269

Stony Desert 269–271, 272–274, 275–276

Diamantina River 277, 284–286

Kings Creek 292–294

Selwyn Range to Gulf of Carpentaria 296–299, 301, 303–304, 308–312

travelling by night 301

turns back 309

Burke splits group at Camp 119 310, 312–313

Camp 119 to Gulf of Carpentaria 310–312, 313–316

Burke and Wills expedition: Cooper's Creek Depot party

Brahe in charge see Brahe, William

Brahe's departure 360–363

Brahe's departure date 344, 359, 361

Brahe's departure preparations 358–359

Burke fails to instruct Brahe regarding Mendindee party 256–257

Burke splits party to drive for Gulf 243–244, 251–252

Burke's instructions about how long to wait for Gulf party 255, 260–262, 263, 331

daily routine 264

Exploration Committee 283

Patten shoes horses 343

Patten thrown from horse 299–300

scurvy 342–343, 352–353

stockade 257, 258, 263, 272

supplies 342–343, 362

Wright's delay 255, 256, 257–258, 261–262, 268

Burke and Wills expedition: Gulf party return

physical condition 317–318

arrival at Cooper's Creek 334–335, 357–358

supplies 318, 320, 329, 332, 345–346, 358, 359

Gulf of Carpentaria to Camp 119 317–321

camels and horses 323–325, 332, 340, 344, 350–351, 607

Camp 119 blaze 320

Camp 119 to Selwyn Range 322–325, 327–329, 330–331

Selwyn Range to Cooper's Creek 332–338, 339–340, 347–349, 353–355

Camp 46R (Plant Camp) 344–346, 616–617

Camp 52R 350–352, 607

Camp 61R 359

food distribution 333–334

illness 324

map 354

rain 330–331, 332

thunderstorms 322–323

Burke and Wills expedition: Cooper's Creek Depot

Gulf party return 363–366

discover Brahe has left 365–366, 369–370

decide against pursuit of Brahe's party 367–368

search for Strzelecki Creek 368–369, 377–380, 388–390, 395–397, 401–402

camels 390, 395–396, 399, 404

return to Cooper's Creek 404, 408–410

Dig Tree see Dig Tree

supplies 368, 399

Yandruwandha assist 380, 384–385, 398–399, 403

Burke and Wills expedition: Cooper's Creek

attempt to reach Mount Hopeless 410–414

turn back to Cooper's Creek 414

celebrate Queen Victoria's birthday 415–416

Nardoo Creek 416, 422–425, 621

hear sound of gunshot 416

Wills returns to Depot 416–417, 419–421

Wills weak and dying 431–434, 436–437

Burke and King leave Wills to search for Yandruwandha 435–438, 440–441

Burke and King bury field notes 440–441

Burke weak and dying 442–445

Burke's death 445–446, 449

supplies 411

supplies burnt in fire 422–423

Burke and Wills funeral
  carriage bearing coffins 581–582
  coffin display 577–578
  coffins lowered into vault 584
  Exploration Committee in procession 582
  Exploration Committee organises 567,
      569–570
  funeral procession 580–583
  grave 585
  mourning carriages 582
  pallbearers 583–584
  public viewing of coffins 577–578
  remains 569, 571–572, 572–576
  St George's Hall public meeting following
      funeral 586–596
  tomb 585
Burke and Wills Historical Society 616–617, 618
Burke electorate (Q'ld) 606
Burke River 294
bush rats 238
Byerly, Frederick John 14, 121

C
Cadell, Captain Francis
  Burke, criticisms of 44, 59–60
  career 34–35
  Dick, proposes reward for 282–283
  Exploration Committee ballot on leadership
      41
  Exploration Committee emergency meeting
      281
  Exploration Committee meeting on retrieval of
      bodies 547
  Explorers Memorial 602
  paddle steamers 306
  proposal Howitt retrieve body 521
  proposal to transport supplies up Murray
      84–85, 94
  supports Warburton 20, 34, 35
Calcutt, Mr 455
camels
  arrive in Melbourne on Chinsurah 39–40
  Bilbarka, go missing at 161–162, 165, 171,
      172
  at Blanchewater station 461
  camel boxes 103
  camel pads 151
  camel rugs 75
  camel saddles 243–244
  camel shoes 75, 207, 218
  caring for 84
  Cooper's Creek Depot party 264
  Cooper's Creek, go missing north of 236–238
  Cooper's Creek party 192, 196
  Darling River crossing 185–187

difficulty in mud 113, 120, 310
  endurance 68
  feet burn from heat 319
  feral population 612
  grooming 134–136
  in Gulf party 253, 323–325
  hospital camel 76
  injuries 158–159, 173–175
  Murray crossing 130
  names 107–108
  racing 612
  responsibility for 80–81
  Royal Park, go loose in 105
  rum for 76, 163
  saddlebags 602
  scab 393
  Selwyn Range ascent 328
  Selwyn Range descent 298–299
  to South Australia 460–461
  speed 148
  suitability for exploration 9, 70–71
  trot 116
  Victorian colony purchases from India 9–10
  weight of loads 102–103, 128, 150, 396, 539
camel handlers (sepoys) see also Belooch Khan
      (sepoy); Dost Mahomet (sepoy)
  attire 107, 116
  Cooper's Creek party 192, 196
  depart Royal Park 107–108
  expedition members ceremony, absent from
      88
  Hindu diet 112
  Hindustani language 69, 120
  Howitt's relief expedition 462
  Indian and Afghani arrive on Chinsurah 40
  Landells selects four 69
  Landell's treatment of Tuttie Khan 50
  leave then return to expedition 136, 139–140
  MOU with 92
  Tuttie Khan 50
  wages 69
Camel's Path 298–299, 328
Canally station 100, 132
Carrawaw (Yandruwandha woman) 459, 488,
      489, 611–612
carrier pigeons 435, 483–484
Castlemaine (Vic) 58–61, 401, 513
  Tableau in Memory of Burke and Wills
      596–597
Castlemaine Police 30, 56–57, 144–145, 581,
      602
Castlemaine Rifle Company 580
Castlemaine Volunteers 581
Catherwood, Dr 16
Chamberlain, Neville 602

Chapman, Justice Henry Samuel 590
Chinese goldminers 29–30
Chinese gong 161
cicadas 294
Cloncurry, 3rd Baron 87, 299
Cloncurry Creek 299, 303–304
Cobb & Co. 510
Cole, William 127–128
Cole's waterhole 142
Cook, Captain James 38, 78, 133
Cooper, Charles 53
Cooper River 11
Cooper's Creek see also under Burke and Wills
    expedition
  Barkly refers to 38
  cattle stations along 622–623
  coolabah trees 617
  Dig Tree see Dig Tree
  fish in 468, 469, 490
  Gregory recommends 11, 55
  Gregory's route 55
  Ngapa Merri billabong 490
  people of see Yandruwandha people
  Sturt describes 221
  Sturt names 53
  water depth 222
  wildlife 221–222
  Wills describes 216
  Yinimingka waterhole 442, 449
Cooper's Creek (Moorehead) 618
Coppin, George 40, 435, 483, 487, 609
Covent Garden 610
Cowen, Owen 61, 92, 104
Creber, Henry 61, 86, 92, 96–98, 99
Creber, John 96
Crimean War 27–28
Curlewis expedition 607

D
Darling, Sir Charles Henry 600
Darling River 144, 155–156, 179, 184 see also
    Menindee (NSW)
Denison, Lady 35, 65
Depot Glen 52
Depot Glen 67 54
Deutschen Verein 51
Diamantina River 277, 284–286
Dick (Barkindji man)
  award for assistance 282–283
  with Burke 188, 201, 202–203, 205
  Curlewis expedition 607
  with Lyons and MacPherson 210, 214–215,
    218–219, 227, 242
  Lyons leaves with horses 231–232

Lyons sends to Menindee 245, 247–248, 264,
    266–267, 268
  Torowoto battle 245–247
  with Wright's supply party 300, 301, 302
Dick, Thomas 129, 558–559
Dickens, Charles xii, 15, 365
Dickford see Drakeford, John
Dig (Clune) 618
Dig Tree
  Brahe blazes DIG, camp number and dates
    363
  Brahe buries his note and supplies 361, 363,
    528–531
  Gulf party finds 365–366, 542
  Burke buries his own and Wills journals,
    a note and pages from notebook
    377–378, 543
  Burke fails to add another blaze 543
  current location 617
  Brahe and Wright fail to dig up cache
    405–408, 409, 529, 532, 543
  Brahe and Wright fail to add supplies to cache
    566
  Wills opens cache, buries fresh note and field
    books of Gulf journey 420
  Howitt fails to open cache 470
  Howitt opens cache 490
  as Yirrbandji 397
dingoes 287–288, 480, 485, 574
Dogherty, Ellen 144–145, 280, 572, 574, 575,
    582, 584, 610, 613
Dost Mahomet (sepoy)
  with Burke 69, 162, 171
  Cooper's Creek Depot party 264, 393, 530
  Cooper's Creek party 192, 196, 205, 244
  later life 606
  Pamamaroo Creek camp 462
  scurvy 398
Drakeford, John 92, 187, 194
Duffy, Constable 30
Duke of Wellington 581

E
Eades, Dr Richard 88, 92, 105, 177, 190, 217,
    281, 520, 571, 573, 584, 586, 595–596
Earl, Dr John 619
eclipse of sun 296–297
Elliott, Mr 61, 547
Eltham Police 608
Embling, Dr Thomas 9–10, 67, 85, 427
emus 277
Endeavour expedition 78
Essendon camp 110–112
Eureka Stockade xi, 14, 41, 55–56

Exploration Committee
  blame 505
  Burke and Wills funeral 567, 569–570, 578
  Burke and Wills funeral procession 582
  Burke and Wills remains 572–576
  disbanded 613
  Dr Wills and 426–427
  emergency meeting 281–283
  exploration expertise 19
  first meeting 5
  Howitt, meeting to discuss retrieval of bodies
    545–548
  Howitt, proposal he retrieve bodies 500, 507,
    521–522, 544, 564
  King and 515
  Landells report on Burke 19
  members 5, 19
  Neumayer's progress report 189–191
Exploration Committee: despatches
  to Burke 125–128
  to Burke about Stuart's progress 176–178,
    191–192, 197–198
    see also Lyons, Trooper Myles
  from Burke 130–131
  from Burke about composition of Cooper's
    Creek party 194–195
  from Burke about Gulf party 254
  from Burke about Wills 250
  from Burke advising he might go on from
    Cooper's Creek 204
  from Burke at Cooper's Creek 216
  from Howitt 491–492, 496–497, 499–500
  to Wright 283, 294–295
  from Wright 267–268, 281–283, 429–430
Exploration Committee: expedition
  address to expedition members 88–90
  applications to join 16–17, 51, 61
  appoints officers 50
  budget see under Burke and Wills expedition:
    funding
  Cadell's proposal to transport supplies up
    Murray 84–85
  composition 13
  funding by public subscription see Exploration
    Fund Committee
  Landells and charge of camels 80–81
  MOU with expedition members 90–92
  Wilkie proposes 1, 4
Exploration Committee: expedition leader
  applications for 33–34
  Bruce–Macadam clique to support Burke
    23–25
  examination of candidates 35–36
  proposed 10–13, 19–20
  vote on candidates 41–42

Exploration Committee's awareness of delay
  553–556, 557
Exploration Fund Committee
  Burke's subscription 31
  establishment 4, 7–8
  public subscription 7–8, 10, 12–13, 15–16, 21
exploration of Australian interior
  to claim land for South Australian colony 613
  to claim land for Victorian colony 67, 595
  to establish telegraph line 6, 613
  to find gold 5
  to find pastoral land 4, 5, 148, 196–197, 270,
    622–623
  interior as 'Australian Sahara' 9
  interior as terra incognita 5
  Macadam sets out reasons for 8–9
  press question reasons for 71
  previous expeditions 3, 52–55
  for science 5, 614
  to settle surplus populations 2
exports 6, 612
Eyre, Edward John 55, 360
Eyre's Creek 254, 260, 275

F
Fawkner, John Pascoe 109
Ferguson, Charles
  autobiography 608
  background xi
  Becker and 134–136
  Bowman and 122
  breaks in horses 83
  Burke and 104
  Burke discharges 136–139
  Burke invites to join expedition 55–56, 61
  Burke's cheque dishonoured 139
  Burke's orders 114
  as foreman 92
  horse-drawn wagons 76
  Landells and 114
  loading of wagons 103
  in Melbourne 172–173, 189–190, 205–206
  obtains a ride to Albury 63–64
  offers to leave expedition 128–129
  refuses to sign Memorandum of Agreement 91
  repairs and reloads wagons 108–109
  rifle training 83–84
  Royal Park expedition encampment 81–84
  salary 81, 129
  wrongful dismissal action 608
Flagstaff Observatory 73
Fletcher, Robert 61, 78, 86, 92, 97, 98–99
Flinders River 308–309, 622
Fort Grey Depot 53, 54

Foster, Superintendent Henry 129, 130, 191–192, 197–198, 353, 508, 509, 602
France 429
Frank (guide to Howitt relief expedition) 466, 475, 476, 484
Franklin, Sir John 434
Fraser, Baldwin 41
Frizzell, John 33, 67
Froomes, William 58–59

G
German Club 51
Germany 615
ghee (Indian butter) 133–134
gibber plains 272
Gillbee, Dr William 178, 179, 281, 515, 521, 547
Gipps Land 291, 608–609
goldrushes 5–6, 14, 29–30
Goningberry Range 279, 287–288
Goowall 141–143
Government House, Melbourne 516–520
Gray, Charley
  background xii, 252–253
  Bilbarka 171
  bush skills 317
  Camp 119 310, 312–313, 319
  in charge of supplies 320
  Cooper's Creek party 196, 205
  death and burial 353–358, 443, 478, 493–494
  Dick and 558–559
  Gulf party 252–253, 274
  hired in Swan Hill 129–130
  illness 325, 334, 347
  King and 252–253, 335–336, 349, 356–357, 509–510
  McKinlay and 493–494, 589–590, 621
  remains 521, 590
  theft of food 335–336
  Wills and 335–336, 337, 349, 354, 356–357, 370, 506–507
Gray's Creek 274, 275
Gregory, Augustus
  Bowman and 121–122, 146
  expeditions 22–23, 55, 57–58, 225
  Landsborough, recommends 455
  Leichhardt, search for 4, 11
  map of expeditions 3
  meat biscuits 74–75
  Mount Hopeless 369, 399, 402
  Plains of Promise 309
  supplies 73
  as Surveyor-General of Queensland 11
  Victorian expedition, invited to lead 10–11
  Warburton, recommends 19
Gulf of Carpentaria 151–152, 313–316

H
Hamilton, Police Inspector George 482
Hampton Court maze 237, 369
Harris-Browne 54
Hassan Khan (sepoy) 69
Haverfield, Robert 533
Heales, Richard 428, 501
Hefferman, Billy 511
Hervey, Matthew (Royal Commissioner) 524, 532–533, 534, 541, 551, 558, 560, 561
HMS *Beagle* 308–309
HMVS *Victoria* 428, 455, 460, 465, 472
Hodgkinson, Clement 19
Hodgkinson, William ('Billy')
  background xii, 118
  Bilbarka 161–162, 173
  Brahe and 391
  Burke, Member for 606
  Burke and 56–57, 118–119, 169, 217
  Exploration Committee despatch for Wright 283
  joins expedition as clerk to Burke 125–126
  Koorliatto Creek natives 376
  Landells and 164–165, 166, 170, 175–176, 183
  later life 605–606
  McKinlay's despatch 496
  McKinlay's relief party 492–493, 494, 495, 542
  Melbourne 279–280, 282
  Menindee camp, remains at 192
  Pamamaroo Creek camp 219–220
  Royal Commission of Inquiry mentions 535, 536, 551, 552, 555, 556, 560
  Scropes Range 207–210, 213–214
  South Australian relief expedition 472
  Wills and 175–176
  Wright and 267–268, 294, 429
  Wright's supply party 300, 302–303, 305–306, 371–372, 380–381, 382, 383
Hodgson, John 19
Holmes, Ray 616
Howitt, Alfred
  background xii, 430
  backpacks 434
  Balranald 461
  Bengora Creek 467
  Brahe and 446–449, 451, 452
  Burke and Wills expedition: views on 291–292, 405
  Burke and Wills expedition, views on failure 609
  Burke and Wills funeral 582, 584
  Burke and Wills remains 569, 571–572, 573, 574
  bush skills 430

Howitt, Alfred *continued*
  carrier pigeons 435, 483–484
  Cooper's Creek 468–471
  Cooper's Creek: Burke 484–486
  Cooper's Creek: King 475–479
  Cooper's Creek: return journey with King
    489–490
  Cooper's Creek: Wills 479–481
  Cooper's Creek: Yandruwandha 486
  Dig Tree 470
  Exploration Committee 427–428, 449,
    451–453
  Exploration Committee despatches to
    491–492, 496–497
  Exploration Committee meeting on retrieval of
    bodies 545–548
  Exploration Committee proposal he should
    retrieve bodies 500, 507, 521–522, 544
  as explorer 291
  fishing, questions Brahe about 468, 469
  Gray's burial site 589–590
  later life 608–609
  leads Victorian Contingent Party 434–435
  leads Victorian relief expedition 452–453
  members of expedition 454–455, 466
  Menindee 496, 503
  Pamamaroo Creek camp 452–453, 461–463,
    466
  Royal Commission of Inquiry 544–545
  St George's Hall public meeting following
    funeral 586, 589
  supplies 452, 456, 461–462, 466
  Swan Hill, Cobb and Co. to 434
  Tarcoola 461
  Yandruwandha people: Carrawaw 611–612
  Yandruwandha people, misunderstanding of
    486
  Yandruwandha people, thanks 487–489

I
Indian Mutiny 84, 166
Indian soldiers (sepoys) *see* camel handlers
  (sepoys)
Indigenous Australians *see* natives
inland sea 52, 54
Innamincka 621
Inverness Hotel 112

J
Johnson, Captain George 170–171
Jupiter's moons 268–269

K
Kalkadoon of Cloncurry 304
Kalkadoon of Selwyn Range 298, 328

Kalkadoon people 298, 304, 328
Kauerau, Mr 51
Kekwick, William 48
Kenny, Colour Sergeant Dennis 58
Kinchega station 179, 186, 188, 208, 210,
  219–220
King, Annie 612
King, Elizabeth 518–520
King, John
  absent from St George's Hall public meeting
    following funeral 589
  appearance 519
  as assistant to Burke and Wills expedition 92
  background xii
  Bilbarka 161–162, 171, 172
  Brahe and 262
  Brahe's departure 365, 366, 367–368,
    476–477
  with British Army in India 40, 166
  Burke & Wills panorama 487
  Burke and Wills funeral 583
  Burke's effects 465
  Burke's last words 444–445, 446, 449
  Burke's remains 578
  as camel-handler 84, 165–166, 187, 252, 408
  Camp 119 310, 312–313, 319
  condition 476–477, 484, 490, 496
  Cooper's Creek party 196, 205, 243–244
  Cooper's Creek to Mount Hopeless 403–404
  craving for food 478
  Darling River crossing 502–503
  descendants 612
  ghee 134
  Gray and 252–253, 335–336, 349, 356–357
  Gulf party 252, 320, 337, 346, 351, 358
  Hindustani language 69
  Howitt, applies to join expedition for retrieval
    of bodies 546
  Howitt, return journey with 489–490
  Howitt's relief expedition 473–479
  illness 334
  later life 603
  monuments to Burke and Wills 600–601
  public reception: Bendigo 510–513
  public reception: Melbourne 506, 515–520
  public reception: reaction 520–521
  public reception: Swan Hill 507–510
  relates his experiences 478–479
  rifle training 84, 458, 460
  salary 84
  testimony to Royal Commission *see under*
    Royal Commission of Inquiry
  tribal name 466
  Wills, returns to 450, 454, 455–456
  Wills and 369

Wills's effects 465, 519
Wills's last words 441, 445, 449
Wills's notebook 537–538
with Yandruwandha 456–460, 463–465,
    466–467
Kings Creek 292–294
Knight, James 58
Knowsley 114–117
Kokriega 197
Kompang 144, 150
Koorliatto Creek 340–341, 371–377, 380–381,
    382–383, 384, 385–388, 398, 399–400,
    410, 414–415
Kurnai people 609
Kyte, Ambrose 7–8, 435, 483, 583–584, 586,
    588–589

L
Lake Bulloo see Bulloo River
Lake Pamamaroo 213, 290–291, 300, 302–303
    see also Pamamaroo Creek camp
Landells, George James
    background xi
    Becker and 154–155
    Beckler and 175, 185, 187–188
    Bilbarka 171
    Burke, resignation to 163, 166–167, 168–169,
        185
    Burke invites to join expedition 61, 159–160
    Burke offers to duel 183–184
    Burke orders to take packhorses 153
    Burke splits the party 141–143, 150
    camels, Exploration Committee gives him
        charge of 80–81, 92
    camels, purchases in India 9–10, 39–40
    camel diet 76, 133–134
    camel loading 102–103, 128
    as camel-handler 70–71, 158–159
    contract and salary 69, 80, 92
    Creber and 96–98
    Darling River crossing 185–187
    Exploration Committee and 427
    Hindustani language 69
    Hodgkinson and 164–165, 166, 170,
        175–176, 183
    as horse-trader 9
    later life 604
    Melbourne 216–217
    Menindee, leaves expedition 193, 195
    Mourara Station 173
    route 68
    Royal Commission of Inquiry 527, 538–539,
        557–558
    Royal Park departure 107

St George's Hall public meeting following
    funeral 592–593, 595
as second-in-command 50, 80, 91
Tarcoola 157
testimony to Royal Commission see under
    Royal Commission of Inquiry
Wills and 158–159, 164, 167–168, 176, 183
Landsborough, William 455, 472, 622
Langan, Patrick 61, 92, 134–136, 138–139, 190
Lawless, Edward 87–88, 299
Leahy, Professor Frank 616
Leichhardt, Ludwig
    disappearance 621–622
    expeditions 4, 54, 225, 250
    map of expedition 3
    Plains of Promise 309
    search for 2, 607, 615
    size of party 621–622
Ligar, Charles 427
lime juice 133
Linklinkwho waterhole 146
literature on Burke and Wills 617–618
Lockhart Morton, William
    camp fires 406–407
    criticism of expedition 615–616
    Exploration Committee meeting on retrieval of
        bodies 548
    Gray and 317
    letters to Argus 355–356, 381–382
    offers reward for vessel to Gulf 329–330
    Royal Commission of Inquiry 568
    Royal Society of Victoria 2, 33–34, 41, 81
    as 'Scientia' 46–47, 88
    Torowoto Swamp station 616
Loddon River 446
Lohmeier, Julius 73
Lyons, Trooper Myles
    54 camp [LIV] 228
    beyond Bulloo 227–232
    Burke's cache at Torowoto Swamp 214,
        218–219
    go back for horses 234–235, 239–240
    half-dry pan camp north of Torowoto
        218–219
    Lake Bulloo 223–225
    later life 608
    leaves Dick with horses 231–232, 234
    leaves Menindee 214–215
    map of search for Burke 230
    northern approaches to Torowoto Swamp 242
    party 214–215
    provisions 214
    retreats 229–232
    Superintendent Foster's instructions 191,
        197–198

Lyons, Trooper Myles *continued*
Torowoto 218–219, 245–249
Wright and 209–210, 214–215, 247–248

M

Macadam, Dr John
ambition 2
Argus, action for libel against 576–577
background xii, 21
Blunder Bay route 67–68
Brahe and 594–595
Bruce–Macadam clique to support Burke as
leader 21–25, 31, 41, 47
Burke and Wills funeral 567, 569–570
Burke and Wills remains 569, 571, 572, 573,
576–577
Burke's will 88
Dr Wills and 498–499, 500
Ellen Dogherty 145, 610
engagements 12
expedition supplies 74
Exploration Committee emergency meeting
281
Exploration Committee secretary 19
Ferguson and 206
Hodgkinson and 279–280
Howitt and 427, 447
King and 515, 519
Landells and 592–593, 595
Landells report on Burke 216–217
later life 614
leadership applications 23–25
Legislative Assembly seat 401
'Macadamised' (term for inebriety) 577
as Member for Castlemaine 20
Neumayer and 189, 190
physical appearance 20–21
as Post-Master General 401
St George's Hall public meeting following
funeral 586, 590–596
sets out reasons for exploration 8–9
Stuart's progress 177, 178, 179
supports Warburton 20, 24
testimony to Royal Commission *see under*
Royal Commission of Inquiry
Welch and 512
Wright and 593–595
macadamia nut 614
Macartney, Very Rev. Hussey Burgh 584, 622
McDonald, Flora 608
McDonough, Thomas
as assistant 92
background xii
at Bilbarka 161–162
with Burke 56, 149, 188, 217

Burke and 393, 397–398
camels 461
Cooper's Creek Depot party 254–255, 341,
342, 344
Cooper's Creek Depot to Bulloo River 384
Cooper's Creek party 195–196, 205
Cooper's Creek scouting parties 233,
235–238, 240–241
later life 606
St George's Hall public meeting following
funeral 594
scurvy 344, 352, 358–359, 362, 393, 398,
414
testimony to Royal Commission *see under*
Royal Commission of Inquiry
Wright and 400
Wright's supply party 395
Yandruwandha people 244
McIlwaine, James 136, 139
McIntyre, Duncan 622
McIver, George 621
McKinlay, John
finds remains near Cooper's Creek 495–496,
541–542, 607
Gray's grave 493–494, 589–590, 621
Hodgkinson and 492–493
rumours of white men near Cooper's Creek
491, 493
SA Burke Relief Expedition 460–461, 466,
472, 482, 491
McLeary, Dr Barry 619
McMillan, Angus 19
MacPherson, Alexander
Burke hires as saddler in Menindee 187
go back for horses 234–235, 239–240
Lake Bulloo natives 223–224
leaves Menindee with Lyons 214–215
northern approaches to Torowoto Swamp 242
Pamamaroo Creek camp 295
remains behind in Menindee camp 192
South Australian Advertiser 306
Torowoto 218–219, 245–249
Wright sends with Trooper Lyons 210
Maljangapa people 198–199
mallee country 131, 142
malnutrition 619–620
Malyyangapa people 245–247
mangrove swamps 313–316
Marks, Mr 127
Marsh Troupe, Bendigo 510, 512–513
Marsilea drummondii see nardoo
matches 73
Matthews, Julia
absent from funeral 583
Burke leaves Essendon camp to see 110

Burke meets xviii–xix
Burke's desire to impress 31, 44–45, 191–192
Burke's locket 501–502
Burke's remains 578
Burke's will 87–88
in *The Eton Boy* 339
letter to Burke 445
oversees career 609–610
stage career xii, xviii, 110
Tableau in Memory of Burke and Wills
    596–597
meat biscuits 74–75
Melbourne (Vic) 5–6, 100–106, 453–454
    public reception of King 506, 515–520
    State Funeral for Burke and Wills 579–580
    see also Burke and Wills funeral
Melbourne Benevolent Asylum 606, 611
Melbourne Club 31, 45, 610–611
Melbourne Cup 497
Melbourne General Cemetary 583, 601
Melbourne Observatory 582 *see also* Neumayer,
    Professor Georg
Melbourne Punch 274–275
Menindee (NSW) 52, 84–85, 496 *see also*
    Pamamaroo Creek camp
    Burke and Wills expedition missing 429
    Burke dumps supplies beside road 188,
        193–194
    Burke splits expedition at 189–190, 192–193
    Dost Mahomet in 606
    expedition reaches 181–183
    map 184
    Paine's Hotel 182, 208, 296, 429–430
Mesembryanthemum see Pig Face
meteor 174
Middle East 612
Middleton, Tom 492–493
Milpulo people 198–199
mirage 271
Mitchell, Sir Thomas 4, 22–23, 201, 602
Mitchell Library, Sydney 611
Mitchell River 291
Montgomery, James 124–125
monuments to Burke and Wills 501, 564,
    600–603
Moolgewanke (steamer) 170–171, 179, 182–183
Moreton Bay (Q'ld) 54
mosquitoes 279
Mount Birnie 297, 503
Mount Doubeny Ranges 197
Mount Hopeless 55, 368–369, 377, 410, 461
Mount Sturt 48
Mourara Station 173, 175
Mueller, Dr Ferdinand 1, 2
    absent from vote on candidates for leader 41

Becker and 49
Burke and Wills funeral 584
exploration expertise 19
Gregory and 11, 73
Macadam and 614
Mueller medal 609
opposes Burke as leader 35, 36
plant specimens 418, 604–605
procurement of supplies 73
route proposed 6
vetoes Blunder Bay route 70
Mumford, William 609–610
Murphy, Sir Francis (Royal Commissioner) 501,
    524–531, 534–535, 538–544, 548–549,
    550, 552, 562, 584
Murray, Dr James 574, 575
Murray–Darling 13, 52, 84–85, 120, 124, 130,
    157 *see also* Darling River
Murrumbidgee River 131, 456
Mutawintji 198–199, 305–306, 307–308

N
Napoleon Bonaparte 429
Nappa Merrie cattle station 490, 617
nardoo (*Marsilea drummondii*)
    Burke, Wills and King survive on 424–426,
        433, 434, 436, 441, 443
    fills the appetite 437
    grinding stones 464
    King finds 411, 416
    method of gathering 464
    nardoo flour paste 422
    preparation 619–620
    seed-cake eaten at Torowoto 242, 248–249,
        264, 278
    seed-cake eaten by Yandruwandha 398,
        403–404
    specimen 605
    stools from 431
    white-fellow 488
    Wills searches for 408–410
Nash, Richard 73, 83, 87–88, 106, 124–125,
    514, 516, 517, 610–611
natives *see also* native guides
    of Attack Creek *see* Warramunga people
    attitude to camels 120, 131
    awards for assistance 282–283
    from below Bulloo River 206–207
    of Bengora Creek 467
    Burke gives handkerchiefs to 286
    Burke gives shirts to 195–196, 202, 255
    of Cooper's Creek *see* Yandruwandha people
    of Darling River: dream of devils of Burke and
        Wills 599–600
    of Diamantina River 285, 286

natives continued
  Exploration Committee's instructions 95, 96
  of Eyre's Creek 260
  fires: camp fires 406–407
  fires: signal fires 384
  of Gipps Land see Kurnai people
  of Gulf 311–312
  Howitt's study 609
  huts 273, 312
  of Kings Creek 292
  of Koorliatto Creek 372–376, 380–388
  of Lake Bulloo 223–224
  McKinlay's relief party and 482, 491,
    589–590
  massacres of 471
  of Menindee see Barkindji people
  from north of Cooper's Creek 235
  plant-based diet see nardoo; Pig Face
  Scropes Range rock art 271–272
  of Selwyn Range and Cloncurry see Kalkadoon
    people
  of Speewa 131
  of Stony Desert 269, 273
  of Terekencom 140–141
  of Terrick-Terrick Plains 120
  of Torowoto 242, 247–249, 319
  of Torowoto: appearance 321–322
  of Torowoto: battle 245–247
  trading routes 622
  water, sink wells for 253–254
  waterbags 290
  yam diggings 311
native guides
  from Menindee with Burke and Wills 188
    see also Dick (Barkindji man); Peter
      (Barkindji man); Smith, John
  from Menindee with Howitt see Sandy 466,
    468–469
  from Moreton Bay on Leichhardt expedition
    54
  Simon at Kompang 144
  from Terekencom 141, 143
  from Torowoto to Cooper's Creek 205
Native Tribes of South-East Australia (Howitt)
  609
Neumayer, Professor Georg
  absent from funeral 582
  background xii
  Brahe and 51
  Burke asks to find him if he should get lost
    150–151
  Burke proposal for vessel to meet him in Gulf
    149–150, 342, 355–356, 381, 426
  Dr Wills and 330, 426

  Exploration Committee despatches to Swan
    Hill 191–192
  exploration for science 5, 13, 18
  in Germany 615
  Howitt's relief expedition 456
  joins expedition as observer 119, 125–126,
    130
  leaves expedition as observer 150–151
  progress report to Exploration Committee
    189–191
  route 68
  Welch and 428
  Wills's instruments 327
  Wills's remains 578
Neumayer Station III, Antarctica 615
New South Wales colony 4, 6
New South Wales Native Police 471
New Zealand War 465
Newton, Isaac 1
Ngapa Merri billabong 490, 617
Nicholson, William 178
Nogoa River 471–472
Norman, Captain William 455, 465, 472
Northwest Passage expedition 434

O
Orkney, James 460, 466, 497–498
O'Shanassy, John 579
Ovens and Murray Advertiser 577
Overland Telegraph Line 6, 12–13, 613

P
Paine, Tom 182, 208, 296
Pamamaroo Creek camp
  Beckler in charge of 290–291, 294
  Burke and Wills expedition 207–210,
    219–220
  Howitt's relief expedition 452–453, 461–463,
    466
  Lyons and MacPherson 264
  Wright's supply party 300–301, 430
Parker, Robert 612
Parry, Samuel 41
Pasco, Captain Crawford 508
Paterson, Aaron 612
Paterson, A. B. 'Banjo' 614, 623
Patten, William
  appearance 258
  as assistant 92
  background xii, 56
  at Bilbarka 173
  Burke and 56, 61, 258
  Cooper's Creek Depot party 263, 264,
    299–300, 343–344, 530
  Cooper's Creek party 196, 205

death and burial 422
scurvy 343–344, 352, 358–359, 362, 393, 398, 400, 414–415, 532
Patten's Creek 296
pemmican 75, 183
Pentridge prison 76
Peter (Barkindji man)
  in Scropes Range 213
  skills 406
  to Torowoto 267, 278, 279, 287–290
Philister, Mr 66
Phillips, Weston 292, 428, 455, 456, 492, 502–503
Philosophical Institute of Victoria 1–4
  becomes Royal Society of Victoria see Royal Society of Victoria
  Exploration Committee see Exploration Committee
  Exploration Fund Committee see Exploration Fund Committee
  receives Royal Charter 17
Phoenix, Dave 606, 618, 619–620, 621
photographs taken by Howitt's party
  of Burke 485
  equipment 430–431
  of Howitt's party on Cooper's Creek 477, 489
  of King 477
  plates 489, 496, 522
  of Yandruwandha people 477–478, 489
Pig Face (Mesembryanthemum) 415
Pitchery (Yandruwandha man) 417, 421–422, 487
Pitt, Colonel 83–84
Plains of Promise 308–309
plant specimens from Scropes Range 213, 418
Poko Tinnamira (Yandruwandha man) 417
Police Commissioner 157–158, 177, 178
politics
  in exploration of Australian interior 5–6
  railway contracts 21
Polygonum Swamp 353–358, 493–494, 541–542
porcupine grass 141
Poria Creek 491–492
Porter, Mr 360
Pratt, Sir Thomas (Chair, Royal Commission) 501, 524–525, 527–528, 544, 549–551, 557, 560
Prungle outstation 140–141
Purcell, William 300, 307, 327, 340, 375, 382, 383

Q

Queensland colony
  Burke and Wills expedition: possible return route 255, 342, 452, 528
  Queensland relief expedition 455, 465, 472

R

railway line 21, 47
Rat Point 422
Richmond Police 49–50
Robert O'Hara Burke Memorial Museum 602
Rowe, Dr (station) 120–121
Royal Artillery 580
Royal Botanic Gardens Herbarium, Melbourne 605
Royal Commission of Inquiry
  Argus view 523
  Becker's letter to Exploration Committee 555
  Beckler on Wright as third-in-command 533
  Beckler's testimony regarding Brahe 533
  Brahe, Beckler's testimony regarding 533
  Brahe, Dig Tree 528–531
  Brahe, findings on culpability 566–567
  Brahe, instigates return with Wright 532–533
  Brahe, Wills's instructions 531
  Brahe, Wright's delay 534, 561
  Brahe and Wills's clothes 561–562
  Brahe as witness 527–533, 561–562
  Brahe in terms of reference 523
  Brahe returns with Wright 532
  Burke's appointment of Wright 525, 548, 565
  Burke's contradictory orders 567
  Burke's decision not to follow Brahe 531
  Burke's despatches 549, 553
  Burke's hasty decision to drive for the Gulf 565
  Burke's splitting of party 565
  Commissioners 501, 524
  Exploration Committee's awareness of delay 555–556
  Exploration Committee's cheques dishonoured 536–537
  Exploration Committee's expenditure 526
  Exploration Committee's failure to urge Wright to move 566
  findings 565–568
  fishing on Cooper's Creek 534–535
  Howitt as witness 544–545
  King and arrival at Depot 542
  King and Burke's decision not to follow Brahe 543
  King and Depot party 543–544
  King and Gray's burial 541, 542
  King and Gray's thieving 539–540
  King and Gulf party supplies 539
  King and McKinlay's find of remains near Cooper's 541–542
  King and return to Depot 540–541
  King and Wright's delay 541
  King as witness 538–544
  Landells 527, 538–539

Royal Commission of Inquiry *continued*
  Landells as witness 557–558
  Macadam 524–527, 535, 536–537, 549,
    562–563, 567
  McDonough 530, 534–535
  Stawell 553–556
  terms of reference 501, 523–524
  Thomas Dick as witness 558–559
  Wecker 535–537
  Wright, despatches to 554
  Wright and Brahe's return 561
  Wright and Lyons and MacPherson 560
  Wright as witness 537, 548–551
  Wright in terms of reference 524
  Wright on Burke's changes of orders 551
  Wright's confirmation of appointment
    535–537, 548–549, 556
  Wright's delay 528, 534, 535–536, 550–551,
    559–561, 566
  Wright's despatches 525–527, 535–537, 552,
    555, 559–560
  Wright's letter 549–550, 562–563
  Wright's literacy 552
Royal Geographic Society 4
Royal Navy 133
Royal Park expedition encampment 71, 81–84,
  86, 96–98, 100–106
Royal Park obelisk 601
Royal Society of Victoria
  cheques dishonoured 536–537
  Exploration Committee *see* Exploration
    Committee
  first meeting of 1861 349–350
  formerly Philosophical Institute of Victoria *see*
    Philosophical Institute of Victoria
  Howitt's photographic plates 522
  inaugural annual dinner 37–38
  membership decline 614
  plant specimens 418
  premises 18, 241, 613
  public funds for expedition *see* Burke and
    Wills expedition: funding
  public subscription for expedition *see*
    Exploration Fund Committee
  Royal Commission of Inquiry 501
Russia 27–28, 429

S
Sadleir, John 44, 56, 100
St George's Hall public meeting following funeral
  586–596
Samla (Hindu sepoy) 69, 112
Sampson, Mr 455
Sandy (guide to Howitt relief expedition) 466,
  468–469, 473, 476, 484

Sarah (Burke's housekeeper) xix
St James Cathedral, Melbourne 569–570
Schmidt, F. 57–58
scientific community 5
scientific information 152
Scropes Range 197, 207–210, 213–214,
  271–272, 302–303, 418
scurvy
  Burke and Wills expedition 54, 75, 133, 326,
    340–341, 343–344, 352–353, 358–359,
    371
  citric acid treatment 414–415
secret ballot 41
Selwyn, Richard 85
Selwyn Range 296–299, 327–329
sepoys *see* camel handlers (sepoys)
Shakespeare, William 66, 79, 441–442, 583,
  585–586
sheep 295
Simon (native guide to Kompang) 144
Sir Charles Hotham Hotel 497
sly-grog shops 104
Smith, James 547, 575
Smith, John 295, 300, 302–303, 307, 327, 375,
  376–377, 382, 384
Smithe, Inspecting Superintendent Peter Henry
  31–32
snakes 239, 324
South Australian colony 38
  Burke Relief Expedition *see* McKinlay, John
  extension of territory to Gulf 613
  Historical Relics Collection 607
  Overland Telegraph Line 6, 12–13, 613
  prize for crossing continent 507, 613
  race to the Gulf with Victoria 148–149,
    171–172, 177, 212–213
  Stuart's public reception 578–579
Sparkes and Cramsie, Messrs 132–134, 139
Speewa 131
squatters in Victoria 5
SS *Chinsurah* 39–40, 68
SS *Firefly* 455, 465, 472
SS *Havilah* 571
SS *Oscar* 460–461
SS *Sir Charles Hotham* 460, 466
Standish, Captain 157–158, 177, 178
Stawell, Lady Mary 67, 106
Stawell, Sir William
  background xii
  Blunder Bay route 67, 70
  Burke and Wills funeral 584
  Burke's pocket books 444–445
  as Chief Justice of Victoria 2, 615
  expedition members address 88

expedition members, address to 90–91
expedition supplies 74, 75
on Exploration Committee 12
as Exploration Committee chairman 19
Exploration Committee emergency meeting 281
Exploration Committee meeting on retrieval of bodies 546, 547–548
King gives Wills's notebook to 537–538
Kyte offers funds for expedition 7–8
leader, Bruce–Macadam clique to support Burke as 31
leader, vote on candidates for 41
photography 430
Royal Commission of Inquiry testimony 553–556
St George's Hall public meeting following funeral 586, 587–589
Stawell Gift 615
Stokes, Captain John 308–309
Stone, Charles 295, 300, 326, 340, 371, 375, 376–377, 383
Stony Desert 53, 229, 254, 269–271, 272–274, 350–352, 353–355
Strangways, Henry 570
Strickland (mayor Bendigo) 510, 513
Strzelecki, Pawel 53
Strzelecki Creek 11, 53, 385, 396, 401–402, 412, 621
Strzelecki Desert 53
Stuart, John McDouall: 1858 expedition
map 3
for South Australian colony 12–13, 18
turns back 22–23
Stuart, John McDouall: 1860 expedition
attacked by Warramunga 171–172, 191
Burke's death 507
Chambers Creek 286, 570
claims for British Empire 48
map 3
public reception 578–579
route 612–613
sets out 32–33, 38, 47–48
sets out again 192
turns back 48, 507
wins prize for crossing continent 507, 613
Sturt, Charles 201
describes Cooper's Creek 221
expeditions 2–4, 22–23, 26, 58, 225, 233
Eyre's Creek 254
hears rocks splitting 416
map of expedition 3
maps he formed 270
names Cooper's Creek 53

Narrative of an Expedition into Central Australia 52–55
natives 622
Scropes Range 197
Stony Desert 272, 273
Stuart and 12, 18, 54
Sturt, Evelyn (Royal Commissioner) 524, 526–527, 529
Sullivan, James (Royal Commissioner) 524, 527, 558
Swan Hill
Burke and Wills expedition 94, 118, 120, 123–132, 187, 191–192, 253
Explorers Memorial 602
Howitt relief expedition 447
King: public reception 507–510
Swan Hill Police 129, 178

T
Tarcoola station 154–155, 161, 162–163
Burke arrives at 144
hired wagons and wagon-drivers dismissed at 157
wagons and punt wagon left behind at 156–157
Tchukulow (Yandruwandha man) 487
telegraph line see Overland Telegraph Line
Terekencom 140–141
terra incognita 5
Terrick-Terrick Plains 119–121
Thackeray, William xii, 15
thunderstorms 254, 322–323
Tirrawarra Swamp 268–269
Tolarno station 179
Torowoto Swamp
Burke and Wills expedition 179, 180, 199–202, 218–219, 242, 322
Howitt's relief expedition 467
Lockhart Morton's station 616
Lyons and MacPherson 264, 278–279, 288, 289, 291
native battle 245–247
Wright's supply party 318–319, 321–322
Tragowel 121–122
transit of Venus 38
tree blazing marks see also Dig Tree
Burke's grave on Cooper's Creek 486
Camp 61 468
Camp 119 320
Exploration Committee instructs Burke to mark route 173
L (for Leichhardt) by Flinders River 622
McKinlay at Gray's grave 494–495
Wills's grave on Cooper's Creek 481
Tropic of Capricorn 292, 293, 296

Turinyi (Yandruwandha woman)
  descendants 612
  King and 463, 466, 489
Tuttie Khan 50

V
VEE see Burke and Wills expedition
Venus corona 433
Victoria, Queen 17, 415–416
Victorian colony 4
  final cost of Burke and Wills expedition 614
  gold wealth 5–6
  grant pension to Ellen Dogherty 610
  grant pension to King 603
  Melbourne to Bendigo railway 21
  proposal to annex Central Australia 595
  provides funds for expedition see Burke and
      Wills expedition: public funding
  provides funds to retrieve bodies of Burke and
      Wills 500, 547
  purchases camels from India 9–10, 39–40
  race to the Gulf with South Australia
      148–149, 171–172, 177, 212–213
  State Funeral for Burke and Wills 500–501,
      507, 579
Victorian Contingent Party 434 see also Howitt,
    Alfred
Victorian Exploring Expedition
  renamed Burke and Wills Exploring
      Expedition 500
  see also Burke and Wills expedition
Victorian Football League 12
Victorian Volunteer Artillery 580, 583
Vining, William 434, 454, 484
von Tempsky, Gustavus 41–42

W
Walker, Frederick 471–472
Wantula waterhole 493
Wanyiwalku people 245–247, 267
Warburton, Major Peter Egerton
  Dr Wills and 481–482, 611
  as 'Justitia' 45–46
  as possible leader Victorian expedition 19–20,
      23–25, 34–36, 41–42, 44, 59–60
Warramunga people 48, 171–172, 191
water 75, 141
  beside native huts 312
  camels and 303
  dingo scratchings for 287–288
  horses and 303, 304–306
  Howitt's relief expedition 467
  Menindee to Cooper's Creek 196–197,
      202–203
waterbags 78

water-bottles 78
Watpipa (native guide) 143
Wecker, Edward 208, 210, 496, 535–537
Welch, Edwin
  background xii
  Brahe and 520
  congestion of retina 456
  Cooper's Creek: Burke 484
  Cooper's Creek: King 473–474, 478, 479
  Darling River crossing 502–503
  Exploration Committee meeting on retrieval of
      bodies 545–548
  Howitt's relief expedition 428, 431, 434,
      454, 467
  King, escorts from Menindee to Melbourne
      503, 508–515
  King, escorts in Melbourne 516, 517
  photography 430–431, 477, 485, 489
  Plant Camp 616
Wheeler, Dr William 455, 476, 484, 575
Wilkie, Dr David 281
  Burke and Wills funeral 570
  Burke and Wills remains 571, 573–574
  Dr Wills and 426, 498–499
  Exploration Committee meeting on retrieval of
      bodies 547
  Exploration Committee treasurer 19, 77, 80,
      537
  Ferguson and 172–173, 189
  proposes expedition to cross continent 1–4
  route 68
  Stuart's progress 178
Wills, Dr William
  accompanies camels to South Australia
      460–461
  background xii
  Brahe and 500, 568
  Burke and 111, 369, 568
  Exploration Committee and 329–330, 425,
      426–427
  Ferguson and 104
  King and 514, 516, 517
  leaves before funeral 572
  Macadam and 498–499, 500
  McKinlay relief party 472, 491
  memoir 568, 611, 617–618
  monuments to Burke and Wills 600
  offers to join search party 428
  Royal Commission of Inquiry 568
  Warburton and 481–482
  Welch and 514
  William and 49, 327
  William's clothes 561–562
  William's death 497–500
  William's effects 519

William's interment 521
William's letter to 438–440, 531
Wills, Harry 434
Wills, Tom 572, 578, 584
Wills, William John
 appearance 117
 background xi, 13–14
 Birnie, friendship with see Birnie, Richard
 Brahe and 176, 261, 365, 367, 467
 Bulloo River, clay pan below 206–207
 Burke and 111, 125, 185–187, 250
 Burke splits the party at Menindee 141–143
 camels and 121
 Cooper's Creek, describes 216, 222
 Cooper's Creek party 196, 197, 205
 Cooper's Creek scouting parties 233,
  235–238, 240–241, 243–244
 Devon monument 602–603
 eclipse of sun 296–297
 expedition departure 112
 Exploration Committee's instructions 64
 Flagstaff Observatory instruments 73
 Gray and 335–336, 337, 349, 354, 356–357,
  506–507
 Gulf party 252, 274
 Hodgkinson and 175–176
 Howitt's relief expedition 479–481, 609
 journal entries 402–403
 Jupiter's moons 268–269
 Landells and 125, 158–159, 164, 167–168,
  176, 183
 letter to father 438–440, 531
 mapping of country 64
 Menindee 182
 meteorological readings 121
 Mount Birnie 297
 Mount Hopeless route 368–370
 Mutawintji 198–199
 naming powers 211
 nardoo 408–410
 natives 201–202
 Neumayer and 13, 14, 127, 217
 photograph of 611
 Pitchery and 417, 421–422
 Plains of Promise 308–309
 Plant Camp: buries instruments 345–346,
  616–617
 Porter and 360
 reasons for joining expedition 36–37
 remains 575–576
 rifle training 84
 role on expedition 16, 18
 as second-in-command 108–109, 200, 212,
  250

 sense of direction 237
 as station hand 385
 Stony Desert 271
 Strzelecki Creek 402
 studies previous expeditions 52–55
 as surveyor and astronomical observer 61,
  64, 92
 Tarcoola 157
 as third-in-command 61, 64, 91
Wilyakali people 198–199
Woodend (Vic) 513, 514
Wright, William
 in Adelaide 586–587
 background xi
 blame 505
 Burke as lost 395, 397–398
 Burke hires 179–180, 186, 188, 192
 Burke's instructions 203–205, 257
 Cooper's Creek Depot, arrives with Brahe
  405–408, 409
 criticisms of abilities 201
 delays in Menindee 208–210, 265–266, 280,
  281, 395, 618–619
 Exploration Committee despatches 294–295,
  429–430
 family at Kinchega see Kinchega station
 Koorliatto Creek to Cooper's Creek 399–400
 later life 604
 Lyons and MacPherson 267, 268
 Macadam and 593–595
 Patten and 422
 returns to Menindee 205, 207
 salary 200–201, 207
 sends Hodgkinson to Melbourne 267–268
 squatters land scout 594
 supply party see Wright, William: supply party
 as third-in-command 200–201, 203, 210,
  213–214, 282, 294–295, 391
 Torowoto, guides Burke to 196, 197, 199
Wright, William: supply party
 Exploration Committee and 350
 Exploration Committee funding 281–283,
  295
 Exploration Committee's instructions 295
 horses and camels 296, 300, 301, 303,
  304–306, 319
 members 295, 300
 supplies 295–296, 393, 395, 398
 Brahe joins up with 391–393
 Bulloo River 340, 346–347, 370
 Burke's tracks 326
 camel search parties 325
 camp names 326
 Pamamaroo Creek camp departure 300–301,
  302

Wright, William: supply party *continued*
   Scropes Range 302–303
   Bilpa to Mutawintji 304–306
   Mutawintji 307–308
   illness 326–327
   Koorliatto Creek 340–341, 398, 399–400
   Koorliatto Creek natives 371–377, 380–381,
      382–383, 384, 385–388
   retreat to Menindee 397–398
   stockade 380–381
   Torowoto 318–319, 321–322
   Torowoto going north 325–327
   Torowoto retreat 388, 393
   water supplies 295–296, 302–303
Wylie, Mr 360

Y
Yandruwandha people *see also* Carrawaw;
   Pitchery; Turinyi
   Aboriginal Story of Burke and Wills 612
   assist Burke and Wills expedition 380,
      384–385, 421–422
   attire 487–488
   Bendigo toast health of 511
   boomerangs 418
   Brahe fires on 283–284, 471
   Burke and King fire on 417–418, 621
   Burke and Wills quarrel story 621

   Burke offers fishhooks to 398–399
   Burke's grave 464
   Christian mission 622
   on Cooper's Creek 232–233, 244, 255, 258,
      263, 283–284, 371, 379
   diet 398, 403
   fishing hooks 332
   frontier conflict 622–623
   Howitt asks about Gray's remains 590
   Howitt thanks 487–489
   Howitt's misunderstanding of 486
   Howitt's relief expedition 468–469, 473–476
   King, farewell to 489
   King with 456–460, 463–465, 466–467
   language 459–460, 463
   names 487
   off Cooper's Creek 424
   photographs of 477–478
   picking nardoo seed 417
   sign language 457
   system of living 464
   tomahawks 465
   white-fellow murder story 620
   Wills, bury clothes 456, 457
   Wills, send away 423
   Yandruwandha–Yawarrawarrka Native Title
      claim 623
   Yirrbandji, coolabah tree 397